The Political Economy of Poverty, Equity, and Growth

Series editors
Deepak Lal and Hla Myint

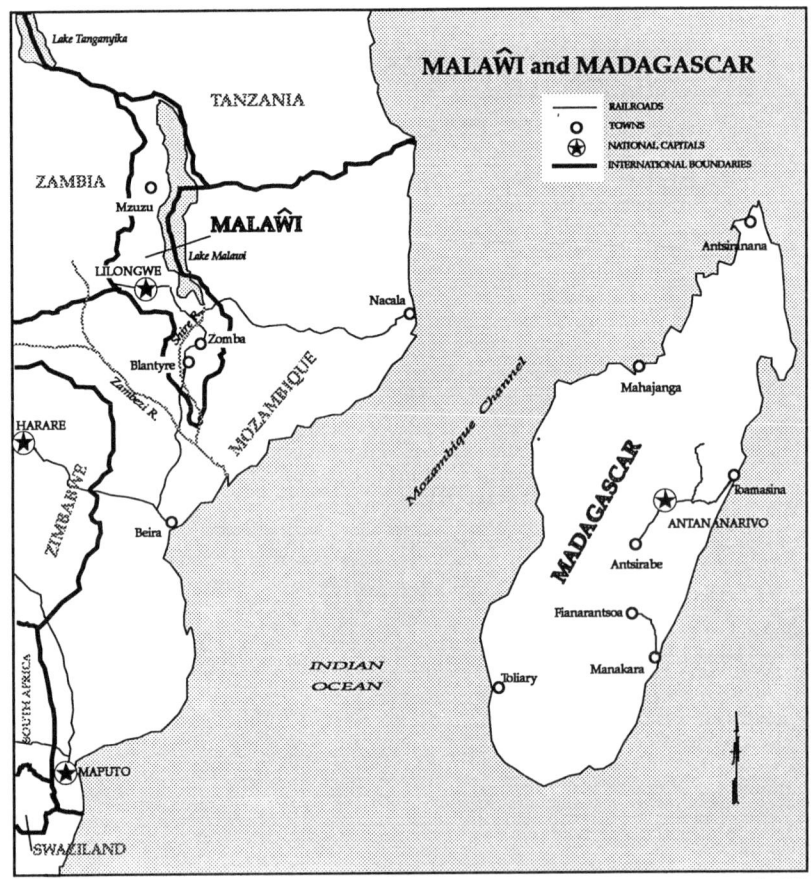

A World Bank
Comparative Study

The Political
Economy of Poverty,
Equity, and Growth

Malaŵi and Madagascar

Frederic L. Pryor

Published for the World Bank
Oxford University Press

Oxford University Press
OXFORD NEW YORK TORONTO DELHI
BOMBAY CALCUTTA MADRAS KARACHI
PETALING JAYA SINGAPORE HONG KONG
TOKYO NAIROBI DAR ES SALAAM
CAPE TOWN MELBOURNE AUCKLAND
and associated companies in
BERLIN IBADAN

© 1990 The International Bank for
Reconstruction and Development / THE WORLD BANK
1818 H Street, N.W., Washington, D.C. 20433, U.S.A.

All rights reserved. No part of this publication
may be reproduced, stored in a retrieval system,
or transmitted in any form or by any means,
electronic, mechanical, photocopying, recording,
or otherwise, without the prior permission
of Oxford University Press.

Manufactured in the United States of America
First printing November 1990

The findings, interpretations, and conclusions expressed in
this study are the results of research done by the World Bank,
but they are those of the authors and do not necessarily
represent the views and policies of the World Bank or
its Board of Executive Directors or the countries they represent.
The World Bank does not guarantee the accuracy of the data
included in this publication and accepts no responsibility
whatsoever for any consequences of their use.

Library of Congress Cataloging-in-Publication Data

Pryor, Frederic L.
   The political economy of poverty, equity, and growth:
Malaŵi and Madagascar / Frederic L. Pryor
      p.   cm. – (A World Bank comparative study)
   Includes bibliographical references and index
   ISBN 0-19-520823-4
   1. Malaŵi–Economic conditions.   2. Malaŵi–Economic
policy.   3. Income–Malaŵi.   4. Madagascar–Economic
conditions.   5. Madagascar–Economic policy.   6. Income–
Madagascar.   I. World Bank.   II. Title.   III. Series.
HC935.P794   1990
338.96897–dc20   90-43293
                                                              CIP

Foreword

This volume is the first of several emerging from the comparative study, "The Political Economy of Poverty, Equity, and Growth," sponsored by the World Bank. The study was done to provide a critical evaluation of the economic history of selected developing countries in 1950–85. It explores the *processes* that yielded different levels of growth, poverty, and equity in these countries, depending on each country's initial resource endowment and economic structure, national institutions and forms of economic organization, and economic policies (including those that might have been undertaken).

The Scope of the Comparative Study

The basic building block of the project is a coherent story of the growth and income distribution experiences of each country, based on the methods of what may be termed "analytical economic history" (see Collier and Lal 1986) and "political economy." Each country study provides both a historical narrative and a deeper explanation of how and why things happened. Each study also seeks to identify the role of ideology and interest groups in shaping policy.

Our comparative approach involved pairing countries whose initial conditions or policies seemed to be either significantly similar or significantly different. Although initial impressions of similarity or difference may not have been borne out on closer inspection, this binary approach offered a novel and promising way of reconciling in-depth case studies with a broader comparative method of analysis.

To provide this in-depth study of individual cases, a smaller number of countries was selected than is conventional in comparative *statistical* studies. We have serious doubts about the validity of inferences drawn from such cross-sectional regression studies about historical processes (see Hicks 1979). Therefore this project, by combining qualitative with quantitative analysis, has tried instead to interpret the nature and significance of the usual quantifiable variables for each country in its historical and institutional context.

To provide some unifying elements to the project, we presented the authors of the country studies with several provisional hypotheses to be considered in the course of their work. These concern the determinant of growth, the importance of historical and organizational factors in determining alternative feasible paths of growth to redress poverty, and the relative roles of ideas, interests, and ideology in influencing decision making.

Our synthesis volume in this series discusses the extent to which these hypotheses were or were not substantiated in each of the country studies. The following list of the country studies and their principal authors suggests the range of the overall comparative study:

Malaŵi and Madagascar	Frederic L. Pryor
Egypt and Turkey	Bent Hansen
Sri Lanka and Malaysia	Henry Bruton
Indonesia and Nigeria	David Bevan, Paul Collier, and Jan Gunning
Thailand and Ghana	Oey A. Meesook, Douglas Rimmer, and Gus Edgren
Brazil and Mexico	Angus Maddison and Associates
Costa Rica and Uruguay	Simon Rottenberg, Claudio Gonzales-Vega, and Edgardo Favaro
Colombia and Peru	Antonio Urdinola, Mauricio Carrizosa Serrano, and Richard Webb
Five Small Economies: Hong Kong, Singapore, Malta, Jamaica, and Mauritius	Ronald Findlay and Stanislaw Wellisz

Many of these volumes will be published in this series by Oxford University Press. In addition, a volume of special studies on related topics, edited by George Psacharopoulos, will also be published.

This Volume

Frederic L. Pryor's study of Malaŵi and Madagascar is the first in the series to be published. Malaŵi and Madagascar have received much less scholarly attention than other countries selected for the project.

There were no full-length studies of these two countries, and their economic statistics were incomplete or unsatisfactory. Pryor, therefore, has had to undertake a considerable amount of basic research in reworking their national income statistics and developing his own data series. He has also presented a comprehensive survey and evaluation of some of the less easily accessible information on the two countries in his extensive notes. As a result, the present volume contains economic histories of Malaŵi and Madagascar that are valuable in their own right, in addition to their contribution to the eventual comparative purposes of the overall study.

Malaŵi and Madagascar were paired for joint study because they represent two low-income East African countries with similar initial conditions of development. They started from different colonial backgrounds, however, and have followed somewhat different policies since independence.

Popularly, Malaŵi is regarded as an example of African capitalism and Madagascar as an example of African socialism. Pryor provides a penetrating analysis of the real nature of their underlying similarities and differences. For example, he shows that Malaŵi may be regarded as more socialistic than Madagascar in its ratio of public expenditure and public investment to gross domestic product. But he also shows that Malaŵi has followed a very businesslike "capitalist" method of running its state-owned enterprises on a strictly profit-earning basis. However, the failure of Madagascar's "socialist" policies of industrialization based on capital-intensive import substitution does not seem to be different from the failures of such policies in other developing countries—whether capitalist or socialist in their philosophical orientation.

The political economy of Malaŵi has been dominated by the figure of Dr. Banda, the Life President of the country since its independence. Pryor's account of Dr. Banda's influence on the theory and practice of Malaŵi's development policies provides some of the most illuminating and entertaining sections of his book. Given his considerable previous knowledge of, and experience with, communist economies, Pryor is also ideally suited to study the socialist policies of Madagascar. He is equally adept at conveying the febrile climate of the "socialist revolution" in Madagascar in the 1970s and depicting Dr. Banda's tough-minded pragmatic approach to economic policy, which went against the development theories in fashion in the 1960s. But he also shows and tries to explain why, despite a (seemingly) impressive record of growth, Malaŵi's success in alleviating poverty has been limited.

In sum, Frederic Pryor has succeeded in putting Malaŵi and Madagascar on the scholarly map.

Deepak Lal and Hla Myint
Series editors

Contents

Foreword   *v*

Acronyms and Abbreviations   *xiii*

Part I. Background   *1*

1. Introduction   *3*

   The Two Countries   *3*
   Theme: Economic System   *6*
   Theme: Economic Development   *9*
   Theme: Poverty, Equity, and the Distribution of Income   *11*
   Theme: Political Economy   *12*
   Approach   *15*
   Notes   *16*

Part II. Malaŵi   *19*

2. Background to the Economy of Malaŵi   *21*

   Geography   *21*
   Peoples   *24*
   Important Historical Developments   *27*
   Important Economic Institutions   *34*
   The Ideological Climate   *36*
   Chances for Success   *39*
   Notes   *40*

3. Economic Growth in Malaŵi   *43*

   The Record of Economic Growth   *43*
   The Crucial Role of Investment   *48*
   The Strategy of Economic Development   *53*
   Summary   *63*
   Notes   *63*

4. Agriculture: Property and Production Policies in Malaŵi   67

Agricultural Intensification and the Land Constraint   68
Small-Scale Agriculture   68
Production Policies for Smallholders: Capital-Intensive Projects   72
Production Policies for Smallholders: Labor-Intensive Approaches   77
Large-Scale Agriculture   80
Summary and Conclusions   92
Notes   92

5. Agriculture: Product and Factor Markets in Malaŵi   97

Product Markets   97
Agricultural Prices   101
The Credit Market in the Rural Sector   109
The Labor Market in the Rural Sector   116
Summary and Conclusions   120
Notes   121

6. Foreign Trade and the Balance of Payments in Malaŵi   124

Trade Orientation and Key Structural Characteristics   124
The Financial Side of Foreign Trade   132
Some Implications for Economic Growth   140
Some Implications for the Distribution of Income   141
Notes   142

7. Manufacturing and Transportation in Malaŵi   146

Manufacturing: Institutions and Policies   146
Price and Wage Controls   154
The Growth of Manufacturing Production   159
Transportation   162
Summary and Conclusions   165
Notes   166

8. The Government Sector in Malaŵi   169

The Size and Operation of the Government Sector   169
Tax, Expenditure, and General Budgetary Policies   172
Microeconomic Effects of Governmental Expenditures:
  Two Case Studies   180
Monetary Policy and the Financial System   186
Summary and Conclusions   189
Notes   190

Part III. Madagascar   195

9. Background to the Economy of Madagascar   197

Geography   197
Peoples   200

Historical Developments 204
Important Economic Institutions 210
The Ideological Climate 212
Chances for Success 214
Notes 215

10. Economic Growth in Madagascar 219

The Record of Economic Growth 219
The Crucial Role of Investment 225
The Strategy of Economic Development 229
Summary 237
Notes 238

11. Agriculture: Property and Production Policies in Madagascar 241

Extensive Agriculture and the Land Constraint 241
Small-Scale Agriculture 242
Production Policies for Smallholders: Capital-Intensive Approaches 245
Production Policies for Smallholders: Labor-Intensive Approaches 247
Large-Scale Agriculture 253
Summary and Conclusions 256
Notes 257

12. Agriculture: Product and Factor Markets in Madagascar 261

Product Markets 261
Agricultural Prices 267
The Credit Market in the Rural Sector 276
The Labor Market in the Rural Sector 280
Summary and Conclusions 282
Notes 284

13. Foreign Trade and the Balance of Payments in Madagascar 287

Trade Orientation and Key Structural Characteristics 287
Trade Policies 292
The Financial Side of Foreign Trade 296
Some Implications 304
Notes 305

14. Manufacturing and Transportation in Madagascar 308

Manufacturing: Institutions and Policies 308
Price and Wage Controls 316
The Growth of Manufacturing Production 318
Transportation 320
Summary 324
Notes 325

15. The Government Sector in Madagascar   328

The Size and Operation of the Government Sector   328
Tax, Expenditure, and General Budget Policies   330
Microeconomic Effects of Governmental Expenditures   336
Monetary Policy and the Financial System   342
Summary and Conclusions   344
Notes   346

Part IV. Broader Considerations   349

16. The Distribution of Income in Malaŵi and Madagascar   351

The Structure of Income   352
Wages   356
The Overall Distribution of Income   361
Poverty   365
Equity   370
Notes   371

17. Explorations in Political Economy   377

Ideology Revisited   378
Economic Interests and Governmental Policies   384
Economic Development and Income Distribution   396
Notes   399

Appendix   403

A. Land Tenure in Malaŵi and Madagascar   403
B. Foreign Trade Patterns in Malaŵi and Madagascar   413
C. The Road Network in Malaŵi and Madagascar   418
D. The Size of the Government Sector in Malaŵi and Madagascar   419
E. Additional Source Materials for Chapter 1   420
F. Additional Source Materials for Chapter 3   422
G. Additional Source Materials for Chapter 5   423
H. Additional Source Materials for Chapter 9   429
I. Additional Source Materials for Chapter 16   430

Bibliography   437

Index   459

Acronyms and Abbreviations

ADD	Agriculture development division (Malaŵi)
ADMARC	Agricultural Development and Marketing Corporation (Malaŵi)
AREMA	Advance Guard of the Malagasy Revolution (Madagascar)
BNM	Banque nationale malgache de développement Madagascar)
BTM	National Bank for Rural Development (Madagascar)
c.i.f.	Cost, insurance, freight
CFA	Communauté Financíere Africaine
CMEA	Council of Mutual Economic Assistance (East European economic agency)
CNAPS	Caisse nationale de prévoyance social
CV	Coefficient of variation
DA	Development area (Malaŵi)
DGP	Direction générale du plan (Madagascar)
EEC	European Economic Community
FAO	UN Food and Agriculture Organization
FIDES	Fonds d'investissement pour le développement économique et social (French foreign aid agency)
FMG	Malagasy franc
FNUP	Fonds national unique de préréquation (Madagascar)
FOFIFA	National Center of Applied Reseach for Rural Development (Madagascar)
GDP	Gross domestic product
GOPR	Groupement opération productivité rizicole (Madagascar)
ICOR	Incremental capital-output ratio
IISS	International Institute of Strategic Studies
IMF	International Monetary Fund
INSRE	Institut national de la statistique et de la recherche économique (Madagascar, now called Banque des donnés de l'état)
ISNAR	International Service for National Agricultural Research
LLDP	Lilongwe Land Development Program (Malaŵi)

xiii

MCP	Malaŵi Congress Party
MTIT	Ministry of Trade, Industry, and Tourism (Malaŵi)
MK	Malaŵi kwacha
MYP	Malaŵi Young Pioneers
NAC	Nyasaland African Congress
NRDP	National Rural Development Program (Malaŵi)
NSO	National Statistical Office (Malaŵi)
OCAM	Organization commune africaine et malgache
OECD	Organisation for Economic Co-operation and Development
OMNIS	Office militaire national des industries stratégiques (Madagascar)
OMPIRA	Office militarie pour la production agricole (Madagascar)
OPR	Opération productivité rizicole (Madagascar)
ORSTOM	Office de la recherche scientifique des territoires d'outre-mer (French government institution)
PADASM	Parti des deshérités de Madagascar
PSD	Parti social démocrate (Madagascar)
RENAMO	National Renewal of Mozambique
SDR	Special drawing rights (of the IMF)
SINPA	Société d'intérêt national des produits agricoles (Madagascar)
SMIG	Salaire minimum interprofessional garanti (minimum wage in Madagascar)
SMOTIG	Service de la main d'oeuvre pour les travaux d'intérêt général (Madagascar)
UDECMA-KMPT	Union de Démocrates Chrétiens de Madagascar (political party)
UNESCO	United Nations Educational, Scientific, and Cultural Organization
UNICEF	United Nations Children's Fund
VONJI-ITM	Popular Support for National Unity (political party in Madagascar)
WHO	World Health Organization

I Background

1 Introduction

Malaŵi and Madagascar are two nations in southern Africa with roughly similar economies: small, poor, and predominantly agricultural.[1] In the popular press in Europe and America the two nations often serve as leading examples respectively of "Afro-capitalism" and "Afro-communism." Such labels are misleading, but they do point out that these countries have followed very different economic policies. In some respects their economic performances have also differed; for instance, from 1960 through 1986 per capita gross domestic product (GDP) increased at a moderate rate in Malaŵi but decreased in Madagascar. In other respects their economic outcomes have been similar; in the same quarter-century, income differentials appeared to widen and poverty seemed to increase in both countries, but especially in Malaŵi.

This analytical economic history of the two nations investigates three basic questions: What economic policies did the two nations follow? Why did they adopt different economic policies? How did these policies influence economic growth and income distribution? Although their colonial periods strongly influenced subsequent economic developments in these two countries, I focus primarily on their postindependence periods from the early 1960s through 1986.

The Two Countries

Malaŵi and Madagascar lie about 1,000 kilometers (620 miles) apart and, as shown in the map on the frontispiece, face Mozambique from the west and the east. The data in table 1-1 indicate that the two nations have roughly similar populations, although Malaŵi has only about one-sixth the area of Madagascar.

Malaŵi, formerly called Nyasaland, was a British colony until early in 1964; from 1954 to 1964, however, it was administered as part of

Table 1-1. Selected Social and Economic Indicators

| | | | Weighted averages ||
Indicator	Malaŵi	Madagascar	31 low-income nations[a]	19 industrialized nations
Population				
Population, 1980 (millions)	6.0	8.7	16.5	37.6
Average annual population growth, 1960–86 (percent)	2.9	2.4	2.5	0.9
Gross domestic product				
Per capita GDP, 1980 ("international dollars")	417	589	562	9,420
Average annual growth of per capita GDP, 1960–86 (percent)[b]	1.6	-1.1	1.0	3.3
Agriculture				
Land used for crops per capita, 1988 (hectares)[c]	0.24	0.25	0.27	0.51
Share of GDP originating in agriculture (percent)	37	36	45	4
Foreign trade				
Exports of goods and nonfactor services as percent of factor price GDP, 1980	30	15	14	20
Average annual change in commodity terms of trade, 1960–84 (percent)[d]	-2.5	-0.3	-0.8	-0.3
Social indicators				
Infant mortality per 1,000 live births, 1980[e]	176	120	130	11
Population per physician, 1980[f]	28,805	9,235	15,846	554
Students in school as percentage of age group, 1980				
Primary	69	100	70	102
Secondary	16	22	19	89

a. The thirty-one low-income nations exclude China and India but include Malaŵi and Madagascar.
b. The separate growth data for Malaŵi and Madagascar are calculated by fitting exponential trends to the data; for the other countries the trends are calculated from endpoint data.
c. For Malaŵi and Madagascar the land data refer respectively to 1978 and 1980.
d. For changes in the terms of trade, the data include only 1967 through 1984.
e. The mortality data for Malaŵi refer to 1977 rather than 1980; for Madagascar, the infant mortality rate increased to roughly 150 by 1985.
f. For Malaŵi the data on physicians include clinical officers.
Source: Appendix, section A of this volume; Pryor (1988a) and (1988b).

the ill-fated Central African Federation of Rhodesia and Nyasaland. Hastings Kamuzu Banda, a former medical doctor who led the struggle for independence, has governed the country since it achieved independence in 1964. He is also the head of the country's only political party.

Madagascar was a colony of France and became fully independent in 1960. Since that time it has experienced several abrupt changes of government. From 1960 to 1972 Philibert Tsiranana, a former teacher and government administrator, was head of state; his party, the Social Democratic Party, was the dominant political force. In early 1972 a military coalition forced him to cede power, and a three-year transition government followed. In 1975 the military appointed Didier Ratsiraka, a former naval officer and diplomat, as president. After forming his own political party, the Advance Guard of the Malagasy Revolution (AREMA), he has won three elections and has served as president since 1975. Madagascar adopted a new constitution at the end of 1975, and the Ratsiraka government is now called the Second Republic. It has been officially recognized by the Soviet Union as a country with a "socialist orientation, " one of the few so designated in Africa or among former French colonies. It is also one of the few nations with this designation that has had a functioning multiparty system throughout most of the period since independence.[2]

The economies of Malaŵi and Madagascar have many similarities. Both share roughly the same climate. Both are overwhelmingly rural—considerably more than 80 percent of their labor forces are engaged in agricultural pursuits, and agricultural products constitute the bulk of their exports. Neither has very much arable land in relation to its population.[3] Interindustry linkages within each country are not extensive, and both nations are highly dependent on imports of capital equipment, consumer goods, and raw materials. Both nations are poor in human and physical capital, technology, and economically exploitable mineral wealth. On many lists, both number among those 10 percent of nations that have the lowest per capita incomes.

The two nations differ substantially in several important respects. Malaŵi is landlocked, while Madagascar is an island. Malaŵi has a much higher population density and richer soil; over time its farm sizes have decreased and its agricultural production methods have intensified. Madagascar has a relatively low population density, and the quality of its soil is much poorer; over time its farm sizes have increased as poorer land has been brought into production. The two nations also differ with regard to foreign trade, which has represented a much higher ratio of total production in Malaŵi than in Madagascar. Moreover, the former has experienced more adverse external shocks during the last few decades, as reflected in a decline in the commodity terms of trade.

6 *Malaŵi and Madagascar*

The few social indicators for the two countries in table 1-1 also reveal wide differences. Infant mortality was much higher in Malaŵi than in Madagascar; this rate increased in Madagascar and fell in Malaŵi, however, so that by the mid-1980s these mortality indicators probably ranged from 150 to 160 per thousand live births in both countries. Malaŵi has fewer physicians per capita and also a lower enrollment rate in the educational system. Social indicators concerning overt interethnic conflicts are not available; nevertheless, such difficulties do not appear severe in either nation. From such a brief review we might conclude that Malaŵi has a greater "economic orientation" and Madagascar, a greater "social orientation." This judgment would be premature, however; in the following chapters, I show that it can only be accepted after considerable modification.

The two countries have had rather different colonial experiences. Malaŵi was a poorer nation, and its conditions at independence were less favorable to economic development than those in Madagascar. In recent decades, however, the levels of per capita production in the two nations have converged. Some evidence suggests that Malaŵi's aggregate economic growth is somewhat overstated, while Madagascar's actual decline may not be as great as the numbers suggest.[4]

A major problem in analyzing the two countries' economies is the relative lack of basic statistics and of previous economic analyses on which to build. It has been necessary to calculate (or to recalculate) not only parts of the national accounts of both nations but also their income distribution, the commodity terms of trade (for Madagascar), indexes of relative agricultural prices, and a number of other crucial series. In many cases my evaluations of economic events in the two countries differ from those of others because of disagreements concerning these basic series. A discussion of the statistics and a description of the estimations are presented in Pryor (1988a) and (1988b).

Theme: Economic System

Official ideological statements about the economic systems of Malaŵi and Madagascar appear to have little correspondence with various measurements of the degree of socialism practiced in either country.

Economic Ideology

The ideological orientations of the two governments have been very different. Various pronouncements by the respective leaders of the two nations reflect these differences. For instance, Malaŵi's President Banda once declared,[5]

In so far as I know Africa, if they [Africans] have any economic system at all, it is not capitalism, it is not communism, it is not socialism, it is definitely not statism, but individualism. Here a man and his wife want first to have a hut of their own, a garden of their own.

In Madagascar official statements such as these appeared after 1975:

To realize a true independence, to attain our fundamental objectives . . . and the development of a just society where exploitation of man by man is banned . . . it is necessary to engage in a drastic, revolutionary transformation; to dynamite the old structures and dynamize a new economic order . . . (Ratsiraka 1975, p. 9)

In order to inculcate in the Malagasy people a new mentality, full of dynamism, of solidarity, and of self-sacrifice, many conditions must be fulfilled. The petty spirit, which only searches for private gain, will no longer be tolerated. (Madagascar, Direction générale du Plan 1977a, p. 18)

Such ideological pronouncements mask more than they reveal, because they draw our attention away from other—perhaps more important—ideological elements, such as nationalism, or more subtle factors such as preconceptions about the nature of governmental management and administration. Further, such pronouncements cannot be taken at face value but require us to determine whether the underlying reality corresponds to such sentiments and also to understand why the official ideological positions have taken their particular directions.

Structural Indicators of the Economic System

According to the data presented in table 1–2, public ownership (as revealed by the share of the total labor force working in facilities owned 50 percent or more by the government) is somewhat higher in Malaŵi than in Madagascar, although the reverse is true if agriculture is omitted. The situation in the modern sector, however, is more complex because the definitions of this sector are somewhat different in each country. In any case, the well-publicized nationalizations and expropriations in Madagascar during the mid- and late 1970s brought public ownership only slightly above the level in Malaŵi, which had experienced a much quieter growth of the public sector.

Table 1-2. Indicators of the Size of the Public Sector

	Percentage of total labor force		Percentage of modern sector[a]	
Sector	Malaŵi 1977	Madagascar 1980	Malaŵi 1977	Madagascar 1980
Economically active in the public and parastatal sectors[b]				
Agriculture	2.6	0.8	32.3	51.9
Mining and manufacturing	12.1	28.0	29.9	54.6
Utilities	65.9	70.2	100.0	70.2
Construction	16.1	9.1	32.9	11.4
Transportation and communication	58.6	27.8	82.6	70.9
Trade and tourism	30.6	13.9	75.9	48.3
Banking and finance	94.5	100.0	63.2	100.0
Other services	45.4	71.1	82.2	79.5
All sectors	6.3	5.3	46.8	63.7
Nonagricultural sectors	26.6	37.7	61.4	66.1
Public expenditures, 1970–82[c]			Malaŵi	Madagascar[d]
Current government expenditures as percentage of GDP			17.2	14.6
Central governmental gross fixed capital investment (excluding parastatals) as percentage of GDP			11.0	5.4
Governmental gross fixed capital investment (excluding parastatals) as percentage of total gross fixed capital investment			47.7	33.9

a. The modern sectors consist of all wage and salary earners included in the governmental surveys of the labor force. They are defined according to legal and statistical criteria that are not completely comparable in the two nations.

b. Estimates of employment in the public sector as a percentage of economically active are quite rough for both countries, and the sectoring principles in the two countries are somewhat different. For Malaŵi employment in the state sector includes the statutory enterprises, the parastatals, and Press (a company owned by the president but technically belonging to the state).

c. GDP data are in factor prices in Malaŵi and in market prices in Madagascar.

d. These public investment data for Madagascar include some small estimations.

Source: Pryor (1988a) and (1988b), section K; and tables 8-1 and 15-1 of this volume.

Another important structural element of the economic system is the relative importance of government expenditures. In this respect Malaŵi appears to have a more important public sector than Madagascar, as measured both by current government expenditures as a share of GDP and by the direct share of investment through the government budget.

These kinds of comparisons lead us to conclude that such terms as "socialism" or "capitalism" do not describe the structure of the economic system of either country very well; for this reason, this study seldom uses them. The official ideologies of Malaŵi and Madagascar have, however, strongly influenced the economic policies each nation has adopted. In this important sense the study of their economic systems reduces to an analysis of the goals of economic development and the means selected to achieve such goals.

Theme: Economic Development

The analysis of economic development focuses on investment, production, and foreign trade strategies. The relative simplicity of the economic structures of the two countries means that most of the prominent models, such as economic dualism, tell us little that we could not learn more directly.

Investment Strategy

From a narrow technical standpoint, two facts may explain the differences in economic growth in the two countries: Malaŵi has had a much higher average rate of investment than Madagascar, and it has been able to obtain a higher increment of production per unit of investment.

The differences in investment ratios are traceable to several underlying factors, including differences in the degree to which the two governments have been willing to tax their populations to finance investment and in the degree to which parastatal enterprises have served as a source of investible funds or as a target for government subsidies.

The differences in production per unit of investment have been due in large measure to the differences in the two governments' investment strategies and to the methods they have used to administer those policies. The Malaŵi government has attempted an incremental approach, with a great deal of emphasis on investment in the rural sector. It has also tried—with limited success—itself to invest and also to encourage private investment in highly labor-intensive projects. Madagascar started out with an investment strategy roughly similar to Malaŵi's, but by the mid-1970s the Ratsiraka government changed the orientation, placing a much larger share of government investment in the urban sector and in highly capital-intensive manufacturing projects. In the late 1970s the government also attempted a big push through its "invest-to-the-hilt" program. The choice of investment projects, however, was often haphazard.

Production Strategy

Both governments pursued a series of policies to influence the structure and quantity of production. Because market elements are very important in both economies, governmental policies for setting prices and import quotas have been crucial. Although price controls and different systems of import controls have existed in both countries, these measures have been much more intrusive in Madagascar than in Malaŵi. Direct government subsidies or indirect types of assistance, such as bank loans to companies operating at a loss, have been more consequential in Madagascar.

A particularly important pricing decision concerns the relative prices paid to agricultural producers and the price they pay for goods from other sectors (the "internal terms of trade"). Higher relative prices of agriculture encourage investments in the agricultural sector for both domestic and foreign markets. In Malaŵi these internal terms of trade have been roughly constant for production by smallholders (peasants and others with rights to farm small plots of land) and have followed world market prices for estate production. In Madagascar the government set these internal terms of trade at a roughly constant level for both estate and smallholder production until the mid-1970s to the mid-1980s, when it lowered relative agricultural prices.

Each government has also pursued a variety of other policies to influence production. Given the overwhelming importance of agriculture in the two nations for both aggregate production and exports, I devote much more analytical attention to production policies in the rural than in the urban sector and to such issues as the relative stress placed on collective agriculture (for example, estates, state farms, and cooperatives) as opposed to individual agriculture and a variety of other agricultural issues, including land tenure policies, the types of credit arrangements offered to farmers, and agricultural extension work.

Foreign Trade Strategy

Until the early 1980s the Malaŵi government attempted to maintain an exchange rate that would keep the balance of payments in equilibrium, and it also strongly encouraged estate production. As a result Malaŵi's exports have grown faster than domestic production. The government also maintained relatively low import tariffs on manufactured goods and imposed few quantitative restrictions. In these important ways it can be said to have had an export-oriented growth pattern. The Madagascar government, in contrast, has pursued a policy of import substitution. It has expressed the desire to reduce its external dependency and has strongly emphasized the necessity of producing once-imported goods at home. From the early 1970s to the mid-1980s the currency was overvalued, and the government showed considerable reluctance to devalue. Import restrictions, both import tariffs and quantitative controls, were extensive. As a result of these policies, foreign trade has increased at a slower rate than aggregate production, and domestic manufacturing experienced considerable surplus capacity because of its inability to obtain needed inputs from abroad.

Theme: Poverty, Equity, and the Distribution of Income

The most important cause for the apparent increase in income inequality in both countries seems to have been a widening of income differentials in the rural sector among smallholders. Neither government intended such results. These income trends have also had quite different underlying causal factors in the two countries, springing from the particular set of agricultural production policies that each has pursued and the basic land tenure arrangements. The transfer of labor from the poorer agricultural to the richer urban sectors, a mechanism Simon Kuznets posited to result in greater income inequality during the course of economic development, was not very important. Counteracting forces—especially the narrowing income gap between the urban and rural sectors in both countries—have not been sufficiently strong to offset widening income differentials in the smallholder sector.

In both countries most of the impoverished live in rural areas, and the increasing poverty must be tied to agricultural policies. Several of the social indexes reported in table 1-1, particularly the high rate of infant mortality, give some indication of the poverty problem in an absolute sense; in Madagascar this rate was increasing in the 1980s. In a relative sense, poverty has increased in both countries, because average real rural incomes have remained roughly the same in both countries, while the rural income distribution has become increasingly unequal.

In this study I discuss the problem of equity primarily in terms of intergroup, rather than intragroup, differences. The topic is difficult because equity has both objective and subjective aspects. In an objective sense, differences in trends in average incomes between certain socially significant groups (for example, regional groups, ethnic groups, or occupational groups) could indicate whether income differentials are widening or narrowing. The people involved, however, may judge the fairness or unfairness of their incomes on quite different criteria such as how far they are above some socially defined minimum. How the populations of the two nations actually perceive equity is difficult to know. Public opinion data, analyses of these topics in the mass media, or other types of public discussion on the matter are not readily available for either country, especially since the early 1970s. I try, however, to bring in certain qualitative information about riots and other political manifestations that appear to relate to equity questions.

Theme: Political Economy

Political economy focuses on the causal forces underlying the choice of particular economic policies. The "old" political economy deals particularly with the role of historical forces, cultural factors, and ideology, while the "new" political economy focuses more on the interaction of important groups (including the government itself) in maximizing their self interests. Both types of approaches are useful for analyzing either market or nonmarket processes, and I draw upon both because neither is sufficient alone to explain the given facts. Several types of problems arise, however, in carrying out such a research agenda.

A key aspect of the political structure of both Malaŵi and Madagascar is their relatively high degree of centralization, albeit of a rather different kind in each country. A brief glance at certain governmental parameters of the two countries may provide some appreciation of the analytical problems that arise. In a formal sense Malaŵi has preserved many of the forms and institutions of the "Westminister model" of government, which in some cases might lead to political decentralization. The constitution also specifies recognition and preservation of the institution of chieftaincy (that is, local authorities of particular ethnic groups). The minutes of the Parliament indicate, however, that debate does not include very diverse points of view. Further, the constitution specifies two extremely important centralizing elements—a single-party state and lifetime tenure of the first president as head of both the government and the single party.

Actual political centralization in Malaŵi is much greater than the formal structure would suggest and is best encapsuled by the "four cornerstones of the government" enshrined in the constitution: unity, loyalty, obedience, and discipline. President Banda's own analysis of his situation provides more insight into the situation:[6]

> I am the boss here. Why beat about the bush? I am the boss. I am responsible for this country, the welfare of the ordinary people in the villages, men and women, boys and girls. Whatever the rules and regulations, practices and usage, etiquette in other countries . . . whatever the etiquette between the officials and politicians, between Permanent Secretaries and their Ministers, whatever the usage in other countries—not here, not here! I am the boss. I am responsible. If anything goes wrong, it's not my Permanent Secretary who is going to be blamed. Therefore, when the opinions of the officials on any subject conflict with my own opinions, my opinions should

always prevail. Any official who does not like that can resign at any time. And that has been my policy all through.

A leader ... who depends on others, even his own officials or outside experts, is a prisoner. And I never want to be a prisoner on any subject, not one. I accept advice from my so-called experts, so-called advisers, so-called specialists only when their advice agrees with my own ideas and not at any other time.

In Madagascar the situation has been rather different. In the First Republic, from 1960 to 1975, the highly centralized French prefectoral system, which the colonial government had installed originally, was enshrined in the constitution. The constitution also provided for a multiparty system, however. During the Second Republic (from 1976 onward) this particular paragraph was dropped from the constitution to further the president's apparent goal to have a single-party state.[7] Further, the constitution of the Second Republic declares that no citizen has the right to oppose the state in its construction of a socialist order (article 14) and guarantees such rights as freedom of the press and assembly only when exercised in conformity with the objectives of the socialist revolution (article 28). The basic administrative principle of the government is specified as "democratic centralism, " which is defined as permitting freely elected local governments to regulate their own affairs and send up suggestions for policy at a higher level, although "the decisions of superior organs are obligatory for the subordinate organs." The prefectoral system of local government was dismantled and a new system was installed, which was based on the *fokonolona*, a traditional self-governing local assembly.[8] Although this was declared to be a step toward decentralization, the principle of democratic centralism would apply to all these local units of government as well.

In a very real sense, however, Madagascar has much less political centralization than this formal institutional evidence might imply. Although the president and his AREMA party profess a Marxist ideology, it is not a vanguard party of the Leninist mold but more like a mass party. Further, a functioning multiparty system has continued to exist, and since 1975 five to seven parties have participated in the parliament (National People's Assembly). Two of these parties (VONJI-ITM and UDECMA-KMTP) do not appear to have a Marxist ideology. In addition, on some issues debate in the National People's Assembly is vigorous.[9] In 1982 the presidential election was contested, and the opposing candidate received roughly one-fifth of the total votes and almost half of those cast in the capital. Unlike in Malaŵi, the newspapers in Madagascar carry a certain amount of guarded criticism of both the conception and execution of various governmental policies. For example, during the 1986 debate in the National People's Assembly about the proposed five-year plan, newspapers reported vigorous criticisms from both the right and the left. Moreover, lower units of government, which appear in some ways to be able to evade the constraints of democratic centralism, have countermanded a number of the president's economic policies. In sum, although political centralization still seems considerable and provides an important explanation for certain developments in the economy, it seems in fact to be less effective than in Malaŵi.

Such centralization raises some interesting questions. For instance, how is political power maintained in the two countries? Why has Madagascar experienced more changes in political and economic policy than Malaŵi? And why did particular governments adopt certain critical policies such as the rural emphasis or, since 1975, the urban emphasis, the nationalization program, and the invest-to-the-hilt program in Madagascar?

All of these questions of political economy present some serious practical problems of research. Political centralization in itself usually impedes the flow of information about what the government is doing and how it has arrived at its decisions. The dialogue occurring in the formation of day-to-day economic policy is usually maintained within the confines of the governmental bureaucracy. Maneuvering of various groups influencing policymaking is difficult for an outsider to understand. Overt public opinion is difficult to ascertain except when spontaneous political manifestations occur. In a real sense "civil society" is stunted in the two nations. The political forces underlying certain key decisions affecting long-term economic policy are often more visible, however, and that is why this study emphasizes these longer term policies.

In a number of cases group preferences must be inferred from the activities of such groups. Further, the existence of certain political actors must be inferred from an analysis of what interests particular policies serve, even though no publicly discernible political group concretely espouses such policies. For instance, in neither country do rural and urban interests appear to be organized in a formal sense, although a struggle between them certainly exists. Rather, the process of formulating economic policy represents a struggle among people who for particular reasons have taken it upon themselves to represent such interests. In both countries, however, the smoke of battle is often too thick to identify exactly which groups and people are involved, so the analysis focuses on the beneficiaries rather than the participants. In this discussion of political economy, however, I try to guard carefully against hypostatizing such group interests into concrete organizations in the belief that "classes" act as unified political entities.

Approach

This book is organized into parallel studies of the two nations. Each begins with a chapter discussing the most important geographic, ethnic, historical, and ideological factors influencing the course of the economy. That is followed by a chapter focusing on aggregative growth. The next five chapters deal with microeconomic issues in the agricultural, industrial, governmental, and foreign trade sectors.

The penultimate chapter of the book analyzes income distributions in both countries. Such results are, of course, critical outcomes of the processes of making and implementing economic policy. At this point, the building blocks are in place for analyzing some crucial issues of poverty and equity.

The final chapter is a speculative venture in which I use the tools of the old and new political economies to draw deeper meaning from the experiences of the two countries. The comparison of these two concrete situations helps answer some crucial questions concerning the nexus between "growth and equity" that have particular relevance to the experience of other nations, and it avoids the airy generalizations found in much of the technical and popular literature on the topic.

This study is not an exercise in normative economics, and my purpose is neither to condemn nor to approve the various policies and actions of the two governments. The French adage, "To understand everything is to forgive everything" is wrong on two accounts: it implies an historic inevitability that does not actually exist, and it implies that judgments about facts can not be separated from judgments about values. The proverb should be rewritten, "To understand everything is to forgive nothing."

Although I make judgments about the relative success of various policies or projects, these are usually made in accordance with the criteria the governments themselves used for taking the particular actions, rather than on the basis of some independent value judgment of my own. My intention is neither to advise the leaders of these countries on which policies to follow nor to distribute responsibility for success or failure among particular people or groups. To argue that particular governmental policies were harmful does not imply that any government interventions in the economy at all are undesirable. The criteria for judgment lie in the types of measures selected and the ways they are implemented; the management capacities of all governments are limited and must be taken explicitly into account.

In sum, this study is an exercise in positive economics. The aim is to try to understand what happened and why and to explain why the goals of well-intentioned plans were not met and how the difficulties experienced in both countries contribute to our general knowledge of economic development. Above all, I try to focus attention on economic policies and their implications for economic growth and income distribution. A more thorough understanding of the connections between these phenomena may help to approach these problems in a way that will assist these two nations, as well as others, in achieving their national economic goals.

Notes

1. The diacritical mark in Malaŵi signifies a Bantu phoneme, which is pronounced roughly halfway between an English "v" and "w." The adjectival form of Madagascar is "Malagasy, " which is also used in this study as the collective name of the various ethnic groups inhabiting the island. These notes use only abbreviated references; full citations are to be found in the list of references at the back of the book. The manuscript was closed at the end of 1987, so only the most important events that followed could be reported.

2. Appendix, section E has a table of the political status of former French and British colonies.

3. Data on the arable land per capita are presented in table 1-1. In comparison with the factor endowment of other nations, as reported by Leamer (1987), both Malaŵi and Madagascar must be considered capital-poor and relatively land-poor nations.

4. An examination of the biases in the national account statistics of the two nations is found in Pryor (1988a) and (1988b).

5. President Banda's speeches are printed in separate folios, and the National Library in Lilongwe has a relatively complete collection of those delivered up until the late 1970s. The citation in the text and other similar sentiments come from his speeches of March 27, 1975, and September 21, 1975.

6. President Banda, speeches of March 11, 1975, and December 11, 1975. In recent years relatively little has been written about either ideology or politics in Malaŵi, but interesting insights are contained in Fyfe and others (1985) and Mtewa (1986).

7. Two key ideological documents of the Second Republic are Ratsiraka (1975) and Mara (1986). The first is enshrined in the constitution as the official ideological statement; the second is a semiofficial description of important developments of the ideology. The definition and application of "democratic centralism" later in the paragraph come from the former source (p. 38); the goal of the single party is stated in the second source (p. 18).

8. The *fokonolona* was an institution of governance in some of the Malagasy ethnic groups in the period before colonialism. Periodically and unsuccessfully the French colonial government tried to resuscitate and harness the *fokonolona* to carry out some of its local policies.

9. On rare occasions the National People's Assembly, which is numerically dominated by AREMA, has voted down a law proposed by the president. In 1987, for example, the Assembly rejected a bill establishing a school of administration separate from the university (which allegedly would have downgraded certain activities of the regional branches of the University of Madagascar). Considerable recent materials are available on party politics in Madagascar; these include Archer (1976), Chaigneau (1985), Covell (1987),

Mara (1986), and de Gaudusson (1985). The most exhaustive sources are Chaigneau (1981) and (1984–85). The nine volumes of his dissertation are available at the university library in Nanterre, a suburb of Paris; the trip is worthwhile because these dissertations provide an invaluable survey of Madagascar politics.

II Malaŵi

2 Background to the Economy of Malaŵi

In the mid-twentieth century the economy of Malaŵi (then called Nyasaland) was highly underdeveloped. The country had a low standard of living, a low level of technology, relatively little domestic manufacturing, inadequate transportation and communications, considerable illiteracy, and poor health conditions. Most of the population worked in agriculture. These unpromising conditions require some further exploration if we are to understand how this country, in the first quarter-century after its independence, was able to achieve a considerably faster rate of economic growth than that of most Sub-Saharan African nations.

Geography

Malaŵi is landlocked and small, with about the same area as Liberia, Guatemala, or Czechoslovakia.[1] In 1985 its population density was about 51 people per square kilometer, which was relatively high by African standards and roughly equal to that of northern Europe. Its major geographical advantages are a mild temperature, a relative abundance of rainfall, and a fairly rich soil. Its geographical disadvantages include a relative shortage of agricultural land, a lack of exploitable minerals, and high-cost transportation links with most of the outside world.

At independence Malaŵi was connected with the Indian Ocean by some rough roads leading eventually to the South African port of Durban, by a railroad to the Mozambique port of Beira, and by the Shire River connecting Lake Malaŵi with the Zambezi River, which in turn flows into the ocean; the Shire River is not completely navigable, however. The high cost of transportation to the coast has been a dominant factor in Malaŵi's economic history until the present day.

The climate of Malaŵi is hot and humid for long stretches of time, and this has given rise to various health problems for both humans and animals. Approximately 12 percent of the country is infested with the tsetse fly, so trypanosomiasis (sleeping sickness) occurs in these areas. Thus raising cattle is problematic, as was ox- or horse-drawn transportation during the early colonial period before railroads and trucks. Hookworm and bilharzia are also found, and malaria is endemic in most parts of the country lying below 1,500 meters (5,000 feet).

Roughly three-quarters of Malaŵi consists of a highland plateau about 750 to 1,350 meters above sea level. This land is suitable for growing tobacco, maize, tea, groundnuts, and coffee. Smaller areas include lowland areas around Lake Malaŵi and the Shire River and different mountainous areas. The varied topography, combined with considerable differences in rainfall in various parts of the country, permits cultivation of both tropical and subtropical crops.

On the average Malaŵi is well watered, having a mean annual rainfall of roughly 1,199 millimeters (47 inches). Year-to-year rainfall variation is slightly greater than in Europe and is among the most moderate in Africa. Thus agricultural catastrophes caused by drought do not often occur. About once every five years, however, cyclones from the Indian Ocean visit Malaŵi and cause considerable economic difficulties in the affected areas. The normal rainfall pattern is monsoonal, with most rain falling in the summer months, from December through March; double-cropping without irrigation appears infeasible. These marked seasonal fluctuations in rainfall have also increased difficulties in obtaining year-round supplies of drinking water, a factor that has led to quite varied population densities within given districts and also to some obvious health problems.

The soils are favorable for agriculture. The most common soils are latosols, which are reddish, friable, freely permeable, and slightly acid. On the plateau the soils are often thin and poor, but they can be enriched. The alluvial soils in the lake littoral area and the Shire valley are particularly desirable for crop production. By African standards Malaŵi soils are usually regarded as fertile, although regional differences are marked; generally, fertility appears to improve as one moves southward from the "dead north." The commonly employed hoe cultivation exposes soil to insolation and leaching, resulting in more decay of organic matter than is desirable. Furthermore, tropical rains falling on the unprotected soil cause excessive runoff and erosion, especially on the slopes. After two or three years of cultivation using traditional cropping practices, the soil may require twenty years or more to regain its fertility.[2] Authorities differ on the severity of such problems as erosion and soil depletion, but these phenomena are certainly very much less severe than in Madagascar.

Overall, about 30 percent of Malaŵi's land is suitable for intensive agriculture, another third is totally unsuitable without great advances in technique, and some of the remainder appears suitable for tree crops or occasional agriculture. Table 2-1 presents some supplementary data on land usage. Of greatest importance is the small amount of arable land per capita, about 0.24 hectares in contrast to 0.38 for Africa as a whole.[3] The potential for expanding agricultural land seems about exhausted, as witness the sharp decline in planted land per capita between 1964 and 1978. If Malaŵi wishes to increase agricultural production, only two major possibilities are available: to draw more of the land now fallowed into production, or to obtain more output per unit of land now farmed. Such intensification of production appears feasible. The staple of Malaŵi is maize, and in comparison to various maize-producing countries throughout the world, average land productivity in Malaŵi has been quite low—a function of the seeds and agricultural practices rather than of the fertility of the soil. Nevertheless, in many parts of the country the decline in farm size has not been offset by increasing productivity; this is a major cause for the increase in poverty.

Other than soil and rock for building materials, Malaŵi has few mineral deposits for commercial exploitation. Four coal fields have been located; although they contain coal of good quality, their depth, complexity of faulting, and in several cases their distance from transportation facilities have prevented large-scale commercial exploitation. Bauxite deposits in the southern region near Mlanje are extensive; although commercial firms have investigated these deposits for possible

Table 2-1. Land Use in Malaŵi, 1964 and 1978

Use	1964	1978
Total land area (thousands of hectares)	9,405.1	9,405.1
Customary land under cultivation[a]		
Total	n.a.	2,875.4
Actually planted	1,287.4	1,332.1
Estates		
Total	98.1	469.0
Actually planted	25.4	58.4
National parks, forest reserves	n.a.	1,883.0
Urban areas and infrastructure	n.a.	1,035.6
Nonarable land	n.a.	3,142.0
Total land area per capita (hectares)	2.483	1.647
Agricultural lands per capita	n.a.	0.586
Actually planted	0.347	0.244

n.a. = Not available.
a. Customary land includes land farmed by smallholders and other land held under traditional tenure arrangements.
Source: Pryor (1988b), table A-1.

investment, they have foreseen many problems in exploiting them, including difficulties in constructing and running a smelting plant, and these deposits remain untapped. Other mineral deposits have been found, but except for vermiculite and strontianite monazite, their export potential seems limited. As a result, the government has not invested much in this sector.[4]

Peoples

For most Sub-Saharan nations, including Malaŵi and Madagascar, charting the country's political economy requires an understanding of the interaction of various ethnic groups. Outwardly, interethnic relations in Malaŵi have been relatively calm and, by and large, have not adversely affected the stability of the government—always a critical factor in economic development. At independence, relative average incomes of various ethnic groups were fairly similar, so difficulties on this account did not arise.

Although Malaŵi's ethnic mix may appear varied, it is not by African standards.[5] As shown in table 2-2, the two largest ethnic groups, the Chewa and Nyanja, constitute somewhat more than 40 percent of the Malaŵi population. Both stemmed from the Maravi, the ancient tribe lending its name to the entire country. The ethnic diversity of Malaŵi has several features deserving brief comment. First, the country does not form any kind of ethnic unity. Because its borders, imposed by the British, cut across various ethnic groups in the region, most groups have ethnic relatives in other countries.

Second, many social differences exist among the various ethnic groups. Although agriculture plays a major role in the food supply of all, fishing and herding are very important among the Tonga and the Ngondi, respectively. Most ethnic groups are polygynous. Most have strong matrilineal clans (more technically, sibs) and matrilineal inheritance, but the Tumbuka and Ngonde have patrilineal clans and inheritance. In most (but not in all) ethnic groups, a newly married couple lives with the wife's relatives or the husband's matrilineal relatives. The traditional communities among the different ethnic groups also vary in structure and size.

Third, not many non-Africans live in Malaŵi. In 1964, when Great Britain gave up political hegemony over the country, British nationals and other Europeans constituted less than 0.2 percent of the population (in contrast with Northern and Southern Rhodesia, where Europeans constituted 1.9 and 4.8 percent of the population in 1964). During the colonial period, the British government also brought a number of workers from India into the colony as soldiers, many of whom remained as merchants. The nation can not be easily classified as a "white settler colony" or as a "white trading colony," because Indians dominated the commerce. Among other things, the small number

Table 2-2. Ethnic Groups, 1966, and Ethnic Origins of Cabinet Ministers, 1964 to 1983, Malaŵi
(percent)

Group	Population, 1966[a]	Cabinet ministers, 1964–83[b]
Chewa	28.3	29.5
Nyanja	15.3	3.3
Lomwe	11.8	6.6
Yao	11.2	16.4
Ngoni	9.0	11.5
Tumbuka	7.4	11.5
Sena	2.8	3.3
Tonga	2.0	8.0
Other	12.2	9.8
Total	100.0	100.0

a. These rough estimates of the ethnic proportions are based on adjustments made to the data on ethnicity from the Nyasaland Protectorate (1946) and to data from Malaŵi, NSO (1969) on languages spoken at home.

b. Ethnic origins of the cabinet ministers are calculated from service-years of cabinet membership; although some ministers hold several portfolios, they are only counted once each year. The "other" category includes members of smaller ethnic groups (including Europeans), members with mixed ethnic backgrounds, and those few cabinet members whose ethnicity could not be determined. The names of the members of the cabinet each year from 1964 through 1967 come from annual editions of *Statesman's Yearbook*; for 1968 through 1983, the names come from Legum and Drysdale (annual). Ethnic origins were identified for me by professional social scientists in Malaŵi.

of British in Malaŵi meant that Nyasaland did not receive the high volume of European investment in economic overhead that occurred in the Rhodesias. This lack of previous investment, in turn, was an important factor underlying the pessimism about Malaŵi's potential for economic development after independence.

The direct impact of ethnicity on the economy is difficult to assess. For instance, colonial administrators seemed to believe that the matrilineal family system was inimical to economic growth because men would never devote much time and effort to improving their farms if the land was not to go to their sons. This dubious belief perhaps tells us more about the British than about the Malaŵians. More sophisticated theories about the problem of ethnic influences on the economy—and vice versa—require specification of the time period under consideration, because the situation was in flux. Certainly after the entry of the British and contact with the world market, little could stop the social order from changing. The colonial government's revival of the chieftainships in 1933 was merely a method of strengthening colonial power through a system of indirect rule and did not serve to stop the forces of change.

An outside observer in Malaŵi senses a strong consciousness of ethnicity. Ethnicity does not mean tribalism, however, because the different ethnic groups are not centrally organized either in a governmental or a party structure. Ethnicity also does not mean "traditional values," which indicate indifference to economic forces, particularly those arising from the activities of the market. Many studies of supply elasticities indicate considerable sensitivity to price changes; sample surveys also reveal an "economic" orientation; and workers from Malaŵi enjoy a good reputation in neighboring countries as hard workers when the economic rewards are adequate.[6] These appear to be important factors underlying Malaŵi's economic performance after independence.

At the time of independence, roughly three-quarters of the population could understand the Chewa language, which was adopted as the national language in 1968. This has aided the nation-building process, because the country has not been greatly burdened with mutual incomprehensibility. Moreover, ethnic identification does not seem sufficiently strong to undermine immediate economic self-interest; for instance, experiments have revealed that tradesmen do not engage in price discrimination against other ethnic groups in favor of their own (Dean 1966, chapter 6). Certain data on intermarriage provide a more intimate indication of ethnic relations in Malaŵi; such data must be obtained primarily from sample surveys from urban areas because nationwide data are not available. For instance, in the area around Blantyre and Limbe—Malaŵi's largest urban area—a 1957 sample survey revealed that a considerable proportion of marriages, 41 percent, occurred between members of different ethnic groups (Bettison 1958).

On the level of day-to-day politics interethnic relations have been more difficult.[7] In Africa, ethnic arithmetic is a crucial political skill, and President Banda has been careful to balance his cabinet with members from different ethnic groups, as table 2-2 suggests. More detailed analyses of high-ranking civil servants, police officers, army officers, members of parliament, and the central executive of the Malaŵi Congress Party for a single year also show a rough balance of positions among the various ethnic groups. Ethnic factors were important in the realm of "high politics, " especially in the first decade after independence, and in the choice of a rural-oriented strategy of development. Nevertheless, property damage, investment uncertainty, or other such difficulties arising from interethnic struggles have not hampered Malaŵi's economic development.

The most overt interethnic frictions in Malaŵi (as well as in Madagascar) have concerned the Asians. In Malaŵi at independence, Asians—primarily Indians—accounted for somewhat less than 0.3 percent of the population, but they were particularly concentrated in various branches of commerce. During the 1970s a number of African countries took measures against Asians. The Malaŵi government was not immune to such currents, forcing the Indians to sell their houses and farms in the rural areas and to confine their economic activities and their residences to the three (later four) largest towns. No other ethnic group received this treatment.

Malaŵi's African population has always been predominantly rural. In 1945 less than 2 percent of the population lived in towns of more than 5,000 people; in 1966 this number had risen to 3.9 percent.[8] This rural preponderance, combined with the relatively low degree of tenancy in the rural sector, has meant that economic classes (defined either in the sense of differential access to the means of production or in terms of occupation) were not highly differentiated. Possibly a more important differentiating factor has been the spatially uneven distribution of the population: in 1966 the shares of the population living in the northern, central, and southern regions were 12, 36, and 52 percent, respectively. The population densities reflecting this uneven distribution were 18, 41, and 65 persons per square kilometer.

During the colonial period a considerable portion of the Malaŵi population, especially males, worked outside the country; this was another indication of Malaŵi's relative poverty. In 1960 roughly 14 percent of the economically active population over 14 years old worked abroad; by 1972 this proportion had reached almost 25 percent. During the mid-1970s the government took measures to reduce this flow, but until that time, more Malaŵians worked abroad than in the modern sector of their own country.[9]

The historical literature on Malaŵi contains considerable debate about how much such short-term emigration harmed or helped the country's economic development. Many observers have argued that such an exodus of males not only reduced the work force available in Malaŵi but also greatly harmed the family structure. Others point out that the matrilineal family structure in many ethnic groups permitted a wife to live with her family during her husband's absence and that the men returned not only with money useful for taxes, a dowry, or investment but also with some experience with the economic gains from hard work, a certain cosmopolitanism, a certain tolerance for the customs of others, and some appreciation of the benefits that the outside world has to offer. Equally important, these men brought home a receptiveness to ideas of nationalism that served to strengthen and broaden the base of the independence movement.

Important Historical Developments

A central political focus of the recent economic history of both Malaŵi and Madagascar has been a struggle to overcome the colonial past. Specifying the exact economic impact of colonialism in the context of the low initial levels of economic development is difficult, however.

Certainly neither of the two countries experienced the kind of imperial plundering the Spanish practiced in colonial Mexico or the Dutch in Indonesia, but in part this is attributable to the fact that neither Malaŵi nor Madagascar offered enormous economic gains for such predatory activities. Nevertheless, at the end of the colonial period, both countries manifested certain similar economic features found in most colonies: a dualistic economy, in which foreigners primarily owned the means of production in the modern sector; transportation and communication infrastructure mainly oriented toward facilitating foreign commerce; a pattern of foreign trade consisting of agricultural and raw material exports to the colonizing country and imports of manufactured goods from that nation; and great disparities of income between foreigners and the indigenous population.

British and French colonialism in Africa were very different in nature, however.[10] To the British, the "empire" was India, and many of the other colonies, especially in central Africa, represented a minor diversion; to the French, selected African colonies—including Madagascar—and Indochina were a major focus of political energies. To the British, the act of asserting sovereignty was the key activity in central Africa; to the French, trade and the *mission civilisatrice* were equally important. Wherever they could, the British relied on indirect rule in Africa, using the local chieftains and spreading their colonial administration very thin; the French, where possible, instituted a dense and centralized administrative apparatus. The British emphasized giving a relatively large number of people a rudimentary education; the French generally spread education less widely but gave a much more thorough (and French) education to those who passed through the system.

The British appeared to be economically less exclusive and allowed many noncolonial nationals to conduct business in their colonies; the French usually tried to obtain more exclusive dealings with the colonies. The British were often more socially exclusive than the French, holding out to the Africans the eventual goal of self-government—dominion status—so they could achieve political, though not social, equality. In contrast, the French had more direct contact with Africans and held out to them the goal of assimilation as French citizens if they could achieve an adequate level of French culture. Both colonizing countries usually created armies from their African subjects; however, British Africans saw relatively little military action in Europe beside English soldiers, while the French used their African forces in faraway places not only in maintaining order throughout their empire but also in fighting in Europe with French soldiers in World Wars I and II.

When the British granted independence, they generally lowered their involvement in their colonies on all fronts; in contrast, the French, after granting independence, tried to hold on politically, militarily, economically, and culturally. The major post-independence program of the British was the Commonwealth, a rather tepid affair noted for the sound of tinkling teacups. The post-independence projects of the French were much more extensive. The French Community included a trade and monetary bloc of countries, all using a common currency (the CFA franc); strong French technical aid and cultural missions; and military cooperation involving French soldiers garrisoned in many former colonies.

Such commonplace generalizations, while useful as a starting place for analysis, only partly explain why the outcomes of the decolonialization process have been somewhat different in the two sets of colonies. For example a much higher percentage of former French colonies have had Marxist governments, and military involvement in the governing of these nations has also been greater than in former British colonies (see Appendix, section E). Historians of comparative colonialism have not yet analyzed the exact historical roots of these and other differences between former French and British colonies. Many important differences between Malaŵi and Madagascar are founded in local circumstances.

A Brief Historical Survey of Malaŵi

Continuous contact with the West began only after 1859, when David Livingstone first visited Lake Malaŵi. In the succeeding three decades settlers from England and a number of Scottish missionaries came to the country. The latter played an extremely important economic role, setting up schools (especially in the northern region) and hospitals and also trying to improve agricultural conditions. Many enthusiastically advanced the notion that the country could become economically developed only by much greater agricultural productivity, an idea of great influence for the future.

In 1891 the British government declared a preemptive protectorate to counter Portuguese interests, suppressed the slave trade, and set up a colonial government. The British financed this colonial venture primarily by hut and poll taxes on the African population, although the short-run African emigration that occurred in response to these taxes ran contrary to the colonists' need to obtain labor for their domestic estates. Direct forced labor played a very minor role in colonial economic affairs.

The Nyasaland Protectorate (as it began to be called) did not flourish. The colonists found no minerals, and the high costs of transporting crops for export discouraged agriculture. Indeed, finding any suitable export proved difficult, and costly attempts were made with various crops such as coffee, before tobacco, tea, and groundnuts proved successful. In 1908, the colonial government attacked the transportation problem by constructing a railway connecting Blantyre, the colonial center, with Chiromo in the south. The intention was to circumvent the rapids on the Shire River so that goods could be shipped to the Zambezi River in Mozambique and thence to the Indian Ocean. Unfortunately, the level of the Shire fluctuates over a long cycle, and as the level of the river fell, the railway had to be further extended to the Zambezi. Transportation on the Zambezi raised other problems, and transshipment of goods across the Zambezi to the railroad on the other side of the river, which led to the port of Beira in Mozambique, was troublesome. By 1935 a railway bridge across the river was completed, allegedly the longest railway bridge in the world at the time.

The economic rationale of this very expensive railway line was questionable. Farmers in Nyasaland found the railway rates much higher than the rates for shipping by water. Also, dubious financial practices characterized a good deal of the decisionmaking regarding its construction. Although Nyasaland finally had a direct, albeit not completely reliable, connection to the ocean, the colonial government of Nyasaland was saddled with some very large debts. Because Great Britain expected colonies serving no important strategic purpose to pay for themselves—and Malaŵi had little strategic purpose after the Portuguese colonial expansion was halted—the colonial government had few remaining resources for health, education, the improvement of agriculture, or the construction of other social overhead capital. For instance, in 1948 the colony had only 8 kilometers (5 miles) of paved road.[11]

In 1924 Sir Charles Bowring declared that Nyasaland was really not suited for large-scale European agriculture; indeed, fewer than 500 British farmers lived in the colony at any one time.[12] Further, industrial development did not appear profitable, and the British introduced very little manufacturing into the country. They even did not pursue their interests in trade very aggressively, and, as the years went by, Asians—primarily from India—came to control more than three-quarters of the colony's wholesale and retail trade.

In sum, the Nyasaland Colony did not evoke much British interest or attention. In 1904 H. L. Duff, a prominent Britisher, observed that "There is perhaps at this day no British possession so little known to the British people" (cited in Mlia 1975), and this statement describes the situation in later years as well. Indeed, Nyasaland is mentioned so rarely in the *Cambridge History of the British Empire* that it could well have belonged to another country. Typical evaluations of British policy conclude that "The story of [Malaŵi's] underdevelopment is one of official neglect" (Pachai 1978) or that "During the colonial period the scope of colonial administrative policies in agriculture were extremely limited, as were the means by which support for change in agricultural practices and production could be mobilized" (Kadzamire 1977). To govern such a colony well or with consistent long-term policies was not imperative. According to one historian, British economic policy in the colony was characterized by "fitful vacillations, contradictory attitudes, and false starts" (Leroy Vail, in Rotberg 1983). I do not agree with some observers that British policies caused poverty in Malaŵi, because the level of development was very low before the British came; but they did little to alleviate the problem.

After World War II, the situation began to change as Great Britain initiated a belated effort to increase aggregate production in Malaŵi.[13] The colonial government and outside interests began to invest in Nyasaland, and from 1954 through 1963 (the earliest years for which consistent national accounts data are available) gross fixed capital formation averaged about 23 percent of the factor-price GDP.[14] Such funds were well spent, because the incremental capital-output ratio was slightly over 3 and the growth rate of GDP averaged about 4.6 percent a year. The government tried especially to encourage agricultural production, a policy complemented by high world prices for Malaŵian exports; from 1948 through 1963 gross crop production grew about 5.6 percent a year. Thus, Malaŵi began its existence as an independent nation with some momentum in economic development, although this important factor was not generally recognized or appreciated at the time.

Despite these efforts, at its independence Malaŵi was one of the poorest countries in the world. Per capita income was still very low. Although transportation links now included about 431 kilometers (268 miles) of paved roads and 470 kilometers (289 miles) of railroads, and other improvements had been made, few modern production techniques were used in manufacturing or agriculture. To obtain foreign exchange the nation was dependent on massive labor emigration and on the export of relatively few products—tea, tobacco, and groundnuts. With few important sources of internal savings, Malaŵi, like many other low-income countries, depended on capital from abroad to increase its fixed capital stock. The level of education was low, and health conditions were appalling.

The Land Question

The "land question" constituted the single most serious conflict of economic interests between Africans and Europeans (see Pachai 1978; and Rotberg 1965, pp. 1–24). A significant number of British colonists had arrived in Malaŵi before the establishment of the colonial government and, through various means, had obtained a large part of the available land; this meant that colonists initially had considerable power over the government. One of the poll taxes the government imposed on Africans was the *thangata*, which they could pay off by performing labor services for the Europeans. By the mid-1950s less than 7 percent of the African population—only those living on European estates—had to pay this tax, but it had become an important and hated symbol of colonialism.[15]

From 1930 onward the extent of European land holdings in Malaŵi fell dramatically as the political and economic situation changed. The high and increasing population density kept tensions over the land problem high throughout the interwar period, and in the aftermath of the Abrahams Report of 1946, the colonial government began to buy land from Europeans to turn it over to Africans. In 1948 land in the European freeholds amounted to 490,000 hectares (1.21 million acres), which was 5.2 percent of the total land area; by June 1954 this percentage had been reduced to 3.7 percent; and by June 1964, to somewhat less than 2 percent, while leaseholds (primarily held by Britishers) amounted to less than 1 percent (see Pryor 1988a, table A-3; and Pachai 1978, pp. 186–87). Almost all these foreign-owned estates were concentrated in the southern region of the country, where they occupied a considerable share of the land most suitable for some important export crops such as tea.[16]

In the years preceding independence the relative importance of African agriculture had been increasing and that of settler agriculture, decreasing. For instance, from 1948 through 1966 the estate-produced share of total gross crop production fell from about 23 to 14 percent and the share of total crop exports fell from about 45 to about 30 percent. At independence the total planted land of the estates was only about 25,000 hectares, although the total estate land was much larger. Such trends certainly did not provide any indication that a strengthening of the estates (albeit taken over and developed by Malaŵians) would prove a key part of the development strategy of Malaŵi in the future.

At independence roughly 87 percent of Malaŵi's land was held as "customary land" (formerly called African Trust Land). Although this land was owned communally, the chief or headman, in consultation with elders of the community, assigned it to individual families. These families had considerable security of tenure as long as they farmed the land, and few families were landless. Only 3 percent of the land was privately owned, and the remaining 10 percent was held as public lands (formerly called Crown Lands), which consisted in large part of forests. No significant African landlord class held either freeholds or leaseholds, and almost all private estates were European owned.

The Nationalist Struggle

Because Nyasaland had no national identity when the British conquered it, nationalism was not an important force in the colony for many years. Although the Chilembwe rebellion of 1915 had a considerable psychic impact on the British, it involved relatively few people. It did, however, indicate an underlying discontent with British rule, a sentiment fostered by the various native associations that began to form after 1911. An outgrowth of these native associations was the Nyasaland African Congress (NAC), founded in 1944 as the nation's first political party. On the surface, however, the political scene remained relatively quiet until discussion of federation with other colonies began.

For a variety of reasons the British fostered the Central African Federation between Nyasaland and the two Rhodesias, which lasted from 1954 to 1964. Almost all supporters of the federation claimed that the arrangement would offer all the countries involved very obvious economic benefits. They supplied little serious evidence to support this claim, however, and a careful analysis of the economic issues by Arthur Hazlewood (1967, pp. 185–291; and Hazlewood and Henderson 1960) demonstrated that the actual economic benefits of federation were small.

Africans in Northern Rhodesia and Nyasaland almost unanimously opposed the federation. They feared the introduction of racist policies into their countries, which—though not free of racial discrimination—had more liberal laws and attitudes than did Southern Rhodesia. To Nyasaland Africans such long-run political considerations were considerably more important than the immediate economic benefits of the fiscal subsidy of £2 million to £5 million—the equivalent of 4 million to 10 million Malaŵi kwacha (MK)—from the federation government in Nyasaland.

Within Nyasaland the NAC led resistance to the federation. Outside the country a strong opposing voice was that of Dr. Hastings Kamuzu Banda, a native of Nyasaland who had studied medicine in the United States and Scotland and who had practiced in London for many years before moving to Ghana. After a series of ineffective political actions against the federation, the fortunes of the NAC sank, its older leadership was discredited, and its younger leaders searched for an older man who could command the respect necessary to lead the movement. They invited Dr. Banda to return, and in 1958, at the age of 60, he came back to his homeland after an absence of forty years.[17]

Dr. Banda proved to be an effective organizer and a spellbinding orator, and he made a deep impression on the people as he toured the country speaking for a breakup of the federation and independence for Malaŵi. Although the party's leaders were primarily intellectuals who lived in the urban areas, Banda made great efforts to organize the party in the countryside. Both before and after Banda's return, the party recruited a number of traditional chiefs; further, Banda's message also impressed many smallholders, especially those who had worked abroad, and they provided considerable support to the party. When working in South Africa or Rhodesia, Nyasaland workers were often housed together, and this undoubtedly give them a certain sense of community, which they previously had lacked. Thus the party had both urban and rural members and developed a relatively broad base of popular support. The absence of strong ethnic divisions and the presence of a dominant language also aided the spread of nationalism. Some British policies, although well-meaning and often appropriate, were enforced in arbitrary and unpopular ways, which reinforced nationalist sentiments.

Political events moved quickly. In 1959 and 1960 the federation government imprisoned Dr. Banda for thirteen months, which only enhanced his reputation in Nyasaland. In 1961, in the first national election, the NAC, now renamed the Malaŵi Congress Party (MCP), swept the lower rolls (the election delegates specified for Africans). Moreover, MCP sympathizers captured several legislative seats in the upper rolls (for Europeans) as well. Dr. Banda assumed ministerial responsibilities for natural resources (which included agriculture) and local government. The British made some ineffective attempts to obtain African support—by doubling the minimum wage, for example—but opposition increased. After considerable agitation, Britain dissolved the federation on the last day of 1963, and in 1964 Malaŵi took its place in the world as an independent nation, with Dr. Banda as its first prime minister.

Malaŵi achieved independence without a civil war and with relatively little bloodshed, but it also had little experience with self-government and multiparty democracy. The high degree of centralization with which the MCP had won the battle was soon extended to the nation as a whole. In July 1966, when Malaŵi became a republic, the MCP, with Banda at its head, was officially recognized as the only legal political party. Furthermore, only party members could be members of the National Assembly. Important constitutional changes in 1971 designated Dr. Banda as Life President, further centralizing political power.

Important Economic Institutions

Nyasaland had a rudimentary governmental framework and a small civil service. Until shortly before independence, expatriates held all leading positions. The colonial government had relatively little control over the economy, especially because somewhat more than half of the protectorate's GDP originated outside the monetary economy. It pursued a grab bag of economic policies. Some, such as the relatively low import tariffs and the absence of export tariffs, were quite liberal; some amounted to little more than petty interference (as in trade); and still others, such as the policies pursued through the crop marketing board, had a certain impact on production.

The colonial government had produced two middle-term development plans that placed top priority on the construction of economic infrastructure. During the entire colonial period various administrators spoke of the necessity for food self-sufficiency in the nation, and in the period following the 1948–49 crop failure, the government enforced land conservation and certain "advanced" agricultural practices by fines and crop destruction. These unpopular practices played an important role in nationalist agitation. In the last development plan, transportation and agriculture received first and second priority, respectively, in the expenditure of development funds; the government never gave much attention to manufacturing.

The foreign sector was not large. Foreign ownership in agriculture was confined to the estates, which produced a declining share of gross agricultural output. Foreign-owned industrial enterprises accounted for about 56 percent of total manufacturing gross output, but this total was very small. Government ownership accounted for 6 percent of output, and private Malaŵian ownership accounted for 38 percent (Blades 1970). Most if not all of the private domestic share was either handicraft or was owned by Malaŵians of Asian descent. Foreign interests owned several commercial banks. Nyasaland had no central bank, and from 1954 to 1964 central bank functions were carried out in Salisbury, the capital of the Federation.

Markets were regulated and stunted. Rural factor markets (land, credit, or labor) were nonexistent or unimportant. Although the colony had no formal system of price controls, certain smallholder crops were marketed through crop export boards. The Native Tobacco Board, founded in 1926, and later the Maize Control Board and a Cotton Marketing Board had monopsonistic powers over exports of particular crops; in 1962 these three boards were consolidated into the Farmer's Marketing Board. Although ostensibly set up to reduce price fluctuations (a dubious claim discussed in chapter 5) they often served as a tool of the foreign-owned estates, one of the few interest groups with influence, against the smallholders. In other ways a variety of petty regulations hobbled retail and wholesale trade (see Wright 1955).

Labor unions were weak in Nyasaland, even though Malaŵians had played important roles in the formation of labor unions in South Africa and Northern Rhodesia.[18] Indeed, a strike led by Nyasaland workers had prompted the state of emergency in 1959 that led to the arrest of Dr. Banda and other political leaders. Nayasaland's first labor union was formed in 1949 (the same year that the first Employers Association was founded), and three more unions were started during the next decade. Nevertheless, competition among Malaŵians for jobs in manufacturing was considerable, and Malaŵi had no industries, such as copper mining in Zambia, from which an active labor union could squeeze extra-high wages.

Minimum wage legislation had been in operation in Nayasaland since the 1950s. For the modern sector various semigovernmental councils, organized according to industrial sector, oversaw wages. Shortly before independence, however, when the tea industry group recommended a considerable wage increase, they became "advisory councils."

The unions did not play a role independent of the NAC in the agitation for independence; indeed, the MCP later suspended two labor union members because they organized strikes and demonstrations without consulting the party leadership. Soon after independence the leaders of the unions were absorbed into the party or civil service, and MCP policies strongly influenced the unions. Top MCP leaders from all sides of the political spectrum—Dr. Banda as well as some of his opponents such as Dunduzu Chisiza, Henry Chimpembere, and Willie Chokani, the first Minister of Labor—were suspicious of labor unions and appeared to fear the emergence of a highly paid and protected group of urban workers. In such an environment labor unions remained small, and by 1967 fourteen unions represented only about 4 percent of the labor force. In Madagascar union membership was much greater.

The educational system was also quite underdeveloped, although roughly half of the children between the ages of six and eleven were in the first six grades of school, a somewhat higher percentage than in other British colonies. Partly, this may reflect the relative scarcity of Europeans in Nyasaland—Africans were frequently employed in jobs whites would have held in Rhodesia or Kenya.[19] The colonial government, however, neglected secondary education; it never established any institutions of higher learning as the French did in Madagascar. On the eve of independence, only about thirty-three Africans had completed a university education, although this may be an undercount.[20]

The Ideological Climate

The roots of nationalism in Malaŵi were relatively shallow. Although the process of independence served as a forge for nationalist ideology, nationalism in the postindependence period focused more on the battle for economic development than on the elimination of foreign influences. Ideological struggles concerning the "isms" were muted during the independence struggle; the postindependence period also saw little public debate about such matters. Much more important were subtler ideological forces concerning the relative roles of rural and urban sectors.

Nationalism

Nationalism can define itself in various ways. In Malaŵi the most important key for understanding such an ideological force is President Banda's strong belief that "You can not have true political independence without economic development."[21] As a result, Banda adopted a conciliatory stance toward the British, even during the struggle for independence. Since independence he has pursued close relations with any country, except Marxist regimes, that might grant Malaŵi aid to assist its development efforts.

The focus of nationalism on economic development has meant that the Malaŵi government has had few qualms about encouraging foreign trade. Until the late 1970s it maintained the tariffs at the low colonial rates; it placed few quantitative restrictions on trade; and it continued to encourage agricultural production and exports, especially from the estates.

Other implications of this particular focus of nationalism deserve mention. At independence Banda declared a policy to replace European expatriates in the government only with equally qualified Malaŵians. In August and September 1964 he faced a bitter dispute within his cabinet that included demands for an acceleration of the rate of indigenization of the government. Banda defeated the opposition; removed these dissident cabinet members, who represented the left wing of the party and who were soon in exile; and continued his policies of slow replacement of Europeans in the governmental bureaucracy.

Under Banda's interpretation, nationalism also did not imply rapid nationalization of foreign-owned assets. Although the Malaŵi government bought out the country's two foreign-owned commercial banks in succeeding years, it did not expropriate most foreign economic interests. Indeed, the government tried to encourage foreign investment and to take advantage of foreign expertise, especially because Malaŵi had too few educated Malaŵians in the early years of its independence to replace the expatriates.

Economic Philosophies

The linkage between colonialism and capitalism was weaker in Malaŵi than in many other newly independent nations because the colonial power did not play a dominant role in commerce or manufacturing. Furthermore, the few educated members of the Malaŵian elite remaining after the intraparty struggle in the fall of 1964 had, for the most part, attended English or American universities during a period when such ideological matters were not burning issues. A market economy was accepted as "natural." As Mtewa (1986, p. 34) dryly remarks, "Socialism, or any of its variations, never seemed to seriously preoccupy the thinking of the Malaŵi leadership before or after independence."

President Banda's economic philosophy has not greatly changed over the years, and statements he made in 1975 were similar to the views he held at independence. In addition to his views on individualism, he had strong ideas about property:[22]

> In Malaŵi we can not have capitalism of the American type where railways, airways, electricity and water facilities, the telephone and telegraph system are all in private hands, to say nothing of shops and industry. . . . On the other hand we could not have the communism of the Russians and the Chinese, where the state owns everything and people are not allowed to own anything at all, not even their own children. . . . So we have to have something midway. The government has to do certain things. Let the government through statutory bodies own the railway, airways, water, electricity. But the people must own their own land on which to have their own houses; people must be allowed to have shops, to have farms and estates.

Not all leaders of the Malaŵi Congress Party shared these sentiments. For instance, before his death in an auto accident in 1962, Dunduzu Chisize, a young colleague of Banda's and a rising star of the MCP, had written: "We pursue happiness by rejecting . . . individualism . . . and by emphasis on a communal way of life."[23] Many of the younger party leaders sharing these ideas were exiled after the intraparty struggle.

Of much greater importance than ideas about capitalism or socialism in themselves were ideas about the relative importance of the rural and urban sectors. President Banda has stated his basic orientation most forcefully: "I am from the village and my first duty is to help the villagers."[24] Among African leaders, Dr. Banda was one of the few who had scientific training and had very successfully pursued a career outside politics. Therefore, he was perhaps more aware of the gaps between the knowledge and skills at hand and those needed to administer a modern industrial system in his country.

Of course, one person can not provide the crucial ideological directions for an entire country. In a carefully argued essay, however, the historian Martin Chanock (in Page 1973, part I, pp. 27–35) noted that the Malaŵian government's emphasis on agriculture and on individualism represented a continuation of the basic ideas promulgated by the early Scottish missionaries, continued by the colonial government, and shared by many Malaŵians, especially those educated in the 1920s and 1930s.

The strong agricultural emphasis also did not go unchallenged, but the leading proponents of urban development and manufacturing, as well as those who were more inclined toward collectivism, were among the dissidents dismissed after the 1964 cabinet crisis. President Banda's long tenure in office has insured a continuity of his emphasis on rural development.

Thus, the dominant ideological beliefs in Malaŵi at independence account in an important way for Malaŵi's agricultural development path. Although other African nations, such as Madagascar, began with that emphasis, such singlemindedness over a period of a quarter-century has been almost unique in Africa. Certain parallels can be found, however, in the Côte d'Ivoire and in the ideas of Félix Houphouët-Boigny.

Chances for Success

Most observers did not give Malaŵi much chance for economic success when that nation became independent. Nyasaland was considered an "imperial slum" and was called the "Ireland of Central Africa—poor, scenic, and with a ready supply of exportable labour."

The skeptics certainly had good grounds for such an evaluation. The country started from such a low level of productivity that the long-run problems of achieving an acceptable level of economic development seemed insurmountable. Short-run problems were also frightening. In the first year of independence governmental finances were in desperate straits, with revenues covering only about half of the expenditures. Although investments in Malaŵi had been rising, domestic saving covered only about one-third of the addition to the capital stock. Many familiar with the nation spoke of its lack of economic viability and of the fact that President Banda was heading an "empty government" in a nation with an "empty economy" and a minuscule educated elite.

In evaluating the prospects for Malaŵi such observers overlooked the economic growth the country had been experiencing for more than a decade, the ideological climate that seemed favorable to development, the capabilities and vigor of Malaŵi's leadership, and the capacity of the population for hard work.

Dr. Banda did not promise his nation easy economic victories, and its early economic successes were quite unexpected to most. They gave his regime legitimacy and stability, however, which allowed it to achieve further economic successes—and further stability. During its first decade Madagascar had roughly the same economic successes but with opposite results. In part this was because initial expectations were very high and were not met and because the domestic political opposition to the government was able to point out the discrepancy between expectations and results in a credible fashion. As a result the Malagasy government lost legitimacy, political instability ensued, and economic decline followed when major economic policies were changed. The disadvantages of colonial neglect were quite apparent in Malaŵi, but the advantages of such neglect turned out to be more important in its economic development.

Notes

1. This section draws heavily upon Pike and Rimmington (1965); Pike (1968); and Kettlewell (1965). The population, area, and density comparisons with other countries are made with data from United Nations, *Statistical Yearbook 1982*. The rainfall data come from various issues of Malaŵi National Statistical Office, *Malaŵi Statistical Yearbook 1982*, p. 2, and cover twenty-seven weather stations for eleven years. Longer series for fewer stations are found in World Meteorological Organization (1971). The comparisons with other countries are made using the same methods presented in Pryor (1985b).

2. The estimate of twenty years' time for soil regeneration is given by Pike (1968), pp. 191 ff. Controversy exists concerning the severity of soil erosion and deforestation: see Kettlewell (1965) or Brunt (1983). Kettlewell, a colonial officer in charge of agriculture, particularly stresses the problem, while Brunt has a much less alarmist view.

3. The estimates of usable agricultural land are based on data presented in Pryor (1988a), table A-2, and represent a dramatic revision of oft-cited data from an earlier year. The data for Africa as a whole are calculated from Food and Agricultural Organization, *1979 Production Yearbook*, tables 1 and 3. These data provide only the roughest of comparisons because the FAO does not specify how it made its estimates. For Malaŵi and Madagascar, at least, the FAO data appear to be considerably off the mark.

4. Malaŵi, Office of the President and Planning (1988), chapter 7, presents a full assessment of the mineral potential. For 1987–96, the government plans to place only 0.5 percent of its total investment in the minerals sector.

5. For simplicity I am omitting the prefix "A" for the ethnic designations and the prefix "Chi" for the language designations in Malaŵi. One measure of ethnic diversity is by language, and Taylor and Hudson (1972), pp. 271–74, present some quantitative rankings. They put Malaŵi only in the 42.5 place (out of 136 nations) in their list of linguistic diversity. The most comprehensive survey of the various ethnic groups composing Malaŵi is by Tew (1950). For this discussion I draw upon Tew and also Murdock (1967).

6. A considerable number of studies dealing with price elasticities of supply or response to other economic incentives are cited in later chapters. Descriptions of ethnic characteristics, especially with regard to work, are often of a dubious quality, but the economic literature of the country frequently mentions the hard-working nature of Malaŵians; see, for example, Kings Phiri, "Production and Exchange in Pre-Colonial Malaŵi, " in Fyfe and others (1985), pp. 3–32, and Liebenow (1982). Brown (1970a) discusses a sample survey taken shortly after independence asking smallholders if they would work more or less if their wages increased; in various samples, 66 to 71 percent said "more," and the remainder said "the same."

Background to the Economy of Malaŵi 41

7. Vail and White (1984) provide a much deeper analysis of the role of ethnicity in modern Malaŵi politics. Although their ideas are interesting, the proper evidence for firm judgments is not yet available. The analysis noted in the text of the ethnic background of a wide range of government officials for a single year is by Joffe (1973), especially the table on page 392 and accompanying analysis.

8. The data in this paragraph come from Pryor (1988b), tables B-4 and B-5.

9. Somewhat conflicting sets of data on the Malaŵians working abroad are presented by Coleman (1973), table 4, and by Boeder (1974). The decline in Malaŵians working abroad in the middle and late 1970s from that in the early 1970s was due in part to the President's ban on work in South Africa in 1974 (modified a few years later to permit a small number of workers to accept such work) and from the return of Malaŵian workers from such countries as Zambia and Zimbabwe, which were experiencing economic difficulties during the 1970s.

10. Much interesting work on comparative colonialism and its later impact has been carried out; for example, see Gifford and Louis (1971), Asiwaju (1976), and Woronoff (1972). Considerable controversy has arisen about the overall differences of French and British colonialism, a dispute occasioned in part by the quite different geographical and historical situations of the colonies. Quantitative estimates of the relative rapacity of selected colonial regimes, as well as the quantitative importance of foreign nationals in various colonies are presented by Maddison (1990).

11. The datum on paved roads comes from a speech of the Governor General Glyn Jones in Jackson (1965), pp. 352–59. For the railroads, Leroy Vail has a detailed discussion in Palmer and Persons (1977), pp. 365–95, presenting an interesting case study in which the interests of settlers and the colonizing government were at odds. A more general analysis of this conflict is presented by Neale (1984). Information on relative water and rail transportation rates is provided by Pachai (1978), p. 23.

12. Mlia (1975) places the highest number of European farmers at 400 in 1921; this appears to have been exceeded in 1956. The information about wholesale and retail trade also comes from Mlia. The statement by Bowring is cited by Barker (1961).

13. According to the last Governor General, "[N]o appreciable sums of money were made available [by the Colonial government] for general development until after the end of the Second World War" (Glyn Jones, in Jackson 1965).

14. All data for this paragraph come from Pryor (1988b), section E. The growth rate statistics are obtained by fitting exponential curves to the various series. To minimize the impact of weather variations, the incremental capital-output ratio is calculated from the change of GDPs of the initial and end years predicted by the regression equation for GDP. The datum for gross crop production represents an estimate and must be accepted with caution.

15. The number of families under the *thangata* system is discussed by Thomas (1985) and by John Iliffe, in Fyfe and others (1985), pp. 243–92.

16. The largest single European estate was a huge area in the north. This estate comprised 1.1 million hectares (2.7 million acres), which amounted to

12 percent of the total land in the protectorate. It was originally held by the African Lakes Corporation and later by the British South Africa Company. During the 1920s this deed was challenged, and in 1930 this entire estate reverted to customary (African Trust) land.

17. This estimate of President Banda's age is based on his school records from the Wilberforce Academy in Xenia, Ohio.

18. This paragraph draws on materials presented by Joffe (1973), Chipeta (1976b), and Short (1974).

19. John McCracken, in Ranger (1968), p. 191. Data on enrollment rates for 1960 can be found in World Bank, *World Development Report 1983*, pp. 196–97.

20. The number of university graduates is often cited but can be disputed. From Malaŵi, NSO (1984), vol. 1, p. 162, we can calculate that roughly 350 people had some university education. How many of these were Africans or how many graduated is unclear, however.

21. The quotation comes from my interview with President Banda, April 22, 1987, but the same idea is expressed in different ways in scores of his published speeches.

22. These quotations are drawn from President Banda's speeches of March 27 and September 21, 1975, on deposit in the National Library in Lilongwe.

23. Chisiza (1963); another statement can be found in his article in Jackson (1965), pp. 1–18.

24. The quotation comes from the interview cited in note 21.

3 Economic Growth in Malaŵi

This chapter analyzes the most important macroeconomic indicators and the development strategy of Malaŵi in order to provide a framework for the detailed examination in the succeeding chapters of the government's economic policies. Four major characteristics stand out. First, Malaŵi had a moderately high rate of growth of per capita GDP from the time of its independence in 1960 until the late 1970s; since 1979, however, its economic growth has slowed markedly. Second, the nation mobilized considerable domestic and foreign resources to carry out an extensive investment program. Third, the effectiveness of investment in raising GDP has declined over time. Finally, Malaŵi's overall strategy of economic development has been appropriate for fast economic growth, given its initial comparative advantage and factor proportions.

The Record of Economic Growth

From 1954 through 1986 Malaŵi's GDP appears to have grown at an average annual rate of 4.6 percent.[1] Because population growth in Malaŵi has been rapid, about 3.0 percent a year, per capita GDP has increased about 1.6 percent annually, which would result in a doubling in about a half-century. This growth rate in per capita GDP appears to be considerably higher than that of most low-income nations of Africa. These estimates are uncertain, however; some respected economists have argued that Malaŵi's actual growth has been slower.[2] We can tentatively conclude that Malaŵi seems to have had a successful but not spectacular record of economic growth, a judgment differing from the standard, rosy view in the economic literature based on outdated national accounts data.

Sectoral Growth

Sectoral growth rates within Malaŵi have varied widely. The largest sector, measured both in labor and contribution to GDP, is agriculture.

According to my estimates, total gross crop production and crop exports grew from 1948 through 1984 at average annual rates of 5.0 and 5.1 percent, respectively (Pryor 1988a, table C-1). Market exchange has made certain inroads into the subsistence agriculture sector. The locus of agricultural production has also changed; estate production rose from about 7 percent of total agricultural value added at independence in the middle 1960s to about 20 percent in the early 1980s.[3] (The data on gross crop production presented in the next chapter reveal an even more dramatic increase in the relative importance of the estates.) Since independence, the agricultural production of estates, in absolute terms, has been the most important source of growth of Malaŵi's economy.

For other sectors, constant price series start at much later dates. Of greatest interest is manufacturing, which grew between 1967 and 1984 at an average annual rate of 5.0 percent. This shows that Malaŵi, though placing its highest priorities on the development of agriculture, has experienced a very satisfactory performance in manufacturing as well. The share of GDP originating in manufacturing is still low, however, having risen from about 11 percent in the late 1960s to 12.5 percent in the early 1980s.

Population Policies

The rate of population growth is an important factor to consider because the unused arable land is almost exhausted, and diminishing returns are an important factor underlying the increase in poverty in Malaŵi during the last quarter-century. From 1901 to 1945 Malaŵi's population grew at an average annual rate of about 2.5 percent a year.[4] With some improvement of health standards and a lowering of infant mortality, population growth increased so that in the early 1980s the growth rate was roughly 3.2 percent a year and, according to government projections, will increase up to the mid-1990s.[5]

Until the early 1980s the Malaŵi government showed little interest in limiting births. The Pharmacy and Poisons Act has made importing certain types of contraceptives difficult. Moreover, until recently President Banda has strongly resisted any birth control program, declaring such measures to be inappropriate for a nation with high infant mortality.[6] In 1982, however, the government included a child-spacing service as part of its maternal and child health program, and many health centers and mission hospitals began to provide contraceptive services. Interest in these programs has greatly increased, and they are being introduced into many more villages. In addition, the statistical service completed a first-rate study of fertility, contraceptive practices, and number of desired children (Malaŵi NSO 1987). This report may well serve as the basis for greater official attention to the population problem.

Periodization

Malaŵi has had three policy regimes since 1948:

- The preindependence period, both the "pure" colonial period from 1948 to 1954 and the period of the federation with Southern and Northern Rhodesia from 1954 to the end of 1963
- The initial postindependence period from 1964 until 1979, which can be subdivided into the period from 1964 to 1968, when the government was primarily concerned with consolidation and restructuring of the economy, and the period from 1968 until 1979, when the government was promoting all-out economic growth
- The period from 1979 through 1986, when the locus of policymaking appears to have shifted from the Life President and his long-time advisors to a younger group of officials and to the civil service (see chapter 17).

This political delineation, however, does not correspond directly to phases in Malaŵi's economic development. Except for the emphasis on estate production after independence, a number of the basic lines of economic policy were relatively similar in the federation period and in the independence period up to 1979. In many cases the major differences were primarily in the way the government implemented such policy lines, rather than in the basic thrust of its policies. Moreover, Malaŵi's growth rate (either of GDP as a whole, of gross crop production, or of crop exports) does not appear to have differed significantly in the federation period and after independence until 1979.[7] For instance, as shown in figure 3-1, GDP exhibits a relatively smooth positive growth except for two periods of decline: from 1962 to 1966, when the federation was breaking down and independent Malaŵi was struggling to its feet, and from 1979 through 1986, when the economy was buffeted by external shocks and policy mistakes and per capita growth declined.

Because comparable national account data series are not available before 1954, we must rely on proxies, such as crop export data, to chart the course of the economy. These show a relatively random pattern from 1948 through 1955, with the early years strongly affected by the serious drought of 1948. Dramatic change occurred, however, during the federation period, when both crop exports and GDP appeared to rise rapidly; certain other indicators, such as the ratio of investment to GDP and secondary school enrollments, also took important upturns.

The most important causal factor for this change in the growth pattern during colonialism appears to have been the enormous fiscal subsidies Nyasaland received from the Federation. From 1954 through 1963, the excess of federation expenditures in the colony over taxes collected from the colony amounted to almost 15 percent of the colony's

Figure 3-1. Indicators of Economic Growth in Malawi

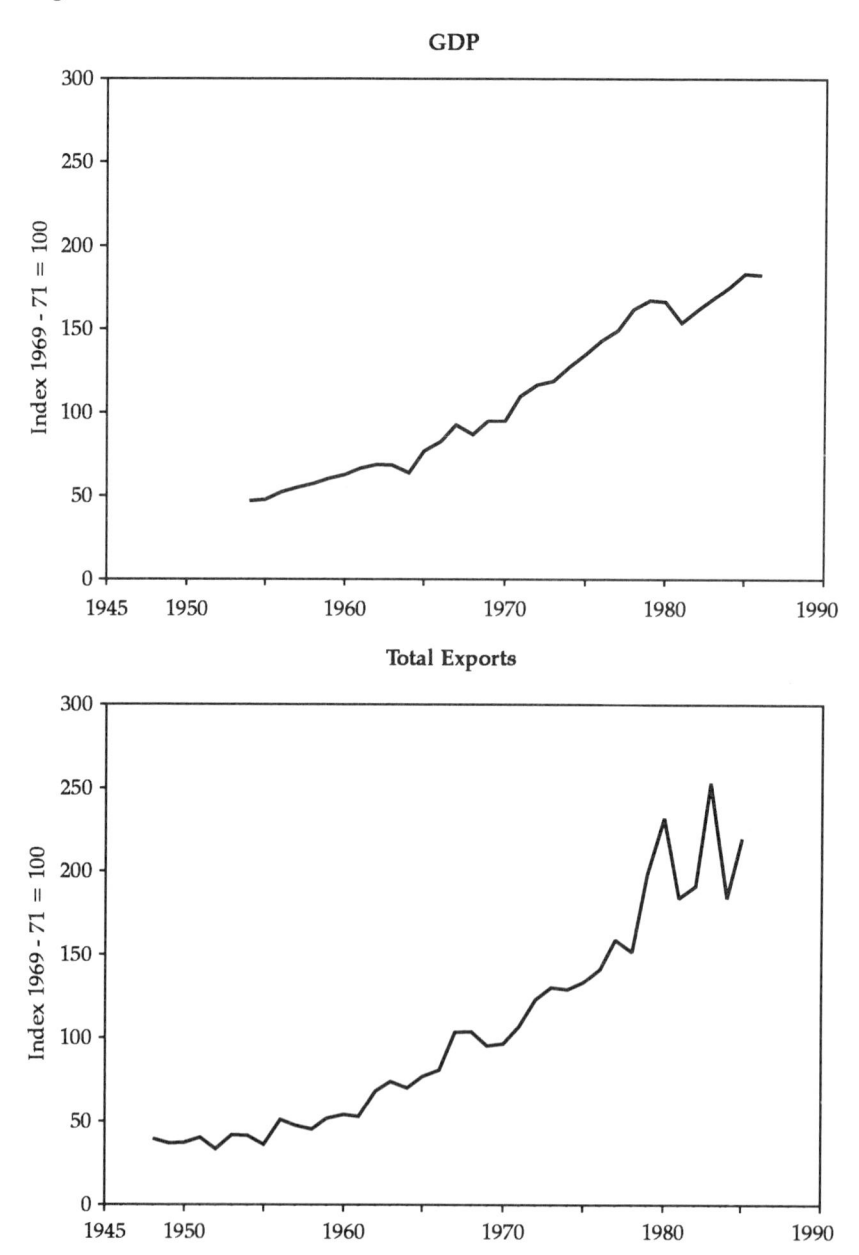

GDP

Total Exports

Note: The export series is estimated by chaining a series for production for agricultural exports for 1948 to 1964 (such exports represented about 90 percent of total exports) and a series of total exports from 1964 to the present.

Source: Pryor 1988b.

GDP and, indeed, was more than its total gross fixed investment during the same period.[8] Although the fiscal subsidy probably overstates the economic advantages Nyasaland received from the Federation, such transfers appear to have set in motion a considerable growth of the economy that carried over for the first decade and a half after independence.

Dissolution of the Federation brought some serious economic problems to Malaŵi, not the least of which was the loss of this fiscal subsidy. In the immediate postindependence years, however, the United Kingdom made a series of grants allowing the Malaŵi government time to consolidate; to establish certain basic governmental institutions, such as a central bank and a planning commission; and to begin mobilizing domestic sources of finance for investment. From 1964 through 1979, the economy grew at an impressive rate. GDP increased roughly 5.9 percent a year, and public and private consumption rose at an average annual rate of about 4.3 percent; the difference in these growth rates reflects a considerable increase in domestic resources mobilized for investment.[9]

The most important internally induced shock to the economy was the 1974 ban on emigration to South Africa for work, which was partially rescinded two years later. At that time the Malaŵian economy was growing fast enough to be able to weather these policy changes without strongly adverse effects.

In the late 1970s and early 1980s, a number of serious external shocks buffeted Malaŵi's economy. The commodity terms of trade (the ratio of export to import prices) fell, not only because of the second oil shock but also because of a relative decline in the prices of the products Malaŵi exports. The major transportation links between Malaŵi and the Indian Ocean—the rail lines running through Mozambique—were disrupted by insurgent (RENAMO) activity, leading to an enormous increase in transportation costs of foreign trade. Also, a partial drought occurred in 1980.

The tobacco estates, which provided a key export, were highly leveraged, and these external problems exacerbated their weak financial conditions, sending many into receivership. The parastatals that had spearheaded Malaŵi's industrialization not only had similar financial problems but others as well; they had grown so fast in the previous years that management controls were insufficient, and they were unable to adapt easily to new conditions. As a result they began to run heavy losses. As international reserves plummeted, the Malaŵi government borrowed heavily in private capital markets, acting on the assumption that many of these difficulties were short run. This assumption was incorrect. It delayed a necessary reorganization of these industries, and on top of the considerable external debt-service charges from previous long-term borrowing, it saddled the government with additional external payments. In the early and mid-1980s investment fell sharply, government expenditures increased considerably (in large part to service the debt), and for several years GDP declined. In the mid- and late 1980s, more than 750,000 refugees from Mozambique flooded Malaŵi, placing additional strains on the governmental budget.

These shocks forced Malaŵi to reschedule its foreign debts. In the first half of the 1980s, the nation also received several structural adjustment loans from the World Bank and agreed to a series of measures that included reducing price controls in the domestic economy; raising prices paid to smallholders in order to encourage more production in that sector; restructuring the parastatals and Press Holding, the largest enterprise in the country (which was almost completely owned by the president); raising public utility rates to reduce deficits in this sector; increasing government revenues to reduce the deficit in the public sector; establishing greater government control over public expenditures and also over the operations of the parastatals; devaluing the currency; and trying to achieve more diversification of exports. The results of these measures were not all as foreseen. The debt service still remained high, the terms of trade declined even more, the devaluations were not of sufficient magnitude to bring about equilibrium in the balance of payments, and per capita GDP continued to fall.

The structural adjustment program was not working, and by early 1988 the economic situation appeared bleak, bolstered only by an important International Monetary Fund (IMF) loan. The fiscal strains induced by the Mozambique refugee flow increased, and higher military expenditures also became necessary to check RENAMO activities in Malaŵi. Further, some inappropriate economic policies (for example, a cumbersome foreign exchange allocation system) acted to prolong the economic stagnation of the first half of the decade.

The Crucial Role of Investment

Malaŵi has been very successful in obtaining investable resources both from external and internal sources, particularly for the public sector. The effectiveness of this investment, however, appears to be declining over time.

The Volume and Financing of Investment

Malaŵi's mobilization of external and internal funds for investment has been impressive according to international norms.[10] The data in table 3-1 show that in the twenty-two years following independence in 1964, total gross investment averaged 23.4 percent of factor price GDP, although this percentage varied widely in individual years during this period. Total investment as a share of GDP rose steadily throughout the

Table 3-1. Investment and Savings Ratios (Current Prices), Malaŵi, 1964 to 1986

(percent)

Year	Gross investment/GDP	Gross national saving/GDP	Gross national savings/gross investment	Government budgetary investment/gross investment[a]
1964	8.9	-1.2	-13.3	65.8
1965	15.0	-0.6	-4.0	53.4
1966	19.1	0.7	3.7	45.8
1967	15.0	-1.0	-6.8	45.9
1968	19.1	0.4	1.9	49.3
1969	21.3	4.0	18.9	51.4
Average	16.4	0.4	0.1	51.9
1970	29.9	12.5	41.8	56.8
1971	22.3	9.8	44.0	48.8
1972	28.6	13.2	46.1	46.4
1973	23.9	13.5	56.6	56.2
1974	29.1	18.7	64.2	42.3
1975	36.1	18.8	52.2	50.8
1976	25.3	15.8	62.7	57.1
1977	26.3	18.0	68.5	51.9
1978	40.7	21.6	53.1	49.3
1979	30.9	7.1	22.9	55.7
Average	29.3	14.9	51.2	51.5
1980	27.6	3.0	10.7	70.5
1981	19.5	6.8	34.9	58.0
1982	23.6	10.4	44.0	39.5
1983	25.3	14.9	58.9	36.6
1984	15.4	13.3	86.8	61.2
1985[b]	16.2	6.2	38.0	58.1
1986[b]	18.2	8.5	46.9	52.7
Average	20.8	9.0	45.7	53.8
Overall unweighted average	23.4	9.3	36.2	52.3

a. Government investments do not include the investments of the parastatals, which are classified as part of the private sector.
b. Preliminary data.
Source: Pryor (1988b), tables E-1 and L-4a.

first decade after independence to reach impressively high levels in the late 1970s.

Gross domestic savings averaged about 9.3 percent of GDP during the period, but this figure also varied widely from year to year. In the immediate postindependence period gross domestic saving was negative, but it rose rapidly and from 1964 through 1986 financed about 36 percent of total gross investment. The remainder of total investment was financed almost equally by grants and loans, which came primarily from foreign governments and international agencies. Private foreign capital flows to Malaŵi have been small, especially so net of profits and remittances abroad. Nevertheless, Malaŵi has been relatively successful in mobilizing foreign funds to aid its development efforts. The time-series data for Malaŵi provide some contrary evidence to the oft-repeated generalization that foreign aid acts primarily to replace domestic saving.[11]

THE PUBLIC SECTOR ROLE. Government investment, either direct or through a few governmental enterprises included in the public accounts (most parastatals are excluded), has amounted to about half of Malaŵi's total investment since its independence. Given the preponderant weight of the parastatals in the modern sector, direct or indirect investment by the public sector may have accounted for two-thirds to three-fourths of all investment in Malaŵi.

The Malaŵi government made a great effort to increase government saving in order to finance investment; indeed, one of Banda's first important economic measures was to take advantage of postindependence euphoria to raise taxes, especially on the urban sector, so as to put governmental finances on a sound basis for the first decade. Subtracting government borrowing (both domestic and foreign) from government investment, the government sector's net saving in an average year amounted to about 3.6 percent of GDP; this rate varied considerably from year to year.[12]

The parastatals have also been an important source of investment funds. In most developing nations the parastatals are a net drain on government resources. In Malaŵi, as shown in table 3-2, this has not been the case. Since independence, the profits of the "public enterprises" (these exclude a considerable number of parastatals that act essentially as private enterprises and are excluded from the consolidated parastatal accounts) have averaged about 1 percent of GDP, another important source of investment finance. The government chartered most of these parastatals as profitmaking institutions and has been cautious in giving them subsidies, unlike the governments of Madagascar and most other Sub-Saharan nations.

Foreign governments and international lending institutions usually channeled their loans and grants through the Malaŵi government.

Table 3-2. Net Profits or Losses of Public Enterprises, Malaŵi, 1964 to 1984
(percent)

Fiscal year	Share of GDP	Fiscal year	Share of GDP
1964	0.4	1974–75	3.3
1965	0.8	1975–76	1.5
1966	0.3	1976–77	4.5
1967	-1.5	1977–78	3.0
1968	1.7	1978–79	-0.4
Average	0.3	Average	2.4
1969–70	2.4	1979–80	-0.9
1970–71	1.6	1980–81	-0.6
1971–72	3.3	1981–82	0.3
1972–73	2.8	1982–83	-0.4
1973–74	3.0	1983–84	-0.0
Average	2.6	1984–85	0.7
		Average	-0.2
		Overall unweighted average	1.2

Note: Percentages are based on current prices. The data on net profits exclude taxes. They cover the "public enterprises," but because balance sheets are not consolidated, they do not cover most of the enterprises owned partly or wholly by public enterprises. These accounts also do not include Press Holding. They do include: ADMARC, Air Malaŵi, Blantyre Water Board, Capital City Development Corporation, Electricity Supply Commission, Kasungu Flue-Cured Tobacco Authority, Malaŵi Broadcasting Corporation, Malaŵi Housing Corporation, Malaŵi Railroads, and a number of smaller public enterprises as well. Because the fiscal year runs from April 1 to March 31, the GDP of the first year mentioned in the fiscal year is the denominator of the ratios.

Source: Up to 1979 the data come from Malaŵi, Minister of Finance, *Public Sector Financial Statistics*, various issues. For 1979 through 1985 the data come from Malaŵi, Office of the President and Planning, Economic Planning Division, *Economic Report 1985*, p. 92. These two sources differ somewhat for the two overlap years. The GDP data come from Pryor (1988b), table E-1.

This, of course, acted to increase public-sector investment and to strengthen the role of the public sector in the economy.

THE PRIVATE SECTOR ROLE. Much information needed to analyze the private-sector role in saving and investment is unavailable; therefore, this analysis must be more speculative than that for the public sector.

A large share of private saving in Malaŵi appeared to come from sources other than private individuals. Certain data suggest that from April 1973 through March 1983 private households accounted for less than a fifth of total saving (World Bank 1985, p. 29). The low share for household saving can be seen in another way. In 1968–69, the last year for which detailed saving information is available for the entire population, net saving was less than 1 percent of income of smallholders or urban families (that is, those living in the four largest cities). In 1979–80, budget data for urban families are also available, and although they do not permit a very exact analysis, net personal saving does not appear to have been a very significant share of total income (Malaŵi NSO 1983b).

Until the end of the 1970s the real interest rates of banks were generally positive, which encouraged savings. Thereafter, price increases regularly began to exceed the interest rate, and private savings appeared to fall (see chapter 8). Another likely factor influencing aggregate saving was changes in the distribution of income (chapter 16), especially an increasing share for property income and a widening of income differentials. If the marginal propensity to save rises with income, this should result in higher aggregate private savings.

Several kinds of investment risks deserve brief mention. Malaŵi does not have the investment risks stemming from rapid changes in government policy that are found in other African countries, in large part because of the unbroken tenure in office of President Banda. The Life President can expropriate any property, however, if in his view the owners have used such property contrary to state interests (see chapter 7). This sequestration provision has been invoked in a number of cases in which Asians and Greeks in business were accused of violating currency and other laws. This power certainly does not encourage industrial investment, either by Malaŵians or by foreigners. In the 1980s two other investment risks became important: manufacturers experienced considerable difficulties in obtaining imported inputs for their production because of overvaluation of the currency and the necessity to license imports, and some private investors also may have been uncertain about policies the government might pursue in a post-Banda era.

Investment Effectiveness

A crude measure of investment effectiveness is the incremental capital-output ratio (ICOR)—the units of investment needed to increase the GDP by one unit.[13] Other things being equal, the lower the ICOR, the higher the investment effectiveness. In Malaŵi from 1954 through 1986 the ICOR was 4.0, which is higher than that found in Southeast Asia or in many economically developed nations but lower than that in many other African nations such as Madagascar, which from 1950 through 1986 had an ICOR of 7.9.

The difference in ICORs between Malaŵi and Madagascar has several explanations. The development strategy Malaŵi pursued appears more appropriate to the conditions of the nation than that in Madagascar. Furthermore, Malaŵi has placed much greater emphasis on using the market mechanism to provide incentives to direct production and investment than has Madagascar, a point analyzed in detail in later chapters. Although much public investment in Malaŵi has not yielded the results initially projected, the economic projects have been sufficiently well chosen and designed so that highly expensive failures have been few, in contrast to Madagascar.[14] The neglect of industrial development in basic consumer goods during the colonial period also left available an attractive range of import-substituting investments.

The effectiveness of investment in Malaŵi has varied considerably over time and reveals a disturbing trend. During the colonial period the ICOR was about 2.8, from 1964 through 1979 the ICOR rose to 3.7, and from 1979 through 1986 it climbed to 9.9. Part of this apparent decline in investment effectiveness can be attributed to a shift in the pattern of investment. After 1963 the new government of Malaŵi invested relatively more than had the colonial government in social overhead and integrated rural development projects, both of which have high incremental capital-output ratios. In the period from 1979 through 1986, moreover, a number of factors unrelated to investment effectiveness itself (especially the external shocks) reduced GDP growth and thereby raised the ICOR.

The Strategy of Economic Development

Strategic and tactical economic policies of Malaŵi's government have contributed to the behavior of the ICOR. By strategic I mean the general orientation toward economic development, in this case, the government's focus on agriculture and export-led growth. By tactical I mean the individual policies and their implementation, which are the focus of the sector-by-sector microeconomic analysis in the next five chapters.

The Initial Approach

Malaŵi's first long-term development plan covered 1965 through 1969 (see Malaŵi Government 1964). It was strongly influenced by the ideas of a highly regarded young politician, Dunduzu Chisiza, who died before the plan was completed. This plan was more a shopping list than an integrated plan and had little subsequent influence on actual governmental policies.

A concurrent plan was the Gwelo No. 2 plan, which Dr. Banda conceived while in Gwelo Prison in the late 1950s.[15] This was more of a political program than a strategy proposal or an integrated planning document. It focused on three major projects: moving the capital from Zomba in the Southern Region of Malaŵi to Lilongwe in the Central Region; constructing an improved road along Lake Malaŵi to aid north-south transportation; and building a university. Later Dr. Banda added the building of a railway spur to the Mozambique border, which would link Malaŵi with the port of Nacala on the Indian Ocean.

Dr. Banda saw each of these four projects as generating enormous positive externalities for the nation as a whole. Moving the capital would shift the economic weight of the country from the overpopulated south to the less populated Central Region (which was also more accessible to the Northern Region). The rail spur would provide a margin of safety from reliance on a single rail connection to the Indian Ocean through the Mozambique port of Beira (few Malaŵians or others suspected that two decades later insurgent action in Mozambique would make both lines almost useless). The lake shore drive would help not only to link the new nation together but also to provide the Northern (and allegedly poorest) Region with better means of marketing its agricultural and other products. The new university would help the nation to begin to solve its acute shortage of educated cadres, part of a series of measures to create a leadership elite. The British government sent the Hill Mission to investigate these projects. The mission decided that all but the university project seemed uneconomic, so no U.K. financing would be forthcoming. Shortly thereafter, however, the Malaŵi government obtained West German aid in building the lake shore highway and South African financial and technical support for the construction of the new capital and the railway line.

The third long-term plan was *DevPol I* (Malaŵi, Office of the President and Planning 1971), a remarkable document published in 1971, which laid out the basic economic philosophy to guide policymaking during the decade. The details of the various development projects for administrative purposes were embodied in a series of rolling three-year plans intended to serve as guides for government administration, although for certain years their operational role has been doubtful. As an official document, *DevPol I* was more a set of principles for planning and policy than a detailed listing of a series of projects and the administrative steps necessary to achieve specific aims; that is, it set forth a strategy rather than a blueprint.[16] In 1988 the government issued *DevPol II* (Malaŵi, Office of the President and Planning 1988), which laid out the basic economic philosophy guiding policymaking for the 1987–96 decade.

DevPol I immediately stressed that development of the agricultural sector was to have the highest priority. The first page of the report justified this decision in terms of factor proportions. It stated,

> The choice of strategy which gives top priority to raising agricultural productivity is dictated not only by the present pattern of economic

activity among the population but also by the nature and distribution of Malaŵi's economic resources. The factors of production with which Malaŵi is relatively well-endowed are land and labour; the factors which are in short supply are capital and high-level skills.

It is therefore no more than common sense to make the maximum use of land and labour and economize on the use of capital and skills. A further point to note about Malaŵi's resource base is the absence of a highly lucrative primary industry, such as copper in Zambia. Even though such industries in less developed countries create serious problems of structural imbalances and maldistribution of income, they do at least provide the capital resources with which development in other sectors can be financed. Malaŵi is not entirely lacking in useful mineral resources, but even the most potentially valuable . . . cannot be expected to provide surpluses for reinvestment during the next ten years. Hence it is only realistic to assume that Malaŵi will continue to require foreign capital to finance development in both the public and private sector throughout the coming decade and this is a further reason for economizing on capital and maximizing labour intensity.

To maximize agricultural productivity *DevPol I* proposed a two-part strategy: several growth-points in the form of large-scale, high-productivity projects, such as irrigation and settlement schemes, combined with a general raising of the level of production through agricultural extension and marketing operations for the nation as a whole. To encourage agricultural production, producers should be paid as high a nonsubsidized price as possible (p. 54); thus the marketing board should not to be used as a medium for raising capital for other purposes. *DevPol I* focused most attention on smallholders; however, it did foresee that estate production would grow faster (annually 6.8 percent) than smallholder production (annually 5.2 percent for market and nonmonetary production combined; smallholder market production alone was supposed to grow 11.4 percent a year). The initial elements of the increasing emphasis on estates production can be seen in the following two statements:

> There is clearly a potential for increasing export earnings and domestic income through more productive use of land under an estate type organization for crops (such as flue-cured tobacco) which requires a high level of working capital and management expertise. [p. 7]

> The emphasis in agricultural policy is on a general rise in agricultural productivity to be achieved quickly and effectively by the most economical means. [p. 34]

DevPol I also specified areas of secondary importance. The next priority after agriculture was the development of transportation, crucial for agricultural marketing and tourism. Because the rail line connecting to Nacala had already been built, the major focus of the document was on constructing roads.

This long-term plan placed only a tertiary emphasis on the development of manufacturing. It made a useful distinction between those industries servicing local demand (which would lead to import substitution) and those industries relying on local supplies of raw materials (which would be export oriented). It advocated the development of both, although with greater emphasis on the latter. The document espoused the selective use of tariffs to encourage domestic manufacturing and emphasized the superiority of tariffs over quantitative restrictions to achieve the desired ends, but it also noted the dangers of such policy tools.

In sum, the aim was to provide incentives for private investment in manufacturing rather than direct government participation. The plan argued against tax holidays to attract new capital but urged the use of investment allowances and the easy repatriation of capital. It saw the necessity of encouraging foreign capital to finance such industries by providing the proper incentives, arguing that a general takeover of existing foreign capital would not be advisable. It also emphasized the necessity of local participation in new industries and pointed toward joint ventures as a way of resolving conflict. To encourage local saving and investment, it advocated indirect taxes on consumption rather than direct taxes on total income. Import duties would be a crucial element initially but would decline in importance as import substitution took place (p. 116).

Although the text of *DevPol I* did not stress foreign trade, various tables did (pp. 22 and 26). Domestic exports were expected to grow more than three times faster than GDP. Increased agricultural exports were to supply most of this growth. Although manufactured exports were projected to grow faster than agricultural exports, they started as a very much smaller share of total exports.

DevPol I was very mindful of the distributional issues that investment programs raise. With regard to manufacturing, it stated,

> The establishment of capital-intensive industries by foreign capital would make little direct contribution to the elimination of poverty or even to aggregate domestic income; if they involve an increase in domestic price as a result of over protection or the closing down of existing labor-intensive Malaŵi enterprises (e.g., brick making, carpentry, and grain milling), their effect could only be to depress the standard of living of the people.
>
> As a general rule, therefore, Malaŵi's development strategy rules out the promotion of highly capital-intensive industry, unless their function is clearly essential and there is no choice of technology. A

high level of protective tariffs would lead to a serious rise in the prices of basic consumer commodities, which would depress real incomes and, probably, reduce the supply of agricultural products for export. The object of tariff policy is to provide a secure domestic market for internationally competitive producers and manufacturers—not to provide shelter for the inefficient or a stimulus to uneconomic investment. The same considerations apply in the case of supply-based industries processing local raw materials in that they are only encouraged if they are able to pay export parity prices for their primary inputs. In this way industrial development in Malaŵi can . . . avoid the effect . . . of concentration of income in the towns at the expense of the rural areas.

The distribution of income between urban and rural areas is an important factor in Malaŵi's incomes and price policy. . . . It would be contrary to this broad policy to create a privileged position for urban wage earners. . . . Not only would this depress the living standards of the mass of the people, but would also act as a disincentive to increased effort in the agricultural sector. . . . High differentials between urban and rural wages also promotes the flow of job-seekers into the town, causing serious social and political problems. [p. 2]

The long-term plan also stressed the importance of not raising the minimum wage on humanitarian or economic grounds (to widen markets).

Experience during the past decade has shown conclusively that this approach is invalid: the result has invariably been to create a small privileged urban class whose consumption has become increasingly import oriented. . . . Any rise in wage costs not related to productivity would adversely affect estate agriculture and jeopardize . . . exports. [p. 3]

DevPol I did give some attention to other social issues such as achieving a more equitable regional distribution of income. This provided a rationale for more equal distribution of investment among the various regions and for moving the nation's capital. *DevPol I* was quite mindful of constraints, however, and did not promise everything to everyone. The ordering of priorities was quite explicit, and the document stated frankly that the objective of financial independence would inevitably limit resources available for social services. The plan also argued that greatest emphasis in education should be placed on secondary, technical, and university education as a means of widening the bottleneck created by the lack of skills, at the expense of greater attention to primary education.

The Realization of DevPol I

The numerical goals and specific policy guidelines *DevPol I* provided invite some comparisons against the subsequent reality. Table 3-3 contrasts the actual and planned shares of government development fund expenditures.

SECTORAL INVESTMENT ALLOCATIONS. The government's major tool for allocating resources among sectors was a special part of the budget devoted to nonrecurrent expenditures (primarily, but not exclusively, capital expenditures), the development account. An examination of this account leads to several tentative conclusions. First, development expenditures on transportation and communications may have had a higher priority than agriculture. Part of this seems to be a classification problem, because a very large part of the transportation

Table 3-3. Malaŵi Development Priorities, Actual and Planned
(percent)

	Average annual shares of government development fund[a]			
	Actual		Planned	
Sector	1957–58 to 1962–63	1968 to 1982–83	DevPol I 1970–79	DevPol II 1987–96
Agriculture and natural resources	25	23	19	23
Transportation and communication	17	37	34	29
Utilities (electricity and water)	5	7	11	17
Social (education, health, community development)	25	9	14	22
Government buildings and new national capital	14	18	13	5
Other (including industry)	14	6	7	4
Total	100	100	100	100

a. The development fund is a special part of the budget of the central government devoted to nonrecurrent development expenditures. The government makes some investment expenditures outside this budget, however, and some expenditures from the development fund finance current expenditures. Further details and sources are given in Pryor (1988b), section C. Other statistical problems are discussed in the Appendix, section F.

Source: The data come from Central African Federation of Rhodesia and Nyasaland, Central Statistical Office (1964). Some sectoral data on total fixed capital investment are available for Malaŵi for the period 1973 through 1979 from Malaŵi, NSO (1983b); and these can be compared with similar data for the federation period. The NSO, however, had some reservations about their accuracy and has discontinued the series; at first glance this series appeared somewhat inconsistent with the data from the governmental development account, but I have no detailed evidence on the matter.

investment was placed in the rural sector and might be classified as agricultural investment. Second, the high transportation expenditures in the postindependence period appeared to be the result of a reallocation of central governmental funds from social projects, reflecting the low priority *DevPol I* accorded education. Third, the relative share of actual expenditures devoted to agriculture and natural resources was roughly the same in the periods before and after independence.

The very rough sectoral breakdowns of total fixed investment in the federation and in the 1973–79 periods reveal few important differences. Imperfect as these comparisons are, they reveal a considerable continuity in basic policy lines. Given that the last years of the federation had witnessed a considerable growth of production, this was a useful initial condition for the newly independent nation.

AGRICULTURE. As *DevPol I* anticipated, production on estates grew faster than on that on smallholdings. The difference turned out to be considerably greater than expected, however, because estate production grew faster and smallholder production slower than predicted. Nevertheless, total agriculture has grown more rapidly than population, and the country can feed itself—a significant accomplishment in comparison to many other Sub-Saharan nations. Food insecurity has, however, existed at this local level in different localities. One important policy stricture in *DevPol I*, namely that the marketing boards should not manipulate prices paid to smallholders to obtain funds for other purposes, was soon violated when real world market prices for certain agricultural goods rose while the government's monopsonistic buying agency continued to pay roughly the same real prices (see chapter 5).

LABOR-INTENSIVE INVESTMENTS. Sufficient data to calculate capital-labor ratios are not available; however, an alternative indicator is the relative growth of the labor force and of value added in the *monetary* sector. From 1968 through 1984 the growth of labor averaged 5.4 percent a year (see chapter 16), while GDP grew at a 5.7 percent rate. A sectoral disaggregation of these data shows that if several capital-intensive sectors, such as transportation, communications, and construction, are omitted, labor grew considerably faster than value added, which reflects a fall in the average wage and in labor productivity. Thus, based on a factors proportions argument, this goal of the plan was achieved, at least on the basis of individual sectors of the economy.

FOREIGN TRADE. Until the early 1980s, when the nation began to experience several balance of payments difficulties, tariff rates in Malaŵi appeared moderate (see chapter 6). The government did not generally impose export taxes or formal quantitative restrictions on imports, although it did maintain certain informal import quotas, mainly through foreign exchange rationing. Exports grew considerably faster than GDP, and thus the policy of export-driven growth appears to have been realized, at least until about 1980.

INCENTIVES. Tax holidays were not given, and repatriation of capital, although not completely free of barriers, has been much easier in Malaŵi than in most other African nations. These policies (and the foreign trade policies) outlined in *DevPol I*, in combination with the parastatals' relatively easy access to credit and the relative lack of governmental micromanagement of industrial affairs (even in the parastatals), were probably responsible in large measure for the growth of manufacturing. The real prices the crop marketing board paid to smallholders remained roughly the same during the first two decades after independence (dipping somewhat in the mid-1970s); they did not move closely with world market prices and provided a considerable source of profits to the marketing board. Thus incentives that might have encouraged faster smallholder production were withheld. In contrast to other African nations, however, a considerable share of the board's profits were reinvested into agriculture, in large part, in the estate sector or agroindustries.

OWNERSHIP. Relatively little nationalization was foreseen, except in critical sectors. During the course of the 1970s the two commercial banks were nationalized, as were the railroads and certain large industrial enterprises. The parastatals carried out such measures primarily by purchasing shares of these firms. In addition, the government continued to buy up European-owned estates. Considerable foreign investment was not touched, however, and many new joint ventures between Malaŵian parastatals and foreign interests were established. The public sector probably ended up somewhat larger than the *DevPol I* implicitly assumed.

EDUCATION AND HEALTH. *DevPol I* placed a tertiary priority on the development of education and health, except for particularly important projects. As discussed in chapter 8, enrollments in primary schools increased only slowly, while enrollments in secondary schools grew at a rapid rate, exactly as foreseen. Bottlenecks in skilled labor slowed replacement of European expatriates in key positions in the government and economy. For certain investments in education and health (particularly the provision of pure water), the government sponsored a series of unique labor-intensive village self-help projects that allowed effective use of the small amount of investment funds going to this sector.[17]

Long-Term Planning in the 1980s

By the late 1970s events had made many parts of *DevPol I* obsolete. In 1981 the government published a five-year development plan for 1981–82 to 1985–86, about which little was heard thereafter. It also began preparing *DevPol II* to cover the next decade. In fact Malaŵi planners told me that the government has made three separate attempts to produce such a plan. Two foundered on the shoals of bureaucratic infighting; the third, a rather bland document, was published in early 1988. During this long gestation period President Banda did not appear in the least interested in its preparation.[18]

DevPol II has some important similarities and differences from *DevPol I*. Aggregate labor productivity is planned to increase only 6 percent during the entire next decade, which suggests continuation of the capital-widening strategy. *DevPol II* also foresees gross fixed capital formation and exports increasing at average annual rates of 4.6 and 5.2 percent, respectively, in contrast to the planned 4 percent average annual increase of GDP. This suggests that policies to increase investment rates and the export orientation will continue as well. The realism of some of the numbers is open to question—for example, the implicit assumption of an ICOR of 3.1, which is considerably lower than that achieved at any period since independence.[19] The most important difference is that the new plan contains much less discussion about broad policy principles. The data in the plan do suggest that the relative share of the public sector in production should remain about the same; the plan also calls for more private participation in agricultural marketing and a flexible exchange rate policy (with some restrictions on obtaining foreign exchange). Despite these and other policy hints, just how the government intends to achieve some of its ambitious goals remains unclear. This discourages taking the plan very seriously.

In the distribution of investment, *DevPol II* places less stress on transportation and communication and on agriculture than did its predecessor. Indeed, agriculture will receive only 16.5 percent of all governmental investment; the rest of natural resource investment is aimed primarily at forestry. Within agriculture, the emphasis on estate agriculture continues: estate and smallholder agricultural production are planned to grow annually 4.9 and 3.3 percent, respectively. *DevPol II* also plans for government to direct relatively more of its investment toward public utilities (of which a significant share is going toward irrigation, which will aid agriculture) and toward education, health, and other social services.

In the mid-1980s the outside observer receives an impression—admittedly vague—that the government's long-term development policies appear to have little central focus. Civil servants in the different ministries, at least in talking with me, seemed to have little awareness of where and how the projects of their ministry fit into the overall thrust of Malaŵian economic development. Several officials shared their impression that in the mid-1980s the civil service seemed to be functioning less effectively than before; this lack of common purpose could well be an important cause.

The Origins of the Development Strategy

The basic thrust of the development strategy of *DevPol I* appears to have come directly from President Banda. B. D. Giles, who served a term as chief economist of the government of Malaŵi, has provided some evidence for this: "Not all the analysis that was done was fed into policy—mainly because, under ... Dr. Banda, it was at best useless and at worst dangerous to put forward any views that conflicted with his known preconceptions" (Giles 1979). Many of the ideas in this long-term plan also received enthusiastic support from the international lending community.

In an interview, I asked President Banda why, in contrast to most other African leaders, he had taken a rural orientation toward development. He replied, "I am from the village and my first duty is to help the villagers." In his speeches he reminisces often about his boyhood on a farm; about how he produced his own maize, groundnuts, and beans by the time he was seven or eight years old; and about his high school agricultural education at the Wilberforce Academy in Xenia, Ohio, from September 1925 to June 1928, when he was taught to plow by actually holding the plow while his teacher led the horse.

Some argue that a political leader's world view is strongly shaped by early successes, and Dr. Banda did well in the various agricultural courses he took at Wilberforce.[20] Shortly after returning to Malaŵi Banda began to speak of his dream of making Malaŵi the "Denmark of Central Africa" and of the need for hands-on agricultural work. Denmark is an interesting model. In the nineteenth century, it, like Malaŵi, had a high population density, few natural resources, and relatively little capital.

In 1962, at a conference organized by the Ford Foundation in Malaŵi to discuss the country's development strategy, Banda forcefully stated his intention to focus primarily on agriculture, much to the chagrin of some leading development economists who had given him somewhat different advice.[21] Certainly Banda did not appear overly impressed with industrialization. He had received his education between the world wars, when industrialization was not viewed as a panacea. Also he had lived for many decades in Western cities, and as a physician in England with a working-class clientele, he was certainly acquainted at first hand with the health problems of the industrial proletariat of the world's first industrial nation. Although *DevPol I* was couched in economic language by an economist (particularly the late Henry Ord of Edinburgh University), it clearly reflected the thinking and beliefs of the Life President and mapped a path much different from that most of the rest of Africa followed.

The emphasis in *DevPol I* on economic incentives and trade also reflects the milieu in which Banda grew up. For instance, the British administrative tradition in Malaŵi, stressing careful administration to minimize subsidies and little attention to grandiose plans for the future, undoubtedly had an important influence on Banda and his colleagues as well.

Summary

Malaŵi's growth rate has been satisfactory, especially for a country that, at its independence, was given little chance for success. Underlying the success was a considerable mobilization of internal funds for investment, especially through the fiscal system; an active and successful search for foreign grants and loans; an investment strategy quite suitable for the comparative advantage and factor proportions of the country; and relatively effective use of investment funds, at least until the end of the 1970s.

In the mid-1980s Malaŵi could not maintain its forward thrust. Its rates of investment and investment effectiveness had fallen. Although the government changed some economic policies, certain of the new measures appear to be inappropriate for sustained growth, as I document in subsequent chapters.

Notes

1. All growth rates reported in this chapter, except for very short periods, are calculated by fitting an exponential curve to the data in order to minimize the influence of the end points.

2. The generalization about the rest of Africa is based on World Bank (1981), annex table 1, p. 143. For the period 1960 through 1979, the weighted average annual growth rate of per capita GDP for "low-income, non-arid" African nations was 1.0 percent. The same source estimates average annual growth of GDP per capita for Malaŵi for the period to be 2.9 percent; my own calculations for the same period place it closer to 2.0 percent.

The uncertainty in Malaŵi national accounts data lies in the estimation of how much smallholder agricultural production is consumed by the producer or never reaches the market for other reasons. The National Statistical Office (NSO) found that its earlier estimates of such nonmarketed production were considerably overestimated, and it completely revised its calculations starting in 1973.

My GDP estimates connect NSO estimates for 1973 through 1984 and my own estimates for the period 1954 to 1973. The latter calculations combine previous

NSO estimates for the monetary sector and my own estimates of the nonmarket production. Details of the regression method I used to make the estimates are provided in Pryor 1988b, section C, which also presents the results of various consistency tests.

The impact of any upward bias in my estimate of nonmarket production is easy to determine. For instance, if the average annual growth of smallholders, nonmarket production had been 3.7 percent rather than 4.7 percent, then the average annual GDP growth would have been 4.3 percent; and if such production had an average annual growth rate of 2.7 percent, then average annual GDP growth would have been 4.1 percent a year. Given this uncertainty about smallholders' production, average annual growth of GDP from 1954 through 1984 was probably between 4.1 and 4.5 percent, and the average annual growth of GDP per capita, between 1.0 and 1.4 percent. Because savings increased during this period, the growth of consumption was somewhat slower; however, consistent series for consumption for the entire period are not available to make an exact calculation.

My rough estimations, revealing a slowly growing per capita production in the smallholder sector, differ from the views of Kydd and Christiansen (1982) and Kydd and Christiansen, in Fyfe and others (1985). They argue that per capita smallholder production has stagnated or declined during Malaŵi's period of independence. Kydd's essay in Fyfe presents a useful history of the calculation of national accounts. Kydd and Christiansen in the same source do not make any quantitative estimates but rely on various qualitative indicators. Given the nature of the underlying data, any evaluation of smallholder production must be viewed with extreme caution. Although I have greater faith in my own estimating methods, their informed conclusions on this matter must be noted.

3. The early data come from Malaŵi NSO (1972), p. 4; the data for the early 1980s are from unpublished data supplied by the National Statistical Office.

4. This rate is based on data for the *de jure* population and come from Malaŵi NSO, *Malaŵi Statistical Yearbook, 1982*, p. 5. The early population estimates do not appear to be very accurate and probably reflect only gross magnitudes.

5. World Bank (March 1986b) has an analysis of these population problems. This publication discusses in considerable detail Malaŵi's recent program for child spacing. President Banda's opposition to population control is discussed by Morton (1975), pp. 46 ff., and by Short (1974), pp. 279 ff. Both sources note the deportation of some Dutch missionaries in 1968 for their advocacy of birth control measures; Short also mentions official Malaŵi claims that the optimum population for the nation is 6 million to 12 million. According to Munger (1969a), President Banda detests the various treaties dating from the late nineteenth century that set Malaŵi's boundaries, and in the years following independence he was not worried about overpopulation because his vision of Malaŵi more closely approximated the very large area of the ancient Maravi empire.

6. The 1987–96 plan foresees the crude birth rate remaining roughly the same during the decade (between 54.6 and 56.9 per 1,000 population).

7. These conclusions were reached by calculating regressions with dummy variables representing the various periods and then testing the statistical

significance of the calculated coefficients for the dummy variables. All data come from Pryor (1988b), table E-1.

8. According to Arthur Hazlewood, in Hazlewood (1967), p. 210, the fiscal subsidy was £77 million (equal to 154 million MK). The data from Pryor (1988b), table E-1, show total gross fixed investment of 133.3 million MK (current prices). For the 1954–63 period, the fiscal subsidy averaged almost 15 percent of GDP.

9. The calculation of public and private consumption is quite rough. It was made by combining GDP data with data on the relative importance of investment in GDP and the share of domestic investment financed by domestic savings (table 4-1). For the entire period from 1964 through 1984 the average annual growth rates of GDP and of public and private consumption were 4.8 percent and 4.0 percent, respectively.

10. My standard for "international norms" is based on the results reported in Chenery and Syrquin (1975). One problem in using these results is that Malaŵi and Madagascar have such low per capita GDPs that the portions of the charts showing these two countries have considerable margins of error.

11. Other anti-aid arguments are that such assistance has an urban bias, focuses only on highly visible projects, or results in a very large growth of governmental current expenditures. Morton (1975) analyzes how these and other arguments do not appear to hold true in the Malaŵian case.

12. Data on these matters come from Pryor (1988b), table K-1a. The data on individual saving in 1968 are presented in Appendix table G-1.

13. The incremental capital-output ratios are calculated by fitting an exponential curve to the GDP data, calculating the change in GDP from the values on the curve corresponding to the relevant years, and then comparing this with gross fixed capital investment during the relevant period. Such a procedure minimizes the impact of the choice of endpoints.

14. Many have criticized as wasteful certain of the Malaŵi government's "service" investments such as construction of expensive presidential mansions in three major cities, an expensive international airport in Lilongwe, a luxury hotel in the north, and the creation of an elite English-type public school.

15. I have been unable to find any written document specifying the Gwelo Plan No. 2, although Dr. Banda discussed it in many speeches. The Gwelo Plan No. 1 was political and focused on breaking the Federation and gaining independence.

16. My assessment of the positive impact of *DevPol I* on Malaŵi's economic development is controversial. One leading specialist on Malaŵi maintains an opposite view, arguing that (a) *DevPol I* was essentially "a prospectus for aid agencies, written by people from an aid agency"; (b) it may not have been effectively communicated to the bureaucracy, especially because few copies were seen in government offices after 1973; and (c) government policy deviated from *DevPol I*, especially with its implicit taxation of smallholders through manipulation of agricultural prices. Without doubt it was a useful document for aid agencies, even though it was very different from similar documents in other countries. This should not mask the fact that the document represented Banda's major ideas and that the strategic thrust, if not the details,

appeared to gain considerable agreement from the bureaucracy so that it gave the impression of pulling together in harness during the 1970s.

17. Chikhula (1984) particularly stresses this aspect of Malaŵi's development strategy.

18. This was a strong impression from my interview with President Banda on April 22, 1987, when I tried to discuss the principles underlying *DevPol II* with him.

19. The ICOR is calculated from data presented by Malaŵi Office of the President (1988), chapter 24.

20. For instance, Barber (1972) wrote an entire book on the proposition: "The best way to predict a President's character, world view, and style is to see how they were put together in the first place. This happened in his early life, culminating in his first independent political success" (p. 6). The biographical details of Banda's experiences in learning about agriculture come from a number of speeches, including those of July 26, 1975, and November 24, 1975. I obtained some information about Banda's grade record at the Wilberforce Academy from Wilberforce University. He began his high school work there in his late twenties. At that time, in this all-black high school, many students were older than high school students today. He had a grade average slightly higher than B, receiving his A grades in one history course and in four agricultural courses (general agriculture, field crops, gardening, and animal husbandry). Banda's gratitude for the education he received is best demonstrated by his $2 million gift to Wilberforce in 1979. By the 1970s Banda was one of the few African leaders who received his higher education in the interwar period; leaders from the same age cohort, such as those in the Côte d'Ivoire and Senegal, had also stressed agriculture.

21. The various papers are presented in Jackson (1965). The advice given to Nyasaland leaders was moderate. Banda's "Closing Address" (pp. 360–68) notes, "[I]f we are to develop Nyasaland in the way it should be developed, we must think in the first place in terms of developing and modernizing agriculture, rather than in terms of developing [manufacturing] industries." One participant at the conference told me that Banda's rejection of much of the advice he had received was considerably stronger than the printed version of his speech. The conference had been organized as a result of a correspondence between Dunduzu Chisiza and Walter Rostow. Chisiza had been greatly impressed with Rostow's book *The Stages of Economic Growth*, which he had read when imprisoned with Banda by the Federation government.

4 *Agriculture: Property and Production Policies in Malaŵi*

Agriculture is Malaŵi's largest economic sector both in labor force and in production. It is also the major source of exports, and its growth has been an important source of dynamism for the economy as a whole. President Banda, who has acted as his own minister of agriculture for much of his long period in office, has repeatedly stressed the importance of this sector.

The government's support of agriculture has raised some general problems of growth and income distribution. What sectors of agriculture should the government encourage, and what are the most effective policy tools to use? To what extent should governmental policies be targeted either at the most productive farmers or at the broad mass of farmers? In the Malaŵian context, the first problem has focused discussion on the relative importance of programs directed toward estate and toward smallholder agriculture and on the government's tilt toward the former through its credit and price policies. The second problem has centered attention on the extent to which the government has taken a stance that could be called a wager-on-the-strong policy (a phrase coming from a policy followed in the waning decades of Czarist Russia).

No valid a priori prescriptions can resolve either policy problem. For instance, although a wager-on-the-strong program widens rural income differentials, it is a defensible development strategy if three conditions are met: if resources channeled to the strong are more productive than if expended on the rest of the agricultural sector; if some benefits trickle down from the wealthier to the poorer part of the agricultural sector; and if the poorer part of the agricultural sector is not disadvantaged by other government policies, by natural conditions, or by its interactions with the wealthier part of the agricultural sector. In Malaŵi, the failure to meet most of these conditions has led to an apparent increase in poverty even as agricultural production has grown. In addition to its economic impacts, the wager-on-the-strong policy has had some obvious and important political and social consequences.

Agricultural Intensification and the Land Constraint

From independence in 1964 through 1986 agricultural production in Malaŵi grew at an average annual rate of about 3.2 percent.[1] Almost all of this growth was in crop production. Total land under cultivation (by smallholders and estates) increased in the same period at about 0.5 percent a year, and the number of agricultural workers increased at an annual rate slightly exceeding 2.0 percent. Thus, both land and labor productivity in agriculture have increased markedly, and Malaŵi's agricultural growth can be considered "intensive." Intensification of both estate and smallholder agriculture provided the explicit orientation for the agricultural policies proposed in *DevPol II*.

The dramatic decline in the average size of smallholder farms after independence and the apparent land shortage also point to increased intensity of cultivation. Estimates suggest that such land scarcities are least in the Northern Region and greatest in the Southern Region. To avoid increasing poverty under conditions of land scarcity, any wager-on-the-strong policy must be supplemented by special programs aimed at those with very small farms.

At any particular time, about 42 percent of the land used for agricultural purposes is cultivated; the rest is fallow or used for other agricultural purposes. In 1978 smallholders held about 86 percent of all Malaŵi's agricultural land (the remaining 14 percent was held by the estates) but farmed about 96 percent of the land under cultivation. Little information is available to help understand why the estates cultivate a smaller portion of their land; for instance, they might lack capital or hold poorer quality land. Undercultivation has been a concern in Malaŵi, and in *DevPol II* the government stated its intention of breaking up those estates not using their land effectively. Even if the estates did cultivate as large a share of their land as the smallholders, however, this additional amount would increase cultivated land only 15 percent—a small part of the calculated land shortage.

Small-Scale Agriculture

The smallholder sector follows traditional land tenure and production practices, its market production has been limited by law to certain crops, and its growth has been slow.

Land Tenure

Traditional forms of land tenure apply to almost all smallholder land. Tenure arrangements are complicated, but in general the following observations prevail (documented at length in section A of the Appendix):

- The distribution of smallholder farms is relatively equal—considerably more so than in Madagascar—and has remained so for the last several decades. Although the number of farms considered too small, using traditional techniques, to support a family has increased, the percentage of such farms has remained roughly the same.
- Landlessness and renting of land are uncommon, in strong contrast to Madagascar. The traditional rights to a piece of land are only validated by farming it oneself. Most leased land is on the estates (the "visiting tenant" system). Little evidence is available that landlessness has greatly increased since independence.
- Land under traditional land tenure can not be sold easily, although some has been leased to estates. A person obtains generalized permission to use particular land from traditional political or family authorities. The lack of a land market, combined with limitations on migration cause land-labor ratios to differ considerably throughout the country. The losses in efficiency from such a misallocation of production factors, however, are less than 5 percent of total production.
- Land tenure arrangements do not appear to have impeded the adoption of new agricultural technologies, at least for technologies that are independent of scale and that require little credit. Economies of scale are probably not very important; the staple, maize, is farmed by hand-hoe techniques, so relatively equal division of land probably has little impact on total production.
- The land tenure system discourages the development of a rural credit market, because land cannot be pledged as security (it would be difficult to transfer to outsiders). Of course, farmers could pledge their future crops, but this raises the creditor's risk and costs of enforcement. Thus, private agricultural credit, if supplied, comes at an interest premium, a subject receiving more attention in the next chapter.
- Agricultural production in Malaŵi has evolved in such a way as to allow the government, by law, to reserve certain cash crops exclusively for either the smallholders or the estates, a situation summarized in table 4-1. This arrangement cannot be justified on efficiency grounds, because smallholders in other nations have successfully grown tea and sugar, or on grounds that certain crops require special technical expertise, because a central technical expert could be assigned to serve many smallholders. In fact, the reservation system reduces allocative efficiency. Crop reservation is an outgrowth of the interwar period and the struggles between

70 *Malaŵi and Madagascar*

Table 4-1. Major Crops Grown by Estates and Smallholders, Malaŵi

Crop	Estates	Smallholders
Division of crops directly determined by government[a]		
Tobacco		
Flue-cured	Exclusively	
Burley	Exclusively until mid-1980s	
Oriental		Exclusively
Fire-cured		Exclusively since 1968
Sun/air cured		Exclusively since 1968
Cotton		Exclusively since 1962
Division of crops arising from other causes[b]		
Tea	Exclusively until recently	
Sugar	Almost exclusively until mid-1980s	
Paddy rice		Exclusively until recently
Groundnuts		Exclusively
Maize		Almost exclusively

a. Direct governmental action includes legislation, administrative directive, or negotiated actions.

b. Other causes include government actions taken for purposes other than the division of crops that, nevertheless, had that end result; examples include offering finance and technical expertise only to producers of a particular crop only in one sector.

Source: Interviews in Malaŵi

foreign estates and the African smallholders; the estates could manipulate the colonial government to obtain economic advantages.[2] In the late 1970s and early 1980s, however, this division of crops began to break down, especially as the smallholders began illegally growing estate-reserved crops. In the middle 1980s the government began formally to grant permission for more smallholders to cultivate burley tobacco and tea. The next chapter discusses the pricing implications of the reservation policy, and how it has acted against the smallholders, who are the poorest segment of the population.

• Since independence a number of laws have been enacted giving the government considerable power to change traditional tenure regulations and transferring specific pieces of land from traditional tenure to estates or to tenants. The government has also tried to encourage land consolidation by registration of land titles, although this program has not moved very far. Traditional land tenure arrangements appear to be quite secure—as long as the land is farmed.[3]

Production Growth of Smallholders

Estimates of the long-term growth of smallholder production must be taken cautiously because the underlying data, particularly for the early years, are uncertain. My estimates suggest that gross agricultural production (both cash crops and crops for home consumption) in the smallholder sector grew about 2.2 percent a year from 1964 through 1986. This rate was slightly faster than the roughly 2.0 percent annual increase in the smallholder population (derived from the 1966 and 1977 censuses). Rather uncertain data on family income tend to support the conclusion that per capita production grew very little. Other observers, relying on qualitative indicators, have suggested that per capita smallholder production and incomes actually have fallen somewhat. In any case, all observers agree that no great increase has occurred.

Perspective on the performance of the smallholder sector can be gained by taking into account several other considerations:

- From 1948 through 1963, in the last years of colonialism, gross crop production of smallholders appeared (we can not be very certain) to grow 6.0 percent a year.[4] In other words, by applying their efforts to a series of small projects in the smallholder sector, the colonial government seems to have had considerably more success in increasing production than has the current government, which has focused more on large integrated projects.

- From 1964 through 1986 gross crop production of the estates increased at an average annual rate of 10.4 percent, almost five times faster than in the smallholder sector. This great discrepancy was not planned, even though *DevPol I* projected a somewhat greater growth of estate than smallholder production, as did *DevPol II*.[5]

- The supply system for smallholders has not functioned smoothly, especially in the 1980s. For instance, although smallholder use of certain agricultural inputs, such as fertilizer, increased considerably, several obstacles discouraged use of these inputs in the late 1970s and early 1980s. The state-owned monopoly distributor of fertilizer had difficulty obtaining the credit and foreign exchange to purchase fertilizer from abroad; rail links connecting Malaŵi with Indian Ocean ports became uncertain and later were cut, which raised the cost of bulk items such as fertilizer; and many farmers could not easily find credit to purchase such inputs.

- Government investment in agriculture did not go into the purchase of agricultural equipment, and total private saving of smallholders did not appear sufficient for these purposes either, although we can not be completely sure.[6] In any case, in the 1980–81 crop season only 3.5 percent of all households owned a plow (which meant that 85 percent of the cultivated land was not plowed but was hand-hoed or tilled in some other way); only 0.7 percent owned a wheelbarrow; only 2.3 percent, a sprayer; only 2.0 percent, a ridger.[7] Slightly fewer than a third of the households applied any fertilizer to any crop. Seeds for about two-thirds of all plots used in growing maize, groundnuts, or pulses were retained from the previous year rather than purchased from the outside, which means that the traditional seeds remained a major input for these farmers. To the extent that labor productivity increased in the smallholder sector, it was due in considerable measure to greater use of fertilizer and improved seeds rather than mechanical equipment.

Production Policies for Smallholders: Capital-Intensive Projects

Although the government's policies effectively emphasized estate production, that was certainly not the original intention. Design problems as well as certain types of administrative constraints prevented a number of expensive projects aimed at smallholders from achieving their desired results.

Large-Scale Integrated Projects

A few years after independence, the Malaŵi government began to place great emphasis on large-scale, integrated rural development projects. This approach was abetted and assisted by various international aid agencies, such as the World Bank, and it contrasted strongly with the agricultural development policies of the colonial government, which had avoided expensive, capital-intensive projects that might strain administrative resources.[8]

In the late 1960s the Malaŵi government launched four integrated development programs: one in the Northern Region (the Karonga Rural Development Project), two in the Central Region (the Lilongwe Land Development Programme and the Lakeshore Project), and one in the Southern Region (the Shire Valley Agricultural Development Project). The projects consisted of considerable investment in the construction of rural infrastructure (roads, marketplaces, boreholes, irrigation, and health facilities) plus numerous land improvement projects, various conservation measures, increased agricultural extension work, supply of services complementary to agriculture, and the provision of credit. The four programs lasted about a decade before they were replaced by the National Rural Development Program.

The basic idea underlying the integrated development programs was simple: Agricultural development requires not only investment in particular production projects but also a series of complementary investments in other areas to enhance the projects' effects. Moreover, administering these projects as entities separate from the formal government apparatus could avoid difficulties in coordinating the activities of different ministries. Further, placing these projects in different parts of the nation would lead to a regional balance of benefits.[9] In contrast to the encouragement of the estates, which were financed primarily through the domestic banking system, financing for these integrated programs came almost exclusively from the government budget or from abroad.

The integrated projects focused on relatively favorable areas. The data in the upper part of table 4-2 show that at the start of the programs, the districts in which the projects were carried out had somewhat larger holdings per family than did the rest of Malaŵi, that the net farm (cash) income per family was about 1.9 times the average for all smallholders in Malaŵi, and that total cash income was about 13 percent higher than for all smallholders. The districts with the projects varied widely in holdings and wealth; for example, the Lakeshore project was in a relatively poor district and the Karonga and Lilongwe projects were in the richest districts.

The costs of the four original projects were high in many respects. The target farmers constituted about 10 percent of all Malaŵian smallholders (about 30 percent of those in the target area). The expenditures per family adopting the new technology amounted to about twenty-two times the average family income of Malaŵian smallholders in 1968 and 1969. The total cost of these four projects was 165.2 million MK, while total governmental budgetary expenditures for natural resources from 1968 through 1978 were about 192.8 million MK. Assuming that about half of the expenditures on the integrated projects would have been spent for infrastructure through other parts of the budget and that agricultural expenditures constituted three-quarters of total budgetary expenditures for agriculture and natural resources, the four integrated projects absorbed almost 60 percent of total governmental expenditures on agriculture.

Although the benefit-cost ratios of these investments appear low, their impact on agricultural production within the areas embraced by the four integrated programs is difficult to assess, partly because the available data are uncertain and partly because the programs changed considerably in size and scope over the years.[10] They obviously had little effect on gross crop production of the smallholder sector as a whole, which at best has grown only slightly faster than the growth of population. An evaluation of the Lilongwe project shows no sustained increase in maize yields and perhaps a decrease in groundnut yields. In the Shire Valley project, the hectare productivity in cotton (the major crop) fell; for other crops it rose only slowly. The scattered data for the Karonga project also show no remarkable results. No evaluation of the Lakeshore project is readily available.

Table 4-2. Data on the Four Major Integrated Projects, Malaŵi, 1968–69 Crop Year

			Separate projects			
Item	All Malaŵi	All projects	Karonga	Lilongwe	Lakeshore	Shire Valley
Initial conditions[a]						
Average size per holding (hectares)	1.5	1.9	1.4	2.2	1.2	1.5
Average net farm income (MK)[b]	9.3	17.4	21.9	18.9	9.0	16.3
Average current cash income (MK)[c]	33.6	37.9	50.7	36.1	21.1	42.3
Costs						
Years covered by cost data	—	—	12	14	10	14
Total costs (million MK)	—	165.2	12.6	22.9	23.3	106.4
Families in target areas (thousands)	—	272.7	41.4	54.6	103.0	73.7
Families adopting technology package (thousands)	—	84.8	4.8	21.0	31.0	28.0
Cost per adopting family (MK)[d]	—	1,948	2,625	1,090	752	3,800

— = Not applicable.

a. The initial conditions data are for districts that are not quite contiguous with the project area.
b. Current farm cash receipts minus current farm cash expenditures.
c. Current farm cash receipts plus other current cash income such as wages, excluding transfers, credit, and capital cash receipts.
d. The cost per adopting farmer is somewhat misleading because the projects contain nonagricultural components and expenditures that may benefit a larger number of farmers. For instance, the Karonga program contains a lake transportation program, a district hospital, and a rice irrigation scheme that serve many more people than just the adopting farmers.

Source: Malaŵi Government (1970), tables D2.1 and D6.1; and Chipande (1983b). The costs per adopting family are my own estimates and differ from those of Chipande.

These disappointing results could have three major causes. First, the technology and credit packages were inappropriate for all but the largest farms (these matters are discussed in detail in the next chapter). Second, the pricing policies of ADMARC, the parastatal monopsony purchasing smallholder products, served as a disincentive for production (a topic also for consideration in the next chapter). Third, the high costs of administration, the difficulties of coordinating the programs, and the use of investment funds for purposes with little direct relation to agricultural production reduced the effectiveness of these programs.

The integrated programs also seemed to widen income differentials among smallholders in several ways. As noted, only the richest farmers could take advantage of the technology package. Moreover, the projects were placed in areas with higher per capita incomes than other farming areas of the country; the heavy capital outlay and the demands on trained personnel precluded their use in the poorest areas of Malaŵi.

In retrospect, the government underestimated the administrative and coordination difficulties inherent in the basic concept of the complementarity of agricultural investment (which is closely related to the notion of the "big push" in development). The administrative separation from the ministerial structure of the government did not prove to be the expected cure-all for such coordination problems; indeed, such gimmicks can seldom overcome the administrative constraints on governments. In addition, turning completed projects back to particular ministries was difficult. In some cases operation or maintenance problems of particular nonagricultural components were so severe as to lead to their partial abandonment after the turn-back (World Bank June 1982). Finally, the intense attention to the four projects led to a neglect of other areas.

Small-Scale Integrated Projects

In 1978, after internal discussion for about five years, the Malaŵi government adopted a different approach toward integrated agricultural development. The National Rural Development Program (NRDP) divided the country into eight agricultural development divisions (ADDs), each of which comprised five development areas (DAs). In rotation each DA would receive special governmental attention for three years so that after twenty years each DA would have been the object of special treatment. This approach concentrates funds on particular areas but ensures long-run equality of treatment if the NRDP completes its planned trajectory. The agricultural extension work and other programs carried out in the DAs not receiving the special treatment during a particular period are supposed to be maintained at current levels.

Some of the guiding ideas behind the NRDP were much different from those of the large-scale projects. Of greatest importance, the program was to be much more closely integrated into the existing governmental structure. Indeed, in some cases administrative boundaries were changed to conform to the ADDs, which were designed to cover specific ecological zones. The investments were to focus less on infrastructure and more on projects directly related to production so that an investment would have a quicker economic payoff. Deemphasizing the multicomponent approach of the large-scale integrated programs was supposed to minimize coordination problems among different administrative agencies. Extension work was also to be stepped up in the ADDS. In addition, the program was supposed to make special arrangements for redistributing income in favor of the rural poor (J. A. K. Kandawêre, in Fyfe 1985, pp. 527–46).

I have been unable to locate data to evaluate the NRDP systematically; indeed, such information may not be available. A preliminary study noted that the cost per family of these programs was roughly the same as for the integrated programs, so the movement from "intensive" to "extensive" investments did not materialize (Kandawêre, in Fyfe 1985; World Bank June 1982). Furthermore, the amount of special aid these projects were supposed to distribute to the rural poor apparently was not very significant. Also, civil servants in Malaŵi told me that the program repeated many of the mistakes of the integrated projects, including the high administration costs, overly complex management system, inflexible administration, inappropriate technology packages, investment expenditures for purposes (such as infrastructure) having little direct relation to agricultural production, and concentration of benefits among too few farmers in the favored districts. In a laconic paragraph in *DevPol II* (p. 27), the government admitted that the impact of the NRDP "has not as yet been as substantial as envisioned." Rather than abandoning the program, however, it was supposed to refocus its efforts even more on those components directly related to agricultural production and marketing in order to make the investment program more labor intensive.

A quite different type of capital-intensive approach was announced in *DevPol II*—the development of irrigation. The most notable project will be a 20,000-hectare scheme in the lower Shire. Given the geography of the country, such irrigation projects are likely to reach only a small proportion of smallholders.

The delays in rectifying the NRDP's problems, which were becoming apparent in the early 1980s, contrasts with the government's policy pragmatism and flexibility in the 1970s, when the difficulties of the integrated projects became apparent. This policy inertia during the 1980s appeared to result in part from the lack of strong leadership as policymaking authority devolved from the Life President to younger governmental officials and the civil service. In any case, the Malaŵi government clearly took important and expensive measures to improve smallholder agriculture and, in large measure, failed. The government's development strategy may be characterized as estate-oriented by default—it has been unable to implement an effective large-scale program for the smallholders.

Production Policies for Smallholders: Labor-Intensive Approaches

To aid smallholders, Malaŵi has followed a variety of labor-intensive projects, many of which are ingenious. Although probably more cost effective than the large-scale programs, their effectiveness has been limited.

Colonial Policies

The British government pursued three types of agricultural policies in the post-World War II era: technology development, extension programs, and small training and development projects.[11] Technology development was a high priority. These programs drew not only from colonial research in other nations but also from several small experimental stations set up in Malaŵi These programs, however, appeared to benefit primarily the European estate owners. Agricultural extension work was supposed to spread the new technologies. The ratio of trained extension workers to African farmers, at roughly 1 to 20,000, limited the effectiveness of these programs. The small-scale projects were aimed at increasing production. They included a master-farmer scheme; the establishment of several agricultural training schools; separate credit cooperatives for estates and smallholders; and certain infrastructure projects, primarily to regulate the water level of the Shire River. How these limited policies (or, for that matter, the agricultural price policies the British followed) led to the very fast growth of smallholder production during the last decade and a half of the colonial era is difficult to understand. To the extent that these programs provided special benefits to estate owners and master farmers, they represented a colonial version of a wager-on-the-strong strategy.

Major Approaches after Independence

The Malaŵi government has also pursued a variety of labor-intensive programs in addition to its integrated development programs. These programs have varied considerably in scope and direction.

TECHNOLOGY POLICY. The relative factor proportions in the agricultural sector have led the government to introduce and stress use of labor-intensive technologies. For instance, it has advocated the use of oxen, not tractors, and labor-intensive agricultural methods such as tie ridging and hand spraying of insecticides. By encouraging use of improved seeds and fertilizer, it has focused more attention on improving land productivity than on raising labor or capital productivity (thus responding in the manner suggested by theorists of induced innovation). An important constraint on smallholder agriculture, however,

78 Malaŵi and Madagascar

is the labor shortage occurring during periods of peak labor demand; encouragement of labor-saving technologies for the tasks carried out at this critical season would have had a high payoff.

EXTENSION AND TRAINING. The extension service has been the government's primary contact with most farmers.[12] In the early 1980s the government fielded about 4,000 extension workers, or about 1 per 250 farm families, but their distribution, at least in the middle and late 1970s, was uneven. The areas outside of the four rural development projects had only one extension worker to about 1,400 to 2,400 families; within the project areas this ratio was much higher. Increasing the number of extension workers for all ADDs has been a goal of the NRDP.

Malaŵi has tried a number of ingenious schemes to increase the effectiveness of its extension work. These include group education projects, which reach about a fourth of the population each year; movies about agriculture; special training courses, which have recorded roughly 70,000 student-days a year; a special farmers' magazine, which had a circulation of 16,000 in the late 1970s; and training in agricultural technology through the Malaŵi Young Pioneers.[13]

Some evidence indicates that the extension service has had a positive effect on production. For instance, in the Lilongwe Land Development Programme, maize yields were directly correlated with the number of visits by extension workers, although such a correlation was less impressive for groundnut production. The government has tried to enhance the effectiveness of extension work by closely linking it with the granting of credit; as discussed in detail in the next chapter, farmers usually can obtain credit only if they follow recommended agricultural practices. Evidence also supports a positive correlation between the number of visits by extension agents and the adoption of new technologies by individual farmers.

Nevertheless, the extension programs are open to some serious criticisms.[14] Some observers have noted that the extension service does not reach certain subsectors of the rural economy; for instance, although women control a significant number of smallholdings, extension worker visits to farms headed by females are fewer than visits to male-headed smallholdings. Other critics have argued that the extension workers have encouraged crops that are inappropriate for Malaŵian conditions. Extension workers are said to direct rather than induce farmers to adopt approved activities. *DevPol II* criticized the extension program for its inability to adapt its advice to the actual needs of smallholders and for its inadequate logistic support of its field workers.

The Malaŵian agricultural extension service has certainly been more active than a similar service in Madagascar. The bald statement in *DevPol II* (p. 29) that extension activities have not had "a significant impact in increasing productivity" is exaggerated, because diminishing returns in agriculture would probably have been more severe without this work. Nevertheless, agricultural extension clearly has not lived up to initial expectations.

RESEARCH. The government has tried to structure close links between the extension service and research but has encountered many problems. For instance, for many years the extension service particularly stressed a special type of high-yield maize suitable for Malaŵi's climate. This hybrid maize, however, is difficult to store under village conditions; it requires fertilizer, which many farmers can not afford (and the most appropriate fertilizer damages the groundnuts, which are used later in the rotation scheme); it can not be eaten green, which is sometimes necessary during the hunger period preceding the harvest; it does not meet the taste criteria of many Malaŵians; it must be grown in pure stands, which are prone to greater pest problems; and it is subject to greater production risks. Indeed, this maize seemed suitable only for the largest farms in the Central and Northern Regions, which have an assured food supply. These problems were evident for more than a decade, but the maize program continued uncorrected.

The attempts made in the 1980s to strengthen the mutual communication between agricultural extension and research (particularly for maize production) appeared hesitant and slow.[15] A good part of the problem stemmed from the research side, especially because the agricultural research budget has been small, accounting for less than 0.5 percent of gross agricultural product. The Ministry of Agriculture has operated eleven different research stations, but only two have had sufficient personnel and resources to implement comprehensive research efforts. Such research work has further been criticized as diffuse and insufficiently focused on the most important problems, especially those the smallholders face. Furthermore, little research has focused on economic and social problems in agriculture to aid governmental policy formation. *DevPol II* proposed the creation of a number of Centers of Adaptive Research, which would carry out experimental work on crop problems specific to each center's particular locality.

INPUTS. The government subsidized certain farm inputs, particularly fertilizers, even though until the late 1980s only the wealthier farmers could obtain the credit to buy such inputs. Since the late 1970s these subsidies have been reduced. The government also established a special parastatal, the National Seed Company, to market better varieties of seeds. For a while it even tried distributing free improved seeds, but experience showed that such seeds were wasted, and this type of project was abandoned.

MASTER FARMERS. The Malaŵi government has also continued the colonial program for master farmers, one of a number of governmental measures designed to create an economic elite to lead the country's development.[16] Such programs channel subsidies and credits to farmers receiving the master farmer designation. In the colonial period the program was quite small and, by 1960, included only 745 smallholders. The Malaŵi government modified, broadened, and continued the program under the rubric of the Progressive Farmer (*Achikumbe*) Program; in 1975 and 1977 the program included, respectively, 63,000 and 76,000 farmers. These farmers can sell their tobacco at auction, rather than through ADMARC, a government parastatal; they also receive special credits and priority for farm inputs, as well as other favored treatment. The hope that such progressive farmers would serve as teachers-by-example to their fellow smallholders has not been realized in certain areas where extraordinary agricultural success is sometimes associated with witchcraft; however, the growth in number of progressive farmers suggests that this belief is becoming less important.[17] The progressive farmer program represents in a very direct form a wager-on-the-strong policy, because it deliberately increases income differentiation in order to increase production. Despite such intentions, some local observers claim it has not appreciably increased agricultural productivity, but no hard data on the matter are available.

The government's overall labor-intensive production policies toward smallholders were probably more cost effective than its large-scale, capital-intensive projects, but they still left much to be desired. Their administration, however, was certainly more efficient than similar programs in Madagascar. In Malaŵi most production programs were channeled through a single ministry; the government tried to a certain extent to work through traditional rural elites, such as the chiefs, so that they would help implement some of the improvement programs; and the extension service was able to reach a considerable share of the rural population, especially through its group programs. The financial and administrative resources available for the smallholder programs were limited, however, because the government focused its major efforts on the large-scale, capital-intensive projects. Some important structural problems, such as the lack of effective two-way communication between research and extension work, also created difficulties. Furthermore, the government proved unable to devise any effective programs to prevent the income fall of the poorest smallholders. Thus, although the government's wager-on-the-strong policy was a deliberate decision, it was also partly inadvertent.

Large-Scale Agriculture

Large-scale agricultural enterprises include both production cooperatives and agricultural estates (plantations). Although the Malaŵi government has promoted various types of input, credit, and marketing cooperatives, it has not encouraged production cooperatives, and as far as I could find out, none was ever established, a marked contrast with Madagascar.

The public and private agricultural estates have played a leading role in the growth of Malaŵi's GDP and exports. The civil service has not played any significant role in the administration of public-sector estates, nor did it have much to do with the private estates until the mid-1980s. Most of the growth of the estate sector has occurred through the aid of credit from banks, which, although state owned, operate autonomously.

A Review of the Estate Sector

Before independence all estates were foreign owned; after independence Malaŵians began to purchase them, especially those producing tobacco. Among the early buyers was President Banda, working through his own Press Holding Corporation and General Farming Company. During the late 1960s and early 1970s President Banda encouraged all leading politicians to follow his example. "Every minister must have an estate. . . . I am right up to my neck in debt, but I will pay the debt one day." "We must impress upon our people the importance for producing . . . by setting concrete and tangible examples ourselves. By this I mean we must do this by opening up gardens, or farm ourselves . . . whether we are Minister, Parliamentary Secretary, Member of Parliament, Party Leader . . . "[18] The state-owned banks provided tangible support for these acquisitions in the form of credit. This policy appeared to be an attempt to create a new class of wealthy Malaŵians, who not only would aid the country by their development efforts but also would owe the president an important political debt.

The banks and parastatal enterprises generously provided the new estates with loans and advice (chapter 8), and government agencies, especially ADMARC, also participated in buying and managing the estates. Given such encouragement, the estate lands owned or leased by Malaŵians increased rapidly during the early 1970s. Developing those estates, which were not simply a takeover of European farms, required clearing the land, erecting buildings, sinking boreholes, and farming where no agriculture had taken place before, a difficult venture in any circumstance. Moreover, even though these estates were not very mechanized, technical problems were still formidable.

Some aggregate statistics are available on the growth and relative importance of the estate sector as a whole (Pryor 1988b, section A). In 1957 "private lands" were usually estates; they consisted of roughly 400,000 hectares (about 1 million acres), of which about 320,000 were freeholds primarily held by Europeans and the remainder were leaseholds. By 1967 freeholds were down to roughly 200,000 hectares, and leaseholds were up slightly to 100,000 hectares. By 1974 the government had purchased most freeholds, some of which were leased back to the former owners and the remainder to Malaŵians. Over time the remaining private freeholds apparently were gradually leased to Malaŵians, and by the mid-1980s estates (leaseholds and freeholds) comprised roughly 600,000 hectares. The process of extending the estate sector was aided by invoking some controversial land laws passed in the late 1960s. These allowed the government to obtain customary lands, which it leased to private individuals. It appears (although complete certainty on the matter is not possible) that such land, taken from the smallholder sector, accounted for the bulk of the newly established estates. For instance, both the SUCOMA sugar estate and the ranch once held by Press Holding Corporation (ranching has now ceased) were operated on lands formerly under customary law. Also, most of this expansion of estates, whether on customary or other lands, appears to have occurred primarily on lands that had relatively little or no previous agricultural use.[19]

In the early period after independence the estates were relatively large and their numbers (owned or leased by private individuals) were few. By about 1980 the estates occupied roughly 14 percent of all Malaŵi's agricultural land, and some claim they hold a much larger fraction of the highest quality land. About 1,200 of these estates (mostly owned by Malaŵians) grew tobacco; 26 (mostly owned by UK nationals) were tea estates; 2 were sugar estates; and a small number were of other kinds.[20] In the 1970s the major growth in estate land had been for tobacco; in the mid-1980s the number of tobacco estates (defined as those permitted to grow burley or fire-cured tobacco) started to increase again as the government began to give smallholders permission to cultivate such crops. *DevPol II* had projected 3,000 burley tobacco estates averaging about 10 cultivated hectares and 58 new coffee estates by the late 1980s. This long-term plan also announced limitations on the increase in the land area held by the estate sector, except where land was relatively abundant.

The public sector has played a significant role in estate production, but the exact share requires some work to determine. I include the president's estates in the public sector, primarily because of his declaration that he holds his companies "in trust for the people of the nation" (he has no direct heirs) and because of legal evidence that, after his death, they will revert to the state. From scattered numbers, I estimate that in the late 1970s and early 1980s, ADMARC, Press Holding, and General Farming held about 30 percent of the estate land used in production and from 20 to 30 percent of all estate land. From still different evidence, I also estimate that in 1977 the public sector provided roughly 32 percent of the employment in the estates, or about 2.5 percent of the total economically active in agriculture (Pryor 1988b, table K-3).

All of the estates owned in the public sector and by the president have been run on strictly commercial lines and have been expected to make a profit. Indeed, this policy aim was met during most of the 1970s, and thus "capitalist" Malawi accomplished an unmet goal of most socialist nations—making state-owned farms profitable.

Management of the new estates raised problems.[21] Many of the new estate owners lacked the requisite technical and managerial skills to run the estates by themselves; further, many were without sufficient personal capital or loans to finance such ventures sufficiently. Some estates were able to obtain as managers young European farmers from Southern Rhodesia who were leaving because of the political unrest in the 1960s, occasioned by that country's Unilateral Declaration of Independence. Because of uncertainties about the abilities of these Rhodesians, a considerable number had short-term contracts (often only two years), which of course limited their perspective. Many appeared to have left Malawi by the late 1970s.

Some critical management problems were not immediately apparent. Tobacco prices were high during the early and mid-1970s, and many estates were able to show impressive profits by riding this tobacco boom. In 1974 and 1975 claims of profit rates of 25 to 30 percent were common. The data in table 4-3 reveal that wages on the estates averaged between 33 and 60 percent of the total value added in the estate sector (with higher percentages recorded in the later years). Assuming land value and capital per worker were triple the wages paid workers, rates of return on investment would average between 22 and 67 percent.[22]

The real structural problems in the estate sector became apparent in the late 1970s and early 1980s, when Mozambique insurgents (RENAMO) began to disrupt Malawi's railway links through Mozambique to the Indian Ocean (they were completely cut in 1983 and 1984). At the same time, export prices started to fall rapidly in relation to import prices (chapter 6). Many estates (including some under ADMARC and Press Holding) began to lose considerable amounts of money, and a number went into receivership or bankruptcy. In essence this increased the size of the state sector in agriculture because by this time the banking sector, which appointed or served as the receiver, was almost entirely government owned. Further, the management of other private estates by the Agricultural Liaison Service (owned by the banks) increased the role of the public sector in managing these estates, even though ownership remained private. In *DevPol II* the government announced its intention of setting up the Estate Extension Training Service to provide additional aid to the estate sector.

As a result of these economic difficulties, considerable restructuring occurred in the estate sector. A survey of the private tobacco estate owners made in 1986 revealed that only 19 percent of the owners

Table 4-3. Comparisons of Labor Productivity of Smallholders and Estate Workers, Malaŵi, 1968 and 1973–80

Year	Estimated labor force, smallholders (thousands of male-worker equivalents)[a]	Value added per worker (MK)[b] Smallholders No adjustment	Rough adjustment	Estates	Annual wage (MK)[c] Average on estates	Minimum (for 300 days)
1968	2,442.6	n.a.	n.a.	n.a.	94.4	69
1973	2,685.3	43.3	56.2	288.1	111.9	75
1974	2,736.7	52.2	67.9	380.9	126.8	75
1975	2,789.0	57.0	74.1	322.6	124.2	75
1976	2,842.3	69.0	89.7	308.0	131.1	75
1977	2,896.7	81.5	106.0	398.8	147.8	75
1978	2,952.1	86.4	112.3	287.0	172.7	75
1979	3,008.6	87.2	113.4	302.3	171.7	75
1980	3,066.1	n.a.	n.a.	n.a.	190.9	90

n.a. = Not available.

a. The estimated labor force of smallholders is an exponential interpolation between the 1968–69 and 1980–81 crop years; the two end points were obtained from Malaŵi Government (1970) and (1984).

b. The total value added in current prices comes from Malaŵi, NSO (1983b), but the statistics were calculated in different prices for the same goods for estates and smallholders. I have, therefore, adjusted the value added of smallholders upward by 30 percent each year (the 30 percent is roughly the average profit of ADMARC on its sales of smallholder products).

c. The data on wages in agriculture come from various issues of Malaŵi, NSO, *Reported Employment and Earnings, Annual Report* (irregular) and Pryor (1988b), section H. The minimum wage data are for "other areas."

were politicians and civil servants (probably a much smaller share than planned), 36 percent of the owners were formerly employed in relatively low-status jobs (smallholding farming and manual labor), and the remainder were roughly split between those with high- and medium-status jobs. About 65 percent resided on their estates, and roughly the same proportion claimed to spend most of their time in activities connected with farming. Only 13 percent could be considered absentee owners, who did not live on their estates, hired estate managers, and did not spend most of their working time on farming concerns; in contrast, various sources indicate that absentee ownership was common in the late 1960s. An overwhelming majority leased, rather than owned, their land in 1986.[23]

The estate strategy was another aspect of President Banda's attempt to create an economic elite to help guide the country. The results of this attempt may not have been entirely successful, at least as indicated by the answers of these estate owners to a question about their profit expectations. The mid-1980s were difficult times because the exchange rate was considerably overvalued, which meant that these owners received low domestic prices for their crop. Only 2 percent of the estate owners said that income from the estate had fully met their expectations; 15 percent replied, "most" of their expectations; 50 percent, "some" of their expectations; and the expectations of 35 percent were not met at all. Given the external shocks this sector absorbed, such results come as no surprise. Capitalist farmers seldom obtain all the profits they wish; nevertheless, in Malaŵi such estate owners seemed particularly disgruntled. If these estate owners are considered as a "new class" or "new rural bourgeoisie, " they appeared a disappointed class, mollified only by pride in their new status as land leasers and the realization that other opportunities for higher incomes were limited.

Production

The government's attempt to link political patronage and rent-seeking to the cause of agricultural development through estate agriculture gave rise to some spectacular results in the early and mid-1970s, when the program took hold. The growth rate of gross agricultural production was 10.4 percent a year between 1964 and 1986, and both land and labor productivities on the estates appear to have been much higher than in the smallholder sector. This can be most easily seen by comparing their share of agricultural inputs and outputs. In the late 1970s and early 1980s the estates employed about 6 percent of the total labor force and farmed about 4 percent of total cultivated land. The data in table 4-4 show that the estates produced 35 to 45 percent of the gross crop production. Although this is much higher than their share of value added (17 to 20 percent), both production and value added are much higher than their share of land and labor inputs.[24] Other evidence comes from crop data presented in *Malaŵi Statistical Yearbook*, which show higher land productivity on the estates for almost all comparable crops. Knowing the degree to which this higher land and labor productivity has resulted from the use of more advanced technology, greater capital inputs (because of the generous loan program), or more use of complementary inputs (improved seeds or fertilizers) would permit computation of the relative costs of production; the requisite data are not available, however.

Time trends are also important to consider. In the period covered by the table, labor hired by the estates increased annually by 4.6 percent, while planted land annually increased by 3.2 percent. Thus the land-labor ratio decreased, although not as rapidly as in the smallholder sector. Comparing input and output trends, both labor

Table 4-4. Data on the Estate Sector, Malaŵi, 1955 to 1984

Year	Average annual number of hired workers (excludes tenants)[a]	Planted land (hectares)[b]	Gross crop production (thousands of 1978 MK)[c]	Estate share (percent)[c] Gross crop production	Exports
1955	54,240	31,467	17,895	18.6	41.7
1956	62,960	31,731	19,074	19.0	32.2
1957	63,390	30,678	18,574	18.3	33.7
1958	61,810	30,936	21,870	20.8	35.5
1959	61,210	29,937	23,084	19.7	36.4
1960	60,300	29,523	24,873	19.6	40.0
1961	57,400	30,682	25,873	19.5	42.7
1962	53,050	27,940	25,487	16.9	29.6
1963	50,023	25,569	23,394	15.5	25.4
1964	49,250	25,355	21,538	16.0	25.9
1965	49,700	25,293	23,351	13.7	24.1
1966	50,150	24,726	25,708	13.7	26.8
1967	50,600	25,522	29,086	14.4	23.5
1968	51,044	24,466	29,672	18.4	29.1
1969	55,821	28,612	31,703	17.8	31.3
1970	62,081	31,521	40,720	21.4	39.7
1971	66,341	35,304	43,501	20.0	41.4
1972	73,699	36,369	49,619	21.2	40.9
1973	88,159	38,779	58,998	26.6	46.8
1974	92,934	41,610	59,091	25.9	52.1
1975	107,551	44,649	76,277	32.9	59.0
1976	120,118	50,839	83,728	31.1	61.5
1977	154,696	53,652	98,597	31.9	63.2
1978	169,334	58,356	101,943	32.0	66.2
1979	182,295	63,150	118,807	34.7	66.1
1980	181,137	67,808	130,408	39.3	65.0
1981	157,195	67,402	128,430	40.7	71.7
1982	158,200	n.a.	151,085	44.3	74.3
1983	197,200	n.a.	160,318	45.0	76.4
1984	177,700	n.a.	151,244	41.9	65.6

n.a. = Not available.

a. Employment data from 1968 through 1984 are from various issues of Malaŵi, NSO, *Reported Employment and Earnings* (annual). The data for 1968 through 1976 have been adjusted to accord with the definitions followed in 1977 and subsequent years. Labor force data from 1955 through 1963, Central African Federation of Rhodesia and Nyasaland (1964). The degree of comparability of these data with the NSO data is unclear, but the orders of magnitudes suggest some comparability. The data from 1964 through 1967 are interpolations between 1963 and 1968.

b. The land data are summaries of crop data of tobacco, tea, seed cotton, sugar, tung, and coffee. For the latter two, I had to make some minor estimates. The data come from Malaŵi, NSO (1970b), (1980a) and various issues of *Malaŵi Statistical Yearbook*.

c. The data on estate sector production and exports come from Pryor (1988b), section C.

and land productivity appear to have risen dramatically, but several interpretative problems reduce our confidence in these conclusions. Data on inputs are lacking. Also, the production of burley tobacco on the estates has been carried out in good measure by tenant farmers, who are not counted as employees. For what it is worth, the joint factor productivity of the reported employees and land appears to have increased at an annual average rate of 5.1 percent, but much of this is probably due to an increase in the capital stock and a change in the composition of output.[25]

Table 4-4 also shows the dramatic increase of estate production in both total gross crop production and crop exports, confirming the oft-made observation that estate production has served as the dynamo of Malawian growth. This is not the end of the story, however, for two vital questions must be answered. To what extent has the rapid growth in estate production led to a widening of income differentials, especially in agriculture (a thesis Kydd and Christiansen (1981b) argue with great vigor)?[26] And to what extent has this growth been at the expense of the smallholder sector?

Impact on Income Distribution

The property income originating from the estates was an important factor in widening nationwide income differentials. Some notion of the relevant magnitudes can be gained from some data for 1973 through 1979 that show total net profits of private estates averaging 4.0 percent of the factor price GDP.[27] Profits were being made in many other parts of the economy, however, and these private estate profits represented only about one-seventh of total profits during this period. Thus the estates' contribution to overall income inequality appears limited, and at least in a direct sense, such profits were not at the expense of the smallholder, although they did have some important indirect effects.

Exploration of the estates' impact on income distribution raises some other questions that are relevant for this study:

- To what extent did work on the estates permit smallholders to escape from poverty? The average income of families on the estates in 1968–69 was roughly twice that of smallholder families (chapter 16). The workers on estates amounted to about 2 percent of the male-worker equivalents of smallholders in 1968 and about 6 to 8 percent in the crop year 1980–81, so the opportunity to work in a higher income sector was available to only a small share of the rural population.

- How was the higher income of estate workers related to the higher labor productivity of the estates? Lacking proper data, only some crude comparisons of productivity can be made by using the value-added data in table 4-3. For the seven years for which data are available, the (adjusted) value added per worker in the smallholder sector ranged from 20 to 40 percent of the value added per worker in the estate sector (the percentage rises during this period). Especially noteworthy is that the value added in the smallholder sector ranged from 50 to 70 percent of the wages of estate workers (the percentages rise from 1973 to 1977 and then fall slightly). The most straightforward interpretation from these data fragments is that average and marginal labor productivity (assuming workers were paid their marginal product) in the estate sector were higher than in the smallholder sector and that part of this higher productivity was translated into higher incomes.[28] Contrary to some assertions, estate wages did not seem to lead, at least directly, to the creation of poverty.

• Why were estate workers paid more than the minimum wage, especially in light of the fact that they were unable to organize into labor unions to obtain a share of any economic rents accruing to the estates? Given the fact that estate incomes were higher than smallholder incomes, estate managers could have enlarged their labor force, which would have reduced worker marginal productivity but would also have lowered the agricultural wage. This question is important, especially because estate owners reported that labor was relatively easy to obtain.[29]

The existing statistics do not allow definitive answers to these questions, but several conjectures can be offered. First, the income differential might reflect a quality difference between the average smallholder and the average estate worker. More specifically, estate workers might require a certain amount of capital or improved land; if these inputs were not available, the labor force could not be expanded easily. Furthermore, the estate owners might be willing to pay high wages to maintain a reliable labor force. Second, the higher wage might represent the reservation wage of the smallholders, who were reluctant to lose their independence. This conjecture suggests that estate owners would have difficulty obtaining labor even at this higher wage, but this does not seem to have been the case. Third, these data, which are uncertain, might overstate the income differentials between smallholders and estate workers. For instance, the income of smallholders might be understated because the data do not include certain types of production for home consumption, or the estates might have overstated the income of workers to reduce tax or other legal liabilities. Of course the gap might be underestimated to the extent that payments-in-kind to estate workers (for example, free housing, water, and certain meals) are not included in their stated income.

• To what extent did the higher labor income in the estate sector contribute to the increase in income inequality? For the nation as a whole, this question can be answered by dividing the sources of income inequality for the nation into that arising from within-group and between-group income differences of rural workers. A transfer of workers from the smallholder sector to the estates probably results in some narrowing of income differences between estate workers and smallholders. Further, the inequality of income among estate workers is less than that among smallholders (chapter 16), so the increase in the number of estate workers puts a larger share of the population in a sector with smaller within-group differences. In both ways, therefore, the hiring of workers from the smallholdings serves to narrow nationwide income differentials.

Qui Bono?

Has growth of the estate sector occurred at the expense of the smallholder sector? Some top decisionmakers in Malaŵi have argued that the two subsectors of agriculture are completely complementary in that estates serve as schools to teach more advanced agricultural methods. Other observers, however, have argued that the estates have grown almost completely at the expense of the smallholders. To a certain extent, the problem pivots around the definition of "expense."

ESTATES AND THE COMPETITION FOR LAND. To what extent did the expansion of the estate sector result in less land for smallholders or landlessness? The evidence presented above suggests that somewhat less than half of the estate land was transferred from the smallholder sector, and most of it apparently had not been used for agriculture previously.

Information about the related problem of landlessness in Malaŵi is almost nonexistent, and this topic has not received much open political attention in the media, which the government controls. In various articles Kydd and Christiansen have argued that the increasing land shortage and resulting impoverishment has forced smallholders onto the estates. Although this proposition contains some truth, the situation is more complicated. The income differentials between the estate and smallholder sectors have also pulled smallholders toward the estates. The degree to which estate workers can be considered landless also depends on several factors. An unknown share of plantation workers have family members with land to which they might return. Further, the system of customary tenure permits the plantation workers to obtain land if they decide to return to smallholding, at least in the northern areas where land is still available. Whether this will remain true in the future, however, as land pressures increase and as traditional ethnic land tenure arrangements begin to crumble is doubtful.

Between 1966 and 1977 (the last two census years) 5 percent of Malaŵi's population moved from rural to urban areas; how many were motivated by landlessness arising from the expansion of the estate sector is not known. Given the fact, however, that estates hold only a small percentage of farm land in Malaŵi, the declining size of holdings because of increasing population is probably responsible for more of the rural-urban migration than is the increase in the size of the estate sector alone.

ESTATES AND THE COMPETITION FOR LABOR. To what extent did the better farmers move from the smallholder land to become workers on estate land? Data on the relative schooling of such workers appear to be unavailable for the two subsectors; as a proxy, however, we can use information on those who have worked abroad, on the assumption that these workers have shown "more initiative" or have had an opportunity to learn more new skills. Actually, the proportion of workers with foreign work experience is higher among the *alimi* (smallholding farmers) than among estate workers.[30] The contrary interpretation—that the less successful smallholders took work abroad because they could not earn a living on the farm in Malaŵi—would not explain why these workers returned to smallholding rather than remaining abroad or joining the urban work force. All that can be definitely said is that the estates have succeeded in drawing off some able-bodied men from the smallholder labor force.

ESTATES AND THE COMPETITION FOR CREDIT. To what extent was the considerable amount of credit the estates received from the banks at the expense of the smallholders? Would or could such credit have gone to smallholders? Some institutional factors deserve consideration here.

Because most smallholders in Malaŵi still hold their land in a traditional tenure arrangement, it can not be alienated or used as collateral for any loan arrangement. Further, administering a series of small loans costs a lender considerably more than administering a few large loans that equal the same amount. Following commercial practices to which they were committed, the banks are unlikely to have extended much credit to smallholders unless the government had guaranteed and subsidized such loans. The government appeared unwilling to back such a program, however, in part because of its lack of personnel to administer it effectively.

The ultimate sources of finance for the estates and smallholders were different. The largest share of finance for the estates came from domestic sources (although domestic banks borrowed some of their resources, in turn, from abroad); the largest share of finance for investment in the smallholding sector, especially for the various integrated governmental development projects, came either from the government or international aid agencies. If these domestic bank loans had not gone to estate owners, they probably would not have been granted to smallholders anyway under existing institutional arrangements (a key premise). To the extent that smallholders were taxed to finance bankruptcies in the estate sector or that such funds were used for investments that would have had a national payoff, then the indirect long-run impact of the credit allocation system has been adverse for the smallholders.

A complicating factor is that parastatals own a number of estates, and these estates are cross-subsidized, either from the parastatals' urban operations or, in the case of ADMARC, from the profits gained by buying and selling smallholder crops. These parastatals have alternative investment opportunities, however, so the loans they were granted were not at the expense of the smallholders. Nevertheless, those ADMARC profits used to subsidize the ADMARC estates did represent a direct burden on the smallholders.

The most basic economic question underlying the direction of credit relates to the relative payoff of such credit in different sectors. Would an alternative institutional arrangement and allocation of capital that spread credit more evenly through the entire agricultural sector have led to a faster overall growth rate? Two conflicting pieces of evidence must be taken into account.

First, the results of the large-scale integrated projects to increase smallholder production were certainly very disappointing (although these results in good part stemmed from the pricing of smallholder products, which was much different than the pricing of estate products). Smallholder production scarcely kept up with population growth, and the administrative apparatus probably was not large enough or experienced enough to administer effectively large-scale credits granted to the smallholder sector. To make the point more directly, administrative constraints prevented effective implementation of alternative investment programs, so if resources had not flowed to the estate sector, Malaŵi's overall growth would have been slower.

Second, in the preindependence period, with relatively favorable prices and relatively modest flows of investment resources, the smallholder sector appears to have grown quite rapidly (table 4-4). Although this growth might be a statistical illusion, we might infer that if the Malaŵi government had followed pricing policies similar to those of the late colonial government and had made credit available, smallholder production growth could have been even faster in the postindependence period. Whether a different pricing policy toward smallholders would have been politically feasible is, of course, a difficult question, but the answer probably has little to do with the estates themselves.

Other Costs

Most of the new estate production focused on tobacco and sugar, and Malaŵi's increasing trade dependency upon these crops provided many problems in the late 1970s, when international prices for these crops began to decline. Recently, the estates have finally started to diversify in a tentative fashion into coffee, groundnuts, macadamia and cashew nuts, and wheat. *DevPol II* stressed the need for crop diversification, although this policy directive is difficult to implement. The estate strategy also diverted attention from the diversification of crops by smallholders, although smallholders in other nations have successfully produced many crops grown by Malaŵian estates. The concentration of resources on the estates may have hindered the growth of smallholder production of these or other crops by directing technology inputs away from these crops.

Summary and Conclusions

Malaŵi apparently did not set out to implement an estate strategy of economic development. It finally adopted such a course, in part, because the government's attempts to increase smallholder production were not very successful. When the potentialities of the estate sector became apparent, top government officials quickly took appropriate measures, such as the provision of credit, to encourage this sector. To a certain extent—we still cannot be sure of the magnitude—the growth of the estate sector has occurred at the cost of lower growth in the smallholder sector; to a considerable extent, however, the success of the estates is also attributable to the provision of high personal economic incentives to produce.

If the requisites of a wager-on-the-strong policy are properly met in the smallholder sector, that approach also will lead to wider income differentials, though not to greater poverty. The Malaŵi government seemed unable to increase productivity among the poorest smallholders, unwilling to raise prices paid for smallholder exports, and inattentive to certain problems of smallholder agriculture such as the labor bottleneck at peak periods of demand. These policy problems, combined with a decline in average farm size, have prevented escape from the effects of diminishing returns, which seem to be the most important factor underlying the apparent decline in real income of the families at the bottom 40 percent of the income distribution.

Notes

1. The production and land data used in this and the following paragraph come from Pryor (1988b), sections A, C, and E.

2. This crop separation policy is discussed at greater length by Ian Livingstone, in Arhin and others (1985), pp. 169–93; by John McCracken, in Fyfe and others (1985), pp. 35–65; and by Christiansen and Kydd (1986). The literature suggests several possible exceptions to the generalization about inefficiency of the crop separation system. For example, one argument is that dark fired tobacco is demanding to grow and offers little scope for mechanization, so it should be limited to smallholders, while flue-cured tobacco requires expensive barns for curing and should be limited to estate production. Neither exception really stands up. Why should estates not grow dark fired tobacco if they find it profitable? What prevents smallholder farmers of flue-cured tobacco from selling their crops to a curer?

3. Public opinion data on this matter revealing considerable security of tenure are presented by Payr (1977). Some useful observations on this topic can also be found in Mkandawêre (n.d.). Clement Ng'ong'da ["Land Reform and Land Dispute Resolution in Malaŵi, " in *Conference on Design* (1985–86)] has noted that the individualization of land titles has not led to a vigorous land market because lenders are still unwilling to accept land as security.

4. All data on gross production come from Pryor (1988b), section C. The data for 1948 through 1963 are very approximate.

5. According to Malaŵi, Office of the President and Planning (1971), p. 134, total smallholder production was supposed to grow during the 1980s by 5.2 percent a year and estate production by 7.0 percent. According to Malaŵi, Office of the President and Planning, *Economic Report 1985*, p. 101, smallholder agriculture was expected to grow 3.8 percent a year between 1986 and 1990, and estate agriculture, 6.7 percent.

6. The data in this paragraph come from Malaŵi Government (1970) and (1984). The savings data are drawn from the former source, table R.6, which provides the only available data on rural savings. Capital disbursements in cash on smallholdings amounted to 3.4 percent of total aftertax income (income including imputations of agricultural products produced and consumed on the smallholding). Credits received from various sources amounted to 1.2 percent of aftertax income, and a residual category—said to consist primarily of dissavings—amounted to 2.3 percent of total income, so net saving appears to have been negative. Data on cash saving or payback of loans and noncash investment are not available, however. The marginal propensity of cash investment out of cash income was about .05, but again this only covers a part of investment and a part of income.

7. On a personal level, half of the households did not own a chair; 65 percent, a table; and 67 percent, a lamp.

8. Outside aid agencies have played a very important role in Malaŵi's agricultural development, an issue discussed by Gondwe (1972), Gordenker (c. 1976), Hewitt and Kydd (1984), McMaster (1974), and Morton (1975).

9. Of course, policies to achieve "regional balance" were also implemented through other means. For instance, according to Robert Lazlett, in Fyfe and others (1985), pp. 381–486, in the late 1970s and early 1980s a second sugar estate at the mouth of the Dwangwa River was financed in part by the parastatals in the name of regional balance; this mill is said to have particularly high costs of production.

10. In this discussion of the production impact of the projects, I draw heavily upon World Bank (1981a), Kinsey (1984), and on various evaluation reports from the World Bank. Some general problems of evaluation of these projects are discussed by Phipps (1976). Lele (1975) provides a general appraisal of a number of integrated agricultural projects in different countries.

11. A major source of information on the colonial period is Kettlewell (1965). Kettlewell was a high colonial administrator for agriculture for twenty-five years, and his description of the problem emphasizes the "bright side" of the colonial program. More than two decades after his departure from Malaŵi, he is still a standing target for criticism by President Banda, who sees him as the symbol of all British mismanagement of the economy. Leroy Vail, in Rotberg (1983), presents quite a different view of the colonial economy, but he does not focus as deeply as Kettlewell on specific policies.

12. For the entire discussion on the extension service I draw on the description by the World Bank (May 1981a) and (1983); P. D. de C. MacDonnell, in Page (1973); and Payr (1977). *DevPol II* (Malaŵi, Office of the President and Planning, 1988, p. 27) lists roughly 1,700 extension agents. The source of the discrepancy with the World Bank datum cited in the text is unclear; the lower figure may refer only to special areas.

13. The Malaŵi Young Pioneers (MYP) was set up in 1964 as a branch of the Malaŵi Youth League to form "the spearhead of rural development." President Banda had been impressed both with the Ghana Young Pioneers and with the agricultural system in Israel, and he invited Israeli technicians to set up an intensive, year-long training program for youth between eighteen and twenty-three years of age in general education, agricultural technology, military training, and leadership. The program has a relatively low cost and features very spartan accommodations for its students. After graduation the MYP members are sent to various settlement and rural development schemes to help introduce modern cultivation techniques and set up youth clubs in secondary schools to teach about agriculture. The farms of MYP members are said to have a productivity about four to five times the average, but some of this undoubtedly reflects the considerable infusion of capital in these projects. Since the mid-1970s this program for a rural elite has graduated about 3,200 young men and 630 young women a year. In certain instances the MYP has also served a paramilitary purpose for the government—for example, in its disputes with the Jehovah's Witnesses. Two interesting discussions of the MYP are found in Wood (1970) and in Madu (1978), pp. 430 ff.

14. For this paragraph and the discussion on hybrid corn in the next paragraph, I draw upon Hirschmann and Vaughan (1984); P. D. de C. MacDonnell, in Page (1973), pp. 53–68; and Louis A. H. Msukwa, in Fyfe and others (1985), pp. 509–26.

15. This discussion is drawn primarily from International Service for National Agricultural Research (ISNAR) (1982) and from interviews in Malaŵi.

16. I draw especially upon Todd (1984). Information about the number of master farmers in Nyasaland (and that they were expected to become "yeoman farmers") comes from Kettlewell (1965). The data on the number of these farmers in the mid-1970s come from Ghai and Radwan (1983), p. 81; these figures are much higher (and more reasonable) than those offered by Todd

(1984), p. 54. The source of the information about relative productivity of these farmers is Chipeta (1976a), p. 10, although he does not supply any supporting data.

17. The diversity of ethnic groups in Malaŵi makes any generalizations about agricultural success and witchcraft accusations questionable. Public opinion data on the matter in the Lakeshore Project, collected by Payr (1977), showed that a considerable number of farmers recognize the role of hard work and ability in making more agricultural income. Dequin (1970) also discusses this issue for the same area and reaches the same conclusions. A somewhat different view is offered by Chipeta (1976a), p. 9.

18. These citations are drawn from the president's speeches in 1971 and 1968, respectively, cited by Williams (1978), p. 283, and by Joffee (1973), pp. 543–44.

19. Some Malaŵian economists, such as Chipanda (1983b), have also made this observation, but data on these matters are very incomplete. See Pachai (1973).

20. The number of tobacco estates is for 1981 and comes from Malaŵi, NSO, *Malaŵi Statistical Yearbook 1982*, p. 76; the number of the other estates is for 1979 and comes from World Bank (May 1981a), appendix 3. These various data on number of estates exclude data on Press Holding and General Farming. The increased number of estates was announced in *DevPol II* (Malaŵi, Office of the President and Planning, 1988, p. 23).

21. My entire discussion of the ownership and operation of the estate sector draws from the extremely useful analysis by Christiansen and Kydd (1986). Other interesting remarks on the topic are made by Ian Livingstone, in Arhin and others (1985), and by Loesch (1983).

22. This assumption is based on impressions gained from scattered data; a wide range of other assumptions also yield very high profit rates.

23. This description of the characteristics of tobacco estate owners in 1986 comes from Pryor and Chipeta (forthcoming 1990). A questionnaire was mailed to 250 tobacco estate owners registered by the NSO; if "estate" is defined more broadly to include those with a license to grow certain types of tobacco, then the NSO estate registry was incomplete. This mailing yielded ninety-four usable replies, a response rate of 37.6 percent representing roughly 7.8 percent of all registered tobacco estates. The survey did not include estates held by Press Holding and General Farming. Fifteen percent of the questionnaires to the owners were returned unopened, which suggests that such estates were bankrupt or in receivership or that the owner had died. Although generally the estate owners were not politicians, it has been suggested to me that they might be close relatives of politicians. We did not pose any question to elicit this type of sensitive information.

24. My calculations of gross crop production of estates and smallholders were made on the basis of assigning crops to particular sectors (see table 4-1) and then calculating indexes. The value-added data come from the national accounts and were calculated more exactly, so the two numbers are not completely comparable.

25. I fitted a Cobb-Douglas production function with a time trend to the data in table 4-4; however, certain obvious problems arise with such a procedure,

96 Malaŵi and Madagascar

beyond the fact that the tenant labor supply is missing. Data on several important inputs (capital, fertilizer) are missing; because these increase over time, their impact must be captured in the trend coefficient. In addition, there is multicollinearity among the independent variables. Another problem is that although the inputs are for a particular year, some of the resulting production takes place in the next year; regression experiments trying to take this into account yielded such nonsensical results that they are not reported. The calculations yielded an estimated marginal gross crop productivity of labor in 1978 of (very roughly) 200 MK.

26. This position has been modified by Ian Livingstone, in Arhin and others (1985).

27. The agricultural profits data come from Malaŵi, NSO, *Annual Economic Survey, 1973–1979* (1985). To eliminate profits of estates in the public sector, I reduced these profits by 30 percent, a rough procedure based on the assumption that the profit rates in the public and private estates were approximately the same. Total property income data come from Pryor (1988b), table E-3.

28. A more rigorous demonstration of this point would require determination of the marginal product of labor, but such an analysis requires the calculation of a production function in the estate sector, which cannot be done with any accuracy because of lack of data on certain key inputs. The rough calculation reported in footnote 25 yields a marginal gross crop productivity for an estate worker of very roughly 200 Kwacha a year; the marginal net crop productivity should, of course, be lower. Average annual estate wages in the same year were about 173 MK. Although these marginal productivity estimates are fraught with uncertainties, workers in the estate sector appear to have been paid very roughly their marginal product.

29. One expert on the economy of Malaŵi doubted this interpretation of my survey results (see footnote 23). He suggested that this ease of finding estate labor was a relatively recent phenomenon and that the situation was quite different during the mid-1970s. Unfortunately, no documentary evidence on this issue is available.

30. Data from NSO (1980b), pp. 4, 316, and 342, permit a calculation of the percentages of all rural workers who have worked abroad and then of all *alimi* with similar work experience. It is also noteworthy that a much higher percentage of rural than of urban workers have worked abroad.

5 Agriculture: Product and Factor Markets in Malaŵi

Different types of market policies in Malaŵi have influenced agricultural production in diverse ways. The practice of allowing estate owners to sell their crops at auction and to receive the full market rate, combined with a policy (until 1980) of maintaining the currency at roughly the equilibrium rate, greatly encouraged estate production. The policy requiring most smallholders to sell many of their crops through the Agricultural Development and Marketing Corporation (ADMARC), a monopsonistic state buying agency, has discouraged their production, especially since the world market price of export products rose while real domestic prices remained roughly the same. A large part of the profits of ADMARC, however, were invested either in estates or agroindustries, in effect transferring resources within the agricultural sector. These pricing policies have acted as a general tax on the smallholders, the poorest segment of the population, although within the smallholder sector, the implicit tax has been progressive in effect.

Rural factor markets, fusing both traditional and modern elements, have been stunted. The credit market has operated to favor the estates and richer smallholders, another instance of the country's wager-on-the-strong policy. The labor markets also have acted to widen income differentials, although through a much different mechanism and not as the result of any specific governmental policy.

Product Markets

Crops grown on the estates have been sold primarily for export. They have been marketed either by private agents or in private auctions to foreign buyers. Malaŵi's exchange rate policy has been a critical component of this arrangement because the country has been a relatively small world producer of most products (except for fire-cured and burley tobacco) and has had little influence on the world price. A restricted group of smallholders—for instance, those designated as progressive farmers and those under special authorities, such as the Kasungu Flue-cured Tobacco Authority—also have been allowed to sell their products at auction. This privilege of selling at auction has permitted the estate owners and richest smallholders to avoid the implicit ADMARC tax, thus further widening overall income differentials.

Most smallholders have had access to two marketing systems: the farmers' markets, where crops are sold on a small scale for domestic consumption at whatever prices buyers are willing to pay, and (until 1987) the markets administered by ADMARC for both domestically consumed and exported products. These asymmetric marketing arrangements for smallholders and estates arose in the late 1920s from initiatives taken primarily by the estate owners (almost all of whom were British), combined with the well-meaning but misguided paternalism of some colonial officials.[1] These predecessors of ADMARC were among the first agricultural marketing boards in Sub-Saharan Africa.

ADMARC was founded in April 1971 to succeed the Farmers Marketing Board. This board had been formed in 1962 to amalgamate the separate tobacco, maize, and cotton marketing boards, which had been in existence for several decades. ADMARC has been a large enterprise, employing between 14,000 and 24,000 people in 1984 (depending on the season) in its agricultural functions.[2] It has handled export crops, such as tobacco, groundnuts (peanuts), and cotton, as well as staple crops, such as maize, that are not exported in significant amounts.

ADMARC's structure is somewhat different from that of the marketing boards in most other African nations. It may be characterized as a quasi-parastatal. The Malaŵi government owns the company and appoints the directors. According to its charter, however, the company operates as a profitmaking organization and thus has considerable autonomy. Unlike marketing boards in many African nations, it has no financial incentives to maintain low food prices for the urban consumer, and it does not serve to raise funds for public investment or other governmental purposes. Nevertheless, the government's Price Commission sets the prices ADMARC offers farmers for their output and the prices they pay for such inputs as fertilizer; the Life President makes or approves the most important of these prices. ADMARC also has carried out certain other governmental functions, including financing maize and fertilizer subsidies and bearing the cost of building up and maintaining the nation's food reserve, an important cause of its severe financial difficulties in the 1980s.

Like many other marketing boards, one of ADMARC's major functions has been to stabilize agricultural prices. It must buy all of the products offered to it at a unified national price, which is announced before the planting season—a mandate that has not always proved possible to accomplish. In the mid-1980s, for instance, when the company suffered from a severe shortage of working capital, it could not make all required purchases. ADMARC has operated through a network that had grown by the mid-1980s to more than 75 permanent and 2,000 seasonal market places. Until 1987 ADMARC dealt directly with smallholders rather than through a system of authorized agents. ADMARC's growing marketing network has undoubtedly reduced transaction costs and encouraged agricultural production.

Although ADMARC has had a monopoly on export sales of smallholder products, private individuals have sold their own maize and other crops. Until the early 1970s Asian traders also bought and sold locally consumed products, and some not completely convincing evidence indicates that they provided sufficient competition to ADMARC and its predecessors to keep the price of maize higher than the government had wanted at that time (Lele 1975, p. 113). In the early and mid-1970s the government restricted the commercial activities of Asian merchants to urban areas and brought this competition to a close. In 1987, however, the government again permitted private traders to buy and sell smallholder crops on a small scale. How this new system will evolve is unclear, although in the rice market, at least, these private market transactions appear important. At no time did the government intervene significantly in the operations of the informal farmers markets.

ADMARC has many other economic activities. It sells farmers various agricultural inputs, such as seeds and fertilizers, for which it has monopoly franchises. By the early 1980s ADMARC owned about twenty agricultural estates and shares in about thirty companies, which included not only a variety of agroindustries but also the Bata Shoe Company, Lever Brothers, the National Bank of Malaŵi, the National Insurance company, the Portland Cement Company, and a metal products company. ADMARC also has acted as a financial intermediary, lending funds to a number of companies for various ventures; its largest investment of this type was a loan of 40 million MK (about $30 million) to Press Holding, which is almost completely owned by President Banda. In the mid-1980s ADMARC experienced some severe financial difficulties with its industrial operations, and further problems beset its banking activities when Press Holding had difficulty in repaying its loans. Under pressure from the World Bank, ADMARC underwent a corporate restructuring. By 1986 its portfolio of nonagriculturally related investments was considerably reduced, and its financial situation appeared to improve.

ADMARC's accountability to the public is maintained through its annual report. Although this report carries extensive financial information on a crop-by-crop basis, the quantity and quality of information on its other activities are less satisfactory.

ADMARC's efficiency has received mixed reviews. Its crop purchasing operations appear to have been conducted with somewhat lower costs than those in other East African nations, but this is not a very high standard for comparison.[3] Its activities not connected with the purchase and sale of agricultural products have led to considerable losses, however.

Because of Malaŵi's high population density and relatively dense network of public transportation, most farmers have relatively easy access to urban centers to purchase farm inputs and consumer goods. ADMARC supplies certain farm inputs to smallholders through its many sales outlets, and Malaŵi's policy (until 1980) of maintaining a relatively realistic exchange rate allowed this function to be carried out in a relatively smooth fashion, unlike in Madagascar. Some indication of the increasing sales of fertilizer is shown in table 5-1; these data contrast strongly with similar data for Madagascar (see table 12-1). During the 1980s, when Malaŵi's exchange rate was overvalued, delivering imported consumer goods to the rural areas became more problematic, which discouraged smallholders from producing for the market to purchase such goods.

When the Asian merchants were required to leave the rural sector in the mid-1970s, they generally tried to sell their retail outlets either to individual Africans or to parastatals. Systematic evidence on the effectiveness of the new marketing agents is not available, although anecdotal evidence suggests some deterioration in the quality of service. In contrast to Madagascar, any lack of consumer goods in the rural sector or any shortage of agricultural inputs to the farmers does not appear (at least until the mid-1980s) to have had much influence

Table 5-1. Fertilizer Sales to Smallholders, Malaŵi, 1960 to 1984

Year	Metric tons	Year	Metric tons	Year	Metric tons
1960	166	1968	9,905	1976	30,471
1961	224	1969	15,559	1977	44,355
1962	454	1970	20,725	1978	43,939
1963	1,018	1971	24,831	1979	43,847
1964	1,995	1972	24,054	1980	49,142
1965	5,596	1973	31,743	1981	57,200
1966	8,586	1974	14,850	1982	41,738
1967	9,828	1975	22,353	1983	63,251
				1984	65,786

Note: From 1966 onward the data refer to the agricultural year. Total fertilizer usage by both estates and smallholders is difficult to determine because data on domestic production and imports are not available for many years.

Source: Malaŵi, NSO, *Malaŵi Statistical Yearbook* (various issues).

on agricultural production, at least insofar as such problems have not become salient in the Malaŵian literature on agriculture.

Agricultural Prices

The setting of domestic prices and the marketing operations of ADMARC are greatly influenced by price trends and fluctuations on the world market. As shown in table 5-2, the weighted average price of Malaŵi's four major export crops, which accounted for almost three-quarters of the value of its exports in the period from 1964 through 1984, increased at an average annual rate of 4.73 percent from 1964 to 1984. This is considerably below the roughly 7.34 percent average annual increase of world export unit values during the same period (IMF, *International Financial Statistics Yearbook*, 1986, pp. 126–27). Similarly the 5.51 percent average annual increase of Malaŵi export prices from 1975 through 1984 was less than that for world export unit prices, 6.02 percent. For a short period during the late 1960s and early 1970s the external commodity terms of trade in Malaŵi rose

Table 5-2. International Price Trends and Fluctuations, Malaŵi, 1964–84 and 1975–84
(percent)

Crop[a]	Average annual price change[b] 1964–84	1975–84	Fluctuations: pseudo-coefficient of variation[c] 1964–84	1975–84
Staple: maize	5.05	2.41	10.25	10.58
Export crops				
Tobacco	5.07	7.46	4.23	2.80
Tea	3.26	5.63	10.20	15.35
Groundnuts	5.32	-3.17	16.98	16.68
Sugar	6.62	2.54	8.42	9.27
Weighted average	4.73	5.51	7.46	8.14

a. The four crops, accounting for about 74 percent of exports in the period from 1964 through 1984, are listed in order of relative importance of export share. The relative values of exports serve also as the weights in the weighted average.

b. The price changes are based on U.S. dollars and are calculated by fitting an exponential trend line to the relevant price data.

c. The pseudocoefficient of variation starts with the absolute value of the deviation of the price for a given year from the trend price in the same year, measured as a ratio to the trend. The statistic presented above is the average of these ratios. In all cases the trend price is measured as the average price for the two previous and two following years. (See also footnote 6 of this chapter.)

Source: IMF, *International Financial Statistics Yearbook*, 1985, pp. 138–41.

somewhat, thus providing the basis of prosperity for estate exports; since that time, however, the external terms of trade have declined almost continuously (chapter 6).

The Intersectoral Terms of Trade: Some General Considerations

The relative prices of goods sold and bought by smallholders—the intersectoral terms of trade—partly reflect governmental agricultural price and production policies, because the government can influence this real price of agricultural goods by taxes, subsidies, and market policies of state monopsonies and monopolies. In poor agricultural nations, differences in average urban and rural incomes are the most important income inequality, and the intersectoral terms of trade have important distributional effects as well (chapter 16).

PRODUCTION EFFECTS. If the intersectoral terms of trade change, the marketed output of agricultural goods also will change; the exact amount will depend on the relevant price elasticities of supply. For Malaŵi this effect should be quite important, based on the results of a number of empirical studies that point to high price elasticities of supply.[4] Several econometric studies, including Colman and Garbett (n.d.), Dean (1966), Gordon (1971), and Minford and Ohs (1976), show that the price responsiveness of Malaŵian smallholders is high for particular crops; indeed, the price elasticity of supply for tobacco in Malaŵi, as calculated by Dean, is roughly the same as that for the same crop in the United States. Less formal statistical studies, such as those by Pearson and Mitchell (1945), Brown (1970a), Channock (1972), Chipeta (1976a), Mills (1975), and Lavrijsen and Sterkenburg (1976), also suggest high elasticities of supply for individual crops. Of course, price elasticities of individual crops give no indication of the aggregate price elasticity of supply of the smallholder sector; nevertheless, because substitutability between crops is limited in the short term, changes in the intersectoral terms of change should have a significant impact on overall market production of the smallholder sector.

Dean also carried out some fascinating controlled experiments at rural markets in Malaŵi to test whether ethnic and other social factors influenced price and found that they did not. Thus in Malaŵi's rural sector, economic forces appear to dominate price setting and social factors do not appear to be important impediments to production.

These various studies of price responses have two important implications. First, if a devaluation should occur and if smallholders benefit subsequently from higher domestic prices for their products, the sector would respond with more production. Second, if the government turned the terms of trade against the smallholder sector in order to obtain investment funds, agricultural production might decline enough to jeopardize the entire investment program. Specifically, agricultural production and exports would fall, and the foreign exchange for obtaining the necessary investment goods would not be available, a simple mechanism that had a devastating impact in Madagascar. In the mid-1980s, neither of these simple propositions seems to have gained much support among Malaŵian policy makers with whom I spoke. The drafters of *DevPol II*, which appeared in 1988, seemed more aware of the problem, possibly as a result of the educative efforts by international lenders such as the IMF and World Bank.

CONSUMPTION EFFECTS. The success of shifting the intersectoral terms of trade to squeeze investment resources from the rural sector also depends upon the degree to which industrial workers change their demand for rural products. If a tax is placed on food and if the urban price elasticity of demand is relatively low (that is, the workers continue to buy almost the same quantity of food despite its higher cost), then the tax acts to transfer resources from workers to the government, which uses those funds to finance investment. If the urban demand is price elastic (for example, if urban workers start growing more of their own food, rather than buying it), then the taxation program would not be very effective in raising revenues for investment and would primarily burden the rural sector, which must accept lower revenues. The information on demand elasticities for either Malaŵi or Madagascar, however, is not sufficiently detailed to judge the impact of such a tax.

The distributional aspects of the terms of trade are much easier to specify. Engels' law says that food expenditures as a percentage of total consumption expenditures falls as income rises, and this hypothesis is confirmed by urban budget studies for both Malaŵi and Madagascar. Therefore, any sales tax on food is regressive to the extent that has a proportionately greater real cost for smallholders, the poorest group in the nation, than for the urban workers, who have higher incomes.

INVESTMENT EFFECTS.

If the surplus available for investment is generated primarily in the urban sector, then turning the terms of trade against agriculture can only generate a surplus for investment if real incomes in both the rural and urban sectors fall (Sah and Stiglitz 1984). Furthermore, such a policy actually can reduce funds available for investment if the marginal propensity to save is higher in the rural area, a proposition for which some evidence exists for Malaŵi (see Appendix, table G-1). Finally, if investment in the rural sector has a lower incremental capital-output ratio (which seems reasonable, although appropriate empirical evidence is not available), the strategy to raise investment funds in fact can lower the growth rate.

Table 5-3. Indicators of Agricultural Producer Prices, Malaŵi, 1948 to 1984

Year	Index of ADMARC prices (1978 = 100)	Intersectoral terms of trade (deflated index of ADMARC prices, 1978 = 100) Index of implicit deflator of monetary GDP	Retail price index	Ratio of ADMARC prices to export prices at official exchange rate (percent) 5 major products	2 major products
1948	—	—	—	—	52.2
1949	—	—	—	—	41.5
1950	—	—	—	—	50.3
1951	—	—	—	—	49.5
1952	—	—	—	—	29.6
1953	—	—	—	—	48.8
1954	—	—	—	—	52.6
1955	—	—	—	—	47.5
1956	—	—	—	—	54.8
1957	—	—	—	—	56.1
1958	—	—	—	—	70.0
1959	—	—	—	—	61.7
Unweighted average	—	—	—	—	51.2
1960	—	—	—	—	59.1
1961	40.71	101.4	—	64.2	60.0
1962	46.32	107.2	—	68.5	71.2
1963	43.85	98.7	—	61.9	61.3
1964	42.97	94.3	—	58.2	54.8
1965	45.68	100.7	—	58.6	57.7
1966	48.06	98.1	—	65.3	61.6
1967	48.85	107.4	—	81.0	79.7
1968	41.93	86.8	86.2	59.2	50.6
1969	48.45	99.7	100.6	56.0	50.7
Unweighted average	—	99.4	93.4	63.5	60.7
1970	57.44	106.2	106.4	48.0	47.9
1971	60.22	103.2	103.2	41.3	40.8
1972	55.32	93.9	91.3	52.7	48.0
1973	62.57	97.1	98.4	48.8	54.0
1974	71.72	95.6	97.7	39.3	44.0
1975	78.43	100.0	92.5	35.4	36.6
1976	90.11	102.7	101.9	31.9	29.2
1977	90.12	88.8	97.8	29.2	22.5
1978	100.00	100.0	100.0	46.3	44.2
1979	102.07	105.7	91.7	44.1	43.7
Unweighted average	—	99.3	98.1	41.7	41.1

(continued)

Table 5-3. Indicators of Agricultural Producer Prices, Malaŵi, 1948 to 1984 *(continued)*

Year	Index of ADMARC prices (1978 = 100)	Intersectoral terms of trade (deflated index of ADMARC prices, 1978 = 100) Index of implicit deflator of monetary GDP	Retail price index	Ratio of ADMARC prices to export prices at official exchange rate (percent) 5 major products	2 major products
1980	108.29	97.9	82.2	46.7	44.4
1981	108.18	80.7	73.4	35.0	28.5
1982	137.41	92.4	84.9	49.7	22.2
1983	176.94	109.6	96.3	49.9	36.4
1984	197.94	113.3	89.8	49.0	44.4
Unweighted average	—	98.8	85.3	46.1	35.2

— = Not applicable.
Source: Based on Pryor (1988b), section C.

The Intersectoral Terms of Trade: Actual Behavior

The data presented in table 5-3 summarize ADMARC's policies and, at one step removed, the policies of the Malaŵi government toward the smallholders. The series showing prices offered to agricultural producers, deflated by an appropriate price index, represents the intersectoral terms of trade. An appropriate deflator is not available, however, so two imperfect substitutes were used as deflators instead, and conclusions drawn from these data must be considered tentative.

The data from table 5-3 suggest no real shift in the terms of trade between smallholder agriculture and the urban sector, at least through 1978. The two series used to deflate the ADMARC average purchase prices yield rather different results in the 1980s, however, a problem resulting from differences in coverage, weights, and methodology of the deflators. Using the GDP deflator, no significant trend emerges for the entire period; the urban cost of living deflator produces a slight long-term downward trend.

Marketed output is an important variable to examine, for it plays a crucial role in the volume of exports or imports of agricultural goods. The relative long-term stability of the intersectoral terms of trade in Malaŵi may explain why the share of marketable output of smallholder production also has remained roughly the same. Smallholders appear to have sold about 15 percent of their total production during the 1950s (Pryor 1988b, table C-1). In the 1960s this ratio rose and then declined thereafter, and by the early and mid-1980s it was roughly the same as during the 1950s.

The ratio of ADMARC prices to export prices for the same commodities, shown in table 5-3, provides some useful evidence on the extent to which ADMARC has served as a barrier between the smallholder sector and foreign markets, preventing smallholders from reaping the benefits of high world market prices. This data series remained roughly constant from the colonial period through the federation period to independence in 1964. From the late 1960s to 1977 the ratio fell; that is, ADMARC's implicit tax on smallholders rose. Since that time the ratio has risen; but in the mid-1980s it was still lower than in the colonial and federation periods, which means that smallholders were more highly taxed after independence than before.

Combining information about relative domestic and foreign prices with the data on intersectoral terms of trade offers another perspective on long-term agricultural price policies. ADMARC set agricultural prices to prevent smallholders from gaining from the price increases on the world market in the 1970s. Although ADMARC's profits fell in the 1980s, real smallholder incomes did not gain at ADMARC's expense, because the overvaluation of the exchange rate meant that domestic currency receipts for export sales were lower than they would have been at an equilibrium exchange rate. Thus currency overvaluation in the 1980s has "taxed" the smallholders just as high ADMARC profits did in the 1970s.

During the 1970s ADMARC used its profits to finance its investments in the estate sector, its various agroindustries, and its participation in certain nonagricultural companies. Undoubtedly the overall effects of such policies were to reduce marketed output of smallholders.[5] The estates, however, could receive the higher foreign prices, which encouraged their rapid growth.

Other Aspects of Agricultural Prices

Several other consequences of price policies deserve attention in that they influence any evaluation of economic events in both Malaŵi and Madagascar.

PRICE AND INCOME STABILITY. Have ADMARC policies served their explicit goal of providing price stability, however enlightened or misguided such a goal may be? In the long run, ADMARC policies in Malaŵi certainly served to stabilize prices for smallholders. Producer prices remained about constant in real terms, while the relative real world market prices for these products first rose and then fell during the twenty-year period following independence. Short-run stabilization effects are more difficult to analyze.

One way of measuring short-run price fluctuations is by calculating a "pseudo-coefficient of variation," which measures variations of prices in a given year from a five-year trend and can be interpreted in the same manner as a coefficient of variation.[6] Using this method I investigated four different annual series: prices paid by ADMARC, foreign trade prices for the same products, and total agricultural revenues calculated with the two different sets of prices. The period covered is 1961 through 1984.

The fluctuations in the index of official prices were considerably less than those in the index of export prices. Fluctuations in agricultural receipts (for the products in the index), based on export (rather than ADMARC) prices, were not much different than when actual domestic prices were used. Insofar as income stabilization is more important than price stabilization alone, ADMARC appears to be focusing on the wrong stabilization target.

Price stability can also refer to prices within a given year. ADMARC does not vary its buying prices over the season, although the prices in farmers' markets do show seasonal fluctuations, lying above or below the ADMARC selling price at different times of the year.[7] Allowing producers and rural buyers to carry out transactions at these market (rather than ADMARC) prices seems irrational unless one or more of the following conditions prevail: (a) ADMARC collection points are so far apart that the ADMARC price plus the local transportation costs do not warrant the transactions at the official price; or (b) ADMARC's buying and selling activities take place only at particular times in the year, which may not coincide with desires of buyers and sellers to make these transactions;[8] or (c) ADMARC does not carry out its mandate to buy all crops offered to it, either for administrative convenience or from lack of cash. Without more detailed information, the relative importance of these factors for explaining deviations between ADMARC and market prices cannot be determined.

PRICE VARIATIONS OVER DISTANCE. In a free market situation the different transportation costs from farm to market in different parts of the country may give rise to spatial variation in prices of both agricultural outputs and inputs. ADMARC's prices are uniform nationwide, both for administrative simplicity and for certain considerations of interregional equity. If ADMARC's price is higher than cost of production plus transportation, this policy encourages farmers far from the markets where particular goods are sold to produce such goods. A lower price encourages them to buy agricultural products from other farmers that, if transportation costs had been properly included in the price, they could have produced more cheaply themselves. Furthermore, the uniform price results in quite different implicit subsidies or taxes in different parts of the country. More specifically, in Malaŵi it benefits the north and disadvantages the south. Certain data relevant to these matters are presented in table G-2 of the Appendix.

FISCAL AND ECONOMIC EFFECTS. ADMARC has usually reported a profit from its crop purchase program. Although caution is advised in using ADMARC's financial data, some important conclusions are apparent (see Appendix, table G-3). During the 1970s and until the mid-1980s, ADMARC's annual trading profits amounted, on average, to 1.8 percent of Malaŵi's GDP. The occasional loss years have specific explanations. For instance, the large loss in the 1985–86 crop year resulted primarily from an increase in producer prices (mandated by the government) that was unmatched by increases in consumer prices; this led to a liquidity problem that prevented ADMARC from purchasing certain crops offered to it.

For the same period, ADMARC's total (trading and other) profits were only about 1.4 percent of GDP. The difference between total and trading profitability indicates that ADMARC's nonagricultural operations have lost considerable money over the years. ADMARC trading profits represented, on average, a markup of 41.7 percent on agricultural purchases. This represents a very high marginal tax, even as it amounts to a relatively small part (4.8 percent) of average smallholder incomes. Nevertheless, it is the marginal, not the average implicit tax that influences production for the market.

The incidence of this implicit tax has been quite different among the various segments of the smallholder sector. The price markup has been greatest on tobacco, followed by groundnuts and cotton, while implicit subsidies have been highest on maize (the staple), followed by general produce (vegetables, coffee, cassava) and rice. The official rationale for the maize subsidy, which appears to pay farmers more than the export price of maize, has been to encourage enough production to ensure self-sufficiency plus a slight surplus to export.[9] Because transportation costs raise the import costs of maize at the border far above export costs, this policy has a certain economic logic. The subsidy seems less reasonable, however, when we note that urban consumers pay a lower price than they would if trade in maize between the rural and urban areas had been totally free.

The incidence of ADMARC's trading profits appears to be progressive among smallholders. Almost all smallholders, especially the poorest, grow maize, and they are better off selling it (and other food crops) to ADMARC than on any possible open market for exports. Although ADMARC profits on tobacco have been high, fewer than 10 percent of smallholders—generally the richest farmers—have been licensed to grow tobacco. This licensing system has been in operation for several decades. Malaŵi is a relatively large world producer of fire-cured and sun- or air-cured tobacco, and because the government believes the elasticity of demand for tobacco is sufficiently low, it limits production to avoid depressing world prices. ADMARC's high profits on tobacco thus represent a tax on the higher income, licensed smallholders rather than the low-income maize producers. In short, ADMARC profits can be considered as a sharing of the economic rent arising from the relative scarcity of licenses for producing tobacco.

The urban consumers' ability to obtain staple foods, especially maize, at a subsidized rate might appear to represent a regressive transfer of income from the rural to the urban sector. The matter is not that simple, however, because some of ADMARC's losses on maize sales have been subsidized from tax revenues paid by the urban population.

Price Policies for the 1990s

DevPol II outlined some specific price policies for the 1987 to 1996 period. The system of preannounced, fixed producer prices is to continue, as is the system of offering private traders a premium for produce delivered to ADMARC depots, which is designed to place the transportation function into the hands of the private sector. The government will endeavor to fix the maize price at the level at which domestic production would satisfy domestic demand, including the creation of a strategic grain reserve. The prices of other agricultural products not entering into foreign trade are to be set so as to insure self-sufficiency as well. Prices for agricultural products traded on the world market are to be set at their export or import prices at the border. This policy appears quite reasonable, assuming that the exchange rate is maintained at the proper level (a dubious assumption).

The Credit Market in the Rural Sector

At independence, Malaŵi had two commercial banks, both foreign owned. Since the mid-1970s the government has owned the banking system (now comprising three commercial banks).[10] Encouraged by the Life President, all of these commercial banks have extended considerable credit to agriculture, especially from the mid-1970s onward.[11] As shown in table 5–4, agricultural loans—mostly to the growing estate sector—have amounted to roughly one-fifth to one-fourth of their total loans, or about 3.5 to 4.0 percent of GDP. When many of the estates ran into financial difficulties in the late 1970s, their borrowing soared, and by 1982 these debts amounted to about 230 MK per hectare or about 1,700 MK per planted hectare (at that time, respectively, about $245 and $1,800). In addition, some estates have been able to borrow from the parastatals; and estates owned by ADMARC have been financed from the profits of the company's trade in smallholder crops.

Table 5-4. Bank Loans to the Agricultural Sector, Malaŵi, 1965 to 1983

	Total bank advances to agriculture			Net change during year	
		As a percentage of			
Year-end	1,000 MK	Total bank advances	GDP	1,000 MK	As a percentage of GDP
1965	1,446	17.7	0.9	—	—
1966	1,196	13.5	0.6	-250	-0.3
1967	1,552	15.0	0.8	356	0.2
1968	1,842	14.6	1.0	290	0.2
1969	1,874	11.1	0.9	32	0.0
Unweighted average	—	14.4	0.8	—	0.0
1970	2,086	9.6	0.9	212	0.1
1971	3,015	10.9	1.0	929	0.3
1972	3,306	10.0	1.1	291	0.1
1973	5,706	19.5	1.7	2,399	0.7
1974	7,763	16.6	1.8	2,058	0.5
1975	13,606	24.6	2.8	5,843	1.2
1976	27,872	38.8	4.8	14,266	2.5
1977	30,190	35.0	4.4	2,318	0.3
1978	53,763	44.5	7.2	23,573	3.2
1979	81,853	48.0	10.4	28,090	3.6
Unweighted average	—	25.8	3.6	—	1.3
1980	92,671	53.8	10.3	10,818	1.2
1981	94,272	49.7	9.4	1,601	0.2
1982	115,128	51.8	10.2	20,856	1.8
1983	138,520	52.4	10.7	23,392	1.8
Unweighted average	—	51.9	10.2	—	1.3
Overall unweighted average	—	28.3	4.3	—	1.0

— = Not applicable.

a. Agriculture includes forestry and fishing. In 1973 the banks changed the way they reported loans to different economic sectors; although this probably did not significantly affect reported loans and advances to agriculture, the series from 1965 through 1972 may not be completely comparable with the years thereafter.

b. Loans and advances to agriculture are compared with loans and advances to the entire domestic private sector, which, in turn, represent roughly one-half of total assets of the commercial banks.

Source: Malaŵi, Reserve Bank, *Financial and Economic Review* (various issues).

Credit to Smallholders

The smallholders have not been able to obtain much credit from money lenders, banks, or the government, although various types of informal credit arrangements have been available to them.

In 1925, the colonial government imposed the Credit Trade to the Natives law to protect Africans in their credit transactions with non-Africans. This law made any such loans unrecoverable unless the African borrower had a permit to contract debts and unless the debt was drawn up in writing and attested by the District Commission (Chimango 1977). The law virtually eliminated smallholders' access to trade or seasonal credit from money lenders. Even after this law was revoked in 1958, the lack of collateral still limited smallholder credit. Land held under customary tenure could not serve as collateral for a loan because it could not be transferred. Most smallholders had no other assets, such as cattle or agricultural equipment, to pledge as collateral; in the crop year 1968–69 only 10.7 percent of smallholder families owned cattle, and only 2.7 percent, a plow (Malaŵi Government 1970, tables R5.3 and R5.6; and Malaŵi Government 1984, tables 6.2 and 7.2). These figures did not change much over the next decade and a half. Most smallholders could offer only their crops as collateral for loans.

In 1968–69 only 2.2 percent of smallholder families reported cash receipts from credit, and the average amount outstanding per family was only 0.89 MK.[12] Smallholders are able to use certain traditional channels of credit, although many such transactions have been more in the nature of reciprocal exchange as part of a smallholder's social obligations. To attempt to separate the market and social aspects of such transactions would lead us too far afield. Nevertheless, the following examples provide the flavor of such arrangements: The *kubwereka* loan is a short-term loan that occurs primarily within kin or friendship groups and requires no interest; millet loans are only for the season and include an implicit interest charge, because the borrower must return more millet than was received; the *katapila* loan has a longer term than the other two types and requires both an interest payment (up to 100 percent) and a guarantor, which eases the collateral problem.

At the end of the colonial period the government took certain steps to provide smallholders with access to credit, but the programs were minuscule and were later abandoned.[13] After independence in the late 1960s the government began to provide limited credit to those participating in the progressive farmer scheme (chapter 4), but only the wealthiest farmers received such credit because a prerequisite for becoming a progressive farmer was holding a considerable amount of land. The government also began to experiment with various ways of channeling credit to a broader group of smallholders and included a credit program as part of the four major land development programs. Table 5-5 presents some data on these credit arrangements.

The government's emphasis was initially on lending to individuals. In 1973, however, the Lilongwe Land Development Program (LLDP) set up credit cooperatives to receive and distribute short-term loans, a program that proved durable. At first the program provided credit to individuals in the group or to the group itself; later the focus was primarily on group credit. In both situations the entire group assumed responsibility for repayment of each loan (Schaefer-Kehnert 1982). On top of the 10 percent interest rate, borrowers placed a sum equal to 10 percent of their loans into a security fund that was used to pay off defaulted loans. If the security fund were insufficient for this purpose, the members of the group might be deprived the next year of farm inputs such as improved seeds and fertilizers. The groups have been composed of ten to thirty neighbors, have often been dissolved and reformed at the end of each year, and have relied on unpaid management.

Group credit schemes seem to have been successful in a limited sphere, spreading from credit cooperatives in the Lilongwe area to "farm clubs" outside the area. From 1972–73 through 1978–79 repayment rates for the various credit programs were extremely high—almost 100 percent for group loans and about 98 percent for individual loans. In most of the other land development programs, similarly high repayment rates are reported. In a bankerly sense, the innovation worked. Nevertheless, these credit programs have remained small (see Malaŵi, Minister of Agriculture and Natural Resources 1980). For instance, in 1980 the four land development programs extended credit to about 45,000 individuals and about 36,000 groups. Thus about 400,000 farmers benefited from such loans, which means that most farm families were still unserved by the program. These numbers do not include the participants in several small credit schemes outside the development areas. The average size of the loans was also very small—30 MK or less—and the term was for less than a year. In 1978, in the LLDP, the 103,600 families included in the program cultivated an average of 1.3 hectares each. The average loan per cultivated hectare was roughly 10 MK, only slightly more than 1 percent of the loans per cultivated hectare on the estates in the same year. During the period covered in table 5-5, the middle-term credits granted (excluded from the above averages) were only a small fraction of the short-term loans.

The credit component of the National Rural Development Program introduced in the late 1970s (chapter 4) was considerably more extensive than the credit program of the integrated rural development projects. I have not, however, been able to obtain enough data to

Table 5-5. Scattered Data on Short Term Credit Flows to Smallholders, Malaŵi, 1968–69 to 1979–80 Crop Years

Short-term credit flows in the development projects (thousands of MK)

					All four projects	
Crop year	Lilongwe	Karonga	Lakeshore	Shire Valley	Total credit	Percentage of GDP
1968–69	5	—	—	—	5	0.00
1969–70	7	—	—	—	7	0.00
1970–71	83	—	89	—	172	0.07
1971–72	329	—	93	—	422	0.15
1972–73	392	1	126	—	519	0.17
1973–74	495	25	188	—	708	0.21
1974–75	736	75	279	—	1,090	0.25
1975–76	859	80	346	—	1,285	0.26
1976–77	1,012	110	357	189	1,668	0.29
1977–78	1,293	186	592	252	2,323	0.34
1978–79	1,461	147	355	213	2,176	0.29
1979–80	2,003	167	461	211	2,842	0.36

Borrower characteristics in the Lilongwe Land Development Project

	Thousands of borrowers					Average amount of loans (MK), all borrowers
Crop year	Total	Individuals	Group members	Number of groups	Borrowers per group	
1972–73	21.2	21.1	—	—	—	18
1973–74	25.7	23.9	1.8	94	19	19
1974–75	25.1	20.5	4.6	242	19	29
1975–76	32.2	24.6	7.6	410	19	27
1976–77	36.7	23.5	13.3	670	20	28
1977–78	42.5	14.6	27.9	1,267	22	30
1978–79	51.3	23.1	28.4	1,217	23	28

— = Not applicable.

Note: These data omit medium-term loans and loans from other programs such as loans to settlers.

Source: Chipande (1983a); Schaefer-Kehnert (1982); and Malaŵi, Minister of Agriculture and Natural Resources (1980).

evaluate this initiative. The Malaŵi government also has several other channels for credit to smallholders (see World Bank 1981a, pp. 150 ff.).

The conditions attached to most credit programs have effectively directed most credit to the farmers with the largest holdings. Many of the loans in the LLDP were tied to innovation packages (seeds, fertilizer, and use of particular techniques). These were of a labor-intensive nature, and their success depended on the timeliness of certain operations. Only households that could provide either family labor or hired labor during certain critical periods could use the package in the manner intended (Chipande 1983a). Furthermore, the innovation packages often specified a minimum farm size—an area sufficient for a specific number of bags of fertilizer. The major constraint on providing farm credit was often not the availability of funds but the availability of borrowers able to comply with the technology package conditions.[14] This helps explain the fact that about four-fifths of the households receiving such credit were growing either tobacco or improved maize—the largest farms. This notion is confirmed in *DevPol II*, which argues (p. 27) that although 8,100 credit clubs existed, they tended to include only the wealthier smallholders.

The strong correlation between size of holding and credit has had other causes as well. The default rate on the loans has been highest among the smallest holdings, so the government has understandably tailored the program to richer smallholders. Survey data also show a large fraction of female farmers claim to have been excluded from receiving credit, but these families, constituting about 30 percent of Malaŵi rural families, generally have small holdings.[15] Finally, requests for credit to provide wages for casual labor during the growing season or credits for farm implements and cattle were generally not considered eligible under these programs. The inability to obtain sufficient labor and capital inputs to meet seasonal requirements has been a major constraint on increasing production in the smallest size holdings.

A crucial component of *DevPol II* is to expand credit availability enough to increase the share of smallholders receiving credit from 16 percent in the mid-1980s to double this amount in the mid-1990s. The government plans to consolidate the existing credit funds, strengthen the credit-granting role of the agents of the Ministry of Agriculture, broaden the conditions for granting credit, and change the credit-technology package to correspond more to the circumstances of the average smallholder. The government also intends to take the simple measure of selling fertilizer in smaller bags so that farmers with smaller holdings will find it worthwhile to request credit. At the same time, however, it plans to reduce interest rate subsidies, so these smallholders will be paying somewhat higher rates on their loans.

The Impact of the Credit System

Although formal credit flows are limited, remittances from abroad and informal credit flows have helped satisfy smallholder demands for credit. Also, ADMARC's policy of stabilizing crop prices over the year may have limited credit demand. What then is the real extent of credit scarcity in the smallholder sector?

Survey data on maize growing provide one piece of evidence on this matter.[16] In 1980–81 about 1.3 percent of all smallholders used an improved local maize seed; of those who did not, 60 percent claimed the reason was the unavailability of money or credit with which to buy it. Only 26 percent of smallholders used fertilizers in the maize plots; of those who did not, 89 percent blamed the unavailability of money or credit. Only 0.6 percent of all smallholders used insecticides; of those who did not, 25 percent attributed the fact to the unavailability of money or credit. For the growing of groundnuts the responses were very similar.

Another indication of a credit shortage comes from financial data. Surveys of the Central Region in 1966 and the Lower Shire Valley in 1967 found that, respectively, 73 and 83 percent of smallholders with savings hid this cash on their farms (Brown 1970a). (These percentages are undoubtedly underreported for fear of theft.) Because cash for transactions purposes is generally not hidden, such drastic "home banking" suggests that smallholders are often unable to obtain needed credit.

An interesting manifestation of the credit constraint is revealed in the decisions about crop specialization by smallholders. Other things being equal, we might expect that farms with a low ratio of available land to labor would specialize in the production of labor-intensive products. This has not occurred; in fact, some data show that smaller farms specialize in land-intensive food crops (Appendix, table G-4).[17]

This "safety first" outlook is not peculiar to Malaŵi, of course, but is found in many other parts of the world as well. The basic argument is simple. If smallholders specialized in a cash crop, such as tobacco, they would face not only the production and price risks of growing tobacco but would also have to purchase the foodstuffs they might have grown at home. If they specialized in food crops, they would face only the production risks of that crop. With this risk factor in mind, it can be easily shown that the lower the land-labor ratio, the greater the specialization in food crops. Any tendency of smallholders to base their planting decisions on factor proportions is overridden by their inability to bear a great deal of risk because of lack of crop insurance, lack of sufficient personal assets to offset any food crop shortfalls, or lack of credit for purchasing food in bad years (Wright 1978, pp. 66 ff.).

The stunted capital market (combined with the stunted land market) has had several other important impacts on production. Product and labor markets have borne the brunt of any economic adjustments in the agricultural sector. Also, smallholder decisionmaking in these two markets has been highly constrained, and some critical allocation decisions have been made simply because the smallholders have neither the income nor the resources available from lending institutions to bear many agricultural risks.

The Labor Market in the Rural Sector

With the stunted markets for land and capital, the labor market and various types of labor exchanges have been the primary mechanisms for allocating resources for greater productive efficiency. Furthermore, wage labor has provided an effective way for those with little land and credit to increase their incomes. Except for various settlement schemes or the establishment of certain projects or development authorities in underpopulated areas, direct or indirect government actions to influence the rural labor markets have been relatively insignificant.

Formal and Informal Labor Exchanges

Malaŵi population censuses show that in the late 1970s the estates hired roughly 8 percent of the rural labor force, and individual smallholders hired another 1 to 2 percent. Through a number of more informal institutions, labor is carried out cooperatively or exchanged through some type of reciprocal exchange mechanism. Chipeta (1982) has analyzed several dozen of these arrangements.[18] He demonstrates empirically that labor productivities vary considerably among these various forms of work arrangements; moreover, among those types of labor for which some type of compensation is given, the relationship between individual effort and payment also varies considerably—in some cases it is quite direct, while in other compensation schemes it is nonexistent. He uses such evidence to explode the common notion in the economics literature that the rural sector features a standard or traditional wage.

A considerable number of Malaŵians have foreign work experience (Malaŵi, NSO 1980b, vol. 2). For instance, in 1977 (four years after the government had cut back on short-term migration to South Africa), about 17 percent of all Malaŵians aged 15 or older had worked abroad at some time. The pattern was much different for the two sexes; about 35 percent of all men, but only 1.5 percent of all women, had worked abroad. From the president of the nation on down, a wide variety of male Malaŵians gained valuable work experience and a broader intellectual horizon from this short-term work abroad. A considerably higher percentage of the rural population (about 18 percent) than of the urban population (11.5 percent) had this experience, evidence for the oft-made suggestion that the major motive for such emigration was to obtain the necessary capital for independent smallhold farming or (for some ethnic groups) to finance payment of a bridewealth (payments to the bride's family).

Migration abroad for work does not necessarily imply internal labor mobility. In Malaŵi in 1977 about 5.0 percent of the population was living in a region, and 16.3 percent in a district, different from the place of birth.[19] The most important migrant stream has been from rural to urban areas, for only 7.8 percent of the total rural population had emigrated from other regions. The pattern of the migration stream to the urban areas ran from the Northern Region to the Central Region, and from the Central Region to the Southern Region. Among the various rural districts, economic elements strongly influenced the flow of migration. Christiansen (1984) carried out a useful regression analysis of this rural migration showing that both push factors, such as high population density, and pull factors, such as differential employment opportunities, are important in this flow.

The government's scant encouragement of migration deserves note. Although the four integrated projects contained rather impressive plans for new settlements, these plans do not appear to have been implemented to any great extent, although roughly a dozen new settlements were set up through the Malaŵi Young Pioneers (chapter 4). The government has also placed a few agricultural projects in rural areas it deemed underpopulated or in need of employment.[20] The number of participants in these various programs has been relatively small. The government's restraint in carrying out large and expensive programs to redistribute the rural population has been appropriate, given the general scarcity of available arable land.

The Functioning of the Labor Market

The most important single consideration for any rural labor market is the season of the year. For instance, a linear programming model of four types of rural households and their input requirements throughout the agricultural year reveals that a major constraint on obtaining farm labor occurs in December and January, the months of peak demand, and that in most other months there is a surplus of rural labor.[21] Seasonal factors are complicated because the two months of peak labor demand occur during the wet season, when poor households not only face severe food shortages but also have high exposure to diseases, such as malaria, which reduce family labor supply. Among other things, this suggests that higher public expenditures focusing on health problems in these few months of great agricultural activity might have a very high payoff in increased production and in reduced rural poverty.

Data in table 5-6 on farm size and labor market behavior provide additional insight into the functioning of the rural labor market. Although these data are rather rough, they show clearly that land per family worker increases with the size of the holding and that net labor flows from the smallholdings decrease as the size of the smallholding increases.

The amount of labor hired in the smallest size holdings, on a hectare basis, is greater than on the larger holdings, a phenomenon Collier (1985) interprets in terms of cash and credit constraints.[22] To explore

Table 5-6. Labor Market Behavior by Size of Smallholding, Malaŵi, 1968–69 Crop Year

	\multicolumn{5}{c	}{Farm size (hectares)}	
Item	Less than 0.81	0.81– 1.61	1.62– 2.42	2.43– 4.85	More than 4.85	Average
Hectares per "man equivalent" of farm family	0.21	0.44	0.66	0.96	1.71	0.56
Cash crop receipts per hectare (MK)	2.55	2.88	3.53	5.56	5.76	4.16
Cash crop receipts as a percentage of total cash receipts	27.7	42.7	49.9	58.0	62.7	50.7
Labor years per hectare						
Hired in	0.04	0.02	0.02	0.02	0.02	0.02
Hired out	-0.78	-0.27	-0.15	-0.11	-0.07	-0.21
Net labor flow	-0.74	-0.24	-0.13	-0.09	-0.05	-0.19
Labor years as percentage of family "man equivalents"						
Hired in (+)	+0.8	+0.9	+1.1	+2.4	+3.7	+1.3
Hired out (-)	-16.0	-11.7	-9.9	-11.0	-11.5	-12.0
Net labor flow	-15.2	-10.7	-8.8	-8.6	-7.8	-10.7

Note: To determine labor hired in and out, it was necessary to convert financial data to labor equivalents. For labor hired out, I used an estimate by Dequin (1970), appendix 28, that the wage rate for casual labor in 1966 was .233 MK a day; for other labor hired in or out, I assumed that the daily pay was equal to the minimum wage. To convert to an annual basis I have assumed a work year of 250 days. For "man equivalents," an adult female worker is counted as 0.8, and a child (either male or female) is counted as 0.3 of an adult male worker. The labor does not include commodity-paid labor or labor obtained through cooperative work arrangements.

Source: Malaŵi Government (1970), various tables.

this phenomenon further, he carried out a regression analysis on thirty-five small, ecologically homogeneous areas and showed that the labor hired per hectare in these various units (the dependent variable) can be explained in large part by their mean cash income per acre (the independent variable); he also demonstrated that the amount of labor hired depends on how that cash is obtained from nonfarm and from farming activities.

The data on labor flow as a percentage of available family labor provide additional insight into the relationship between farm size and labor market behavior. In-hired labor increases and out-hired labor decreases as farm size increases. Because the smaller holdings grow fewer cash crops and, as shown in the table, obtain less of their total cash receipts from the sale of cash crops, workers from these smaller farms are more likely to hire themselves out than are smallholders with larger farms. Most of this work off the farm is carried out by men and is away from the agricultural sector, which probably prevents them from efficiently allocating their time between the two types and places of work. At planting or harvesting times, when traditional mechanisms for work exchange will not produce enough suitable labor (that is, when the work requires more hands or strength than is available on the farm), the person operating the farm must hire casual labor. Collier is certainly correct in asserting that these farmers, who have income from work outside of agriculture, also have more cash (in relation to the area farmed) with which to hire labor. They also may have more need to hire such labor, however.

Part-time work on the estates or on other farms has not appeared to be a viable option for most smallholders who are employed away from their own farms. The estates have arranged their tasks so as to maintain a fairly steady labor force; quarterly employment statistics show the labor force during the busy season (first quarter) is only one-third larger than in the slack season (third quarter). Detailed income data show that nonfarm work is what provides most of the cash income of smallholders.

Labor market income was almost 30 percent of the family income of smallholders in 1968–69, and it appears to have declined in real terms to roughly 10 percent of smallholder family incomes in 1984–85 (chapter 16). A considerable portion of this apparent decline (the data do not permit complete certainty) seems to reflect diminishing opportunities for work abroad and for temporary employment in the urban sector. The temporary urban jobs probably have gone to former rural dwellers, who now live permanently in shanty towns around the urban areas. This conjecture is based on considerations of relative population change in different areas. Between the census years 1966 and 1977, urbanization grew about 8 percent a year, while formal nonagricultural employment grew roughly 5 percent a year.[23] Although

120 Malaŵi and Madagascar

formal urbanization is overstated because of boundary changes of the cities, the informal sector in these cities must have been growing rapidly.

This decline in off-farm income has two obvious and important implications for the increase in income inequalities of the nation as a whole. First, the smaller chance of the poorest smallholders to supplement their incomes with wage work widens income differentials in the rural areas. Second, the lower incomes of any segment of the rural population lead to a widening of income differentials between urban and rural areas.

These phenomena can be viewed from a different perspective. Even though the fall in the real minimum wage should have encouraged greater employment of low-skilled rural workers for short-term jobs, the presence of an urban informal sector has crowded them out. In an important sense the rural sector has become an inadvertent victim of the success of the urban sector.

Summary and Conclusions

Market factors have influenced the growth of agricultural production in several ways. The government's reluctance to tax estate production and the state-owned banks' generous provision of credit to the estates have encouraged estate production. In contrast, the government and ADMARC have discouraged agricultural production by smallholders both by the high implicit marginal tax imposed through the system of agricultural producer prices and by relatively small credit flows to smallholders.

Three major factors have acted to widen rural income differentials. First, smallholders are the poorest segment of the population, and the government's pricing policies for agricultural goods, implemented through ADMARC, have lowered their incomes and discouraged their production for the market. Second, the credit and technology package the government offered to the smallholders has proven suitable primarily for those with the largest farms and highest incomes; the poorest smallholders have received relatively little technological help or credit. Third, the apparent drying up of opportunities for smallholders to earn income through temporary off-farm jobs, especially in the urban areas, has widened income differentials within the rural sector and also between urban and rural families. The first two of these factors are part of the government's wager-on-the-strong strategy; the last has not been a consequence of any particular government policy.

Farmers in any country have difficulty organizing themselves as a political force to advance their economic interests. In poor countries, such as Malaŵi, the low average level of education in the countryside compounds the problem. High government officials in Malaŵi, from the Life President on down, are extremely sympathetic to the plight of the smallholder, but they also have other goals and problems to consider. Until the mid-1980s, international lending institutions acquiesced to the pricing policies toward smallholders. The end result was a set of market policies that encouraged and aided the estates while discouraging production by smallholders, lowering their incomes, and widening income differentials.

Notes

1. Bates (1984), pp. 126 ff. has a more general and extended discussion of this point with regard to many African nations. Analysis of the political factors in Malaŵi that led to this situation can be found in the essays by John McCracken and by Megan Vaughan, in Fyfe and others (1985).

2. Malaŵi, NSO, *Reported Employment and Earnings Annual Report, 1982–1984*, p. 16. This datum excludes employment in companies in which ADMARC holds shares.

3. Some financial comparisons between ADMARC and the crop marketing organizations of several other African nations are made by Bose and others (n.d.).

4. References for these and other studies are given in the Appendix, section G. The study by Dean (1966) referred to later in the paragraph is one of several market experiments carried out in Malaŵi; Nyirenda and others (1959) reports on another.

5. Other aspects of the problem can be investigated by comparing ratios of official purchase prices to realized prices of export crops of other African nations. For 1960 through 1984 the average unweighted ratios of official prices to export prices of groundnuts in Malaŵi was 0.547. A similar unweighted average ratio for nine other African nations (for which data for more than ten years are readily available) is 0.573. The data come from Hesp (1985). In another experiment with the same data set, I computed the unweighted averages of the official prices of maize for seven countries, converted them into U.S. dollars at the official exchange rate and compared them with similar unweighted averages for Malaŵi. Prices in Malaŵi were roughly 20 percent below those in the other countries. Because of certain incomparabilities, these comparisons seem less trustworthy than the first experiment. Nevertheless, in this restricted sense we can say that smallholder production has been relatively discouraged in Malaŵi.

6. More specifically, I calculated the average value of the variable under investigation for the two previous and the two following years (a "donut average"), determined the ratio of the difference between this donut average and the value of the variable for the middle year of the series in question, and then squared the ratio. The square root of the average of the sum of these ratios is the pseudo-coefficient of variation, which represents a ratio of deviations to an average. For Malaŵi I used five-product price series, weighted with the same quantity weights as in table 5-3. For experiments on income I compared the current value of agricultural revenues assuming that domestic and

then export prices applied. The pseudo-coefficients of variation discussed qualitatively in the text are agricultural export prices, 18.2 percent; domestic agricultural prices, 8.8 percent; agricultural revenues calculated in export prices, 22.8 percent; and agricultural revenues calculated in domestic prices, 22.9 percent. My conclusions regarding income stabilization are somewhat different from the ideas advanced by Brown (1970b) that the predecessor to ADMARC actually destabilized smallholder incomes, but his data were from an earlier period. E. D. Silumba, in *Conference on Design* . . . (1985–86), has presented some interesting data suggesting that price fluctuations of smallholder products were greater after independence than before.

7. Some data on these matters are presented in Malaŵi, Minister of Agriculture and Natural Resources, *Agro-Economic Survey* (November 1977, February 1979) and in working papers numbers 4 (May 1983) and 5 (September 1983) of this same Agro-Economic series.

8. Free market seasonal price fluctuations also suggest two additional hypotheses. One is that real interest rates and storage costs (of spoilage, for example) are sufficiently high in these rural areas that the existing price variations make intertemporal arbitrage unprofitable. In this regard Collier (1985) cites Salmond (1957) showing weight losses for storing untreated maize of almost 20 percent after eighteen months' storage. The other hypothesis is that intertemporal arbitrage may not take place because no one is willing to assume this function. This might have occurred for a short while after the removal of Asian merchants from Malaŵi during the 1970s and before Africans fully assumed their trading functions (This could well have corresponded to the period to which these data apply.) Both conjectures suggest that product markets were not completely efficient.

9. A natural market for Malaŵian maize would be Zimbabwe whenever that country faces a maize deficit. Malaŵian officials told me, however, that for political reasons Zimbabwe has chosen to import its maize in these emergency conditions from the Democratic People's Republic of Korea.

10. The two British banks merged in 1971 to form the National Bank of Malaŵi, and in 1977 Malaŵian parastatals bought a majority interest. In 1970 the Commercial Bank of Malaŵi was formed with a majority interest held by Portuguese investors, but in 1974 Malaŵi parastatals bought the majority interest. Also in the early 1970s the Malaŵian government and several foreign governments set up the Investment and Development Bank.

11. In 1973 the Malaŵi government also submitted a proposal to the World Bank for establishing the Agricultural Development Bank of Malaŵi, which also would have provided loans to the estates. This project was turned down on the grounds that the benefits would accrue only to the higher income farmers. This matter is discussed briefly by Christiansen and Kydd (1986). As shown in table 5-4, agricultural loans—mostly to the growing estate sector—have amounted to roughly one-fifth to one-fourth of these banks' total loans, or about 3.5 to 4.0 percent of GDP. When many of the estates ran into financial difficulties in the late 1970s, their borrowing soared, and by 1982 these debts amounted to about 230 MK per hectare or 1,700 MK per planted hectare (at that time, respectively about $245 and $1,800). In addition, some estates have been able to borrow from the parastatals. ADMARC-owned estates

have been financed from the profits of the company's trade in smallholder crops.

12. Malaŵi Government (1970), p. 30. Collier (1985) discusses traditional lending practices in Malaŵi, and Pryor (1978) has a more general study of credit transactions as an element of precapitalist economies.

13. Dequin (1970), pp. 40 ff., and World Bank (1981a), pp. 150 ff., survey colonial attempts to channel credit to African smallholders.

14. A fuller statement of these matters is contained in Chipande (1983b). This is one of the two best technical studies of particular economic problems of Malaŵi.

15. The share of women as heads of smallholding households is given in Malaŵi Government (1984), tables 1.2 and 1.3.

16. The data in this paragraph come from Malaŵi Government (1984), tables 2.21, 2.23, 2.24, and 2.26. These data are actually stated in percentages of total plots; for simplicity, I have substituted smallholders for plots.

17. I draw especially on the argument of Collier (1985), who applies to Malaŵi an analysis that he and Lal (1986) had previously made for Kenya.

18. Chipeta does not indicate, however, the relative importance of these various labor exchanges to total labor requirements or whether informal labor exchanges are increasing or decreasing in relative importance.

19. The conclusions presented in this paragraph are based on the 1977 population census (Malaŵi 1980b, vol. 1).

20. Several projects—for example, a second sugar estate at the mouth of the Dangwa River—were justified in part in the name of a regional policy. This particular example proved an expensive method of creating jobs, a situation discussed by Robert Lazlett, in Fyfe and others (1985), pp. 381–406.

21. This discussion is based on results by Chipanda (1983a) and (1983b). His fascinating linear programming model of smallholder decisionmaking brings out very clearly the production constraints facing four different kinds of smallholders.

22. Collier and Lal (1986) offer a similar interpretation for Kenya. My interpretations of these phenomena are somewhat different from Collier's. Chipande (1983a) and (1983b) has another explanation.

23. The data on urbanization come from Pryor (1988b), table B-4; the labor force data are for 1968 through 1977 and come from Malaŵi, NSO (1969 and 1980b).

6 Foreign Trade and the Balance of Payments in Malaŵi

From Malaŵi's independence to the end of the 1970s, four trends characterized its foreign trade sector: agricultural exports, particularly from the estate sector, increased more rapidly than GDP; the import regime was relatively liberal; the exchange rate policy was to maintain a rough equilibrium in the balance of payments; and the foreign-held government debt of Malaŵi steadily increased, although debt-service payments were relatively low. From the end of the 1970s through the mid-1980s, a significant reversal occurred. The volume of exports remained roughly the same, import restrictions increased greatly, the exchange rate was overvalued, and debt-service problems became increasingly severe.

Many of the foreign trade problems in the 1980s arose from a series of external and internal shocks to the Malaŵian economy. From the mid-1970s through the mid-1980s the terms of trade became increasingly adverse. In a major policy error in the late 1970s, the government considerably increased its foreign borrowing, mistakenly believing its balance of payments problems to be short term. In the early 1980s Malaŵi's low-cost links to Indian Ocean ports were cut, which sharply increased the transportation costs of foreign trade. In addition, the financial authorities were slow to devalue the currency when it became overvalued in the 1980s. All of these shocks led, in turn, to a balance of payments crisis, several debt reschedulings, and a partial restructuring of the economy in the early and mid-1980s under the prodding of international lending agencies. As of the late 1980s, however, many of Malaŵi's foreign trade difficulties appeared to persist.

Trade Orientation and Key Structural Characteristics

In poor agricultural nations, export-led growth generally provides a source of expansion for the entire economy. At the same time, it raises the relative income of the agricultural sector, which mainly provides the exports and which contains the poorest part of the population. Because various policies in Malaŵi have favored estate over smallholder agriculture (chapters 4 and 5), the links between the encouragement of exports, especially agricultural, and the distribution of income are complicated to analyze.[1]

The Degree of Openness

According to the data presented in table 6-1, Malaŵi's exports averaged 22.5 percent of factor price GDP (in current prices) from 1964 through 1986. Its "trade openness" in 1975, measured by this relationship, was more than 25 percent greater than the average of sixteen Sub-Saharan nations with roughly similar populations and levels of economic development in the same year.[2] More sophisticated experiments using such data for larger samples of comparison nations yield somewhat mixed results.[3] Nevertheless, Malaŵi's foreign trade appears to be somewhat higher than one would expect from a nation with similar per capita income and population.

Examination of the ratio of trade to aggregate production over time provides a more dynamic approach to the measurement of trade openness. Table 6-1 shows that exports became a greater share of GDP (in both current and constant prices) during the period covered in the table. This phenomenon suggests export-led growth. At the same time, the share of imports to GDP fell. Such divergences in export and import trends were brought about by dramatic changes in the terms of trade. During the 1967–84 period Malaŵi's terms of trade worsened at an average annual rate of 3.4 percent a year. This trend reflects the relative fall in world market prices of Malaŵian exports, the rise in transportation costs (tantamount to a decline in the terms of trade), and the two oil shocks of the 1970s (Malaŵi imports all of its petroleum products). The transportation cost increases originated from the RENAMO insurgency in Mozambique, which disturbed and eventually (1983) cut the rail links from Malaŵi to Indian Ocean ports in Mozambique. These costs were the cause of the divergences in the f.o.b. and c.i.f. import series beginning in the late 1970s.

The data in table 6-2 offer a different perspective on Malaŵi's export performance. From 1954 through 1984 its export volume grew at an average annual rate of 5.5 percent, while its constant factor price GDP grew 4.7 percent a year (Pryor 1988b, table E-1).[4] In the federation years (1954–64) exports grew roughly 6 percent a year, and between 1964 and 1979 they increased at an average annual rate of 5.8 percent. From 1979 through 1985, however, exports grew only 0.6 percent a year, a decline caused by the financial difficulties of the estates and a possible shift in the intersectoral terms of trade against agriculture (see table 5-3), abetted by an overvalued exchange rate.

Table 6-1. Trade as a Share of GDP, Malaŵi, 1964 to 1968

Percentage of factor price GDP

	Current price			Constant price	
Year	Exports	Imports f.o.b.	Imports c.i.f.	Exports	Imports f.o.b.
1964	18.4	21.1	23.8	23.0	n.a.
1965	17.2	24.4	28.1	20.9	n.a.
1966	18.8	29.2	33.0	20.6	n.a.
1967	20.9	25.7	29.3	23.4	32.0
1968	20.9	29.7	35.0	25.0	35.4
1969	20.6	28.6	33.3	21.2	28.4
Unweighted average	19.5	26.5	30.4	22.4	31.9
1970	21.3	29.3	35.4	21.3	29.3
1971	20.4	25.9	30.8	20.4	27.2
1972	20.8	28.7	33.1	22.1	28.3
1973	23.4	29.1	33.6	23.0	26.3
1974	23.4	32.1	36.4	21.2	25.0
1975	24.7	39.0	44.2	20.7	27.0
1976	26.2	28.7	32.6	20.6	18.6
1977	26.4	24.2	30.7	22.3	20.7
1978	21.0	30.2	38.3	19.7	25.1
1979	23.1	32.2	41.3	24.8	24.6
Unweighted average	23.1	29.9	35.6	21.6	25.2
1980	25.3	28.7	39.6	29.1	22.6
1981	24.4	23.1	31.3	24.4	20.0
1982	22.4	18.6	28.6	24.7	18.5
1983	22.3	18.0	28.1	31.6	17.9
1984	29.2	15.0	25.0	22.0	13.7
1985	23.8	16.4	27.3	25.1	16.7
1986	22.3	15.7	n.a.	n.a.	n.a.
Unweighted average	24.2	19.4	30.0	26.2	18.2

n.a. = Not available.

a. The constant price data are calculated from trade volume indexes based on 1970 and adjusted for the GDP price basis so that current and constant price shares are the same for 1970.

b. Includes reexports.

Source: Pryor (1988b), tables E-1, F-1, F-2a, and F-2b.

Table 6-2. Important Foreign Trade Series, Malaŵi, 1954 to 1986

Year	Real effective exchange rate	Exports	Imports	Terms of trade	Balance on current account	Long-term capital flow and debt relief	Tariff revenues as a percentage of imports (c.i.f.)
	Indexes (1970 = 100)				Percentage of factor price GDP		
1954	122.5	43.34	n.a.	n.a.	n.a.	n.a.	n.a.
1955	126.2	37.57	n.a.	n.a.	n.a.	n.a.	n.a.
1956	120.0	53.03	n.a.	n.a.	n.a.	n.a.	n.a.
1957	116.8	49.69	n.a.	n.a.	n.a.	n.a.	n.a.
1958	117.4	47.48	n.a.	n.a.	n.a.	n.a.	n.a.
1959	116.9	53.81	n.a.	n.a.	n.a.	n.a.	n.a.
1960	117.8	56.36	n.a.	n.a.	n.a.	n.a.	n.a.
1961	114.7	54.79	n.a.	n.a.	n.a.	n.a.	n.a.
1962	116.7	71.11	n.a.	n.a.	n.a.	n.a.	n.a.
1963	122.3	77.33	n.a.	n.a.	n.a.	n.a.	n.a.
1964	120.6	72.87	n.a.	n.a.	4.1	1.6	n.a.
1965	118.1	80.17	n.a.	n.a.	1.3	1.3	10.4
1966	118.6	84.46	n.a.	n.a.	-9.2	4.5	12.7
1967	107.0	107.32	106.70	86.63	-5.0	6.4	15.6
1968	100.2	107.76	110.83	89.98	-10.9	10.1	13.8
1969	97.3	99.27	96.83	92.89	-10.9	11.1	14.0
Unweighted average					-5.1	5.8	13.3
1970	100.0	100.00	100.00	100.00	-12.5	11.4	12.9
1971	100.0	111.14	107.37	102.07	-9.4	9.4	16.4
1972	95.2	127.50	118.76	93.41	-12.2	9.2	14.3
1973	86.1	135.40	112.39	89.70	-6.4	10.3	14.6
1974	88.8	134.29	115.18	84.23	-6.3	11.2	12.0
1975	83.0	138.28	130.89	81.22	-13.3	9.6	10.3
1976	88.9	146.43	95.73	79.32	-7.6	7.0	11.1
1977	92.7	164.79	111.51	94.06	-4.9	9.9	13.2
1978	86.8	157.55	146.52	84.68	-14.8	9.9	14.4
1979	74.3	205.61	147.90	66.60	-21.3	10.7	16.3
Unweighted average					-10.9	9.9	13.6
1980	69.2	240.53	135.31	56.56	-18.6	18.3	21.4
1981	75.8	190.84	113.90	68.78	-7.8	3.6	27.0
1982	73.2	198.20	108.34	69.86	-8.2	4.1	26.5
1983	75.8	262.71	108.82	64.04	-10.4	4.7	n.a.
1984	78.5	190.86	86.79	66.79	0.8	5.4	n.a.
1985	n.a.	228.00	109.99	57.03	-6.7	0.4	n.a.
1986	n.a.	n.a.	n.a.	n.a.	-3.6	3.3	n.a.
Unweighted average					-7.7	5.7	25.0

n.a. = Not available.
a. Exports before 1964 represent only production for exports of agricultural products.
Source: Pryor (1988b), tables E-1, F-1, F-4, and F-6.

The volume of Malaŵi's imports from 1967 through 1984 grew about 1.0 percent a year. From 1967 through 1979 imports grew only 2.3 percent a year, and from 1979 through 1985 they declined 6.5 percent a year. The differential in growth rates of exports and imports was not enough to prevent balance of payments difficulties arising from large debt-service charges, however. *DevPol II* projected that from 1987 through 1996 exports would grow faster than GDP, which in turn would grow faster than imports; unfortunately, this planning document does not spell out very clearly how such successful results could come about.

Trade Policies: Quantitative Restrictions and Taxes

For a given level of protection, quantitative restrictions have a much more adverse impact on trade than do tariffs.

QUANTITATIVE RESTRICTIONS. *DevPol I* argued strongly against the use of quantitative controls in trade. In a formal sense this approach appears to have been followed not just for its intrinsic merits but also because of the lack of trained bureaucratic personnel to administer such a program and the president's possible desire to avoid setting up a situation that would encourage corruption.

Informally, however, the system of import licensing administered by the Minister of Trade, Industry, and Tourism has acted as a system of quantitative restrictions. Although in most years this system did not play a very important role, the ministry at different times has placed restrictions on imports from particular countries or on particular products. Moreover, in the mid-1980s the balance of payments came under severe pressure, and the use of foreign currency for imports required prior approval by the Reserve Bank, which strengthened the system of informal quantitative restrictions in a very important way.

Given the informality and, in the case of Reserve Bank requirements, nontransparency of the two systems of import licensing, their overall effects are hard to judge and appear to have varied over time. Some critics of the government, such as T. David Williams (1978, p. 289), have argued that in the 1970s the import licensing system gave the government opportunities to favor particular private or public firms, and to become corrupt. The degree to which this actually occurred during that period is unclear because such regulations did not appear to be very important except during short periods of foreign exchange shortages. For the first decade and a half after independence quantitative restrictions did not seem greatly to influence the volume of trade.

The situation has been much different during the 1980s. The central bank's currency allocation system has lasted for a number of years and has been highly restrictive. During a visit to Blantyre in 1986 I heard a litany of complaints from importers and manufacturers and an endless stream of anecdotes about favoritism in foreign exchange allocations; none of these, of course, could be independently verified. Nevertheless, the scramble for foreign exchange licenses appeared to give rise to expensive bureaucratic maneuvers.

These import restrictions did damage domestic manufacturers, who were left with idle capacity because they were unable to import critical intermediate inputs during balance of payments difficulties. The extent of such damage appears to have varied over time. David Wheeler (1983) tried to measure this phenomenon statistically for the 1970s. His data for Sub-Saharan nations show that Malaŵi ranked among the most favorable with respect to maintaining the level of these vital imports. For the 1980s, however, the situation appears different. A number of Malaŵian manufacturers complained bitterly to me that the foreign exchange allocation system had led both to considerable excess manufacturing capacity and to uncertainty in enterprise planning because they could not anticipate particular import decisions by the Reserve Bank.

Shipping goods out of the country has also required licenses, but according to the foreign traders I interviewed, the licenses have taken only two or three weeks to obtain and have not noticeably discouraged exports. *DevPol II* announced that in the future the government would try to encourage exporters by giving them preferential access to foreign exchange during periods of foreign exchange shortages.

TAX TREATMENT OF EXPORTED AND IMPORTED GOODS. Malaŵi officials have had little sympathy with negative tariffs, that is, holding down a domestic price if the foreign price has increased. They have also shown no hesitancy about passing higher prices of imports on to consumers. For instance, the rise in oil prices on the world market led to a roughly equivalent increase in the domestic price of oil. Indeed, when balance of payment problems increased shortly thereafter, the price of gasoline rose more than proportionately as tariffs on oil products were raised.

The available tariff data permit easy calculation of nominal tariff rates (that is, tariff revenues and import surcharges as a percentage of the value of imports) for the major categories of imports. Such statistics must be used cautiously because they do not take into account those goods for which tariff rates had been sufficiently high to discourage all or almost all imports.

In the 1960s the average nominal tariff rate was about 13 percent, low in comparison with other developing nations, but the structure of tariffs was similar to that of these other nations. More specifically, tariffs were highest for oil products (about 45 percent), "other intermediate products" (about 25 percent), and consumer goods (about 20 percent). They were lowest for plant, machinery, and equipment (about

2 percent); raw materials (about 3 percent); and transport equipment (11 percent) (Pryor 1988b, section F).

This kind of tariff structure reflected the desire of policymakers to encourage domestic production of consumer goods and other intermediate products, and (as shown in chapter 7), this goal has certainly been achieved. Also, by setting increasingly higher tariff rates on imported goods closer to the final stages of production, policymakers have attempted to raise effective tariffs with the stage of processing. The disadvantage of this structure, compared with a flat-rate tariff, is that it encourages capital-intensive methods of production in that domestic prices of imported capital equipment become relatively lower than prices of other goods or the price of labor. Given the relatively constant labor-output ratios found in the manufacturing sector, however, this effect does not appear very strong in practice. Further, because Malaŵi is many years away from having its own heavy industry, such tariffs have not had any great disincentive effect on domestic production. In sum, given the factor proportions existing in Malaŵi up to now, especially the lack of skilled workers and employees, tariff incentives probably have not changed the final structures of trade and domestic manufacturing to any considerable degree.

As shown in table 6-2, overall tariff rates remained roughly the same from the late 1960s to the late 1970s. In 1979, however, when the balance of payments problems of the several previous years were seriously exacerbated by the second oil shock, Malaŵi policymakers roughly doubled the average tariff rate. They maintained the same tariff structure, however. In 1981, the highest import taxes were on oil products (91 percent), transportation equipment (34 percent), consumer goods (31 percent), and other intermediate products (25 percent). Average nominal tariffs were relatively low on plant, machinery, and equipment (10 percent) and on raw materials (4 percent) (Pryor 1988b, table F-4).

In the name of discouraging unnecessary imports, the Malaŵi government abandoned its relatively liberal trade principles after the 1970s. Although no detailed evidence is available on how the decision to raise tariffs was reached, this policy apparently had the dual purpose of raising government revenues and improving the balance of payments situation; protectionism alone did not appear to be a motive, although this was the end result. *DevPol II* decried "unnecessary protection" and argued for tariff reforms to reduce tariff rates and make them uniform across all imports (p. 63).

Data on effective tariffs (that is, on tariffs as a percentage of value added in domestic production) would provide a much better measure of trade protection, but the lack of a detailed input-output table prevents us from making such calculations for all goods. Some rough sample calculations show very much higher effective tariffs for certain goods, because the share of value added in their manufacture is relatively small in relation to total sales (Chamley and others 1985, table 2-3). Thus the relatively low nominal tariffs may be deceptive, and Malaŵi should probably be considered a country with middle-range protection, which increased significantly in the late 1970s and early 1980s. Unlike many African nations, Malaŵi has not taxed exports, except in 1986, when it taxed estate exports of tobacco and tea. Nevertheless, the overvalued exchange rate during the 1980s has acted as a tax on exports.

The structure of export and import taxes can also influence the degree to which imports adjust to changes in export receipts in a symmetrical fashion. In most countries imports rise and fall when export receipts change, because of income effects. If imports increase more during upswings in exports than they decrease during downswings of exports, the nation will have some severe balance of payments problems. David Wheeler (1983) tried to measure this asymmetrical response phenomenon in his econometric study of trade data for a number of Sub-Saharan nations. Of the thirty nations in his sample, Malaŵi had the third most favorable import responses; that is, Malaŵi had one of the best records in the sample of nations in avoiding asymmetrical responses of imports to export changes. I suspect this is because, during this period, quantitative restrictions on imports were not important and because the tariff structure and exchange rate policies allowed price effects to dampen such asymmetries; conclusive proof of this conjecture, however, would require more intensive quantitative analysis.

Trade Regime: Favored Sector Approach

A truly comprehensive approach toward the trade regime must take into account not only tariffs, quantitative restrictions, export promotion, and exchange rate policies but also domestic taxes, production subsidies, and monetary policies. Did this policy package favor the export sector, the import-competing sector, or the sector producing goods and services only for domestic markets?

A crude but useful empirical approach is to examine trends in the relative prices of export, import-competing, and nontraded goods. If we consider the agricultural sector as the export sector, the mining and manufacturing sector as the import-competing sector, and the other sectors (utilities, construction, distribution, commerce, finance, housing, and services) as the nontraded goods sector, we can use implicit price deflators from the national account statistics to determine how domestic policies affected the three sectors.

Although some data problems arise and we must be cautious, our estimates suggest that Malaŵi's export sector has had a slow but steady increase in relative prices (that is, in comparison to the GDP deflator).[5] The estimates also reveal a steady but slower rise in the relative prices of import-competing goods, at least until 1980, when the relative price series leveled off. Both these price increases have been at the expense of the domestic nontradables, for which relative prices have slowly and steadily declined.

These data, combined with previous information on the declining terms of trade, suggest that Malaŵi has managed its economic affairs to favor both the export and the import-competing industries, to the detriment of the nontradable goods industries. That is, its trade regime has permitted an adjustment to the declining terms of trade by discouraging imports and encouraging exports, the type of adjustment a functioning market economy would make in such circumstance to bring its balance of payments into equilibrium. The relative rise in the prices of tradables compared to nontradables has also favored property-intensive (that is, capital- and land-intensive) industries over labor-intensive industries, and this appears to have had an important impact on the distribution of income (chapter 16).

The Financial Side of Foreign Trade

Exchange Rate Policies

The institutional history of the exchange rate in Malaŵi has a number of interesting aspects.[6] For our purpose, however, indexes of trade-weighted nominal and real effective exchange rates are more important. Up to the end of the 1970s, the government generally acted to maintain the nominal value of the Malaŵi kwacha at about 90 to 100 percent of its 1965 value. Real effective exchange rates can be calculated by adjusting the nominal exchange rates with the implicit GDP deflators of each trading partner to derive an index of Malaŵi trade prices relative to the rest of the world. These data are presented in table 6-2.

The real effective exchange rate declined almost steadily from 1964 to 1980. By 1980 it had reached a low of 57 percent of the 1964 real value. Since then it has risen slowly. Such changes in the real effective exchange rate have been the result of the exchange rate policy combined with conservative monetary and fiscal policies, which have kept domestic prices from rising as fast as prices abroad.

These calculations suggest that during the 1970s the Malaŵi government avoided the practice in many developing nations (especially former British colonies in Africa) of permitting a currency to remain highly overvalued. At first glance, the Malaŵi kwacha appears undervalued, but with the terms of trade turning steadily against Malaŵi, such a fall in the real effective exchange rate was necessary to achieve balance of payments equilibrium.

For the 1980s, however, several developments indicate that the currency has been considerably overvalued. The quantitative restrictions on imports and the slow growth of exports have been the most obvious signs. Moreover, the government was far from allowing a free exchange of its currency. Citizens were not permitted to hold foreign bank balances or currencies and were restricted in the amount of domestic currency they could take out of the country. Immigrants were also limited in the amount they could transfer abroad at any one time. To encourage foreign capital and skilled foreign workers to come to Malaŵi, however, expatriates in Malaŵi could remit a considerable fraction of their earnings abroad, and repatriation of foreign capital has been relatively simple.

Given these signs of continuing disequilibrium, the data in table 6-2, showing that the real exchange rate appreciated slightly from 1980 through 1984, are disturbing. Furthermore, from 1984 through 1988 the currency fell at an average annual rate of about 17.3 percent against the dollar (and 22.1 percent against the SDR), while the consumer price index rose at an average annual rate of 19.5 percent. Thus the real value of the Malaŵi kwacha did not greatly change (IMF, *International Financial Statistics*, February 1989). The exchange rate restrictions were a response to the overvaluation and have given rise to a black market in kwacha in neighboring countries. The ratio of the black market rate to the officially quoted rate has fallen rather steadily since 1973, and it took a particularly sharp dip in 1981. During the 1980s this ratio has averaged between 50 and 60 percent of the official rate (Pryor 1988b, table G-2).

Equilibration Mechanisms

During the 1960s and 1970s the Life President seemed willing to follow the recommendations of foreign advisors and international agencies and to maintain an equilibrium exchange rate. In the 1980s, as economic policymaking devolved more on the ministers and the civil service, governmental views on the advisability of any kind of devaluation to achieve this goal have changed.

In talking with junior civil servants in Malaŵi in 1987, I was struck with their pessimism about the possibility that further devaluation would aid the balance of payments problem; their views appeared to reflect those of more senior officials as well. Some argued that agricultural production would not respond to the higher prices, a claim that flies in the face of all empirical studies of price responsiveness in agriculture. Others maintained that the main recipients of the benefits of a devaluation would be the large multinationals operating within Malaŵi (an argument I show in the next chapter to be wrong). Still others declared that a devaluation would create too many short-term problems and that a slow depreciation via a lower increase of domestic than foreign prices would be far preferable. This governmental pessimism served as a bedrock to withstand pressure from foreign lenders to carry out a significant devaluation. Although *DevPol II* advocated a flexible exchange rate policy, it did not spell out what this means, and it also foresaw future exchange rate shortages; such an orientation toward exchange rate policy does not bode well for the future.

As far as I know, the impact of a devaluation on the Malaŵian economy has not been studied in detail. Certain factors would seem crucial in analyzing such a policy measure, especially as a response to deteriorating terms of trade. As a very small country, Malaŵi surely has had very little impact on world prices (except for fire-cured and burley tobacco). A number of different types of adjustments might occur in response to devaluation.

PRICE EFFECTS. A devaluation would raise the domestic price of Malaŵi's exports and the domestic prices of imports and import-competing goods as well. The impact on the balance of payments would depend not only upon the obvious production effects both on agricultural exports (chapter 5) and on import-competing goods but also upon the degree to which domestic consumers would switch their consumption toward nontradables and domestically produced import-competing goods.[7] The evidence presented above on relative prices in these three sectors shows that incentives for such substitutions of consumption did indeed occur in the 1970s.

These price effects are not automatic, and many other factors can counteract them. For instance, policy errors, such as an inflationary financing of the governmental deficit, could raise domestic prices of exports, or wage increases in the nontradable sector could prevent consumption from shifting to these goods and services. So far, the monetary policies followed during most of the postindependence period, the weakness of labor unions, the lack of wage indexation, and the government's actions in moderating its own wage increases and in dampening general wage increases have prevented such offsets. Nevertheless, governmental price policies in agriculture or foreign exchange allocation policies that discourage or prevent producers of exports or of import-competing goods from increasing production could offset the mechanisms equilibrating the balance of payments. In the mid-1980s such counteracting forces to a balance of payments adjustment might have been important, especially with regard to import-competing manufactured goods.

INCOME EFFECTS. A devaluation that led to a lowering of domestic incomes would reduce domestic consumption of tradable goods (assuming, of course, that such tradables are not inferior goods). Such a reduction in income can come about in several ways.

Unemployment. One mechanism, occurring in industrial economies after devaluation, is an increase in unemployment. Although appropriate time-series data are not available, joblessness probably was not increasing in Malaŵi.

Real wage decline. Real wages can also decline after devaluation, either absolutely or, if productivity is increasing, by rising at a slower rate than productivity. Average real wages appear to have declined in Malaŵi (chapter 16), so this adjustment to a balance of payments disequilibrium must have occurred. By maintaining the level of domestic prices at roughly the same level, real income can also fall with the decline in the terms of trade and the devaluation because of the absolute rise in the domestic prices of imports. To a certain extent, this also appears to have occurred.

Changes in the income distribution. A different type of income mechanism occurs after devaluation with the shift in the relative prices of tradables and nontradables. Because of different factor intensities in the two sectors, such a shift might act to lower the share of wage income and increase the share of property income.[8] This quite likely occurred in Malaŵi. Such a mechanism leads to a reduction in imports of consumption goods by the receivers of labor income and an increase in imports of consumption goods by the receivers of property income. With certain types of savings schedules, this shift in the distribution of income would lead to increased savings and lower overall consumption of goods and services (that is, to less absorption of domestic resources), and this would aid balance of payments equilibration.[9] The situation is complicated, however, because changes in the relative consumption of tradable and nontradable goods must also be taken into account, a matter on which little information is available.

ABSORPTION EFFECTS. Any mechanism encouraging production to grow faster than consumption would aid the equilibration of the foreign exchange market following a decline in the terms of trade or a devaluation. A faster increase in the supply of exports and import substitutes than in the growth of imports would achieve the same goal. In Malaŵi exports have grown faster than GDP, as has manufacturing production—the import-substitution sector (chapter 7). Monetary and fiscal policies are also important here. Deficit spending by the government has made equilibration of the balance of payments more difficult, but during the 1970s the conservative monetary policy with positive interest rates aided such equilibration by reducing real private spending.

In sum, certain economic mechanisms appear to be at work in the Malaŵi economy that would lead to an equilibration of the balance of payments in cases of foreign exchange shortages if the government carried out a real devaluation of the currency. The pessimism of the Malaŵian civil servants seems unwarranted.

The Balance of Payments

Several important structural shifts have occurred in Malaŵi's balance of payments accounts. The data in table 6-2 make apparent some trends in the major components of the balance of payments, defined as shares of GDP.

Merchandise balance. In the late 1960s and most of the 1970s the merchandise balance (exports minus imports of goods) was usually in deficit from 4 to 14 percent of GDP. Following the severe readjustments of the late 1970s and early 1980s, the merchandise balance turned positive, ranging from 3 to 12 percent of GDP during the first five years of the 1980s.

Service balance. Nonfactor service payments (for example, transport, insurance, and tourism) have turned increasingly negative in the years since independence, rising from about 5 percent of GDP in the late 1960s to about 11 percent in the 1980s. In great part this represents the rise in transportation costs of foreign trade. Net outflows of factor payments (interest, profits, and wages) behaved erratically, but from 1980 through 1984 they averaged about 7 percent of GDP. Much of this, of course, represented interest payments to finance the growing foreign indebtedness and the profit repatriation permitted in order to attract foreign investment.

Transfer payments. Total transfer payments amounted to 9 to 14 percent of GDP in the first years after independence. For the most part this represented transition grants by the British government to assist Malaŵi's government in establishing itself. After these were phased out in the early 1970s, such transfers fluctuated between 1 and 5 percent of GDP, depending upon the success of the government in attracting grants from other nations.

Taken together, these trends in the major parts of the current account balance resulted in a negative balance that ranged from –5 to –13 percent of GDP from 1966 through 1977; deepened rapidly to –22 and –20 percent in 1979 and 1980, the years when the economy was hit by the second oil shock, a drought, and drastically rising transportation costs; and then improved in the mid-1980s.

In most years long-term foreign credits to the government (and, in the early 1980s, debt relief) primarily financed the trade deficit. The imports for many governmental investment projects have been financed this way (chapter 3). The role of the public sector in the trade deficit becomes apparent if we subtract from the current account all the credit to the government and government enterprises; the residual deficit looks considerably less dangerous, ranging from +3 to −7 percent of GDP from 1965 through 1978. The serious problems of 1979 pushed this nongovernmental deficit percentage up considerably, and it remained high until the mid-1980s, when the situation seemed somewhat more secure. This exercise shows that a major causal element in the current account deficit has been borrowing by the government and some of its enterprises.

Thus the public sector has had rather conflicting roles in Malaŵi's balance of payments problems. During many years in the 1970s the negative balance on the current account was in good measure a result of borrowing by the government and the public enterprises. The government aided the equilibration process, however, by its relatively conservative monetary policies, which permitted automatic mechanisms to influence the operations of both the private and the parastatal sectors. In the 1980s the government did not make the proper exchange rate corrections and, instead, resorted to more direct measures to balance the international accounts. This attack on the symptoms, rather than on the basic causes, left the balance of payments problems still unresolved by the end of the decade.

EXTERNAL INDEBTEDNESS. Servicing the foreign-held debt has been a major burden on the Malaŵi economy during the 1980s. The balance of payments data and, more directly, data on the foreign debt itself testify to the enormity of the problem. The data in table 6-3 summarize the major trends. External indebtedness measured in dollars increased at an average annual rate of 13 percent from 1970 through 1986. Taking into account the rise in U.S. prices, the average annual rise of real indebtedness has been about 7 percent. As a proportion of GDP, Malaŵi's foreign indebtedness rose from 44 to 83 percent in the same period.[10] This was accompanied by an increase in the debt-service (debt repayment and interest payments) share of exports from 7 percent in 1970 to 40 percent in 1986.

The composition of the debt has also changed considerably over time. The share of debt held by multilateral agencies, especially the World Bank Group, rose from 14 percent in 1970 to 69 percent in 1986, while the share for bilateral creditors fell from 59 percent to 24 percent. The major sources of bilateral loans have been the United Kingdom, followed by the United States, South Africa, and the Federal Republic of Germany. In 1979 the United Kingdom converted many of its loans to grants, and the Danish and German governments followed suit shortly thereafter. The private financial market financed a considerable share of the 1977 through 1979 surge in foreign indebtedness, raising its share from about 20 percent to almost 30 percent of total external debt. Because these loans were made for shorter periods and at higher rates, they put a heavy strain

Table 6-3. Malaŵi's Outstanding Foreign Debt, 1970 to 1986

Year	Total	Outstanding disbursed debt at year end ($ millions) Official creditors Multilateral agencies	Bilateral agencies	Private creditors[a] Suppliers	Financial markets	Average interest rate, commitments (percent)[b]	Debt-service ratio (percent)[c]	Average maturity, commitments (years)[d]
1970	122.4	16.9	83.8	4.6	17.1	3.8	7.1	29.2
1971	140.8	25.9	94.1	4.1	16.7	2.5	7.2	28.7
1972	164.5	36.7	104.8	8.4	14.6	1.6	7.6	30.1
1973	201.8	46.4	128.4	7.8	19.3	2.9	7.7	38.4
1974	229.6	54.4	147.2	6.9	21.2	2.2	7.8	40.4
1975	257.1	66.3	157.5	5.7	27.6	2.7	7.9	32.5
1976	294.8	77.8	165.2	4.1	47.7	4.8	8.5	24.7
1977	368.8	107.4	175.8	3.1	82.5	5.5	10.0	23.8
1978	503.9	144.3	220.8	13.6	125.2	4.5	17.0	29.4
1979	510.2	188.2	149.5	18.3	154.1	8.8	17.7	16.2
1980	643.6	237.9	212.1	20.6	173.0	5.8	20.3	23.4
1981	674.8	287.0	197.4	18.0	172.4	6.7	26.8	29.9
1982	704.0	334.7	205.2	12.4	151.6	3.5	23.5	33.6
1983	712.9	371.0	200.4	7.7	133.9	3.1	23.2	37.6
1984	740.2	447.5	162.0	7.5	123.3	3.9	21.4	38.2
1985	804.1	516.5	189.5	8.0	90.1	1.8	29.2	44.8
1986	909.7	631.3	214.2	6.9	57.4	3.2	40.0	27.3

a. Includes only publicly guaranteed debt.
b. Based on loan commitments. Includes low-interest and interest-free loans.
c. Ratio (expressed as percentage) of interest and amortization to the dollar value of exports of goods and nonfactor services. This series has a very slight incomparability between 1979 and 1980.
d. Based on loan commitments.
Source: EPD data bank, World Bank, External Debt Division, January 1988.

on the balance of payments. By 1986, however, the private market share of the external debt was only 7 percent. The rise in Malaŵi's international debts in the late 1970s eventually proved too much to service and led to three international loan reschedulings in 1983 and 1984, amounting to $113 million. Nevertheless, the average interest rate on these debts remains very low (negative in real terms).

FOREIGN ASSISTANCE. Although the political economy of "foreign aid-mongering" has yet to be written, brief inspection of the available data reveals several trends relevant to this discussion.[11] Countries with relatively small populations appear able to obtain relatively more foreign assistance per capita than other nations. Furthermore, aid givers apparently prefer making grants or loans to countries with a record of success that is good enough to convince the donors that their funds might be well spent. Because Malaŵi is small and has a reasonable record of success, we would expect it to have been quite successful in obtaining bilateral foreign assistance. In reality, this does not seem to have happened.

On an average annual basis from 1977 through 1983, Malaŵi was able to obtain about $25 per capita a year in bilateral aid; this includes total net disbursements of international financial flows from all sources. It is little better than the $21 per capita obtained by the thirty-six least developed countries and the $24 per capita obtained by all developing nations.

The United Kingdom has been an important source of development funds for Malaŵi since its independence; recently the United States has provided significant aid as well. Nevertheless, financial flows to Malaŵi from the OECD countries during the 1977 through 1983 period were about $14 per capita, in contrast to $18 for developing countries as a whole. Malaŵi has been able to tap some unusual bilateral aid sources. For instance, South Africa has helped to finance the building of the new capitol and the construction of the second rail link to the Indian Ocean, and Taiwan has aided some agricultural projects.

Malaŵi's relative failure in aid-mongering has had several causes. The wealthy nations giving foreign economic aid have not viewed Malaŵi as having much strategic potential. Furthermore, Malaŵi is little known outside of Africa and, where known, has been viewed as one of the few African nations with extensive diplomatic relations with South Africa and Portugal (when it was still a colonial power). Thus aid givers obtain little domestic cachet by extending aid to Malaŵi. Moreover, Malaŵi has not been able to make much of a splash in the world media. Although it has carried out some interesting experiments in economic development, it has not received the publicity given to Tanzania for its *ujaama* villages or to Grenada for its new international airport.[12]

The international lending agencies are well aware of Malaŵi's existence and have apparently been particularly impressed by the country's progress. Of course, such agencies are not hampered by the domestic political constraints of individual lending governments.

Emigration and Emigrant Remittances

Since the turn of the century many Malaŵians have emigrated to other countries for various periods of time to obtain higher paying jobs and occupational training or education. The short-term impact of such emigration on the balance of payments arises from emigrant remittances. Contrary to some opinions, however, these do not seem very important.

Kydd and Christiansen (1981) estimate that more than 76,000 Malaŵians abroad sent remittances home in 1977.[13] Many Malaŵians emigrated permanently, however, and those taking their families with them would not send home many remittances. Furthermore, many immigrants into Malaŵi were also sending remittances back to their homelands. Net emigrant remittances probably were not very great or were unlikely to have had much impact on the balance of payments; IMF estimates of the balance of payments arrive at the same conclusion.

Some Implications for Economic Growth

On general theoretical grounds, because Malaŵi has a relatively high ratio of exports to GDP, the expectation might be that it could take advantage of the world division of labor to achieve greater static and dynamic efficiency than could a more autarkic nation such as Madagascar. Although greater participation in trade would certainly make a one-shot improvement in static economic efficiency, a higher trade-GDP ratio would not necessarily lead to a higher growth rate unless one of the following three circumstances prevails:

• The nation saves and invests more as a result of greater foreign trade.

• The greater static efficiency brought about by trade leads to more effective investment, helps overcome X-inefficiency, or provides other positive externalities such as a greater stock of technological knowledge or a reduction in "organizational dualism."[14]

• Foreign competition encourages domestic producers continuously to increase their productivity and production.

Although conclusive evidence is lacking on these three factors for Malaŵi, during the last decade or so, nations with export-led growth have generally grown much faster than those with an import-substitution policy. When Malaŵi's entire foreign trade regime (fiscal, monetary, trade, and foreign exchange policies) is considered, the country has had an export orientation, at least until the 1980s. The foreign trade regime appears to have been an important factor in Malaŵi's economic growth in the 1960s and 1970s, and the changes in this set of policies with the subsequent overvaluation of the exchange rate and the system of trade regulations seem an important reason for its slow growth in the 1980s.

These general considerations do not exhaust the nexus between trade and growth. For instance, based on general economic considerations, perhaps a lower degree of export diversification would lead to a lower degree of economic growth, because the economy would be subject to greater variations in export receipts. Although Malaŵi's exports are highly concentrated in four products, some evidence suggests that world market price fluctuations of these exports do not appear especially great.[15]

Some Implications for the Distribution of Income

Trade policy can act to raise prices of tradables relative to nontradables. Under certain conditions this can, in turn, raise property incomes relative to labor incomes, making the distribution of income more unequal.

Because agricultural goods make up the bulk of Malaŵi's exports, trade also influences the relative incomes of the urban and rural sectors. Certainly, some major benefits of maintaining an equilibrium exchange rate have accrued to estate owners who have been able to increase their production marketed abroad. Estate workers benefit only insofar as their wages remain higher than their potential earnings in the smallholding sector. On the basis of the same logic, the estate sector was hurt by the overvalued exchange rate in the 1980s because it received fewer units of domestic currency for its goods.

ADMARC acted as a barrier that prevented smallholders from reaping the benefits of higher world market prices for their products. Major exceptions included those wealthier ("progressive") farmers who could obtain licenses to plant tobacco or who could export outside of ADMARC. The overvalued exchange rate also hurt the smallholders because if ADMARC wished to avoid loosing money on exporting smallholder products, it had to pay the farmers a lower price.

In the urban sector the determination of gainers and losers associated with exchange rate policy is more difficult. The economic burden of the policy of maintaining an equilibrium exchange rate during the 1960s and 1970s was on urban consumers because they had to pay higher prices for imported consumer goods. When the exchange rate was overvalued, however, those groups of urban consumers able to obtain foreign exchange to purchase imports were major gainers. Some urban producers—especially those producing import-competing goods—gained from a realistic exchange rate and lost from an overvalued exchange rate because a low exchange rate made domestic production profitable. Which of these sets of forces were stronger for any subgroup of the urban population depends on that group's particular circumstances. Higher civil servants, however, would appear to be unambiguous gainers from an overvalued exchange rate because their incomes were not greatly affected and because they can generally obtain foreign exchange to purchase imports.

The increase in transportation costs arising from the cutting of rail lines in Mozambique lowered the domestic prices of exporters and raised the domestic prices of importers. Although this would seem to benefit producers of import-competing goods, overvaluation and subsequent exchange rate shortage created considerable surplus manufacturing capacity and nullified the potential gain. Again, the only clear economic winners were those groups who could obtain the rationed foreign exchange.

The export of labor (emigration) might have had some influence on the distribution of income in Malaŵi. On this problem Kydd and Christiansen (1981, p.1) raise some interesting issues:

> We also argue that the rapid decline in the opportunities for migration, which took place in the 1970s, by itself made the distribution of income less equitable. Further, there is evidence that the sharp increase in real wages paid to the greatly reduced number of migrants working as miners [abroad] exacerbated inequality.

I believe Kydd and Christiansen are quite correct in claiming that the emigrant remittances narrowed family income differentials. Household budget data show that female-headed rural families tended to have lower domestic incomes than families with both members working at home; obviously, the remittances they received from their husbands working abroad raised these low incomes. For rural households in 1968–69 we also have data with which to compare measures of family income inequality including and excluding such remittances. All measures show increases in income inequality when such remittances are removed from income.[16] Although such data are not available for urban households, the same pattern probably occurred.

Other aspects of Kydd and Christiansen's claims appear more dubious. Because the wages of migrants are not included in the calculation of the distribution of income, emigration alone should not directly influence any measures of inequality. Assuming with Kydd and Christiansen that most of these emigrating workers were from the rural areas and returned to their homes, it is unclear how income differentials would be widened. Much depends on whether these workers would have numbered among the poorer or richer smallholders if they had not emigrated, and this is unknown.

The empirical investigation presented later (chapter 16) allows us to distinguish how the narrowing of the urban-rural income differentials and the widening of income differentials within the rural sector affected the nationwide income distribution. It cannot, however, separate the rural income effects attributable to trade alone or to other agricultural policies. For this reason the impact of foreign trade on the distribution of income is impossible to determine exactly; we must rest content with the qualitative conclusion that trade has probably acted to narrow urban-rural income differentials, even while its net influence on intrarural differentials is unclear.

Notes

1. Section B of the Appendix addresses the structure of exports and imports and the direction of trade, two important aspects of trade that are not directly relevant to the major themes of this study.

2. To obtain a comparison sample for 1975, I selected nations with a population size ranging from 50 percent less than Malaŵi's to 50 percent more than Madagascar's. I followed a similar rule with regard to per capita GDPs, drawing data from two sources: Summers and Heston (1984) and World Bank (1983). Unfortunately, the GDP estimates in these two sources differ considerably (indeed, the exact meaning of the World Bank estimates is unclear), which left a number of subjective judgments to be made. Of the seventeen nations in the world that fit the population and GDP criteria, sixteen were in Sub-Saharan Africa. These were used for the comparisons, although for particular variables discussed in the text, data were not available for all nations. The sample includes Bénin, Burkina Faso, Burundi, Cameroon, the Central African Republic, Chad, Ghana, Guinea, Mali, Mozambique, Niger, Rwanda, Senegal, Sierra Leone, Somalia, and Zambia.

Trade openness is sometimes described as trade dependency, and a curious literature, in the German language, severely criticizes Malaŵi for such trade dependency (see, for example, Braun and Weiland (1980)). The concepts of openness and dependency are not the converse of each other, and separate study of the problem of dependency is useful (although not for this study). Our understanding of the problem is not aided by Braun and Weiland's hidden assumption that Malaŵi is the only developing country in the world and must be judged, therefore, by the performance of the industrialized nations.

3. A regression for thirty market economies ranging from the United States, the Federal Republic of Germany, and India to Malaŵi and Kenya is:

$$\log \frac{E}{Y} = 5.524 - 0.1982 \log P - 0.03610 \log \frac{Y}{P}$$
$$(0.0692) \qquad (0.10439)$$
$$R^2 = .2380$$

where E/Y is the average ratio of exports of goods and nonfactor services to the factor price GDP in 1974–76; Y/P is per capita GDP in "international dollars" for 1975; P is the population; and R^2 is the coefficient of determination. The E/Y data are calculated from data from World Bank (1983), and the Y/P data come from Summers and Heston (1984) and from Kravis and others (1982). The sample includes only the market economies (and excludes Luxembourg).

A regression for forty-seven developing nations with populations ranging from 1 million to 15 million and with per capita GDPs ranging from $250 to $2,000 is:

$$\log \frac{E}{Y} = 3.682 - 0.2746 \log P + 0.2984 \log \frac{Y}{P}$$
$$(0.1098) \qquad (0.1067)$$
$$R^2 = .2777.$$

The data on E/Y and P come from the same sources as above; the per capita GDP data come from World Bank (1983).

The first regression shows Malaŵi's export ratio to be about 5 percent of the predicted level, while the second shows this ratio about 65 percent higher.

I suspect that the income range is too broad in the first sample and that some nonlinearities are present.

4. From 1954 through 1984, exports appear to have grown at an average annual rate of 5.9 percent, while GDP rose 4.8 percent. The export index for 1955 through 1963 covers only agriculture, however.

5. Although constant price national account data are readily available, comparable current price GDP data by sector are available only for the period from 1973 through 1979 from Malaŵi, NSO (1983b). These series can be extended to cover the period from 1967 through 1983, but their reliability declines; such data come from earlier national account reports of the NSO and from various World Bank reports since 1983.

6. Section B of the Appendix contains a brief discussion of institutional aspects of Malaŵi's exchange rate policies. Pryor (1988b) table G-2 presents a series for the nominal exchange rate. Real effective exchange rates are usually calculated with cost-of-living, retail price, or wholesale price indexes rather than implicit GDP deflators. The retail price indexes of both Malaŵi and Madagascar have some serious problems for this purpose, however. Also, neither nation estimates wholesale price indexes. Thus the only usable price indexes are the implicit GDP deflators. For Malaŵi, my calculations for the real effective exchange rate are quite similar to those presented by May (1985), p. 13.

7. The high world price elasticity of demand for most exports from Malaŵi obviates the need for "elasticity pessimism" deriving from Marshall-Lerner considerations.

8. The theory behind the impact of changing income shares and relative prices is discussed by Lal (1986). Complications arise when the initial price shock occurs for imports or exports alone and when these two sectors have different ratios of property income to labor income. Underlying the argument in the next sentence of the text is the reasonable assumption that production of export goods is more property intensive than is production of nontradables.

9. Household budget surveys, such as that in Malaŵi Government (1983), do not show that the share of possible imported goods is very much greater for the wealthy households who are the recipients of property income than for the average household (the wealthy spend a larger share of their income on services). An input-output study by Gondwe (1977) has the reverse conclusion, but this part of his analysis has a problematic data base; he could well be right, however.

10. The shares in GDP are calculated by converting the dollar debt to kwacha and then using the factor price GDP data as a base. Data on net factor payments as a share of GDP are from Pryor (1988b), tables E-1, E-3, F-3a, F-3b, and G-2.

11. These generalizations, as well as the data presented in the next two paragraphs, are based on an empirical analysis of foreign aid data from OECD (1984), esp. p. 28. Frey and Schneider (1986) present an interesting new approach to foreign aid-mongering, although their ideas do not provide much insight for Malaŵi and Madagascar.

12. A description of the kind of publicity campaign Grenada needed to obtain large amounts of foreign aid is found in Pryor (1986).

13. IMF estimates of net emigrant remittances are presented in its *Balance of Payments Yearbook,* various issues.

14. The argument about organizational dualism is made by Hla Myint, in Meier (1987), pp. 107–51.

15. My discussion on tables 5-2 and 12-2 offers some information on export fluctuations. Gulhati and Atukorala (n.d.) present evidence that import instabilities have actually been somewhat greater in Madagascar than in Malaŵi. The linkage between economic growth and trade concentration seems questionable in the light of the study by MacBean (1966) of a much broader sample of nations, which shows little linkage between economic growth and fluctuation of exports.

16. These inequality statistics were calculated from data presented in Pryor (1988b), table I-1, which shows that such remittances amounted to about 2.7 percent of total smallholder incomes or about 5.4 percent of total cash incomes. In the budget survey for urban households, transfers are not separated into transfers from abroad and domestic transfers, so a similar calculation could not be made; however, emigrant remittances should be a much lower share of total or cash income.

7 Manufacturing and Transportation in Malaŵi

In its manufacturing and transportation sectors, Malaŵi's policies differed considerably from those of Madagascar and achieved much more impressive results. Although the government of Malaŵi has pursued an agriculturally oriented strategy of development, the nonagricultural sectors have grown faster than agriculture. For instance, from 1967 through 1986, the average annual growth of production by the primary sector (agriculture, forestry, and fishing) was 3.0 percent; that of the secondary sector (manufacturing, mining, utilities, and construction) was 4.4 percent; and that of the tertiary sector (transportation, communications, commerce, and services) was 5.0 percent (Pryor 1988b, table E-2).

Manufacturing: Institutions and Policies

The growth of manufacturing in large measure is attributable to Malaŵi's success in maintaining its economic infrastructure—especially transportation—and until 1980, in following an appropriate set of foreign trade policies. Contrary to reports in the popular press and the impression given by the relatively low import tariffs in the 1970s, the growth of manufacturing did not represent a triumph of private enterprise in a laissez faire economy. In fact, the government owned much of the manufacturing sector and carried out a deliberate industrial policy, including an extensive system of price and wage controls.

Institutions

The ownership and operation of the most important industrial enterprises in Malaŵi have been heavily concentrated in parastatals and a few large foreign multinational firms.[1] The public sector has comprised four types of organizations:
 • Public enterprises, including the water boards, the railroad, AD-MARC (Agricultural Development and Marketing Corporation), and

MDC (Malaŵi Development Corporation). Although run on commercial lines, some have been expected to fulfill certain public functions as well (for example, ADMARC's input subsidies to smallholders). The taxes of these public entities have been lower than those of private corporations and are calculated in a different manner.[2]

• Press Holding Corporation, the largest enterprise in the country. This institution must be placed in a special category. The Life President has held almost all its shares "in trust for the people of Malaŵi"; and its classification as a parastatal is controversial, especially because relatively little information is released about its operations. Since the reorganization of the company in 1983, the government has had a share in its profits and its management. Some legal opinion holds that upon the president's eventual death, formal ownership will convey to the government; this eventuality is also controversial and unclear. My rough estimates suggest that Press Holding employed almost 6 percent of the labor force in the modern sector in 1977; much more informal estimates for the early 1980s indicate that such employment had increased to about 10 percent of the modern sector (Pryor 1988b, table K-3).

• Parastatals of the first degree, or those enterprises managed as wholly owned subsidiaries of the public enterprises or Press Holding. These have operated according to the same laws as privately owned firms. In certain cases their undistributed profits have not appeared in the consolidated income and loss statement of the public enterprise, and only their net assets (rather than their gross assets and liabilities) were included in the consolidated balance sheet.

• Parastatals of the second order, or those enterprises in which the majority share is owned either by the public enterprises or by other parastatals (minority shares are privately held, either by Malaŵians or foreigners). These institutions have had a management independent of the public enterprises and have been run as totally separate operations. Their undistributed profits or losses have been excluded from the financial statements of the parastatals, and their gross assets and liabilities usually have not been included in the consolidated balance sheet.

In the public sector as a whole, the five most important commercial enterprises have been: Press Holding, established in 1960; ADMARC (discussed in chapter 5); MDC, founded in 1964; the Import and Export Company of Malaŵi (IMEXCO), established in 1971 and owned jointly by MDC and Press; and the Industrial Development Bank (INDEBANK), established in 1972, of which ADMARC has owned about one-fifth and governmental banks in the United Kingdom, the Federal Republic of Germany, and the Netherlands and the International Finance Corporation (of the World Bank Group) have owned the rest.

Although each of the five leading parastatals started out with a very specific purpose, each rapidly branched out into many different industries during the late 1960s and 1970s. Press Holding grew from printing the party newspaper to running tobacco estates and a variety of commercial and manufacturing ventures. ADMARC moved from crop trading to many different agroindustrial and manufacturing activities. IMEXCO has functioned not only as an export and import company but also has operated a considerable number of the Chipiku wholesale stores (an attempt to replace the Indian traders in the rural areas by Malaŵian nationals), a truck assembly plant, and an electrical contracting service. Only MDC and INDEBANK have stayed close to their original charters, although MDC's mandate is very broad and it has interests in many different industries.

At the end of the 1970s the activities of any of the five large parastatals were difficult to characterize. Herein lay one of the important causes of the severe financial difficulties that several began to experience, namely, that their scarce managerial talents were spread over too many disparate ventures in which they had little expertise.

In the early 1980s the three largest government-owned enterprises, ADMARC, MDC, and Press Holding, were all in serious financial condition. The problems of Press Holding were unusual. It was highly leveraged through loans from the commercial banks (owned by the government) and from other parastatals such as ADMARC. Also, part of its funds were siphoned into a noncommercial account, from which the Life President has financed many activities, including building the Kamuzu Academy (an elite boarding school), various gifts to hospitals and schools in Malaŵi, the support of particular projects of the Malaŵi Congress Party and the Women's League, and a $2 million gift to Wilberforce College in the United States in 1979 (*The Forcean Quarterly Briefs: The Alumni Publication of Wilberforce University*, May 1979).

By 1983, Press Holding was the largest single debtor in the country, with a negative net worth of tens of millions U.S. dollars. Many of its debts were to the two commercial banks in which it held an interest. Under a 1983 restructuring plan worked out as part of the framework of a World Bank structural adjustment loan, the government assumed certain debts of Press and much greater control over the company; the Life President's control over the company was correspondingly diminished (although he will receive an annual fee said to be 1 million MK); several subsidiaries were sold off; some key personnel changes were made; and the organization of the company and many management practices were changed.

MDC and ADMARC were also reorganized and brought on sounder footing in the middle 1980s, although ADMARC's financial problems persisted because of the drain on the company's resources for supplying certain quasi-governmental services. The three companies also began to exchange their shares so that each could consolidate its holdings and regain control over its investments. ADMARC wound up with a major portion of its portfolio in agroindustrial enterprises; Press Holding concentrated its attention on a number of enterprises producing goods using relatively standard technologies; and MDC began to focus its efforts more on entrepreneurial ventures, including the introduction of new technologies into Malaŵi, mineral exploitation, development of sources of alternative energy, and operation of hotels.

Foreign ownership has also been important in the manufacturing sector, but such enterprises have most often been jointly held with the parastatals. In such arrangements the foreign multinationals have supplied management and technical services and some capital, while the parastatals have supplied additional capital plus expertise on Malaŵi. The most notable of these multinational investors have been Carlsberg (beer), Lever Brothers (vegetable oils and chemicals), and Lonrho (a British multinational with interests in sugar refining and other industries, including shared ownership with the Malaŵi government of the textile company, David Whitehead and Sons).

The relative importance of the public sector in Malaŵian manufacturing is difficult to determine. In the modern sector in 1977 about 30 percent of jobs in manufacturing were held in the public enterprises, Press Holding, or parastatals of the first degree; the number of jobs in the parastatals of the second degree is not known.[3] Aside from their role as owners of enterprises, the parastatals have also played important roles in identifying and appraising promising industrial projects. Moreover, they have often influenced project selection by means of loans and technical support. Jerome Wolgin and his associates (1983) spoke with some accuracy when they noted that "the private sector is alive and well in Malaŵi and owned by the government." The prominence of government-owned factories will probably continue in the future, given the belief expressed in *DevPol II* (p. 62) that "the number of Malaŵian entrepreneurs willing and able to undertake industrial ventures of any size has been very limited."

This institutional structure has influenced the manufacturing sector in several ways. Most striking, enterprises in the modern sector have been few and relatively large, a feature linked with the centralizing role played by the parastatals.[4] For instance, in 1975 the modern sector in manufacturing (at that time comprising all enterprises employing twenty or more employees) included 115 enterprises employing 28,004 workers. Of these, the six enterprises with more than 1,000 employees employed 36 percent of the reported labor force and the eight firms with 500 to 999 workers employed an additional 18 percent.

In comparison with economically developed nations in Europe, the share of the labor force employed in such large enterprises is high in Malaŵi. Centralization within the manufacturing sector has had two important impacts. First, the rural area has had few small, labor-intensive factories to provide off-farm employment for smallholders. Second, the parastatals have reinvested their profits rather than distributing them to individual Malaŵians; thus this property income has led to a high rate of investment untied to income inequalities.

These public and parastatal enterprises have operated along commercial lines, with the government expecting them to make a profit (see table 3-2). This commercial orientation has led to careful selection of investment projects, and up to the mid-1980s Malaŵi had not invested in any extremely large white elephants (World Bank, May 1981c, p. 8).[5] Of course, some of the individual projects these parastatals undertook have not been successful, but the failure rate has not been high and the financial difficulties of several of the largest parastatals appear to be short term.

Although this record may not be worthy of excessive praise, in comparison with other African nations, such as Madagascar, it is quite unusual. The reinvestment by the publicly owned enterprises shows in still another way that "capitalist" Malaŵi has achieved a means of expansion of the public sector unrealized in most of the socialist African nations.

Government Policies and Instruments

The direct operational role of Malaŵi's central government in the manufacturing sector has been minimal. The government has chosen instead to exercise its influence through a variety of direct and indirect constraints and incentives.[6] The Ministry of Trade, Industry, and Tourism (MTIT) has been the most important agency involved in these policies because it administers the surveillance of imports and exports (chapter 6), investment licenses, price controls, and, in part, wage and salary controls.

Malaŵi's industrial policy has been complex. For purposes of discussion, its goals can be classified into three groups: encouragement of investment, direction of investment, and acquisition of needed skills.

GENERAL ENCOURAGEMENT OF INVESTMENT. By setting up MDC and INDEBANK, the government tried to provide private entrepreneurs with a source of capital and expertise. It also attempted to encourage manufacturing by indirect incentives, including special depreciation allowances and write-offs before and during start-ups, accelerated depreciation, limited special protective tariffs, certain exemptions on paying tariffs on imported goods used for exports (drawbacks), and certain rebates on tariffs on products used as intermediate goods. In accordance with the guidelines of *DevPol I*, these incentive measures have not included tax holidays.

The accelerated depreciation provision broadly defined costs that might be written off (for example, expenditures incurred before and during start-up). After operations have begun, allowable depreciation rates also have been liberal. Moreover, to encourage more intense use of labor, these rates increase with the number of shifts worked. For a single-shift operation, the fiscal authorities have permitted a 10 percent depreciation rate on buildings and a 20 percent rate on equipment after start-up.

Manufacturers of new products have been able to apply for special tariff protection, although to qualify, firms had to satisfy local demand for the product, to meet certain quality requirements, and to price their products within a particular range of the c.i.f. cost of imports. The government has been cautious in granting special import protection, however, and has seemed fully aware of the dangers of local monopolies in the domestic market. Moreover, most of the special protective tariffs have generally been limited to five years; that is, infant industries are expected to grow up and become competitive adults.

One disincentive for manufacturing investment has been the expropriation policy. The constitutional protection of property is overridden by the legal right of the Life President to expropriate property without payment if, in his view, the owners have used such property contrary to the interests of the state. As noted in chapter 3, manufacturers in Malaŵi have mentioned this disincentive effect to me in connection with some projected bilateral and multilateral deals, but beyond this anecdotal evidence its real impact is uncertain.

DIRECTION OF INVESTMENT. The government of Malaŵi has tried to control the establishment of new enterprises in order to prevent (a) the construction of industrial establishments considerably below optimum size, (b) production of goods with low local value added and high import content, and (c) concentration of industry in any particular region. Although the relatively low import tariffs may have furthered these goals, the major instrument for these purposes has been an annual licensing system. All firms with ten or more workers or employees or with machinery having a 25-horsepower or higher rating must annually renew their licenses. Renewal has been automatic for firms continuing or expanding their present lines of business—applicable to most manufacturing investment—a policy that *DevPol II* said would be continued. The procedure may have discouraged some new ventures; only fifteen to twenty new licenses have been issued each year (World Bank, May 1981c, pp. 238–40).[7]

In the late 1970s MTIT usually took about four to six weeks to process new license applications and rejected less than 10 percent of applicants. Applications apparently were discussed informally before being formally submitted. The ministry claims to assess projects according to financial viability, competence of management, the importance of Malaŵian raw materials used in production, and the strategic importance of the project (World Bank May 1981c, pp. 35–36). It can cancel existing licenses if the holders violate laws, fail to produce in a reasonable time as promised, or attempt to sell or transfer the license. In nine special cases before the mid-1970s, the ministry granted licenses allowing the holder an exclusive right to produce a certain product for a specified time up to five years; since then, it has discontinued this practice.

OBTAINING NEEDED SKILLS. Malaŵi has emphasized secondary and technical education, rather than primary education, to widen its skills bottleneck (chapters 3 and 8). Furthermore, the nation has not hesitated to employ foreigners. In the late 1970s expatriates held about half of the top-level jobs in the private sector, especially in manufacturing (see also chapter 8, footnote 14). For instance, in 1985, they held the directorships of both Press and MDC, as well as other parastatals such as the airline. This reliance on expatriates to manage manufacturing enterprises has probably aided economic development in the short run. Although the use of foreigners to fill leading positions in the economy has diminished during the last two decades, Malaŵi's dependency on them will undoubtedly continue for some time. Their presence is also a sign of Malaŵi's inability to educate a group of Malaŵian entrepreneurs and managers at a sufficient rate to fill the leading positions.

The lack of detailed information on how these industrial policies have operated makes full assessment difficult. Certainly the general encouragement of investment in manufacturing has not been successful, judging from the decline of such investment after 1975 and the general stagnation of manufacturing production after 1980. The extent to which the licensing system has encouraged or constrained investment is unclear. The government's ability to maintain an appropriate exchange rate (at least up to 1980) so as to avoid discouraging exports has probably been a much more important influence on manufacturing than have these regulations. The skills bottleneck has also proved an intractable policy problem.

In sum, the various industrial policies discussed so far probably have not had a markedly positive impact. More importantly, however, most have not discouraged initiatives within the manufacturing sector or biased investment in particular directions. The administrative framework of the governmental bureaus dealing with industry appears orderly and stable, and the government does not appear to have taken measures far beyond its competence to administer in reasonable fashion.

Special Aid to Small Enterprises

Malaŵi should find small enterprises attractive. They are highly labor intensive; many can be located in rural areas to serve as a source of additional income for poor smallholders; they are usually based on local raw materials; and they can provide a useful training experience for budding entrepreneurs and managers. In 1985 Malaŵi's small and medium-size enterprises employed almost 30 percent of all manufacturing workers (excluding workers in the informal sector).[8]

In the 1970s the government took some steps to encourage these enterprises; for example, in 1975 it founded the Rural Trade Schools. In the 1980s it stepped up efforts to provide technical aid and finance; for instance, in 1981 INDEBANK founded the Special Development Fund (INDEFUND) for assisting small businesses. In 1983 the European Economic Community also sponsored the founding of the Small Enterprise Development Organization of Malaŵi (SEDOM), which was designed to provide financial and technical help to small businesses and craftspeople in the urban areas. Other relatively recent institutions founded to aid small businesses include the Malaŵi Export Promotion Council; the Vocational Training Institute; the Development of Malaŵian Trader Trust (DEMATT), which trains retailers; the Malaŵi Entrepreneurial Development Institute (MEDI), which provides training for small businessmen and craftsmen; and the Malaŵi Union of Savings and Credit Cooperatives (MUSCCO).

Evaluation of the work of these institutions raises problems. Certainly various indexes of their work appear impressive. For instance, after three years of operation SEDOM had made more than 1,100 loans, given business and technical training to those receiving such loans, and claimed to have generated 6,500 jobs. Its projects covered a wide range of activities such as ox cart repair, insecticide preparation, and sheet metal work. Repayment rates on SEDOM loans also appeared to be satisfactory.[9] The various agencies aiding small business have operated primarily in the Southern Region and have been relatively limited in scope; *DevPol II* promised that both of these shortcomings would be resolved.

Assessing the overall impact of these programs raises some difficulties. Scattered data on small and medium-size business are outdated, but they suggest that these firms are accounting for a rising share in total manufacturing employment, which implies some success in encouraging these enterprises.[10] The payoff of the most recent programs to encourage small manufacturing and craft operations is quite uncertain, for much depends upon the ability of the program administrators to identify or develop proper candidates for this assistance.

Two additional factors complicate any kind of overall assessment of these small business programs. First, after the government took over the two commercial banks during the 1970s, the investment they financed shifted from small urban businesses to estates and various parastatals. Thus the recently created institutions listed above serve a function previously performed, in part, by the banks. Second, the expulsion of Indian merchants from the rural communities and the confinement of their business activities to the urban areas did not appear to result in a significant upsurge of private African activity in rural trade (Johnathan Kydd, in Fyfe and others 1985, pp. 293–380). Instead, the parastatals took over much of this trade. The remainder seems to have been abandoned; in the Malaŵi countryside, one often sees former Indian retail establishments showing no signs of current use.

Price and Wage Controls

Neither the price nor the wage controls have fulfilled their original purposes. They have not, however, had a greatly adverse effect on the economy.

Price Controls

The Malaŵi government has used several arguments of questionable validity to justify the imposition and maintenance of price controls. These include prevention of inflation and overvaluation of the currency; protection of the real incomes of the poorest segment of the population; provision of a climate of economic stability; and prevention of high profits accruing to import-competing enterprises, especially those that are foreign owned.

The price control system has had two distinct phases. ADMARC and its predecessors have administered a monopsonistic pricing system for certain agricultural products (chapter 5). Also, since the late 1960s MTIT has administered a system of price controls for manufactured products, consulting with the Economic Planning Division (of the president's office) and the Ministry of Finance on the national impact of particular measures or on technical issues such as cost calculations.

Formal laws and regulation have fixed maximum ceiling prices on certain mass-produced, fairly homogeneous commodities, such as cement, fertilizer, maize meal, petroleum products, sugar, and vegetable oils, and both maximum selling prices at the retail level and controls at the wholesale level on certain consumer goods that allegedly compose an important part of low-income budgets. During the late 1970s price control legislation covered only beer, fuel, matches, hoes, infant foods, meat, medicines, milk, and sugar. The MTIT, however, also set up price controls by decree for a wide variety of other goods. This system began innocently by requiring notification of planned price increases for governmental statistical purposes; during the 1970s the ministry began to "comment" on these prices. Soon, medium-size and large firms hesitated to raise prices on goods, even though they were not under price controls, without receiving a notice of "no objection" from MTIT. Eventually the ministry developed a system of formal price controls.

For both industrial and consumer goods, the government set maximum selling prices on a cost-plus basis. For locally produced goods, the basis was the direct manufacturing cost with a variable markup, which was higher for new products or for those with special selling risks. For import-competing goods, the basis was the c.i.f. cost plus a fixed markup.

Because Malaŵi has generally had only one or a few domestic producers for any particular good, few problems arose because of different fixed prices on the same good produced by different manufacturers, as happened in Madagascar. Nevertheless, administration of the price control system appeared cumbersome in many instances. Although MTIT claimed its cost investigations were relatively objective and efficient, in some cases it took up to a year to make decisions (World Bank, May 1981c, p. 39). Documentation of the cost calculations, investigation of the company's efficiency by using various technical and financial coefficients, and examination of the company's profit picture all influenced the granting of price increases, and these procedures are time consuming.

As a condition of receiving World Bank structural adjustment loans in the early 1980s, Malaŵi dismantled its price control system for manufactured goods over the course of several years. The law of December 16, 1985, left formal price controls only on meats, sugar, fuel, fertilizer, and motor vehicle spare parts. Scattered information indicates that some informal price consultation between firms and MTIT officials still continues.

The data in the top part of table 7-1 provide some idea of the coverage of the price controls. These have an upward bias because of the broad specification of the goods in the lists used for the estimates. Except for the highest income groups, about half of the purchased goods—mainly food and clothing—came under the controls. The percentage of consumption goods on the market (in contrast to home-produced goods) rises as income increases, and if we recalculate the percentage of price-controlled goods as a percentage of total income, the controls appeared most important for the middle-income rather than the poorest or richest families.

The degree to which these price controls actually influenced prices is also of interest, and the data in the bottom part of table 7-1 give some indication of this. The first column presents the retail price index of all goods and services; the last column, the price index of goods with

Table 7-1. Data on Price Controls, Malaŵi, 1980 and 1986

Price-controlled goods and services as a percentage of family expenditures

Total annual family expenditures	By formal law only, c. 1980	All controlled prices c. 1980	All controlled prices 1986
Less than 240 MK	1.7	49	9
240–479 MK	3.9	52	9
480–839 MK	4.6	49	9
840–1,199 MK	6.5	50	10
1,200–1,679 MK	8.0	46	9
1,680–2,399 MK	6.6	49	10
2,400–4,799 MK	6.0	39	8
More than 4,799 MK	4.7	25	6
Average	5.2	34	7

Retail price indexes (Blantyre low-income weights)[a]

Year	Total	By formal law only, c. 1980	All controlled prices c. 1980	All controlled prices 1986
1979	100.0	100.0	100.0	100.0
1980	118.3	113.2	127.9	117.1
1981	132.3	129.0	164.3	131.0
1982	145.3	123.6	153.9	127.1
1983	165.0	136.2	189.5	135.2
1984	198.0	173.9	221.2	173.2
1985	218.8	197.2	247.0	205.5
1986	249.5	220.5	271.4	214.9

Note: Because some goods under price control are specified very broadly, these data are rather uncertain and may have an upward bias. Some of the categories of price controls have been specified by law; others have been specified by decrees of the Ministry of Industry, Trade, and Tourism.

a. The price indexes cover twenty-five goods whose prices were controlled in 1980.

Source: The information about goods under price control regulations comes from information supplied to the World Bank by the Malaŵi government and from *The Malaŵi Government Gazette*, 1437, vol, 22, no. 69, December 16, 1985. The family budget data refer to Blantyre residents in 1979–80 and come from Malaŵi Government (1983). The underlying price series and weights come from the National Statistical Office.

controlled prices throughout the entire period. Although differences appear in these two indexes, especially in 1982 and 1983, by the end of the period they were relatively similar. In other words, the behavior of controlled prices paralleled closely the behavior of the prices of all goods and services covered by the retail price index. The middle two columns present price indexes of goods and services that were controlled in 1980 (by formal law and by both law and governmental decree). Price controls on a majority of these goods had been lifted by the end of the period, and the price index (of all controlled prices) had risen 13 percent above the retail price index as a whole.

This exercise suggests three tentative conclusions. First, price controls led to somewhat lower prices of the goods in question than would have resulted in a totally free market. Second, after the initial dampening of price increases, the controlled prices rose at the same rate as the prices of noncontrolled goods. Third, with the lifting of price controls, prices rose faster than the general index; we may conjecture that once the decompression effect has been completed, these prices will follow the trajectory of the general price index.

In 1987, after the price regulations had been scrapped, junior civil servants in Malaŵi argued to me that any devaluation would increase the profits of the multinational monopolies in that country. Because these companies have usually participated in joint ventures with the government, and shared in the profits, this was a curious complaint. Their hidden assumption that these multinationals were not maximizing their profits after price controls were lifted also seems strange.

The degree to which Malaŵi's price controls have distorted incentives in manufacturing is difficult to judge. Several Malaŵi manufacturers have told me that controls adversely influenced investment, but the extent of such disincentives cannot be determined. The degree to which controls have prevented import-competing firms from gaining windfall profits is also unclear. Manufacturing firms' profit rates after taxes were lower than in the rest of the economy, at least from 1973 through 1979, but the economic desirability of this situation is questionable.

Wage Controls

Malaŵi's labor unions have been organized along industrial rather than craft lines; furthermore, they have been weak and have exercised little influence on wages. Their political role has been small. They did not play a particularly important role in the drive for independence (chapter 2), and the government removed a number of their experienced leaders in the mid- and late 1960s. The unions' lack of militancy and economic influence has resulted from the availability of a ready pool of workers from the countryside to occupy unskilled jobs and from the low economic rents in industry for owners and workers to share (as in the case of the copper mines in Zambia). The unions do not appear to have played a leading role in wage negotiations and according to some observers, the government has relied upon the employers' associations to make the case for wage increases before the government's wage control committee.

The Malaŵi government has viewed wage controls as a second line of defense against a potential wage-price spiral. The system began relatively late in the colonial era, during the early 1960s, with the introduction of Wage Councils in various industries. These had certain powers to recommend wage levels and increases, but the colonial government became disenchanted with the idea in 1963, when the wage council for the tea industry recommended a substantial wage increase for the tea estate workers. The government of independent Malaŵi (1964) was also unhappy with this particular proposal, and in 1965 it considerably reduced the powers of the Wage Councils.

More important institutional changes occurred in 1969, when the government introduced its "National Wages and Salaries Policy." This policy document outlined two aims: to contain wages, especially of the unskilled and semiskilled workers, in order to encourage the establishment of labor-absorbing firms and agricultural estates; and to restrain domestic inflation in order to maintain Malaŵi's competitiveness in international markets.[11] The government's own wage practices were to set an example. Furthermore, the government would not grant general public-sector wage and salary increases but rather would adjust wages only to attract scarce skills. It has generally followed this policy. Average government wages and salaries appear to have remained roughly the same percentage of total average wages and salaries from 1968 to the present (chapter 16). This also means that average real government wages and salaries have declined. Moreover, in most industries, average wages in the government sector have been considerably lower than in the private sector (Pryor 1988b, table H-3). *DevPol II* announced the government's intentions of continuing these policies.

The minimum wages were to be kept low in order to encourage employers to adopt labor-intensive techniques. A tripartite organization of representatives of employers, labor, and three independent members appointed by the government (one of whom chairs the board) proposes changes in minimum wage levels to the National Wages Commission. The Minister of Labor chairs this commission, which has included the representatives from other government agencies, such as the treasury, as well as representatives of employers and employees. Real minimum wages fell slowly during the 1970s and in 1983 were roughly 61 percent of their 1969 level (Pryor 1988b, table 4-4). Although the minimum wages have placed a floor on wages, they seem to have placed few restrictions on employers and most likely have encouraged them to adopt labor-intensive technologies.

Private employers have been restrained from raising the general level of wages. If such increases amounted to more than 5 percent a year, the employers had to apply to the Wages and Salary Restraint Committee for approval. Chaired by the Secretary to the President and

Cabinet, this governmental committee has included representatives from the ministries of labor, trade, industry and tourism, and treasury, as well as the Office of Planning and Development. The employer has had to demonstrate that the wage increase would be matched by increases in productivity so that a subsequent price increase would not occur. The committee has also examined whether the requested wage increase would result in the substitution of capital for labor, whether it was really needed to attract scarce skills, and whether it was in line with other wages in the economy. This system of controls broke down during the inflation of the mid- and late 1980s.

Under wage controls nominal wage increases have been moderate and the average real wage has fallen (chapter 16). Given labor market conditions in Malaŵi and the weakness of its unions, this would probably have occurred without the wage-setting mechanism. The government has admitted that the wage control procedure has sometimes been destabilizing (Malaŵi Government, Minister of Finance and Economic Planning Division 1983). For instance, in the late 1970s real wages fell to such an extent that the Wage and Salary Restraint Committee granted a substantial wage increase for a large share of the labor force at one particular time, which caused some difficult adjustment problems in trade and other sectors.

The Growth of Manufacturing Production

The manufacturing sector in Malaŵi started with a number of handicaps: a small domestic market; a shortage of skilled workers, technicians, and managers; and uncertain transportation links that have required manufacturers to maintain large stocks of inputs to serve as buffers against shipping delays. The average inventories in manufacturing were twelve-week supplies—the range was from four weeks to sixteen weeks.[12] As a landlocked country, Malaŵi has particularly high transportation costs; moreover, for political reasons Malaŵi has sometimes lacked access to markets for manufactured goods in neighboring countries. On the positive side, Malaŵi producers have enjoyed a natural tariff caused by the high transportation costs of imports competing with domestic goods.

Manufacturing production in Malaŵi has increased dramatically, as shown in table 7-2. From 1970 through 1986 the production (output) index increased at an average annual rate of 6.0 percent, while value added in manufacturing rose at an average annual rate of 4.1 percent. The two indexes yield rather different results for several reasons, including different deflation methods, different treatments of inputs in the production process, different weights, and somewhat different coverage. Detailed information is not available to weigh the relative importance of each factor.

Table 7-2. Indexes of Manufacturing Production, Malaŵi, 1967 to 1986

(1970 = 100)

					\multicolumn{5}{c}{Industries producing mainly for domestic market}
		Total manufac- turing produc- tion index				\multicolumn{4}{c}{Consumption goods}
Year	Total value added in manufac- turing		Export industries	Total	Inter- mediate goods	Total	Food, beverages, tobacco	Footwear, clothing, textiles	Other goods
Weights	—	—	20	80	18	62	33	14	15
1967	88.3	n.a.	n.a.	n.a.	n.a.	n.a.	n.a.	n.a.	n.a.
1968	90.2	n.a.	n.a.	n.a.	n.a.	n.a.	n.a.	n.a.	n.a.
1969	93.1	n.a.	n.a.	n.a.	n.a.	n.a.	n.a.	n.a.	n.a.
1970	100.0	100.0	100.0	100.0	100.0	100.0	100.0	100.0	100.0
1971	100.4	110.6	108.7	111.0	103.1	113.2	112.3	118.1	110.8
1972	117.8	122.0	125.4	121.3	122.9	120.9	127.6	118.8	108.0
1973	119.3	147.4	137.7	149.9	147.6	150.4	169.4	115.2	142.4
1974	133.1	156.0	131.6	162.1	129.0	171.7	192.1	120.1	175.1
1975	156.3	180.0	154.0	186.5	157.6	194.8	225.7	130.2	187.3
1976	150.7	178.3	172.3	179.8	128.6	194.6	238.6	109.9	176.8
1977	155.1	199.1	207.3	197.1	142.9	212.8	259.8	126.2	190.2
1978	163.4	219.9	217.3	220.6	166.8	236.2	274.4	148.3	234.3
1979	170.5	220.7	220.2	220.8	172.4	234.7	273.9	169.2	205.2
1980	169.4	223.9	201.6	229.5	150.4	252.5	292.9	149.4	259.7
1981	176.0	246.9	180.6	263.5	124.3	303.9	374.5	170.6	273.0
1982	173.2	232.3	199.8	240.7	99.9	281.7	370.1	181.4	180.8
1983	188.0	268.6	194.3	288.2	110.8	339.7	428.4	187.6	286.7
1984	192.3	262.1	234.7	269.0	109.2	315.3	404.0	175.3	251.0
1985	191.2	264.0	242.3	269.4	107.0	316.5	408.3	182.6	239.6
1986[a]	189.9	268.3	204.1	284.4	105.3	336.4	436.8	171.5	269.4

— = Not applicable.
n.a. = Not available.
Note: The exact components of the various industrial subindexes are not specified in any NSO publication I have seen.
a. Preliminary data.
Source: The value-added index comes from Pryor (1988b), table E-2; the manufacturing index is from Malaŵi, NSO, *Malaŵi: Monthly Statistical Bulletin*, various issues.

The balance *DevPol I* foresaw between manufacturing production as a substitution for imports and as a component of exports appears to have been maintained—both have grown at roughly the same rate. The value of export manufactures amounted to roughly one-fourth that of manufacturing for domestic consumption. Nevertheless, its growth indicates that the efforts Malaŵian policymakers made to blunt inflation and maintain a competitive currency during the 1970s had a positive impact on domestic manufacturing for export. The differential growth of the four series for goods for the domestic market gives some indication of the pattern of import-substituting investment; the different classification of the production and trade data, however, impedes the exploration of import substitution in any depth. Although *DevPol II* claimed (p. 62), without presenting evidence, that most viable import-substitution possibilities have been used up, examination of Malaŵi's imports suggests that this judgment may be premature; for instance, in the mid-1980s the country still imported some vegetable oils for making soap.

Malaŵi's manufacturing growth has been relatively labor intensive.[13] Reliable constant price data on the capital stock are only available for 1973 through 1979 and show a constant capital-labor ratio. For a much longer period, employment in manufacturing has grown at roughly the same rate as output. This suggests—but does not establish—that the aggregate capital-labor ratio has remained roughly constant for some time and that the overall growth can be characterized as extensive. The evidence is mixed on whether production increases have been highest in the most labor-intensive branches of industry, and until more disaggregated data are available, the question cannot be answered definitively.

Although growth has been somewhat uneven from year to year, absolute declines have occurred in only a few years. Specification of those years is difficult because in several cases the value-added and the production indexes yield different results. Manufacturing growth slowed markedly in the mid-1980s for several underlying reasons. Investment in manufacturing has fallen considerably since the mid-1970s; since the early 1980s the exchange rate has been overvalued, which has increased the difficulty of exporting, competing with imports, and obtaining necessary inputs for production; and transportation costs to the Indian Ocean have increased, which may have encouraged import-competing industries but discouraged manufacturing for export.

Given the factor proportions in the country, a pattern of extensive growth is desirable. It economizes on the scarce factor of production (capital) and uses the abundant factor (labor) to the fullest. Moreover, this pattern leads to a more equal distribution of income by narrowing income differentials between urban and rural areas. More specifically, the willingness of manufacturers to draw their labor from the vast pool of unskilled agricultural workers inhibits the growth of a labor elite that obtains high wages for itself and forces the manufacturer to adjust for these higher labor costs by substituting capital for workers.

This rather rosy picture of manufacturing growth does not seem sustainable in the long run unless some important policy changes are made. This can be most easily seen by examining some financial data for the sector as a whole.[14] From 1973 through 1979 manufacturing accounted for 17 percent of total employment in the modern sector and about 17.5 percent of net profits. Profits plus surtaxes and excises in the economy amounted to 36 percent of the book value of fixed assets, slightly more than for the modern sector as a whole. This sector was more heavily taxed, however, so that net aftertax profits were 24 percent of the value of fixed assets, in contrast to 30 percent for the economy as a whole. In real terms, investments in manufacturing reached a plateau in 1975 and declined quite rapidly thereafter, falling 72 percent by 1979 and even more in the early 1980s. Clearly the government needed to reexamine the profit incentives in manufacturing carefully, but appropriate measures were delayed for the good part of a decade until *DevPol II* announced a tax simplification and reduction of marginal rates to be carried out in the late 1980s. Given the statement that manufacturers will be expected to bear an "equitable share of taxation, " a significant tax decrease for the manufacturing sector does not appear likely.

Transportation

In its massive investment programs on transportation facilities, the Malaŵi government had three goals: to open up new areas of the country for agricultural production, to narrow the economic differences between the three regions, and to strengthen transportation links with the outside world. Such measures, of course, reduce transactions costs and help to integrate markets.

Domestic and International Transportation

At the time of Malaŵi's independence in 1964, both internal and external transportation links were limited. In a country 825 kilometers (515 miles) long, paved roads extended about 431 kilometers (267 miles) and reached no farther north than Zomba, the old capital. The country also had about 465 kilometers of rail lines, which extended from Salima (a town near the southern part of Lake Malaŵi) in a southerly direction through Blantyre and Nsanje (formerly Port Herald) and thence out of the country across the Zambezi River (about 40 kilometers south of Malaŵi) and another 325 kilometers south to the Mozambique port of Beira (see map, frontispiece).[15]

In the twenty-one years following independence, the kilometers of paved roads quintupled, increasing at an average annual rate of 7.9 percent (*DevPol II*, p. 92). The government placed primary emphasis on upgrading the current road system rather than increasing its extent. The Northern Region is still inadequately served with all-weather roads. The problems with rail connections to the Indian Ocean in the early 1980s led to the construction in the mid-1980s of the Northern Corridor, a gravel road connecting Karonga with Ibanda, Tanzania, which provided access to the Tanzania-Zambia railway line. *DevPol II* proposed to upgrade this route, and maintenance and improvement of the domestic road network has continued to be a significant part of the government's economic overhead expenditures.

The transportation linkages of Malaŵi with the rest of the world have been an important focus of political activity from the early years of Nyasaland until the present.[16] Malaŵi was dependent upon a single port, Beira in Mozambique, which in some years had high surcharges and was subject to delays of up to 200 days; this port, moreover, has limited expansion potential because it lies on a sandy part of the coast. In the early 1960s, as part of his Gwelo No. 2 Plan, Dr. Banda proposed a second rail line to the Indian Ocean.

The crucial choice of route lay between running a line in an easterly direction and connecting with a Mozambique line, which in turn led to Nacala, a deep-water port capable of expansion, and running a line north along the lake to connect with the proposed Tan-Zam railroad to Dar-es-Salaam. The much higher cost of the latter option, combined with political tensions with Tanzania during the first years of independence, led to the choice of the first option. After Great Britain refused to fund the project in 1965, the South African government stepped in to help finance the construction of the 90 kilometers in Malaŵi and some of the additional 65 kilometers of track in Mozambique.

This was not the only step taken to ensure greater transportation security. The Malaŵi government has since built a 130-kilometer extension of the railway from Salima westward through Lilongwe to the Zambian border to connect with a spur that the Zambian government planned but did not complete. In the late 1970s insurgents in Mozambique (RENAMO) began to disrupt both railway links connecting Malaŵi to the Indian Ocean; maintenance on these lines also deteriorated. In 1983 and 1984 RENAMO cut the train lines in Mozambique almost completely, and from that time to the late 1980s these lines carried relatively little traffic. Malaŵi was forced increasingly to use the port of Durban in South Africa for its foreign trade, and in 1985 and 1986 this port handled 96 percent of Malaŵi's foreign trade tonnage. The average rail journey through Mozambique had been roughly 700 kilometers; in the mid-1980s traffic had to move an average of 3,150 kilometers, largely by road.

Transportation costs in Malaŵi's foreign trade have always been high. From 1964 through 1976 imports measured c.i.f. have averaged about 15 percent more than imports measured f.o.b. (in most countries this ratio is less than 10 percent). Furthermore, these transportation costs have been much higher for particular bulk items, amounting, for instance, to one-third of the f.o.b. costs for imported photocopy paper from Rotterdam, one-half of f.o.b. costs for steel from Durban, three-fourths of f.o.b. costs for a 1-ton Datsun pickup truck from Japan, and almost 100 percent of the costs for superphosphate fertilizer from Durban. From 1976 through 1980 c.i.f. costs of imports averaged 31 percent higher than f.o.b. costs, and from 1981 through 1984, when the Mozambique railway lines were almost completely out of commission, the c.i.f. costs were 56 percent higher.[17] The Northern Corridor route will probably reduce these transportation costs only a modest amount. To reduce costs even more, *DevPol II* announced a priority project to develop nationally owned trucking firms capable of long-distance freight hauling to carry Malaŵi's foreign trade.

In sum, because of international forces totally beyond its control, costs of transportation between Malaŵi and the outside world have skyrocketed. This has acted both to lower real incomes and to put enormous strain on the balance of payments (chapter 6).

Regional Policy

The Malaŵi government took its most important policy step in the late 1960s by moving the capital from Zomba in the Southern Region to Lilongwe in the Central Region.[18] Because the Southern Region was economically the most developed and had the highest population density, this move could provide a growth point in another area. The Blantyre-Limbe area in the Southern Region generated two-thirds of Malaŵi's monetary GDP, and emigration from the "dead north" to the south brought about continually greater regional differences in population density. Even colonial officials were worried about the problem.

Another argument for the move was that the existing governmental buildings in Zomba were highly inadequate and would have to be rebuilt (five of the fourteen ministries were also located in Blantyre). Thus the marginal expenses of the move would not be so great as they would be if usable buildings had to be abandoned.

Political considerations may also have played an important part in the decision. For instance, some believed that moving the capital would bring the government closer to the citizens in the Northern and Central Regions and would help consolidate the new nation. Other commentators pointed out that the new capital would also be in the major area occupied by the Chewa, the ethnic group of President Banda.

Moving the capital to Lilongwe occasioned a major thrust of road improvement in the Central Region in order to link the new capital with the other regions along all-weather roads. Certainly this change also had an important impact on the distribution of the urban population. Between 1966 and 1977 Blantyre's population share fell from

54 percent to 47 percent (Pryor 1988b, table B-4).[19] Moving the capital slowed internal immigration into the Southern Region and quite likely encouraged certain investments in the Central and Northern Regions, which might not have occurred otherwise. Although solid evidence on this conjecture is not available, certainly these measures were an important part of the policy bundle that led to the marked increase in growth of the Central Region. The extent to which moving the capital affected economic growth depends upon the possible alternative uses of funds, a tricky problem to consider.

The construction of the new capital was expected to cost 80 to 90 million MK. Although the actual costs are not known, they were probably considerably higher. In addition, the construction of a new international airport in Lilongwe, the only airport able to accommodate some of the new jumbo jets, was budgeted at another 100 million MK. In the two decades following independence gross fixed investment for the entire nation averaged about 125 million kwacha a year. If we make the very rough assumption that half of the total planned costs represented the marginal costs of the project, we are considering an investment amounting to about three-quarters of the country's total investment in an average year.

In the mid-1980s the Malaŵi government began considering some other major transportation investments to open up other parts of the country, particularly in the north. These included an expensive new international airport in Mzuzu. These projects appear to have been victims of the nation's deepening financial crisis and have not been carried forward.

Summary and Conclusions

Although Malaŵi has followed a growth strategy with primary emphasis on agriculture, it also experienced an impressive growth of manufacturing production until the early 1980s. Many of the basic causes of this growth and its slowdown are the same as those affecting similar developments in the agricultural sector, especially the foreign trade policies.

The government owned a considerable share of the manufacturing sector and also carried out an extensive industrial policy with both direct and indirect policy tools. Potentially the most influential policies were price and wage controls. Because the price controls were administered with considerable attention to market forces, they probably did little to change growth, guide the allocation of resources, or influence the distribution of income. The wage controls, in contrast, may have constrained wage increases, although the weakness of labor unions was also an important factor. Some evidence suggests that the impact of the indirect measures to encourage or guide investment in manufacturing also was not very great. Policies directed toward transportation within the country appear to have aided manufacturing production, although the evidence is uncertain. Nevertheless, the fact that manufacturing enterprises had a great deal of independence from the government, that the government's direct interference was relatively light, and that profitability criteria generally guided industry decisions undoubtedly accounts for much of the successful growth of the manufacturing sector.

The rapid growth of manufacturing, especially in labor-intensive industries, provided employment at a higher income than agriculture and reduced the numbers living below the poverty line, even though the usual measures of income inequality showed an increase (chapter 16). Malaŵi's manufacturing growth, intensified by its recent emphasis on small and medium-size enterprises, has followed such a pattern.

Notes

1. For factual information this section draws heavily upon World Bank (May 1981c); Jerome Wolgin and others(1983); Malaŵi, Ministry of Finance and Economic Planning Division (1983); Christiansen and Kydd (1986); and annual reports of some of the parastatals in Malaŵi. Still other information comes from interviews with business leaders in Malaŵi.

2. Taxation of these enterprises is reported in Malaŵi, Minister of Finance, Public Sector Financial Statistics (annual). In the nine fiscal years from 1973–74 through 1980–81, total net taxes amounted only to 13.5 million MK; 13.3 million MK of these were ADMARC tax payments in 1977–78 and 1978–79.

3. More detailed estimates can be found in Pryor 1988b, table K-3. A list of all major firms and their ownership is provided by Dilg (1973).

4. The data on enterprise size come from World Bank (May 1981c), p. 8; data on the size distribution of enterprises in a number of OECD nations come from Pryor (1973), p. 185.

5. Jonathan Kydd, in Fyfe and others (1985), pp. 293–380, has pointed out a number of projects outside the productive sectors that he believes wasteful. These include large-scale presidential houses in Blantyre and Lilongwe (which supplement the presidential mansion in Zomba) and the construction of Kamuzu Academy (which cost about 40 million MK for the education of only 400 secondary school students).

6. This section draws heavily upon World Bank (May 1981c) and a useful booklet by Price Waterhouse and the Malaŵi Development Corporation (1985) containing a summary of regulations and tax legislation pertaining to business.

7. Williams (1978) sees a manifest political purpose behind the licensing scheme, especially because the ministry's decisions are not subject to appeal. Of course, a government can use any licensing scheme to punish its enemies and reward its friends, but I have found no evidence that such political purposes have outweighed the economic purposes of the licensing system.

8. These data come from estimates presented in United States, AID (1986), which provides an excellent review of the small and medium-size enterprise sector. The discussion that follows draws heavily upon this source.

9. Information about SEDOM activities was gathered in interviews with officials of the agency in Blantyre.

10. Robert E. Christiansen, in Fyfe and others (1985), pp. 407–70. The estimates of small-scale manufacturing used in the paragraph come from B. P. Kaluwa, in Fyfe and others (1985), pp. 623–41. Ettema (1984) estimates total small-scale businesses in 1977 at 25,094; this embraces all sectors, not just manufacturing.

11. Government of Malaŵi, "A National Wages and Salary Policy for Malaŵi" (Zomba, September 19, 1969), cited by Sierra (1981), p. 21. The discussion on the wage-setting institutions relies heavily on Sierra's study as well.

12. Such data are reported in Malaŵi, NSO, *Annual Economic Survey*, various years, and are analyzed in World Bank (May 1981c).

13. Data on capital stocks and employment can be obtained from Malaŵi, NSO (1983a). These data do not permit an aggregation according to the same classification as in the table on manufacturing production, and my experiments along these lines were inconclusive. The data do explode one myth about Malaŵi's manufacturing growth. A number of observers have praised the large share of this growth that comes from the food and beverage industries, which process domestically produced goods. The substantiating data for this claim come from the industrialization table of the world development indicators in World Bank, *World Development Report* (annual). The NSO places the share of food and beverage industries at about 30 percent of value added in manufacturing during 1973–79; for inexplicable reasons the World Bank places this share very much higher, thus allowing misleading comparisons with other nations for which the data are accurately reported.

14. The statistics in this paragraph are derived from Malaŵi, NSO (1983a), p. 38; and the *Annual Economic Survey* for 1980–81, p. 27.

15. The underlying data on the road network discussed in these paragraphs come from section C of the Appendix. The data for the colonial period come from Nyasaland Protectorate (1962). Various commentators have quite different estimates of the length of the Malaŵi railway lines; the data mentioned in the text are considerably greater than the lineal distances measured on a map.

16. The early years of the railroad are described by Leroy Vail, in Palmer and Persons (1977), pp. 365–95. The tangled politics of Malaŵi's relations to the construction of the Tan-Zam railway are described by McMaster (1974). Difficulties with the port of Beira are discussed by Munger (1969b).

17. These differences between c.i.f. and f.o.b. data come from Pryor (1988b), table F-2b. The individual examples are drawn from World Bank (May 1981c), p. 42. My quantitative appraisal of the problem differs considerably from that of Malaŵi, Office of the President and Planning, Economic Planning Division, *Economic Report, 1985*, p. 43, which estimates that in 1983 the cost of using alternative transportation routes was 35 million MK. Total imports (f.o.b.) were 233 million MK, and c.i.f. costs normally should have been 35 million MK (that is, 15 percent of the f.o.b. value); however, the total difference between c.i.f.

and f.o.b. values was 131 million MK. I would conclude that the Economic Planning Commission made a mistake; that the balance of payments data (Pryor 1988b, table F-2b) are wrong; or that the cost of using alternative routes was really 96 million MK (that is, about 7.8 percent of the factor price GDP for the year).

18. This discussion draws heavily from Mlia (1975). The colonial worries about high population densities in the Southern Region are discussed by Megan Vaughan, in Fyfe and others (1985), pp. 67–92. This discussion of regional policy is not complete because I was unable to obtain a copy of Malaŵi, Office of the President and Cabinet, Department of Town and Country Planning (1986).

19. The data come from Pryor (1988b), table B-4. Some of this increase, however, must be attributed to changes in the areas included as "urban."

8 The Government Sector in Malaŵi

Malaŵi's government budget has played a key role in the economic growth of the country. The ratio of government expenditures to GDP has been high, even in comparison with much richer countries. This is attributable both to a considerable flow of foreign loans and grants channeled through the government sector for investment purposes and to a remarkable mobilization of domestic resources by means of taxes and other government revenues. The budget appears to have been relatively efficiently administered and has not supported a disproportionately large civil service. Until the 1980s, an imbalance in the budget of the central government was not a source of inflation and also the central bank carried out monetary policy so as to dampen inflation and mobilize domestic savings.

The impact of the budget on income differentials is difficult to determine. Although the level of taxes is high, their incidence has been mildly progressive. An overall evaluation of the incidence of public expenditures is not possible. Some types of expenditures—for instance, for health—appear to be progressive and have greatly benefited the poor. Expenditures for education, however, have not been used for redistributional purposes nor were they especially targeted toward the poor; their incidence is either neutral or regressive, depending on how these concepts are defined. Still other types of expenditures, such as the agricultural expenditures discussed in previous chapters, have had a regressive incidence.

The Size and Operation of the Government Sector

The data show Malaŵi as a country with a large and growing public sector, at least until the early 1980s. In contrast to the industrialized nations, where the mainspring of public expenditure growth has been an increase in social welfare expenditures, Malaŵi's expenditures for these purposes, measured as a percentage of factor price GDP, rose only 1.5 percentage points. In Malaŵi increasing governmental expenditures for economic purposes underlay the growth of the public sector.

Overall Parameters

In 1983 Malaŵi had roughly 1.3 state workers and 0.7 government employees per hundred population (Heller and Tait 1984).[1] In comparison with other nations in Africa, these ratios are relatively low. Time-series data reveal that the share of the labor force working in the state sector rose until the early 1970s and has remained roughly the same ever since; the share of government workers in the modern sector has actually declined. In recent years local governments have employed only about 10 percent of all government workers, so in this respect the governmental sector is quite centralized.

Total expenditures of the central government (including current and capital expenditures, interest, debt repayments, and other types of financial transactions, plus transfers to local governments) ranged in the second half of the 1960s between 25 and 30 percent of GDP before rising to 35 to 40 percent for most years in the early 1980s. This is a remarkably high level for a developing nation. From independence through the 1970s the share of current expenditures (including transfers and interest payments) to GDP fell as government directed a growing share of its budget to investment. This trend was reversed in the 1980s, when economic growth slowed and Malaŵi began to have difficulty servicing its foreign debt. Local governmental expenditures have averaged about 2.5 percent of GDP during the postindependence period, but local taxes covered only about one-fifth of these expenditures.

Gross fixed capital investment financed through the government budget averaged about 9 percent of GDP from independence through 1984. This represented about 45 percent of total gross fixed capital investment during the period.[2] During the 1980s, the share of government investment in total gross fixed capital investment rose, while the proportion of such investment to GDP declined, thus revealing the considerable cutback in government investment and an even greater cutback by the parastatals and the private sector.

Efficiency of the Government Sector

Have Malaŵi's public expenditures been made in an effective or efficient manner? Unfortunately, this question cannot be easily studied by outsiders, and we must rely on pointillistic evidence suggesting a positive answer.

According to B. D. Giles (1979), an expatriate who served as the chief economist for the government in the mid 1970s and who became quite disenchanted with the Life President,

The absence of decisions produces uncertainties, stagnation, or even deterioration. . . . The great merit of Malaŵi as compared, for example, with Lesotho—was that decisions were taken quickly, usually by the President.

Paradoxically, there was probably more de facto coordination of economic policy in Malaŵi, where central planning was derided, than in Zambia, where it was ostensibly an article of faith.

Another indication of administrative efficiency can be found in a World Bank cross-national study of the use of plant and equipment for road maintenance in developing countries (World Bank, *World Development Report 1983*, p. 45). In 1981 only three nations in the sample had capital (plant and equipment) utilization rates of more than 50 percent, and of these, only Malaŵi was able to achieve a level of 75 percent, which is considered a reasonable rate. Still another piece of evidence comes from interviews with various aid donors to Malaŵi (Canada, the European Economic Community, Great Britain, the United States, and the World Bank). Donors were generally pleased with the way the Malaŵi government spent their funds, pointing to good planning and implementation, even though many of the results (for example, the integrated rural development projects) were not particularly successful (Jonathan Kydd, in Fyfe and others 1985, p. 307).

My own impression, gained from talking with those engaged in business in Malaŵi, is that the level of corruption in the Malaŵi government is relatively low but that in the 1980s the level of administrative effectiveness has declined. Such anecdotal and subjective evidence accords with similar impressions gained by other visitors to that nation.

The Life President was eager to maintain the quality of the civil service and has been very cautious about Africanization. "I do not want to dismiss any European just because he has a white skin. . . . Our African Civil Servants . . . must be patient, they must be trained, they must become efficient before they can expect me to promote them into jobs now occupied by Europeans" (Baker 1977). Objections to this policy were an important cause underlying the most severe political crisis of the nation, the "cabinet crisis" of 1964, which occurred several months after the country gained its independence. When Malaŵians did replace the Europeans they apparently received lower salaries (Kydd and Christiansen 1981, p. 30). This technique simultaneously reduced government expenditures and narrowed income differentials.

Although none of this evidence can be considered conclusive, it suggests a certain degree of administrative efficiency in the Malaŵi government. There has been room for improvement, of course, and some of the important conditions of the World Bank's structural adjustment loans during the early 1980s were aimed at implementing

172 *Malaŵi and Madagascar*

a series of administrative changes. These included strengthening the ministries carrying out planning and budgetary functions, establishing a Department of Statutory Bodies to gain greater control over these activities, and increasing the flexibility of the tax system. Some of the proposed administrative reforms—for instance, the establishment of an intragovernmental committee to coordinate investments—were not successfully implemented, so some of the identified administrative weaknesses were not corrected by the late 1980s.

Tax, Expenditure, and General Budgetary Policies

In general, colonial governments tried to maintain a balanced budget to avoid any need to provide fiscal subsidies; they also considered encouragement of exports to be a major goal for governmental expenditures.[3] This generalization appeared true for Malaŵi's colonial period. After independence, however, budgetary policies changed considerably.

Public Expenditures

Table 8-1 presents data on the pattern of public expenditures in Malaŵi.[4] General services (administration, defense, justice, and police) as a share of GDP initially rose after independence, then fell during the early 1970s, and by the early 1980s had risen higher than the initial levels. Almost all of this increase has been in defense expenditures. Until 1973 these amounted to roughly 0.5 percent of GDP; by the early 1980s this share had more than quadrupled, and it continued to rise through the mid 1980s as the actions of the RENAMO insurgents of Mozambique on Malaŵian territory required ever-increasing defense expenditures. The number of army personnel rose from about 1,600 in the early 1970s to about 4,650 in the early 1980s, or about 1 in 1,378 of the population (International Institute of Strategic Studies, various issues). Of course, even the 1980s level is small in comparison with Madagascar and other African countries. Data on police personnel are unavailable.

DevPol I explicitly gave social expenditures (education, health, and community development) a low priority in its growth strategy, and as a result the ratio of these expenditures to GDP rose only slowly until the early 1970s and then fell in the late 1970s. A number of studies showed that Malaŵi was lagging most other African nations with regard to various social indicators, and this criticism apparently received local support. Although Malaŵi began to suffer some severe economic difficulties at the end of the 1970s and in the early 1980s, social expenditures as a share of GDP began to rise again and soon surpassed previous levels. Educational expenditures, which were

Table 8-1. Public Expenditures of the Central Government as a Share of GDP, Malaŵi, 1964 to 1984–85
(percent)

Year[a]	General services[b]	Health, education, welfare[c]	Natural resources	Transportation and communication	Debt charges	Other economic and miscellaneous
1964	5.8	5.5	2.1	2.9	4.8	6.5
1965	6.0	5.4	2.0	3.3	2.7	5.4
1966	6.0	5.8	2.4	4.1	2.1	5.6
1967	5.4	5.5	2.7	2.8	2.0	6.5
1968	5.4	6.5	3.4	4.1	2.1	6.8
1969	5.2	6.4	3.9	4.2	2.3	6.3
Unweighted average	5.6	5.9	2.8	3.6	2.7	6.2
1970–71	4.9	6.6	4.2	8.9	2.9	7.7
1971–72	4.5	5.4	4.2	3.3	2.8	7.8
1972–73	4.2	5.4	3.9	3.1	3.2	7.0
1973–74	4.6	5.6	4.3	3.0	3.1	6.5
1974–75	4.6	5.2	4.3	3.7	3.2	5.4
1975–76	5.4	4.8	4.1	8.3	2.9	5.7
1976–77	5.2	4.4	3.5	5.0	2.7	5.1
1977–78	5.7	4.4	3.7	5.8	2.5	4.9
1978–79	6.8	5.5	3.5	9.1	2.7	6.5
1979–80	7.2	5.7	4.4	6.6	4.7	9.7
Unweighted average	5.3	5.3	4.0	5.7	3.1	6.6
1980–81	6.6	6.2	4.5	8.5	6.3	10.4
1981–82	7.0	6.7	5.0	5.9	9.3	5.7
1982–83	7.4	6.7	5.2	4.3	6.9	6.5
1983–84	7.3	6.9	5.2	3.8	6.3	13.2
1984–85	6.6	6.8	4.0	4.4	10.3	10.8
Unweighted average	7.0	6.7	4.8	5.4	7.8	9.3

Note: Expenditures include current, capital, transfer, and all other expenditures of the central government.
a. The fiscal year begins on April 1; however, the GDP of the calendar year of the April to December period is used as the denominator of the base.
b. Includes general administration, defense, justice, and police.
c. Includes community development.
Source: Pryor (1988b), tables E-1 and K-2a.

about 3.5 percent of GDP in the mid- and late 1960s, followed an undulating pattern but then rose to more than 4 percent by the early 1980s. Health expenditures as a share of GDP rose in an irregular pattern throughout the period, from 1.5 percent of GDP in the 1960s to 2.0 percent in the early 1980s. Community development expenditures as a share of GDP followed a highly irregular pattern around a roughly constant upward trend.

The overall rise in social expenditures as a share of GDP was not the major cause of the increase in the relative size of government expenditures. A different type of social expenditure (financed from various parts of the budget) became increasingly necessary for the Malaŵi government when refugees from Mozambique began to pour into the country.

The most dramatic increase of public expenditure has been for interest and debt repayment, which reached somewhat more than 10 percent of GDP in fiscal year 1984–85. Despite some restructuring and cancellation of debt, the foreign-held debt has been large enough to entail high service charges (chapter 6). Because Malaŵi has had little room for further increases in taxes, these debt-service payments have adversely affected both investment and other governmental programs, which in turn has had an unfavorable impact on growth. According to *DevPol II*, debt-repayment charges are not expected to decline until the 1990s, an optimistic forecast that implies that government debt will not increase in the interim period.

Public Revenues

In the early years of the new nation Dr. Banda repeatedly emphasized the need for bringing government revenues into alignment with expenditures so as to reduce Malaŵi's dependence on British subsidies. Shortly after independence he raised taxes, taking advantage of the postindependence euphoria, his personal prestige, and his political clout. This turned out to be one of his most important and successful economic policy actions. The population accepted this and later tax increases relatively calmly.[5]

The data in table 8-2 show that in the twenty-year period since its independence Malaŵi has made a remarkable domestic fiscal effort, with taxes rising from roughly 7 percent to about 18 percent of its GDP. In comparison with other developing nations, direct taxes have been relatively high, amounting overall to about 42 percent of total taxes, although this share has gradually declined.[6] Indirect taxes have averaged about 52 percent of total taxes and have risen over the period, especially in the 1980s, when tariff revenues assumed a more important role in the tax system. In contrast to most developing nations, Malaŵi has not taxed exports, except briefly in 1986.[7] Of

Table 8-2. Selected Data on Public Revenues, Malaŵi, 1964 to 1984–85

(percent)

Year	Total/GDP	Direct taxes	Indirect taxes	Other taxes	Foreign grants and loans/ GDP[b]	"Covered" expenditures/ GDP	"Uncovered" expenditures/ GDP
		\multicolumn{3}{c}{Taxes[a] — Percentage of total taxes}		\multicolumn{2}{c}{Public expenditures[c]}	
1964	7.3	50.6	37.0	12.4	14.8	26.6	1.1
1965	7.1	43.5	46.7	9.8	13.7	24.6	0.3
1966	9.1	37.1	51.7	11.2	9.7	22.0	4.1
1967	10.0	42.3	50.0	7.7	9.4	23.2	1.9
1968	11.2	46.5	46.3	7.3	9.3	24.9	3.4
1969	11.6	46.0	46.1	7.9	10.8	26.7	3.2
Unweighted average	9.4	44.3	46.3	9.4	11.3	24.7	2.3
1970–71	12.5	40.7	52.5	6.8	16.9	34.6	0.7
1971–72	12.9	37.7	54.1	8.2	8.7	25.6	2.4
1972–73	12.8	40.8	53.4	5.8	7.2	24.9	2.0
1973–74	13.0	41.8	51.8	6.4	7.9	25.9	1.0
1974–75	12.6	39.9	55.3	4.8	6.7	24.3	2.2
1975–76	13.6	45.5	50.2	4.3	9.9	27.8	3.4
1976–77	12.9	47.3	47.2	5.5	7.5	23.1	2.8
1977–78	13.3	47.5	48.5	4.0	9.8	26.3	0.8
1978–79	16.5	46.6	50.4	3.0	13.1	32.5	1.7
1979–80	18.6	40.6	55.9	3.5	11.2	34.3	3.9
Unweighted average	13.9	42.8	51.9	5.2	9.9	27.9	2.1
1980–81	18.5	39.0	58.8	2.3	11.8	33.8	8.6
1981–82	18.0	34.4	62.6	3.0	14.8	36.7	3.0
1982–83	18.3	38.8	59.0	2.2	10.3	31.6	5.5
1983–84	18.6	39.2	57.6	3.1	11.4	33.4	2.0
1984–85	18.7	39.3	56.7	4.1	9.6	32.5	3.8
Unweighted average	18.4	38.1	58.9	2.9	11.6	33.6	4.6

Note: These data refer only to the finances of the central government. Some of these series (other taxes, foreign grants and loans) are defined somewhat differently than the series presented in Pryor (1988b), table K-1a.

a. Direct taxes comprise those on both households and enterprises; indirect taxes comprise import taxes, surtax (sales tax), and excise duties; other taxes comprise a variety of unspecified taxes.

b. Foreign grants and loans include transfers (current and capital) plus borrowing abroad.

c. "Covered" public expenditures include those financed by taxes, other government revenues, and foreign grants and borrowing; "uncovered" government expenditures are those financed by domestic borrowing or drawing down of cash reserves.

Source: Various issues of Malaŵi, Minister of Finance, *Public Sector Financial Statistics*. The GDP series comes from Pryor (1988b), table E-1.

course, ADMARC's pricing policies toward smallholder export crops have acted as a tax, but such funds were not channeled to the central government.

Tax Incidence

A number of aspects of tax incidence can be examined, but for our purposes the progressivity or regressivity is the most important problem.[8] The unexpected conclusion is that Malaŵi's governmental revenues are mildly progressive. The analysis requires a separate examination of direct and indirect taxes.

DIRECT TAXES. According to household expenditure studies in Malaŵi for fiscal year 1968–69, direct taxes averaged about 6 percent of pretax family income for the entire population. The difficulties of collecting direct taxes in a nation with low general literacy levels should be apparent. As a result, direct taxes have been an amalgam of a head tax (used in the rural areas) and an income tax (used in the urban areas).

The data in the top part of table 8-3 show that among smallholders, for 1968–69, the direct tax rates are first higher and then lower as family income increases. The net result was that the aggregate measures of income inequality presented in the lower part of the table for pretax and aftertax incomes in the rural sector appear only very slightly progressive. In contrast, the data show considerable progressivity in the urban areas, especially in the top income brackets, and therefore the overall measures of inequality for both 1968–69 and 1979–80 show a marked reduction in inequality after taxes.

Thus the system of direct taxes should be considered progressive as a whole. This progressivity, however, must be attributed primarily to the urban taxes rather than to overall differences between the urban and rural tax systems, for in comparing urban and rural families with the same total incomes (monetary and nonmonetary), the average tax payments as a percentage of income are roughly similar.

The degree of progressivity of the urban taxes was probably roughly the same between 1968–69 and 1979–80. The Gini and Theil coefficients show about the same degree of decline for both pretax and aftertax incomes; however, the log variance measure shows somewhat greater progressivity in the earlier fiscal year. Although some believed that the tax changes in 1969, which reduced the tax rates in the upper income brackets in order to encourage savings, would result in a regressive tax structure, such fears proved baseless.[9] Since 1979 certain changes in Malaŵi's tax structure allegedly have been regressive, but their real impact is not yet known. The incidence of taxes on businesses is also unknown.

Table 8-3. The Incidence of Direct Personal Taxes, Malaŵi, 1968–69 and 1979–80

Tax rates by income group

Smallholders, 1968–69		Large towns, 1968–69		Large towns, 1979–80	
Average annual income in income class (MK)	Tax/income (percent)	Average annual income in income class (MK)	Tax/income (percent)	Average annual income in income class (MK)	Tax/income (percent)
59.03	1.15	71.9	2.12	189.7	2.47
63.14	1.43	144.4	2.75	354.7	1.93
76.00	2.51	193.0	2.59	644.1	1.94
80.70	3.21	263.2	2.21	1,002.3	1.98
86.38	3.28	342.3	2.25	1,402.3	2.35
93.08	3.22	461.0	2.28	1,987.9	2.12
102.30	3.25	688.9	2.58	3,279.3	2.60
110.13	3.53	1,138.9	3.91	12,823.3	11.25
127.88	2.87	4,689.6	12.27		
166.94	2.91				
391.15	2.46				
Average					
86.42	2.44	907.6	9.21	2196.3	7.41

Aggregated statistics of inequality

	Before taxes			After taxes		
Year and group	Gini coefficient	Log variance	Theil coefficient	Gini coefficient	Log variance	Theil coefficient
1968–69						
Smallholders families	.203	.118	.113	.199	.115	.111
Families in four large urban centers	.660	1.494	.884	.644	1.422	.829
All families[a]	.448	.317	.796	.425	.304	.694
1979–80						
Families in four large urban centers	.632	1.219	.806	.617	1.170	.754

Note: The 1968–69 data are for the entire year, while the 1979–80 data are for a single month multiplied by 12.

a. Includes not only smallholders and residents of the four large urban centers but also families on the estates and in small towns.

Source: Calculated from data presented in various tables in Pryor (1988b), section I.

INDIRECT TAXES. Derick Kanyerere Gondwe (1977) has written the most sophisticated report available on the incidence of indirect taxes in Malaŵi. His study takes a computable general equilibrium approach, using a 1972 input-output table.[10] Gondwe's important conclusion is that indirect taxes fell primarily on goods that were produced by urban workers and that had a high ratio of labor to capital inputs; therefore, he argues, the overall ratio of wages to rents would rise if all indirect taxes were removed. Because he included smallholders' income as part of rental income, indirect taxes narrow the income differentials between urban and rural workers. He also shows that the indirect taxes on intermediate production have a greater impact on the final pattern of production than the indirect taxes on goods consumed by final users.

Assuming that all indirect taxes were shifted completely forward (that is, their incidence fell completely on the consumer), the tax system acted in a progressive manner. This occurred despite the fact that higher income families spent a larger share of their income on utilities and services, which had no indirect taxes placed upon them at all. The progressivity came about as the result of three important offsetting factors: (a) home-produced goods were much more important in the budgets of low- than of high-income families, and these were not taxed; (b) agricultural goods, which also accounted for a much higher share of expenditures of low- than of high-income families, were very lightly taxed; and (c) the most highly taxed items were imported consumer goods, which were a much larger share of total expenditures of high- than of low-income families.

If no distinctions are made between the differential consumption of imported goods by higher income families and if the results of Gondwe's general equilibrium calculations are used instead of the assumption about complete forward shifting, then the indirect tax system appeared roughly proportional. Gondwe emphasizes, however, that he believes the results obtained with the assumption about forward shifting of taxes are more realistic, that is, the system had a progressive incidence.

GENERAL REMARKS. These results for the direct and indirect taxes suggest that the overall impact of Malaŵi's tax system was probably somewhat progressive. Given the difficulties in administering a tax system in a country such as Malaŵi, this has been a remarkable feat. Because the current tax system represents a continuation of the British system, its progressivity has been an important legacy of the colonial period.

The fiscal system also has not discriminated in favor of the urban sector at the expense of the rural sector; indeed, the indirect taxes on imported luxuries and the higher direct taxes on high-income urban incomes reduce the urban-rural differentials, which have been the most important source of income inequality in Malaŵi. Given the Banda government's announced policy of favoring the rural sector and minimizing urban-rural differentials, this greater taxation of the urban sector was probably an important reason why it did not tamper significantly with the fiscal system it inherited from the colonial government.

The Balance of Expenditures and Revenues

In most years the Malaŵi government has run relatively large budgetary deficits. From 1964 through fiscal year 1982–83, we can calculate (from the data underlying table 8-2) that 55.4 percent of government expenditures were covered by taxes and other payments to the government; 15.2 percent, by foreign gifts; 20.3 percent, by foreign loans to Malaŵi; and 9.0 percent, by domestic borrowing and other domestic financial transactions of the government. A useful distinction is between public expenditures covered by taxes, gifts, and foreign loans, and uncovered expenditures financed by domestic loans, drawing down of cash reserves, and similar sources. Uncovered public expenditures have averaged about 2.8 percent of GDP, rising from 2.1 percent in the 1970s to 4.6 percent in the 1980s.

The rapid rise in foreign grants and loans starting in the late 1970s, combined with the rise in the relative importance of the uncovered public expenditures, requires special attention to two important features of Malaŵi's economy during the decade of the 1980s:

- A considerable portion of the government deficit was financed by borrowing abroad, a fact that the distinction between covered and uncovered expenditures conceals. From 1964 through 1979 annual foreign loans averaged 5.7 percent of GDP; and from 1980 through 1984, 7.8 percent of the GDP. Although this borrowing was mostly for investment, the GDP growth resulting from the investment has been declining (the incremental capital-output ratio (ICOR) has been increasing), and debt service payments have been taking an increasingly large share of GDP and require correspondingly higher taxes to finance.

- The government has changed its position from net saver to net dissaver, in part because of the parastatals' deficits. Hence, in the 1980s the public sector has become a fiscal drain on the rest of the economy (chapter 3).

By the mid-1980s the fiscal problems of the early 1980s showed little sign of being surmounted by appropriate budgetary policies. Indeed, the additional social and military expenditures resulting from the political insurgency in Mozambique and the high debt-service payments were increasing the budgetary strain. The economic future of Malaŵi appears ominous because the rise in the money supply, occasioned by uncovered government expenditures, may fuel inflationary forces.

Microeconomic Effects of Governmental Expenditures: Two Case Studies

The overall incidence of public expenditures is very much more difficult to study than is the incidence of taxes. Nevertheless, case studies of public expenditures for education and health, supplemented by some relatively abundant physical data, allow us to gain some idea of the impact of this side of the budget on the distribution of income. Education and health, according to *DevPol II*, are high priority sectors for government expenditures in the 1987–96 plan period. Malaŵi's policies toward these two sectors also provide a considerable contrast with those of Madagascar.

The government of Malaŵi has had a particular type of basic needs orientation, which President Banda has called his FCR doctrine: sufficient food, adequate clothing, and a roof for all. In practice this has meant that the major thrust of policy has been toward raising incomes, rather than redistributing income through governmental expenditures on education, health, or welfare. The education system has been relatively meritocratic; the health system has had an important progressive impact on the distribution of real income.

Education

The colonial government of Nyasaland followed a "low triangle policy" in education; that is, it provided considerable public education at the primary, but not a higher, level.[11] In 1950 the enrollment rate (the number of students in school as a percentage of the appropriate age group) in primary school was higher than in many other African nations such as Madagascar. During the 1950s, however, Malaŵi's primary school enrollment rates fell. The enrollment rates in secondary schools were very much lower than those for primary schools and rose only slowly during the 1950s. Few Africans from the Nyasaland Colony received a higher education, and the colonial government appears to have tried to avoid creating an educated or assimilated elite.[12]

Shortly after independence, enrollment rates in the primary schools (defined in this discussion as grades one through six) fell rapidly, from 50 percent to a low of 35 percent in 1966 and 1967, and then began to increase slowly, reaching about 70 percent by the early 1980s. In contrast, enrollment rates for the secondary schools (grades seven and above) were less than 3 percent until 1960; since then they have climbed relatively steadily, reaching a high of 18 percent in the early 1980s. The government also founded the University of Malaŵi and several other institutions of higher learning, which enrolled about 1,850 students in the early 1980s.

Although this expansion in education is certainly commendable, by international standards these enrollment rates are relatively low.[13]

Furthermore, a much higher percentage of boys than of girls have received some education. For instance, in 1968 girls constituted only about 36 percent of primary school students; fifteen years later this figure had risen only to 42 percent (Pryor 1988b, section L). Malaŵians became concerned because the absolute number of illiterates appeared to be increasing, even while the percentage of illiterates was slowly decreasing (Pryor 1988b, table J-2). In 1986 the Malaŵi government began to attack this problem with a nationwide literacy program; no evidence on the success of this project is yet available.

QUALITY OF EDUCATION. Probing beyond these enrollment data reveals some somber aspects in the educational picture. The ratio of students to teachers has risen. In the colonial period up to independence the primary schools had roughly forty-three students per teacher; in the early 1980s this ratio was more than sixty to one. The percentage of teachers considered unqualified or temporary has declined only slightly. *DevPol II* projected that the student-teacher ratio would gradually decline from sixty-eight in 1987 to fifty by 1996.

This rise in the student-teacher ratio reflects the decline in real governmental expenditures per student throughout the period. The high ratio also suggests that the quality of education has suffered. Some evidence for this conjecture can be found by comparing Malaŵi with other nations participating in the International Assessment of Educational Achievement (Heyneman 1981, p. 7 ff.). Malaŵian students in the eighth grade (standard) scored lower in reading comprehension but somewhat higher in science and sentence comprehension than students in the fourth grade in other developing nations. Part of this disparity came about because Malaŵi's students took the test in English, the language of instruction in their schools, which still provided difficulties for them. Nevertheless, the comparisons suggest some serious educational problems in Malaŵi's primary schools.

IMPLICATIONS FOR GROWTH AND THE DISTRIBUTION OF INCOME. In trying to explain differences in income inequality among nations, cross-section regressions have shown that such inequalities are less in those countries placing considerable resources in education, other factors held constant (see, for example, Papanek and Kyn 1986). This approach, however, is too aggregative for our purposes, which require some microeconomic evidence.

The strategy in *DevPol II* focused primarily on the development of secondary, technical, and higher education as a means of widening the nation's skills bottleneck. It also placed a higher priority on investment in particular productive sectors at the expense of primary education (chapter 3). Enrollments in postprimary education have not qualitatively or quantitatively begun to match the needs of the economy and thus have not significantly reduced the economic role of the expatriates in the nation. Although the share of senior civil service positions held by expatriates declined from 47 percent in 1971 to 16 percent in 1979 (the absolute number fell only from 899 to 677), in the private sector expatriates still held about 51 percent of the top-level jobs in 1979 (Wolgin and others 1983).[14]

In contrast to Madagascar, unemployment among the educated in Malaŵi has not appeared to be a severe problem, although suitable data are not available for making a firm judgment. The education system has tended over time, however, to widen income differentials, a phenomenon quite apparent from data in different years showing the correlation between income and education (Pryor 1988b, table J-3). Nevertheless, this does not seem to be increasing intergenerational inequalities. In most Western industrialized societies, parents' education is strongly correlated with the education their children receive, as measured by examination performance. In Malaŵi, however, the relationship between academic performance or earnings and parental education has been close to nil, other things being equal. Indeed, regressions of determinants of earnings in Malaŵi show the most important factor to be years of schooling, followed by academic achievement and then school quality; the parent's socioeconomic status ranks fifth (Heyneman 1981).

Thus the educational sector of Malaŵi appears to operate in a meritocratic fashion, at least within the urban sector; or, to view the matter from a different angle, educational achievement is not reinforcing class distinctions. Whether educational expenditures can be said to have a progressive or regressive incidence depends on the concept of incidence that is applied. If we consider "merit" as randomly distributed in the population, then the beneficiaries of educational expenditures by the government are also randomly distributed and the incidence is neutral. If we consider that "meritorious" individuals will always have higher incomes, other things being equal, then distributing education according to merit widens income differentials in the future, so such expenditures are regressive. Because those living in urban areas are more likely to have access to education than those in rural areas, who have lower incomes, expenditures for education can be considered regressive from this standpoint as well.

To what extent has Malaŵi underinvested in education? On the basis of social criteria, any primary school enrollment rates that are less than 100 percent indicate underinvestment, a viewpoint strongly held in such countries as Madagascar. From a strictly economic viewpoint, however, the returns to education are of primary relevance. Some rough estimates of the annual social and private returns to education investments are 21 percent and 50 percent, respectively. Although these estimates may well have an upward bias, they indicate that the economic return is considerable (Heyneman 1981).[15] Malaŵian families also appear to be aware of the high return to education, and some budget studies show an income elasticity of expenditures on education greater than unity, although more recent preliminary evidence suggests these income elasticities are too high. Nevertheless, this rather scattered evidence suggests that even from an economic viewpoint Malaŵi is underinvesting in education and that it could increase its growth rate by allocating more resources to primary and secondary education.[16]

Health

Malaŵi has followed a rather unique health strategy, placing considerable emphasis on health programs requiring relatively unskilled labor and much less emphasis on health care programs requiring highly trained specialists and expensive buildings and equipment (see Brown 1981). Madagascar, which had a much better health situation than Malaŵi at independence, has followed a directly opposite health strategy. By the mid-1980s, however, the health indicators for the two countries had practically converged.

The Malaŵi government has proposed the slogan, "Health for all by the year 2000," which reveals its cautious approach toward policy and its disdain for setting dramatic but unrealizable goals. Currently the health situation appears grim. As discussed in chapter 16 in considerable detail, infant mortality is very high and the average life expectancy is correspondingly low. Morbidity is also very high: 54 percent of the children in an educational survey had received medical treatment for malaria; 21 percent had received treatment for bilharzia; 46 percent reported a fever at least once a month; and 72 percent said they had frequent headaches (Heyneman 1981). *DevPol II* is highly critical of the health situation.

Modern medicine arrived only slowly in Malaŵi. Although a number of medical missionaries came to Malaŵi in the nineteenth century, during the entire colonial period modern medical care was extremely limited. Table 8-4 reports some data on health inputs that, in comparison with Madagascar (table 15-4), are very low. For example, although the ratio of population to hospital beds has improved continuously, even by 1985 Malaŵi had not reached the level that other former colonies, such as Madagascar, had achieved in 1950.

Modern medical services have been far removed geographically from much of the population.[17] For instance, at the end of 1980, 63 to 73 percent of the rural population lived more than 5 kilometers (3 miles) from any medical dispensary—a long walk for a sick person. The dispensaries had supporting hospitals, but to centralize specialists and equipment, these were in the urban centers, which were even less

Table 8-4. Health Inputs, Malaŵi, 1954 to 1985

Year and input	Population per hospital bed
1954	841[a]
1963	783[a]
1966	781[a]
1968	652
1970	611
1977	577
1981	549
1985	581

Medical worker	Population per medical worker		
	1973	1978	1983
Medical officers	46,632	49,224	54,512
Clinical officers[b]	86,719	60,745	29,057
Medical assistants[c]	3,313	2,910	2,375
Other medical personnel	5,013	2,945	2,194
Population per total medical workers	1,872	1,389	1,076

Note: Data are not available for all years.
a. Estimated.
b. Includes dentists.
c. Includes nurses and midwives.
Source: Pryor (1988b), tables B-1 and J-7.

accessible to the villages. *DevPol II* foresaw a considerable increase in these primary health centers in the 1987–96 period to relieve this problem.

Malaŵi has had very few highly trained medical practitioners, and the ratio of population to physicians, which was very high in 1973, has risen even more. Especially disturbing is that a high proportion of physicians in Malaŵi appear to be expatriates. Malaŵi has no medical school, and most of the Malaŵians training in foreign medical schools have chosen to remain abroad. As a result, only twenty Malaŵian doctors practiced medicine in the entire country in 1981 (compared with thirteen in 1973). Of the sixty medical and dental students studying abroad in 1974, only a few had returned by 1981. This has meant that less-trained medical personnel, such as clinical officers who have received only a four year postsecondary school training course, perform the same tasks, including surgery, as trained physicians in other countries. Malaŵi has made efforts to increase the number of less skilled health practitioners, and as a result the ratio of population to total medical personnel has declined more than 40 percent in a decade. In the mid-1980s the government began to take preliminary steps to establish its own medical school.

Malaŵi has also pursued other labor-intensive medical programs. For instance, the vaccination program was of sufficient scope that in the early 1980s, 86 percent, 66 percent, and 68 percent of children under one year of age had received, respectively, BCG, DCT III, and Polio III vaccinations (UNICEF 1986). These figures compare favorably with those of many other developing nations such as Madagascar. Some other Malaŵian efforts to provide labor-intensive medical care have been handicapped because, according to one observer, it is "difficult to imagine that the rural population would accept preventative health care activity in the absence of an effectively operating curative sector" (Vivian M. Thunyani, in Fyfe and others 1985).

Of the various public health programs in Malaŵi, the most notable has been the clean water program.[18] It started in 1968 with the identification of pure water sources. Individual villages must make the decision to undertake the project, at which time the government supplies the necessary technical advice, pipes, and other equipment. The villagers must dig the trenches and set up and maintain the system. This self-help program has attracted international attention and, by 1980, about 79 percent of urban dwellers and about 50 percent of the rural population had access to safe water. Latrine building has been another labor-intensive public health measure, and by the early 1980s 55 percent of the rural homes had latrines (see WHO and others 1984, p. 91). The government has been complementing this work of the villagers with the construction of boreholes and shallow wells. The final goal of safe water and sanitary waste disposal for the entire population by 1990 has been postponed; nevertheless, *DevPol II* projected an increase in the proportion of the population covered by various systems providing water of acceptable quality to 77 percent by 1996.

In brief, in the field of health the Malaŵi government has focused its efforts on the widespread use of semiskilled medical and public health personnel and on public health programs that reach a large number of people. These programs have had a progressive impact on the distribution of income, and a more extensive program along the same lines would increase this progressivity, because it is the poorer segment of the population that suffers most severely from inadequate health care. Certainly the low levels of health have a detrimental impact on economic growth, and more expenditures on health care would be a high-yielding investment.

Monetary Policy and the Financial System

Although strongly influenced by governmental budgetary policies, monetary policies have played an independent role in Malaŵi's economy. In contrast to many former British colonies, the central bank and the monetary system of Malaŵi were not the source of serious economic difficulties, at least until the 1980s. Until the 1980s, the amount of domestic borrowing (uncovered expenditures) by the government was relatively small and the monetary authorities in Malaŵi were relatively responsive to market forces.[19]

Money

As a first approximation, a crude quantity theory of money may be used as a predictor of the relationship between money and prices. The rise in Malaŵi's money supply (M1) has been moderate in comparison with that of many other developing nations.[20] From the end of 1965 to the end of 1984 the average annual rate of increase was 10.6 percent. Nominal GDP during the same time period rose at an annual average rate of 12.1 percent. (To complete the picture, real GDP grew at an average annual rate of 4.5 percent, and the GDP deflator, at an annual average rate of 7.7 percent.) From 1984 through the middle of 1988, however, the situation became alarming: M1 increased at an average annual rate of 27 percent, while the consumer price index increased at an average annual rate of 19 percent (IMF, *International Financial Statistics*, February 1989).

Over time, the income velocity of money in Malaŵi has averaged about 5.4, which is relatively high in comparison with other nations. Because of the relatively low monetization of the economy (that is, the large subsistence sector in the rural areas), much less money is needed for a given amount of GDP. The velocity of money has declined slowly over time, reflecting increasing monetization, as revealed in the national account data by the declining ratio of production in the subsistence sector to total GDP.

The broader money aggregates behaved somewhat differently. M2 and M3 grew at average annual rates that were roughly 3 percentage points more than M1, which means that their income velocities were very different. This phenomenon could have two, not mutually exclusive, explanations. It could reflect the increase of the market sphere, while the subsistence sphere declined because it could not provide an asset with the semiliquid properties of time and savings deposits; or it could also reflect the simple fact that time and savings deposits provided all sectors with an earning asset having a positive real return and relatively little risk. The behavior of M2 and M3 supports the first explanation, but some evidence provides support for the second as well.

From independence to 1980 the real "bank rate" (essentially the discount rate the central bank charges the commercial banks, minus the rate of inflation) was slightly positive. Time and savings accounts, paying 2 to 3 percentage points above the bank rate, provided depositors with a real positive return at very little risk, because the government owned (and implicitly guaranteed) the major banks. The subsistence sector could not provide a liquid asset that would be safe and would provide a positive real return. Hiding money in the ground would yield no positive return, and various types of inventories, which might provide a positive return, would not be safe. The availability of an asset with both safety and a positive return, such as a time deposit, may well account for the lower velocity of the broader money aggregates. Unfortunately, data on personal financial assets are lacking.

For most of the 1980s the real interest rate was negative, even though several times the central bank increased the discount and deposit rates in small increments. Between 1984 and the middle of 1988 the Malaŵian treasury bill rate increased from 11.00 to 15.75 percent, which seemed to indicate some awareness of the inflation problem, but consumer prices increased at the higher average annual rate of 19 percent during the period (IMF, *International Financial Statistics*, February 1989). The discount and deposit rates of interest were increased to about 14 percent in 1987 and then inexplicably were reduced in 1988 to 11.00 percent and 12.75 percent, respectively, in a year when consumer prices were increasing roughly 29 percent. Such a policy discourages saving and encourages borrowing, which can only feed the inflation. Such policies belie the brave monetary policy announced in *DevPol II* to offer savers an "adequate return on their savings," and they will certainly offset any incentive effects of the plans announced in that document to introduce a new saving facility allowing tax-free interest payments on special deposits.

Credit

The money supply is connected closely to the credit system and the financing of the government debt. If the government is running a large deficit, the central bank is not responsible for the rise in credit and can only make sure that interest rates are high enough to induce the public to hold government bills and bonds rather than converting them into cash. The extent to which Malaŵi's public debt fed inflation depends on the monetization of that debt, that is, the degree by which the fiscal deficit of the central government, not financed from abroad, has increased the growth of M1.

A crucial indicator is the share of the internally financed debt that is matched by a rise in the money supply. From the fiscal year 1966 to

1982–83, only about 30 percent of the Malaŵi government's internally financed uncovered expenditures was reflected in a rise in M1; this percentage was much higher in the 1960s.[21] Thus citizens and institutions in Malaŵi appeared willing to hold government bonds as an asset. The underlying reasons for this portfolio behavior cannot be easily investigated because time series data on interest paid on government debt are not readily available (and must still be constructed). Nevertheless, scattered evidence suggests that the positive real interest rates paid on government debt reflect the willingness of the central bank in Malaŵi to adapt its interest rate policy to changing inflation rates.

All of this indicates that a "virtuous circle" was present in Malaŵi, at least in the 1960s and 1970s. The adaptability of the monetary policies to changing circumstances (especially the positive real interest rates) and the relatively low rate of domestic inflation permitted the economy to adjust to the declining terms of trade and the government to follow a relatively liberal trade policy (chapter 6). These responses, in turn, led to higher economic growth, which kept inflation rates low by increasing demand for transactions balances of money.

The Reserve Bank of Malaŵi (the central bank) has attempted to influence the credit market by certain direct controls, such as liquidity ratios for banks, and by moral suasion, for example, asking lending agencies to direct more credit toward agriculture rather than consumers. I have been unable to find any studies evaluating the effects of such policies. According to central bank officials, the discount rate and open market operations have not been important tools of monetary policy.

Although little detailed information is available on other aspects of Malaŵi's financial markets and credit system, the ratios of various credit aggregates of the banking system to total GDP offer some insight.[22] The ratio of total assets of the financial sector (that is, the sum of net claims on foreigners, on the government, and on state bodies, and gross claims on the private sector) to the current price GDP rose from 17 percent in 1965 to 30 percent in the following decade; thereafter, it fluctuated around this higher level. The ratio of domestic credit to GDP, alone, rose continuously, from 6 percent in 1965 to almost 50 percent by the early 1980s. These figures show increasing financial intermediation in the first decade; thereafter, the financial sector balanced its increasing domestic assets of government and private debt with increasing foreign liabilities—that is, it financed a growing share of domestic debt by borrowing abroad. As long as foreign credit sources are available and government can meet its debt payments, the system works fine; if not—and if changes are not made in the fiscal system—the government must finance itself by resorting to the printing press. Of course, as the ratio of foreign debt to GDP rises, foreign lending to the country becomes more reluctant, which in turn increases the linkage between domestic budgetary deficits and inflation.

The inflation of the 1980s had several roots, including the uncovered deficits in the budget and the external shocks to the economy, which exacerbated internal structural weaknesses. The actions of monetary authorities abetted the inflationary process. Real interest rates were negative, and the government debt became increasingly monetized because strong incentives to hold excess cash balances or savings in the bank no longer existed. Domestic prices rose with the increase in the money supply, and Malaŵi's virtuous fiscal-monetary circle of the 1970s became a vicious circle instead.

Summary and Conclusions

In the 1970s the high level of government investment and of other expenditures in the economy certainly aided Malaŵi's economic growth, even though the relative neglect of expenditures on education and health retarded it. Cautious monetary policies at that time also aided growth. In the 1980s an increasing share of government expenditures went to service externally held debt or to finance military and social programs occasioned by the political turbulence in Mozambique. These strains, combined with an inability to raise taxes to cover expenditures, a negative real interest rate that discouraged private savings, and an overvaluation of the currency, have been important factors underlying the stagnation of GDP.

On the whole, the tax side of the government budget appears to have had progressive impact on the distribution of income. Some governmental expenditures, such as those on health, also had a progressive impact. The distributional consequences of other expenditures, such as those for education, appear to have been neutral or regressive, depending upon the concept of incidence. The lack of complete information on incidence precludes overall evaluation of the distributional impact of the government budget.

To what extent is the fiscal behavior of the government to blame for Malaŵi's current economic straits? In recent years a number of economists have argued that the government sector is a self-interested agent and that the expansion of the public sector shows aggrandizement by politicians and civil servants that will eventually lead the government to bankruptcy.[23] This hypothesis seems too crude. Certainly the Malaŵi government was self-interested. Nevertheless, especially in the early years after independence, it adopted a number of policies, such as high taxes and low expenditures on social services, that were bound to be unpopular. Little evidence exists that the public sector expanded primarily to increase the power of the government and civil service, particularly because President Banda carried out some of his important programs outside of formal governmental channels, for instance, the expansion of the estate sector through the banks.

Others have argued that the behavior of the government sector reflected a profound discontinuity stemming from the process of decolonializing. More specifically, colonial economic policy had been cautious, both in keeping the budget in balance and in maintaining governmental expenditures at a relatively low level so they could be administered effectively. The new African states preferred to "gamble on growth," impelled "by the political need to demonstrate progress, to reward supporters and to employ growing urban populations" (Fieldhouse 1986, p. 245). This approach does little, however, to explain Malaŵi's predicament. The Malaŵi government certainly did not take a heedless plunge into bankruptcy during the late 1960s and 1970s. Its goals were relatively modest, and its administration was relatively effective. Although it mobilized considerable resources for government investment by borrowing from abroad, it also mobilized considerable internal resources for this purpose. President Banda did not need foreign funds to demonstrate progress, and he took measures, particularly through his wage policies, to retard the growth of the urban sector and to avoid the need to have a rapidly growing civil service in order to employ a growing educated elite.

The fiscal difficulties of the Malaŵi government in the 1980s had more mundane causes than public-sector aggrandizement or a gamble for growth. The system received some severe external shocks, and the government made some serious domestic policy errors in agriculture and foreign trade and in financing a larger than prudent share of the government deficit from external loans in the late 1970s. The most important cause, however, may be an internal structural change. In the 1980s economic policymaking devolved in considerable part from the Life President and his long-time, like-minded associates, such as John Tembo, who served many years as the head of the Central Bank, to the civil service and to younger officials, who had quite different ideas about economic policy. No person or group had both the political will and the power to bring about some painful fiscal reforms of the kind that President Banda had carried out in the mid-1960s. Buffeted by severely adverse external events, the government lacked sufficiently strong leadership to break the vicious fiscal circle in which it found itself in the mid-1980s.

Notes

1. The rest of this discussion is based on the data presented in section D of the Appendix and Pryor (1988b), section K.

2. About 40 percent of total gross fixed investment was financed through the government (state and local) sector during the federation period (1954–63).

This datum was calculated from Central African Federation of Rhodesia and Nyasaland, Central Statistical Office (1964).

3. Birnberg and Resnick (1975) argue that this was a general policy of colonial governments. For Malaŵi, qualitative evidence can be adduced to show that such principles were in operation in the Nyasaland colony—for example, in the building and the financing of the railroad.

4. Analyzing Malaŵi's budgetary policies raises a minor difficulty—the central government operates on two budgets: the revenue account, which covers current expenditures for the "traditional" functions of government, and the development account, which covers capital expenditures and the nontraditional functions of government. About 10 percent of the government's gross fixed capital formation comes from the revenue account, while roughly one sixth of its social expenditures are financed through the development account. This dual budget has several political purposes; one is to permit the government to show that it finances the revenue account totally from domestic sources and therefore uses most foreign aid to cover capital expenditures. For this discussion, I have consolidated the two budgets.

5. In trying to understand this relatively passive acceptance of higher taxes, adherents to the ideas of the *Steuermentalität* school might be interested in knowing that the Lomwe (an ethnic group in the southern part of the country) have a creation myth claiming that taxes were one of the first inventions of humankind after the world was formed. Moreover, the animals in the forests are descendants of men who tried to escape these taxes by moving away from the villages. Schoffeleers and Roscow (1985), pp. 22–23, analyze this story.

6. A number of studies using tax data from the IMF, *Government Finance Statistics Yearbook*, have shown Malaŵi's relatively high share of direct taxes. Chamley and others (1985) show that Malaŵi has had a high tax "effort" in comparison to other countries with a roughly similar level of per capita GDP.

7. Bates (1984) stresses the important role of export taxes in most African nations.

8. Another incidence question is whether the increased taxes have reduced private savings or consumption. Chhibaer (n.d.) has argued that taxes fell primarily on savings, but this macroeconomic study used aggregative data from Malaŵi before results of the major revision in the national accounts were available. This particular incidence question is far from closed.

9. This issue was raised by Short (1974). It must be noted, however, that my data for the two years are not completely comparable because the 1968–69 data were collected on an annual basis and the 1979–80 data, on a monthly basis. The direction of the bias in the comparisons is not clear, however. Chamley and others (1985) documented the changes in Malaŵi's tax structure since 1979 that have decreased progressivity.

10. This subsection on the impact of indirect taxes is based completely on Gondwe's analysis, which without doubt is one of the two best technical analyses I have seen on the Malaŵi economy; unfortunately, it has received little public attention. Gondwe's calculations are based on a ten-sector 1968 input-output table for Malaŵi, which he updated to 1972. He presents both tables and claims that the original table had been estimated by Malaŵi, NSO,

Annual Economic Survey 1968. His citation is vague, and he indicates neither how the original table was estimated nor the limitations of the data. In any case, this table has apparently not been published, and my inquiries at the NSO were met with the blanket assertion that no such calculations had ever been made. Inspection of the 1968 table reveals some anomalies, especially with regard to indirect taxes in the transportation and communication sector. Some of these were corrected in Gondwe's 1972 update. The two tables are also not completely comparable because the 1968 table includes imports as a row (with the value added rows), while the 1972 table presents imports as a column in the final demand quadrant (with the import duties distributed in the indirect tax row). Because some of Gondwe's assumptions (especially his high export and import elasticities) are subject to serious question and some of his data are uncertain, I believe his results should be reported qualitatively rather than in tabular form.

11. Information on the Nyasaland educational system is drawn from Speck (1967), p. 41; and Isaac C. Lamba, in Fyfe and others (1985), pp. 149–86. All data on enrollment rates in this section come from Pryor 1988b, section H.

12. Some claim that only thirty-three Africans in Malaŵi had university degrees at independence. The 1966 census gives a total of 360 with some university education, but this may have included non-Africans. Those with university training in the mid-1970s numbered roughly 3,500 (Malaŵi, NSO, 1984, vol. 1, pp. 158, 162).

13. The Malaŵi government's efforts in education are understated by such statistics, because in the 1950s somewhat fewer than half of the children were in "assisted" (that is, publicly supported) schools. By the late 1960s enrollments in such schools had risen to more than 80 percent of all enrollments, and they continued to rise, to about 93 percent in the early 1980s. Thus, the education of a larger share of children has been financed publicly, rather than privately in the bush schools. This implies an improvement in the quality of education as well, because these bush schools provided very inferior training.

14. I have calculated these percentages by omitting unfilled jobs. An interesting analysis of Africanization in the period from independence up to the early 1970s is found in Baker (1972). Some critics claim that the slow Africanization is designed to permit members of the president's own ethnic group to obtain these positions; initially they had lower average levels of education than those from other ethnic groups (particularly in the north). I have seen no evidence that this is happening. Much more can be said about replacement of expatriates by Malaŵians, because the process requires more than just finding a local person with the same formal qualifications. For the purposes of this study, however, the quantitative indicators in the text must suffice.

15. These estimates may be upwardly biased because of excessive estimates of expected earnings of Malaŵians with particular qualifications.

16. In the early 1980s, expenditures per student at the primary level were 12 MK; at the secondary level, 209 MK; at government boarding schools, 546 MK; and at the university (which has roughly 8.5 students per teacher), more than 3,000 MK per student. The data come from Thoboni (1984) and, for government boarding schools (Kamuzu Academy), Jones (1982). In comparison to other countries, these differentials appear excessive. The datum for primary schools

appears low because it excludes local government expenditures and the value of investments in the form of free labor (during "work weeks"). The datum for government boarding schools also appears low; according to Jonathan Kydd, in Fyfe and others (1985), pp. 293–380, Kamuzu Academy, which was completed in 1981, cost 40 million MK (with endowment) and educates 400 students a year. The opportunity cost per student, assuming a 10 percent interest rate, is thus 10,000 MK a year—the cost of educating 800 students in primary school. Also, Thoboni's figure of 2,926 MK for a university student excludes room and board, as well as amortization costs of the buildings and equipment.

17. Malaŵi Government (1984), vol. 3, p. xiii, reports that 37.1 percent of the rural population lived farther than 8 kilometers from any medical dispensary, while another 54.6 percent were 2 to 8 kilometers away. The higher estimate in the text was made by assuming that the population density was constant from 2 to 8 kilometers around the dispensary; the lower estimate, by assuming that the population density was twice as great in the circle from 2 to 5 kilometers around the dispensary as in the circle from 5 to 8 kilometers.

18. The water program in Malaŵi is discussed by Liebenow (1981) and by Bharier (1980). More recent studies include Warner and others (1983) and various reports by L. A. H. Msukwa and his colleagues at the Centre for Social Research in Zomba. Data for the water program are contained in these sources or are from WHO (1986) and UNICEF, *The State of the World's Children 1986*. The range in the text reflects differences in these estimates. One rural Malaŵian observer described the system as follows: "God provided the water, the Kamuzu [President Banda] provided the pipes, and the villagers provided the labor." The government also provides a concrete slab around the top of the well, as well as technical and administrative aid. The vaccination data for both countries come from the UNICEF publication. Data on rural latrines come from a survey cited by WHO and others (1984), p. 91.

19. All data on money, interest, credit, and investment discussed in this section are from Pryor (1988b), section L.

20. M1 includes currency and demand deposits; M2 includes M1 plus private time and savings deposits; and M3 includes M2 plus private deposits in nonbank financial institutions (a definition slightly different from that used elsewhere).

21. These data on uncovered expenditures come from the sources underlying table 8-2. I exclude uncovered expenditures in the first three months of 1970.

22. The data in this discussion are from Pryor (1988b), section L.

23. This literature is summarized by Ronald Finley and John D. Wilson, in Razin and Sadka (1987).

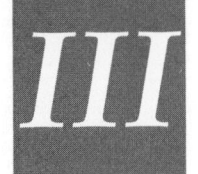

III Madagascar

9 Background to the Economy of Madagascar

In the mid-twentieth century Madagascar exhibited the major characteristics of economic underdevelopment: a low level of technology, a small domestic manufacturing sector, inadequate transportation and communication, and relatively poor health conditions. Most of its population worked in smallholder agriculture. Because of considerable investment during the colonial period, however, per capita production was somewhat higher than in Malaŵi, and both French and Malagasy political leaders believed that the island had substantial potential for rapid economic growth.

Geography

Madagascar is the fourth largest island in the world and is roughly equal in area to Kenya, France, or Afghanistan; it has more than six times the land area of Malaŵi.[1] The overall population density is low, in part because large parts of the island are unsuitable for cultivation. The major geographical advantages for economic development are a mild temperature, a relative abundance of rain in many parts of the island, and a diversity of climate. The disadvantages include considerable environmental degradation, fairly poor soil, and rugged landscape.

The most prominent geographical feature of the island is the central highland area, extending almost the entire length of the island and ranging in height from 700 to 2,500 meters (2,300 to 8,200 feet). This hilly topography, which covers more than half of the country, makes agriculture difficult and also presents many transportation problems. The country must rely on a small network of roads and railroads to cover a large area, and the lack of maintenance of this fragile transportation infrastructure in the late 1970s and early 1980s was a major contributing factor to the decline in Madagascar's marketed agricultural production (chapter 12).

On the whole Madagascar is a well-watered country, with an average annual rainfall of 1,560 millimeters (61.4 inches), but regional variations are considerable; roughly 15 percent of the country—in the south and southwest—does not have enough rain to support agriculture without irrigation. The year-to-year variation of rainfall is relatively low, about the same as in Malaŵi, which means that agricultural catastrophes from drought do not happen often. Many cyclones cross the island, however, and once every few years they cause a good deal of destruction not only to crops but also to the economic infrastructure.

Seasonal rainfall variations are considerable in the central highlands but are much less in coastal areas, where year-round agriculture is possible. The different climatic conditions define several distinct natural areas, which support a greater range of agricultural products than can be grown in Malaŵi; as a result, Madagascar's agricultural exports are more diversified. The climate is conducive to malaria, however; further, bilharziasis occurs in the southwest, and tuberculosis, in the highlands. Trypanosomiasis (sleeping sickness) is not a serious problem in Madagascar, and cattle raising is much more important than in Malaŵi.

The soils of Madagascar appear to be considerably less suited for agriculture than Malaŵi's. An old cliché about Madagascar is that it has the shape, color, and fertility of a brick. Roughly two-thirds of the island, especially the highlands and some parts of the east coast, are covered by depleted ferruginous or ferrallitic soils with relatively low fertility. In the extensive highlands the hillsides cannot sustain production on an annual basis; only the more fertile valley-bottom soils permit intensive agriculture. The soils in the arid south are sandy and are also not very fertile. Although soils in the western part of the island are potentially more fertile than soils elsewhere on the island, development of these areas would require considerable investment. Only on the east coast of the island have the relatively fertile alluvial soils been developed.

Ecological problems also appear to be much more severe in Madagascar than in Malaŵi. The land fertility problem, has been compounded by a form of slash-and-burn agriculture called *tavy*, a technique practiced for many centuries.[2] Roughly a million hectares of land are burned deliberately each year. Fire has destroyed a good part of the woodlands, and deforestation has become a severe problem. Moreover, on the slopes, which cover a large part of the island, the vegetation is burned in order to plant rice for a season and then is left fallow for up to twenty years, a practice leading to considerable soil erosion. In the flat lands also vegetation is burned to increase the short-run suitability of the land for temporary pasturage. This practice has caused erosion and depletion of the natural organic materials and also has eliminated many plants and grasses suitable for grazing, allowing thorny scrub and rougher grasses to take their place. Aside from its direct impact on the soil, the burning of vegetation has been an important cause of some serious floods, especially in the west; these floods, in turn, have washed away more valuable soil.

Only 4 percent of the land on the island is actually under cultivation. Although some claim that another 9 percent of the land is suitable for agriculture, these estimates must be taken very cautiously, given the rudimentary statistics on land usage (Pryor, 1988a, section A). The land cultivated per farmer is increasing at the same time that land productivity is falling; that is, the farmers are operating on the "external margin" of cultivation (see chapter 11). Bringing more land into agricultural use requires expensive investments, especially because much of this potentially fertile land is far from population centers, so farmers must be relocated long distances, land settlements built, and roads constructed.

Statistics on land usage in Madagascar are rather uncertain. The census data presented in table 9-1 appear the most reliable statistics available on the topic. Whatever measure is used, the cultivated land per capita is low. Most agricultural lands are farmed by smallholders, and rice is the major staple. In comparison with other rice-producing countries in the world, the average land productivity for rice in Madagascar is relatively low, although it is somewhat higher than is maize-growing productivity in Malaŵi compared to other maize-producing countries.[3]

Table 9-1. Land Usage in Madagascar, Crop Year 1984–85

Total land area (thousands of hectares)	58,704
Customary land under cultivation[a]	1,918
Actually planted	1,723
Estates and cooperatives	125
Actually planted[b]	75
Other	56,660
Total land area per capita (hectares)	6.044
Agricultural lands	
Customary and estate lands	0.208
Actually planted[b]	0.183

a. Customary land includes land held under traditional tenure arrangements and land farmed by smallholders.

b. The planted land on the estates *(grandes exploitations)* includes only land for irrigated and nonirrigated temporary crops and land for tree crops. These data are less inclusive than the data presented in Pryor (1988a), table A-2, which show planted land per capita of 0.237 hectares for 1984–85.

Source: Pryor (1988a), table A-1; and Madagascar, Ministère de la production agricole et de la réforme agraire (1986).

Madagascar's mineral deposits are more important to its economy than are those in Malaŵi. Such resources do not appear to be an important source of wealth, however, and in recent years raw materials have accounted for less than 10 percent of all Madagascar's exports. The most important minerals include bauxite, chromium ore, gemstones, graphite, mica, and uranium ore. Other known minerals include low-grade iron ore deposits and phosphate resources. For many of these minerals, intensive exploitation does not appear economic. Oil is present, but its commercial possibilities are not yet proven. Capital shortages have prevented Madagascar from intensively using its principal energy resources: hydropower, coal, lignite, and oil sands.

Peoples

Conflicting theories abound about the earliest history of the peoples of Madagascar, but certain facts are generally accepted. Sometime during the first millennium, Madagascar was populated by peoples from Southeast Asia. The Malagasy language spoken today is classified as a Malayo-Polynesian language; some claim its closest linguistic affinity is with Maayan, a language spoken in south-central Borneo (Murdock 1959, chapter 27). The Southeast Asians intermarried either with the original African inhabitants of Madagascar or with the African peoples (Bantu) who subsequently emigrated to the island. In later centuries Indians and Arabs also came to the island. The present population is primarily an admixture of Asian and African racial groups, with those of Southeast Asian extraction more likely found in the highlands. The culture of the island also combines elements from both groups, for instance, the irrigated rice agriculture from Asia along with some cattle cults from Africa.

Malagasy population statistics specify some eighteen ethnic groups. Table 9-2 lists the most important numerically. This numeration appears to be partly an administrative convenience, however. Using criteria of subjective ethnic identification, French ethnographers have distinguished forty-eight different ethnic groups.[4] The various ethnic groups have certain important social-structural differences (although not nearly so great as in Malaŵi). For instance, some of the groups are highly stratified socially, while others are quite egalitarian; most have ambilineal inheritance (roughly equal inheritance of both sexes from both parents), and only a few have patrilineal inheritance; some have bridewealth, and others do not; most have monogamy, but a few are polygynous. Some of these variations can be found even within the same ethnic group.

The cultural unity among the various groups appears of much greater importance than such social-structural differences.[5] Practically all of the Malagasy peoples speak the same language, and most share

Table 9-2. Ethnic Groups and Ethnic Origins of Cabinet Ministers, Madagascar
(percent)

Ethnic group	Rough estimate of population proportions, 1970	Ethnic background of cabinet ministers, 1968–83[a]
Merina	26.1	32.0
Betsimisaraka	14.9	19.3
Betsileo	12.0	8.0
Tsimihety	7.2	9.2
Sakalava	5.9	13.0
Antandroy	5.3	0.8
Antaisaka	5.1	0.0
Antaimoro	3.4	2.7
Bara	3.4	0.8
Other[b]	16.7	14.2
Total	100.0	100.0

a. The ethnic origins of the cabinet ministers are calculated from person-years of cabinet membership; although some ministers hold several portfolios, they are only counted once each year.

b. Includes members of smaller ethnic groups (including Europeans), members with mixed ethnic backgrounds, and those few cabinet members whose ethnicity could not be determined.

Source: Estimates of ethnic proportions are from Nelson (1973), p. 61, citing from Madagascar, INSRE, (1971). The names of the members of the cabinet each year for the period from 1968 through 1983 are from Legum and Drysdale (annual). The identifications of ethnic origins were made for me by professional social scientists in Madagascar.

important common cultural traits such as monotheism, veneration of ancestors, and elaborate funeral rituals. Furthermore, some of the ethnic groups have achieved ethnic identification only within the past few centuries and as a result of political events, rather than from social-cultural differences. According to Jean Poirier (cited in Chaigneau 1985, p. 19), "If the population is divided in several dozen ethnic groups, it is significant to note that they present between each other less cultural divergence than the French 'ethnic groups' of the 19th century." Although this may be slightly exaggerated, ethnic identification certainly appears much weaker in Madagascar than in Malaŵi.[6]

New ethnic groups have played an important role in the recent history of the island. The most important has been the French. At the beginning of 1962, a year and a half after Madagascar's independence, all foreigners accounted for 2.1 percent of the population, including 62,000 people from metropolitan France (0.9 percent of the population) and 42,000 French citizens from other colonies (0.7 percent of the population, primarily from the Comoros and Réunion) (France, Ministère de la cooperation, 1963; and Bunge 1983). In Malaŵi the British composed less than 0.2 percent of Nyasaland population, which illustrates in a dramatic fashion the differences between French and British commitment to these two African colonies.

As in Malaŵi, ethnicity in Madagascar does not mean tribalism. Although relatively little scholarly work has been carried out on the influence of ethnic factors on economic activity, traditional values apparently have not greatly deterred economic development.[7] Of course, such values have led to some actions adversely affecting growth—for instance, food taboos have caused neglect of certain nutritious foods, and irrigation pumps have been shut down on work-free religious holidays. Nevertheless, in many important aspects of the economy, such as sensitivity of production to price changes, traditionalism does not seem important.

Ethnic relations in Madagascar have many harmonious elements. For instance, intermarriage, although apparently less frequent than in Malaŵi, occurs often. In 1966 about 10 percent of all marriages were between men and women of different ethnic groups (Madagascar, INSRE, n.d.[c], pp.53–55). The degree of exogamy varied, however, from roughly 4.5 percent among the Merina or the Antandroy to about 24.5 percent among the Sakalava.

Ethnic frictions do exist, however, and have a strongly regional focus. In "high politics" the most important cleavage is between the peoples of the highlands (primarily Merina and Betsileo) and the rest of the island (the coastal peoples, or the *côtiers*) (see Spacensky 1970). Aside from the racial differences between these two groups, these cleavages are accentuated by a number of important economic and cultural factors. Average rural incomes vary considerably among ethnic groups and also among regions (Appendix I, tables I-1 and I-2). A much higher percentage of the Merina live in urban areas, especially in Antananarivo Province, which contains the capital of the nation as well as about half of the island's industry. The Merina also have a higher average educational level than other ethnic groups.

Ideological differences between the Merina and the *côtiers* include religion (Protestantism is stronger among the Merina in the highlands; Roman Catholicism is stronger among the *côtiers*) and the Merina's stronger economic interest in an urban-oriented development strategy directed from the capital. The composition of the two major postwar governments and the two leading parties reflects these ideological differences. Philibert Tsiranana headed the First Republic from 1960 to 1972; his Social Democratic party, the principal political party on the island, was dominated by *côtiers*. The Merina have played a much more important role in the government of the Second Republic, which from 1975 to the present has been headed by Didier Ratsiraka and his AREMA party. Although table 9-2 suggests that the ethnic balance in the cabinet roughly parallels population shares, these aggregative data mask the fact that the Merina increased their share in the cabinet from 18 percent during the First Republic to 36 percent in the governments that followed. The manifestation of the Merina's gain in political strength has been the change in economic policies, particularly the shift from a rural to an urban focus of development. In deference to the delicate nature of such regional conflicts, the government of the Second Republic made some well-publicized attempts to gain support of the *côtiers* by narrowing the differences in educational opportunities between the highlands and coastal regions; the results have been somewhat different from the stated intentions, however (chapter 16). These interregional rivalries also led to considerable rivalry over the allocation of investment funds and have led to some location decisions that have raised production costs.

The most overt interethnic frictions in Madagascar (as well as in Malaŵi) have concerned recent Asian residents. In Madagascar in 1962 Asians—primarily Indians, Pakistani, and Chinese—accounted for somewhat less than 0.4 percent of the population. The explicit measures directed against Asians in many African nations during the 1970s found little resonance in Madagascar. Nevertheless, some general policies have affected Asians disproportionately. For example, in the mid-1970s the Madagascar government nationalized almost all foreign trade and much domestic trade, especially wholesaling and crop purchasing; although this economic policy extended to all nationalities, it was particularly adverse for the Asians, who were strongly concentrated in these types of commerce. In the mid-1980s restrictions against crop buying and other types of internal trade were liberalized, and Asians returned to their former commercial work. In 1987 riots against the Indo-Pakistanis (but not the Chinese, who were more assimilated) occurred in a number of Malagasy cities; although the causes are not clear and may have resulted from domestic political factors, many of the rioters were said to resent the alleged excessive profits the Asians realized as a result of the liberalization of trade.

Madagascar has been predominantly rural; in 1966 about 12.6 percent of the population lived in urban areas—more than double the percentage in Malaŵi at the same time (Madagascar, INSRE, n.d. [c]). The population has also been unequally distributed among rural areas, in good part because of differences in agricultural conditions. For instance, although the average population density for the island as a whole was 10.6 per square mile in 1966, it varied from 27.1 in the province of Antananarivo (in the highlands) to only 4.4 and 5.0, respectively, in the provinces of Toliary (Tuléar) in the south and Mahajunga (Majunga) in the west.

In contrast to Malaŵi, Madagascar has experienced little emigration for the purpose of work. Indeed, the island has received immigrants, especially from the Comoros and Réunion, to obtain work or land; in recent years, however, this inflow has ceased.

Historical Developments

Madagascar's first contact with the West appears to have occurred in 1500, when Portuguese ships were blown off course and sighted the island. In the following two centuries the Portuguese, Dutch, British, and French explored the coasts and attempted to set up small missions or settlements. Considerable European attention focused on the island at an early date. A history of the island was published in France in the midseventeenth century, and Daniel Defoe wrote a novel about the island in 1729; since then many books have been devoted to various aspects of the island.[8]

During the seventeenth and eighteenth centuries the island began to experience a certain degree of political coalescence. Of particular importance were the Sakalava empire and the Betsimiraka kingdom on the east and west coasts, respectively. In the late eighteenth and early nineteenth centuries the Merina conquered most of the island under the leadership of King Andrianampoinimerina (1787–1810) and his son Radama I (1810–28); this kingdom lasted until the French conquest. The Merina were a highly stratified society that developed an able administrative apparatus. They established a unified legal system, carried out land reclamation, and began a slow modernization of the army. Although considerable European penetration of the island began during this period, the Merina royalty were able to maintain the independence of their island nation, which was recognized by many leading countries of the world, by playing off the British and the French, who competed for political, economic, and religious influence (French Catholic missionaries were particularly active in the coastal areas; British Protestant missionaries, in the highlands). Among the positive accomplishments resulting from this balancing act was a great upsurge in education; by the end of the Merina reign, 135,000 Madagascar children (roughly 7 percent of the population) were learning to read and write, mostly in mission schools. A negative aspect of the European presence was the deliberate neglect of road building in a futile effort to hinder any type of Western invasion.

Madagascar's political independence began to wane after a war with France from 1883 to 1885 and subsequent territorial concessions; the treaty of 1886, which marked the end of this war, also gave the French a vague reason to believe they had established a protectorate over the island. In 1890 the French and British ended their rivalries on the island with an agreement recognizing a French "protectorate" over

Madagascar in return for similar French recognition of British political designs in Zanzibar. In 1894, when the French tried to formalize their protectorate, the Merina Queen Ranavalona III refused to recognize the claim. In 1895 a French expeditionary force quickly conquered the Merina capital, Antananarivo, and the island became a French colony the next year. The French quickly began making social changes, first by freeing the half-million slaves, roughly one-quarter of the population.

In 1896 General Joseph Galliéni arrived to serve as the second Resident General; all historians of the island regard him as a remarkable administrator and the true founder of the island's modern development. He took six years to quell the fierce Ménelàmba resistance against the French, and in 1904–05, shortly before he left the island, he was forced to subdue a smaller scale rebellion as well.

Galliéni was a coldly rational man ("I have never been moved by the emotions") with boundless energy, a contempt for bureaucracy, and remarkable toughness ("Kindheartedness is worth nothing to anyone; it is too often taken for weakness").[9] He defined his mission as "to make Madagascar French, to undermine the British influence, and to bring down the Hova [the ruling caste of the Merina] pride and power." Fiercely devoted to developing the island economically, he admonished his subordinates to "ensure that those whom you administer tremble only at the idea of your leaving."

Galliéni built roads connecting Antananarivo with both the north and south coasts of the island as well as other centers; he began construction of a railroad from Antananarivo to Toamasina (Tamatavy) on the coast; he installed urban sewer systems; he built more than 100 hospitals, dispensaries, maternity units, and leprosaria; he established the Academie Malgache and encouraged agricultural experimentation, extension work, and reforestation; he reorganized and supported a school of medicine, which had been established by British missionaries in 1886; and he supported primary and secondary education, especially by subsidizing the mission schools, and also set up a vocational training school and a college for public administration.

Financial problems in Galliéni's Madagascar were severe, and many of his accomplishments had their darker side. Soon after taking power he introduced forced labor for most males from sixteen to sixty years of age, a system replaced after a few years by various methods of "persuasion" when labor was needed. Although much of this labor was used in his public works program, some forced laborers were rented out to agricultural settlers from France. Galliéni also introduced a system of poll and cattle taxes to force peasants to participate in the market economy by selling their agricultural produce or their labor. These taxes were an important source of public revenue until 1973, and their abrogation at that time caused some severe budgetary difficulties. Galliéni managed to redirect most of the island's trade to France and also induced a flow of French farmers and business people to the island; the latter engaged in trade and in a variety of mining (mica, gold) and other commercial ventures as well. With this impetus from Galliéni, Madagascar started much more rapidly down the road toward modern economic growth than did Malaŵi under various British administrators.

Galliéni's successors were less capable and less farsighted than he was. In following the new French policies of reducing subsidies to their colonies and of separating church and state, the colonial administrators of Madagascar reduced financial support to the missionary schools, a policy leading to a reduction of primary education, especially in the coastal areas. The island's government did continue to support some secondary schools, which provided sufficiently advanced schooling to create a small educated elite, thus continuing the French policy of assimilation. French citizenship was given to any Malagasy who could speak French and fulfill certain other requirements; by 1939 some 8,000 Malagasy had achieved this status.

Galliéni had also instituted a *politique de race* to strengthen local political institutions and, more indirectly, the position of the *côtiers* against the Merina. Galliéni's successors, however, were not so concerned about ethnic balance. For instance, after the decline of the mission schools, they were contented to have most of the postprimary schools centered around Antananarivo, a policy benefiting the Merina more than other ethnic groups more distant from the capital. Also, their greater wealth enabled the Merina elite to send their children to France for further education. The net result was a Merina domination of civil service posts at independence.

In 1925 the colonial government instituted a labor law with detailed wage and hour regulations, which helped settlers obtain a pool of low-wage workers. In the next year the colonial administrators also reorganized their system of "persuading" men to work on public works projects by establishing a civilian labor army of young conscripts of military age (SMOTIG: Service de la main d'oeuvre pour les travaux d'intérêt général), which lasted in one form or another until the end of World War II. Although SMOTIG never comprised more than 10,000 Malagasy men before World War II, it became symbolic of colonial oppression, as had the *thangata* in Malaŵi.

The colonial government began economic planning efforts in Madagascar shortly after the end of World War I, but these early efforts were tentative. In its first half-century of rule, excluding the period of Galliéni, the French government invested relatively little in Madagascar in comparison with some other African colonies such as the Maghreb.[10] Such public investments in Madagascar were still considerably more than British governmental investment in Malaŵi. Although

French private capital apparently did invest proportionately more in Madagascar than in other colonies in Black Africa, this investment was also much less than in Indochina or the Maghreb (Thompson and Adloff 1965, p. 306).

After World War II the colonial government stepped up its efforts at economic planning. In 1947 Maurice Rotival, a Franco-American visionary, worked out a rather unrealistic ten-year plan. Several five-year plans followed, and these focused primarily on public investment in economic infrastructure.[11] Although the French government financed a considerable share of these public investments, the share of total gross fixed capital investment in Madagascar's GDP was relatively low—an average of about 14 percent (chapter 10). Moreover, this investment did not quickly increase production, because the incremental capital-output ratio was high. A large share of the public funds were used for highly capital-intensive transportation investments or for repairing the damage arising from the insurrection of 1947 and its savage repression, events that cost the island from 2.5 to 5 percent of its population and apparently a considerable amount of its capital stock as well.[12]

During the 1950s the behavior of the macroeconomic aggregates was unclear to contemporaries. Subsequent estimates revealed that from 1950 through 1960, GDP was growing at an average annual rate of 2.4 percent a year, while per capita growth was only 0.7 percent a year (or less—population estimates for the early 1950s are rather uncertain). Thus the newly independent nation, in contrast to Malaŵi, did not start with a particularly strong momentum of economic growth.

At independence in 1960 Madagascar had a somewhat higher per capita GDP and degree of urbanization than Malaŵi; however, the economy still was at a very low level of economic and technological development. It did have a small manufacturing sector, which employed about 9 percent of the work force in the modern sector (or about 0.7 percent of the total labor force), but the country obtained foreign exchange primarily by exporting a diverse array of agricultural products and several mining products. The transportation infrastructure was still rudimentary. The island, which was 1,580 kilometers long, had only 1,290 kilometers (801 miles) of paved roads and 815 kilometers (506 miles) of railroads in two unconnected systems (see figure 1-1).

The Land Question

The "land question" was as inflammatory an issue in Madagascar as in Nyasaland; however, it was handled in a somewhat more orderly fashion, primarily because private land companies did not reach the country before the colonial government. Although some French companies had obtained large land concessions before the formation of the colony, this land was not developed until afterwards. The system of land administration, which was put into place in the 1890s, was modeled after the Torrens Land Law in Australia and defined three land tenure systems: traditional land holdings, where land was allotted according to the customs of the particular area (which varied considerably from place to place); the land registered in the land cadasters, which were introduced around certain population centers and which were open to both Malagasy and foreigners; and the land concessions made to French companies or individuals.

At the time of independence European colonists farmed roughly 6 percent of all land under cultivation. This land represented only a small fraction of the land they owned; the remainder was used for grazing, was not arable, or was arable but left idle (see Appendix, section H). The foreign holdings were spread over the entire island and produced a great variety of agricultural crops, unlike the British estates in Malaŵi, which at independence were confined primarily to the Shire highlands and produced only a few types of plantation crops. Two-thirds or more of Madagascar's planted areas of such important export crops as tobacco, cotton, sugar cane, cacao, and sisal came from the "grand concessions" owned either by French or Malagasy, which were located in the coastal areas.

Land leasing (in contrast to ownership) by Europeans was much less important than in Malaŵi. Furthermore, the foreign farms in Madagascar were much smaller on the average than the British estates in Malaŵi. Land renting to smallholders, however, was considerably more prevalent, although in the early 1960s less than 10 percent of all farmland was leased out, primarily by Malagasy landlords.[13]

Although the overwhelming majority of the rural population in both countries held its land according to traditional rules of tenure, registered land ownership was greater among the Malagasy (many of whom appeared to be members of the former Merina elite) than among the indigenous population of Malaŵi. Thus Madagascar began independence with a small but important indigenous landlord class, which Malaŵi had lacked.

The Struggle for Independence

Unlike Malaŵi, Madagascar had a previous national identity when it became a colony and thus had a greater sense of nationalism. The "pacification" of Madagascar was much more difficult than in Malaŵi, and its insurrection of 1904 and 1905 was much more widespread and violent than the 1915 Chilembwe uprising in Malaŵi. The organizational network against the French also seemed more extensive. In 1913, for example, a secret nationalist organization, the vvs, was founded; the arrest in 1915 of some 300 to 500 intellectuals suspected of belonging to the organization and the sentencing of the alleged leaders for an imaginary plot has had a very strong symbolic significance for the Malagasy people.[14] Nationalist feelings subsequently bubbled to the surface on various occasions, for instance, during the riots in Antananarivo in 1929. The culmination of these nationalist sentiments was the extremely sanguineous 1947 insurrection, a cataclysmic event with no parallel in Malaŵi.[15]

Malagasy hopes of self-rule began to rise during World War II, especially after the Gaullists issued the Brazzaville Declaration of 1944, which established the principles of colonial representatives sitting in the French parliament and of local representative assemblies. The Constituent Assembly of the Fourth French Republic in 1945–46, attended by official Malagasy representatives, did not offer the Malagasy national self-determination but merely full French citizenship and a set of provincial assemblies. After the failure of the 1947 insurrection, domestic political agitation in Madagascar was dormant for almost a decade.[16]

In the mid-1950s the initiative for independence came from the French and was not triggered by any type of political agitation such as that occurring in Malaŵi. Therefore no single leader could gain the prestige that Banda had earned for leading the Malaŵi people to independence. The independence process in Madagascar began in 1956, when Guy Mollet's socialist government in France promulgated the *loi cadre* (enabling act) granting France's overseas territories considerable internal autonomy, as well as universal suffrage and a single electoral roll (thereby abolishing a special European roll).

Thereafter, domestic Malagasy politics began to ferment. Madagascar had a certain tradition of party politics, and a number of the political groups that became parties after the *loi cadre* had homologues among various political parties in France, which offered them advice and financial assistance (see Chaigneau 1985, p. 28; Spacensky 1970; and Thompson and Adloff 1965). At one point Madagascar had thirty-five political parties, and the multiparty system became an integral part of Malagasy political life. Indeed, such a system was later enshrined in the first constitution, and political pluralism appeared to have a bright future.

In 1958 President Charles de Gaulle offered a referendum to the peoples of the African colonies: either full independence from France or restored nationhood with links to France maintained within the French Community. In Madagascar the latter option received 77 percent of the votes, and events moved swiftly as France granted full sovereignty to members of the Community.

On June 26, 1960, Madagascar became fully independent. Philibert Tsiranana, the founder (in 1957) and leader of the Parti Social Démocrate, was the nation's first president. His government was to last twelve years, during which time the French presence remained strong. A former French civil servant in Madagascar bluntly stated, "The French continued to take the initiative and to assure the functioning of the administrative machine until 1963–64. Afterwards they were reduced to the role of advisors. . . . The French [had the public image] of being everywhere and of continuing to direct the country" (Deleris 1987). He might have added that the French maintained a considerable military presence on the island as well. Following the fall of Tsiranana, French influence fell dramatically as the succeeding Malagasy governments moved to the left and either renegotiated or renounced many of the agreements so carefully worked out in the late 1950s and early 1960s to maintain France's position.

Important Economic Institutions

The Merina government was quite centralized, as was the succeeding colonial government. The French generally held the top positions in the colonial government, but a cadre of Malagasy civil servants with considerable experience was in place at lower levels. Many civil servants, including the first president of the new nation, had been trained in the school of public administration that Galliéni had established. The colonial government had also adopted many of the cumbersome French governmental structures, including a number of dirigistic devices for influencing the economy. Unlike Malaŵi, however, Madagascar did not have any state marketing board for agricultural exports.

Most of the modern sector, which embraced foreign and domestic trade as well as manufacturing, utilities, and transportation, was in foreign hands. The most important such firms were two major French merchant houses, the Compagnie Lyonnaise (founded 1897) and the Compagnie Marseillaise (founded 1898), and two lesser French companies, the Société Rochefortaise and the Société de l'Emyrne (founded in 1911).[17] The data on 415 of the largest commercial establishments in 1968–69 reveal an interesting picture (Madagascar. INSRE, n.d.[e]). In wholesaling, importing, and manufacturing, French-owned firms accounted for 70 to 75 percent of total business, while another 8 percent (importing) to 23 percent (wholesaling) was accounted for by Malagasy of Asian descent. In wholesaling and importing, firms of native Malagasy accounted for 2.3 and 1.5 percent, respectively; in manufacturing, they accounted for about 14 percent.[18] Clearly colonialism and capitalism were strongly linked, but what is surprising is that the share of Malagasy firms was so high. A nascent Malagasy commercial and manufacturing class was developing, in contrast to Malaŵi, where Africans had practically no ownership participation in the modern sector.

Because Madagascar belonged to the Franc Zone, it had no independent central bank. This function was handled by a department of the French central bank, which limited the amount the new Malagasy government could borrow. The French guaranteed the convertibility of the currency (the CFA franc) with the French franc. Foreign interests owned all of the island's commercial banks.

Despite considerable commercial activity, markets were far from free. Galliéni had introduced a set of foreign trade regulations favoring trade with France, and these persisted in various forms throughout the colonial period. In 1936 the colonial government also introduced a system of controls of industrial and wholesale prices, which remained intact over the next half-century, although it was modified many times over the years (de Bandt and others 1984). During World War II a rice marketing office also forced peasants to sell quotas of rice at low prices, but this office was deeply resented and was abolished after the war. In general, however, land and labor markets in rural areas were stunted.

In the years following World War II the colonial government introduced the French minimum wage system (SMIG: Salaire minimum interprofessionnel garanti), which featured a complicated set of wage grades; it has been maintained ever since. Although labor guilds existed during the Merina empire, the formation of modern labor unions did not begin until 1937, when a French labor law was extended to Madagascar. By 1952 branches of the important French labor unions were battling for dominance in Madagascar. Although these Malagasy unions broke their formal ties with their French counterpart unions in 1957, they did maintain their ties to various political parties within Madagascar, as do French unions in France. By 1960 three labor confederations had enrolled more than half of the labor force suitable for unionization.[19] Although these unions appeared to be much more important than those in Malaŵi, they never became an important political or economic force in Madagascar's postindependence period because they were dominated by the political parties or by political and economic events beyond their control. Employers also formed a number of syndicates, which gained more than 1,200 members, but these had a limited economic role.

Roughly half of the appropriate age groups were attending primary school in 1960, and 26,700 children—about 4 percent of the relevant age group—were in secondary school (Pryor 1988a, section J). The University of Madagascar was established in the mid-1950s, in cooperation with a number of French universities; by 1960 723 students had enrolled, a number that would increase fiftyfold in the next quarter-century (Madagascar, Ministère de l'enseignement superior, 1985). In addition, a number of Malagasy had received or were receiving a university education in France. The country also had its own medical school and a network of hospitals, staffed by Malagasy personnel trained either at home or abroad.

In contrast to Malaŵi, Madagascar at independence was a country with a set of modern political and economic institutions and with sufficient educated elite to be able to chart its own future.

The Ideological Climate

Nationalism has a much different meaning in Madagascar than in Malaŵi. Furthermore, views toward capitalism and socialism, as well as urban versus rural development, were also quite different in the two countries.

Nationalism

Nationalism in Madagascar had deep historical roots and in many respects was clearly a stronger force than in Malaŵi. France also played a much more intrusive role in Madagascar, both before and after independence, than the British did in Malaŵi, and nationalist feelings against the colonial power were also stronger.

Nationalism in Madagascar took on the form of increasing demands for economic independence from France. This meant agitation for rapid indigenization of the government and for reduction in French control over the nation's economy. Such nationalism also harbored a deep suspicion of foreign trade, because this sector seemed to represent the main channel of foreign dominance, and in contrast to Malaŵi few Malagasy intellectuals viewed exports as a leading sector for development. The growing cadre of educated elite in the country felt frustrated by French tutelage and by French occupation of leading positions they thought they could—and should—fill.

The nationalist movement was to culminate in the steps the governments of Gabriel Ramanantsoa (1972 to 1975) and Didier Ratsiraka (from 1975 onward) took to resign from the French-sponsored regional organization, OCAM (Organization commune africaine et malgache), and from the Franc Zone; to establish a national currency; to force the removal of French soldiers from Malagasy soil; and to expropriate a considerable share of French commercial, banking, business, and agricultural interests. The economic policies of the Malagasy governments from 1972 through the mid-1980s paid relatively little attention to foreign trade, and the ratio of trade to GDP fell during the late 1970s and early 1980s.

Economic Philosophies

Because colonialism was associated with capitalism, these former colonies might be expected to have a certain distrust of the market and their leaders to advocate some type of socialism. In Madagascar, however, these ideological currents were not so simple.

At independence, almost all of Madagascar's educated elite had studied in France, where ideas about socialism and Marxism were much more prevalent than in English and American universities. Philibert Tsiranana's Parti Sociale Democrate had strong ties with Guy Mollet's SFIO party (Section francaise de l'internationale ouvriere) in France.

According to an analysis by Pascal Chaigneau (1985, p. 24), Tsiranana's Malagasy socialism was "a pragmatic philosophy scarcely encumbered by ideological nuances." Tsiranana appeared to have mixed opinions about the previous dirigism of the economy, employing many of the ideological phrases and ideas of the SFIO but, at the same time, pointing to the advantages of a private sector unfettered by government bureaucrats. The following statements illustrate his approach to the traditional socialist program of nationalization:

> Our socialism is restrained and is adapted to our country. The world of business fears nationalizations and if it learns that one has nationalized a hotel, a factory, no more investment capital will come. (cited by Chaigneau 1985, p. 24)

> For us, "nationalize" means to create enterprises where private initiative does not operate ... As for placing our hands on that which has been created by the private sector and which is flourishing, we will not do it for we do not want to commit a theft. (cited by du Bois de Gaudusson 1979)

Alain Spacensky (1970, p. 302) examined some of the government's attempts at land reform and concluded, "The socialism of the P.S.D., in fact, was essentially rural." Tsiranana also inveighed against "communist subversion," maintained no diplomatic relations with Eastern Europe, and attempted to maintain firm bonds of friendship with France. He was a confirmed pluralist, and although his party dominated politics for a decade, he took no steps toward establishing a one-party state.

Three years after the fall of Tsiranana, Commodore (*capitaine de fregate*) Didier Ratsiraka became President. His ideological views were rather different from those of Tsiranana:

> We are not exactly Marxist-Leninists, but we take from Marxism-Leninism the thinking behind our economic projects and all our philosophy, and we try to adapt it to Malagasy realities. (du Bois de Gaudusson 1985, citing *Afrique Asia*, December 1977, p. 32)

> Socialism in Madagascar is not in contradiction with the Bible. I am a convinced and unshakable socialist. I accept Marxism in its economic approach because Marx was a man who fought for freedom. But I also believe firmly in God and my faith is unshakable. (cited by Mara 1986, p. 16)

It is only when the individual peasant economy will be transformed by the socialist revolution in the countryside that one will be able completely to liberate the peasants from ignorance, sickness, and misery. (cited by Mara 1986, p. 31)

The constitution of the Second Republic of Madagascar (December 31, 1975) embodied these principles. It declared that public ownership of the principal means of production is the primary way to achieve economic progress, that work is a duty and an honor, and that each should give according to his ability and should be paid according to the quality and quantity of his work.

President Tsiranana's economic policies were perceived to have failed, and this discredited many economic policies believed to be "liberal." Marxism was part of the academic atmosphere in the training of the elite, who also stood to obtain desired positions of economic management if nationalization occurred. The military held political power after Tsiranana's downfall, which created incentives for a revolution from above (according to the same dynamic that occurred in Benin). Although none of these factors is sufficient in itself to turn the dominant ideology leftward, each increased the probability that such a change would occur. Thus the turn of events guided by Didier Ratsiraka in 1975 and the years following represents a logical evolution and not so great a discontinuity in Madagascar's political-economic development as some have argued.

Economic policy after the fall of Tsiranana also shifted toward urban development. In his first inauguration speech, Tsiranana spoke of himself as "the son of a peasant, an old cowherd" (Spacensky 1970, p. 40). This moving speech was more than political rhetoric. Although many of his economic development policies were similar to those the colonial government followed, he did reorient government investment and efforts to increase production much more toward agriculture than before. The Ratsiraka government and the young politicians of his group were much more inclined to support urban projects. The real price farmers received for agricultural goods declined, government investment turned away from agriculture and toward industry, and the share of current governmental expenditures going to the agricultural sector was reduced.

Chances for Success

In the first years after independence economic expectations for Madagascar were very high.[20] The country had an educated elite, it had a social infrastructure with many modern institutions, it had unused land that was believed to be fertile, and it had a dedicated group of French technicians and Malagasy civil servants to aid the process of economic development. Optimism reigned. Foreign and domestic commentators seemed to overlook the fact that the level of per capita production had been increasing only very slowly during the last decade before independence, that the investment rate was very low, and that the economy still consisted mostly of a rural sector with very low productivity.

In his twelve years in power Tsiranana managed to increase economic growth so that the GDP was growing at a moderate rate—roughly the same rate as in Malaŵi—but this growth fell far short of expectations. In the two years before he lost office, the island was hit by some short-term disasters—a cattle plague, a drought, and a very severe cyclone—and agricultural production, especially in the south, declined considerably. Tsiranana's economic policies were popularly believed to have failed, and this belief, combined with his illness, the split in the PSD, and the rioting that broke out in the south, contributed to his fall from office. Tsiranana's successors reversed many of his policies, and these changes led to a dramatic decline of per capita income; only in the mid-1980s did the government start to come to grips with economic realities.

In Malaŵi expectations were low, and the moderate economic successes of the government led to political stability and more economic successes. In Madagascar expectations were high, and the moderate economic successes of the government led to political instabilities, governmental changes, and the eventual deterioration of the economy. Such contrasting outcomes provide more evidence to support the adage that when humans speak of the future, the gods smile.

Notes

1. This discussion draws particularly upon Bastian (1967); Nelson (1973); and World Bank (June 1983), annex I. The comments on rainfall are drawn from annual data on rainfall for twenty-five years from seventy-one weather stations covering the entire country. For a special computer run to derive these unpublished data, I would like to thank the Service Météorologique. See also chapter 2, footnote 1.

2. In this discussion on ecological problems I draw especially upon Battistini and Richard-Vindard (1972), Jolly (1980), Razafimahefa (1986), and Dumont (1959, 1961).

3. This generalization is made on the basis of land productivity data drawn from Food and Agricultural Organization (annual).

4. The data on ethnic identification come from Jean Poirier et Jacques Dez (1963). Apparently a version of this essay by Poirier alone appeared in *Revue française d'études politiques africaines* 100 (April 1974). Murdock (1967) presents comparable social-structural data for the Merina, Tanala, Antandroy, and Sakalava. Although no extensive ethnographic survey of the island has been made in recent decades, several important intensive studies of particular

ethnic groups have been published, for instance, Althabe (1969), Bloch (1971), Kottak (1980), and Pavageau (1981).

5. Turcotte (1981) presents evidence that even in the two least similar dialects of the Malagasy language, more than 60 percent of the words are the same.

6. I received an interesting confirmation of the relative unimportance of ethnic identity. For Malaŵi, the data on the ethnic background of cabinet members were easy to collect, and few informants were required; for Madagascar, this task was much more difficult, and I needed to talk with a considerable number of people before the list was complete. In many cases, I received regional identifications, rather than the needed information: "I don't know his ethnic group, but he comes from the northwest." Traditional ethnic leaders (analogous to the chiefs in Malaŵi) seem to play a political role only at the local level.

7. The only scholarly work I have seen specifically devoted to the topic is Dez (1962). Although he presents a number of interesting examples of clashes between requirements for economic development and traditional values, they do not appear to be of sufficient seriousness to warrant alarm with regard to the problems I discuss. For instance, traditional values would suggest low price elasticities of supply of agricultural production. In the two statistical studies for Madagascar that I could locate (Ahlers and others 1984, annexe B; and Berthélemy and others 1988), the various supply elasticity estimates for paddy and coffee seem within the range of such elasticities for other countries as presented by Askari and Cummings (1976).

8. The first two references are to Etienne de Flacourt's *Histoire de la Grande Ile de Madagascar* and to Daniel Defoe's *Madagascar; or Robert Drury's Journal, During Fifteen Years Captivity on That Island*. The most remarkable works about Madagascar were thirty-eight folio volumes covering all aspects of the country, which were written by Alfred Grandidier and his son Guillaume in the late nineteenth and early twentieth centuries. For the historical description of Madagascar that follows, I have drawn heavily on Ralaimihoatra (1962), Heseltine (1971), and Thompson and Adloff (1965).

9. The first, second, and last citations of Galliéni come from Stratton (1964), pp. 144 and 220–21; the third citation comes from Heseltine (1971), p. 142. Galliéni's imaginative administrative methods were also illustrated at the beginning of World War I when he mobilized Paris taxis to take French troops to Battle of the Marne in the absence of other transportation. One of his aides in Madagascar was Louis Lyautey, later to become a famous field marshall, who said of Galliéni, "That man has a joy of living. Conqueror, explorer, a great warrior, he is the opposite of the military martinet. 'Good form,' reports, cliché's, even hierarchies do not exist for him. His results correspond to his aims; he uses means of infinite suppleness and many different instruments" (Ralaimihoatra, 1962, p. 211).

10. Pourcet (n.d.), especially pp. 161 ff., provides a useful analysis of French public investments in Africa. This study is the best single source on the early economic history of Madagascar.

11. Gendarme (1960) discusses these early planning efforts and dissects the Rotival plan in detail. He concludes (p. 140) that "The abundance of maps, drawings, histograms and the remarkable use of colors give this volume

a serious appearance. The author knew admirably how to utilize modern printing techniques, but this is the only scientific value of the work."

12. Responsible estimates of Malagasy deaths range from 100,000 to 200,000. The French Haut-commissaire, Pierre de Chevigneé, stated that "more than 100,000 died." Other estimates I have seen range from 11,200 to 300,000. Tronchon (1982) discusses in detail this problem of estimating the number of victims (pp. 71–72). His own astonishment that such deaths were not reflected in the administrative population censuses should not be taken seriously, because such population data were highly inaccurate. Tronchon also presents considerable anecdotal evidence of the destruction of property and the abandonment of farms by French colonists. Although the overall extent of this destruction and flight of human capital is unknown, it seems highly likely to have played a role in Madagascar's slow economic growth during the 1950s. I have been unable to find any reliable evidence either to support or to discredit this proposition.

13. Overall data on land renting come from Madagascar, Ministère des finances et de commerce and INSRE (1966), p. 66. Thompson and Adloff (1965), p. 32, present data showing that 80 percent of the 150,000 hectares of the rented land farmed by smallholders was owned by Malagasy—not French—landlords.

14. The initials stand for *Vy Vato Sakelika* (iron, stone, and shoots), to which various authors have given different symbolic significance. Ralaimihoatra (1962), pp. 250–60, provides a Malagasy perspective on the VVS.

15. Crucial facts about this political action, exactly how it started and why, are not known with precision. Opinions vary enormously, even about such simple matters as the relative roles of Merina and *côtiers*. The primary source is Tronchon (1982).

16. Thompson and Adloff (1965), Spacensky (1970), and Chaigneau (1985) provide an extensive analysis of political events from the end of World War II to independence.

17. Gendarme (1960), pp. 138–39, presents a diagram showing the various administrative links of three of these companies with their various interests.

18. I estimated the midpoint of the size groupings as the average turnover for each class in order to arrive at these estimates. The data on industrial establishments (manufacturing, mining, and utilities) come from INSRE, *Recensement industriel 1967*. In all of these censuses the nationality of the top manager is used as a proxy for ownership, an assumption that is not entirely accurate.

19. Thompson and Adloff (1965), pp. 457 and 463, give the number of union members as 72,000. The sectors most suitable for unionization were calculated by taking the total number of wage earners and subtracting domestic service, government workers, liberal professions, and trade and banking. Cadoux (1969), p. 67, estimates that union membership rose from 50,000 in 1961 to 100,000 by the end of the 1960s.

20. The Malagasy popular press reveals this optimism: economists, who should have known better, were similarly infected, however. The Société d'etude pour le développement économique et social (1971) forecast for the period from 1966 through 1985 an annual average growth of 4.40 percent for

real GDP, 2.25 percent for population, 4.90 percent for exports, and 1.73 percent for the real per capita standard of living. Other experts spoke authoritatively of Madagascar poised for the "takeoff" into self-sustaining growth. Madagascar was merely an extreme example of the economic optimism sweeping many African states, analyzed by Fieldhouse (1986), pp. 86–90. A fascinating document showing the dashed hopes resulting from such high expectations is Madagascar, Ministère d'etat, Chargé des finances (1971). In this volume numerous technocrats and intellectuals gave their views on economic problems and possible solutions for the future. Many of the utopian ideas of the French student uprising of 1968 found resonance in these speeches.

10 *Economic Growth in Madagascar*

This chapter analyzes the most important macroeconomic indicators and the growth strategy of Madagascar and yields four major conclusions. First, per capita GDP has declined over a period of three decades, with the major deterioration taking place after 1970. Second, the investment rate has been low, and the nation has not been able to mobilize internal resources for an extensive investment program. Third, the effectiveness of investment has been low, declining markedly after the mid-1970s. Fourth, the initial growth strategy focusing on agriculture seemed suited to the country's comparative advantage and factor endowments, and the government's shift in emphasis to investment in the urban sector and in capital-intensive heavy industries after 1975 was a key factor in the stagnation of production.

The Record of Economic Growth

From 1950 through 1986 Madagascar's GDP grew at an average annual rate of about 2.0 percent (Pryor 1988a, section E).[1] This rate was slightly below the annual average population increase of 2.2 percent, so per capita income declined about 0.2 percent a year. Madagascar's highest level of per capita GDP was achieved between 1969 and 1971; in the 1950–52 and the 1984–86 periods, per capita GDP was about 17 and 28 percent, respectively, below this high point.

Such calculations give rise to the same problems that bedevil the data of Malaŵi, in particular, in estimating production for home consumption in the smallholder sector. In the late 1970s and early 1980s the quality of the basic statistics also deteriorated, and some evidence indicates that the official data, on which the above estimates are based, may exaggerate the actual economic decline.[2]

Sectoral growth rates varied widely from 1950 through 1986 (Pryor 1988a, table E-2). Agriculture, forestry, and fishing (the primary sector) grew at an average rate of 1.3 percent. Manufacturing, mining, utilities, and construction (the secondary sector) increased the fastest

220 *Malaŵi and Madagascar*

with an average annual growth of 3.2 percent; however, most of the growth of this sector was in the first half of the period. Transportation and communication, trade, finance, and governmental and private services (the tertiary sector) grew at an average annual rate of 2.1 percent.

POPULATION. The rate of population growth has had an important influence on the level of per capita GDP. Between 1900 and 1950 Madagascar's population increased only about 1.4 percent a year.[3] The population began to increase at a faster rate after 1945, when the colonial government undertook a series of extensive public health measures to reduce the incidence of certain diseases such as malaria, which was a much greater problem in this nation than in Malaŵi. By the early 1980s the population of Madagascar was increasing about 3.0 percent a year, even though the infant mortality rate was rising.

The Malagasy government has not shown much official interest in limiting births. It has retained the 1920 French law prohibiting the distribution of birth control devices without a physician's prescription. The twenty-two-year plan of the Ratsiraka government was constructed on the explicit assumption that births would not be limited. In recent years, however, the government has allowed a planned parenthood group (Association pour la famille heureuse) to carry out a birth control campaign, but this program has reached only a minuscule part of the population. I was told by a Malagasy public health official that, as a result of ignorance about family planning, more than 10 percent of all recorded pregnancies end in self-induced abortions.

The alarm some demographers and other specialists raised when the nation's population passed 10 million in 1986 found little response in official quarters. Kornfeld (1986, p. iii) quotes President Ratsiraka expressing the government's ambivalence about a population policy:

> It is really necessary to double or triple the active population in order to satisfy the needs of development. We do not have a problem of overpopulation except in the provincial capitals such as Antananarivo, perhaps also Toamasina, because people have a tendency to go to the cities to settle. . . . I think that in Madagascar we should have a population of 10 million, but as that will come quite quickly, it would perhaps be necessary, after the year 2000, to control births. Perhaps we ought to begin before the year 2000 to plan births and to plan education of these children. I am against abortion but favor population control methods such as family planning. It is better to encourage the population to control its growth than [to have the situation] in India where there is too great a population.

If the rate of population increase in the decade preceding this statement continued to the year 2000, Madagascar's population would be almost half again as large as the 10 million limit the president mentioned.

Periodization

Madagascar has experienced several important changes in government in the last two decades and, in contrast to Malaŵi, the most appropriate economic periodization parallels these political changes. Figure 10-1 presents GDP and export series for the entire period, but the series are so irregular that a statistical analysis is more revealing.

THE PREINDEPENDENCE ERA. During the last decade of the colonial period (1950–60) Madagascar's GDP grew at an average annual rate of 2.4 percent. The actual population growth rate for this early period is somewhat uncertain, but it appears relatively slow—about 1.7 percent a year—as the effects of the new public health problems were just beginning to have an impact. The average annual per capita GDP growth rate of 0.8 percent (or less, if population growth is underestimated) during this decade was below the growth rate in the first part of this period. Exports were growing about 1.8 percent a year, while the terms of trade were declining.

THE TSIRANANA ERA. The second period spans the government of Philibert Tsiranana, from independence in 1960 to its downfall in 1972. The average annual GDP growth rate rose to 3.1 percent. The population growth rate also increased, however, so per capita GDP rose only 0.9 percent a year, roughly the same rate as during the colonial period and not much different from Malaŵi's growth rate during the 1960s. A greater share of the growth came in the first years of Tsiranana's government, giving the appearance of a loss of momentum in the final years of his rule. As a share of GDP, investment (in fixed prices) declined during the Tsiranana era, but the effectiveness of such investment was greater than in the colonial period. Exports stepped up considerably, increasing at an average annual rate of 4.5 percent, while the terms of trade leveled off.

Tsiranana's government fell in 1972, in part because of a number of short run economic problems such as a drought and famine in the agricultural districts in the south, a cattle plague, and some very severe cyclones that caused considerable property damage. The 1971 revolts in the southwest in the regions around Toliary (Tuléar) and Betroka were suppressed at the cost of considerable bloodshed, and this military action left a residue of ill will. Few data on regional economic conditions are available to investigate the economic background of these difficulties more thoroughly. Important political unrest also occurred in the capital, brought about by the illness of the president; the weakness in the ruling party and its internal power struggles; and an unaccustomed rise in retail prices in the previous few years, combined with a freeze in public-sector salaries. A final blow to the government

Figure 10-1. Indicators of Economic Growth in Madagascar

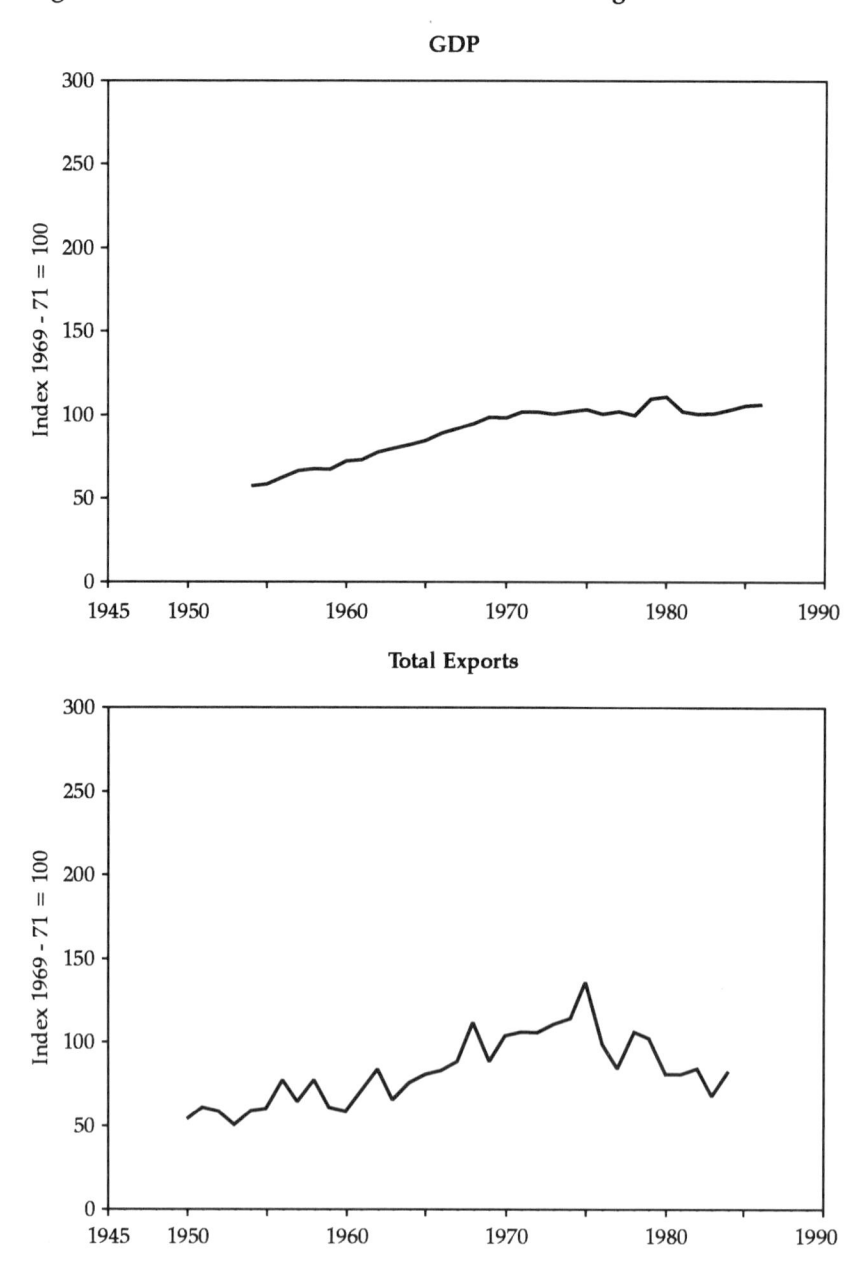

GDP

Total Exports

Source: Pryor 1988a.

came as a student strike, occasioned in part by growing unemployment of university graduates, brought about severe reprisals and still larger demonstrations against the government by a broader coalition of people.

THE RAMANANTSOA AND RATSIRAKA ERA. The third period began in 1972 with the three-year government of General Gabriel Ramanantsoa. He undertook a number of important changes in economic policy aimed at ameliorating the most current economic problems, undoing the alleged mistakes of the previous government, and reducing the economic influence of the French. The subsequent government of Didier Ratsiraka (1975 to the present) intensified these changes.

The country's economic performance during this period did not measure up to that of the two previous periods. Per capita GDP declined at an average annual rate of 2.4 percent a year from 1972 through 1986, accompanied by a fall in consumption and by a rise in infant mortality and other poverty indicators. In the early and mid-1980s domestic order also began to break down. In the countryside, praedial larceny (crop stealing) and other crimes rose sharply; the crime rate also appeared to increase in the urban areas, encouraged in part by a nearly year-long police strike in the capital and its aftereffects.

Three major sets of economic policy changes undertaken during the Ramanantsoa government contributed to these economic difficulties:

- In 1972 the government abolished the poll and cattle taxes in the rural sector, a monetary tax originally imposed by Joseph Galliéni early in the colonial era to "educate" the Malagasy to market either their goods or their labor. In 1962 these taxes amounted, on the average, to about 6.2 percent of total rural incomes or 13.3 percent of their total monetary incomes (Francois and others 1967, p. 41).[4]

  Abolishing this tax led both to financial difficulties for the government and to a decline of agricultural production. The causal mechanism underlying the production fall is straightforward. A certain amount of agricultural production was marketed to pay taxes, so farmers responded to the removal of such taxes by increasing their leisure and producing less for the market.[5] In economic jargon, the removal of the tax was a pure "income effect" and, other things being equal, would result in a reduction of work (that is, production). Although the government appeared to be aware of the problem and raised prices paid to agricultural producers at the same time, such a price increase (in real terms) lasted only for a few years and did not provide a long-term offset to the income effect.

- In 1973 Madagascar left the Franc Zone. France no longer guaranteed the convertibility of the Malagasy currency, and dividends from foreign investments in Madagascar were no longer freely transferable abroad. After Didier Ratsiraka became president in 1975, the government reduced the French role in the economy even more by taking over French companies.[6] His government quickly nationalized the banks, the insurance companies, and the movie theaters; it also confiscated several of the large French trading companies, which controlled a large share of the commerce and manufacturing on the island; and it obtained majority ownership in an important maritime shipping company, an oil refinery, and other enterprises. In the following two years, additional nationalizations occurred, and by 1978 an overwhelming share of the manufacturing sector was state owned (table 1-2).

These measures to achieve economic independence from France had several highly adverse economic effects. Most obviously, they discouraged direct foreign investment in Madagascar not only by the loss of currency convertibility but also because a new investment code limited foreign participation in particular sectors of the economy so that overall investment declined. The exodus from the Franc Zone also led to some short-term balance of payments difficulties, which were exacerbated by increasing the rigor of the foreign exchange rationing system rather than devaluing the currency to raise agricultural prices and encourage production. This approach, which lasted throughout the 1970s, led to greater difficulties in obtaining agricultural inputs (as well as consumer goods for the farmers), and this in turn induced a decline in agricultural exports and an even greater shortage of foreign exchange.

• In the mid 1970s the government set up nationalized enterprises *(sociétés d'intérêt national)* to purchase crops, to displace the private rural traders and French commercial enterprises, and to carry out certain foreign trade functions. This system did not function very smoothly and brought about a literal "disintegration" of agricultural markets (chapter 12). Farmers experienced severe difficulties in selling their crops, in purchasing agricultural inputs, and in buying consumer goods. Thus they had less ability and also little incentive to produce for the market.

As a result of these policy measures, total and marketed agricultural production declined. The lack of productive inputs also led to a decline in manufacturing production, which increased the need to import manufactured consumer goods and added to demand for foreign exchange. Thus a downward spiral began. From 1972 through 1984 the volume of total exports decreased at an average annual rate of 3.8 percent a year.

In 1978 the government announced an invest-to-the-hilt policy, which caused investment almost to double and triggered still more economic difficulties. This program, financed by relatively short-term government borrowing abroad, quintupled Madagascar's foreign debt in three years. Most of the large projects in this program were ill-chosen and had little impact on production. Combined with a fall in exports, a massive default on these foreign loans was inevitable. In 1979, with the second oil shock, the foreign exchange problem worsened, but the overall terms of trade did not greatly change, because prices of certain Malagasy exports rose. Madagascar suffered much greater economic dislocations in the late 1970s as a result of its internal economic policies than occurred in Malaŵi as a result of the external shocks; as a consequence, Madagascar's per capita GDP declined more than Malaŵi's in the first half of the 1980s.

Under the prodding of international lending agencies, which stepped in to help in the early 1980s, the government undertook a number of important recovery measures, including a series of devaluations starting in 1980 that culminated in a 50 percent devaluation in June 1987. In the mid-1980s the government also undertook to dismantle domestic price controls, gradually eliminate the rationing of foreign exchange and return to market allocation of foreign exchange, reduce production bottlenecks with targeted investments (for example, the improvement of roads to get agricultural produce to market), liberalize the rice market, increase agricultural prices to encourage production and exports, restructure a number of public enterprises, and reform the banking sector.

These reforms produced some successes. For instance, the government deficit fell, the deficit on current account declined, and agricultural production increased considerably in the 1986–87 harvest. The implementation of many of these reforms did not proceed unimpeded, however; for instance, in the mid-1980s local governments subverted some of the central government's important agricultural measures.

A FOURTH ERA? When fully implemented these reform measures may lead to a fourth economic period, which will be an upswing. At the time this manuscript was closed, however, it was too early to judge the success of these liberalization measures.

The Crucial Role of Investment

Madagascar has not been very successful in mobilizing either internal or external resources for investment. As a result, its domestic savings and investment rates have been relatively low. Further, such investable funds have not been used effectively.

Table 10-1. Investment and Savings Ratios, Madagascar, 1950 to 1986
(percent)

Year	Gross investment/GDP	Gross national saving/GDP	Gross national saving/gross investment	Government budgetary investment/ to gross investment
1950	18.0	n.a.	n.a.	n.a.
1951	19.2	n.a.	n.a.	n.a.
1952	20.5	n.a.	n.a.	n.a.
1953	16.5	n.a.	n.a.	n.a.
1954	13.8	n.a.	n.a.	n.a.
1955	14.7	n.a.	n.a.	n.a.
1956	9.5	n.a.	n.a.	n.a.
1957	11.8	n.a.	n.a.	n.a.
1958	9.5	n.a.	n.a.	n.a.
1959	10.2	n.a.	n.a.	n.a.
Unweighted average	14.4	n.a.	n.a.	n.a.
1960	11.0	n.a.	n.a.	n.a.
1961	9.5	n.a.	n.a.	n.a.
1962	7.9	-5.8	-72.6	n.a.
1963	10.6	-3.4	-31.7	n.a.
1964	11.1	-3.0	-27.0	n.a.
1965	10.2	-1.2	-11.8	n.a.
1966	13.4	1.9	14.3	n.a.
1967	14.6	5.3	36.7	n.a.
1968	16.2	7.2	44.1	n.a.
1969	16.9	7.9	46.8	n.a.
Unweighted average	12.1	1.1	-0.2	n.a.
1970	15.6	9.9	63.2	n.a.
1971	17.6	9.3	53.0	n.a.
1972	13.6	6.9	50.9	n.a.
1973	14.0	8.5	61.0	n.a.
1974	13.6	11.3	83.1	n.a.
1975	12.8	8.0	62.6	44.5
1976	12.8	8.6	67.5	57.7
1977	12.9	8.5	66.3	55.4
1978	14.5	8.2	56.5	59.2
1979	25.3	10.6	41.6	51.6
Unweighted average	15.3	9.0	60.6	53.7

(continued)

Table 10-1. Investment and Savings Ratios, Madagascar, 1950 to 1986 *(continued)*

(percent)

Year	Gross investment/GDP	Gross national saving/GDP	Gross national saving/gross investment	Government budgetary investment/ to gross investment
1980	23.5	8.3	35.1	65.6
1981	18.1	5.3	29.2	57.8
1982	13.4	3.3	24.7	55.5
1983	13.2	9.9	74.9	36.8
1984	13.6	9.3	68.1	46.4
1985	14.0	n.a.	n.a.	n.a.
1986	13.8	n.a.	n.a.	n.a.
Unweighted average	15.7	7.2	46.4	52.4
Overall unweighted average	14.3	5.9	36.4	53.1

n.a. = Not available.

Note: Ratios are based on current price data.

Source: Data for the first three columns come from Pryor (1988a), tables E-1b and L-4; data for the last column are from Madagascar, Ministère des travaux publics (1985), p. I-49. The latter source does not specify whether investment of local governments and parastatals is included.

The Volume and Financing of Investment

The data in table 10-1 show that from 1962 through 1984, investment averaged about 14.6 percent of market price GDP. This is almost 10 percentage points lower than the investment-GDP ratio in Malaŵi.[7] Other things being equal, this seems an important source of the differences in GDP growth rates in the two nations.

Gross domestic savings in Madagascar averaged about 5.9 percent of its GDP during the period from independence to the mid-1980s and financed about 36 percent of total investment. As in Malaŵi, roughly equal shares of externally financed investments were grants and loans; a somewhat higher share, however, came from private sources—chiefly from France.

During a good part of its postindependence period, Madagascar did not actively encourage foreign grants and loans, and foreign capital inflows had a much lower ratio to GDP than in Malaŵi. In the late 1970s the Malagasy government began to take greater interest in foreign borrowing, especially after a number of economists (particularly from the World Bank and the International Monetary Fund) emphasized repeatedly to the government that the investment rate was low and that Madagascar was favorably placed to borrow on the world market because its foreign debts were also quite low. This advice, plus the hope that the coffee boom benefiting Madagascar would persist, were important reasons for undertaking the disastrous invest-to-the-hilt campaign.

PUBLIC-SECTOR ROLE. For the period covered by the data in table 10-1, roughly 50 percent of total investment was carried out through the government budget, about the same proportion as in Malaŵi. If investment by Madagascar's parastatals (which became important after 1975) were included, the share of government in total investment would be much higher.

Of crucial importance is the degree to which the government acted as a net source of investable funds. Although the proper data to make such calculations are not available, I have found no indication in the economic literature suggesting that the government was a net saver. The Tsiranana government was unwilling or unable during the postindependence euphoria to raise taxes to finance more public investment, and the succeeding governments were not able to carry out those fiscal measures necessary for government to serve as an important source of net savings. Although we cannot be certain, the government appears to have used most of the foreign aid it has received in recent years for financing current rather than capital expenditures.

Scattered qualitative evidence suggests that up to 1972 the small parastatal sector did not require much subsidization. From 1975 through the mid-1980s the enlarged parastatal sector incurred substantial losses. The government nationalized a number of enterprises on the brink of bankruptcy in order to save jobs—the familiar process of "lemon socialism." Also, the government was loath to raise prices of parastatal-produced goods to avoid exacerbating the inflation; this policy, of course, brought further financial difficulties to the parastatals. Moreover, the new managements installed in the parastatals often lacked experience and made many mistakes. To cover their current expenses, the parastatals became major borrowers from the state banks in the late 1980s. In contrast with Malaŵi, the parastatal sector in Madagascar has been a sink for, not a source of, savings.

PRIVATE-SECTOR ROLE. Detailed data on private savings are not available for Madagascar. Real interest rates to savers, at least those offered by banks, have been negative (chapter 15). This suggests that the Malagasy population had few financial incentives to save. Further, the shift from labor to property income did not seem as important as in Malaŵi (chapter 16), so this structural change would not have led to an increase in private savings.

Investment risks in Madagascar also discouraged private savings. Certainly the nationalizations after 1975 had a negative impact on additional private investment and saving. Further, the rationing of foreign exchange, lasting from 1973 through the mid 1980s, increased the risk associated with any project dependent upon foreign imports, because these inputs might not be available when needed. More than two-fifths of capacity in manufacturing was idle in the early 1980s (chapter 14), in great part for lack of inputs. The cumbersome governmental price controls on domestically produced goods (chapter 14) also increased the possibilities of financial losses in a period when the prices of imported inputs were rising.

Investment Effectiveness

In Madagascar from 1950 through 1986 the incremental capital-output ratio (ICOR) was about 7.9, in contrast to 4.1 in Malaŵi from 1954 through 1986.[8] This lower degree of investment effectiveness appears to have two explanations. First, after 1975 Madagascar chose a development strategy that was not appropriate to its comparative advantage, factor proportions, or administrative abilities of the government, a factor particularly evident in the invest-to-the-hilt campaign. Second, certain types of investment, particularly in roads, were much more capital intensive than those in Malaŵi, primarily because of Madagascar's more rugged topography.

The ICOR in Madagascar has varied considerably over time. From 1950 to 1960, during the colonial period, the ICOR was 8.0. From 1960 through 1972, during the Tsiranana government, it fell to 5.1; this reflected the Tsiranana government's reordering of investment priorities from the transportation sector toward sectors more directly related to production. From 1972 through 1986, during the Ramanantsoa and Ratsiraka governments, the ICOR reached the extraordinary level of about 55, which reflected the downward spiral of growth occasioned by the impact of foreign exchange, tax, price, and investment policies on agriculture; the failure of the invest-to-the-hilt program; and the wave of nationalizations with their resulting economic disorganization.

The Strategy of Economic Development

The colonial government of Madagascar promulgated a number of economic plans in the period following World War II, but a sectoral breakdown of actual investment flows under these plans is only available for the funds spent by FIDES (Fonds d'investissement pour le développement économique et social, the French foreign aid agency). These accounted for about three quarters of the total "extraordinary

230 Malawi and Madagascar

budget" during the 1950s and about one quarter of total known investments in Madagascar (Madagascar, Commissariat général au plan, 1961, pp. 251–56).

The data in table 10-2 show clearly that the colonial government placed its first priority on investment in transportation and commu-

Table 10-2. Madagascar's Development Priorities as Revealed by Investment Data
(percent)

Sector	1947–60, FIDES[a]	1964–1968[b] Planned Total nation	Planned State budget	Actual state budget	1975–84[c], Total public	1986–90 plan Total nation	1986–90 plan Government
Agriculture, forestry, fishing	28.7	23.4	29.9	35.1	21.4	32.2	38.7
Mining and manufacturing	0.2	13.6	2.1	3.0	4.0	17.3	15.2
Transportation and communication	54.5	34.6	41.8	34.9	31.3	20.7	25.1
Education and health	12.7	6.0	13.6	} 6.9	12.7	} 13.8	} 2.3
Housing	1.8	14.7	3.9		0.0		
General and administration	1.6	4.0	6.3	19.1	17.9	16.0	18.7
Utilities	0.5	3.6	2.4	n.a.	12.7	n.a.	n.a.
Total	100.0	100.0	100.0	100.0	100.0	100.0	100.0

n.a. = Not available.
Note: The data in the various columns are only very roughly comparable. The sectoring principles are somewhat different, and lack of sufficient details prevents making complete adjustments. Also, the type of included investment (for example, land purchase, inventories, buildings, equipment, human capital) is often not specified very clearly. Detail may not add to 100 percent because of rounding.

a. FIDES (Fonds d'investissement pour le développement économique et social) was the major channel of the French government's foreign aid.

b. Total national investment includes all public and private investment; the state budget includes only the central governmental budget and excludes the public and semipublic organs.

c. The degree to which "total public investment" includes local governments or public organs outside the state budget is unclear.

Source: The FIDES data come from Madagascar, Commissariat général au plan (1961), pp. 251–52, and are rearranged for greater comparability with the other data. The 1964–68 plan data come from Madagascar, Commissariat général au plan (1964), p. 33. The fulfillment data for the same plan come from Madagascar, Commissariat général au plan (1969), p. 11; these data are adjusted for comparability with the plan data. The 1975–84 data come from Madagascar, Ministère des travaux publics (1985), p. I-49. The 1986–90 plan data come from Madagascar Government, *Journal officiel de la République Démocratique de Madagascar,* no. 1775, July 26, 1986.

nications; such investment is generally capital intensive. Agriculture had the second priority, but the impact of this investment on the smallholder sector is unclear. Some agricultural investment funds were used to settle colonists from other French dependencies (for example, from Réunion), and a much larger share was used to finance various village development projects (chapter 11). Popular Malagasy belief suggests that a significant part of these investments aided the French-owned estates, but no serious quantitative evidence has yet been adduced to support this claim.

After independence the governments of Malaŵi and Madagascar had very different "styles" of planning, which had some impact on subsequent developments. Madagascar's middle- and long-range plans were generally worked out in much greater detail and were more specific in their designation of particular goals and projects than was Malaŵi's *DevPol I*. The Malagasy plans usually gave much less attention to the policy framework or to the general goals of policy with regard to such subsidiary questions as income distribution, the capital-labor ratio of new investments, the dangers of rapid urbanization, the problem of providing proper incentives for private enterprise, and the necessity for trade-offs among goals.

The planning efforts of the Malagasy government also showed much less awareness of the constraints on government administration and of the need to administer resources efficiently than did those of the Malaŵi government. This difference was apparent in the much higher goals of the Malagasy plans and in the Ratsiraka government's hope of dramatic institutional changes to achieve economic objectives.

These different planning styles had several sources. Madagascar's independence was accompanied by much greater optimism than was Malaŵi's. Furthermore, the Malaŵi government consciously used economic incentives to motivate people, while the Madagascar government has sometimes considered moral incentives and institutional change as interchangeable tools of administration. The two approaches reflected in good measure the contrasting planning styles of the British and French, as well as their different administrative traditions (chapter 17).

The Initial Approach

In 1962 the Tsiranana government produced a document detailing certain planning options, but it was neither as broadly focused as *DevPol I* nor did it consider in detail the types of economic policies necessary to implement the various proposed approaches.[9] The first five-year plan covered 1964 through 1968. It was a highly detailed, quantitative exercise, focusing primarily on a very specific set of projects rather than on the complementary economic policies concerning tariffs and taxation, credit, or education that must be considered at the same time.

232 Malaŵi and Madagascar

Analyzing this plan to determine the government's planning preferences is made especially difficult by the number of ad hoc plan adjustments that had to be made because performance fell so far behind the goals. Nevertheless, several aspects of Tsiranana's original five-year plan stand out clearly.

Investment share. The plan projected a rise in the share of investment in GDP of roughly 14 to 21 percent from 1960 to 1973. Given the other assumptions in the plan, supporting this investment increase would have required the share of taxes in the GDP to rise roughly four percentage points during that period. The plan discussed the fiscal implications of the investment program only in broad generalities, however, and did not squarely face the significant increase in taxes it implied.

Sectoral breakdown. The division of planned investment by the central government, as shown in table 10-2, was quite similar to that in Malaŵi's *DevPol I* and to the FIDES approach. Transportation and communications were still to receive the greatest share of investment, although their share was lower than before independence; this decline in share was picked up by increases in investment in manufacturing and services. Planned agricultural investment had about the same high share before and after independence. The planned share of agricultural investment to GDP was much lower in Madagascar than in Malaŵi because total investment was lower in Madagascar; moreover, much of the planned private investment in Malagasy agriculture did not materialize.[10] Nevertheless, in a rough way both nations originally had the same basic orientation in the years immediately following independence.

Trade. A preliminary plan document considered two possibilities for increasing Madagascar's "economic independence": export-led growth, and growth based on import substitution. The planners argued that export-led growth is not viable where the market for export goods is narrow and depends on a single major buyer, two conditions they believed to be characteristic of Madagascar. The published five-year plan adopted the import-substitution option, expecting total trade turnover to grow at about the same rate as overall production. This, of course, was much different than the Malaŵi plan.

Regional issues. The plan stressed the importance of looking at the development process from a regional perspective. The planners did not appear to follow their own advice, however. Except for the transportation part of the plan, they did not break down much new investment by region or analyze in detail the regional impacts of such expenditures.

Actual economic performance fell far short of the highly optimistic plan goals. The long-term plan projected average annual growth of aggregate production between 1960 and 1973 at 4.9 percent and an ICOR of 2.5.[11] In reality, production grew at about half the projected rate; total investment (in contrast to the investment from the budget) was about 60 percent of that planned, and the ICOR was roughly double the forecast. Such underfulfillment, of course, nullifies the whole coherence of the plan.

Transitional Plans: 1967–77

At the close of the 1964–68 plan, the Tsiranana government produced the *Programme des grandes opérations*, which focused attention on a small number of priority investment projects; in agriculture these included the large development authorities discussed in the next chapter. This was followed by a three-year plan for 1972 through 1974. In 1974 the successor government of General Ramanantsoa produced a four-year plan for 1974 through 1977. These last two plans had little influence on the economy. The three-year plan suffered from the decline in political effectiveness of the government in the years before Tsiranana fell; before the four-year plan could be implemented, Ramanantsoa was replaced as president. All of these transitional programs and plans gave even higher priority to the agricultural sector than had the 1964–68 plan. The 1972–74 plan discussed the need for agrarian reform, farmer training, and higher prices to the agricultural sector (U.N. Fund for Population Activities 1979). The 1974–77 plan expressed alarm about an allegedly widening income gap between rural and urban populations and reversed the customary investment priorities by allocating 41 percent of state investment to agriculture and only 39 percent to transportation and communications. The Ratsiraka government sharply reversed this policy emphasis, however.[12]

The Ratsiraka Government: 1975 through 1985

In 1977, after two years in office, the Ratsiraka government produced both a three- year plan and also a statement (*Fundamental Options*, hereafter *FundOp*) outlining the framework of the nation's economic development up to the year 2000 (Madagascar, Direction générale du plan, 1977a). In contrast with the previous governments, the Ratsiraka government very clearly spelled out the policy guidelines underlying its plans. The *FundOp* was an enormously ambitious document and announced so many goals and guidelines that they often seemed conflicting (for example, it placed great emphasis on establishing both capital- and labor-intensive industries).

On the production side, *FundOp* declared the development of a heavy industrial base as the most important goal and foresaw the eventual development of forward linkages. The first stage, from 1978 through 1984, would feature construction of industries producing the basic primary products—energy, fertilizer, cement, and iron. At the same time, the level of consumption would remain relatively unchanged so the results of increased productivity could be reinvested. The second stage, from 1985 through 1992, would see the absorption of the unemployed and the underemployed into the labor force and an increase of per capita consumption. At the same time, metal and metalworking industries would be developed and light industry would diversify. The third stage, from 1993 to 2000, would bring full employment, a further increase in the level of per capita consumption, and the development of a broad and integrated industrial structure.

This vision was accompanied by ambitious quantitative goals. During the twenty-two-year period up to the year 2000, total GDP would grow at an average annual rate of roughly 6.1 percent.[13] Trade turnover would increase at a slightly slower annual rate (6.0 percent), with exports growing faster than imports so as finally to eliminate imbalances between exports and imports. Gross fixed capital investment would increase 9.3 percent a year, and ultimately the planned ICOR would be about 3.0.

The concrete manifestation of these ideas was the three-year plan for 1978 though 1980, which projected a 5.5 percent annual growth rate for real GDP.[14] This document had several curious features. The planned annual growth of foreign trade turnover was 6.3 percent, but ways to achieve this export growth or to resolve the balance of payments problems received very little discussion. The large investment program in the basic manufacturing industries was more prominent in the three-year plan than in *FundOp*, and furthermore it would be carried out in the enterprise sector rather than through the government budget. The primary sector was to grow at an annual average rate of 4.3 percent—faster than it had grown in years—but its planned share of investment through the government was actually smaller than that achieved during the 1964–68 period under Tsiranana. The invest-to-the-hilt campaign, promulgated about a year after the three-year plan was published, was not foreshadowed in the plan at all.

The mixed metaphor serving as a slogan of the plan—agriculture is the base, industry is the motor of economic development—was interpreted so as to neglect agriculture in favor of industry. The share of public investment in agriculture from 1975 through 1984 would be lower than at any time since independence (see table 10–2).

Both the three-year plan and *FundOp* placed considerable emphasis on the human side of economic development and on the institutional aspects of building socialism. The percentage that parastatals were to contribute to value added was roughly the same at the beginning and end of the plan period, which suggests that the major wave of nationalizations from 1975 through 1978 fulfilled most of the government's long-term nationalization goals. The share of value added by cooperatives and their members was to rise considerably, however; for instance, the share for crop raising was expected to increase from 10 percent in 1980 to 72 percent in 2000. Both plans spoke of the need for substantial improvement in levels of education, health care, and housing in general and in the real incomes of the poorest in the society in particular. Productivity would be enhanced, not by closer attention to economic incentives, but by education and a change in the attitudes and behavior of workers and managers, whose efforts would be channeled through a new type of participatory administrative system (see Ratsiraka 1975, and Madagascar Government 1980). In the countryside this change in "mentality" was to follow a strengthening of the role of the *fokonolona*, a traditional unit of local government; where *fokonolona* did not exist, they would be created. These village councils, in turn, would work to strengthen the agricultural cooperatives the government was to establish. In the urban sector the government set up thirteen "socialist enterprises" in 1979 (chapter 14); these were governed at various levels by councils comprising representatives of the state, workers, and management. This new management system was to be extended gradually to all state-owned enterprises.

The *FundOp*, the three-year plan, and the invest-to-the-hilt campaign were based on two critical assumptions: that Madagascar had sufficient managerial resources to translate the plans' macroeconomic goals into specific projects and to implement these projects in such a way as to realize the aggregate goals; and that the international economic environment would remain the same (with high coffee prices). Neither assumption proved valid. Furthermore, the government invested in a series of ill-conceived manufacturing projects, which took years to bring into production and which were not closely related to domestic conditions (chapter 14). For instance, the government built wheat and soya mills in the interior of the country, even though wheat and soya beans are not extensively grown on the island; also it chose projects with inappropriate technologies such as a $100 million urea fertilizer plant using an outmoded process with high-cost inputs.

The decline in exports, the ever-increasing external debt-service charges, and the long delays in completing planned investments led to a debt default. The goals of the invest-to-the-hilt program met with catastrophic results.

The Future

In the mid-1980s, under the prodding of international lending agencies, the Ratsiraka government announced a number of important liberalization measures. The president began to emphasize repeatedly the necessity of increasing agricultural production in order to eliminate food imports. He also announced an export-to-the-hilt campaign.

The five-year plan for 1986 through 1990 reflects this recent shift in development strategy. It also contains scathing criticism of the previous growth policies (Madagascar, *Journal officiel de la République Démocratique de Madagascar*, no. 1775, 1986). The overall goal for GDP growth is relatively modest, about 3.1 percent a year. The major plan goal is agricultural self-sufficiency and, as shown in table 10-2, investment priorities shift dramatically toward agriculture. Furthermore, rural investment will turn from the large state farms and toward the smallholders. For all sectors the plan stresses rehabilitation of existing investment rather than new investment.

Nevertheless, indications are that many Malagasy government officials do not take this new plan very seriously. The plan was not widely diffused to the population; it was not published in pamphlet form and remains accessible only in the official law journal. To implement the plan effectively would require considerable reorganization of the institutional apparatus for carrying out the new government policies. At the end of 1987 such a massive reorganization had not yet occurred (the neglect of administrative constraints has been a leitmotif in Malagasy planning). Scattered evidence suggests that lower levels of the bureaucracy subverted a number of the plan's policy goals (for instance, informal foreign exchange allocation continued for some time). In several interviews, knowledgeable Malagasy not working for the government speculated that the primary purpose of the plan was to please the World Bank in order to obtain more loans.

The Origins of the Investment Strategy

As was the case in Malaŵi, the thrust of Madagascar's investment strategy seemed to originate with the political leader of the country.

Philibert Tsiranana received his higher education in the interwar period and during his presidency (1960–72) tried to maintain a close relationship with the French in order to obtain maximum aid in developing the country. He grew to maturity in a rural area, and his political base was strongest in the coastal agricultural areas. Thus his emphasis on agriculture as the leading sector, which intensified the French colonial government's focus on this sector, should come as no surprise.

Didier Ratsiraka's training and background are quite different from Tsiranana's.[15] Although born in a rural area, he grew up in cities and received most of his education after World War II, when industrialization was seen as the key for overcoming economic underdevelopment. He attended the elite Lycée Henri IV in Paris, focusing particular attention on mathematics; and he took his higher education at the Ecole navale at Brest and the Ecole supérieure de guerre navale. He certainly had little or no exposure to agriculture during his formative years. Ratsiraka served as a naval officer and later as a military attaché in Paris. From the Ramanantsoa administration he received a sudden promotion to Minister of Foreign Affairs. In this capacity he renegotiated the various treaties with France to reduce that nation's presence in Madagascar and established Malagasy diplomatic relations with a host of socialist countries the Tsiranana government had cold-shouldered.

After 1972 young planners and government officials in Madagascar began to replace the French expatriates. Like Ratsiraka, many had grown up in urban areas (particularly Antananarivo) and had received their higher education in France during the heady decades of the 1950s and 1960s. Thus the urban orientation of Ratsiraka's policies signaled a generational change in the Malagasy leadership, a change in ideology, and also a change in political dominance from the *côtiers* to the Merina (chapters 9 and 17). The Merina were also the major beneficiaries of the new urban orientation and emphasis on manufacturing, and they have been major supporters of Ratsiraka, at least until the early 1980s. He, in turn, drew much more extensively than Tsiranana upon Merina to serve in his cabinet.

Summary

In terms of its goals, the macroeconomic performance of the Malagasy economy has been disappointing. Per capita production, which had shown moderate improvement from 1960 through 1970, declined considerably thereafter as a result of a relatively low investment rate and a declining rate of investment effectiveness.

A major cause of the low investment rate has been insufficient domestic savings. The public sector has not served as an important source of net savings, and incentives for private saving have not been attractive. Explanations of the low rate of investment effectiveness are more complex. The choice of a development strategy based on capital-intensive, urban-oriented investments did not correspond to administrative capabilities or domestic factor proportions; the production disincentives for agriculture, a sector serving to absorb labor and to provide most exports, led to a decline in exports; and the poor selection of investment projects, particularly during the invest-to-the-hilt program, wasted investment resources. Although Madagascar did not suffer the external shocks that Malawi experienced, the foreign sector also contributed to slow growth and low investment effectiveness, but in good measure these adverse effects are attributable to domestic policy that embraced a cumbersome foreign exchange allocation system and an overvalued exchange rate.

Notes

1. See footnote 1, chapter 3, for method of calculating growth rates.

2. Two particular types of offsetting errors beset the calculation of GDP. First, Madagascar's administrative estimates of population show a population growth rate higher than mine for the 1950s. If my estimates of population growth are too low, then my estimated per capita GDP growth is overstated. Second, the GDP estimates for 1950 through 1970 are my own and are quite uncertain for the period from 1950 to 1960. Internal evidence suggests that I might have underestimated GDP growth in the last decade of colonial rule, that is, that my estimated per capita GDP growth rates are understated. After 1960 discrepancies between income and production data (discussed in Pryor 1988a, section I) suggest that the growth in agricultural production might also be understated. More specifically, some estimates of living standards in physical terms, such as those by Pourcet (1987) show that consumed calories per capita have increased (although consumption of some types of nutrients have declined) since the early post World War II years; these estimates rest on uncertain population estimates for 1950.

3. Early population data come from various administrative censuses and are reported by Rafrezy and Iarivony (1985), p. 20. They must be considered as reflecting only gross magnitudes. My own population estimates from 1950 to the present are given in Pryor (1988a), appendix B.

4. I have removed farming expenses from income before calculating the cited percentages. These poll taxes were said to be hated by all. Although I have no direct evidence on such attitudes, a literary reflection occurs in a short story by Herison Victor Andriamihafy (Club des amis de la S.T.A.R. 1971, pp. 7–25), which relates the adventures of a young fisherman who had not paid his poll tax and fled the implacable tax collector, just as Jean Valjean tried to escape Inspector Javert. The many parallels between Hugo's novel and Andriamihafy's short story do not appear accidental. Althabe (1969) provides some sociological glimpses into the collection of these taxes.

5. Kottak (1980), p. 163, emphasizes the importance of selling goods to pay taxes. Guy Pourcet, a long-time observer of Malagasy, has suggested to me that part of the decline in marketed agricultural production during this period resulted from social change within the villages. The notables, who dominated the village up to the early 1970s and who used their political power over the other villagers to obtain a certain amount of marketable agricultural surplus, were replaced when the Ramanantsoa government began to strengthen the traditional rural institutions. This meant that the original producer could consume more of the marketable surplus. I have been unable to obtain any information to test this intriguing hypothesis.

6. The Ramanantsoa government did not nationalize any important companies. Nevertheless, it did acquire ownership interests in all of the commercial banks and achieved majority ownership of Air Madagascar. Archer (1976), p. 84, discusses these policy steps.

7. A problem in comparing the investment-GDP ratios for Malaŵi and Madagascar arises because the GDP denominators have different price bases. Because import taxes on machinery are much higher in Madagascar than in

Malawi and because investment in Madagascar is reported in market prices, I have chosen to minimize the impact of such taxes by using GDP in market prices rather than in factor prices (as in Malawi). Using the same price base for the GDPs of the two countries would yield a more misleading comparison.

8. This incremental capital-output ratio is calculated by the method described in footnote 13, chapter 3. For Madagascar, the capital share is an estimate of the gross fixed capital investment rather than total investment.

9. The key documents are Madagascar, Commissariat général au plan (1962), which lays out certain important options; and Madagascar, Commissariat général au plan (1964).

10. Comparing these data on planned government investment with Malawi's development expenditures, shown in table 3-3, Madagascar appears to have placed somewhat more relative emphasis (both in its plan and in the actual implementation of the plan) on agriculture. These two sets of data are not completely comparable, however, because of differences in sectoring principles. For instance, for Malawi much of the investment in rural roads is classified in "transportation"; for Madagascar some of this investment may be in "agriculture."

11. The plan only presents "production intérieure brute," which omits certain kinds of services. I assumed that the entire GDP would grow at the same rate and compared planned investment to overall growth to arrive at this estimate of the ICOR.

12. Although the changes in the sectoral mix of government investment proposed by the Ramanantsoa government represented a continuation of ideas current during the last years of the Tsiranana government, preliminary steps taken under Ramanantsoa culminated in the Ratsiraka government's widescale changes in the institutional framework. For the rural sector the 1974–77 plan stressed the importance of strengthening the *fokonolona* as a means of increasing agricultural production. The government also declared certain other sectors, such as banking, insurance, energy, mining, transport, and foreign trade, as "commanding heights" *(secteurs clefs)*, in which the state would eventually become the "sole master." In addition, the government in 1973 promulgated a new investment code reserving certain areas of investment exclusively for the state and setting up new criteria for tax concessions for foreign investment; these criteria included employment creation, location in less developed regions, and a net gain for Madagascar in foreign currency. This code also did not offer the security of the 1962 code with regard to safety of investment (foreign or domestic) or repatriation of profits. The law is contained in *Journal officiel de la République Démocratique de Madagascar*, no. 73-057 (September 21, 1973); Andriamananjara (1974) has an interesting commentary on it.

13. The GDP growth had to be estimated by adding to the published aggregate production the value added by the government and the household services sectors. I have estimated the incremental capital-output ratio by assuming constant growth of gross fixed capital investment and then summing over the relevant period.

14. The plan's misprints and small arithmetic errors required recalculation of all average annual growth rates. Also, some technical aspects of the plan

are questionable—for instance, the assumption that export prices would rise 12 percent a year.

15. The biographical information comes from Kornfeld (1986), footnote 6; Chaigneau (1985), p. 246; and Robert Archer (1976), p. 74. The three sources differ slightly in the names of the schools attended. I have been unable to obtain Ratsiraka's academic record to compare with Banda's.

11 Agriculture: Property and Production Policies in Madagascar

Agriculture is Madagascar's largest economic sector. It is the major source of exports, and its slow growth has adversely affected the rest of the economy. Much less is known about the performance of agriculture in Madagascar than in Malaŵi, in large part because the quality and quantity of agricultural statistics are poorer.

The government of Madagascar has faced some general problems of growth and income distribution in formulating its agricultural policies. What sector of agriculture should the government encourage, and what are the most effective policy tools to use? To what extent should governmental policies be targeted at the most productive farmers or at the broad mass of farmers? Debate on the first question has focused more on alternative crop policies, an issue far from the major theme of this study, than on the relative importance of different types of farms such as estates and smallholdings. The second question has not really been raised in a clear form. Although the government has followed various wager-on-the-strong policies for most of the postindependence period, this has not been a deliberate choice but rather the inadvertent result of ignoring the distributional impacts of various agricultural policies.

Extensive Agriculture and the Land Constraint

Production in Madagascar's agriculture, herding, forestry, and fishing (primary) sector grew at an average annual rate of about 0.6 percent from 1960, at independence, through 1986.[1] This was considerably slower than the average annual population growth of 2.5 percent. In roughly the same period the estimated planted area of major crops increased about 2.2 percent a year, and the rural population, at an annual average rate of 1.8 percent. These data show that both land and labor productivity in agriculture were declining, while the land-labor ratio was increasing. This agricultural growth pattern may be described as "extensive and combined with adverse productivity trends," which suggests that land of poorer quality was being brought into production (diminishing returns on the extensive margin). These aggregate data, however, hide very marked differences in the degree of extensive agriculture in various areas.

Because of Madagascar's rugged topography and substantial soil degradation, only 4 percent of its land has been used to grow crops. In 1960 about 60 percent of this agricultural land was planted with crops or tree cultures; by 1985 this proportion had risen to about 85 percent.[2] Some estimates, which cannot be taken too seriously, suggest that the amount of unused land potentially suitable for agriculture is about double the land in use, but the quality of this potential cropland has yet to be determined. The extensification that has occurred in the last quarter of a century may be less attributable to the availability of land on the external margin than to the unavailability of such inputs as fertilizer, pesticides, and better seeds, which would permit more intensive use of the existing land. If fertile land is still available, the policy problem is to move people to this land and to provide them with sufficient economic overhead to permit production.

In addition to crop production, animal husbandry has been quite important. In the early 1970s the cattle population appeared to be roughly equal to the human population on the island. From 1960 through 1984 the stock of animals grew at an average annual rate of about 1.0 percent (Pryor 1988a, section C). The amount of meat produced per animal has been low throughout the period.

Small-Scale Agriculture

Smallholders have held and farmed about 95 percent of the land used for crop raising in Madagascar. Unlike in Malaŵi, roughly similar portions of the land in the estate and smallholder sectors are under cultivation. Madagascar's crop system also differs from that of Malaŵi in that about half of the land is irrigated and rice rather than maize is the major food staple.

Land Tenure

Traditional land tenure regulations within Madagascar differ from one ethnic group to another.[3] In most groups, however, a Malagasy family receives permission from village authorities to farm a particular piece of land, and the family can pass this right of usage (guaranteed by the community) down from generation to generation. From a different perspective, this system amounts to a quasi-private appropriation of lands, especially by families in the highlands; such appropriations have usually occurred early in the formation of a village.

For the purpose of this discussion we must be content with some broad generalizations about the tenure system. The Appendix, section

A, discusses the tenure situation at greater length and documents the observations that follow:

- In contrast to land tenure practices in Malaŵi, people in Madagascar need not farm the land themselves in order to maintain their land rights. In the early 1960s less than 10 percent of the total farmed area was rented, and by the mid-1980s the situation was much the same.[4]

- As a result of the Malagasy system allowing a family to accumulate land without farming it, the distribution of land holdings in the smallholder sector was considerably less equal than in Malaŵi; at independence, the distribution of smallholder incomes was also less equal.[5] In contrast to Malaŵi, inequalities of land distribution appear to have decreased over time.

- Under the traditional tenure system, some land-use rights appear secure, at least as long as someone in the family farms the land and as long as the peasant community remains relatively stable. Cadastral surveying and registration of land titles have been proceeding together, and the government hopes to complete the process by the end of the century.[6] Insecurity of tenure has occurred under conditions of breakdown in the traditional peasant community, which enforced land claims; breakdown in domestic order in the countryside, which in the early 1980s gave rise to praedial larceny; and confusion in areas of recent inmigration where the exact claims of the migrants on the land were unclear. Any increase in tenure insecurity obviously has an adverse impact on agricultural production.

- In contrast to Malaŵi, the Malagasy government has not distinguished between smallholder and estate crops, nor does it license production of certain crops; farmers are free to grow whatever they wish.

President Ratsiraka stressed the importance of land reform and redistribution in his 1975 political platform (Ratsiraka 1975, p. 86). His government has not, however, redistributed much land to individual smallholders and also has not touched the system of traditional land tenure through any kind of land reform.

The government's attempts to increase the actual land under cultivation were not sufficiently comprehensive to have had a major effect on land distribution and tenure.[7] These various projects have also suffered from management problems and have been very costly. The government has experimented with various combinations of five separate approaches to the problem:

- The eight major agricultural development authorities have opened up areas of land not previously farmed.

- The government has encouraged labor transfer to new areas in various settlement schemes in unfarmed areas.

- The Battle of Rice campaign in the 1970s attempted to increase farmed areas in individual districts.
- The government made large investments in irrigation infrastructure, especially in the Morondava and Mangoky areas, as well as in a series of microhydraulic projects to increase land use.
- The army through its Office militaire pour la production agricole has tried, with the help of North Korean technical assistance, to increase the land area used for rainfed rice cultivation.

The government has generally chosen which branches within agriculture to give the most support for increasing production on the basis of type of crop rather than type of tenure (smallholder or estate). More specifically, Malagasy policymakers have approached the problem in terms of deciding the relative priority to give to production of domestically consumed crops (primarily rice) as opposed to export crops.

Production

Until 1974 the policymakers appeared to emphasize measures to increase production of export crops (coffee, spices), raw material crops to be processed by domestic industries (cotton, sisal, tobacco, sugarcane), and meat. In the mid-1960s, however, the government launched a large operation to increase the production of rice, and production during the Tsiranana era appeared to keep up with the growing population. By design or not, the government seemed to follow a balanced approach.

From the mid-1970s to the early 1980s the entire agricultural sector was relatively neglected. Policies toward various crops featured considerable incoherence, with different policymakers stressing either food or export crop production. In the early and mid-1980s the crop policy again became more balanced, although I have been unable to find any indication that the means used to encourage particular crops are closely designed to achieve this balance.

For the most part, only indirect evidence is available about smallholder production. Official production data are too aggregative to be of much use (the particular components of the primary sector are not separated), and calculating special indexes of smallholder and estate production is not possible. We do know, however, that a much larger share of estate production than of smallholder production has been in export crops and that agricultural products have constituted the overwhelming part of total exports. These two facts allow us to use comparisons of aggregate production and trade data to distinguish roughly the production trends in the smallholder and estate sectors (Pryor 1988a, sections E and F).

During the 1950s, the last decade of the colonial period, total production by the primary sector and total exports grew at respective annual rates of 2.9 and 1.8 percent, which suggests that smallholder production was growing faster than total agricultural production. Smallholder production was also increasing faster than the population, which indicates rising labor productivity. Thus smallholder production seems to have been an important source of growth for the economy as a whole at this time.

During the Tsiranana era (1960 through 1972), total average annual growth of primary sector production fell to 1.2 percent, while that of exports increased to 4.5 percent. Apparently labor productivity in the smallholder sector declined, while labor productivity on the estates appears to have increased dramatically. This conclusion is consistent with the thrust of agricultural policy during that time.

From 1972 through 1986 (covering both the Ramanantsoa and Ratsiraka governments) total production by the primary sector increased at an average annual rate of 0.75 percent, while in a slightly shorter period exports declined at an average annual rate of 3.8 percent. Under very conservative assumptions, we can say that smallholder production rose less than 1.9 percent, compared with a rise in the rural population of roughly 2.0 percent a year.[8] Thus the trends of declining smallholder labor productivity and declining smallholder production per unit of total population, which started at independence, probably continued through the mid-1980s.

A number of indicators show that the technical level of farming has been very low (although higher than in Malaŵi).[9] For instance, in 1962 only 15 percent of the smallholders used fertilizer (in these years roughly three-quarters of the fertilizer was used for cotton and sugar cane production), and in the 1984–85 crop year, only about 21 percent of smallholders had plows. The only farming input in general use seems to have been irrigation water; in 1962, about 54 percent of smallholder land was irrigated, while in 1984–85 this decreased to about 51 percent.

Production Policies for Smallholders: Capital-Intensive Approaches

Tables 8-1 and 15-1 show that governmental current and capital expenditures on agriculture from the early or mid-1960s to the early or mid-1980s averaged about 3.8 percent of GDP in Malaŵi and about 2.5 percent of GDP in Madagascar. Furthermore, in Madagascar the programs aimed at the rural sector declined from about 32 percent of the state budget in 1975 and 1976 to a low of 11 percent in 1982 before rising somewhat, to 13 to 15 percent, in 1984 and 1985.[10] This reflected the Ratsiraka government's policy shift toward industry. The programs described in this chapter, therefore, affected a much lower share of total agricultural production and, in this narrow quantitative sense, had a smaller impact than the programs in Malaŵi.

During the late 1960s and early 1970s the Tsiranana government placed considerable emphasis on large-scale, integrated development projects in the rural sector. Such projects were pursued on a much smaller scale than in Malaŵi and had a rather different evolution. In the early 1960s the government began to set up a series of state farms to serve as experimental stations. It also established five major integrated development authorities (*Sociétés d'aménagement rural*, sometimes called *Grands périmètres*); the number of development authorities has since increased to eight.[11] Initially the government founded most of these as mixed public-private organizations. Somewhat later, most became parastatals with considerable autonomy from the Ministry of Agriculture. They were encouraged and also financed in good part by external sources such as the International Development Association (part of the World Bank Group), the Fonds européen de développement (of the European Economic Community), and the Fonds d'aide et de coopération (Government of France).

Most of these development authorities attempted both to expand the available land under cultivation and to increase land productivity. Most also administered an irrigation system, focused their major efforts on a few crops or on cattle, and provided a bundle of technical and other services to the farmers who owned land in the administered area or who rented land (on a sharecropping basis) from the development authorities. Data on the total funds allocated to these development authorities are not available, but their relative share in total agricultural development expenditures in the twenty-five years following independence seems to have been considerably less than that of their counterparts in Malaŵi, especially with the government's apparent reduction of financial support to these authorities during the 1970s and 1980s.

The development districts in Malaŵi covered a total of approximately 800,000 hectares, while the Madagascar development authorities covered a total cropland of very roughly 100,000 hectares (this estimate is merely an order of magnitude based on very scattered data), or about 5 percent of the total cultivated land. For 1980 one source estimated that smallholders located in these development areas accounted for about 10 percent of total smallholder production (ISNAR 1983, p. 8).[12] Even if accurate, we cannot tell if development authorities realized their goal of raising land productivity, because data for the period preceding the creation of the development areas are not available. The work of the capital-intensive development authorities was supplemented by a number of labor-intensive "opérations," such as GOPR, OBM, and l'Opération Café.

The activities of these eight development authorities cannot be evaluated systematically because of the lack of suitable data, but the experience of one of them, SOMALAC, for which considerable information is available, is instructive. SOMALAC has administered a rice-growing area around Lake Alaotra and has been one of the most important of the development authorities. Unlike most of the others, the Tsiranana government established it on expropriated land and gave it directions to redistribute land to the peasants as part of a "mini" land reform. By the mid-1980s, however, most of its land was only rented to smallholders.

SOMALAC does not appear to have met the high technical expectations for it (Blanc-Pamart and others 1984). Although land productivity in the SOMALAC area has exceeded the country's average because of the richness of the soil, the authority has introduced little technical change; for instance, in groundnut production, less than 5 percent of the farmers have adopted the suggested technological package, and less than 1 percent of the farms use fertilizers. Water management of the authority has been poor, and by the mid-1980s the water distribution system needed considerable rehabilitation. As a result of the uncertainties of the water supply, more than half the farmers still plant by broadcasting their rice seed rather than using the more land-intensive practices the authority advocates. From 1973–74 to 1982–83, production or productivity changed very little in the SOMALAC area.

SOMALAC's financial situation was precarious in the first half of the 1980s for a variety of reasons such as the unavailability of vital inputs, low prices for its products, and an inability to recover the costs of services and water provided to the farmers (a situation occurring in a number of the other development authorities as well). SOMALAC appeared in great need of an infusion of new funds to rehabilitate the irrigation system. The weak financial status of SOMALAC in the mid-1980s was similar to that of a number of other development authorities such as SAMINGOKY. Although detailed analysis of SOMALAC's financial problems is not possible, the available literature suggests that poor internal management was responsible for many of them.

In sum, the large-scale, capital-intensive projects by which Madagascar planned to raise smallholder productivity have been much smaller, less integrated, and more narrowly defined than those in Malaŵi. As in Malaŵi, they also cannot be considered very successful, especially because of administrative problems.

Production Policies for Smallholders: Labor-Intensive Approaches

In the last years of the colonial era the most important thrust of French policy toward smallholders was the construction of a considerable amount of economic infrastructure, particularly roads. Apart from these measures, however, opinion within the colonial government about how to revitalize and modernize the rural sector differed considerably, and during the 1950s a dizzy whirl of institutional changes and new bureaucratic initiatives occurred.[13]

This luxuriant foliage of bureaucratic agencies hides the fact that, according to the conventional wisdom, their work was not well-coordinated and they did not follow a common plan of action. In good part, many of these changes represented bureaucratic maneuvering for the control and direction of rural development within the colonial government. On a technical level, the various policies set in motion have received considerable criticism; for instance, the well-known French agronomist René Dumont accused the CRAMs of encouraging the "insanity of tractors" (*folie du tracteur*) because such machinery was difficult to maintain or use on the small plots (Dumont 1959).

Major Approaches after Independence

A considerable amount of institutional creation and reshuffling occurred after independence as well, and many of the existing agencies, such as the CARS, CRAMS, and SOS, were reorganized and received new names (Desjeux 1979). The new government also launched some new agencies for particular purposes; for instance, in 1963 the Ministry of Agriculture started the AIR (Associations d'intérêt rural) to organize the input and marketing cooperatives.

The government's agricultural extension activities were of greatest importance. It sponsored "intensive agricultural extension" (or *grande opération*), which either focused on specific crops or worked through the development authorities to seek out farmers to help, and "diffuse agricultural extension," which was general farming aid delivered mainly at the request of the farmers.

A key development in intensive agricultural extension occurred in 1965–66 when the Ministry of Agriculture started OPR (Opération productivité rizicole), a large project aimed at increasing rice production, primarily on the high plateau. This project had several roots, the most important of which was the colonial system of tying agricultural extension work on a particular crop to a crop research station. Local units were to administer the grass-roots work of OPR. In a long process of negotiation with the French financiers who were funding it, the project was removed from control of the ministry and local groups and was administered instead by a new, semiautonomous agency, GOPR (Groupement opération productivité rizicole). Because the program had a strong fertilizer component, it entered into large-scale distribution of certain agricultural inputs (chapter 12). The government also set up other semiautonomous operations such as L'opération café in the coastal area or the Opération Befandriana-Mandritsara in the Majunga Prefecture.

In pursuit of its diffuse agricultural extension work, the government in the early 1960s established the Animation rurale, which lasted about a decade. In 1965 a special agricultural extension service (Service de la vulgarisation) was set up to coordinate extension work among the smallholders; this service has continued in one organizational form or another ever since. In recent years, however, such extension work has been splintered among a number of different organizations, including the eight development authorities.

As a result of this fragmentation of administrative responsibility, the actual number of extension workers is difficult to determine. In the early 1980s, the Ministry of Agriculture had roughly 5,000 to 7,000 extension staff—1 per 240 to 335 rural families (World Bank June 1983, p. 75) When the number of extension workers in other governmental agencies is included, the program appears still larger. As measured by the ratio of agricultural extension workers to rural families, the program is larger than that in Malaŵi.

The quality of this agricultural extension work is quite another matter. The problems of coordinating the extension work with that of other kinds of rural-aid programs have persisted since the colonial period. Furthermore, the productivity of rice cultivation, in contrast to maize, appears to be considerably more sensitive to technical factors—use of the right kind of seed, timely use of other inputs, and correct regulation of water—so disorganization of any governmental effort to supply inputs has a highly adverse effect on production (Bray 1986). Thus the activities of GOPR, which appeared to have some success in diffusing technical knowledge about growing rice, were nullified after the mid-1970s by shortages of such agricultural inputs as fertilizers and by inefficient crop purchasing (chapter 12).

Despite some successes in the diffusion of agricultural technology, much of the grass-roots extension work has been very ineffective. Based on his experience in the field, one prominent Malagasy sociologist, Bertin Razafimpahanana (1972), commented about this work in the 1960s:

> If it is shown that such [extension] efforts were, in general, crowned with success from a technical point of view, that is not the same thing from the point of view of agricultural extension. Their centers are infrequently visited by the peasants and, in the majority of cases, the peasants are unenthusiastic toward them. One could say that in general there is practically no diffusion of new techniques among the mass of peasants. . . . We have been impressed by that colossal effort of the responsible authorities, an effort balanced by a more or less resounding stalemate. [p. 12]

Razafimpahanana also speaks of some peasants making symbolic visits to the extension agent in order to "look good" to the authorities.

They would take the proffered plants and plant them, but they would not use the new agricultural techniques they were taught. He argues that the ever-rising figures on number of plants or fertilizer sold do not reflect any important reality.[14]

Strong criticism of the extension service has continued in the Ratsiraka era. A conference in the mid-1980s focused on such problems as the urban background of the agricultural agents, their inability to integrate themselves into peasant life, and their hermetic working environment.[15] Another source noted that in the early 1980s the work of the extension agents suffered from unclear objectives; further, they had no set program of activities, no training, little mobility, and little logistic support. The training programs for farmers declined in importance in the early 1980s with the closing of the *Lycées agricoles*.

Problems of personnel and program management were not the only difficulties the extension program has encountered. The published information gives no evidence that the system has attempted mass diffusion of technological knowledge in the ingenious ways the Malaŵians devised. Furthermore, although the Malagasy government devoted special efforts to agricultural training and extension work among the young, such programs did not prove successful (for reasons not entirely clear), in strong contrast to Malaŵi's Young Pioneers.

Some Malagasy observers also argue that during the Tsiranana era most technical aid to the rural sector was aimed primarily at the richer farmers with a crop surplus to sell. This version of the wager-on-the-strong strategy was part of the government's stress on increasing marketed agricultural surplus. During the 1972–75 period, the government claimed to have taken steps to broaden the targets of its extension work; unfortunately, I could not find data on recipient characteristics to determine whether such a shift actually occurred.

The extension work has not been closely tied to agricultural research, which raises its own set of issues (ISNAR 1983). In the early years of French occupation the colonial government began an agricultural research program. From independence to 1974 most agricultural research was carried out by branches of two French governmental institutions: ORSTOM (Office de la recherche scientifique des territoires d'outre-mer) and GERDAT (Groupement d'études et de recherches pour le développement de l'agronomie tropicale). Staffed mainly by expatriates, they focused particular efforts on export crops and on the technical support needed to create a modern agricultural sector through estates, state farms, and the development authorities with their various irrigation projects.

In 1974 the Ramanantsoa government, as part of its program to reduce French influence on the island, asked these agencies to leave. Since that time the agricultural research program has undergone a number of reorganizations and is now split among a number of institutes, of which the most important is probably FOFIFA (National Center of Applied Research for Rural Development; the initials stand for the Malagasy name). In the mid-1980s the number of research workers (specialists and technicians) was higher than before, but the quantity and quality of research had declined considerably, exacerbated by a fall in funds devoted to research. Furthermore, many of the existing research programs did not appear to correspond to clear development priorities. For instance, although Madagascar's staple is rice, by the mid-1980s it had not yet introduced for general use any of the "miracle rice" that has so dramatically raised productivity in the Asian rice economies.

Technology policy has not provided realistic guidance to this extension and research work. According to the prevailing factor proportions, efficient allocation of Malagasy government funds should lean toward labor-using agricultural technologies. Technology policies, however, have not quite worked out this way. The strong emphasis of colonial agricultural agencies on mechanization has been modified, but a technology policy was implemented only in fits and starts and was aimed more toward the estates than the smallholder sector. For instance, in the late 1970s 1,000 Soviet tractors were imported, primarily for agricultural use by the military; however, they proved hard to keep in repair and in some cases were too heavy for their intended purpose. A number of more suitable, labor-intensive technologies, such as rotary hoes or mechanical rice transplanters, are available; the former were produced but only in very low numbers, and the latter were not yet introduced by the early 1980s (World Bank June 1983, pp. 272 ff.). A 1973-74 survey of farmers showed that their most important stated need was equipment (followed by credit and effective extension services).

Until the mid-1980s the government did little to address this problem of appropriate technology. Indeed, in many respects the availability of appropriate inputs into agriculture worsened in the 1975-85 decade; proper fertilizers, improved seeds, and insecticides became less available to smallholders as the scarcity of foreign exchange increased, leading to a downward spiral in which declining export production further reduced foreign exchange earnings (chapter 9).

An official statement from the 1986-90 five-year plan summarizes the shortcomings in Madagascar's agricultural policies:

> The organization of agricultural extension and the work of the extension agents has been poor because of the lack of sufficient financial means. Agricultural research was practically annihilated. The link between research and extension work was quasi-nonexistent . . . the system of management and of maintenance of the irrigation canals had ceased to function, occasioning a rapid degradation of the system. As for agricultural inputs, the system of expanding and distributing of high grade seeds is defective. The

problems of insufficiency of fertilizer have been aggravated by the inefficiencies of the distribution system. [Madagascar 1986, *Journal Officiel*, no. 1775]

Selected Management Issues

The administrative structure of government organizations dealing with agriculture has been much more complex in Madagascar than in Malaŵi (World Bank June 1983). In the early 1980s Madagascar had eight regional development authorities, fifteen production units (primarily state farms), fourteen marketing organizations, forty agroindustrial enterprises, four input producers and providers, ten support services (to provide, for example, price stabilization and agricultural research), and eight *opérations* for various crops or areas. The overlap in function among these different governmental units was considerable. For instance, prices for different agricultural products were set by the Ministry of Industry and Commerce, the Ministry of Agriculture, and local authorities; the price stabilization boards themselves were under the joint tutelage of the Ministry of Commerce and the Ministry of Finance.

Many of the agencies dealing with agriculture, such as the Office militaire pour la production agricole, which administered a highly mechanized and large rice project, were completely independent of the Ministry of Agriculture, and many had only a tenuous connection with the ministry. A conservative estimate places the number of staff members of the various governmental organizations dealing with agriculture but outside of the Ministry of Agriculture at 50,000—several times the number of staff within the ministry. Furthermore, the Ministry of Agriculture was unable to practice effective oversight over some agencies formally under its control. For instance, of the thirty-three parastatals reporting to the ministry, twenty-seven lost money between 1976 and 1980, with total losses amounting to about 2 billion FMG (about $8 million). Although the 1986–90 five-year plan placed great emphasis on agriculture, the government made no significant organizational changes at the time of its promulgation to implement the new policies better.

Two obvious difficulties arise. First, the problems the French colonial government faced in coordinating the work of various agencies dealing with agriculture appear to have multiplied manyfold. For instance, a series of expensive investments in agroindustries, made in the late 1970s and early 1980s, did not receive enough agricultural raw materials to operate profitably (chapter 14). Second, such splintered authority led to ineffectiveness. For instance, because a certain agricultural extension service has been carried out not only by the Ministry of Agriculture but also by regional authorities, by agricultural *opérations* (for export crops, such as coffee, pepper, clovers, and cocoa, and for sugar and rice), and by the development agencies, smallholders had to deal with a variety of agents for different crops and purposes. Although this system focuses more expertise on a single problem, it also means that each extension agent has more superficial contact—and less influence—with individual smallholder families.

An important part of the government program after the fall of Tsiranana in 1972 has been the strengthening of the *fokonolonas*, the traditional structures of village governance, and the decentralization and devolution of functions from the Ministry of Agriculture and other central organs to local authorities. Various levels of local government have been given authority over local irrigation systems, regulation of land tenure, marketing of certain agricultural products, administration of particular agricultural programs such as the veterinary service, gathering of some statistics, and road maintenance. In addition, they have participated in decisions about granting credit. Much of this devolution of power—however desirable it might be—was carried out too quickly and without sufficient preparation, and serious problems arose. Many of the local authorities had neither the financing nor the expertise to maintain roads, collect statistics, or perform other assigned functions in a satisfactory manner. The effectiveness of the veterinary service, which must carry out programs on a nationwide scale, was particularly vitiated by the decentralization. In 1982, several of the devolved programs, including the veterinary service, were recentralized in the Ministry of Agriculture.

Reorganization without full consideration of the consequences has had adverse results. For instance, during the colonial regime, the central government maintained the larger irrigation systems, while the farmers took care of the smaller systems. By transferring responsibility for both types of systems to the development authorities and to local governments, which lacked adequate funds for the task, the irrigation systems were not properly kept up.

Large-Scale Agriculture

Large-scale agricultural units include production cooperatives and estates, both in the public and private sectors. The Tsiranana government supported various types of input, credit, or marketing cooperatives but paid little official attention to large-scale production efforts, except for a few "precooperatives" on communal lands. Policies changed under the presidency of Gabriel Ramanantsoa (1972–75). Beginning in 1972, the Madagascar government began to nationalize the large estates, especially those owned by foreigners, and during the next five years took over about 166,000 hectares; the degree to which it compensated owners is unclear.[16] Thereafter some of this nationalized land apparently was either abandoned or only partly used. The total area of the large estates (private and public) fell by 50,000 to 87,000 hectares, but no significant share was officially distributed to the smallholders. The nationalized estates that maintained their land were turned into producer cooperatives and state farms.

The top political leadership had considerable interest in agricultural producer cooperatives. In 1975, early in his term of office, President Ratsiraka wrote:

> The socialist transformation of the old relations of production in the villages and countryside is the number one objective of the Malagasy revolution. The essential element in the socialist transformation of the old relations of production is the cooperativization of the rural economy. It is only when the individual peasant economy will be transformed by the socialist road in the countryside that one will be able:
>
> • to liberate the peasant completely from all exploitation, ignorance, sickness, and misery.
>
> • to develop agricultural production rapidly and in a planned fashion
>
> This should be especially easy for us to realize since in Madagascar a tradition of secular communitarianism favors such an evolution (the *fokonolona*). [Ratsiraka 1975, p. 64]

In 1978 the long-term plan projected production growth in the primary sector at an average annual rate of 4.7 percent to the end of the century. Further, by the year 2000 about 72 percent of those engaged in this sector would be members of, or connected with, cooperatives, while only 10 percent would remain individual farmers (Madagascar, Direction générale du plan, 1977a, pp. 24 and 34).

From 1976 through 1980 a number of producer cooperatives were formed, primarily in the coastal areas, on farms oriented toward export production (see Camacho 1982). Although some were created by action "from below," most were set up by the government. Fifty cooperatives received some kind of credit from the Ministry of Agriculture, and more unrecognized cooperatives were said to exist. Although data on their sizes are not available, at one time their operations probably covered 20,000 to 40,000 hectares.[17] Early successes were trumpeted; for instance, according to the Ministère du développement rural et de la réforme agraire (1979), in the cooperative of Lohafasika the former estate workers' incomes doubled in two years. Official optimism soared. Borrowing from the experience of East Europe, the government worked out a system of several types of cooperatives that differed in the degree to which profits were shared and work was carried out collectively.

The high expectations for these producer cooperatives were soon dashed. Exactly what happened is difficult to say because the readily available published materials are not very specific. The cooperatives encountered many technical difficulties, as well as problems in management, financing, incentives, and discipline. One analyst emphasizes also the micropolitical problems arising from the introduction of such cooperatives within the lineage societies of some ethnic groups and the struggles between the members of the cooperatives and the traditional elites. These fledgling production cooperatives needed considerable support; although the government supplied some credit, the total amount of aid given in various areas appears to have been insufficient. By 1984–85 only eighteen production cooperatives, farming 10,251 hectares (about 0.5 percent of the total cultivated area), still existed (Madagascar, Ministère de la production agricole, 1986, p. I–46).

The reasons for the paucity of governmental aid to the production cooperatives are not completely clear. Ratsiraka's statement cited above suggests that the government did not foresee the magnitude of the problems that would arise. Furthermore, the organizational changes in agriculture were occurring at the same time as the invest-to-the-hilt campaign, which drained off both funds and personnel. This cooperativization program is but one of a series of projects of the Ratsiraka government in which administrative constraints thwarted the government's ambitious intentions.

Most of the estates had been owned and administered by French *colons* and produced both domestic food crops and export crops. On the average, they were considerably smaller than the British estates in Malaŵi. In 1984–85 the 612 estates in the modern sector covered 79,500 hectares and averaged 130 hectares.[18] State farms held 41 percent of the estate land area; private and public corporate farms, 20 percent; associations, 16 percent; cooperatives, 2 percent; and individual farms, 22 percent. Only a small part of the lands on these estates had been rented or obtained from the local government.

State participation in agriculture was not confined to state farms. The government also held shares in some of the corporate farms. For the most part the Ministry of Agriculture supervised these government farms, many of which the Tsiranana government had established as experimental stations. Other ministries managed certain farms such as the large mechanized estates, which the military administered.

Management and financial problems have been severe on these new state-owned farms (World Bank June 1983, annex 2). Financial constraints were so acute that in the early 1980s some of the farms were basically out of operation. Supervision of these farms suffered from fragmentation and overlapping of supervisory responsibilities. Agricultural techniques still remained at a low level. Although quantitative details of the situation are not available, one telling event may illustrate its severity. In the mid-1980s the government asked 300 French *colons* that it had nationalized to resume ownership and management of their former estates; only about 30 showed interest (Glenshaw and Harmon 1985). In the same period the government made agreements with foreign firms to improve some of the nationalized estates; for instance, SOFINCO, a Franco-Belgian company, contracted to rehabilitate 4,500 hectares of an abandoned coffee plantation.

Production patterns and productivity of the estates and smallholders have differed considerably. The estates have been much more heavily involved in production for export than has the smallholder sector. For some export crops, such as sugar, cotton, tobacco, soya beans, and sisal, the estates have accounted for a significant share of total exports. Smallholder production has been large in such major export crops as coffee, vanilla, and cloves. In the mid-1960s the estates accounted for about a fourth of all agricultural exports.[19] The estates generally had higher land productivity than the smallholder sector (ISNAR 1983, p. 8).[20] In 1980, for instance, the large estates accounted for roughly 4 percent of total planted land but produced roughly 18 percent of total agricultural output. Some part of this difference was attributable to more fertile lands in the estates; another part, I suspect, reflected the price structure that favored estate production.

In the survey of smallholder production, I pointed out that exports grew faster than agricultural production during the Tsiranana era; thereafter, exports declined while agricultural production continued to rise, albeit at a relatively slow rate. All of this strongly suggests—but does not prove—that estates grew faster than the smallholder sector as a whole during the Tsiranana period and more slowly thereafter. In this limited sense, estate agriculture was a leading productive sector from independence until 1972 and a retarding factor from 1972 on. The uncertainty and administrative chaos in the estate sector engendered by the government's nationalization program and agricultural price policies for export crops have been the most general causes of this disappointing performance of the estate sector in recent years.

Summary and Conclusions

Madagascar has experienced an extensive growth of agriculture, accompanied by declining productivities of labor and land. This has occurred in a situation in which smallholders, in large part operating under traditional tenure arrangements, have occupied the overwhelming share of land.

Government expenditures on agricultural development have been a much smaller share of GDP than in Malaŵi. Although the government emphasized capital-intensive rural integrated projects to aid smallholder production, the area these projects covered was much smaller and the projects were less all-embracing than in Malaŵi. Also, these projects have not been well administered, especially from the early

1970s on. More labor-intensive policies to increase production included agricultural extension work and agricultural research; neither program appears to have been very effective. The Malagasy have had the same difficulties as the Malaŵians in designing and administering programs to improve agricultural conditions in the smallholder sector.

During the mid-1970s the Malagasy nationalized many of the French estates. The government soon abandoned its attempts to turn some of them into production cooperatives, because it did not commit the necessary financial and administrative resources to make the system work. The remaining estates did not function well under state ownership, and the estate sector appears to have been a weight on economic growth.

The distribution of smallholder income was more unequal in Madagascar than in Malaŵi because of the greater inequality of land distribution arising from the different traditional land tenure arrangements. Rural income inequalities in Madagascar appear to have been exacerbated, not by a change in the distribution of land but rather by the government's policies with regard to the marketing of agricultural inputs and outputs.

Notes

1. Population and production data come from Pryor (1988a), sections B and E. Two generally useful studies on agriculture in Madagascar are Pourcet (1987) and Szal (1987). Szal does not see an overall crisis in Malagasy agriculture, because in the mid-1980s per capita rice consumption was still higher than in the 1950s; my conclusion, taking into account the entire agricultural sector (including exports), is much less sanguine.

2. The land data for earlier years come from Pryor (1988a), section A; for later years, from Ministère de la production agricole et de la réforme agraire, and FAO (1988a), volume II. These data are not completely comparable, and changes in land utilization may not have been as great as the text indicates.

3. By far the most complete discussion of Madagascar land tenure is in Rarijaona (1967). An interesting early study is a typescript found at the Bibliothèque nationale, "France, Madagascar et dépendences: Services des domaines et de la propriété foncière," *Rapport* (Paris, 1922). Case studies of tenure arrangements in specific areas are found in the ethnographic literature, for example, for the Merina and the Betsilio, Bloch (1971) and Kottak (1980).

4. Ministère de la production agricole et de la réforme agraire and FAO (1988a), table LXXX, showed that 4.9 percent of total land is rented, while another 7.9 percent is held under "other" forms of land tenure (including squatting and mixed forms). These results are quite surprising in light of the conventional wisdom in Madagascar before the census results were released that land renting had increased. Indeed, when I visited the island, the major disagreements seemed to be about whether this alleged increased tenancy resulted from land buying by the urban population, the extension of

cultivation into less fertile areas claimed by the notables of the villages, or the rise of a *kulak* class in the countryside. Clearly the tendencies the various Malagasy observers saw occurring in specific areas of the country were not characteristic of the country as a whole. The statistics on the hiring of labor are too incomplete to determine whether landlessness, as manifested in the greater amount of hiring of agricultural labor, has increased. I have not seen any convincing evidence that this phenomenon has occurred.

5. In Malaŵi the Gini coefficients of inequality of land distribution in the smallholder sector in 1968–69 and 1984–85 were .369 and .381, respectively; in Madagascar such coefficients for smallholders in 1960 and 1984–85 were .445 and .380. The Madagascar data are not quite comparable in these two years because the earlier figure apparently refers to all agricultural land, while the latter is only for area under cultivation. This means that the increase in equality in land holdings in Madagascar is undoubtedly overstated. The raw data for Malaŵi come from Pryor (1988b), table A-5; the raw data for Madagascar come from Pryor (1988a), table A-4, and Ministère de la production agricole et de la réforme agraire and FAO (1988b), table VIII.

6. Information on recent land registration was obtained from Mme. Rahantamalala, Chef du service des domaines.

7. This is the evaluation in World Bank (June 1983), p. 26, which seemed to be accepted by the few Malagasy with whom I discussed the subject.

8. I have assumed that smallholders produced only for the domestic market, that estates produced only for export, and that smallholder production constituted 80 percent of the total in the initial period.

9. The data for 1962 and for 1984–85 cited in this section come respectively from Madagascar, Ministère des finances et du commerce, and INSRE (1966) and Ministère de la production agricole et de la réforme agraire and FAO (1988c), table XLVIII. These data on equipment are quite different from a preliminary version of the census found in Ministère de la production agricole et de la réforme agraire (1986).

10. These data come from unpublished tables supplied by the Ministère du développement rural et de la réforme agraire.

11. These authorities include SOMASAK (Société malgache de la Sakay), founded 1961—meat and crops; SAMINGOKY (Société pour l'aménagement et la mise en valuer de la vallée du Bas Mangoky), founded 1961—rice and cotton; SOMALAC (Société malgache pour l'aménagement du Lac Alaotra), founded 1961—rice; FIFATO (formerly SEDEFITA, Société d'études et de développement des périmètres de Fiherenana de la Taheza), founded 1962—rice, cotton, legumes; FIFABE (formerly COMENA, Comité d'expansion économique de la plaine de Marovoay), founded 1964—rice, cotton, groundnuts; SODEMO (Société pour le développement économique de la région de Morondava), founded 1972—rice and sugar; FAFIFAMA (Fampivoarana ny fiompiana amin'ny Faritra Andrefani Madagasika), founded 1976—livestock; SOAMA (Société pour le développement de la région d'Andapa), founded 1979. Some discussions of development authorities exclude SOMASAK but include HASYMA (Hasy Malagasy, formerly Compagnie française de développement des fibres textiles)—cotton; ODEMA (Office de développement de Moyen

Ouest), founded in 1965; or FANALAMANGA (Société pour l'aménagement sylvicole de la zone de Mangoro), founded in 1975—timber. The line between "opérations, " state farms, and development authorities is rather hazy. Five of these development authorities (SOMALAC, FIFABE, SODEMO, SAMINGOKY, and SOAMA) embrace large irrigation schemes comprising about 84,000 hectares.

12. The original source of the ISNAR information is not clear as to whether this refers to net or gross production or exactly how such an estimate was derived.

13. In 1949 and 1950 the government began to set up CARs (Collectivités autochtones rurales; after independence these became the Communes rurales), an organ through which the government and villagers carried out agricultural and village development projects with funds ultimately coming from the French foreign aid agency. A mechanization component was added to some in 1956, and these were renamed CRAMs (Communes rurales autonomes modernisées). The CARs and CRAMs paid particular attention to agricultural production for export, in which the French colonists on the island were heavily engaged. Although local groups and the central government were supposed to administer these institutions jointly, technicians from the colonial government appeared to play a leading role in their operations. The CARs and CRAMs were not under the authority of the Agricultural Service (later to become the Ministry of Agriculture), and during the 1950s the Agricultural Service, in order to guide its own programs in the countryside, set up the SPs (Secteurs de paysannat; after independence these became the Secteurs de développement rural). Then, in 1956 the Governor-General began to establish SMDRs (Sociétés mutuelles de développement rural) to guide rural development in still different administrative channels. In addition certain French companies and institutes (such as Compagnie générale des oléagineux tropicaux, and the Institut de recherches du coton et des textiles exotiques) came to the island to focus on particular crops and to aid in agricultural extension work. Other institutional innovations must go unmentioned. Two studies that view the French colonial experiments from quite different standpoints are Desjeux (1979) and Thompson and Adloff (1965).

14. Althabe (1969), pp. 48–56, has a somewhat different type of analysis of the unimpressive impact of extension work in the 1960s.

15. Seminaire national sur la vulgarisation agricole, Fianarantsoa (1983), p. 34. Other information comes from World Bank (June 1983).

16. The estimate of total nationalized land area, 166,000 hectares, comes from Madagascar, Direction générale du plan (1978), p. 173. In 1984–85, according to the preliminary results of the agricultural census, the area of estates and cooperatives was 125,409 hectares (Ministère de la production agricole 1986). According to the final census results, the total area of the modern sector was 79,543 hectares (Ministère de la production agricole and FAO, 1988a, table LXXXIV). I have found no explanation of the discrepancy between the two sets of figures for the mid-1980s or of the fate of the 50,000- to 87,000-hectare difference; some knowledgeable Malagasy suggested to me that part of this missing land was taken over by the landless or by government officials. A pamphlet from Madagascar, Ministère de la production agricole et de la réforme agraire (1980) places the total estate area at 189,941 hectares in 1974–75 but claims only 73,612 hectares were nationalized. President Ratsiraka (1975),

pp. 36 and 64, said quite plainly that the redistribution of land was to be accompanied by a change in the organization of the land and the creation of producer cooperatives.

17. Camacho (1982) lists fifteen cooperatives with an average area of 277 hectares. The cooperatives existing in 1984–85 had an average area of 570 hectares. If we assume sixty-five cooperatives existed at the high point (of which ten survived) and an average area of the nonsurvivors between 200 and 400 hectares, the total area could have ranged from 20,000 to 40,000 hectares. The surviving cooperatives averaged only 149 hectares.

18. The data in this paragraph come from Ministère de la production agricole and FAO (1988a), table LXXXIV. The preliminary census results from Ministère de la production agricole (1986) list a minimum of 716 estates covering 115,158 hectares and averaging 161 hectares. Of the land area, corporate farms accounted for about 52 percent; family estates, 25 percent; state farms, 13 percent; various types of partnerships, 9 percent; and other legal forms, 1 percent. The sources of the differences between the two sets of census data are unclear.

19. Data from Madagascar, INSRE and République française (1970), pp. 9 and 75, suggest that in the mid-1960s the estates (the modern sector) exported about three-quarters of their production but accounted for only about one-quarter of all agricultural exports.

20. ISNAR does not specify whether production is measured gross or net.

12 Agriculture: Product and Factor Markets in Madagascar

Rural income inequalities have increased in Madagascar (chapter 16). The most likely source of this change is the government's product and factor market policies, because the distribution of land holdings has become somewhat more equal (chapter 11). A qualitative appraisal of the impact each of these policies had on the distribution of income is important, even if precise quantitative information is lacking.

Madagascar's specific product and factor market policies have depended very much on the government in power. President Tsiranana pursued a policy of maintaining the traditional market structures as well as roughly the same intersectoral terms of trade between agriculture and the rest of the economy (real agricultural prices). Agricultural production responded by rising at a modest rate. In his first decade of power President Ratsiraka turned the intersectoral terms of trade against agricultural producers. He established a state-owned marketing system that proved incapable of functioning adequately in purchasing crops and supplying farmers with agricultural inputs and consumer goods. As a result, rural markets literally "dis-integrated" (became misaligned with each other), total agricultural production stagnated, and agricultural exports plummeted. This market disintegration lowered incomes more among the poorer farmers than among the richer ones. Since the mid-1980s, the Ratsiraka government has been trying to liberalize rural markets, but evaluation of the impact of this policy reversal on production is not yet possible.

Labor and capital markets, fusing both traditional and modern elements, have been stunted. Governmental policies in the labor market have had little impact. The various rural credit programs have been relatively small and have been administered in a manner to favor the estates and richer smallholders.

Product Markets

Madagascar's product markets have evolved into a complex amalgam of state and private institutions operating with quite different degrees of effectiveness—and with different degrees of legality.

Markets for Domestic Sales

The Madagascar government, unlike that of Malaŵi, has followed the same pricing and marketing rules for both smallholders and estates. Since the early 1960s the government has specified official producer prices for agricultural products; however, the products subject to these official prices and the degree of price enforcement have varied over time. Certain agricultural products have been sold either in farmers' markets or urban parallel markets, in which prices have not been controlled at all. In 1983 the government slowly started to liberalize rice and other markets, but the most important changes did not begin until 1986.

Government participation in marketing crops and agricultural inputs has varied not only over time but also by product.[1] During the Tsiranana era crops and inputs were sold primarily through free markets. From the early 1970s to the early 1980s several different state agencies took over most, but not all, of the marketing of crops and the selling of goods to farmers. Starting in the mid-1980s the government again permitted private traders to purchase crops and sell agricultural inputs. The rice market provides an instructive example.

Rice is Madagascar's most important food staple, and the island has moved from being a rice exporter during the late colonial years to an importer from the early 1970s to the mid-1980s. Until the early 1970s private agents—many of whom were of Chinese, Indian, or Pakistani origin—marketed rice at the farm-gate level; they also supplied credit and sold agricultural inputs and consumer goods. In 1973 the newly installed Ramanantsoa government set up a new parastatal, SINPA (Société d'intérêt national des produits agricoles), which was mandated to intervene actively in rice marketing. In 1975 the government made SINPA the official monopoly for buying and selling rice, groundnuts, and maize and gave other organizations the right to set SINPA prices. Only several large-scale, state-owned development authorities, such as SOMALAC and FIFABE (chapter 11), which administered certain rice-growing districts and marketed the crops grown therein, could circumvent SINPA and sell directly to the public.

SINPA did not carry out its commercial functions in a satisfactory manner, and the produce markets began literally to dis-integrate (see table 12-4). After a financial scandal in 1977, SINPA lost its monopoly position and had to share its rice-buying functions with other parastatal agencies authorized to purchase agricultural crops, with village governmental agencies, and with certain cooperatives. Even during this period of more flexible institutional arrangements, however, many problems arose; for example, the share of rice sold through official channels fell from roughly 12 percent of total production in 1975–76 to 5 percent of production in 1982–83 at the same time that rice sales through the parallel (black) markets appeared to increase.[2] Given the fact that in the early 1980s many parallel market prices were more than double the official prices, this decline in the importance of official markets is not surprising.

The mismanaged parastatal buying activities from the mid-1970s through the mid-1980s probably widened income differentials in the rural areas because only the estates and richer smallholders could afford to transport their crops and take other measures necessary to participate effectively in the booming parallel market for foodstuffs.

In the 1983–84 crop season private trading in certain crops, including rice, again became legal, at least to a limited extent. In the early years of the liberalization local governments responded by stepping up their role in rice marketing, often setting the prices at which rice was to be purchased in their areas of jurisdiction or limiting the number of licenses issued to private traders. In the four years following 1983, however, the central government progressively cut back on the various restrictions on private trading, limited its rice imports and allowed domestic prices of rice to rise, and began to implement a buffer stock program to moderate price fluctuations in rice. The latter program was supported by the World Bank and other aid donors. The various liberalization measures were too complex and contradictory to discuss in detail here, but Berg (1989) and Shuttleworth (1989) provide useful and sensitive analyses.

Retail prices of rice almost doubled during this transition period. Domestic food producers appeared to respond, the land under rice cultivation increased, and production rose. By the late 1980s, however, the retail price of rice had fallen. Whether these effects will be permanent and whether the liberalization will continue remain to be determined.

Markets for Export Sales

Madagascar has many crops that have been primarily exported, rather than consumed domestically. At the time of independence some large exporting firms (mostly French) and a group of private middlemen handled the exporting arrangements with relatively little governmental intervention. Between 1956 and 1962, however, the government set up separate price stabilization funds for most major crops, especially those for export, directed by representatives of the government and the farmers.[3] Their functions have included setting minimum prices the commercial agents paid farmers for particular crops, facilitating marketing, and providing some production aid.

The nationalization of the major French-owned commercial houses in 1976–77 and their replacement by four parastatals (SOMACODIS, ROSO, COROI, and SICE) led to some complicated institutional arrangements. These parastatals carried out certain major export functions for such crops as coffee, cloves, and black pepper. Actual export negotiations for various crops were handled not only by the parastatals but also, in some cases, either by the stabilization funds, by a department of the Ministry of Commerce, or by private companies acting as agents of the government. The parastatals bought some crops directly from the farmers, and private traders acting as agents of the parastatals purchased others.

The marketing situation was further complicated by the fact that the Ministry of Industry and Commerce set the official domestic price for some crops, while the local governments set prices for others. Neither the Ministry of Agriculture nor the buying agencies, such as SINPA, had authority in price setting. This splintering of authority and function meant, among other things, that the government followed no uniform set of price or marketing policies for the different crops. Different agencies followed quite different rules in setting prices; in many cases, determining exactly what rules were in force is difficult. Furthermore, the various commodity price stabilization funds and boards had rather different objectives. Some placed greater stress on price stabilization; others had a much more important role in supplying funds to the government; still others focused more on encouraging production or self sufficiency. This and the many other examples of governmental intervention were so complex that effective policy coordination were almost impossible.

The most fundamental change in the system for marketing export crops occurred in 1977 as a result of soaring prices in the world market for coffee, Madagascar's most important export. The government set up a special agency, FNUP (Fonds national de péréquation), to receive export receipts, to allocate funds to the stabilization boards and other sellers of export crops to cover their expenses, and to channel the remaining funds to the government. With this change the agricultural sector lost control over profits arising from differences between export and domestic prices. Rather than flowing automatically back into agriculture, the government used these profits to finance such programs as the construction of regional branches of the university and the rice subsidy to urban consumers. In 1980 and 1981 these subsidies were greater than the total operating and investment budget of the Ministry of Agriculture for the same period. As part of the structural adjustment program in the mid-1980s, the government removed the rice subsidies.[4]

Markets for Selling to Rural Consumers

Selling products to rural producers and consumers is also an important function of the agricultural marketing system. Madagascar's population density is much lower than Malaŵi's, so the physical difficulties in getting farm inputs and consumer goods to the rural sector have been greater. The problem was greatly exacerbated in the decade following 1975 because many of the rural roads were allowed to deteriorate to a point that getting crops out or agricultural inputs and consumer goods in was difficult (chapter 14). The breakdown of the transportation routes discouraged production. It also may have widened overall income differentials because many, perhaps most, of the richest smallholders lived close to the cities or to the main roads and were well integrated into the market economy. Within those outlying areas where the transportation links had deteriorated the most, however, income inequalities may have narrowed because the richer farmers there were as handicapped as the poorer farmers in selling their crops or obtaining agricultural inputs.

Additional distribution problems arose from another side of the market. In the 1960s the conduits of agricultural inputs and consumer goods to the rural sector included the private crop buyers serving both buying and selling functions; certain parastatals, such as GOPR (chapter 11), which were originally set up to encourage production but which began to sell farm inputs, especially fertilizer; and other parastatals, such as Magasins M, which supplied certain consumer goods. The activities of Magasins M, however, began to decline in the late 1960s. In 1975 the private traders lost their sales function to a great extent when many of their buying activities were discontinued to create SINPA's monopoly; in the same year, GOPR sales of farm inputs were suppressed. In later years SINPA and offices of the Ministry of Agriculture tried to supply the key agricultural inputs and consumer goods directly to the farmers. Neither SINPA nor the Ministry of Agriculture performed their marketing activities very well, however, and in many parts of the island farmers were unable to obtain such goods readily.

The country's foreign exchange shortage led to a cutback of imports of consumer goods and agricultural inputs, which exacerbated the rural supply problem. Imported consumer goods were rationed informally, and the rural consumers did not seem to get their fair share. Imported agricultural inputs also stagnated; for example, fertilizer imports (shown in table 12-1) were far below their 1970 peak, in contrast with those of Malaŵi (table 5-1), which rose steadily.[5] A parallel market for fertilizer also developed.

These problems of selling goods to the agricultural sector adversely affected production. The farmers were less able to produce crops and

Table 12-1. Fertilizer Sales, Madagascar, 1950 to 1984

Year	Metric tons	Year	Metric tons
1950	1,953	1970	30,364
1951	2,562	1971	22,916
1952	3,986	1972	7,787
1953	4,008	1973	15,460
1954	5,752	1974	12,760
1955	3,871	1975	16,825
1956	6,732	1976	14,104
1957	6,632	1977	12,024
1958	7,090	1978	24,304
1959	4,186	1979	19,319
1960	4,974	1980	21,426
1961	4,153	1981	10,558
1962	2,792	1982	30,815
1963	2,220	1983	19,116
1964	4,383	1984	20,468
1965	6,830		
1966	6,591		
1967	12,076		
1968	22,195		
1969	22,564		

Note: These data are for imports because Madagascar had no domestic production of fertilizer during the period. Separation of sales to smallholders and to estates in order to make the data comparable with the Malaŵi series shown in table 5-1 was not possible. The data are slightly overstated because reexports, which were quite small, are not removed.

Source: For 1950 through 1980 the data are from various issues of Madagascar, Ministère des finances, *Statistiques du commerce extérieur de Madagascar* (annual). For 1980 through 1984 the data are from World Bank (March 1986a), p. 145.

had less incentive to market their products. In a very important study Berthélemy and others (1988) provide econometric evidence showing quite clearly that in the late 1970s and early 1980s the declining supply of consumer goods and agricultural inputs to the rural sector played an important role in the decline in marketed output of rice and coffee.[6]

Although no empirical evidence is available, problems in marketing agricultural inputs also may have widened income differentials within the rural sector. Those smallholders with higher incomes, especially those close to transportation routes, were in a better position than the poorer smallholders to obtain inputs and could pay considerably more than the official prices if necessary.

Agricultural Prices

Price trends and fluctuations on the world market have greatly influenced the setting of domestic prices and the marketing operations in Madagascar. Table 12-2 presents some international price data for Madagascar's staple crops and its most important export crops.

The world prices of Madagascar's five most important exports, which accounted for about three-fifths of the total value of its exports from 1960 through 1984, rose at an average annual rate of 8.13 percent. This rate of increase exceeded that for world export unit values, a fortunate occurrence persisting even after the second oil shock. Madagascar was able to reap high profits from the coffee boom in the mid-1970s and a remarkable increase in the price of cloves during the entire period. Thus the world environment has favored export

Table 12-2. International Price Trends and Fluctuations, Madagascar, 1960 to 1984 and 1975 to 1984
(percent)

Crop	Average annual price change[a] 1960–84	1975–84	Fluctuations: pseudocoefficient of variation[b] 1960–84	1975–84
Staple: rice	4.85	2.01	15.61	17.73
Export crops[c]				
Coffee	7.94	7.76	14.66	19.42
Cloves	12.46	5.94	16.70	12.12
Vanilla	6.23	14.93	7.57	7.45
Sugar	6.62	2.54	8.42	9.27
Sisal	5.44	1.91	24.69	14.39
Weighted average	8.13	7.86	13.95	15.40

a. The price increases are in U.S. dollars and are calculated by fitting an exponential trend line to the relevant price data.
b. The pseudocoefficient of variation starts with the absolute value of the deviation of the price for a given year from the trend price in the same year, measured as a ratio to the trend. These data are the averages of these ratios. Trend price is measured as the average price for the two previous and two following years.
c. The crops are listed in order of relative importance of exports. The relative values of exports serve also as the weights in the weighted average.

Source: Except for cloves and vanilla, all data are based on commodity prices presented in International Monetary Fund, *International Financial Statistics: Yearbook, 1985*, pp. 138–41. The price data for cloves and vanilla come from average unit price data for Madagascar exports of these commodities, converted into dollars by the average exchange rate of that year, and drawn from the sources described in section C of Pryor (1988a).

marketing in Madagascar much more than in Malaŵi. The nation as a whole was not able to derive many long-term advantages from these rising export prices, however, and the evidence presented in chapter 16 suggests that rural incomes declined.

As table 12-2 indicates, the rise of external agricultural prices was accompanied by considerable short-term price fluctuation in Madagascar, much more so than in Malaŵi (table 5-2). Because Madagascar is a relatively small world producer in most of its crops, except vanilla and cloves, these fluctuations should parallel changes in farmers' incomes, unless their incomes were buffered by some type of compensating mechanism, a subject receiving remarkably little discussion in the economic literature on Madagascar.

Intersectoral Terms of Trade: Some General Considerations

Examination of the relative domestic prices of agricultural and nonagricultural goods provides some important insights into the functioning of the Malagasy economy.

PRODUCTION EFFECTS. When the government changes the terms of trade, the marketed output of agricultural goods responds, the exact amount depending on the relevant price elasticities of supply. Few economists have paid much scholarly attention to these supply elasticities for Madagascar. The two studies I found (Ahlers and others 1984 and Berthélemy and others 1988) show price elasticities of supply of rice and coffee similar to those in the rest of the world.[7] These results run contrary to the conventional wisdom that social-cultural factors have operated in Madagascar with sufficient strength in the villages to make production rather insensitive to price.

The rise in parallel markets for foodstuffs reflected a widening difference in prices in official and in parallel markets in the decade following the mid-1970s. In the urban areas the parallel market prices for rice, at least from 1983 through 1985, were 50 to 100 percent higher than the official prices; differentials for other foodstuffs, such as sugar and flour, in April 1985 were 50 to 60 percent.[8] In the early 1980s the price differentials for rice induced farmers to sell more through the parallel market than to the official buying organizations.

Careful econometric evidence on the impact of a change in the intersectoral terms of trade on aggregate agricultural production is not available. Nevertheless, the evidence from the two available supply elasticity studies for particular goods suggests that if the terms of trade turned against agriculture, the production response would be considerable because the rural sector would redirect more of its efforts toward production for home consumption and toward leisure. This response undoubtedly played a major role in what actually happened. Marketed agricultural production for exports fell continuously from 1972 to the mid-1980s, especially after the significant fall in real agricultural prices after 1978. This jeopardized the government's entire investment program as foreign exchange to obtain the necessary machinery and manufacturing inputs became increasingly scarce.

CONSUMPTION EFFECTS. No reliable data are available to explore the resource side of this issue; however, some information can be found on the distributional aspects. The data from Malagasy household budget studies show that rural family incomes have been much lower than those of urban families (chapter 16). When the government paid low prices for agricultural products in order to deliver inexpensive foodstuffs to the cities, the urban poor benefited, but the smallholders—the poorest group in the nation—were hurt. Thus the distribution of income for the nation as a whole became more unequal.

FISCAL EFFECTS. The Malagasy government has relied on indirect taxes, especially on exports and imports, for most of its revenues. When the government turned the intersectoral terms of trade against the rural sector so that exports—and later, imports—declined, so did tax receipts from these important sources of revenue.

INVESTMENT EFFECTS. No reliable data on these matters are available for Madagascar. For reasons given in the discussion about Malaŵi (chapter 5), turning the intersectoral terms of trade against agriculture probably slowed GDP growth by reducing savings and raising the incremental capital-output ratio.

Intersectoral Terms of Trade: Actual Behavior

Although data on official prices in the colonial period are not available, scattered data on actual sale prices of six major commodities suggest the real intersectoral terms of trade declined roughly 40 percent from 1950 to 1960.[9] Considering that the resources obtained from the rural sector in this fashion were not used for economic development, this colonial policy lowered incentives for greater agricultural production without providing any compensating advantage—another example of how the colonial administration undercut future economic development in the new nation.

The data presented in table 12-3 summarize the official prices farmers received for their crops from 1960 to the mid-1980s. The price series deflated by an appropriate price index represents the intersectoral terms of trade. Because such a deflator is not available, prices in the table were adjusted by using two imperfect substitutes as deflators. The results, therefore, must be interpreted cautiously.

During the period of the Tsiranana government (1960–72) the intersectoral terms-of-trade series were roughly constant, except for a

Table 12-3. Indicators of Agricultural Producer Prices, Madagascar, 1960 to 1984

		Deflated index of official agricultural prices (intersectoral terms of trade)		Official agricultural prices/ foreign trade prices of eleven commodities (percent)		
Year	Index of official agricultural prices	Index of implicit deflator of GDP	Cost of urban living index	Total	Excluding sugar, vanilla	Excluding sugar, vanilla, rice
1960	52.8	68.4	72.3	29.4	42.6	41.5
1961	53.1	67.8	69.9	30.2	41.1	41.0
1962	55.5	69.3	74.0	28.6	38.9	37.4
1963	57.1	69.5	76.6	29.5	40.3	43.4
1964	65.3	76.3	85.1	36.4	48.8	42.7
1965	64.4	72.0	83.0	32.0	42.6	39.0
1966	60.1	65.4	74.7	26.2	34.8	29.9
1967	61.7	66.5	74.9	27.3	36.4	38.9
1968	62.0	66.2	71.5	27.1	36.1	45.7
1969	66.1	68.0	74.0	30.8	41.2	47.0
1970	100.0	100.0	100.0	44.3	59.4	41.1
1971	76.4	72.5	71.3	34.4	47.1	43.1
1972	76.9	69.1	71.3	34.5	51.2	41.2
1973	78.3	66.3	64.7	29.0	39.9	44.3
1974	111.7	77.4	74.6	19.1	31.3	44.9
1975	131.3	83.6	83.6	24.0	39.2	50.8
1976	131.9	80.5	82.8	26.9	36.3	36.1
1977	149.4	88.5	87.4	32.2	42.4	24.9
1978	151.8	84.3	85.0	32.7	42.1	29.0
1979	165.3	80.5	75.2	35.2	47.8	31.1
1980	189.8	78.2	76.7	34.0	53.3	30.4
1981	213.0	67.2	73.9	23.7	41.8	33.8
1982	250.1	60.0	65.5	32.7	45.7	30.9
1983	277.3	55.6	63.1	28.4	43.1	22.8
1984	315.1	57.6	63.0	25.2	38.2	19.4

Note: For all indexes, 1970 = 100. Foreign trade prices are based on official exchange rates.

Source: Sources of data and a description of the calculation methods are presented in Pryor (1988a), section C.

bizarre jump for 1970, when the government increased the price of rice; this action was later rescinded. During the Ramanantsoa government (1972–75) and the first few years of the Ratsiraka government thereafter, the intersectoral terms of trade turned in favor of the rural sector. This phenomenon might have reflected Ramanantsoa's strong ideas about the importance of agriculture and desire to aid this sector. Also, an increase in agricultural prices was necessary to maintain production when the lifting of the capitation taxes reduced incentives to produce in order to meet tax obligations (an argument made in detail in chapter 10).

The Ratsiraka government's urban orientation was revealed after 1978, when it allowed the intersectoral terms of trade to turn markedly against the rural sector. This policy was implemented by simply raising official producer prices of agricultural goods at a slower rate than prices in other sectors and by masking the domestic price that rural exporters should have received by maintaining an increasingly overvalued exchange rate.

The price policy, the exchange rate policy, and the decline in the availability of consumer goods to the rural sector were the most important elements in the rapid decline of agricultural exports and the very low growth rate of total agricultural production. The continuous fall in both the real price of rice and the share of marketed rice production were obvious responses (see Pryor 1988a, table C-2).[10]

As part of the policy reversal after 1983, real prices paid to the agricultural sector seem to have considerably increased. Different prices were paid for the same agricultural goods, however, and I have been unable to find reliable average price data with which to gauge this policy reversal quantitatively.

The potential for a favorable shift in the intersectoral terms of trade toward agriculture has been considerable, as shown by the ratio of official agricultural prices to foreign trade prices. This ratio rose slightly during the Tsiranana period and subsequently fell; by the mid-1980s it was lower than in the colonial period, especially if rice (which was never exported in great amounts) is excluded from the calculation. The fall in the ratio is even more apparent if sugar and vanilla (two crops with some special features) are also excluded.

These statistical exercises have two important implications. First, the agricultural export sector has not shared in the long-term buoyant international market for its products. Second, the average annual decline in exports (primarily composed of agricultural goods) of 3.8 percent a year between 1972 and 1984 becomes more understandable. Indeed, by 1983–84 the fall in real prices of certain export products, such as coffee, made production unprofitable at the official price when all costs were taken into account (World Bank December 1984, pp. 47–48). In other words, FNUP, which has collected most of the difference between domestic and foreign prices, placed a high implicit tax on the rural sector, thereby lowering real rural incomes.

The liberalization from 1985 onward led to a considerable rise in the real price paid to rice producers. Preliminary estimates for 1987 show a bumper rice crop, which some have attributed to the liberalization. Other explanations are possible, however, so evidence from later years is needed before a firm judgment can be made.

More perspective on the government's producer price policies can be gained by comparing Madagascar's ratios of producer to export prices with similar ratios for the same crops in other African nations. On the whole, the Malagasy ratios have been lower, which in this restricted sense provides more evidence that the price policies of the Madagascar government have been discouraging agricultural production.[11]

Other Aspects of Agricultural Prices

The available price data for Madagascar permit evaluation of several important aspects of governmental price policies for agriculture.

PRICE AND INCOME STABILITY. Although tables 5-2 and 12-2 show individual foreign trade prices of major agricultural products varying more in Madagascar than in Malaŵi, the aggregate price series show roughly the same variations in both countries. This means that the price fluctuations of individual commodities are more closely correlated in Malaŵi.

I examined short-term price fluctuations from 1960 through 1984 by calculating pseudocoefficients of variation for four annual series: prices paid by the government to producers, foreign trade prices for the same products, and total agricultural revenues using the two different sets of prices.[12] In Madagascar the annual fluctuations in the index of official prices were considerably less than those in the index of export prices, although the difference was not as great as in Malaŵi. The fluctuations of agricultural receipts using actual export prices were somewhat greater than the actual fluctuation of such receipts calculated by using official producer prices, so the various price stabilization measures apparently acted to stabilize agricultural revenues, even though the explicit purpose of many of these boards in Madagascar was to stabilize domestic prices, not agricultural incomes. This aggregate income stabilization may have had a small positive benefit for growth for those farmers that diversified their crops. Aggregate income stabilization based on a market basket of crops was irrelevant for individual farmers specializing primarily in one crop unless considerable income or credit transfers took place between the "winning" and "losing" segments of the agricultural sector—which was not the case.

PRICE VARIATIONS OVER DISTANCE. Transportation and other costs cause agricultural prices to differ among various areas unless the government enforces a uniform price or some other price structure that ignores cost factors. For Madagascar market price data for different crops are available for different areas and for a number of years; these permit measurement of changes in price uniformity (if differences in market prices among areas are less than their free market level) and market disintegration (if such differences are greater than their free market level).[13] Table 12-4 presents some evidence of market disequilibria—especially for rice.

These data suggest that from 1973 on, average rice prices in these rural markets were generally above the official buying prices but below the official selling prices. Until 1974 the import price of rice was roughly the same as the domestic selling price, but in the year following the first international oil shock, the import price of rice rose 50 percent above the official selling price and generally remained higher than the official price until 1982–83, when liberalization of the domestic rice price began.

Particularly striking is the evidence on the spatial dispersion of prices. A weighted coefficient of variation (CV) of prices in these markets widened dramatically during the period when SINPA and its successor agencies began to replace the private traders and to purchase the crops itself. The CVs rose over time, which means that the rural markets were literally disintegrating; the arbitrage that previously had kept prices roughly in line in various parts of the country ceased to function with the nationalization of crop purchasing. Alternative mechanisms to keep prices in line are certainly available; for instance, in Malaŵi, market integration of the rural areas appeared to increase with the extension of ADMARC's network of trading outlets. Nevertheless, such alternative mechanisms were not put in place in Madagascar.

One economic impact of any such market disintegration is to encourage production of particular crops in areas having no comparative advantage in their production. Such a misallocation, of course, lowers overall production. The impact on the distribution of income is more difficult to specify, especially because the poorest farmers generally market a lower share of their production and are therefore less affected by pricing policies.

The CVs also can be used to analyze the short-term impact of the liberalization of the rice markets. Using some confidential monthly data supplied by the Ministry of Agriculture on average market prices of rice in the six provinces (Faritany), I calculated an unweighted coefficient of variation for the period from January 1983 through November 1985. A true liberalization would have caused the CV to decline; in actuality, it rose until about January 1985 and then fell, but to a level somewhat higher than at the beginning of the period. This provides quite concrete evidence to support the claim that the local governments were subverting the liberalization of the rice market, at least through 1985. The apparent rise in the real price paid to the farmers since then suggests that by 1987 the central government was

Table 12-4. Indicators of Agricultural Market Disequilibria, Madagascar, 1960 to 1984

			Rice prices (FMG/kg)[c]			
	Ratio of weighted prices on farmers' market to official prices (percent)[a]	Weighted coefficients of variation of prices in farmers' markets (percent)[b]	Official			Average farmers' market price
Year			Purchase price	Selling price	Import price	
1960	n.a.	n.a.	11.0	27.0	25.44	n.a.
1961	n.a.	n.a.	11.0	27.0	26.76	n.a.
1962	n.a.	n.a.	12.0	26.0	30.14	n.a.
1963	n.a.	n.a.	12.0	28.0	31.19	n.a.
1964	n.a.	n.a.	14.0	28.0	26.20	n.a.
1965	n.a.	n.a.	14.0	30.0	31.05	n.a.
1966	n.a.	n.a.	12.6	37.0	32.30	n.a.
1967	n.a.	n.a.	13.0	35.0	37.26	n.a.
1968	n.a.	n.a.	13.4	34.0	41.94	n.a.
1969	n.a.	n.a.	13.6	34.0	35.80	n.a.
1970	n.a.	n.a.	24.2	34.0	32.87	n.a.
1971	101.1	6.4	15.0	34.0	29.69	15.6
1972	93.9	9.5	15.0	34.0	24.11	14.0
1973	140.9	17.8	15.0	38.0	40.43	24.4
1974	134.4	26.4	25.0	62.0	93.16	37.2
1975	120.1	30.7	30.0	65.0	85.35	38.1
1976	111.9	22.5	30.0	65.0	82.54	34.5
1977	110.2	24.2	35.0	56.0	56.23	39.3
1978	116.5	25.6	35.0	55.0	65.83	42.5
1979	111.5	23.3	39.0	55.0	62.63	44.9
1980	130.0	26.7	43.0	60.0	56.52	58.5
1981	142.1	20.8	47.0	70.0	95.71	70.4
1982	n.a.	n.a.	57.0	116.0	98.74	n.a.
1983	n.a.	n.a.	65.0	145.0	106.33	n.a.
1984	n.a.	n.a.	75.0	228.0	136.45	n.a.

(continued)

able partly to enforce its liberalization policies so that this interregional spread of prices probably declined.

Market disintegration also has an important impact on the distribution of income. The richer smallholders probably benefited more from these differences in prices because they had the working capital to pay higher transportation costs if higher product prices occurred at some distance; poorer smallholders did not have that option.

Although liberalization of the market would narrow income differences arising from a disintegrated islandwide market, this would oc-

Table 12-4. Indicators of Agricultural Market Disequilibria, Madagascar, 1960 to 1984 *(continued)*

n.a. = Not available.

Note: The farmers' market prices are the arithmetic average of the maximum and minimum prices for various products in seventeen subprefectures *(Fivondronana)*, as reported by agricultural agents; the original source contains a warning about the quality of these data.

a. Estimates cover four products: rice, coffee, cloves, and groundnuts. Data for a number of minor products are available but are not included; data for certain major products such as cassava (manioc) and sugar were available, but the product definitions appear different for the official and farmers' market prices and, for this reason, they are also not included in the above index. For each commodity the individual prices were weighted by the production of that subprovince in 1970; for the overall percentage, the weighted average prices for individual products are weighted by the total production in 1970 and are compared to a similarly weighted value of official prices.

b. Estimates cover nine products: rice, coffee, cloves, cassava (manioc), groundnuts, sugar, maize, bananas, and sweet potatoes. For each product, weighted coefficients of variation of prices are calculated, with 1970 production in each subprovince as the weights. These weighted cvs are then weighted by the 1970 value of production to obtain a value. An index is calculated using the average values for 1971 through 1973 as the base.

c. Prices are for ordinary, not luxury, rice. The selling price is for *riz usiné* BC2.

Source: The farmers' market prices come from various issues of Madagascar, Ministère de la production agricole et de la réforme agraire, *Statistiques agricoles: Annuaire* (annual). The other price data come from materials supplied by the Direction générale du plan.

cur only in the long run because market relations take time to reestablish. Simon Razafimandimby (1987) has provided some interesting evidence for the Lac Alaotra area that the first impact of the liberalization was actually to widen rural income differentials. The (now legalized) private crop buyers first focused their efforts on the richest areas producing the most rice, so producer prices in these areas rose much more than in the poorer areas, where less rice was offered for sale and where distance from market made transportation more costly.[14] If the Malagasy government loses its courage and acts to limit the "unjust" profits of these middlemen, the private tradesmen may never reach distant, poorer areas, and the high short-run rural income differentials will be frozen into the system for a long period.

OTHER EFFECTS. For Madagascar some financial data of the crop marketing boards are publicly available (World Bank December 1984 and June 1983, annex 1). These are so scattered, however, that not much can be done with them. Pascal Chaigneau (1985) supplies some interesting (though unattributed) qualitative evidence about the operations of these parastatal purchasing agencies, pointing out that they sometimes paid for rice with notes, rather than cash, which the farmers could discount only at very high rates. This reduced rural incomes and further discouraged both the production and the marketing of farm produce.

Although the rice subsidy to urban consumers lowered the prices smallholders received and was thus regressive in effect, the subsidy appears to have been progressive in the urban sector because rice purchases absorbed a higher share of the total expenditures of low-income than of high-income families. Nevertheless, the rice subsidy was a more cumbersome method of urban poverty alleviation than others that were available, and the rise in urban rice prices in the mid-1980s burdened low-income consumers more than high-income consumers.

The Credit Market in the Rural Sector

Factor markets in Madagascar are stunted, which can be shown easily for the credit market. Credit flows to the rural sector were small; in addition, they were skewed toward the estates and wealthier smallholders.

The Formal Structure

At independence in 1960 Madagascar had four commercial banks, largely owned by French banking interests, and a government investment bank (the BNM). All five lent to the agricultural sector, although mainly to the estate sector (except the BNM). In 1975 the government nationalized the four commercial banks and two years later reorganized the state banking sector into three banks, each respectively to specialize in loans to agriculture, industry, and commerce. This division of labor has not been inviolable, however. Although the National Bank for Rural Development (BTM) was to focus on agriculture, roughly half of its commercial loans have gone to commerce and industry; furthermore, the other two banks have cooperated with the BTM in financing particularly large agricultural operations such as rice marketing.

The data in table 12-5 show that the agricultural sector received very roughly one-fifth to one-fourth of all loans, at least until the mid-1970s, and these loans have amounted to roughly 3.5 to 4.0 percent of GDP. Smallholders consistently have received only a small share of agricultural credit, although the specific percentage has varied widely from year to year.

Credit to Smallholders

Because Malagasy smallholders have been unable to obtain much bank credit, they have had to rely on informal credit arrangements or loans from various government programs, as in Malaŵi. Although

Table 12-5. Bank Loans to the Agricultural Sector, Madagascar, 1965 to 1985

	Loans to the agricultural sector			Loans to smallholders		
		As a percentage of			As a percentage of	
Year	Million FMG	Total loans	GDP	Million FMG	GDP	Total agricultural loans
1965	n.a.	n.a.	n.a.	127	0.08	n.a.
1966	n.a.	n.a.	n.a.	102	0.06	n.a.
1967	n.a.	n.a.	n.a.	114	0.06	n.a.
1968	7,168	17.3	3.4	126	0.06	1.8
1969	8,350	18.7	3.7	191	0.09	2.3
1970	11,781	22.8	4.7	286	0.11	2.4
1971	10,774	19.3	4.0	242	0.09	2.2
1972	11,103	19.0	4.0	323	0.12	2.9
1973	11,745	20.3	3.9	418	0.14	3.6
1974	16,999	23.7	4.6	121	0.03	0.7
1975	13,993	20.4	3.5	645	0.16	4.6
Unweighted average		20.2	4.0		0.09	2.6
1975	19,749	n.a.	5.0	645	0.16	3.3
1976	13,886	n.a.	3.3	802	0.19	5.7
1977	12,517	n.a.	2.7	2,377	0.51	19.0
1978	14,314	n.a.	2.9	2,242	0.46	15.7
1979	25,220	n.a.	4.2	243	0.04	0.9
1980	n.a.	n.a.	n.a.	561	0.08	n.a.
1981	n.a.	n.a.	n.a.	1,291	0.16	n.a.
1982	n.a.	n.a.	n.a.	673	0.07	n.a.
1983	n.a.	n.a.	n.a.	493	0.04	n.a.
1984	n.a.	n.a.	n.a.	780	0.06	na.
1985	n.a.	n.a.	n.a.	1,628	0.10	n.a.
Unweighted average			3.6		0.17	8.9

n.a. = Not available

Note: Data on loans vary considerably from source to source; because definitions are seldom given, reconciling differences is difficult. The two sources for total loans give different results for 1975 and may not be completely comparable.

Source: The loan data for 1968 through 1975 come from Madagascar, Minister of Finance and Planning (1977), pp. 149–51. Data on total agricultural loans from 1975 through 1979 include only the loans of the BNM (Banque nationale malgache de développement) and its successor, the BTM (the National Bank for Rural Development); these data come from various issues of Madagascar, Ministére de la production agricole et de la réforme agraire, *Annuaire statistique agricole.* Data on loans to smallholders come from the same source, as well as from information supplied by the BTM.

traditional tenure arrangements discouraged using land as loan collateral, cattle could serve this function. Often the crop buyers were also the moneylenders and took crop liens. In the 1950s a number of French economists, generally having a leftist viewpoint, harshly criticized these middlemen, strongly objecting to the rural interest rates, which ran between 25 and 30 percent a year (in the mid-1980s, however, this was only slightly higher than the rate government banks charged small businesses).[15] Before independence the private lenders were primarily Chinese and Indian merchants. Lending by governmental functionaries and local elites gradually replaced private lending from these sources, and with the nationalization of marketing in the mid-1970s, this form of credit extended by crop buyers declined further.

Various types of traditional money lending also have been available to finance agriculture, as well as important ceremonies. In the high plateau and middle west, kin groups have provided capital for the fattening of cattle in exchange for a share of the final sale proceeds. In some areas migrants have left funds with their traditional chief, who loaned such funds at high rates to people outside the village; when the migrants returned, they reclaimed their original funds plus a certain share of the interest payments.

In Madagascar the government has played a much smaller direct role in channeling credit to smallholders than has the Malaŵi government. Instead, the banking system has either made such loans directly out of its own funds or administered governmental programs (which appear as part of the banks' portfolio of loans). As shown in table 12-5, bank loans to smallholders from 1965 to 1985 have been rather modest, averaging about 0.13 percent of GDP, a much lower rate than in Malaŵi during most years (see table 5-5). In the early 1950s the government started several programs to provide significant amounts of credit to smallholders. From 1963 to 1977 the BNM administered most of these programs, lending to regional development agencies and to farmers' associations.[16] A direct program for bank lending to smallholders (the FMR program) was begun in 1972. The BTM, which took over the BNM's investment portfolio in 1977, continued this smallholder credit program. It has offices throughout the country (the highlands and east coast, which are the wealthier areas, appear to be the regions best served) for its various agricultural loan programs.

The FMR program allocated credit mostly to individuals, but within the context of the *fokontany* (village government) institutions. To be eligible, borrowers could have no more than 5 hectares under cultivation. The interest rates were 1 percent a month, and loans ran from one to ten years. Loans were approved by a credit committee with representatives from the village and the BTM. Its decisions allegedly were based on directives from the Ministry of Agriculture specifying general lending policies, financing plans, and the responsibilities of the extension and other services of the ministry. The *fokontany* bore the major responsibility for administering the program, and in the 1980s the BTM began to withdraw credit from particular *fokontany* in which repayments were poor. Several observers in Madagascar claim, although their basis of evidence is not clear, that by and large only the richer farmers have been able to obtain this bank credit, contrary to the intent of the program (Rouveyan and Chauaney, n.d.).[17]

Loan recoveries of the FMR program have been unsatisfactory. In 1975, the recovery rate was 80 percent; in 1980, it was 70 percent; and in 1981, 41 percent (World Bank June 1983, annex 5). Such poor performance was attributable in part to the political nature of the village credit committees and in part to poor technical supervision by the BTM. In 1981 the BTM began a new program to lend to farmers in *fokontany* closed to FMR credit and in new *fokontany*, where such credit had never been received. This new program, the Integrated Rural Development Operation (ORDI), was expensive to administer, especially because it required a socioeconomic survey of families in the entire area. Because administrative costs were lower on loans to more prosperous smallholders, these loans soon seemed to flow primarily to them.

The Director of the BTM, M. Henri, in a June 1986 interview told me that in the mid-1980s, the rural credit programs to smallholders were in bad shape. The bank had tried various experiments to increase the level of repayments, including tying credit to extension aid, lending to groups rather than individuals, and applying "draconian restrictions" on future farm inputs for delinquent borrowers. The BTM appears to have tried almost all the various measures Malaŵi used successfully, but without Malaŵi's successful results. In part, this is because the government has had no overall credit policy and has not coordinated credit policy with the overall national plan. The smallholder credits have not been provided in the context of an integrated package of technical, marketing, and input aid, and the rural populace has not understood the credit programs well. The breakdown of law and order in the countryside also has hindered repayment.

The Impact of Rural Capital Flows

Quantitative evidence with which to evaluate the impact of the rural capital flows is not available for Madagascar. Indeed, identifying a credit shortage is difficult, especially because the scarcity of agricultural inputs during the last decade, rather than the scarcity of credit, has appeared to be the major problem. In FOFIFA surveys of various rural areas, availability of credit has sometimes been mentioned as a problem of secondary importance, but the main complaints have focused on such concerns as the lack of agricultural inputs.

The Tsiranana government appeared to channel credit primarily to those farmers who sold considerable amounts of crops to the domestic or foreign trade networks, and bank administration of the FMR program suggests that the bias toward lending to the richer farmers continued after 1975.

The Labor Market in the Rural Sector

With markets for land and capital stunted, the labor market could be an important mechanism for allocating resources to increase production and for providing an effective way for those with little land and credit to increase their incomes (chapter 5). Assessing the actual impact of the labor market on either growth or distribution in Madagascar is difficult because of the lack of relevant information. Except for various settlement schemes and similar projects to encourage migration (chapter 11), the Malagasy government has taken few direct or indirect actions to influence the rural labor flows or markets.

Formal and Informal Labor Exchanges

In 1980 the estates hired roughly 1.6 percent of the rural labor force.[18] This is considerably smaller than the figure for Malaŵi. Malagasy smallholders also used a certain amount of nonfamily labor, but the share that was hired is unknown.

The rice economy of Madagascar has featured a number of different kinds of traditional labor exchanges and group labor arrangements. These appear necessary not only because operating and maintaining the irrigation system require cooperative work but also because for any given rice field certain tasks seem to be best performed in a short time period and thus require a labor force beyond the immediate family farming the plot. Various informal labor exchanges have also been used for farming other crops.[19]

The sources of recruitment to work teams differ according to crop (for example, from kin groups, for traditional crops; from village groups, for nontraditional crops); according to the sex of the person organizing the work (a wife recruits from her relatives; a husband, from his); and according to the degree of monetization of the local economy, the availability of migrant workers, and other such factors. The labor productivity of group labor has also varied according to the composition of the group; in the south, for instance, the productivity of kin groups has been relatively low. Poor peasants participated in labor exchanges more frequently than others. Although the quantitative importance of mutual labor exchange is difficult to estimate, the ethnographic literature has implied that it is quite important, an inference reinforced by the common sight of large groups of people knee-deep in water sweeping through a rice field.

Migration and Labor Supply

Unlike Malaŵians, few Malagasy have worked abroad, because Madagascar is more geographically isolated from the rest of Africa. We might also expect less internal migration of labor in the rice economy of Madagascar than we find in the maize economy of Malaŵi. In wet rice agriculture much more investment is tied up in the preparation of the rice paddies, and in the initial years of a newly constructed rice paddy, fertility is lower than in later years. Moreover, diminishing returns occurring with an increase in the farmer-land ratio are believed to be less important in paddy rice production than in many other crops (see Bray 1986).

In fact, however, Madagascar's internal labor migration data are not much different from those of Malaŵi. In 1975 about 5.1 percent of the population lived in a province different from their place of birth; about 13.8 percent lived a significant distance from their place of birth (Madagascar, INSRE, n.d. [f]).[20] A major difference from Malaŵi is that a considerable share—about 9.5 percent of the resident rural population in Madagascar—have moved from one rural area to another. This provides some evidence for the claim that overcrowding of land has occurred in Madagascar but that it has been a local phenomenon (chapter 11).

The major migration pattern has been from south to north. The greatest outmigration occurred in the province of Fianarantsoa (and, to a much lesser degree, the province of Toliary); the greatest inmigration occurred in the provinces of Antsiranana (Diégo Suarez) and Mahajunga. Although outmigration tended to be from provinces with low urbanization to those with higher urbanization, this migration pattern had no obvious relationship either to average rural income in 1962 or to population density, despite qualitative information suggesting strongly that scarcity of fertile land in areas with a suitable climate is an important factor underlying outmigration. No rigorous push-pull type of analysis of migration patterns is available, but I have few doubts that such a study would show migration flows to be strongly influenced by very simple economic factors.

The Malagasy government has tried to encourage migration in several different ways (see Rabes and Rakotoanost 1979). Many of the development authorities brought unused land under cultivation and introduced new settlers to the area. The government also encouraged immigration to various new settlements in underpopulated rural areas such as the middle west section of the country. In 1974 a government decree gave high priority to such settlement schemes and, as a result, four such projects were undertaken with financial assistance from foreign aid donors. The Ministry of Population and Social Welfare also started a rural village for unemployed urban youth. The 1977 policy initiative, the "Battle of Rice," was still another approach; it motivated enlargement of rice land in a variety of different areas, thereby encouraging short-distance rather than long-distance migration.

For the most part these projects must be judged expensive failures. Costs have been high—up to $5,000 to $10,000 per family (World Bank November 1980). Furthermore, a large share of the original migrants left quickly because of lack of proper infrastructure and amenities, social conflicts with those already living in the area, or disillusionment with the achieved results. Although such programs had a certain economic justification, the government proved incapable of administering them effectively. In the 1980s the government appears to have dropped most of its formal migration plans and to have allowed migration to take place spontaneously with relatively little or no official support.

Functioning of the Labor Market

From the scattered information on rural labor markets, only several of the most important parameters can be established. In 1962 an average smallholder farm used sixty-one work days of occasional work from people outside the immediate household (Madagascar, Ministère des finances et du commerce, and INSRE, 1966).[21] Assuming an average labor force per farm of 3.7 (which was the average number economically active per farm in 1975) and a 250-day work year, such labor constituted about 6.6 percent of all farm labor; on the basis of cultivated area, this in-hiring amounted to 0.23 work years per hectare. Although these data include informal labor exchanges (the Malaŵi data reported in chapter 5 do not), labor exchange or purchase in Madagascar appears to have been a much more important phenomenon than in Malaŵi. A large part of the difference is probably attributable to the different characteristics of the major crops in the two countries.

In 1962 these episodes of in-hiring were for short intervals—about three days per occasional worker. Furthermore, the method of payment varied considerably: 47 percent of the work was paid in cash; 9 percent, in goods; 10 percent, in cash and goods; 29 percent, in reciprocal labor; and 5 percent, in reciprocal labor and cash. The average daily payment was 89 FMG, which at the legal minimum wage represented about seven hours of work in a day; the actual number of work hours is not known.[22]

Summary and Conclusions

Several product market factors have influenced the growth of agricultural production in Madagascar. The intersectoral terms of trade appear to have declined in the last years of the colonial period, and the fact that they were not raised thereafter for any significant period of time undoubtedly has retarded growth. The further decline of relative agricultural prices in the late 1970s reinforced these tendencies. An important reason underlying the Malagasy government's agricultural price policies from the mid-1970s to the mid-1980s was the top leadership's fundamental distrust of material incentives. For instance, an important official document from the late 1970s (cited in chapter 1) speaks of the need to tolerate no longer the "petty spirit, which only searches for gain."

Such ideological beliefs did not prevent the government from raising official food prices in the mid-1980s and from liberalizing the rice market in order to encourage food production, nor did they prevent the president from declaring in his 1986 New Year's speech to the nation that his advisors had pressed such measures upon him and that he had never really been in favor of the liberalization. Such differences between policies and values make prediction of future governmental actions difficult; present price policies may well be reversed in the future when the island is not so dependent on foreign loans tied to liberalization. In any case, the impacts of these more liberal policies regarding agricultural prices and markets are too recent to permit evaluation.

Other market factors also adversely influenced agricultural production. From the mid-1970s to the mid-1980s, the breakdown in the marketing of agricultural inputs and consumer goods to farmers lessened the potentiality and the incentive for growth of agricultural production. The disintegration of the product markets for domestic foodstuffs certainly did not improve the situation. The small flows of credit to the agricultural sector probably served to retard production growth, although solid evidence on this matter is lacking.

A number of factors widened rural income differentials. The disintegration of the product market and the growth in importance of the parallel markets for agricultural products favored the richer smallholders, who could take advantage of the situation. Similarly, the shortages of agricultural inputs undoubtedly affected most adversely the poorer smallholders, who did not have the resources to obtain such vital commodities in black market channels. The credit system also seemed to favor the richer farmers both before and after 1972.

The adverse intersectoral terms of trade in the late 1970s and early 1980s also widened the average income gap between the rural and urban sectors. Malagasy farmers seemed less reticent in expressing their discontent with governmental policies than were their counterparts in Malaŵi; the series of rural *jacqueries* in the 1980s, for instance, in Toliary (Tuléar) in 1982 and in Antsiranana (Diégo Suarez) in 1984, seemed related to the adverse impact of such policies on the rural sector (Chaigneau 1985, p. 197). In the long run, the liberalization of rural markets may lead to a narrowing of such income differentials, but in the short run, intrarural income inequalities may increase, and this in turn may jeopardize the liberalization. The dramatic shift in agricultural market policies will be difficult to implement.

Notes

1. This discussion of marketing institutions in Madagascar draws heavily on five sources: Berthélemy and others (1988); Dethier and Stryker (1985); France, Ministère de la cooperation (1986); World Bank (June 1983); and World Bank (December 1984).

2. Relevant data are presented in Pryor (1988a), section C. A problem with these data is that a considerable amount of rice is marketed through unofficial channels. Ahlers and others (1984) show that for 1981 through 1983, farmers sold from 2.5 to 4.3 times more rice through the parallel markets than to official price purchasing organizations.

3. For export crops, these have been called *Caisses de stabilisation*; for domestic crops, Bureaux de commercialisation et de stabilisation des prix. The stabilization funds have covered aleurites (later terminated), cassava, cloves, coffee, cotton, groundnuts, manioc, pepper, rice (later terminated), sugar, and vanilla.

4. The rice subsidies are an interesting chapter in Madagascar economic history that cannot be analyzed here. Pourcet (1987) and Hugon (1987) have interesting discussions on the topic.

5. Malagasy smallholders have less need to buy fertilizers than do the Malaŵi smallholders because animal fertilizers are much more available. Nevertheless, the vast differences between the fertilizer sales (especially on a per capita basis) in the two countries in the later years delivers an important message about the effectiveness of the system supplying agricultural inputs to the farmers. Ahlers and others(1984), p. 7, briefly discusses parallel markets for fertilizer in Madagascar.

6. Berthélemy and Morrisson (1987) provide data illustrating this point for a number of countries.

7. Askari and Cummings (1976) report on various studies of supply elasticities for rice and coffee throughout the world. Although Berthélemy presents elasticities for vanilla as well, I could find no comparable elasticities for other countries. Some problems arise in making such calculations for such products as rice because of the existence of parallel markets. How the two supply elasticity studies handled this problem is unclear, so these results must be considered tentative. The value of the supply elasticities possibly could depend on the degree of integration of peasants with the market economy. A farmer selling a small amount of rice to obtain cash to pay his taxes might increase his sales to the market if the price fell, especially if he had no other sellable crop. Although this mechanism may occur in individual cases, I found no evidence for Madagascar suggesting that this has influenced overall supply elasticities.

8. Price data for the parallel markets come from Hirsche (1986) and Glenshaw and Harmon (1985). The data from these two sources are somewhat different.

9. An index with five commodities is presented in Pryor (1988a), section C. The data are not completely comparable with those in table 12-3, however.

10. Although data on marketed production of other domestically consumed products are available, they are of questionable reliability.

11. Such conclusions are based on rough comparisons made with data presented by Hesp (1985).

12. The method of calculation is given in footnote 6, chapter 5. For Madagascar I use an eleven-product series, and the price series are weighted with the same quantity weights as in table 12-3. For the income series I used the current value of agricultural revenues assuming first that domestic prices and then that foreign trade prices applied. The pseudocoefficients of variation discussed qualitatively in the text for Madagascar are for agricultural export prices, 18.8 percent; domestic agricultural prices, 12.6 percent; agricultural revenues calculated in export prices, 22.0 percent; and agricultural revenues calculated in domestic prices, 15.2 percent. Official prices paid to farms did not vary during a given year; however, those prices paid by private traders did reflect seasonal variations.

13. Local agents of the Ministry of Agriculture in the seventeen *préfectures* outside of Antananarivo have collected annual data on the maximum and minimum producer prices for a variety of goods. Such prices presumably reflected conditions on the farmers' markets and activities of various types of crop purchasers, including agents of different levels of the government; such information is only available in the form of arithmetic averages. Although the quality and quantity of this information leave much to be desired, the data reveal a picture of interspatial variations in price that is consistent with our expectations.

14. Razafimandimby (1987) does not make any distinction between short-and long-run effects and is considerably more alarmed at this widening of income differentials than the interpretation in this text implies. Other publications, such as France, Ministère de la coopération (1986), p. 84, argue without much evidence that the liberalization has widened income differences because the richer farmers can get high prices for their surpluses, but they appeared to be selling a large share of these at black market prices previously.

15. Attention has focused mostly on the role of moneylenders and is coupled with thundering denouncements. A typical description of these moneylenders is given by Gendarme (1960), pp. 125 ff. I have found very little scholarly attention to traditional lending institutions, although some useful information comes from World Bank (June 1983), annex 5. Guy Pourcet, in a letter, graciously supplied me with considerable information on informal credit arrangements.

16. In this discussion I draw heavily upon World Bank (June 1983), annex 5.

17. A version of this paper appeared in *Revue économique de Madagascar* 5, January–December (1970), pp. 137–234.

18. This datum comes from information on agricultural labor in the modern sector and on the total agricultural labor force, presented in Pryor (1988a), section K.

19. Althabe (1969), Bloch (1980), and Kottak (1980) provide useful recent information about cooperative labor. Jacques Charmes for OSTROM and Guy Pourcet have written several reports on labor exchanges in the high plateau and in the south, but these were not available to me except in summary form.

20. These data include only resident population and exclude those coming from abroad. The original source does not specify how great a change of residence constitutes a "significant change of residence." Migration might be underestimated because of a possible error of calculation in the census (seen by comparing tables 37 and 38 of the data source), which counted only the rural-urban migration that is also interprovincial. Deschamps (1959) has an extensive earlier study on migration.

21. Whether the in-hired labor also includes cooperative group labor is unclear. For 1985 Ministère de la production agricole et de la réforme agraire (1986) presents some data on permanent production workers (who apparently work on some of the state farms and other estates) and temporary agricultural production workers (9.4 million man-days). These temporary workers probably do not include all of the various labor exchanges that take place.

22. Minimum wage (SMIG) data for agricultural work in the Toliary area come from Pryor (1988a), section H. I assume that the data for 1960 applied for 1962 as well. I have no evidence that the SMIG was used—or could even be enforced—in the casual hiring of labor in rural areas; rather, this datum serves simply as a baseline.

13 Foreign Trade and the Balance of Payments in Madagascar

From independence until the mid-1980s the performance of the foreign trade sector in Madagascar was unimpressive. From 1960 to the mid-1970s the volume of exports and imports rose at about the same rate as GDP; thereafter, the trade volume fell so that the ratio of foreign trade to GDP was significantly lower in the mid-1980s than it was in 1960. Many of the country's foreign trade difficulties can be traced to the overvalued foreign exchange rate prevailing from the early 1970s until 1987, when a drastic devaluation took place. To maintain some semblance of balance in the foreign exchange accounts, the government administered an increasingly rigorous system of import restrictions.

Madagascar's trade difficulties were largely self-induced. Although the commodity terms of trade fluctuated considerably in the short run, they did not greatly change over the long run. A rapid fall in agricultural exports from the early 1970s to the mid-1980s, combined with the precipitous increase in foreign-held debt and debt-service payments after the invest-to-the-hilt program in the late 1970s, led to a balance of payments crisis and several debt cancellations and reschedulings in the first half of the 1980s. In the mid-1980s, in conjunction with several structural adjustment loans from international lending agencies, the government devalued the currency and restructured foreign trade incentives.

Trade Orientation and Key Structural Characteristics

The overwhelming bulk of Madagascar's exports have been agriculture-based. An increase in exports, therefore, should lead not only to higher growth for the economy as a whole but also to a narrowing of average family income differences between the rural and urban sectors, because smallholder crops are an important part of exports. For most of the postindependence period, however, the government has not given much encouragement to exports.

In this chapter I explore Madagascar's trade performance and the signs of export policy neglect from several different standpoints: the ratio of trade to GDP; the various types of trade policies; and the differential price changes in the export, import-competing, and nontradable goods sectors. The structure of exports and imports and the direction of trade, two important aspects of trade not directly relevant to the major themes of this study are discussed in section B of the Appendix.

The Degree of Openness

According to the data presented in table 13-1, the average ratio of exports to factor price GDP (in current prices) in the colonial period (from 1950 through 1959) was 16.4 percent; after independence, it was 14.2 percent—less than two-thirds of the corresponding ratio for Malaŵi. In the early 1980s the ratio for Madagascar fell considerably below the long-term average. Madagascar's "trade openness" in 1975 was about 11 percent below that of a comparison group of sixteen Sub-Saharan nations.[1] More sophisticated experiments with larger samples of nations yield somewhat mixed results; nevertheless, Madagascar's trade seems to have been somewhat lower than might be predicted for a nation with its per capita income and population.[2]

The ratio of Madagascar's exports to its GDP was roughly the same in 1978 as in 1950, although the behavior of this ratio during this period varied somewhat, depending upon whether current price or constant price series are examined. After 1978, both series show a collapse in exports. The ratio of imports to GDP during the 1950 to 1978 period remained roughly the same in current prices but declined slightly in constant prices. In the early 1980s, the import ratio began to fall as the government struggled to reduce the trade deficit.

The data in table 13-2 provide a different perspective. The volume of exports grew during the colonial period at an average annual rate of about 1.8 percent and during the Tsiranana government (1960–72) at 4.5 percent. From 1972 through 1984, however, export volume decreased at an annual rate of 3.8 percent. The result was a downward spiral of trade and GDP (chapter 10).

In 1972 the government of Gabriel Ramanantsoa removed the poll and cattle taxes Galliéni had imposed on the rural sector in the early years of the colonial period to encourage market production of agricultural products. The Ramanantsoa government seemed aware that this particular type of tax relief would discourage production (chapter 12) and raised real agricultural prices for about five years. This price incentive was not sufficient to elicit more production, however, especially in light of other agricultural policies. A few years later, the Ratsiraka government reduced real agricultural prices below their former level, and marketed agricultural production declined even more.

Foreign Trade and the Balance of Payments in Madagascar 289

Table 13-1. Trade as a Share of GDP, Madagascar, 1950 to 1984

	\multicolumn{4}{c}{Percent of quasi-factor price GDP[a]}
	Current prices		Constant prices	
Year	Exports c.i.f.	Imports	Exports c.i.f.	Imports
1950	16.0	19.8	15.4	27.7
1951	16.7	28.7	16.8	35.1
1952	18.8	26.9	16.7	29.8
1953	16.3	24.9	13.8	28.8
1954	16.6	24.9	16.5	32.0
1955	15.8	23.7	16.4	29.5
1956	15.5	22.0	19.8	28.6
1957	15.5	24.9	15.5	27.3
1958	17.2	22.5	18.4	24.8
1959	15.8	25.0	14.5	25.9
Unweighted average	16.4	24.3	16.4	28.9
1960	13.8	20.5	13.0	21.5
1961	14.3	19.0	15.6	20.1
1962	15.8	20.4	17.5	21.5
1963	13.4	20.8	13.2	22.6
1964	14.2	20.9	14.8	22.6
1965	13.6	20.6	15.5	20.7
1966	13.3	19.3	15.0	20.3
1967	13.3	18.6	15.4	20.2
1968	13.7	20.2	19.1	22.2
1969	13.0	21.1	14.4	22.5
Unweighted average	13.8	20.1	15.4	21.4
1970	16.1	19.0	17.0	20.0
1971	15.2	22.0	16.8	22.5
1972	15.0	18.5	16.8	20.2
1973	14.7	14.8	17.8	16.6
1974	15.7	17.9	18.0	15.2
1975	16.4	19.6	21.2	16.2
1976	15.7	16.3	15.8	13.8
1977	17.7	18.2	13.3	16.5
1978	17.9	20.5	17.1	18.5
1979	14.1	22.7	15.0	23.2
Unweighted average	15.9	18.9	16.9	18.3
1980	12.3	18.4	11.8	19.5
1981	10.9	18.8	12.8	16.4
1982	10.9	14.9	13.5	14.6
1983	10.4	13.7	10.8	16.0
1984	14.0	15.5	12.9	14.9
Unweighted average	11.7	16.3	12.4	16.3

a. "Quasi-factor price GDP" is GDP minus most but not all net indirect taxes.
Source: Pryor (1988a), tables E-1, E-2, F-1, F-2, and F-3.

Table 13-2. Important Foreign Trade Series, Madagascar, 1950 to 1984

	Index (1970 = 100)				Percentage of GDP		Tariff revenues as percentage of imports (c.i.f.)
Year	Real trade weighted exchange rate	Exports	Imports	Terms of trade	Balance on current account	Long-term capital flow and debt relief	
1950	n.a.	52.1	79.5	145.3	n.a.	n.a.	12.0
1951	n.a.	58.6	103.8	121.5	n.a.	n.a.	14.9
1952	71.3	56.5	85.7	125.1	n.a.	n.a.	12.4
1953	72.0	48.4	86.2	137.3	n.a.	n.a.	14.1
1954	66.6	56.6	93.2	129.1	n.a.	n.a.	19.6
1955	74.0	57.8	88.1	119.4	n.a.	n.a.	19.6
1956	71.2	74.4	91.2	101.9	n.a.	n.a.	22.5
1957	80.2	61.9	92.8	109.6	n.a.	n.a.	22.2
1958	83.3	74.5	85.3	102.7	n.a.	n.a.	23.7
1959	90.1	58.4	88.4	112.7	n.a.	n.a.	25.8
Unweighted average	76.1	59.9	89.4	120.5	n.a.	n.a.	18.7
1960	87.6	56.3	78.8	110.6	n.a.	n.a.	26.5
1961	91.2	68.1	74.3	96.3	n.a.	n.a.	29.4
1962	91.5	80.7	84.3	95.3	0.8	0.9	29.3
1963	96.5	63.3	92.0	110.2	-2.4	1.3	28.0
1964	97.3	72.8	94.1	103.0	-1.8	2.0	30.5
1965	99.1	78.0	88.6	88.6	-2.5	3.2	28.4
1966	97.7	79.7	91.4	92.9	-2.2	2.1	28.2
1967	99.1	84.8	94.5	94.0	-0.5	0.4	29.0
1968	97.5	107.7	106.8	79.4	-1.7	0.9	28.3
1969	102.2	84.7	112.7	96.8	-2.8	3.0	28.8
Unweighted average	96.0	77.6	91.8	96.7	-1.6	1.7	28.6
1970	100.0	100.0	100.0	100.0	-0.6	3.7	27.9
1971	102.5	102.3	115.9	91.8	-4.6	4.7	27.7
1972	102.2	101.5	103.9	97.4	-3.0	4.1	26.9
1973	98.7	106.4	84.4	92.5	-2.3	3.2	26.1
1974	99.1	109.9	78.9	74.1	-2.0	1.6	19.8
1975	100.7	130.7	85.1	63.9	-3.4	1.6	19.2
1976	103.2	94.8	70.2	84.1	-1.6	0.9	24.1
1977	105.4	81.0	85.6	121.0	-1.0	1.3	27.3
1978	107.0	101.8	93.6	94.7	-3.8	3.1	23.8
1979	103.8	97.9	129.0	96.1	-14.2	10.7	23.6
Unweighted average	102.3	102.6	94.7	91.6	-3.7	3.5	24.6

(continued)

Table 13-2. Important Foreign Trade Series, Madagascar, 1950 to 1984 *(continued)*

	Index (1970 = 100)				Percentage of GDP		Tariff revenues as percentage of imports (c.i.f.)
Year	Real trade weighted exchange rate	Exports	Imports	Terms of trade	Balance on current account	Long-term capital flow and debt relief	
1980	101.5	78.0	109.3	110.3	-17.0	13.6	27.7
1981	98.5	78.0	85.0	74.3	-12.5	10.9	20.0
1982	95.5	81.3	74.6	78.8	-10.5	6.3	20.3
1983	93.9	65.4	82.7	113.6	-8.7	7.2	20.2
1984	109.7	79.6	78.1	104.0	-7.4	7.5	20.1
Unweighted average	99.8	76.5	85.9	96.2	-11.2	9.1	21.7

n.a. = Not available.
Source: Pryor (1988a), tables E-1a, F-1, F-2, F-3, and F-4.

Because agriculture has dominated exports, total exports fell as well, and for the first time Madagascar began to import rice, its staple, on a massive scale.

In 1973 the government withdrew from the Franc Zone, so France no longer guaranteed the convertibility of the currency. This discouraged investors, who now faced greater uncertainty in repatriating their profits, and Madagascar experienced considerably increased pressure on its balance of international payments. In the late 1970s the government began a massive investment campaign, financed in large part by short-term borrowing on the world market. The program did little to increase output, and the debt-service burden this borrowing entailed exacerbated the nation's balance of payments difficulties.

These balance of payments problems, combined with the government's refusal to devalue the currency to bring its foreign exchange situation back into equilibrium, led to a reduction in imports of a number of vital intermediate goods. These included products of great importance to manufacturers of import-competing goods, so the demand for foreign exchange to import goods that normally could have been made in Madagascar increased. These input shortages also included such goods as fertilizer (table 12-1), which led to a reduction of agricultural production and agricultural exports. A fall in the consumer goods available to the rural sector further reduced incentives to produce for the market (chapter 12). These problems intensified the severity of the balance of payments problem, and the spiral turned downward again.

The terms of trade data in table 13-2 reveal a considerable decline between 1950 and 1960 and a roughly constant overall trend since that time, with considerable variations from trend in particular years such as after the first and second oil shocks. The prices for Malagasy exports have risen sufficiently to offset these import price shocks. The international economic environment has been much more benign for Madagascar than for Malaŵi.

Trade Policies

For a given level of protection, quantitative restrictions in Madagascar, as elsewhere, have had a more adverse impact on trade than have tariffs. In addition, various domestic policies have had repercussions on the country's foreign trade.

Quantitative Restrictions

Various types of quantitative controls have been in operation in Madagascar for decades. A system of import licensing existed before independence. After independence, as part of the arrangements with France guaranteeing the convertibility of the Malagasy currency, a joint Malagasy-French committee decided upon annual quotas on imports from all countries not members of the European Economic Community and outside the Franc Zone.[3] The Malagasy government also issued licenses for certain imports from within the Franc Zone that competed with domestic manufactures. These administrative regulations were supplemented by relatively high import duties and also by total prohibitions of particular imports, the number of which increased to more than 100 during the 1970s. To control the flow of foreign currencies, certain exports also required licenses. The administrative control of trade increased further after Madagascar left the Franc Zone. Since then, the relative importance of administrative regulations of trade has fluctuated according to the balance of payments situation.

The system of licensing foreign exchange has also acted as a quantitative restriction. In mid-1981, an ad hoc committee of representatives from the Ministry of Finance, the central bank, and certain state-owned commercial banks attempted to increase the stringency with which the limited supply of foreign exchange was allocated. Long delays in obtaining foreign exchange were common, and requests, if granted at all, often elicited only a small fraction of the desired amount. To obtain foreign exchange during the early 1980s manufacturers first had to apply to the Ministère de l'industrie et l'énergie et des mines and thereafter to the central bank, so their foreign exchange requests could be reduced sequentially by two different agencies.

After 1984, following the conditions for receiving World Bank structural adjustment loans, the government began to move away from quantitative controls and toward greater reliance on tariffs to maintain balance of payments equilibrium. Considerable delay in obtaining permission to import was still common in 1986, however, at least among most of the business people with whom I spoke. In January 1988 the government further liberalized the import licensing system and made it considerably more uniform and transparent, tying changes in the exchange rate to differences in the demand for foreign exchange through the licensing system and the available supply.

Madagascar also has had a system of export restrictions. During the 1970s every specific good exported required a license; in the early 1980s the system was overhauled to extend export license coverage to a broad range of goods. Nevertheless, in the mid-1980s I still heard horror stories from business people about the bureaucratic difficulties they encountered when exporting. One specialist I interviewed suggested that because particular export licenses specifically benefited particular regions, interethnic political factors might have played an important role in licensing decisions; I could find no evidence to support this conjecture. Additional problems in exporting arose because the central bank required remittance of export proceeds within thirty days of shipment. This meant that foreign buyers had to pay even before they received the goods rather than after the usual sixty to ninety days; clearly such a policy restricted export sales. Furthermore, the Malagasy government gave some parastatals a monopoly on exporting certain products, particularly agricultural products, which also reduced trade by breaking long-standing trade relationships between Malagasy companies and foreign buyers. After January 1988 the government reversed itself and dropped almost all barriers to exporting.

Tax Treatment of Exports and Imports

Relatively little information is available on this topic; for instance, on a visit to Madagascar in the mid-1980s I attempted in vain to find an up-to-date and complete tariff schedule. Analysis of foreign trade taxes is further complicated because the government, in an effort to dampen inflation, maintained a subsidy system to keep the domestic prices for some products relatively constant; when foreign prices rose, the subsidies provided negative tariffs.

The data on the ratio of tariff receipts to the total value of imports (table 13-2) imply that the relatively high import duties during the later years of the colonial period persisted after independence.[4] In a special study of roughly seventy products, Maxwell Stamp Associates (1986) found a nominal posted tariff of about 50 percent. Problems arise in interpreting these calculations, because actual tariffs collected (ex post tariffs, which are not published) were considerably less than the posted tariff rates (ex ante tariffs). The exact reasons behind this discrepancy are obscure; corruption, "negotiated tariffs," special exemptions, and administrative errors probably contributed. Stamp Associates also calculated effective tariffs for its sample. These ranged from -2 percent on paper products to more than 900 percent on textiles; effective tariffs for most major groups of commodities were between 70 and 160 percent.

The Ministère de l'industrie de l'énergie et des mines has claimed that its tariff policy is designed to promote the use of indigenous resources, develop industrial exports, and encourage the production of intermediate goods in Madagascar. Stamp Associates' detailed examination of individual rates indicated that the tariff structure was totally at odds with these three goals. Because that study was based on confidential information, the calculations underlying this conclusion cannot be presented; nevertheless, the analysis was carefully executed and deserves confidence. In any case, the Madagascar import tariff rates appear high and provide further evidence—if any more is needed—of Madagascar's inwardly directed development strategy.

Madagascar has also had a formal system of export taxes. Moreover, since 1977 the Fond national unique de péréquation (FNUP) has collected most of the difference between the actual prices paid for agricultural exports and official domestic prices to producers (chapter 12). Although data on FNUP finances are scattered, in the early 1980s the total export taxes plus FNUP profits appear to have exceeded import taxes.

The combined system of quantitative restrictions and tariffs has hindered the economy's adjustments to changes in the trade situation. One indication is provided by David Wheeler (1983), who measured the degree of symmetry with which imports adjust to changes in export receipts. In most countries imports rise and fall when export receipts change because of income effects. Balance of payments problems occur if imports increase more during upswings of exports than they decrease during downswings of exports. Of the thirty nations in Wheeler's sample, Madagascar revealed the most asymmetrical responses of imports to changes in exports and, as a result, had the greatest balance of payments problems arising from such pressures.

Another measure of the flexibility of the foreign trade system is the degree to which nations are able to keep importing the intermediate goods they need to maintain domestic production during balance of payments difficulties. Because imports in general are reduced during balance of payments difficulties, maintaining the supply of intermediate products requires a much greater cutback of consumption and investment goods. In Madagascar in the early 1980s the lack of such flexibility resulted in considerable unused manufacturing capacity. This situation was exacerbated by the unwillingness of certain enterprises to part with any inventories of raw materials or intermediate products, even though they did not currently need them, because of their fear of being unable to obtain such products in the future. David Wheeler tried to measure this phenomenon econometrically. Madagascar was among those nations in his sample that had the worst record for maintaining inflows of intermediate goods.

On both of these measures of trade inflexibility, the calculations for Madagascar stand in stark contrast to the results for Malaŵi (chapter 6), which during the 1970s had a much different system for regulating trade.

The Favored-Sector Approach

A truly comprehensive approach toward the trade regime must take into account not only tariffs, quantitative restrictions, export promotion, and exchange rate policies but also domestic taxes, production subsidies, and monetary policies (chapter 15). Did this package favor the export sector, the sector producing goods in competition with imports, or the sector producing nontraded goods and services?

A crude but useful empirical approach is to examine trends in relative prices in these three sectors. Similar to the classifications for Malaŵi (chapter 6), agriculture is considered the export sector, the mining and manufacturing industries are the import-competing sector, and the other industries (utilities, construction, distribution, commerce, finance, housing, and services) are the nontradables sector.[5]

From 1960 through 1972, the Tsiranana government appeared to favor the import-competing sector at the expense of the nontradables sector in that relative prices in the former rose and in the latter declined. These changes were not very great (and perhaps were a function of the appreciating real effective exchange rate). After 1972 the apparent prices in the export sector rose at the expense of nontraded goods and services, while relative prices in the import-competing sector remained the same. The actual real agricultural prices paid to the producer began to decline in the mid-1970s, however, so agricultural producers never received these higher export prices; FNUP absorbed the difference. After the fall of Tsiranana, therefore, the regime was not encouraging trade—it failed to stimulate exports by allowing producers to enjoy higher prices and had no impact on import-competing goods.

The difference between Madagascar and Malaŵi, where both import-competing and export prices rose in relation to the prices of nontraded goods and services, is striking (see chapter 6). This is, of course, just one more indication of Madagascar's relative neglect of the foreign trade sector and of the difference between its development strategy and that pursued in Malaŵi.

The Financial Side of Foreign Trade

The basic import-substitution strategy Madagascar's governments followed from independence through the mid-1980s became particularly inappropriate during the 1980s because it gave domestic manufacturers more reasons not to invest. Investing in plant and equipment would have increased their surplus capacity even more. Moreover, those that relied on imported intermediate products could not be assured of obtaining the foreign exchange to purchase such goods, so the financial results of any investment were uncertain.

Exchange Rate Policy

At independence Madagascar was in the Franc Zone. The French central bank guaranteed the convertibility of the Malagasy franc and it was formally tied to the French franc (see section B of the Appendix). In 1973 Madagascar broke the formal link between its currency and France's and established a nationally owned central bank, which controls its own foreign currency reserves. The proximate cause of this change was a policy disagreement arising from Madagascar's desire to place currency controls on all current transactions in the balance of payments; the ultimate cause was the nationalistic desire to rid the country of French tutelage and interference in domestic economic affairs. The most curious aspect of this dramatic change is that Madagascar continued to peg its currency to the French franc at a fixed ratio for another nine years, long after such an exchange rate parity was suitable. Thus Madagascar had all the obvious disadvantages of leaving the Franc Zone but did not use the main advantage—devaluing when necessary.

The trade-weighted nominal exchange rate depreciated during the colonial period and then remained roughly stable from 1960 until 1980; thereafter, a rapid depreciation occurred.[6] The real effective exchange rate shown in table 13-2 reveals a somewhat different pattern; it appreciated 33 percent between 1952 and 1972 and remained roughly constant from 1972 through 1984. From 1984 through 1986 the real effective exchange rate was level against the dollar.

How great was the overvaluation of the Malagasy franc? In a strict sense the Malagasy franc was overvalued during the entire independence period until 1987 because its value was propped up by tariffs and quantitative controls. From 1960 through 1972, however, real exports grew an average of about 4.5 percent a year—a very respectable rate—while imports increased at an average annual rate of 3.0 percent. This suggests that the appreciation in the real rate of exchange during the last decade of the colonial period represented a response to a relatively undervalued currency in 1950.

The currency was certainly overvalued after Madagascar left the Franc Zone, because this important structural change made foreign investors less willing to invest in Madagascar or to finance any of its balance of payments deficits. Quantitative estimates of the degree of overvaluation during this period are difficult to make and vary considerably according to the methods used. One confidential report indicated that from 1970 through 1985 the exchange rate, on average, was overvalued by 25 percent; another indicated that in 1986 the degree of overvaluation was almost 100 percent. The estimates are controversial and are less important than the qualitative conclusion that the overvaluation was significant and played an important causal role in the country's marked decline of exports beginning in the early 1970s.[7] Certainly the roughly constant real effective exchange rate from 1980 until 1987 was inappropriate.

From 1984 through 1988 the Malagasy franc depreciated at an average annual rate of 24 percent against the dollar and 33 percent against the SDR, in great measure because of its dramatic devaluation in June 1987 from 803 FMG to 1,379 FMG to the dollar.[8] During the same four years, Madagascar's consumer price index increased at an average annual rate of roughly 15 to 16 percent. This devaluation, however, provides no guarantee of economic success. Although the devaluation in 1987 was certainly a vivid sign that the government (under considerable pressure from international lending institutions) had finally decided to begin to take important steps to deal with part of its foreign trade problem, the monetary authorities must coordinate future exchange rate decisions with domestic price increases. Philippe Hugon (1987) has argued that the successive small devaluations during the first half of the 1980s created inflationary expectations that may undermine the impact of the new foreign exchange rate policies and that we can only wait to see if increasing domestic prices lead to an appreciation of the real exchange rate.

Why was the government so slow to devalue? I posed this question to almost all those I interviewed in Madagascar and received several different answers:

- The government did not realize that the Malagasy franc was overvalued. Given the fact that Madagascar has some very competent government economists, this does not seem very plausible; furthermore, certain obvious signs, such as the foreign exchange rationing system, must have made the situation apparent to a large circle of influential individuals.

- By continuing to maintain parity with the French franc, Madagascar was demonstrating to foreign bankers that it could manage its own currency quite well without interference from the French. Combined with a conservative fiscal policy until the late 1970s, which also made an important impression abroad, this strategy certainly was successful in that the government was able to borrow considerable money from foreign bankers to finance its invest-to-the-hilt campaign at the end of the 1970s.

• The government was not under political pressure to devalue, because few important economic interests would have benefited. For instance, devaluation would have raised costs of importing inputs; given the clumsy price control system, domestic manufacturers would have had difficulty raising their prices to recover these higher costs. This situation, according to manufacturers with whom I spoke, lasted through 1986 despite the liberalization program. Exporters of agricultural goods would also not have benefited, because the domestic prices of their products would have remained the same.

• As previously noted, widespread nationalization took place from 1975 through 1978. The new managers of these state-owned enterprises had little incentive to increase production after a devaluation, even if they could have passed on the higher costs of imported inputs, because their compensation did not appear to be closely tied to production or profits. Furthermore, the ready availability of subsidies to enterprises with losses did not encourage managers to press for devaluation.

• An effective devaluation would require the Ratsiraka government to dismantle many of its controls over the economy and rely on automatic market mechanisms, which it deeply distrusted, especially in foreign trade matters. Because insularity is so embedded in the Malagasy culture, most top decisionmakers have paid little attention to external constraints or conditions.

• The elite did not urge devaluation, even though they might have benefited in many ways, because sending their children to France for university training would have become more expensive.

The devaluation of June 1987 reveals either a dramatic change in the constellation of interests governing Madagascar or a profound change in public and governmental opinion. These matters are deferred to chapter 17 for discussion.

The direct impact of the currency overvaluation on exports and import-competing goods should be clear. With an ever-increasing shortage of foreign exchange, necessary imports for domestic Malagasy production became scarcer and, as a result, surplus production capacity increased. This brought about the need to import more final goods and to ration foreign currency even more strictly, still another aspect of the downward spiral the country experienced. As table 13-3

Table 13-3. Capacity Utilization in Malagasy Factories, August 1983
(percent)

Industry	Capacity in use
Mining	
Salt	85
Food and kindred products	
Beef processing	70
Milk	50
Fruit juices	33
Sugar	85
Biscuits/chocolate	50
All vegetable oils	15
Cotton and peanut oils	50
Beverages	50
Tobacco products	
Tobacco	65
Textile mill products	
Cotton ginning	70
Spinning and weaving	90
Apparel	
Clothing	60
Lumber and wood products	
Lumber	50
Paper and allied products	
Paper	40
Printing and publishing	
Printing	50
Leather and leather products	
Leather	60
Stone, glass, clay products	
Cement	75
Bottles	25
Fabricated metal products	
Corrugated roofing	10
Electric and electronic	
Batteries	50
Miscellaneous manufacturing	
Candles	50
Pens	40
Matches	40
Weighted averages	
Total	57
Agricultural processing	61
Processing of local non-agricultural raw materials	63
Processing based primarily on imported inputs	41

Note: The various branches of industry are assumed to represent entire industries; as a result the overall results are rough.

Source: Capacity data are from Dethier and Stryker (1985). Weights for estimated averages are value-added aggregates from the 1979 input-output table supplied by the Direction générale au plan.

shows, by 1983 only about 57 percent of domestic mining and manufacturing capacity was in operation, and capacity utilization in processing industries based primarily on imported inputs had dropped to 41 percent.

Equilibration Mechanisms

Madagascar's heavy reliance on quantitative trade restrictions to equilibrate its balance of payments left little scope for other equilibrating mechanisms to operate.[9]

INCOME EFFECTS. The most important automatic equilibrating mechanism was the fall in average real per capita incomes, which reduced demand for imports. This fall was reflected in the urban areas by both a decline in real wage levels and a rise in unemployment (chapter 16).

PRICE EFFECTS. Considering the relative constancy of the real effective exchange rate from the early 1970s until the mid-1980s, changes in relative prices were not very important in equilibrating the balance of payments.[10] The shift in relative prices of tradables and nontradables was much smaller than in Malaŵi. Furthermore, price controls in both the rural and urban areas prevented many price shifts in the international sphere from being transmitted to the domestic economy, so production—especially in agriculture—was not greatly affected. Governmental price interventions also resulted in a negligible shift in consumption from tradables to nontradables (see Pryor 1988a, table E-2).

The lack of significant price effects from the devaluations in the early 1980s and the continual stagnation of exports during that period require special comment. For a devaluation to work (that is, to send the correct signals to the economy), it must be accompanied by a series of liberalizing domestic economic measures so that markets can respond. Clearly the Malagasy government's attempts to carry out complementary measures took much longer to implement than anticipated. Part of this delay undoubtedly reflected certain ambivalencies in the top leadership toward the liberalization; some part was also attributable to considerable resistance by various interests at lower levels. Little documentation is available on these concerns, however.

ABSORPTION EFFECTS. Certain forces that in Malaŵi slowed the growth of consumption more than that of production did not seem very significant in Madagascar. For instance, shifts in income from labor to property did not take place because of an increase in capital-intensive exports did not occur. Furthermore, the government did not pursue a monetary policy that would encourage people to save (chapter 15). Fiscal policies were also relatively conservative until the late 1970s, and large government deficits were not a major cause of balance of payments problem until the invest-to-the-hilt campaign, which caused economic difficulties in many sectors of the economy. Even until the late 1980s the government's combined monetary and fiscal policies were not rigorous enough to stimulate production more than consumption.

The Balance of Payments

Some major aspects of the balance of payments developments in Madagascar are presented in table 13-2 and can be summarized quite simply.[11] From the early 1960s through 1978 the balance on current account was generally negative, but it did not often exceed 3 percent of GDP. Although both the merchandise and service balances were negative, in most years the nonfactor service account and the net factor payments (interest, profits, and wages) were the major sources of this negative balance. An important offsetting item was net transfers to the government, which kept the current account imbalances quite low, especially in comparison to those of Malaŵi. The data in table 13-2 show clearly that such imbalances in the current account were generally matched by an inflow of long-term capital. Given the relatively small size of these capital flows, foreign indebtedness in Madagascar was not so severe a problem as in Malaŵi, at least until the late 1970s.

The invest-to-the-hilt campaign changed everything. Between 1978 and 1979 the balance on current account jumped from -3.8 percent of GDP to -14.2 percent and then to -17.0 percent in 1980 before declining gradually to -7.4 percent in 1984 and still less by the beginning of 1987. The major cause was a severe imbalance in the merchandise account as large amounts of capital goods, financed by credit, flowed into the country. This process was accompanied by a jump in the nonfactor service balance (the exact causes are not entirely clear) and a steadily rising outflow of factor payments, especially interest, to service the ever-rising debt. Transfers to the government increased during the period, but they could not offset these large imbalances. Although both Malaŵi and Madagascar showed roughly similar current account deficits in the early 1980s, the imbalance in Madagascar caused more severe dislocations throughout the economy because of its heavier reliance on administrative controls.

During the invest-to-the-hilt campaign, foreign bankers did not take these problems very seriously because most of the capital inflow had been placed in productive projects that they expected would soon start producing. The most important projects in the campaign, however, took much longer to come on stream than planned (chapter 10), and in many cases production costs were very much higher and actual production was much lower than expected. Thus Madagascar was unable to produce its way out of this crisis.

In sum, Madagascar's balance of payments problems were primarily self-induced and maintained by a series of policy failures in a number of different fields: exchange rate policies, the system of rationing foreign exchange, domestic price control policies, and the mismanagement of state-owned industries. The structural adjustment loans from the World Bank and other loans from the IMF began to bring about some important changes by 1985. Only with the massive devaluation in the summer of 1987 and the introduction of more transparent import controls in the beginning of 1988 did the Malagasy government take measures that would establish a certain consistency in the various liberalization steps and permit the structural adjustment measures to take full effect. At the time this manuscript was closed, evidence was not yet available that would help determine how long the Malagasy economy would take to respond to such measures and whether the government can maintain this economically painful program until the economy has readjusted.

External Indebtedness

Table 13-4 shows that Madagascar's external indebtedness, measured in U.S. dollars, increased at an average annual rate of 25 percent from 1970 through 1986. This increase was quite slow until 1978; indeed, Madagascar's foreign debt during this time was only 60 to 80 percent of Malaŵi's. The invest-to-the-hilt campaign, however, quintupled Madagascar's foreign debt, and by 1986 it was almost three times larger than Malaŵi's. As a percentage of GDP, Madagascar's foreign indebtedness rose from 10 percent to 99 percent between 1970 and 1986, and if the value of the FMG had been in equilibrium, this ratio would have been even higher (Pryor 1988a, tables E-1, F-4a, and G-2). Net factor payments abroad as a share of GDP rose from 3.0 percent in 1970 to 5.6 percent in 1986.

The table also shows that the composition of the debt changed considerably. Until 1978 multilateral and bilateral governmental agencies held most of Madagascar's foreign debt. The government financed the invest-to-the-hilt program in large part by borrowing from the financial markets, often for short periods and at high interest rates. Thus the average interest rate rose, and the average maturity decreased.

When the expected domestic production to pay for these debts did not materialize, the balance of payments experienced considerable strain. During the early 1980s the debt-service ratio was rising quickly and might soon have reached 90 percent without debt rescheduling. Rescheduling and refinancing of private, governmental, or both kinds of debt occurred each year from 1981 to 1984; several conversions of debt to grants also occurred after 1980 (Pryor 1988a, table F-4b).

Table 13-4. Madagascar's Outstanding Foreign Debt, 1970 to 1986

Year	Total	Multilateral agencies	Bilateral agencies	Suppliers	Financial markets	Average interest rate, commitments[b] (percent)	Debt-service ratio[c] (percent)	Average maturity, commitments (years)
1970	89.4	11.4	73.4	0.8	3.8	2.3	3.5	38.6
1971	103.2	17.0	79.9	0.1	6.3	4.1	4.0	10.2
1972	89.8	22.5	55.2	3.7	8.5	1.2	3.4	33.0
1973	118.2	38.5	67.5	3.2	9.0	3.6	5.2	31.9
1974	138.7	51.5	76.3	2.7	8.1	2.3	3.6	36.9
1975	167.3	80.0	77.9	2.3	7.0	0.7	3.1	25.1
1976	183.3	95.7	79.2	2.3	6.1	1.9	4.0	39.4
1977	224.4	107.6	86.6	17.6	12.6	4.1	3.8	23.1
1978	296.4	136.3	105.0	34.1	21.1	5.6	4.5	17.0
1979	609.6	156.0	222.9	115.6	115.1	5.7	7.1	16.1
1980	954.6	219.6	388.9	180.6	165.6	5.3	11.1	17.9
1981	1,435.2	264.7	677.2	169.9	323.4	5.3	15.6	20.7
1982	1,649.8	326.8	865.1	162.2	295.8	4.4	18.1	28.3
1983	1,783.3	379.2	953.9	156.1	294.1	3.7	12.8	29.7
1984	1,875.3	414.1	1,054.5	131.5	275.3	4.2	11.1	32.6
1985	2,260.3	500.6	1,282.1	139.5	338.0	4.2	29.9	29.8
1986	2,635.6	645.6	1,484.1	149.4	356.5	2.4	n.a.	36.7

Columns show: Outstanding disbursed debt at year end ($ millions), Official creditors (Multilateral agencies, Bilateral agencies), Private creditors[a] (Suppliers, Financial markets).

a. Private debt includes only that publicly guaranteed.
b. The average interest rate includes concessionary and interest-free loans.
c. The debt-service ratio is the ratio of interest and amortization to the dollar value of exports of goods and nonfactor services. The series on debt service has a very slight incomparability between 1979 and 1980.

Source: "EPD Data Bank" of the World Bank, External Debt Division. For 1982 through 1985 these data diverge from estimates presented by France, Ministère de la coopération (1986).

Foreign Assistance

Developing nations with relatively small populations generally have been able to obtain relatively more foreign assistance, on a per capita basis, than other nations. Furthermore, as a country maintaining fairly close ties with France and yet having a "socialist orientation," Madagascar might be expected to tap considerable aid from both East and West. In reality, however, foreign assistance to Madagascar has not been unusual. On an average annual basis from 1977 through 1983, Madagascar was able to obtain total net disbursements of international financial flows from all sources combined of about $30 per capita; the thirty-six least developed countries received $21 per capita, and all developing nations averaged $24 dollars (OECD 1984).

Madagascar's largest foreign aid donor was and continues to be France. Although the stream of French aid continued to flow, after 1972, with Madagascar's withdrawal from the Franc Zone, the negotiations to remove French troops, and the nationalization of French firms (often without compensation), the level dropped as Madagascar became much lower on France's aid priorities.

Madagascar's strategic position is allegedly more important than Malaŵi's because it is located along the lanes for shipping Middle Eastern oil to Europe; moveover, many claim that Madagascar can serve as a "permanent aircraft carrier" off the coast of Africa. This argument appears to have carried little weight with aid givers. Like Malaŵi, Madagascar has been unable to make much of a splash in the world press and elicit aid in this fashion. Grants and loans for economic purposes from the CMEA nations (East Europe plus several other socialist nations) also have not been abundant, and the available data suggest that, despite Madagascar's ideological stance and its pattern of voting in sympathy with CMEA positions in international organizations, these nations have played an extremely minor role in Madagascar's total foreign aid picture.[12]

Table 13-4 shows that international agencies were quite generous to Madagascar during its period of economic difficulties in the early 1980s. That nation's dirigistic economic policies and its relative neglect of agriculture, however, have been out of step with the more liberal doctrines recommended by these agencies. Their leverage on Madagascar during its painful recovery from the invest-to-the-hilt program was undoubtedly an important explanation for its change in trade policies.

Some Implications

The trade policies of the Tsiranana government had relatively little impact on growth and income distribution. The policies of the Ratsiraka government—at least until the mid-1980s—slowed growth and widened income differentials.

Economic Growth

Because Madagascar's ratio of exports to GDP has been much lower than that of Malaŵi, it might appear to have failed to take advantage of the world division of labor to achieve greater static and dynamic efficiency. Although this general argument has merit, other aspects of the nexus between economic growth and foreign trade are also relevant.

The most important impact of trade on growth has been its role in the downward spiral in which Madagascar's overvalued exchange rate and its agricultural pricing policies brought about a fall in agricultural exports, a shortage of intermediate inputs and consumer goods to the agricultural sector, surplus capacity in manufacturing and production difficulties in agriculture, slow GDP growth, and further pressures on the balance of payments. Furthermore, its quantitative controls and other types of currency rationing in trade have given rise to greater uncertainties in production, more difficulties in enterprise planning, and disincentives for domestic private investment.

Other linkages between trade and growth were of secondary importance. For instance, a lower degree of export diversification allegedly reduces economic growth by subjecting the economy to greater swings in export receipts. Although export diversification in Madagascar was considerably greater than in Malaŵi, this mechanism did not operate as hypothesized in that Madagascar experienced somewhat greater fluctuation in exports (see footnote 14, chapter 6).

The Distribution of Income

Trade can have several influences on the distribution of income. In agricultural exporting countries, encouragement of trade can especially raise the income of the smallholders, the poorest segment of the population; until the mid-1980s, however, the Malagasy government did not seriously encourage such exports. The shortage of intermediate inputs caused by the overvalued exchange rate benefits those who are willing and able to profit from such scarcities, including government officials who distribute foreign exchange licenses, dealers in the parallel economy, producers with sufficient working capital to obtain such scarce inputs, and urban consumers; in Madagascar these beneficiaries have not included the poor smallholders. Higher foreign debt resulting from trade policy can lead to higher taxes falling unequally on the rich and poor; sufficient information on the incidence of taxation is not available to evaluate this possibility (chapter 15). Such considerations suggest that Malagasy trade policies have widened, not narrowed, income differentials up to the mid-1980s.

Notes

1. Footnote 1, chapter 6, details the sources and methods used in this comparison; in this exercise Madagascar's trade-GDP ratio in 1975 was 30 percent below the prediction.

2. Footnote 2, chapter 6, presents the sources and methods used in this comparison; in this second equation Madagascar's trade-GDP ratio was about 4 percent above the predicted value.

3. Information on the foreign trade regime during the first two decades of independence come from International Monetary Fund (1971), p. 7; Lefebre (n.d.); United Nations (1974); and France, Ministère de la coopération (1986).

4. These data may not include several minor kinds of duties, so the total import tax could have risen. Furthermore, the import tariff structure was discriminatory; for more than a decade after independence it differentiated between goods from France (and the EEC) and from the rest of the world.

5. Of course, mining products are not import-competing, but the comparable current and constant price data needed to remove mining products from the index are not readily available. The import-competing sector also includes construction and utilities, which should really be the nontradables sector. The national accounts data appear to be set up to compare relative prices in the three sectors quite easily; unfortunately the current price data by sector include tariffs from 1950 up to 1970 and exclude such tariffs thereafter. This break in the series dictates caution in interpreting the results. The data for 1970 to the present come from Pryor (1988a), tables E-1a and E-2; the 1960 to 1970 data are drawn from the sources cited in appendix E.

6. Relevant data on the nominal exchange rate are presented in Pryor (1988a), table G-2. Sylviane Guillaumont Jeanneney, in Rose (1985), p. 182; Martin Godfrey, in Rose (1985), p. 177; and May (1985), p. 13, have made other estimations of real and nominal exchange rates. Their nominal exchange rate estimates are roughly similar to mine; their real exchange rate calculations are also roughly similar until 1982–83, when they show greater appreciation. Most of these studies calculate such rates just for imports; furthermore, several use the consumer price indexes as deflators. Because these authors do not specify how they made their calculations, other sources of the differences are not entirely clear.

7. The ratios of black market to quoted rates for the Malagasy franc provide an interesting sidelight on the overvaluation (data are presented in Pryor (1988a), table G-2). Surprisingly, such ratios are much the same as those for the Malaŵi kwacha. Most likely, the official Malagasy currency controls permitted a larger legal outflow of the currency than took place in Malaŵi, so a proportionately higher share of funds left Malaŵi in illegal ways. Less probable explanations are that the degree of overall balance of payments disequilibrium was the same in the two countries (which does not seem likely); the supply and demand functions for black market currencies in the two countries have had quite different elasticities (although a case can be made for this argument, it seems strained); or the data are either incomparable, incorrect, or both (accurate black market data are scarce).

8. The data cited in this paragraph come from various issues of IMF, *International Financial Statistics*. The increase in the consumer price index is a rough estimate; midyear 1988 data were not available when this calculation was made.

9. Jean Coussy, in France, Ministère de la coopération (1985) presents a much more detailed analysis of the Malagasy balance of payments and foreign exchange rate. He particularly stresses the impact of certain structural factors such as Madagascar's economic dependence on foreign countries and the "internal dis-articulation" of its economy, arising in part from economic

dualism. I am not convinced that such a structural analysis provides more insight into the problems under examination than the more orthodox approach that I pursue.

10. In a very peculiar way, price effects destabilized the balance of payments. More specifically, the government undertook the invest-to-the-hilt campaign in part because of the (incorrect) belief that the high coffee prices on the world market would continue and that any decline in this price would be temporary. Top governmental decisionmakers did not realize the true state of affairs until much too late in the investment program.

11. Economic studies of Malagasy balance of payments problems include Hugon (1986); Sylviane Jeanneney, in Rose (1985); and Ramahatra (1986). My analysis and Ramahatra's, the most extensive, differ on a number of points, primarily in our basic data. His sources of data are sometimes not clearly specified; my data and sources are found in Pryor (1988a), section G.

12. According to Chaigneau (1985), p. 157, Madagascar received some Soviet military aid in return for use of certain military facilities on the island. I could find nothing about this in any other sources. A large Soviet economic loan in the mid-1980s, which included shipments of a considerable amount of rice, was also announced, but I have found few details about its purposes, its conditions, or its dates of disbursement.

14 Manufacturing and Transportation in Madagascar

From Madagascar's independence in 1960 through 1986 the secondary sector (manufacturing, mining, utilities, and construction) grew at an average annual rate of only 1.9 percent, compared with 6.2 percent during the colonial era. In different periods its growth rate was inversely proportional to the priority top policymakers granted it. From 1960 through 1975, when the Tsiranana and Ramanantsoa governments focused their attention primarily on agriculture, the secondary sector grew at an average annual rate of 5.5 percent; from 1975 through 1986, when the Ratsiraka government placed its highest policy emphasis on the growth of industry, the secondary sector declined at an average annual rate of 3.9 percent; the rate of decline for manufacturing alone (through 1985) was 3.2 percent a year (Pryor 1988a, table E-2).

Manufacturing: Institutions and Policies

The colonial and the Tsiranana governments used indirect incentives to encourage manufacturing and generally avoided direct intervention. In contrast, the Ratsiraka administration expropriated or nationalized a large number of foreign-owned manufacturing firms and began to play a much more direct role, not only in investment but also in decisions about current production. Price controls and other government directives led to financial losses by the nationalized enterprises, and the overvalued exchange rate led to considerable surplus capacity. As in agriculture, nationalization placed severe strains on administrative resources, and foreign exchange restrictions discouraged investment and created production bottlenecks. In transportation the Ratsiraka government shifted expenditures for maintenance to more exciting investment projects, and the transportation network deteriorated considerably.

Institutions

Foreign (almost exclusively French) companies owned a dominant share of Malagasy manufacturing until the mid-1970s.[1] At the end of the nationalization drive, which gained full force from 1975 to 1978, during the early years of the Ratsiraka government, publicly owned enterprises employed about 57 percent of the labor force in the modern sector of mining and manufacturing and 28 percent of the labor force in the sector as a whole (including crafts and other traditional production establishments).

Initially the various nationalized manufacturing and mining enterprises were placed under the tutelage of various ministries, which did not follow any standard set of policies toward these enterprises. As a result, some enterprises could act relatively independently, while others were subject to more active management by the relevant ministry. In 1978, in order to standardize administrative practices, the government announced plans for an administrative structure for these parastatals, which can be characterized as "classical corporatism" or "syndicalism." Although these plans were never implemented, they provide considerable insight into the guiding ideas of the Ratsiraka government.[2]

The basis of the new system was to be a series of *entreprises socialistes*, each headed by a director responsible to (and nominated by) a *comité de gestion* (management committee) within the enterprise. This committee was to comprise the enterprise director and representatives selected by the government and the workers. A workers' general assembly would ultimately empower the worker representatives and would also elect three commissions to oversee economic and financial affairs, social and cultural affairs, and personnel matters. In addition, the general assembly would appoint representatives to joint worker-management committees on discipline, health, and security. If an enterprise were composed of several establishments, each would have a parallel structure.

An outside *conseil d'orientation* would oversee a group of enterprises in the same industrial branch, serving the same function as the board of directors of a large cartel. This council would formulate the most important policies for the various enterprises, map out branch investment policies, and oversee the integration of newly nationalized firms into the branch. The council would be composed of representatives selected by the government, by the legislature (*Assemblé nationale populaire*), by the various management committees of the subordinate enterprises, and also by workers in these enterprises. Sixteen councils were to be established eventually, six in manufacturing and the remainder covering all other sectors of the economy. The various decrees did not specify the government's role in guiding the councils; on paper, the councils appeared to be self-governing, with no formal relations with the planning office or other governmental organs. The profits of each firm would be divided among the shareholders (some private shareholders might remain), the workers, and the government.

In 1979 the government established thirteen socialist enterprises, and by 1986 the number had grown to twenty-nine. By the beginning of 1988, however, the government had not yet established any orientation councils, and the transitional system of ministerial tutelage continued. The Minister of Industry, M. Rakotomavo, noted that the syndicalist structure of industrial organization has not been abandoned and "remains on the agenda to be implemented in the future." He added that the workers and managers were not yet prepared for the introduction of such a difficult change.[3] Given the rapid liberalization of industry during 1987 and 1988 and the reprivatization of a certain number of state enterprises, these plans probably have been scrapped.

The present legal foundation of the parastatals is complex. These enterprises have a number of different legal forms.[4] Until the mid-1980s administrative controls were also complicated by the fact that the government had no statistical oversight over the enterprises; no centralized source collected information on their finances, personnel, assets and liabilities, or even their exact number. In 1986 the World Bank began a multiyear project to provide this information.

In sum, the nationalization program gave rise to administrative chaos. Furthermore, most of the French expatriates and some of the experienced Malagasy factory managers left the country. Many were replaced by civil servants who had little experience in industrial management. The salaries of the new managers generally were tied to the civil service pay scale, so their incomes were not dependent upon the success of their firms. In some cases the new managers applied governmental accounting methods to industry (for example, they ignored depreciation allowances), and these proved quite inadequate for industrial management.

Government Policies and Instruments

The policies and instruments of the Malagasy government in the manufacturing sector have varied considerably.[5] During the First Republic (1960–75), the government carried out industrial policy primarily in the form of indirect incentives such as tax and tariff concessions; during the Second Republic direct ministerial involvement has been important.

The framework of the system of incentives for manufacturing investment during the Tsiranana government was the 1962 investment code, which provided for a series of tax and tariff concessions granting certain types of import protection plus exemption from paying certain types of import duties for inputs. It promised security of capital and repatriation of profits. The tax structure at that time also allowed double depreciation, which encouraged capital-intensive industries. This appeared inconsistent with the plans of the period in which labor-intensive branches were supposed to grow faster.[6]

A new manufacturer faced considerable uncertainties because some of these concessions had to be negotiated; for instance, some concessions depended upon the "national importance" of the project. Nevertheless, the system did lead to a stream of applications from foreign and domestic investors, and the government approved about twenty investment projects under the code each year. The government also created new sources of financing for the manufacturing sector, as well as a number of auxiliary institutions to aid this sector in other ways. These included the Société nationale d'investissement, a type of holding company founded in 1962 that was to function in part as a financial intermediary; the Banque national malgache de développement, founded in 1963; and the Bureau de développement et de promotion industrielle, founded in 1966 to help set up new factories. Despite such governmental efforts, the growth of production in the secondary sector during the Tsiranana era did not increase greatly in comparison to the last decade of the colonial period.

The Ramanantsoa government (1972–75) promulgated a new investment code in 1973, which reserved particular branches of the economy for the state, declared other branches would eventually belong to the state, removed the safeguards for security of capital and repatriation of funds, and made the various trade and tax concessions to new investors considerably more difficult to obtain. These and other policies, combined with the country's withdrawal from the Franc Zone in 1973, added to investment uncertainties and led to a decrease in investment project applications for special treatment under the code to about eight a year.

These steps did not completely discourage investment by foreigners. In the late 1970s, during the invest-to-the-hilt campaign, investment from abroad took a new form—loans to the government or to the parastatals or, in a few instances, participation in joint ventures. The consequences for the balance of payments were unfortunate (chapter 13).

Divergences between the goals and the actual policies both the Ramanantsoa and Ratsiraka governments pursued to encourage manufacturing have been a major problem. For instance, in a study of industrial policy Maxwell Stamp Associates (1986) found no evidence that the tariff policies influencing manufacturing were consistent with the particular goals of industrial policy promoting production using indigenous raw materials, import substitution, or industrial exports, which the investment code and governmental pronouncements had set forth. Certain of the government's policies, such as the push toward capital-intensive investments during the invest-to-the-hilt program, also seemed to lead to an inefficient allocation of resources. None of the Malagasy governments developed a very coherent set of ideas.[7]

A number of governmental policies external to the manufacturing sector itself also began to have an adverse influence on manufacturing production. The idle manufacturing capacity resulting from the overvalued exchange rate has already received quantitative examination (see table 13-3). Another instance was the new labor legislation; although it led to greater job security for workers, it also meant that manufacturers had more difficulty in reducing their work forces to adjust to adverse circumstances. By the mid-1970s many private enterprises were in severe financial straits, and many were nationalized to save the jobs of the workers; this, of course, was "lemon socialism."

Since independence the Malagasy government has had difficulties in selecting profitable manufacturing projects for investment. During the Tsiranana period, when the government devoted only a relatively small share of funds to manufacturing, it had some difficulty in selecting profitable projects (du Bois de Gaudusson, in Constantine and others 1979, p. 208). During the first decade of the Ratsiraka government, when considerably more resources were available for this sector, the government's investment in manufacturing and mining became even more politicized, and the relatively inexperienced personnel staff of many of the planning offices of the new government were unable to prevent some very costly mistakes. Some examples are in order.

The government constructed two modern and expensive flour mills and two soya-pressing mills; because Madagascar grew relatively little wheat or soya, most of the raw materials would have to be imported. (This is an interesting example of urban bias in investment; white bread, a consumption item of the urban elite, was an important product of the flour from these mills.) A modern leatherworking factory the government built used imported raw materials rather than the domestic products the factory had previously used; furthermore, it displaced a large number of domestic leatherworkers and added capacity, in an industry in which manufacturing capacity was already underutilized before the new factory was built.

The single most costly error of the government was a $100 million fertilizer (urea) plant that was to be oriented primarily toward export (Malagasy farmers used other types of fertilizers). The factory uses a naphtha technology (a high-cost feedstock), and most outside observers doubt it can compete with the less expensive urea fertilizers other countries produce from a natural gas base.

The choice of location of many new factories was also questionable. Most of the flour and soya mills were sited so that transportation to the ports was expensive. A new slaughter house required long transportation (and hence loss of weight) of animals. The government built CIMA, a cement factory, near Antsirabe, which has very poor transportation links with the rest of the island; furthermore, according to some reports, the nearby raw materials for its cement contain too much alumina to be useful for many purposes; and, according to one confidential financial analysis, its imported inputs costs have been higher than the costs of importing the finished cement. Other problems of location have arisen because of the lack of a suitably trained labor force in the area surrounding the enterprise and because of the social impediments to transferring trained labor from one location to another.

Many other examples exist of large-scale investment projects with serious financial problems. In reviewing twenty large investment projects (representing 51 percent of the total number of large ongoing projects in the public investment program), a World Bank technical team in 1984 classified ten as warranting "serious doubts" about their commercial viability and an additional five as worthy of "moderate doubts" (World Bank November 1984).

How could such inappropriate decisions ever have been made? In some cases problems arose because foreign experts or domestic bankers conducted the preliminary and final studies, and neither group was sufficiently familiar with local conditions and constraints in the chosen locations to avoid some important mistakes of project design. In other cases domestic political considerations dominated the choices of investment projects. Interviews with some participants in the decisionmaking process revealed that government technicians raised strenuous objections to particular projects or location decisions and pointed out quite accurately the difficulties that would ensue. Nevertheless, authorities at the highest political levels overruled them, apparently influenced by ethnic or regional considerations. The decisionmaking process can only be understood in a broad political economy context, the subject matter of chapter 17.

After the wave of nationalization, many of the parastatals began to run into severe financial difficulties, caused in certain measure by their undercapitalization and poor management. In addition, the government sometimes directed these enterprises to undertake unprofitable social tasks, for instance, serving as leaders in the battle against inflation by selling at prices lower than their costs; or serving as a purchaser of last resort of certain agricultural goods; or, in the case of the water and electricity company, JIRAMA, solving a series of general urban problems on top of its own production and distribution problems. In a number of cases the state enterprises could not obtain imported inputs, and their overseeing ministry did not permit them to reduce their labor forces as their production declined, which meant that their average costs soared. The degree of overstaffing is difficult to determine, but a figure sometimes mentioned (without any supporting evidence, however) is 30 percent. The Minister of Industry explained to me that the government was reluctant to release workers because of the scarcity of employment opportunities open to them.

By the mid-1980s the parastatals had received considerably more than 50 percent of the total short-term credit the banks had authorized; about 90 percent of these loans were classified as "at high risk" (World Bank March 1986a). The procedures for closing a parastatal were extremely complicated, and the possibility of bankruptcy was not generally admitted. Failing parastatals, therefore, required increasing funding through subsidies or by loans that would never be repaid. By the end of 1987 the limited program to sell certain unprofitable state enterprises was not proceeding very fast. Many of their basic problems were probably not resolvable until the plant managers could have some flexibility, which would require much further liberalization of the economy; many experienced entrepreneurs left after 1975, leaving only a few on the island; and still fewer of these entrepreneurs had the capital or could obtain the credit to purchase the companies.

In June 1985 the Ratsiraka government promulgated a new investment code that liberalized constraints on investment by both Malagasy and foreigners. The government promised five-year exemptions on certain import duties, reduction in some taxes, particular deductions in calculating revenues for tax purposes, and priority allocations of foreign exchange. Nevertheless, according to a report specifically focusing on the investment climate at that time, the chances of attracting new private investment looked bleak because changes were slow. Even after promulgation of the code, governmental authorization for a new investment project required permission from several ministries; and the year-long delays occurring in past years, especially for relatively small investments, showed no sign of being shortened. "Business formation and regulation is complex, fraught with a plethora of petty and unclear regulations and subject to the whims of many minor officials" (Glenshaw and Harmon 1985, p. 2).

The unfortunate state of manufacturing in the mid-1980s had several other explanations. The surplus capacity problem was not yet solved. Manufacturing uncertainties arising from difficulties in obtaining necessary intermediate inputs also continued up to that time. Furthermore, the government was not consistently implementing many of its policies affecting manufacturing. For example, price control measures, which had not yet been fully removed, were not tied to the investment strategy; tariff measures were not coordinated with overall policy; and the investment funds to aid private businesses were very scarce because most bank credit appears to have been allocated to the parastatals in financial difficulties. A dramatic sign of the deteriorating investment climate occurred in a well-publicized but fruitless

1986 government program to interest French investors in Madagascar. In the following years, however, the government appeared to take some steps to simplify the investment process; the impact of these new measures cannot yet be determined, however.

Despite the government's good intentions and specific measures to encourage private investment in manufacturing, it appeared to place the major thrust of its drive to increase manufacturing in the state sector and in projects approved at the top political levels. This policy incoherence suggests either highly limited administrative capacities or strong differences on all these policy matters at the highest governmental levels.

Special Aid to Small Enterprises

For Madagascar, small and medium-size enterprises should be an attractive government investment for the same reasons as in Malaŵi. They are usually highly labor intensive; many can be based in rural areas to serve as a source of additional income for poor smallholders; many use local raw materials, and they can provide a useful "school" for budding entrepreneurs and managers.

The government of Madagascar did not focus much serious attention on these industries, at least until the mid-1980s (see Glenshaw and Harmon 1985). The government had established a number of institutions to aid small business; these include the Fonds national d'investissement, the Centre economique et technique de l'artisinat, the Bureau de développement et de promotion industrielle, the Institut national de formation-promotion, the IMI (Institut malagasy d'innovation), and CENAM (Centre national de l'artisans malagasy). Some of these organizations strayed considerably from the task of aiding small-scale industries and artisans. For instance, the IMI exhibited a prototype Malagasy automobile and has begun to build the first half-dozen; it has also worked on designs for a Malagasy airplane and a Malagasy computer. The resources might have been better used, I believe, to design new kinds of hand-held agricultural equipment and other capital goods for small-scale production rather than to launch these technologically ambitious projects.

Most of the government's small-industry programs have been very limited in scope, and in recent years a number of these institutions are said to be either inactive or ineffective. No special efforts appear to have been aimed at the informal sector in the cities. Small industries had difficulty in obtaining credit; special institutions to provide such credit were not successful, and in the mid-1980s official bank interest rates for small businesses ranged from 20 to 25 percent.

Official policy statements in Madagascar in the mid-1980s began to stress the importance of small and medium-size private manufacturing, and this policy is enshrined in the 1985 investment code. Given the government's limited administrative capability and its priority on keeping afloat the various large-scale manufacturing parastatals, the neglect of small-scale manufacturing is understandable. Again, a chasm separates governmental policy pronouncements and actual policy implementation.

Price and Wage Controls

Madagascar has had price controls for more than a half-century. They have not, however, been administered so as to encourage economic growth. Wage controls have seemed more benign.

Price Controls

The Malagasy government had several motives for imposing and maintaining price controls. It wanted to prevent inflation and inadvertent overvaluation of the currency, protect the real incomes of the poor so that they could purchase necessities at low prices, and create a climate of economic stability. The system proved inflexible and dysfunctional, however, and by the mid-1980s the government began to abandon it.

The price control system began in 1936, when the colonial government established fixed prices on both industrial and wholesale goods (see de Bandt and others 1984). Since that time the system has undergone a variety of changes, including a major extension in 1951 with the establishment of provincial and local price authorities. By the 1980s the system fixed prices on a variety of goods covering all sectors of the economy. The kind of quantitative information on the extent of the system that was used in describing the Malaŵi price control system is not available, but Jacques de Bandt and his colleagues (1984) provide a useful qualitative description of the Malagasy system:

> [T]he regulation of prices is simultaneously a set of economic regulations which controls the sale of agricultural products, the sale of [industrial] products ... the control of inventories ... and the importation and the exportation of goods. [p. 37]

The price-setting system required enterprises to submit requests, backed by various types of evidence about costs, for permission to change prices of each individual good. The price office treated this cost information in arbitrary ways; for instance, it disallowed higher transportation costs caused by deterioration of roads. It also applied different principles of price fixing in different industrial sectors. Moreover, the principles it applied and the concessions it offered often seemed to differ among enterprises in the same industrial branch. One-month to two-year delays between request and action sometimes led to disastrous results; for instance, following the oil price rise in 1979 the cement plant in Amboanio was unable to obtain quick permission to raise its prices in order to pass on the higher cost of imported energy, and as a consequence, the firm went bankrupt. According to de Bandt and his coauthors,

> Price regulation is thus a source of inequality between industrial enterprises since difference in treatment between enterprises is not determined in any way—neither in principle nor in fact—by priorities or options of the industrial strategy. The regulation of price is not integrated into any system of allocation of resources according to priorities. In other words, the administration of price is not— apparently it was never—utilized as an instrument of industrial policy.
>
> The system of price setting, evidently established to keep prices [and profits] under control and to adapt the structure of prices to the objectives followed [by the government], have not, in fact, prevented either high prices, or inflation, or even high profits. [pp. 132-34]

Presently available evidence is not sufficient to determine the degree of price distortion or the resource misallocation that price fixing produced. Certainly the system gave rise to an active black market; for instance, in April 1985 the ratio of black market prices to official prices was 1.6 for blue jeans, 2.2 to 3.0 for leather jackets, 3.0 for shirts, and 3.3 for deodorant (Glenshaw and Harmon 1985).

As a condition for receiving structural adjustment loans from the World Bank, the Malagasy government began to dismantle the price control system. In July 1984 it decontrolled 30 percent of industrial prices, and two years later 70 percent of manufacturing value added was said to be free of such controls. According to several business people with whom I discussed the matter in 1986, many of their prices were totally free and for others the delays in approval for changes were only a month (in contrast to licenses for foreign exchange, which often took four to five months to obtain).

Wage Controls

Labor unions in Madagascar have been weak and have exercised little influence on wages. As in Malaŵi, this weakness can be traced to the structure of the economy itself. Workers from the countryside have been readily available for unskilled jobs. Also, workers could not easily share in the large economic rents in the manufacturing sector by driving up wages, because to the extent that price increases ensued, domestic production would lose ground to imports. In the 1950s the labor unions did not play an important role in the drive for independence, and the various political parties have not depended on the labor unions for support in gaining or maintaining power. In the mid-1980s the labor movement in Madagascar included somewhat more than a quarter of the labor force in the modern sector.[8] The different labor federations have had ties to different political parties, so membership has been splintered; 40 to 50 percent of all federation members belong to the largest two federations. As in France, several different labor federations may represent workers in a single factory.

The minimum wage system in Madagascar (SMIG) has the same structure and many other similar features (including the name) as in France. More specifically, the government establishes a base minimum wage and then applies a set of prescribed coefficients to determine the minimum wage in different parts of the island and for different levels of skill. The real minimum wage in Madagascar has fallen continuously since 1978; by the mid-1980s it was roughly at the same level as in the early 1950s (Pryor 1988a, section H). Little empirical evidence is available on the relationship of actual wages to the minimum wages for particular jobs. Anecdotal evidence suggests that in the mid-1980s actual wages in manufacturing around Antananarivo were sometimes twice the minimum wage, which meant that for these industries the SMIG has not served as a constraint on enterprise decisionmaking. Some of the gains labor achieved in the early 1970s, such as increased job security, have been weakened in recent years. The 1975 labor code, which included generous fringe benefits, has not been implemented by appropriate legislation. Furthermore, the Ratsiraka government has discouraged strike activities; in 1979 the major unions signed agreements with the government, I was told, to "support the triumph of the Malagasy socialist revolution."

The Growth of Manufacturing Production

The manufacturing sector in Madagascar has suffered a number of the same handicaps as that in Malaŵi: a small domestic market; a shortage of skilled workers, technicians, and managers; and uncertain transportation links with the outside world (arising, however, from quite different causes).

Table 14-1 presents detailed data on manufacturing production from 1970 to 1985.[9] The overall production index rose slowly from 1970 through 1979 and then in the next six years fell far below the 1970 level as Madagascar struggled to overcome the foreign exchange and other economic difficulties occasioned by the invest-to-the-hilt program of the late 1970s. From 1970 through 1985 manufacturing production fell at an average annual rate of 1.3 percent (or, on a per capita basis, almost 4 percent a year), an important reason for the surplus manufacturing capacity. The situation was more complex, however, because surplus manufacturing capacity appears to have been endemic since the late 1960s.[10]

The different branches of industry have performed quite differently over time. Information from input-output tables allows comparison of the characteristics of those branches showing positive and negative growth in production; such statistical exercises raise certain problems, but this application points to several tentative generalizations.[11]

- The capital-labor ratios for the fastest and slowest growing branches exhibited few significant differences.

- A certain amount of import-substituting industrialization occurred. The fastest growing branches of industry were those that produced goods for which imports had supplied a relatively large share of domestic consumption. Any favorable impact on the balance of payments, however, was counterbalanced in part by the fact that these fastest growing branches of industry also used a much higher share of imported than of domestic inputs.[12] Manufacturing exports constituted only a very small fraction of Madagascar's total exports, and this share did not increase very much over time. Of twenty-eight major manufacturing projects under construction in 1980, only seven had any real potential for export production. Thus, the pattern of change in the manufacturing sector apparently has done little to alleviate Madagascar's foreign exchange problems.

- A higher share of the products from the fastest growing branches served as intermediate inputs rather than going to final consumers. The user industries may have aided the supplier industries in their quest for scarce foreign exchange by providing an ally in the battle with foreign exchange allocators.

Import-substituting industrialization had both negative and positive features. On the negative side, analysis of the profits of the 350 enterprises covered in the annual industrial censuses reveals that net investments were increasing only at a minuscule rate (for example, between 1983 and 1984, at 0.6 percent).[13] For most years since the mid-1970s the manufacturing sector apparently could not have generated enough surplus to finance new investment, even if it had wanted to increase capacity (de Bandt and others 1986, pp. 20 ff.). On the positive side, a brief glance at the list of imports reveals many simple types of commodities that Madagascar could make; certainly it has not yet completed even the first step of import substitution. Changes in the governmental exchange rate, foreign trade policies, and industrial policies could do much to encourage domestic manufacture of these products.

In sum, table 14-1 contains little indication of serious implementation of the brave plans outlined in *FundOp*'s twenty-year perspective or in the three-year plan of 1978–80 (chapter 10). Immediate economic problems simply overwhelmed the long-run goals.

Table 14-1. Indexes of Manufacturing Production, Madagascar, 1970 to 1985

(1970=100)

Year	Total	Mining	Food and beverages	Tobacco	Textiles	Clothing	Wood products
1970 weights		3.90	37.99	3.76	19.50	7.42	1.78
1970	100.0	100	100	100	100	100	100
1971	104.6	102	93	108	122	84	132
1972	106.6	98	93	119	132	112	86
1973	105.9	138	85	128	133	111	72
1974	114.7	138	91	127	162	116	66
1975	108.0	180	87	128	152	121	54
1976	111.3	171	89	137	156	113	56
1977	113.5	152	90	146	157	114	77
1978	115.0	115	96	164	156	115	78
1979	117.0	119	94	164	165	118	74
1980	115.3	137	89	161	158	131	68
1981	98.4	91	77	138	149	121	62
1982	84.9	57	60	144	144	90	58
1983	93.6	54	72	125	149	102	67
1984	85.2	43	60	141	136	93	71
1985	87.2	78	66	147	130	95	52

Note: The data for 1970 through 1982 come from one set of calculations; the data from 1982 through 1985, which are spliced onto the first series, come from another set. Although the weights and components of these two sets of calculations are somewhat different, such a procedure serves as a first approximation.

Source: Pryor (1988a), table D-1.

Transportation

The inadequate transportation network has been a serious impediment to growth in Madagascar's agricultural and manufacturing sectors. In contrast to Malaŵi, however, these problems were caused for the most part by the government rather than by external forces. Although I have not found any evidence of a comprehensive transportation plan, the government appears to have followed the common goals of constructing a network to reduce transportation costs and to open up new areas of the country for agricultural production. The implementation of transportation policies, rather than the policies themselves, has been the root of the problem.

Paper products	Printing	Leather products	Rubber products	Chemicals	Petroleum refining	Construction materials	Transport equipment, metal products
2.27	3.64	0.75	0.35	4.64	4.78	7.39	1.83
100	100	100	100	100	100	100	100
108	80	103	103	154	94	113	128
101	87	216	120	130	98	96	114
136	91	259	133	140	116	70	95
169	93	332	157	149	110	65	88
172	72	287	169	159	125	51	90
147	79	246	178	172	93	43	86
187	81	297	171	187	88	42	86
205	79	333	175	201	63	47	83
212	78	379	216	213	59	44	81
197	81	345	227	173	89	42	112
147	87	307	140	124	63	31	52
151	78	293	82	94	61	33	14
162	76	279	144	109	33	33	18
149	79	326	116	121	10	34	23
156	80	279	138	118	52	26	19

Domestic and International Transportation

Madagascar's road network is about 2.5 times longer than Malaŵi's.[14] Madagascar is also much larger in area, however, so in roads per square kilometer, its total network has half the density of Malaŵi's; the network of paved roads in Madagascar has about 75 percent of the density of that in Malaŵi. Madagascar's terrain is also much more mountainous, so road building is considerably more difficult than in Malaŵi. Even up to the present day, no paved roads connect certain of the largest cities such as Toliary and Antsiranana (Diégo Suarez).

From independence to the start of the Ratsiraka government in 1975, Madagascar focused its efforts on upgrading the existing network rather than building new roads. The mileage of paved roads increased at an average annual rate of 8.6 percent. Although estimates are not available for the years after 1975, a number of observers have pointed out that the government has invested relatively little in the road network, which deteriorated considerably, especially in the first part of the 1980s. According to the Director of the Planning Office, the government "forgot" to provide normal funds for road maintenance; such mundane matters were undoubtedly of less interest than the exciting investment projects being undertaken in the invest-to-the-hilt program.[15] As a result, weather damage to roads has not been satisfactorily repaired. Rasomoelina (1978, p. 103) noted that peasants have set fields on fire as a protest against the government and that such fires have damaged both bridges and roads, but the extent of this activity is not known.

A World Bank report (December 1984) gives a flavor of what has happened to the domestic road network.

> Many areas of smallholder production remain almost impassable. ... In other areas bridges have collapsed or have been rendered impassable by cyclone damage and structural deterioration. In the Mananjary region, the only outlet open to some coffee growers was to send their crops down river by canoe. ... One coffee processor in Toamasina claims that the journey along the coastal highway to Maroansetra which in 1951 took one day now normally takes four. Deterioration of road surfaces has caused abnormal damage to vehicles and has led some processing/storage companies to ban their drivers from using many rural roads. [p. 169]

Three ministries (Transport, Supplies, and Tourism; Public Works; and Industry and Commerce) have administered transportation services. Problems of overlapping authority gave rise to a number of surface transportation problems, which contributed to a decline in marketed production, particularly in agriculture. For example, the government failed to allocate enough foreign exchange for spare parts for trucks, and for about five years after 1979 it also refused to allow the private sector to import new trucks. As a result, about 50 percent of privately owned trucks were out of commission by the mid-1980s, and the truck stock averaged ten to twelve years in age (Berthélemy and others 1988). At the same time, the government imported 1,000 new trucks from the German Democratic Republic (and 400 from other countries) but allocated these primarily to government ministries and parastatals. These new trucks proved too heavy for the fragile and undermaintained rural roads, however, so they could not easily be used to collect agricultural produce.

To encourage the parastatal in charge of truck transportation, the government set freight tariffs so low that many private truck companies went out of business. Furthermore, the new freight tariffs did not sufficiently differentiate between good and bad roads to reflect the different transportation costs on the two kinds of roads. These unrealistic tariffs pushed the parastatal companies into financial difficulties, and they were loath to take over the business of the failing private companies, especially in areas served by bad roads.

In general, the transportation parastatals were unable to replace the private transportation services. Some private companies that were able to obtain spare parts carried on a type of black market road transportation by evading official tariffs and charging what they wanted; Indian merchants from the west coast were said to have been especially active in this trade. During the middle 1980s the government began to reassess and reverse these policies, but by the end of 1987 the results of this policy reassessment were not yet clear.

At the time of independence Madagascar's railroad network was 860 kilometers long and consisted of two unconnected lines (shown on the map on the frontispiece). Since independence neither line has been essentially extended. During the first part of the 1980s maintenance of these lines suffered as a result of the general economic decline, so service has not been completely reliable.

Other domestic transportation systems have different problems. Most rivers do not provide very long stretches suitable for transportation throughout the entire year. All governments since independence have focused considerable attention on domestic air transportation, both for passengers and small freight. In 1980 the country had fifty-three airports, seventeen of which were all-weather facilities (Bunge 1983, p. 98). This has been an expensive mode of transportation.

Madagascar has several ports open to international traffic. The largest is Toamasina on the east coast, followed by Mahajunga on the west coast. These are supplemented by fifteen or so smaller ports taking international traffic. Many of the current port facilities were constructed as part of the colonial government's large-scale public works projects, especially in the 1930s.

By all accounts facilities in all ports are inadequate, and they are plagued by shortages of equipment, poor management, and theft. Throughout the entire postindependence period labor productivity has been low.[16] In the early 1980s productivity in containerized shipping (as measured by containers filled and transferred per work hour) in Toamasina port was less than 3 percent of that of West African ports (World Bank December 1984, p. 65). Long delays for unloading have been common and have occasioned increases in freight rates. The uncertain operations of the Toamasina port and railroad connections to the highlands have caused important dislocations for highland industry. For instance, a former cabinet minister told me that one order of needed imported fertilizer could not be moved from the ports to the farmers for two years, resulting in a great deal of spoilage.[17]

Regional Policy

Although regional policies have an obvious interaction with the transportation system, relatively little public discussion has focused on regional policy goals. Roughly half the island's industry is in the relatively wealthy province of Antananarivo, the location of the capital city. All postindependence governments have recognized the importance of dispersing manufacturing over the island in order to equalize economic development among the various regions. Indeed, one of the goals of the 1964–68 plan was the development of a regional policy; the 1973 investment code (but not the 1985 investment code) established location in less industrialized areas as a criterion for judging projects. The theme of regional dispersement was also popular in speeches of leading political figures at that time.

Exactly what policies the government actually pursued is unclear, however, as are the quantitative goals for regional policy. Certain wisps of evidence on this matter are available. For instance, in 1977 and 1978 officials in the BTM (National Bank for Rural Development) increased the share of loans going to the poorest provinces (especially Mahajunga and Toliary) and reduced the share going to the province of Antananarivo (Direction générale du plan 1979a). In the name of regional policy, certain projects have been assigned to particular regions. Further, a glance at a map of recent industrial projects shows a spread throughout the entire island (France, Ministère de la coopération, 1986, p. 136).

The degree to which such decisions were made on economic grounds (either short or long range) or purely political criteria is impossible to determine. Why, for example, did the government locate some new factories that must rely on imported inputs in the highlands at the end of a railway that has operated in an uncertain fashion rather than in poorer areas in port cities that have little industry?

Even if the government loosely considered regional comparative advantage in siting new factories, its transportation network decisions have not been well coordinated with its factory location decisions. As a result, some of these new production facilities do not have proper transportation links with their sources of raw materials or their markets.

Summary

Governmental policies in Madagascar have strongly influenced the performance of its manufacturing and transportation sectors. The Tsiranana government (1960–72) relied primarily on indirect incentives, such as tax reductions and tariff concessions, for the manufacturing sector, and production grew at a relatively satisfactory—but not spectacular—pace. The Ramanantsoa government (1972–75) promulgated an investment code reserving certain activities for government investment and reducing incentives for new private investment. The Ratsiraka government (1975 to the mid-1980s) took a much more direct role in production, nationalizing the bulk of the manufacturing sector and participating in both investment and management decisions, and production declined.

The government administered the system of price controls on industrial goods with little attention to market conditions, and many enterprises ran into financial difficulties as a result. The various price, tariff, and transportation policies influencing manufacturing production were not consistent with each other or with any general goals. The overvalued exchange rate and the lack of foreign currency to obtain intermediate inputs further discouraged production. The strategy of heavy-industry investment proposed in the *FundOp* and the actual choice of projects, especially during the invest-to-the-hilt campaign, were not appropriate given existing factor proportions and the administrative constraints of the economy. In transportation, the overlapping authority of several ministries made policy coordination difficult, and the lack of proper maintenance led to degradation of the road network.

These various policies also have had important implications for the distribution of income. Rapid growth of manufacturing, especially in labor-intensive industries, could provide employment for the rural population at a higher income than agriculture. This has not occurred in Madagascar. Furthermore, the breakdown in the transportation system has meant that certain areas—especially the poorer areas ill-served by road transportation—suffered disproportionately.

Notes

1. For the discussion on manufacturing in this chapter I draw from de Bandt and others (1986); France, Ministère de la coopération (1986); Rabier (1986); and World Bank (March 1986a, November 1984, October 1984, November 1981, and December 1976).

2. Details on the proposed administrative structure are taken from Madagascar Government (1980). In interpreting this legislation as "corporatist, " I differ considerably from Jean du Bois de Gaudusson, in Constantine and others (1979), p. 256. Chaigneau (1985), pp. 66 ff., discusses briefly the syndicalist elements of the Ramanantsoa government.

3. Interview with the author, April 16, 1987.

4. These include *entreprise socialistes* (discussed in the text); *establissements public à caractère industriel et commercial* (EPICs), which have no equity capital and are under both the administrative control of a specific ministry and the financial control of the finance ministry; *sociétés d'économie mixte* (SEMs), which have equity capital and were set up to attract foreign participation; *sociétés*

d'intérêt national (SINs), which were set up to replace the SEMs and which possess their own equity capital and enjoy ostensible—but not actual—autonomy from the government; *sociétés d'état* (SEs), which are rather vaguely defined and include state-owned enterprises with quite different statutes; and *sociétés anonyme* (SAs). which are a standard corporate form in the private sector, but in this case the government owns all or part of their equity capital.

5. For this section I draw especially upon Glenshaw and Harmon (1985), World Bank (July 1979), and other World Bank reports cited in footnote 1. The data on investment applications come from World Bank (December 1976). The data on growth in this sector come from Pryor (1988a), table C-2.

6. Some evidence can be drawn from tables 16 and 19 in Petitjean (1978).

7. A former consultant with the Malagasy government told me that for many years the Ratsiraka government resisted formulating a technology policy because officials believed that producing "at international standards of quality" required using a particular technology, leaving the government little choice in production methods.

8. This discussion of labor unions draws heavily on Glenshaw and Harmon (1985). They place the number of union members in the mid-1980s at 100,000; Bunge (1983), p. 73, places union membership in the late 1970s at 132,000.

9. The Institut d'emission malgache, *Rapports annuels d'activité de l'IEM*, presents an industrial production index for an earlier period.

10. For the late 1960s, the World Bank (December 1976) and Petitjean (1978), pp. 60–111, present evidence. The latter source provides by far the best available historical summary of Malagasy industry.

11. The generalizations discussed below are based on a three-part calculation. First, production indexes were calculated for ten branches corresponding to sectors defined in Malagasy input-output tables; second, these branches were divided into expanding and contracting sectors; and third, various statistics for these two sectors were calculated by aggregating data from input-output tables for 1966 and 1979. The estimated capital-labor ratios are particularly uncertain because they are based on ratios of amortization to wages, and these ratios showed some variation among different input-output tables. The source of the 1966 table is Madagascar, INSRE, and République française (1970); the 1979 table comes from unpublished materials supplied by the Direction générale du plan.

12. A detailed investigation of the magnitudes of the net effect on the balance of payments can only be carried out with a relatively recent input-output table, which was not available.

13. Madagascar, Banque des données de l'état (n.d.). Data on profits do not appear to be very reliable.

14. Roughly comparable data on the road networks are found in section C of the Appendix. Madagascar's 13,000 kilometers of rural roads may just include tertiary roads. According to the Madagascar, Direction générale du plan (1977b), p. 169, there were 38,000 kilometers of road, which suggests that quaternary roads comprised 11,000 kilometers. Much of the discussion in the rest of this section draws from World Bank (February 1983).

15. Jean Robiarivony (Directeur général du Plan) in *Afrique-Asie*, July 1, 1985, as cited by Deleris (1987), p. 77.

16. Gendarme (1960), p. 93, provides evidence on port productivity in the 1950s.

17. World Bank March (1986a) presents some evidence on the difficulties port problems have caused for other sectors.

15 The Government Sector in Madagascar

Although Madagascar is a country with a "socialist orientation," its tax level, its share of governmental expenditures in the GDP, and the volume of investment it has financed through the public budget have been less than in Malaŵi. The operational effectiveness of the governmental administrative apparatus, through which these resources flow, has been declining, at least as of the mid-1980s, and inappropriate monetary policies often exacerbated the inflationary pressures arising from deficits in the government budget.

Little is known about the incidence of Madagascar's taxes, but its expenditures appear to have had a progressive impact on the distribution of income. Unlike the situation in Malaŵi, social programs have had an important place in the Malagasy state budget. The rise in school enrollment has been particularly noteworthy, although school graduates have had difficulties in finding jobs commensurate with their educational credentials. The government based its health programs on the use of capital-intensive (both human and physical) technologies; although these programs have been far reaching, they have resulted in little improvement of various indicators of the level of health.

The Size and Operation of the Government Sector

In 1980 Madagascar had roughly 1.1 state and local governmental employees per 100 population. Although this ratio was higher than in Malaŵi (chapter 8), it was relatively low in comparison to other nations in Africa; it also appeared to be commensurate with the relatively low level of government expenditures in Madagascar (Heller and Tait 1984, pp. 40–41). Incomplete time series data suggest that employment in the government sector increased roughly 7.6 percent a year from 1973 through 1984, more than double the rate of overall labor force increase (Pryor 1988a, table H-1).

From 1960 through the early 1980s total expenditures of the central government (excluding transfers to local governments) averaged about 18.5 percent of GDP, a much lower share than in Malaŵi.[1] Furthermore, with the exception of a few years in the late 1970s, total and current public expenditures remained roughly the same percentage of GDP throughout the period. In the 1960s local taxes financed a good part of local government expenditures, which averaged between 3.5 and 4 percent of GDP. After the elimination of the poll tax and cattle taxes in the rural areas in 1972, the local governments relied primarily on transfers from the central government.

Governmental investment expenditures averaged about 4.3 percent of GDP during the period; this ratio was much lower than in Malaŵi. It rose from the end of the 1960s to the end of the 1970s but fell rapidly back to its former level as the economy struggled to regain economic equilibrium after the invest-to-the-hilt campaign. Budget-financed gross fixed capital investment averaged about 28.5 percent of all such investment, also a much lower share than in Malaŵi.

How effectively has the government administered its economic policies, and how efficiently has it used public funds? The conventional wisdom is that at the time of independence, the civil service had a number of well-trained Malagasy administrators and functioned relatively effectively, that the level of government administration remained relatively high until the last years of the Tsiranana government, and that administrative capabilities began to decline thereafter.

Pursuing these matters in greater depth is difficult because relatively little statistical information on the management of the government exists, and the information that is available is both incomplete and outdated. For instance, in 1987 the government had not yet officially closed its books on fiscal year 1981, largely because it was using an outmoded fiscal accounting system inherited from the colonial government. Of course, this lack of current information on government expenditures and taxes is itself one indication that administrative effectiveness left something to be desired; also this lack of information reduces the public accountability of the various governmental entities.

Although the evidence on government efficiency is mainly impressionistic, it would include the general decline in the quality of the work of the central statistical office (chapter 1); the administrative chaos accompanying the nationalization drive in the mid- and late 1970s (chapters 10 and 14); the loss of estate land in the takeover of French properties (chapter 11); the ineffectiveness of the work of the agricultural extension agency (chapter 11), the problems in governmental purchasing of agricultural crops, and the financial scandal in SINPA (chapter 12); the difficulties in administering the distribution of agricultural inputs (chapter 12); the awkward system for allocating foreign exchange (chapter 13); the number of unfortunate decisions made in the government's invest-to-the-hilt campaign (chapter 14); the administrative rigidities of the price control system (chapter 14);

the undermaintenance of roads (chapter 14); the peculiar pattern of retrenchment of government expenditures, which has led to shortages in complementary goods and supplies to government workers (see below); and the inappropriateness of many health and education expenditures (see below).

A recent report on the investment climate, based on extensive interviewing in Madagascar, claims that corruption in the government has increased considerably as the economy has stagnated in the last decade (Glenshaw and Harmon 1985). This problem occurred at both low and high levels of government and added considerably to the costs of business. For instance, starting a new business in the mid-1980s required payoffs ranging from 50 to 150 percent of normal start-up costs.

In brief, both the efficiency and the honesty of the governmental bureaucracy in Madagascar seem to have declined markedly, at least until the mid-1980s. Whether the governmental apparatus can effectively oversee the liberalization policies of the mid- and late 1980s remains to be seen.

Tax, Expenditure, and General Budget Policies

Most colonial regimes directed government expenditures toward the promotion of exports and also tried to maintain a balanced budget. The French in Madagascar did not appear to be an exception to these generalizations. After independence the situation changed greatly as the government aimed public expenditures at a broader range of goals.

Public Expenditures

Table 15-1 shows the general pattern of public expenditures in Madagascar after independence. These annual data are not completely comparable and are also incomplete in that they exclude most (if not all) of the social expenditures channeled through the social insurance system, Caisse nationale de prévoyance sociale (CNAPS), as well as some debt-service payments.[2]

Throughout the period covered in table 15-1, general services (administration, justice and police, defense, and science) remained roughly the same share of GDP, except for a short-term rise in the late 1970s. They were considerably higher than similar expenditures in Malaŵi, a feature that can be traced to the much larger military expenditures in Madagascar. Army personnel increased from about 4,800 in the early 1970s to about 21,000 in the early 1980s; that amounts to one member of the armed forces per 438 population (in contrast to 1,378 in Malaŵi). In addition, members of the paramilitary *gendarmerie* numbered about 8,000 in the early 1980s.[3] This increase in personnel raises doubts as to whether the data on general services presented

Table 15-1. Central and Provincial Government Expenditures as a Share of GDP, Madagascar, 1961 to 1982
(percent)

Year	General services[a]	Health, education, welfare[b]	Agriculture	Other economic services[c]	Other expenditures	Total
1961	6.1	5.3	—————8.1—————		2.2	21.6
1962	5.8	5.1	—————7.8—————		1.8	20.5
1963	6.1	5.5	—————8.1—————		1.9	21.6
1964	6.5	5.6	1.8	4.4	2.0	20.2
1965	6.7	6.0	2.1	6.8	2.4	24.0
1966	6.4	5.5	2.1	6.8	1.8	22.7
1967	6.2	5.5	2.2	7.0	2.0	22.9
1968	6.2	5.9	2.9	7.6	1.9	24.6
1969[d]	6.4	6.0	3.6	8.6	2.4	27.1
1970[d]	5.6	5.8	2.6	7.2	2.3	23.5
1971	4.9	4.9	—————9.7—————		3.0	22.5
Unweighted average	6.1	5.6	2.4	6.6	2.2	22.8
1975	5.2	4.9	1.9	2.5	1.2	15.7
1976	6.4	6.4	2.7	3.6	1.2	20.3
1977	5.6	5.6	2.7	2.6	1.8	18.3
1978	9.6	7.8	2.9	3.8	2.0	26.1
1979	9.0	7.4	4.0	3.4	2.1	25.9
1980	8.8	8.6	3.1	4.8	1.3	26.7
1981	7.8	5.8	1.3	1.3	2.1	18.3
1982[d]	6.1	5.9	1.3	1.8	2.1	17.3
Unweighted average	7.3	6.6	2.5	3.0	1.7	21.1

Note: All data include capital expenditures, except the data for 1961 through 1971, which omit capital expenditures of the provincial governments. The inclusion of the provincial governments and the apparent omission of certain price subsidies make the totals differ from those reported in section D of the Appendix. I have been unable to locate or to calculate comparable statistics for the 1972–74 period or for years after 1982.

a. Includes expenditures for general administration, justice and police, defense, and science; in later years certain military expenditures may be excluded.
b. May or may not include the expenditures of the social insurance system.
c. The comparability of the earlier and later series is not certain.
d. Planned, rather than actual, budget.
Source: Pryor (1988a), table K-3b.

in the table include all military expenditures; I have found estimates of the magnitude of "true" defense expenditures for the early 1980s ranging from 3 to 6 percent of GDP.[4]

The health, education, and welfare expenditures show a continual rise, at least to the early 1980s. Despite the much more extensive system of education in Madagascar, the percentage of GDP devoted to these purposes has not been much greater than that in Malaŵi. Two explanations can be offered. First, these data are incomplete and exclude some or all expenditures of the social insurance system, the university, and other important components of the health, education, and welfare system.[5] Second, much of the teaching in primary schools has been carried out by young Malagasy on their national service duty, which has been financed through another part of the budget.

Economic expenditures show considerable contrast with those of Malaŵi.[6] The share of GDP going into governmental expenditures for agriculture has been relatively low, as has the share of expenditures for other economic purposes. From 1970 through 1983 expenditures for debt repayment and for "other" purposes (apparently financial transactions and price supports) have risen from 1.9 percent of GDP to 4.2 percent. Despite this overall increase, explicit repayments of the Malagasy government debt have been a considerably lower share of GDP than those in Malaŵi, even though in the mid-1980s Madagascar's per capita foreign debt was much greater. The explanation is that a higher share of the Malagasy debt was owed by the parastatals, and their debt repayments were off-budget. Many of the parastatals were in a precarious financial situation and receiving governmental subsidies, so much of Madagascar's foreign debt-service expenditures appeared indirectly in the budget under the category of subsidies to parastatals. Regardless of budgetary niceties, debt service in Madagascar, as in Malaŵi, will severely strain governmental finances for many years to come.

The ratio of government expenditures for goods and services to the wages and salaries of government personnel has declined dramatically from about 70 percent to 15 percent in the post-independence period. In other words, the government retrenched its budget expenditures by cutting supplies and equipment much faster than personnel. This reaction by Malagasy budget officials is very understandable; in many cases, however, the effectiveness of government personnel was sharply limited by the lack of complementary equipment and supplies, such as transportation, computers, and medicines (in the health sector), a story frequently heard when interviewing Malagasy civil servants.

Public Revenues

Three major policy problems are immediately evident: the difficulty of increasing tax revenues, the regressive nature of many taxes, and the large government deficits in the late 1970s.

LEVEL AND TREND. Table 15-2 presents some data showing the importance of various types of government revenues. Like total government expenditures, total receipts rose in the late 1970s and then fell back to their 1970 level by the early 1980s. A longer time series focusing just on taxes shows the total tax share of GDP rising from 14.1 percent in 1960 to 17.7 percent in 1970, a very modest increase, especially in comparison to Malaŵi (Pryor 1988b, table K-2). Indeed, the most important increases in taxes occurred under the French colonial government, which raised the share of taxes to GDP from 7.5 percent in 1950 to 14.1 percent within a decade.

Table 15-2. Selected Data on Public Revenues, Madagascar, 1971 to 1983
(percent)

		Taxes				Fiscal balance/GDP	
		Percentage of all taxes[b]			Foreign	Covered	Uncovered
Year	Total receipts/GDP[a]	Direct taxes	Indirect taxes[c]	Other taxes	grants and loans/GDP	expenditures	expenditures
1971	17.3	16.7	72.8	10.6	1.2	18.9	-0.1
1972	16.1	16.3	73.1	10.6	1.1	17.8	1.6
1973	15.8	22.8	68.8	8.4	1.4	17.5	1.9
1974	14.6	18.5	70.2	11.3	0.9	15.9	2.0
1975	14.1	13.8	73.0	13.1	1.4	16.2	0.7
1976	16.7	13.5	69.0	17.5	1.0	16.2	3.3
1977	21.7	15.8	72.9	11.3	1.0	23.1	0.1
1978	21.4	19.4	71.8	8.8	1.8	23.6	2.2
1979	19.5	17.5	72.8	9.7	6.3	26.6	7.1
1980	17.7	18.5	71.4	10.1	7.3	26.2	10.8
1981	15.7	22.4	63.0	14.5	7.5	26.2	4.9
1982	15.3	18.8	70.1	11.0	5.2	24.2	0.2
1983	n.a.	17.5	67.7	14.8	n.a.	n.a.	n.a.
Unweighted average	17.2	17.8	70.5	11.7	3.0	21.0	2.9

n.a. = Not available.

Note: These data refer only to the finances of the central government and are the most inclusive public finance data available for this sector. It is not clear whether they include social insurance expenditures.

a. Total receipts include receipts of FNUP (Fonds national unique de péréquation), which channels the difference between domestic and foreign prices of agricultural exports to the government for financing the rice subsidy and certain investments.

b. Total taxes are somewhat smaller than total receipts.

c. Includes export and import taxes, excise taxes, and turnover taxes.

Source: Pryor (1988a), table K-1.

Tsiranana's greatest economic error may have been his failure to adjust tax revenues and public expenditures so as to be able to finance more development projects. This judgment might be considered too severe if a tax increase was politically infeasible, even in the post-independence euphoria, but I have found no credible evidence suggesting that Tsiranana's power base was so precarious.

The structure of taxes has followed the usual pattern found in developing countries (Malaŵi excluded)—the overwhelming share has come from indirect taxes. Direct taxes counted for only one-fifth to one-sixth of total tax revenues. In the early years of independence the most important indirect taxes were from imports. In recent years export taxes (including the profits from agriculture obtained by the Fonds national unique de péréquation (FNUPs), which were channeled into the government budget) have become increasingly more important than the import taxes. This reliance on foreign trade taxes is quite understandable; they are easy to collect on an island, where all exports and imports enter or leave via a limited number of ports or airports. A disadvantage is that governmental revenues are highly sensitive to the volume of foreign trade and to the foreign exchange and other policies that influence such trade. With the dramatic decline in foreign trade in recent years (chapter 13), the Malagasy government has had increasing difficulties in financing its expenditures.

TAX INCIDENCE. Little professional attention has focused on the incidence of Malagasy taxes. The only extensive empirical evidence regarding direct taxes is for the rural sector in 1962; these data, presented in table 15-3, show an average tax rate more than double that for the rural sector in Malaŵi. A large share of such taxes were the poll taxes and cattle taxes Joseph Galliéni imposed early in the colonial era to force the farmers to sell produce on the market or to work for wages for French colonists. These taxes were highly regressive, which the table makes obvious. They were also highly unpopular, especially when they were collected during the famine in the early 1970s after rural cash revenues had fallen. Such resentment undoubtedly played a role in the rural insurrections that brought about the fall of the Tsiranana government in 1972. The severity of the production effects arising from the removal of these taxes by the succeeding Ramanantsoa government is discussed in chapter 11; the fiscal effects are also important to consider.

These capitation taxes raised a considerable share of the revenues of the local and provincial governments. Their abolishment required the central government to replace them, which led both to greater integration of the budgets of the different levels of government and to an additional strain on the revenues of the central government, already under stress because of the decline in foreign trade. One response was

Table 15-3. Incidence of Direct Personal Taxes, Malagasy Rural Sector, 1962

	Average income in income class (thousands of FMG)	Ratio of tax to income (percent)
	22.8	0.0
	30.6	5.0
	44.5	8.1
	55.3	7.0
	68.3	6.3
	84.6	5.2
	110.9	4.3
	166.2	3.8
	315.6	3.6
	833.4	3.0
Average	60.9	5.6

Aggregated statistics of inequality

Income measure	Gini coefficient	Log variance	Theil coefficient
Before taxes	.290	.220	.194
After taxes	.296	.226	.203

Source: Pryor (1988a), section I.

to establish FNUP in 1977 to obtain a large share of the profits that the boom in coffee prices was producing for coffee exports.

The available data on household expenditures for urban areas do not permit determination of the incidence of either direct or indirect taxes. For instance, in small towns (secondary urban centers) in 1980 the shortfall between family incomes and expenditures (which include savings, direct taxes, taxes for CNAPS, loan repayments, and other financial transactions) amounted to roughly 20 percent of total revenue, but details on the various individual items are not available.[7] I suspect that before 1971 direct taxes were less of a burden for urban than for rural families, that is, that the tax system was regressive not only within the rural sector but also between the rural and the (wealthier) urban sectors. After the removal of the capitation taxes in the rural area, this was probably no longer the case.

The reasons that the Malagasy government did not place a greater share of the tax burden on the urban sector are difficult to determine. One conjecture is that it was quite unaware of the real burden of taxation on different parts of the population, just as we are today.

336 Malawi and Madagascar

Until the Malagasy government directs its statistical agencies to collect the relevant information to determine the impact of taxes, the question of incidence must remain unanswered.

Still other research problems arise concerning the incidence of indirect taxes. Such taxes fell both on consumer goods and on machinery and intermediary products, but in an irregular pattern (Maxwell Stamp Associates 1986). Although an input-output table is available for analyzing the incidence of these taxes, the form of the tax data make this task too difficult to attempt here.

The Balance of Expenditures and Revenues

Over the long run, governmental expenditures and revenues have not been greatly out of balance. From the data underlying table 15-2 we can calculate that 74.4 percent of government expenditures were covered by taxes and other receipts; 13.0 percent, by foreign grants and loans; and 12.5 percent, by internal borrowing and other domestic financial transactions of the government. This means that the government expenditures that were financed by internal borrowing and money creation averaged only 2.9 percent of GDP.

These "uncovered" expenditures have varied considerably from one period to the next, however. They were very low at the end of the Tsiranana era but rose considerably as the government deficit increased during the invest-to-the-hilt program. By 1982 the government was able to reduce its uncovered expenditures practically to zero, an act of political courage and ability because it was taken at the end of more than a decade of decline in living standards. Comparable information about uncovered expenditures since that time are not available, but the government seems to have maintained budgetary discipline, for the most part by raising taxes.[8] The increase in civil service employment slowed down considerably in the mid-1980s, and—equally important—the average real wages of civil servants fell at an annual rate of about 7.8 percent in the same time, a significant real saving in personnel expenditures.

Microeconomic Effects of Governmental Expenditures

Although our knowledge of the incidence of taxes is quite incomplete, we can study the incidence of the expenditure side of the government budget by examining two particular kinds of governmental expenditures. The Malagasy government has placed considerable emphasis on raising economic welfare directly, that is, by providing education, health, and welfare services rather than investing in the economy to raise the level of per capita income, which was Malawi's strategy. The final outcomes on the distribution of income, however, differed from the expected results.

Education

Different aspects of the educational system serve to widen or narrow income differentials. For instance, Madagascar's efforts to provide universal primary education probably led to a narrowing of income differentials because a segment of the rural poor gained the skills to earn more income. The dramatic fall in illiteracy among women also probably narrowed income differentials for the society as a whole. The important role of private secondary schools and also of university training abroad, however, has probably increased income inequality in that only those families with higher incomes can afford such high-quality education.

QUANTITY OF EDUCATION. In 1950 enrollment rates (number of students in school as a percentage of the appropriate age group) in both primary and secondary schools were considerably lower in Madagascar than they were in Malaŵi (Pryor 1988a, table J-2). Indeed, the enrollment rate—5.4 percent—was lower than in the precolonial period.[9] In the 1950s, however, enrollment rates in primary schools (defined here as grades one through six) and secondary schools (grades seven and above) rose considerably. By 1960 primary school enrollment rates were roughly equal to those in Malaŵi, and secondary school enrollment rates were higher. Furthermore, during the colonial period a much higher percentage of Madagascar's than of Malaŵi's high school graduates studied at universities. As a result, Madagascar had a larger educated elite to take control of its government after independence—a direct result of the colonial policy of assimilation.[10]

During the Tsiranana administration, enrollment rates in primary schools rose steadily, from about 52 to 78 percent, and his government planned to achieve universal primary education by the mid-1980s. The Ramanantsoa and Ratsiraka governments gave further support to education, and Madagascar allegedly achieved this goal by 1976. Illiteracy in this year was also much lower than in Malaŵi, and with universal primary education, it should decline significantly in the coming decades.

Nevertheless, the attempt to broaden educational opportunity has not worked out quite as planned, because the regional impact has been uneven. For instance, a comparison of the degree of illiteracy among the rural population of different age groups in 1984–85 shows that the greatest declines in illiteracy did not occur in Toliary, the province with the highest degree of illiteracy, but rather in Antsiranana, which had about the median degree of illiteracy (Appendix, table I-3). Furthermore, illiteracy in Antananarivo province appeared to increase slightly. The most positive result of the program was the great decline in illiteracy among women, which narrowed the differences in the educational levels of men and women.

The enrollment rate in secondary schools rose dramatically from 4 percent at independence to 32 percent in 1984; roughly 55 to 60 percent of these secondary school students attended private schools. The University of Madagascar, which was founded in 1955, has also expanded rapidly, enrolling 37,181 students in the academic year 1984–85 (Madagascar, Ministère de l'enseignement supérieur, 1985). The number of university students per capita in Madagascar was roughly thirteen times higher than in Malaŵi by the mid-1980s.

Certainly the Malagasy educational effort is impressive. An important motive in the expansion of the system was the attempt by the Ramanantsoa and Ratsiraka governments to equalize economic conditions in different parts of the country by providing all provinces with the necessary human capital for economic development, a vital part of President Ratsiraka's apparent desire to increase the representation of *côtiers* in the civil service. The level of primary education was already relatively high in Antananarivo Province and also the university is located there. Expansion of education, then, required universalizing primary education and establishing branches of the university in all provincial capitals, which occurred in 1977.

QUALITY OF EDUCATION. Trends in student-teacher ratios are difficult to establish because of the fragmentary nature of the data, but the ratio appears to have declined in the elementary schools from roughly 65 per teacher in the early 1970s to roughly 38 per teacher in the mid-1980s.[11] The fall in the student-teacher ratio does not appear to have led to an increase in the quality of education, however. Many of the teachers at the primary school level, especially in the rural areas, have been young men and women fulfilling their national service (VSN) duties, an interesting social innovation of the Ramanantsoa government in 1972. Few of these neophyte teachers had much beyond the primary level of education themselves, and before taking up their teaching duties, they received only five to twelve weeks of teacher training.

Secondary schools have similar problems with the quality of the teaching staff. A UNESCO survey found 75 percent of the teachers unqualified. Although data from standardized international tests are not available, other indicators—for example, the percentage of students passing particular examinations—imply that the quality of education has fallen over time.

A similar problem occurred at the university level. From 1981 through 1984 the ratio of graduates of the university to total student body hovered between 4 and 5 percent, indicating that a high proportion failed their exams. Many must have continued their education, however, because governmental financial support of students at the university level has been quite high. Outside observers have also noted that the knowledge of French has been rapidly declining since the 1970s, when Madagascar began to make the Malagasy language the official language of instruction at the primary and secondary levels.

IMPLICATIONS FOR GROWTH AND THE DISTRIBUTION OF INCOME. I have found little indication that the educational system at the secondary and university levels was consciously geared to meeting Madagascar's needs for skilled personnel. For instance, in speaking of both the secondary and higher levels of education in the mid-1980s, UNESCO (1984a and 1984b) reported,

> Employers in the public, parastatal and private sectors find among the graduating students fewer and fewer employees who have the knowledge and the know-how to become productive workers quickly.

The government has placed the most emphasis on a formal academic education and the creation of impressive academic credentials. The teaching of technical skills useful for a creating a cadre of skilled workers appears to have languished. Some private-sector establishments, I have been told, train their own technicians, thus filling some of the educational lacunae. Although the data are too fragmentary to assess properly the relationship between the educational needs of the economy and the educational system, the amount of relevant technical training appears to be considerably below that in Malaŵi.

The absorption of workers with educational credentials has been low in the fifteen years of economic stagnation since the early 1970s, and many young Malagasy have had great difficulties in finding suitable employment. For instance, in 1975 only about 40 percent of those leaving school could find jobs requiring their formal education.[12] Estimates for later years are not readily available, but because of slow economic growth, the situation probably has not improved. In the Antananarivo airport, you can have some interesting conversations on modern French literature with college graduates working as glorified porters helping tourists through the highly complicated customs system.

A legacy of the colonial era was the important role of expatriates in the Malagasy economy, especially in the early years after independence. A study of the 191,620 jobs in the modern sector in 1965 revealed that 73 percent of the 6,020 cadre supérieur were non-Malagasy (33 to 60 percent in the public sector and 86 percent in the private sector); of the 17,900 *cadre moyen*, 29.5 percent were non-Malagasy (Hugon 1976, p. 32).[13] Indigenization of these jobs was much higher on the political agenda in Madagascar than in Malaŵi, and the rapid exodus of French nationals after 1972 suggests that the process has been quite rapid since then, even though many of the Malagasy replacements did not have the requisite education and have had to learn on the job.

To what extent has Madagascar overinvested in formal education? From a social perspective, one can argue that all such expenditures are justified to realize human potentials. Apparently, no one has made an estimate of the economic returns to education, but the inability of many high school and university graduates to obtain appropriate jobs suggests that the social return has been low and may continue so until the educational system is more oriented toward the economic needs of the country.

Health

The Malagasy government has placed a much greater emphasis on formal health care programs than has the Malaŵi government. Madagascar's larger expenditures on formal programs (and health inputs of highly skilled personnel) has not been matched by greater effectiveness, however. At independence Madagascar had a much higher average level of health than did Malaŵi, as measured by infant mortality rates and life expectancy. By the mid-1980s, the health situation in Madagascar had deteriorated so much that important health indicators were almost the same in the two countries.[14]

Madagascar has had a rather unique heritage in modern medicine. English missionaries founded a medical school in the 1880s, which the French colonial government supported thereafter (chapter 9). At independence (per capita) medical inputs of hospital beds, physicians, and health personnel were quite impressive. Table 15-4 provides some data on trends in health input ratios.

Population per hospital bed was quite low in 1950 but has risen somewhat since that time. Modern medical services are still remote for much of the population, and most can only reach such facilities by walking (World Bank October 1986). For instance, in the early 1980s, about 55 percent of the rural population lived more than 5 kilometers (3 miles) from any medical dispensary. The supporting hospitals for these centers are located in urban centers to centralize the specialists and expensive medical equipment. The rural primary health care centers have been highly underutilized; in the early 1980s they averaged only nine to ten consultations a day, partly because of insufficient medicines, equipment, supervision, and trained personnel. In an interview, the Minister of Health appeared to place more emphasis on the political importance of the presence of these primary health centers than on their medical effectiveness.

Although the ratio of population to physicians has risen slightly, Madagascar has been far better off in this respect than Malaŵi. It has a lower ratio of population to health workers in every major category, although the relative differences narrow with the amount of training of the personnel. Madagascar's emphasis on training the highest skilled

Table 15-4. Population per Unit of Health Inputs, Madagascar, Selected Years, 1950 to 1985

	Type of input			
			All medical personnel[a]	
Year	Hospital beds	Physicians	Narrow definition	Wide definition
1950	411[b]	n.a.	n.a.	n.a.
1955	410	n.a.	n.a.	n.a.
1956	n.a.	8,686[b]	1,997[b]	1,037[b]
1960	407	n.a.	n.a.	n.a.
1964	379	n.a.	n.a.	n.a.
1967	n.a.	9,619	1,770[b]	920[b]
1970	354	n.a.	n.a.	n.a.
1973	367	n.a.	n.a.	n.a.
1977	403	9,425	1,322	825[b]
1981	490	n.a.	n.a.	n.a.
1985	n.a.	9,132[b]	1,255[b]	627[b]

n.a. = Not available.

a. The exact composition of the narrow and wide definitions of medical personnel are not entirely clear. I have had to make a number of small estimations to achieve comparability from year to year by using ratios of narrow to wide definitions of such personnel in other years (not included in table).

b. Estimated.

Source: Pryor (1988a), tables J-4 and J-5.

medical personnel is also revealed in its decision in the early 1970s to close down the school for paramedics serving as "bush doctors," because it wanted all Malagasy doctors to have the same medical education as physicians in France.

This emphasis on formal health care programs coexists with a relative neglect of health measures that require only lesser skilled labor. In the mid- and late 1970s, for instance, about 80 percent of the urban population but only 7 percent of the rural population had access to safe water, a sharp contrast to the rates in Malaŵi (UNICEF, annual-1986, p. 85; but see Ratsiraka 1975). The government has placed little emphasis on vaccination programs, which also use relatively unskilled labor; for instance, in the early 1980s only 13, 35, and 3 percent of infants under one year of age had received vaccinations, respectively, of BCG, DPT III, and Polio III, all much lower percentages than in Malaŵi. Latrine building, another labor-intensive public health measure, has progressed about equally in the two countries; in Madagascar in the early 1980s, only 47 percent of the rural homes had such facilities (Madagascar, Ministère de la population et la condition sociale, n.d.).

In sum, the Malagasy government has given considerable attention in its policy statements to improving the state of health but has not used its resources efficiently. Formal health inputs have been much greater than in Malaŵi, but the system is achieving only minimally better results in such indicators as infant mortality.

Low levels of health have a detrimental impact on economic growth. Countries with inadequate public health systems usually have wider income differentials because the inadequacies of the system have the greatest impact on the low-income groups. Quantifying this impact in Madagascar would require more detailed data, however.

Monetary Policy and the Financial System

Although strongly influenced by governmental budgetary policies, monetary policies also play an independent role in the economy. To a certain extent the central bank has contributed to Madagascar's economic problems. The amount of governmental borrowing (uncovered expenditures) has been small in most years, but the monetary authorities have not been particularly responsive to market forces.[15]

Money

The rise in the money supply (M1) has been moderate in comparison with that in many other developing nations.[16] In Madagascar from the end of 1962 to the end of 1984, the average annual rate of increase was about 10.4 percent, roughly the same as in Malaŵi. Nominal GDP during the same time period rose at an average annual rate of 10.0 percent. (To complete the picture, real GDP grew 1.2 percent annually; the GDP deflator, 8.9 percent.) From 1984 through 1988 M1 increased only a little faster, 13.4 percent a year.

Because the income velocity of money remained about the same throughout the period, the crude quantity theory of money is a useful tool to analyze monetary events. The average velocity was about 4.6, considerably lower than that of Malaŵi. The difference appears to stem from the greater relative importance of the monetary sector (conversely, the smaller share of the subsistence sector) in GDP. This view would be reinforced by tracing the relative stability in income velocity to the relative constancy in the share of agricultural production for home consumption in rural incomes; in fact, however, this share seems to have decreased (see table 16-1). Without more information about monetary transactions in rural areas, we cannot provide a satisfactory explanation.

More inclusive definitions of money supply behaved somewhat differently from those in Malaŵi. More specifically, in Madagascar M2 grew at roughly the same rate as M1. The structure of interest rates provides some insight into this phenomenon. In Madagascar the nominal discount rate was constant during the 1970s; the real discount rate averaged –3.7 percent (Pryor 1988a, tables L-3a and L-3b). In the 1980s the real discount rate remained negative; indeed, in the spring of 1985, the central bank lowered the nominal discount rate from 13.5 to 11 percent despite accelerating price increases, and this lower rate prevailed until the end of 1987 (IMF, *International Financial Statistics*). Although not a great deal of information is available on interest rates paid on time deposits, they appear to have been much the same as the discount rate and thus were also negative.

One might expect the average velocity of money to be higher in Madagascar than in Malaŵi because depositors were losing real purchasing power and should have been less willing to hold their assets in the form of cash balances. This factor was offset by other forces, however, including the lesser importance of agricultural production for home consumption; the role of strict exchange controls in preventing capital flight from Madagascar; the difficulties in purchasing certain tangible assets such as land; the wave of nationalizations in the mid-1970s, which increased the risk of investing in alternative assets; and the decreasing reliability of the supply system in rural areas since the mid-1970s (in addition to the usual risks because of the weather). All of these factors may well have made liquid forms of wealth the best possible asset choice, even though the real interest rate was negative. Appropriate personal financial assets data needed to investigate these matters in detail are not available, however.

Credit

Increases in the money supply generally feed inflation. These increases are connected closely to the credit system and to the financing of government debt. If the government is running a large deficit, it uses its credit to finance its expenditures and causes a net increase in the money supply. To neutralize the resulting inflationary pressure, the central bank can only try to keep interest rates high enough to induce the public to buy and hold government bills and bonds rather than spending the increase in money. To see how this process operated in Madagascar, one must determine the amount of monetization of the government's debt, that is, the degree to which the internally financed fiscal deficit of the central government fed the growth of M1.[17] From 1971 through 1984 roughly 84 percent of the Malagasy government's debt was translated into a rise in M1.[18] This percentage is much higher than that in Malaŵi and shows the Malagasy much less willing to hold government bonds as an asset.

The underlying reasons for this differential portfolio behavior are difficult to identify, but some scattered data suggest that the government was not willing to pay a sufficiently high interest rate on its debt to encourage people and institutions to hold its bonds. The discount rate of the central bank was also relatively low, so the real interest rate on government bonds in most years, as far as I can ascertain, was negative (Pryor 1988a, table L-3b).[19] The situation was exacerbated in years when the crop-purchasing agencies, such as SINPA and ROSO, paid the farmers for their crops in government bonds rather than money. In the late 1970s these bonds could be liquidated only at deep discounts, which supports the notion that government debt was not a popular asset among most Malagasy and that it was monetized more readily than in Malaŵi.

This set of circumstances created a vicious circle in Madagascar from the mid-1970s to the mid-1980s. The negative interest rates led to high monetization of the debt, which increased inflation and led to internally generated pressures on the balance of payments; these pressures, in turn, led to a lower volume of foreign trade, which reduced the government's revenues and increased its need for internal borrowing. One interesting time-series analysis by Olivier Ramahatra (1986, p. 145) shows that during that period the deficit in the governmental budget was almost the same as the current account deficit in the balance of payments.

Central bank officials in Madagascar were unwilling to discuss matters of credit policy with me, and the available data permit examination of only a few other relevant aspects of the credit market.[20] The ratio of total assets of the financial sector (that is, net foreign claims plus net claims on foreigners, on the government, and on the private sector) to current price GDP rose from about 20 percent in 1962 to a high of 33 percent in the late 1970s and then fell to about 6 percent by 1984. The ratio of net claims on the domestic economy to GDP rose continuously, from 10 percent in 1962 to about 52 percent in 1984. Foreign debt of the financial system has increased so fast since the late 1970s—primarily as a result of the invest-to-the-hilt campaign—that it almost equals domestic financial assets. These events have raised enormous problems in servicing foreign debt and also have imperiled the ability of the banks to lend domestically.

Summary and Conclusions

In an aggregate sense, the government budget in Madagascar has not served as important a role in economic development as did the budget in Malaŵi. As a share of GDP, Malagasy government expenditures for economic purposes have been lower than those of Malaŵi, and the ratio of fixed investment financed through the budget to total fixed investment has been lower as well. Monetary policy has not served growth effectively because the negative real interest rates have encouraged monetization of the public debt and inflation whenever the government has run a deficit not financed from abroad. Expenditures for education and health should have been growth enhancing, but the education system seems ill designed to produce workers with the proper skills for the economy. The inputs or financial resources devoted to public health by the mid-1980s have not yielded commensurate results. Other governmental expenditures have acted to retard growth; for example, military expenditures have probably slowed the growth rate, even though the government has tried to reduce the trade-off between military expenditures and economic development (guns versus butter) by involving the military in civil engineering, agriculture, and mining and manufacturing. The lack of effectiveness in administering government expenditures and the foreign debt burden created through governmental fiscal policies are other growth-retarding factors.

The current incidence of the tax system is unknown. On the expenditure side, universal primary education has undoubtedly narrowed income differentials in that all children on the island have an opportunity to receive such services. The health expenditures should also have narrowed income inequalities, but the administrative failings of the public health system have fallen disproportionately upon the poor.

Chapter 8 raised two conjectures about the behavior of the public sector in Sub-Saharan Africa: (a) the government sector has acted in a predatory or self-aggrandizing fashion to increase its size and power; and (b) the top political leaders have tried to break away from their colonial past by gambling on economic growth, impelled "by the political need to demonstrate progress, to reward supporters and to employ growing urban populations" (Fieldhouse 1986, p. 245). To what extent do these conjectures apply to Madagascar?

As in the case of Malaŵi, the self-aggrandizement hypothesis does not take us very far. Unlike many developing countries, the share of government expenditures in GDP has not greatly changed in Madagascar, so self-interest on the part of the politicians and the civil service does not seem greatly evident. Of course, the size of the public sector has been severely constrained by difficulties in obtaining tax revenues, which was in good part due to the link between taxes and foreign trade and the decline in exports from the early 1970s through the mid-1980s. Nevertheless, the aggrandizement hypothesis appears too crude to serve as a useful explanation for most public-sector activities in Madagascar.

The gamble-for-growth hypothesis has more relevance, but not for the Tsiranana government, which followed conservative fiscal and monetary policies and experienced a certain degree of economic success. The Ratsiraka government's invest-to-the-hilt campaign in the late 1970s, financed by high domestic and foreign borrowing, appears to be a much better illustration of this gamble, especially because it did reward supporters (a theme discussed in detail in chapter 17). Given the capital-intensive nature of Ratsiraka's early economic programs, redistributional or employment goals were quite secondary.

Madagascar's gamble also involved a number of other policies toward agriculture and trade, which are analyzed in previous chapters. Certainly Madagascar's difficulties in the 1980s can be traced much more easily to governmental policies than to external forces.

Notes

1. The data in this and the following paragraphs come from section D of the Appendix and Pryor (1988a), section K.

2. CNAPS, founded in the late 1950s, has provided certain funds for pensions, accidents, and family allowances for most modern-sector workers; contributions have amounted to 14 percent of wages. Madagascar's data on public expenditures are also not completely comparable with Malaŵi's (table 8-1) because the sectoring principle is somewhat different and because the Madagascar data include both central and local governmental expenditures.

3. The data on military personnel come from various issues of International Institute of Strategic Studies (IISS) (annual). For 1980 Chaigneau (1985) has a lower figure; and Covell (1987), p. 116, cites an anonymous source (J. P. D., "Madagascar: une économie en crise, " *Sudestasie* 26, 1982, pp. 32–44) claiming that the actual number of soldiers is nearly triple the official figure. One confusion is that the National People's Army includes the Development Army, which carries out civil engineering projects, as well as OMPIRA (Office militaire pour la production agricole), which was given responsibility for the "100,000 hectares" rice project and which has received extensive aid from the Democratic People's Republic of Korea; and OMNIS (Office militaire national des industries stratégiques), which administers certain mine and harbor facilities. The degree to which the personnel in these organizations are included in the total count of armed forces personnel is unclear.

4. The lower military expenditures datum comes from IISS; the higher, from Chaigneau (1985), p. 138, and from France, Ministère de la coopération (1986), p. 169. None of these sources provides the bases of the estimates.

5. Hugon (1976), pp. 258 ff., presents somewhat higher numbers for governmental expenditures on education.

6. The statistics in the next two paragraphs are drawn from table 15-1 and Pryor (1988a), section K.

7. The data on revenues and expenditures come from Madagascar, Banque des données de l'état (1987a), p. 1, and (1987b), p. 45. Neither source discusses in any useful detail differences in the family income and expenditure data.

8. France, Ministère de la coopération (1986), p. 65, provides more recent, but not comparable, data. Tables 2.3 and 8.2 in that source give data on personnel in the government sector and on average salaries.

9. According to Hugon (1976), p. 63, 135,000 children were in school in 1895 and 175,000 in 1931. Using population data for these two years from Rafrezy and Randretsa (1985), plus a short extrapolation to 1895, we can see that the ratio of pupils to population declined from 7.5 percent in 1895 to 4.7 percent in 1931.

10. Shortly before independence, 576 Malagasy were in French universities and another 1,103 were studying at the University in Antananarivo, according to Madagascar, Commissariat général au plan (1961), p. 41. In the mid-1970s those with university training numbered roughly 19,000, according to Madagascar, INSRE, *Analyse des données socio-économique, Mileau Urbain* (n.d.[b]), pp. 40–43.

11. Considerable data on teachers and students come from Minister of Finance and Planning (1977), but recent data are much more scarce. The student-teacher ratio cited in the text comes from data from UNESCO (1984a, b). The next paragraph draws heavily from these UNESCO sources, from which the citation also comes. Chaigneau (1985), pp. 211–19 also discusses the declining educational standards at the university.

12. According to the United Nations, Fund for Population Activities (1979), p. 19, of 54,000 students leaving school, only 20,000 could find jobs that required their degree of formal education.

13. Hugon's table contains an error, so the number of non-Malagasy in the public sector cannot be determined exactly; in the text the lower and upper limits are bracketed. The meaning of "non-Malagasy" is not clear; it may include those from the Comoro Islands and Réunion whose ancestors came to Madagascar several generations ago.

14. World Bank (October 1986) has the most complete survey of the health system.

15. All data cited in this discussion come from Pryor (1988a), section L; or IMF, *International Monetary Statistics*, February 1989.

16. M1 includes currency and demand deposits, M2 includes M1 plus private time and savings deposits, and M3 includes M2 plus private deposits in other financial institutions (a definition slightly different from that of M3 used elsewhere). For growth rate calculations, I do not take into account the changes in definition of monetary aggregates in 1979, but any resulting error should be very small.

17. All data in this section are drawn from Pryor (1988a), section L.

18. The data on uncovered expenditures come from table 15-2. The funds involved in various treasury operations are included in the deficit.

19. Some information on payment in bonds comes from private sources.

20. The cited statistics are only for the "narrow definition" of credit specified in appendix L of Pryor (1988a). The same trends appear using the "broad definition."

IV Broader Considerations

16 The Distribution of Income in Malaŵi and Madagascar

Income differences widened and poverty increased in the two decades following independence in both Madagascar and Malaŵi. To a considerable extent changes in the structure of incomes in the rural sector, influenced by a combination of governmental policy and diminishing returns to agricultural labor, brought about these trends. The mechanisms underlying such trends, which appeared especially marked in Malaŵi, were somewhat different in the two nations.

In poor agricultural nations the distribution of income can become increasingly unequal for three reasons:[1]

- The disparity in average incomes of families in the urban and rural sectors widens. In both Malaŵi and Madagascar, however, this disparity narrowed, primarily because real family incomes in the urban sector fell considerably.

- The relative number of families increases in the urban sector (as long as the urban sector accounts for less than half of the population), where average incomes are higher. Although such a population movement occurred to a limited extent in both countries, it did not have an important impact on the overall distribution of income.

- The income inequalities within the urban or rural sectors widen. As the available data suggest, this was the key factor underlying the overall increasing income inequalities in both nations.

Before beginning the detailed analysis, I must emphasize the tentative nature of the income statistics, which are pieced together from a variety of family income surveys in different sectors at different times and adjusted to make them as comparable as possible. A brief survey of factor income shares, urban-rural income differences, and wage trends may help develop some understanding of the most important components of income. Because income statistics are most uncertain at the lowest income levels, poverty is best studied by examining physical indicators of well-being, especially health. Questions of equity in both nations seem to have focused primarily on the brute facts of malnourishment and starvation rather than on differences in relative incomes of the population as a whole.

The Structure of Income

Despite the paucity of data, considerable insight can be gained on shares of different types of income, the behavior of wages, and various types of income inequality in Malaŵi and Madagascar.

Relative Shares of Labor and Property Income

Malaŵi witnessed a dramatic rise in the share of property income and a corresponding fall of labor income. More specifically, during the period of federation, the share of property income from the modern sector in the total national income fluctuated between 5 and 10 percent; after independence it rose to a high of 23 percent in 1977 before falling to 15 percent in 1979, the last year for which such data are available (Pryor 1988b, table E-3). Underlying the general rise in property income were two major factors: the increase in profits of the estates, which were expanding rapidly and which accounted for an increasingly larger share of total agricultural exports and production; and the rising profits of public and private enterprises. Given the large public-sector presence in the modern sector (table 1-2), a considerable share of these profits must have gone to the government, which means that only part of the profit share acted to widen family income differentials. Appropriate data to determine the relative public and private shares of such property income are not at hand, however.

Data on factor income shares are not available for Madagascar. Qualitative evidence suggests, however, that the share of national income classified as property income going to private Malagasy citizens has not changed greatly. Most modern-sector profits that French nationals received in the 1960s went to the Malagasy government after the nationalization and expropriation programs of the mid-1970s. Total profits may have declined thereafter as these nationalized firms ran into financial difficulties.

Two mechanisms discussed in the economic literature offer some help in understanding what happened to factor income shares in the two countries. One, a variant of the Stolper-Samuelson hypothesis, indicates that in a competitive economy any rise in relative prices of traded goods (that is, export or import-competing goods, in contrast to goods and services not entering into foreign trade) that producers receive leads to a rise in the relative share of property incomes in the total national income because the traded goods are generally more capital intensive than nontradables (Lal 1986).[2] The price increase can result from events on the world market or from domestic circumstances (such as a devaluation combined with an increase in exports). In Malaŵi the domestic prices of traded goods rose more rapidly than nontraded goods and services (chapter 6), while in Madagascar these trends were much less apparent (chapter 13), especially because agricultural producers did not receive any share of the higher world market prices for their products.

The second mechanism is Arthur Lewis' model of economic growth with "unlimited labor." This formulation suggests that in any economy in which a nonmonetary traditional sector furnishes labor for the modern sector and real wages stay roughly the same, total profits rise in step with the growth of the modern sector. If the modern sector is growing faster than the traditional sector, profits as a share of national income rise. This mechanism could have been operating in both countries, although it would not explain the fall in wages that occurred.

Although the two mechanisms give some understanding of the economic forces at work, neither provides a complete explanation. Other types of mechanisms could be added, but they have even less explanatory power.

Differences in Monetary and Nonmonetary Incomes

The focus on formal property and labor incomes omits rural incomes, which are often nonmonetary and which consist of an inseparable amalgam of both property and labor income. An increase in the relative importance of nonmonetary income can indicate either a widening or a narrowing of the distribution of income, depending upon other circumstances. For instance, if the fall in monetary income reflects a restriction of opportunities for poor smallholders to supplement their farm income with wage work or if it means that urban workers have lost their jobs, then income distribution is becoming more unequal. If the fall in monetary income arises from a decline in receipts from cash crops, which provide a greater share of income of wealthy than of poor farmers, then income distribution is becoming more equal.

The estimates in table 16-1 of total family income (including homegrown crops for consumption and most types of fringe benefits) yield some useful information about these matters, even though their uncertain quality requires cautious interpretation.

For Malaŵi the share of wages and salaries in total family income has declined over time among both smallholders and residents of the four major towns.[3] For rural residents this relative fall in monetary income appears to have been associated with increasing income inequality, in large measure because poor smallholders increasingly were prevented from supplementing their incomes by taking jobs in urban areas (chapter 5). For urban residents, "other monetary income" (which includes profits from the modern sector) remained roughly the same

Table 16-1. Monetary and Nonmonetary Components of Family Income, Malaŵi and Madagascar, Selected Years

Survey group	Year	Thousands of families	Wages and salaries	Other monetary	Non-monetary	Total income
Malaŵi				*Malaŵi kwacha*		
Smallholders	1968–69	885.0	24.34	13.03	49.05	86.42
Smallholders	1984–85	1,252.0	45.4	—386.9—		432.3
Estates	1968	28.0	95.34	11.71	33.25	140.31
Small urban areas	1968	11.0	411.96	163.55	31.42	606.93
Four major towns	1968	42.6	748.82	128.00	30.83	907.65
Four major towns	1979–80	121.5	1,486.2	322.9	391.9	2,201.4
Madagascar				*Malagasy franc*		
Rural sector	1962	1,076.2	—31,754—		29,192	60,946
Rural sector	1980	1,542.9	—114,098—		78,702	192,900
Small urban areas	1962	36.6	—153,600—			153,600
Small urban areas	1980	227.3	—299,208—		56,992	356,200
Six major towns	1962	98.9	—173,000—		26,300	199,300
Seven major towns	1980	140.3	—462,700—			462,700

Note: These data are estimates and contain a number of uncertainties; moreover they are not completely comparable, either between countries or between years. For Madagascar, "Estimate A" (the estimates without adjustments for comparability with the national account data) is presented; "Estimate B" (discussed in Pryor 1988b) reveals a greater disparity between average urban and rural incomes.

Source: Section I in both Pryor (1988a) and (1988b).

percentage of family income, which suggests that a considerable share of the rise in property income went to public enterprises. The fastest growing segment of family income was nonmonetary income—the most difficult type of income to estimate.

In Madagascar monetary income appears to have become a larger share of agricultural income.[4] This trend probably was accompanied by a rise in income inequality in rural areas, because it seems to have resulted from sales on the parallel market, an opportunity more open to wealthy than to poor smallholders (chapter 12).

Differences in Urban and Rural Incomes

A very important feature of the structure of income in both countries has been the large differences between average incomes in the urban and rural sectors, and the narrowing of such differentials over time. The data presented in tables 16-1 and 16-3 show that in Malaŵi the ratio of average family incomes in the urban sectors (just large towns) and in rural areas (just smallholders) was 10.5 in 1968–69 and 7.5 in 1984–85. In comparison with other African nations, these ratios appear to be very high. Some validation is obtained by calculating the per family GDP originating in agriculture and in the remaining sectors.[5] In Madagascar the ratio (of average income in major towns to that of the entire rural sector) was much lower than that for Malaŵi—3.3 in 1962 and 2.4 in 1980.

These considerable differences between the two countries arise in part as statistical artifacts. More specifically, the income data for Madagascar are not consistent with national accounts data; if adjustments are made (estimate B in Pryor 1988a), the urban-rural differences would be twice as great. Furthermore, the Malaŵi data include income of expatriates in the urban sector, while the Madagascar data exclude it. If the data were made comparable this way, the Madagascar ratio of average urban to rural incomes would be more similar to the Malaŵi ratio.

These comparative urban-rural income data also reflect some real differences between the two countries. One colonial legacy deserves note. The French colonists were much more dispersed through the countryside in Madagascar than were the English in the Nyasaland colony (chapters 2 and 9). France, in order to aid its colonists, invested considerably in rural infrastructure all over the colony; to a certain extent, this investment also aided the Malagasy smallholders. In Malaŵi governmental investment in the rural sector was relatively small until after World War II.

The narrowing differences between average urban and rural incomes in both countries require further investigation. In Malaŵi between 1968–69 and 1984–85 average smallholder family incomes increased roughly 6 percent, while average incomes in the major towns declined about 25 percent.[6] Smallholders' real family incomes from wages and salaries (off-farm employment) declined about 42 percent. The estimates of total smallholder incomes are quite rough; the urban income data are more reliable and reflect wage trends. In Madagascar between 1962 and 1980 average family incomes in the rural sector remained about the same, while incomes for the Malagasy in the major towns declined about 27 percent.[7] Again, the rural income data are quite rough, especially because they may not include income from the parallel market; the urban income data seem more reliable and reflect wage trends. Such large urban-rural income differences imply quite unequal distributions of income for the country as a whole. Furthermore, they direct our attention to problems of migration from the rural to the urban sector and of urban unemployment.

Although urbanization has increased in both Malaŵi and Madagascar, the rates were considerably less than many other developing countries have experienced (table B-4 in both Pryor 1988a and Pryor 1988b).[8] In Malaŵi between 1966 and 1977 the total population grew at an average annual rate of 2.9 percent, while population in the urban areas increased somewhere between 4.7 and 8.0 percent. In Madagascar between 1966 and 1985 the population grew at an average rate of 2.5 percent a year, while population in the urban areas was increasing at 6.1 percent. In both countries the urban population was increasing somewhat faster in the smaller urban centers than in the large cities (where average incomes have been relatively higher). Economic simulations with income distribution data suggest that this migration factor accounted for very little of the overall change in the inequality statistics.

Wages

In both countries the decline in real wages was an important component of the decline in urban incomes. For Malaŵi considerable data on employment and wages in the modern sector are available; for Madagascar such data are scattered, and few available series of any length are available.

MALAŴI. The modern-sector labor force increased at a rate of about 6.2 percent a year from 1968 through 1985, slightly more than double the rate of population increase.[9] In the modern urban sector, however, the labor force grew about 4.9 percent a year in this period, while that in the modern rural sector grew about 8.0 percent. This underscores the important role of estate agriculture in Malaŵi's economic development.[10]

From 1968 through 1985 the ratio of wages and salaries in the rural to the urban sector averaged 26.5 percent; from the early 1970s through the first half of the 1980s this ratio remained roughly the same. The aim of *DevPol I* (chapter 3) to keep the rural-urban wage disparity low so as to discourage migration to the urban areas was obviously not realized; however, the difference in average wages does not tell the entire story.[11]

The key trend in Malaŵi was the fall in average real wages of about 3.8 percent a year between 1968 and 1985. Part of this decline reflected a shift in the composition of the labor force in which lower paid agricultural workers constituted a larger share of employment in the modern sector. In the urban and rural sectors separately, however, real wages have fallen, respectively, 3.2 and 2.4 percent a year.

The most likely explanation for a major part of the fall in real wages was a shift in the composition of the labor force toward jobs paying less than the average wage (Sierra 1981, p. 28).[12] For instance, between 1969 and 1976 three-fourths of the newly created private-sector jobs were unskilled jobs at low wages; this composition effect would lower average wages over time, even if real wages for every specific job remained the same. Scattered evidence also suggests that as Malaŵians began to fill high-income jobs previously held by European expatriates, the salaries of those jobs were reduced. What is really needed to resolve this issue is salary data for specific jobs, but such information is not readily available. I suspect, however, that real wages for most specific jobs probably declined over the period, but at a relatively slow rate.

Other forces impinging upon the average wage level also provide some important clues about changes in the structure of wages. Unemployment alone probably was not responsible for any fall in average real wages, because the rate of joblessness was low throughout the period. At the time of the census in 1977, unemployment amounted to about 4.8 percent of the economically active in the urban sector and 1.9 percent of those in the rural sector (Malaŵi, NSO, 1984, vol. I, p. 167). A smaller scale survey carried out in Blantyre in 1972 also showed a similarly low unemployment rate: 3.7 percent of the labor force, with poorly educated workers composing the bulk of the unemployed (Sierra 1981, pp. 17–18). Among other things, these unemployment data suggest that Malaŵi was able to adjust successfully to a relative increase in the number of available workers when short-term emigration to obtain work in South Africa, Zambia, and Zimbabwe declined. This adjustment was not completely automatic but was aided by some small-scale training programs.

Unemployment among poorly educated workers may well have had an important impact on wages at the low end of the scale.[13] Unlike many developing nations, Malaŵi has not had much unemployment among the educated, which can probably be credited to the growth spurt in the 1970s; during this time the demand for educated or trained personnel in the urban sector outpaced the supply, which increased rather slowly. This phenomenon also occurred in the cities, where the wages and salaries of those with more education rose faster than the wages of other workers between 1966 and 1977 (Pryor 1988b, table J-3).[14] Thus the difference in average rural and urban wages was much greater than the difference in wages received by an unskilled worker in the two sectors.

The difference in average income between smallholders and workers in the modern sector was considerable (chapter 4). This suggests that employers could draw upon a large pool of unskilled workers for replacement or for additional workers, a factor that probably moderated wage increases in the modern sector, especially on the low end of the scale. It also provides one important explanation for the weakness of labor unions in Malaŵi.[15]

The fall in the real minimum wage probably affected the wage structure very little. During the colonial period from 1954 until 1967, the minimum wage more than doubled; from 1967 through 1983, however, it declined 42 percent and by 1983 was only about one-fifth higher than in 1954 (Pryor 1988b, table H-4). Furthermore, from 1958 to the mid-1980s the ratio of the minimum wage to the average wage was roughly constant at less than 30 percent. Thus, throughout the postindependence period the minimum wage provided little effective constraint on wages.

MADAGASCAR. From the scattered labor market data that are available several important trends in the labor market can be discerned. First, employment in Madagascar's modern sector increased from 1960 through 1984 roughly 2.3 percent a year, considerably slower than the 6.1 percent annual rise in population in the urban areas; the informal-sector growth these data imply has been directly documented by others. Second, in marked contrast to Malaŵi, the growth of the wage employment in the estates in Madagascar did not appear to be an important source of growth for the entire modern sector, in marked contrast to Malaŵi. Indeed, in Madagascar the fastest growing segment of the modern sector was the government sector, most likely in the urban areas. Third, real wages seem to have fallen throughout the entire independence period. From 1960 to 1970 real average annual wages in the private sector declined about 0.8 percent a year; from 1966 through 1984 average annual wages of industrial workers fell about 2.3 percent a year (Pryor 1988a, section H). Real urban wages appear to have declined more slowly than those in Malaŵi, even though per capita income was falling in Madagascar and rising in Malaŵi. This suggests a widening of income differentials within the urban sector between the wage workers and workers in the informal sector; unfortunately, the estimating procedures for calculating the overall income distribution could not take this into account.

The most important economic force at work was unemployment, which was much higher in Madagascar than in Malaŵi.[16] For instance, in Madagascar in 1980 the unemployed in the urban areas registered as seeking work amounted to more than 8 percent of the labor force outside of agriculture; from 1970 to the mid-1980s the number of the registered unemployed tripled. Actual unemployment appears to have been much higher than registered unemployment. One reliable source estimated unemployment in Antananarivo, the largest city, to have been more than 30 percent in the early 1980s (UNICEF 1984, p. 12).[17] Unemployment undoubtedly exercised a downward pressure on wages. The relatively slow fall in real wages probably was more the result of governmental resistance to lower wages than of opposition by labor unions, which were more oriented to job security and working conditions.

As in Malaŵi, the legal minimum wage probably was not instrumental in raising unemployment. From 1970 through 1984 real minimum wages decreased at an average annual rate of 3 percent. Moreover, the minimum wage fell from 46 percent of the average industrial wage in 1966 to 34 percent in 1982, almost the same percentage as in Malaŵi (Pryor 1988a, table H-2).[18] In sum, this minimum wage did not constrain employment.

WAGES IN THE GOVERNMENT SECTOR. Malaŵi average wages and salaries in the government sector and in the state-owned enterprises did not seem to have been greatly out of line with other wages in the economy.[19] Furthermore, average government wages appear to have fallen slightly in comparison to private-sector wages from 1968 through 1984 (Pryor 1988b, tables H-2 and H-3). The Malaŵi government has had a conscious policy of keeping government wages and salaries roughly in line with the private sector.

Consistent time-series data are not available for Madagascar. Information from the 1960s suggests that government wages were high in comparison to the private sector.[20] After 1976, however, average wages and salaries in government appeared to fall in comparison to other urban wages (Pryor 1988a, p. 40; and France, Ministère de cooperation, 1986, table 8.3).

Regional and Ethnic Income Differences

Differences in average incomes among regions and among ethnic groups are extremely sensitive political topics in both Malaŵi and Madagascar. The generalizations presented here are based on evidence discussed at length in section I of the Appendix.

In Malaŵi in the late 1960s average smallholder incomes in the three regions of the country were roughly equal. The policy concern about the "dead north" was misplaced. Although this area was less urbanized than the rest of the country, average smallholder incomes were about the same. Since that time smallholder income differences have widened; average incomes have fallen in the Southern Region and have risen at about the same rate in the Central and Northern Regions. Because the south has been the most densely populated and has had the smallest average size farms, this income decline probably reflected diminishing returns in agriculture. Various social indicators differ considerably among the regions; for instance, the literacy rate was much higher in the Northern region than in the other two regions where the politically dominant ethnic group (Chiwa) was located. Because of their higher level of education, the northerners dominated the civil service until the mid-1980s.

In Madagascar rural income differences among regions appear to have been somewhat greater than in Malaŵi in 1960 and somewhat less than in Malaŵi in 1985. One of the richest provinces and the one with the highest levels of urbanization and literacy was Antananarivo, where the largest ethnic group (Merina) was located; the Merina also have dominated the civil service.

Deliberate Incomes Policies

I have found little evidence that the Malaŵi government consciously intervened to change the distribution of wage income. The government's basic needs strategy has focused more on raising income levels than on distributional issues alone (chapter 8). The wage control program also was aimed more at average wages in particular sectors than at the structure of wages (chapter 7).

In Madagascar the situation was quite different. The lifting of the poll and cattle taxes in the rural sector in 1972 was the government's most dramatic step to improve the lot of the lowest income group. From 1977 to 1979 the government took three additional steps: it raised the minimum wages in the lowest wage categories at a faster rate than in higher categories; it revised its own pay scale to favor the lowest paid workers (and to freeze the pay of the higher civil servants); and it began to subsidize sales to the urban sector of such basic products as rice, the main staple and the largest single item in the budgets of the poor. These actions were progressive with regard to urban income distribution, but they may have had a regressive effect for the income distribution of the nation as a whole. The rural sector essentially financed such subsidies in that farmers (especially those producing for export) received prices lower than free market prices for their crops.[21] This acted to offset the gain the rural sector achieved when the government removed the poll and cattle taxes. The subsidy on food consumption of the urban population was eliminated in the mid-1980s as part of the liberalization program, a policy step fraught with danger to the government.

Both nations have had only limited scope for direct redistribution of income through the government budget (on either the tax or expenditure side). In certain cases deliberate government policies to aid the poor have been counterproductive. For instance, the Malagasy government's attempt in the 1980s to contain prices for edible oils and condensed milk (two important commodities in the household budgets of the poor) simply led to a decline of domestic production, which meant that these items were more difficult for the poor to obtain. Of course, the government can have a substantial indirect effect on income distribution by such policies as encouraging or discouraging foreign trade or agricultural production.

The Overall Distribution of Income

Any estimates of income distribution in Malaŵi and Madagascar must be used cautiously. Neither country has carried out a complete income survey, and the available data for individual sectors must be adjusted with the aid of numerous assumptions based on qualitative information (see section I in both Pryor 1988a and 1988b). For this reason, all the conclusions in the discussion below are hedged with qualifiers.

For Malaŵi a number of studies contain estimates of income distribution at a single point in time, but Kydd and Christiansen are the only economists who have studied trends in the distribution.[22] They state their conclusions very bluntly:

> In Malaŵi, it is our view that a peasant dominated agricultural sector leads to a more equitable distribution of income. It is also our view that the growth of the estate sector relative to the peasant sector in the post-Independence period has reversed this trend in income distribution. . . . We are also of the opinion . . . that real incomes for the greater [sic] majority of households have not increased significantly. It is our view that these changes are a direct consequence of the government's de-emphasis of the peasant sector in favour of the estate sector. . . . We also argue that the rapid decline in the opportunities for migration, which took place in the 1970's, by itself made the distribution of income less equitable. Further, there is evidence that the sharp increase in real wages paid to the greatly reduced number of migrants working as miners [abroad] exacerbated inequality. [p. 1]

For Madagascar several estimates of the income distribution are available, but they are only for 1960.[23] As far as I can determine, no income surveys were made in that year, so these estimates are based on tax and national account statistics. Although my estimates leave much to be desired, they are based on more appropriate evidence, namely, household budget surveys.

Table 16-2 presents the Lorenz curves of income inequality for the two nations at two different points in time. For Malaŵi the data are for the "best estimate" and are available for 1968–69 for income both with and without direct taxes. Estimates A and B for Madagascar define the limits of the "best estimate"; unfortunately, Estimate B cannot be made for 1980 with much accuracy.

The average standard of living in both countries is close to what people in the West might consider "subsistence, " and around this average, family incomes are distributed quite unequally. In both countries the poorest 20 percent of families received somewhere between 4 and 8 percent of total income, while the richest 10 percent of families received one-third to one-half of total income.

Table 16-2. The Size Distribution of Income, Malaŵi and Madagascar, Selected Years
(percent)

	Cumulative share of gross family income					
	Malaŵi			Madagascar, before direct taxes		
Cumulative share of population arranged in order of increasing incomes	1968–69		1984–85, Before direct taxes	1962		1980, Estimate A
	Before direct taxes	After direct taxes		Estimate A	Estimate B	
20	8.2	8.6	3.3	8.1	7.0	5.0
40	18.8	19.7	9.5	18.6	16.2	13.7
60	30.9	32.3	19.1	32.8	28.5	27.1
80	44.6	46.4	34.3	51.0	42.5	47.6
90	53.8	55.9	47.6	64.2	57.3	62.9
95	61.1	63.4	58.0	74.3	68.0	73.7
99	74.6	77.4	75.8	88.9	85.8	91.1
100	100.0	100.0	100.0	100.0	100.0	100.0

Source: Table I-5 in both Pryor (1988a) and (1988b).

To what extent has the growth—or decline—of per capita income influenced the income of the poorest segment of the population? One method of studying the problem is to define the poverty line as the income of families in the fortieth percentile in an early year and then to determine the percentage of families with incomes (adjusted for changes in prices) below this poverty line in a later year. Using this relativistic procedure, we find that the percentage of those in poverty increased in both countries.[24]

Contrary to expectations based on general considerations of the nature of economic growth, poverty has increased considerably more in Malaŵi, the country with the higher growth of per capita income. (To a certain extent this may be a statistical illusion, because my estimates could not fully take into account changes in the distribution of urban income in Madagascar.) Certainly the largest cities in Malaŵi exhibit less malnutrition and human misery than those in Madagascar. For instance, I found no evidence in Malaŵi of groups of people living on the food at the garbage dumps, which Camacho (1986) described as occurring in Madagascar.

Table 16-3 presents additional statistical comparisons of income inequality in the two countries. The data show average family incomes of major population groups and three measures of income inequality for particular population groups and for the overall population. The measures of income inequality, assuming constant group incomes,

Table 16-3. Income Inequality Statistics, Malaŵi and Madagascar, Selected Years

Family type or residence	Number (thousands)	Average total income[a]	Inequality coefficients[b] Gini	Theil	Log variance
Malaŵi, 1968–69					
Smallholders	885.0	86.42	.203	.113	0.118
Estates	28.0	140.31	.187	.093	0.110
Small towns	11.0	606.93	.466	.417	0.651
Four major towns	42.6	907.65	.660	.884	1.494
Total	966.5	130.03	—	—	—
Aggregate	—	—	.448	.796	0.317
Aggregate assuming all incomes in group = mean of group	—	—	.317	.432	0.274
Malaŵi, 1984–85					
Smallholders	1,252.0	358.2	.453	.348	0.607
Estates	89.2	425.1	n.a.	n.a.	n.a.
Small towns	34.2	2,157.1	n.a.	n.a.	n.a.
Four major towns	98.5	3,235.4	.621	.776	1.065
Total	1,473.9	596.2	—	—	—
Aggregate	—	—	.599	.944	0.860
Aggregate assuming all incomes in group = mean of group	—	—	.365	.447	0.361
Madagascar, estimate A, 1962					
Rural	1,076.2	60.9	.290	.194	0.220
Secondary urban centers	36.6	153.6	n.a.	n.a.	n.a.
Largest six towns	98.9	199.3	.500	.466	0.806
Total	1,211.7	75.0	—	—	—
Aggregate	—	—	.391	.371	0.352
Aggregate assuming all incomes in group = mean of group	—	—	.168	.106	0.125
Madagascar, estimate A, 1980					
Rural	1,542.9	192.9	.435	.329	.517
Secondary urban centers	140.5	356.2	.487	.399	.747
Largest seven towns	227.3	462.7	n.a.	n.a.	n.a.
Total	1,910.8	237.0	—	—	—
Aggregate	—	—	.489	.426	.628
Aggregate assuming all incomes in group = mean of group	—	—	.154	.065	.096

— = Not applicable.
n.a. = Not available.

Note: Estimates for the two countries are not quite comparable. For each country, however, the results are roughly comparable over time.

a. Income data for Malaŵi are in kwacha; those for Madagascar are in Madagascar francs.
b. All of the coefficients become larger when inequality increases. The Gini coefficient lies between 0.0 and 1.0; the others are unbounded.

Source: Section I of both Pryor (1988a) and (1988b).

permit a separation of the various impacts of intergroup and intragroup differences; this procedure is not exact, however, for the Gini coefficient.

In the 1960s in both countries the single most important factor underlying the overall inequality of income was the difference in average income between urban and rural populations. This can be seen by comparing the income inequality coefficients for the entire economy without adjustments with those for which all incomes in a particular population group are assumed to be equal to the mean. In most cases the income differences in group means account for roughly half of the total income inequalities.

Because of the way the Madagascar data are estimated, the overall inequality coefficients for the two countries cannot be compared initially. When the data are made more comparable, however, income inequalities within the rural sector of Madagascar appear to be greater than those in Malaŵi. This undoubtedly reflects the more unequal distribution of land in Madagascar, a phenomenon attributable to the different land tenure arrangements in the two countries (chapters 4 and 11). Madagascar probably had a greater overall equality of income, however, primarily because of its narrower urban-rural income differentials.[25]

Both countries exhibit the same important trends. Income appears to have become more unequally distributed. The trend toward inequality was particularly evident in the rural sector, which also had the lowest average income; in the urban sector, the inequalities seem to have remained roughly similar.[26] The influences of the relative increase in size of the urban sector (a factor widening income inequalities) and the narrowing of the urban-rural income differences (largely because of the decrease in the real average wage) cancelled each other out—that is, the inequality coefficients assuming all incomes in a group are equal to the mean of the group did not greatly change between the earlier and later years.

The increasing inequality of income among smallholders in Malaŵi can be traced to the government's wager-on-the-strong policy (chapters 4 and 5). More specifically, only those smallholders with larger farms could apply the government's technology package, primarily had access to credit, and could sell their export crops at auction prices rather than the lower ADMARC prices. Also, the government generally conducted its integrated development programs in areas that were wealthier than average. These factors did not greatly influence the distribution of land, but they differentially influenced production and income from smallholdings of various sizes. These factors were quite independent of the greater encouragement of estate agriculture, which most Malaŵi observers emphasize. Malaŵi thus provides an important counterexample to the oft-made but careless generalization that a development strategy based on agriculture or on labor-intensive industries leads to a more equal distribution of income.

The increasing inequality of income among smallholders in Madagascar has occurred for several different reasons (chapters 11 and 12). In its later years the Tsiranana government also followed a wager-on-the-strong approach toward agriculture. It channeled most of its technical aid and credit to those farmers producing on a scale sufficient to permit the generation of investment funds by means of crop sales for internal or foreign trade. Some observers have argued that village leadership and the distribution of governmental aid changed considerably from 1972 to 1975, with more aid going to smaller farms; this hypothesis is difficult to confirm. After 1975, inequalities in rural income distribution appeared to widen. The government was still providing most agricultural credit to the richest farmers; the deterioration of the roads was most adverse for the smallholders in the outlying (poorest) areas; and the nonprice rationing of agricultural inputs and the rise of parallel markets for agricultural products gave greater opportunities for gain to the richest farmers, because only they had enough working capital to take full advantage of this situation. These various factors more than offset any income-equalizing effect of the apparently diminishing inequalities in land holdings.

Poverty

The direct measures of both countries to alleviate the worst effects of poverty are difficult to quantify. Furthermore, some of the most important actions, such as the food security measures, are too recent for proper evaluation.

Determination of the extent of poverty also raises many problems because neither the Malaŵi nor the Malagasy government has published any extensive studies on the subject. Malaŵi has no official poverty line, and in my interview, President Banda quickly dismissed my suggestion that poverty had increased. The Malagasy government has been more conscious of the problem, particularly for the urban areas, and has tried to gain some idea of its magnitude. It does not appear to have followed a consistent approach, however; the income level at which a two-person family falls into the "absolute poverty" category has varied over the years from about 25,000 FMG a month in 1981 to 54,000 FMG in 1985 (in constant, 1985 FMG).[27]

Poverty Indicators

Given the uncertain nature of the income data at lower levels, the extent of poverty can be explored best by examining a series of physical indicators of well-being that are particularly sensitive to real incomes of the poorest segment of the population. With the exception of mortality data, such indicators are only available for single points in time.[28]

According to these indicators, the extent of poverty appears to be much the same in the two countries. This information, combined with knowledge about the higher average per capita income in Madagascar, implies that income inequality is greater in Madagascar than in Malaŵi and that the inequality statistics presented in the discussion above do not capture an important aspect of the income distribution. Evidence based on poverty trends points to the same conclusion.

INFANT MORTALITY. Although at independence Malaŵi and Madagascar had quite different rates of infant mortality, the rates converged considerably by the mid-1980s. In Malaŵi infant mortality declined from about 204 per 1,000 live births in 1967, to 176 per 1,000 in 1977, and to roughly 160 per 1,000 in 1982 (Pryor 1988b, table J-5).[29] This does not necessarily indicate a fall in poverty as measured by income, because infant mortality has decreased in many African nations where poverty has not decreased; it does, however, show an increase in physical well-being.

For Madagascar, information about infant mortality rates is much more uncertain.[30] For 1975, estimates range from 68 per 1,000 (the official census datum) to 160 per 1,000 (based on fertility rates and age distribution data). For 1985, my own estimate is that the infant mortality rate was roughly 150 per 1,000, although this estimate may be on the high side. Considerable evidence indicates that infant mortality rates increased from the late 1970s through the mid-1980s; only a part of this rise is attributable to improvements in the system of collecting mortality information.

BIRTH WEIGHT. Aggregative information on the birth weight of infants is a common measure of the nutritional condition of women bearing children.[31] In Madagascar a nationwide sample survey in 1984 revealed that 14.4 percent of the infants had a birth weight of less than 2,500 grams (about 5.5 pounds); smaller scale studies record higher percentages. Only partial data on birth weights are available for Malaŵi. One survey of all babies born in Malaŵi hospitals and health centers in July 1964 (admittedly only a fraction of all newborn babies) showed that 16.5 percent had birth weights lower than 2,500 grams. Although the difference in these percentages between the two countries appears significant, the quality of the data are poor, so the results are subject to question.

WEIGHT AND HEIGHT OF CHILDREN. Anthropometric data on children that reveal undernourishment are increasingly used as measurements of absolute poverty.[32] Restricting the sample to children under five years of age minimizes the influence of racial factors; most well-nourished children in all countries appear to have the same age-specific height-weight pattern until their sixtieth month, an hypothesis explicitly confirmed in a special study of Malaŵi (unfortunately no such study is available for Madagascar). The anthropometric data suggest few important differences in the two countries.

For Malaŵi, height-weight data are also available from an impressive national survey of children of smallholders, which was carried out in conjunction with the 1980–81 National Sample Survey of Agriculture. A considerable number of smaller scale studies is available for Madagascar; table 16-4 shows data from three of them. The three areas covered are relatively prosperous, so a nationwide study probably would show greater undernutrition. The table also includes similar information for other countries.

A weight-height ratio below 90 percent (or roughly two standard deviations) of the international norm indicates acute undernutrition. Using this criterion, Malaŵi and Madagascar probably have roughly the same degree of acute undernutrition, which is somewhat higher than in most of the other African nations. For Malaŵi, some expected differences appear when comparisons are made before and after the harvest, and the highest acute undernutrition occurs in the Southern Region, where family incomes have been lowest.

The height-age norm presents some ambiguities as a measure of chronic under-nourishment. Furthermore, some controversy exists on the cutoff point to designate undernutrition. Some experts place the cutoff point at 85 percent, or three standard deviations, which would reduce the count of the chronically undernourished roughly by half.

About 50 percent to 60 percent of the children in both Malaŵi and Madagascar appear to have a high decree of chronic undernutrition, and this level is very much higher than in the other African nations. Either the children in the two countries suffered from repeated spells of illness, which meant that they might not have been acutely undernourished at any single time but that the long-run impact of such sickness led to a cumulative stunting; or the ages of the Malaŵian and Malagasy children were considerably overestimated.

The weight-age criterion is the most popular method of measuring chronic protein and calory undernutrition, but it is also the most ambiguous of the three measurements of poverty. It is quite sensitive to estimates of age, and among a population with considerable illiteracy, age estimates in months are often rather uncertain. Furthermore, different investigators define undernutrition at different levels and place the level of "moderate undernutrition" anywhere from 75 to 90 percent of the World Health Organization norms. The presence of edema may make weight levels misleadingly high. Also, children with low weight-to-age ratios do not necessarily have marasmus; if

368 Malaŵi and Madagascar

Table 16-4. Evidence on Undernutrition, Selected African Nations

Country	Ages of subjects (months)[a]	Acute under-nutrition[b]	Chronic under-nutrition[b]	Underweight condition (percent)[b]
Malaŵi rural,				
1980–81[c]	0–60	2.3	57.8	31.0
North	0–60	1.4	64.6	30.8
Central	0–60	1.8	61.4	31.1
South	0–60	2.8	53.0	31.0
Madagascar, 1984				
Antsirabe rural	0–60	0.8	60.8	34.1
Antsirabe urban	0–60	0.6	51.5	28.8
Toamasina urban	0–60	3.5	33.0	38.0
Cameroon, 1978	3–60	1.0	22.1	21.1
Egypt, 1978	6–72	0.6	21.2	14.8[d]
Lesotho, 1976	3–60	1.1	22.7	22.0
Liberia, 1976	0–60	1.6	18.0	24.0
Senegal, Sine-Saloum region, 1982	0–60	4.4	26.1[e]	n.a.
Sierra Leone, 1978	3–60	3.0	24.2	30.5
Swaziland, 1983	3–60	0.4	16.6	12.4
Togo, 1977	6–72	2.0	18.8	30.3

n.a. = Not available.

a. Dash indicates "up to but not including."

b. Condition definitions refer to World Health Organization norms, which are as follows: acute undernutrition, less than 80 percent of median weight for height; chronic undernutrition, less than 90 percent of median height for age; underweight, less than 80 percent of weight for age.

c. Includes only children from smallholder families. Percentages are averages based on measurements taken before and after the main harvest; these were originally presented in standard deviations from the normed median but are adjusted here to the percentage definition by a procedure described in section J of the Research Notes.

d. Originally presented as standard deviation from the normed median but adjusted here to the percentage definition by a procedure described in section I of the Appendix.

e. Includes only children from 3 months up to 60 months of age.

Source: Pryor (1988b), table J-6; Pryor (1988a), section J; Serdula and others (1987).

they are short, their low weight may be appropriate for their height, which seems to be the case in Malaŵi. A special problem arises in the estimates for Malaŵi because these data do not use an international standard; they use a norm based on the Malaŵi median in order to take racial differences into account. If fewer than 50 percent (which seems to be the case) of the nation's children are undernourished, however, this use of a Malaŵi norm does not affect comparability.

These data suggest that about one-third of the children in Malaŵi and Madagascar were undernourished, a somewhat higher proportion than in the other African countries. Although this evidence on undernutrition is somewhat conflicting, it suggests that the critical problem in both Malaŵi and Madagascar has been chronic rather than acute undernutrition and that roughly one-quarter or more of the children in the samples suffer from some degree of undernutrition.

These indicators reveal a mixed picture for different regions of Madagascar. Data for Antsirabe, a wealthy area, suggest lower undernutrition than in Malaŵi, while the data from Toamasina, a poorer area, suggest the reverse. Weight-age data for other areas from some less complete studies not shown in the table suggest that undernutrition is somewhat greater in Madagascar than Malaŵi (Pryor 1988a, table J-3).

Poverty Trends

The decrease in infant mortality in Malaŵi does not provide unambiguous evidence that poverty has declined, because infant mortality has fallen in Africa generally. It does reflect in considerable measure the gradual improvement of Malaŵi's public health service, the cautious step-by-step changes discussed in chapter 8. Until other indicators, such as comparable nutrition data, are available for several points of time, we cannot say whether the data on physical well-being consistently reflects the increase in poverty detected in the income data.

The increase in infant mortality in Madagascar strongly points to an increase in poverty, an impression supported by scattered data showing that in the 1980s a higher percentage of children admitted to some hospitals showed signs of undernutrition.[33] Starvation also appears to have increased in recent years, although little reliable information on the subject is available. For instance, an opposition leader, Monja Jaona, noted in a speech in October 1986 that about 47,000 people had recently died from hunger in three areas in the southern part of the island; the government officially denied the number but did accept the fact that many such deaths had occurred. These data reinforce the impression gained from the income data of a rise in poverty.

The increase of poverty in Madagascar is due in greatest measure to those governmental economic policies that led to a reduction in average income after the fall of the Tsiranana government. These include the shift in relative prices against the agricultural sector that has discouraged agricultural production for the market, the invest-to-the-hilt program, the foreign trade policies leading to general shortages of productive inputs, and governmental expenditures directed toward maintaining a large armed force rather than toward other purposes.

Some have argued that poverty in Madagascar has risen in the mid-1980s as a result of many of the structural adjustment policies such as scaling back government expenditures, reducing import controls, and eliminating the rice subsidy to urban consumers. The analysis in previous chapters, however, suggests that the government could not have continued to run a deficit of the size experienced in the early 1980s; that the new import rules have a better chance of raising production than the old restrictions; and that, although the rice subsidy did aid urban dwellers, the policies associated with it led to an impoverishment of the countryside—a much larger share of the population.[34]

Equity

How fair is the structure of income in these two countries? Some people define equity in terms of the extent of absolute poverty. Others speak of equity in terms of the distribution of income, defining income quite broadly.[35] The discussion in this chapter has presented considerable evidence for these approaches, which focus on objective standards. Equity could be defined, however, in terms of the distribution of income between "socially significant" groups—a subjective standard that defines fairness as the inhabitants of the country itself view it.

A socially significant group is one that a large portion of the population recognizes as a distinct group. In an industrialized nation such groups are defined by ownership of the means of production or by position in the hierarchy of units of production (for example, management and workers). In countries as poor as Malaŵi and Madagascar, however, such social strata are not distinctly separated from the rest of the population, and the most socially significant groups are often defined either by ethnicity or by urban-rural residence. Furthermore, in neither country have I seen any overt indication that public opinion defines equity in terms of interethnic, intersectoral, or any other type of intergroup income differences.

The distribution of income itself does not appear to have great political salience in either nation. Albert O. Hirschman (1973) has argued that tolerance for income inequality changes and that inequality is often more bearable if all incomes are rising. Because income inequalities have been increasing, not decreasing, the situation would seem to be fraught with discontent not only in Madagascar, where average incomes have been declining for more than a decade, but also in Malaŵi, where per capita incomes have slowly declined since the beginning of the 1980s. The Malaŵians and Malagasy did not appear to have viewed this as the most important equity problem, however. Furthermore, the public in Madagascar did not even seem to view the partial breakdown of law and order in the rural areas in the context of equity.

In Madagascar in the early years after independence, equity discussions seemed to focus on the high incomes of the remaining French expatriates on the island, but by the 1980s this factor was no longer of political importance. The scattered evidence suggests that since then the key issue is the extent to which the incomes of certain people have fallen below a social minimum. Most of the overt manifestations of discontent in Madagascar have appeared in the rural areas where the absolute incomes are lowest.[36] The government of Madagascar has placed greater verbal emphasis on a socially just economic policy than has the government of Malaŵi, but these pronouncements have proved of scant comfort to the large number of Malagasy whose real incomes have fallen during the last decade and a half. To the minimal extent that discontent about relative incomes has received political expression in Madagascar, the important groups have been those in the city whose relatively high incomes have fallen in comparison with parvenu groups such as the Asian merchants who benefited from the liberalization in the mid-1980s.

In Malaŵi the fact that the government carried out a nutrition study, albeit under pressure from international aid givers, suggests that absolute income levels of the poorest segment of the population also have importance in the internal political discussions about equity. I was not able to find indications of wide-scale public discussion of these problems, however. Furthermore, no public manifestations of discontent about the high incomes of Asian or other groups seem to have occurred.

In sum, Malaŵians and Malagasy seem to consider malnutrition and starvation as the crux of the equity question, not the distribution of income alone. Such problems are much more serious in the countryside because the rural populations in both countries have the lowest average incomes and have experienced an increasing inequality of income. This absolute increase in rural poverty has serious, long-term political consequences. The governments of both nations will have to focus their development goals for the agricultural sector, as well as the implementation of the various policies to achieve these ends, with this grave problem clearly in mind.

Notes

1. These ideas draw deeply upon the approach of Fields (1975), who noted that "Without exception the results emerge that variations *within* sectors or regions are much more important in accounting for inequality than variations *between* sectors." This does not appear true in a static sense for either Malaŵi or Madagascar, but it does describe the trends of income for both.

2. The assumption that tradables have a higher intensity of nonlabor factors (either capital or land) than nontradables appears reasonable for both Madagascar and Malaŵi.

3. Jonathan Kydd has suggested to me that the wage data from the smallholders in the 1984–85 crop year are underestimated because the field workers of the survey did not collect expenditures data in order to cross-check income and expenditures estimates and because the agencies paying for the survey did not have much interest in such income data and did not place much emphasis on its collection. Although these arguments have merit, the differences between 1968–69 and 1984–85 data are so great (in real terms) that the qualitative conclusions drawn from the data appear reasonable. Kydd (1982), pp. 105 ff., also has a useful discussion of the fall in the ratio of off-farm work to total labor in the smallholder sector.

4. These data are rather uncertain. They suggest, however, that the "flight into self-sufficiency," which raised so much concern, did not characterize the entire rural sector but merely the poorest segment, at least until 1980. If these results are merely statistical artifacts, then the data problems might arise either from underestimating total income or from overestimating monetary income. Section I, Pryor (1988a), discusses issues about these estimations of rural income in greater detail.

5. To the extent that the GDP calculations are based on these income surveys, this type of comparison does not provide additional information. It is difficult to determine why these urban-rural income differentials are so much higher in Malaŵi than in other African nations or why wages in the rural sector have stayed about one-fourth the level in the urban sector. The reason rural incomes are so low should be clear; the difficult question is why urban incomes have been so high. Part of the answer may be found in the lack of the salary compression in the public sector that has occurred in other Sub-Saharan nations; another factor might be the role of the wage-setting boards in determining wage rates in the rural and urban areas.

6. Discussions of the rural income data and of the retail price index used to deflate them are found in sections I and E-1 of Pryor (1988b).

7. Two problems arise in determining real income changes for Madagascar: The GDP and the retail price indexes changed somewhat differently between 1962 and 1980; and the original income data showed an increase in average rural incomes, while production data showed a decrease of about the same amount. I have averaged these two sources to arrive at the conclusion that between these two dates, average real rural incomes did not change much. The price data come from table G-1, Pryor (1988a); the income data are from appendix I. The methodologies of the two surveys are not described in sufficient detail to determine whether the income data are completely comparable.

8. Measuring changes in urbanization in Malaŵi is difficult because of changes in the boundaries of the towns, which now include considerable rural area. In the range of growth rates presented in the text, the lower estimate is the rise in employment in the modern sector in the towns; it understates urbanization insofar as growth of the informal sector in the towns has been faster than that of modern-sector employment. The higher estimate is based on the official estimates of population in the urban areas and overstates the actual growth of urbanization, because the boundaries of the towns were also expanding.

9. The labor force and wage data come from Pryor (1988b), section H.

10. The increase in employment on the estates came from the smallholder sector and also, during the 1970s, from some Malaŵians returning from work abroad. I have seen no convincing evidence that the growth of the estates has led either to an absolute decline of men working in the smallholder sector or to an important skewing of the male-female ratio in smallholder workers, as some economists have argued. This matter is discussed in greater detail in section I of the Appendix.

11. A curious puzzle arises in interpreting data on rural-urban wage differences in the colonial period from the Central African Federation of Rhodesia and Nyasaland, Central Statistical Office (1964), which has a table showing labor force and average wages. The data on employment appear roughly comparable with the samples taken by the NSO starting in 1968; indeed, in the previous discussion of estate labor (chapter 4), I use these data to extend the series back to 1954. The wage data in the "modern" agriculture sector (that is, the estates) appear somewhat high and the wage data in the modern urban sector appear somewhat low in comparison to the data in 1968; and the ratio of rural to urban wages is about 50 percent. This could mean that the relative wages in agriculture took a massive fall between 1964 and 1968 or that the wage data are not comparable because of differences in definition. The latter interpretation seems closer to the truth, especially since the NSO stresses this interpretation as well. During the colonial period the modern sector maintained roughly the same employment, and the ratio of rural to urban workers remained roughly the same as well.

12. The Stolper-Samuelson approach provides another explanation of this trend. This mechanism might be operating not only to raise the share of profits but also to lower real wages. Although this might explain part of the decline in real wages, it does not explain why the disparity between rural and urban wages did not close more quickly.

13. Lyn Squire, in World Bank staff working paper 336, cited by Sierra (1981), p. 20.

14. In the late 1960s, according to Jones and Robinson (1976), Southern Rhodesia had even greater wage and salary inequalities than did Malaŵi, even though it had a much greater pool of skilled labor on which to draw. Some of these inequalities may lie less in education than in nonmarket forces.

15. Humphrey (1973) argues that the government has discouraged unionization as well as such union actions as strikes. Work days lost in strikes declined from roughly 22,000 in the mid-1960s to less than 500 by 1969–70 and then rose to about 1,900 in 1972, after which the government apparently stopped collecting these statistics.

16. As previously noted, the change in relative prices of traded goods and nontraded goods and services was much less apparent in Madagascar than in Malaŵi, so the Stolper-Samuelson mechanism probably did not exercise a very strong influence on real wages.

17. This estimate is said to be low because it does not include underemployment; no source is cited. Unemployment data in Madagascar are quite fragmentary. Such data do not appear in the 1966 census, and the 1975 census shows urban unemployment of only 15,090 (Madagascar, INSRE, n.d. [f],

Mileau urbain, p. 17), which could be greatly underestimated, because it is little higher than those registered as looking for work in that year (see Pryor 1988a, table H-3).

18. In making wage comparisons, I have assumed a work year of 2,000 hours for those receiving the minimum wage.

19. These data on wages in the Malaŵi public sector are somewhat misleading because they do not include certain nonmonetary benefits such as housing allowances for civil servants. These allowances are a relatively important part of income, especially for those in the higher grades.

20. Certain data are available showing wages in the public and private sectors, but these data generally pertain to the 1960s and omit the salaries of the higher civil servants and of the employers in the private sector. For instance, Lecaillon and Germidis (1977), p. 155, report some such data. More general data, such as that presented by Morrisson (1968), p. 76, suggest that wages and salaries in the public sector were relatively high, but these data also refer to the 1960s.

21. Quisumbing and Taylor (1989) present a general equilibrium model showing that only in particular circumstances do food subsidies to urban groups lower rural incomes. This is one such case, because urban wages (and hence the price of urban goods) were not tied to food prices. Moreover, the subsidies were financed in large part by the profits of monopsonistic state agencies that purchased various crops.

22. Other of Kydd and Christiansen essays on the topic include Kydd and Christiansen (1981a) and (1982); see also Kydd in Fyfe and others (1985), pp. 293–380.

23. In general, these estimates of inequality are higher than mine (see Pryor 1988b, section I) because, for other reasons, they include the income of expatriates.

24. Using data from tables I-4 and I-9 from Pryor (1988b) and applying graphical interpolation methods, I found that families in the fortieth percentile had an annual income of roughly 70.5 MK in 1968–69. In 1984–85 an income of 70.5 MK corresponded to a real annual income of 333 MK, which was roughly the income of a family in about the sixtieth percentile. Using data from table I-4 (estimate A) and table I-8 in Pryor (1988a), I found that in 1962, families in the fortieth percentile had an annual income of roughly 47,400 FMG. In 1980 this income corresponded to a real annual income of about 146,400 FMG, which was roughly the income of a family in the forty-fifth percentile. The estimates for both countries are particularly sensitive to the assumptions made to calculate changes in average incomes of smallholders.

25. The estimation procedure understates any adverse changes in Madagascar; moreover, the income inequalities in the cities probably increased in the mid-1980s, when unemployment rose and the rice subsidy was removed.

26. I have based my generalizations on the estimate B inequality coefficients presented in table I-6 in Pryor 1988a, which are much more comparable with the Malaŵi results than are the estimate A coefficients.

27. According to Madagascar, Ministère des travaux publics (1985), pp. 3–38, this limit (in current prices) was 13,000 FMG and 28,000 FMG a month in

1981 and 1985, respectively. Madagascar, Direction générale du plan (1979b) reports different monthly poverty lines: 9,317 FMG in 1971, 13,658 FMG in 1975, and 15,000 FMG in 1977. The figures reported in the text draw from this series, deflated by a retail price index from Pryor (1988a), table G-1. This kind of estimate, as well as calculation of the number of families living below this limit in various years, is highly sensitive to the prices of the major food staples and, of course, family size. Rouveyran (1972) has an interesting qualitative discussion of poverty in Madagascar.

28. For Malaŵi, Msukwa (1986) cites data for 1970 through 1984 on the weight-age ratios of children. Although interesting, such data are insufficiently comparable for trends to be discerned. The same may be said for the nutrition data presented in Pryor (1988a), table J-3.

29. Malaŵi, NSO (1987) places the infant mortality rate in 1983 at 154 per 1,000; it also presents some anthropometric data.

30. Pryor (1988a), section J, discusses various estimates of infant mortality, including my own, in much more detail. World Bank (October 1986), appendix II, presents some data on rising fetal and neonatal mortality from 1978 through 1984. Some annual data on the number of malnourished children can be found in Rabemiafala (1984), p. 445.

31. The Malaŵi data come from Malaŵi, Ministry of Health, WHO, and UNICEF (1986), p. 46; the Madagascar data come from WHO (n.d.). The statistics reported in these two sources are considerably higher than the 12 percent for Malaŵi and 10 percent for Madagascar reported by UNICEF, annual-1986. Other birthweight data for Madagascar are discussed in Pryor (1988a), section J.

32. The discussion of measurements of undernourishment in this section is based on Charlotte G. Neumann, in Jelliffe and Jelliffe (1979), pp. 299–327; Jelliffe (1966); and conversations with Dr. Nancy Binkin, a nutrition specialist of the Center for Disease Control in Atlanta, Georgia. The literature on undernutrition and anthropometric measurements has not quite settled certain key issues, however, especially how race relates to height and weight. Chimwaza (1982) made anthropometric measurements of Malaŵian children in a rural area (Dowa) and in a middle class urban area (Lilongwe) and concluded from the latter sample, "For height, weight, and arm circumference, the results obtained in the present study seem to indicate that the international standards used are appropriate for assessing growth of the Malaŵian children" (p. 229). To my knowledge, no similar study has been made in Madagascar, which is racially quite different from Malaŵi. My conversation with specialists in Madagascar on this question did not reveal any indication that international norms were inappropriate.

33. Such data were shown to me by officials of the Catholic Relief Service in Antananarivo.

34. Certain Malagasy officials who have opposed the structural adjustment program have also argued that an increase in general poverty has occurred because the average household size increased from 1975 to 1985, thus indicating a doubling up of families. The available data, however, suggest that the average household size was about the same in 1966 as in 1985; official analyses of the 1975 census (INSRE, *Recensement 1975, Série études et analyse: Les ménages*,

p. 7) suggest that the ostensible fall in average household size in 1975 was a statistical artifact arising because the question of household size was posed somewhat differently than in 1966. Thus, the alleged rise in household size between 1975 and 1985 is probably a statistical artifact as well.

35. In neither country is the income situation greatly muddied by nonmonetary income in the form of privileges such as access to special stores. Malaŵi's housing subsidies to civil servants are a possible exception.

36. Ramanandraibe (1987) briefly discusses hunger riots in Madagascar. The more publicized riots against the Indo-Pakistani community in 1987 had a different cause.

17 Explorations in Political Economy

The previous chapters have explored the degree to which some important economic policies brought about the increase of per capita GDP in Malaŵi, the decrease of per capita GDP in Madagascar, and the widening of income differentials in both nations. Analyzing why the two countries adopted these policies is a difficult endeavor; it leads us away from the immediate economic events and facts, which are themselves ambiguous, and toward a higher level of generalization at which clashes of interpretations are not easy to resolve. Nevertheless, such generalizations give the analyses in preceding chapters significance for broader issues of economic development and the distribution of income.

In this chapter I approach this problem by focusing on three critical issues: the importance of ideology in policymaking, the role of economic interests in policy formation, and the degree to which the clash of ideologies and interests still allows policymakers enough alternatives to achieve economic growth with greater income equality.

Analysis of ideological factors underlying policy is a task for traditional political economics. The key question is easy to pose: Why have the ideological currents influencing policymaking in the two nations taken such different directions? Possible explanations include their colonial histories, the education and background of their top leadership, the relationships between their economic expectations and outcomes, and certain traditional values.

Analysis of the economic interests underlying policy is a key concern of the new political economics. Some difficult problems arise because interest groups, in the sense of well-defined organizations representing people in roughly the same economic situation, are not prominent in either country. Two important questions are what are the relevant groups engaged in the policy process, and why have the two countries differed so much in the interplay between urban and rural interests and the patterns of day-to-day politics, both of which are important factors in policymaking?

Analysis of more general economic issues, particularly the relationships underlying the alleged trade-off between economic development and increasing income equality, is critical for understanding policy alternatives. With the information gained from the examination of the roles of ideology and of economic interests, we can begin to determine the degree to which policymakers in these two nations—and in other developing nations—have genuine policy choices to make.

Ideology Revisited

Ideology in the broadest sense of the term—perhaps *mentalité* is a better word—is the way leaders see the world, analyze the motivations of their fellow citizens, and view their moral responsibilities as leaders. The political elites in Malaŵi and Madagascar have differed significantly not only in their attitudes toward capitalism versus socialism and in their conceptions of nationalism but also in their ideas about methods of administering and managing their policies. These ideological factors have been important determinants of the economic policies they adopted.

Capitalism and Socialism

Why has the dominant ideology in Malaŵi remained on the right for so long and only gradually begun to shift leftward, while the dominant ideological currents in Madagascar have shifted from right to left and then back toward the middle during the postindependence period?

BASES OF IDEOLOGICAL ATTITUDES. Three important factors have helped create the intellectual atmosphere in these two countries. First, during the colonial period the ideological currents in the two imperialist nations themselves were fundamentally different. The Marxist movement played a much more important role in France than in England or the United States, especially during the years when the first wave of future leaders of the two African nations received their education and developed their personal political beliefs about capitalism and socialism. The political and economic ideas of students in France during the turbulent year of 1968 also found particular resonance among the younger members of the Madagascar elite, whose education took place in the postindependence period and whose teachers had studied in France.

Second, a perceived linkage or parallelism between colonialism and capitalism was much stronger in Madagascar than in Malaŵi. Great Britain had a relatively small political and economic involvement in its Nyasaland colony; indeed, many economic activities of the colony's minuscule modern sector were carried out by Indians and other non-British nationals both before and after independence. In Madagascar the French colonial government was more intrusive, and French business interests dominated the economy. Moreover, the substantial French presence on the island—political, military, and economic—in the decade after independence gave the Malagasy the perception that the French were manipulating economic policy behind the scenes in order to satisfy their own (capitalistic) interests (chapter 9).

Third, the prevailing ideology receives support or opposition to some degree according to the perceived success of those economic policies having a strong ideological basis, where success is defined in terms of fulfilling previous expectations. Of course, the relevant support, opposition, and expectations are those of the particular urban groups in a position to topple the government; the ideological attitudes of the vast number of people living in the countryside are usually of secondary importance because of the difficulties in organizing the rural population for political purposes.

Expectations of Malaŵi's economic success were hopeful but pessimistic. The pessimism was generated in good measure by the common belief, or fear, in both Great Britain and Africa that Malaŵi would not be economically viable after the breakup of the federation with Northern and Southern Rhodesia. The fact that the country's economic performance exceeded the very low general expectations stabilized the new government and gave respectability to the ideology and development strategy of President Banda, which was generally labeled "capitalistic" (chapter 3). The slow turn to the left in the early 1980s resulted, in part, from the realization that the previous development strategy was no longer working; the policies of the early 1980s did not work well either.

In contrast, expectations about the economic future of Madagascar were generally optimistic, reflecting in good measure the rosy views of the French. In its first decade after independence Madagascar's macroeconomic performance was moderately successful, and roughly the same as Malaŵi's, but it fell far short of expectations (evidence is provided in chapter 10). This perceived policy "failure" and a series of short-term economic and political setbacks toppled the government in 1972. The policies and ideology of President Tsiranana lost credibility, and ideological currents changed direction. Despite his party label as a social democrat, Tsiranana was viewed as representing the right, both because of his pragmatic approach toward economic policy and because of his close ties with France. Therefore, a sharp turn to the left was an attractive alternative, both as a model of economic development and as an ideology. By the same token, the failure of the Ratsiraka government to achieve economic growth from the mid-1970s to mid-1980s has undoubtedly influenced the ideological shift back toward the right.

IMPLICATIONS OF IDEOLOGICAL ATTITUDES. Clearly, ideology cannot be easily translated into obvious structural characteristics of the economy and polity, as seen in the comparisons of the size of the Malaŵian and Malagasy public sectors (chapter 1). Nevertheless, beliefs about capitalism and socialism have influenced the methods, direction, and scope of structural measures, such as nationalization, as well as various long-term policy measures, such as the choice of a development path, or even short-term measures such as price and exchange rate policies.

The Malaŵi government viewed public enterprise more as a means toward economic development. In most cases it considered decisions to extend public ownership on relatively pragmatic, rather than programmatic, grounds. The government also attempted to accelerate the development of an African entrepreneurial class by encouraging the private estate sector (chapter 4) and later, small businesses (chapter 7). Although it nationalized certain enterprises by buying out the foreign owners, it also worked with foreign entrepreneurs in a series of joint ventures and until the 1980s provided appropriate incentives for such ventures, notably, relatively easy repatriation of profits.

In Madagascar the situation was entirely different. In the December 1975 Constitution of the Second Republic (Chapter I, Article 7), public ownership of the means of production of key industries was declared essential for economic progress. The government viewed public ownership as an end in itself and carried out a dramatic nationalization program, in many cases by expropriation without compensation. As a consequence production suffered considerable disruption. Since 1972 Madagascar also has been less willing than Malaŵi to allow foreign investment, and despite the new investment code in 1985, the investment climate for private entrepreneurs—either Malagasy or foreign—did not appear promising.

Ideological beliefs about capitalism and socialism influence the boundary between markets and government administration of an economy. Although neither Malaŵi nor Madagascar completely opened its economy to market forces, capitalist and socialist ideologies influenced how the government modified these forces. For instance, both had extensive price controls for industrial goods (chapters 7 and 13) and, by means of monopsonistic marketing boards and other devices, imposed price controls on major agricultural goods as well (chapters 5 and 11). In comparison to Madagascar, however, Malaŵi's price controls introduced fewer deviations from the prices the market would have produced. Moreover, until the 1980s Malaŵi generally had lower tariffs on imported products and fewer quantitative restrictions; even more important, the government demonstrated a greater willingness to set its foreign exchange rate at levels that would maintain a rough equilibrium in its balance of payments so as to take advantage of the world market (and also to aid the agricultural sector). During the 1970s Malaŵi also made greater efforts to set its interest rates so as to avoid the need for capital rationing. In these ways, Malaŵi revealed a greater market orientation than Madagascar, where policymakers proclaimed on a number of occasions after the mid-1970s their basic mistrust of autonomously operating markets.

Ideological attitudes about capitalism and socialism also influenced each country's path of development. Malaŵi chose a development strategy that focused on agriculture and export trade; this seemed appropriate to the factor proportions existing in the economy and seemed to have the highest economic payoff, defined in rather narrow terms. On pragmatic grounds, the Tsiranana government in Madagascar followed a development strategy path roughly similar to Malaŵi's (an important exception was foreign trade policy) during the 1960s and early 1970s. In keeping with its Marxist orientation, however, the Ratsiraka government adopted an approach that was consciously patterned after the Soviet industrialization experience. Its plan was to create a capital-intensive heavy industrial base in the urban areas and to reserve investment in labor-intensive light industry until a later date.[1] Its timing was unfortunate, however, because its investment program began at the end of the boom in coffee prices and only a year before the second oil shock; poor selection of projects and inadequate implementation also encumbered the program (chapters 10 and 14). In the mid-1980s the government made an intellectual about face by adopting a totally different strategy of development in its long-term plan for 1986 to 1990; this latest plan stressed agriculture and light industry. Whether the plan can or will be implemented remains to be seen.

Ideological factors also have influenced the extent to which the public sector financed programs have achieved a mix of economic and social goals. The first long-term development plan in Malaŵi noted a trade-off between these two sets of goals and explicitly chose to support programs to achieve greater growth at the expense of social goals, relying in good part on a number of locally financed, self-help programs to realize various social aims. The Malagasy government placed a much greater emphasis on public expenditures to achieve social goals, as shown, for example, by its drive in the 1970s to raise school enrollment rates. The two nations' health strategies also reflect these ideological differences. Malaŵi relied much more on inexpensive measures, such as pure water facilities, sanitation measures, and inoculations, accomplished by unskilled labor, while Madagascar focused its efforts on more costly programs using highly skilled health personnel (chapter 15).

Nationalism

Madagascar had a much more intense nationalist struggle than did Malaŵi (chapters 2 and 9), although in the last years of colonialism the anticolonial struggle in Malaŵi was more overt. Both countries achieved independence without a civil war. Nationalism has remained an important aspect of the political ideology in both countries, but the focus of this nationalism has been different.

Because the British maintained a relatively low-keyed presence in its Nyasaland colony, Malaŵi after independence, for the most part, did not direct its nationalism against the British. Rather, it was turned inward and defined in terms of the battle against economic underdevelopment. Thus Malaŵi has been quite willing to accept foreign participation in the productive sectors (except for financial institutions) and to accept the aid of expatriate technocrats. Underlying this approach was President Banda's oft-stated belief that without economic development a country could never achieve true political independence.

Nationalism in Madagascar had a much different orientation, in large measure because this country, unlike Malaŵi, was a nation before it was colonized. It had experienced a series of anticolonial uprisings throughout the period of occupation, culminating in the bloody insurrection of 1947, and France participated intrusively in Malagasy affairs after independence. An important factor in Tsiranana's downfall in 1972 was a nationalism turned outward to reduce French influence. Madagascar's withdrawal from the Franc Zone, the removal of French technicians and soldiers, and the nationalization of French economic interests were among the important—and economically costly—policies motivated by such nationalism.

The different types of nationalism have also influenced ideas about the proper role of foreign trade.[2] Before colonization the various ethnic groups in Nyasaland traded among themselves, and little emotional distinction was drawn between local and foreign trade. During colonial times foreign trade was relatively limited, and after independence political leaders had few anxieties about economic dependence on foreign countries. Instead, Malaŵi's development strategy rested on the notion that it could enhance its economic growth by taking advantage of the international division of labor and by fostering a faster growth of exports than of GDP, aided by complementary monetary, fiscal, and exchange rate policies.

In contrast, Madagascar was self-consciously insular before colonization, and the government discouraged entangling trade relations with foreign nations. During colonial times foreign trade became symbolic of exploitation by France, and after independence Malagasy political leaders had a fear of economic dependence on other countries.

As a result, from independence to the mid-1980s all Malagasy governments emphasized the importance of import-substituting industrialization, and their long-term economic plans assumed roughly equal growth of foreign trade and domestic production. From the early 1970s until the mid-1980s the Madagascar government adopted a foreign trade regime with an overvalued exchange rate and widespread trade controls.

The Ideology of Management and Administration

This ideological element is more subtle and difficult to define than those discussed above. It concerns the methods the government chooses to carry out its economic activities and policies. Any such ideology is grounded on some basic notions about human motivations and about how to influence and control people and organizations to carry out policies and orders effectively.

The origins of administrative ideologies lie deep in the national culture. In precolonial times Malaŵi had little political or economic centralization, while the Merina empire in Madagascar exhibited a certain amount of political centralization and possessed a trained cadre of state administrators. Colonial influences were also important; in many respects the diverging views of Malaŵi and Madagascar toward public administration reflect the differences in views toward such matters found in England and France in the 1930s.

In Malaŵi the administration of the government has been more limited and, at the same time, more open than in Madagascar. The organization of Malaŵi's government has been relatively simple and without overlapping authority. The financial affairs of various state entities, at least in many important cases, have been open to inspection by the general public (indeed, this study has drawn upon many of their reports). The government has been cautious in taking on particular economic functions that might overstrain its limited administrative abilities (the price and foreign exchange controls of the 1980s were important exceptions), and it has been willing to delegate many key economic decisions to the private and the parastatal sectors. Furthermore, most of the Malaŵian parastatal sector has been relatively free of direct government intervention and has been charged with the humble task of making a profit without having to implement various social goals as well. The government also has structured incentives so that most investment projects in the state sector were chosen to achieve a profit.

The structure of governmental administration in Madagascar has been more complex, with many overlapping functions; an example is the wide participation of various government agencies and organs in agricultural policy (chapters 11 and 12). Its financial affairs have been less open to inspection, and an outsider, even with the greatest of efforts, has difficulty in obtaining a clear view of what has happened. In many cases the appropriate data for control and understanding simply have not been collected. In contrast with Malaŵi, the Malagasy government has been more willing to take on a broad range of functions that have severely strained its administrative resources; one instance was the invest-to-the-hilt program combined with the attempt to create agricultural cooperatives. The Malagasy government has charged many parastatals with a variety of social as well as economic goals. This is one reason many of the parastatals have incurred high financial losses and yet have been continually subsidized rather than allowed to go bankrupt.

Economic Interests and Governmental Policies

Extensive analysis of the role of economic interests in governmental policymaking requires certain kinds of detailed information on policy formation. Because of the political centralization in both Malaŵi and Madagascar, such information is extremely difficult to obtain. The modest mission of this brief analysis is simply to outline the major issues that require further investigation.

Interest Groups

Neither Malaŵi nor Madagascar has a highly organized and formal set of interest groups lobbying the government for particular economic policies. The various ethnic groups have no formal political structure, and formal organizations representing industrial workers, industrial employers, trading organizations, and rural interests do not appear to have much political influence. Also, social class formation in a modern sense is not sufficiently advanced in either country to provide a very useful explanation of events.

In both countries the influences of economic interests on policymaking appear to have been informal and not highly structured. In Madagascar, where such problems have been studied more closely, interest groups center around personalities and families. Representatives of particular family groups are placed in many different kinds of activities, for instance, the armed forces, agricultural estates, trading companies, and manufacturing. Thus the military or industry seldom develop a single position on certain issues of public policy because these organizations are composed of representatives from many families (see Archer 1976, Covell 1987, and Chaigneau 1981 and 1984–85).[3] Nevertheless, for analytic purposes several broad and important groupings of interests can be delineated.

THE EDUCATED URBAN ELITE. The most important asset of the educated urban elite is not physical wealth but rather human capital; that is, their education and the positions they have achieved because of their education have been the major source of their relatively high income and power.[4] They are active economic agents, with their influence arising from their positions in some organizational hierarchy or from their professional skills. The educated urban elite includes entrepreneurs; higher level technocrats; and employees, politicians, and professionals in both the public and private sectors. In both countries, their hold on the civil service has been particularly important. In Malaŵi a disproportionate share of the educated urban elite has come from ethnic groups in the north, where education has been more widespread; in Madagascar a disproportionate share has come from the Merina, the ethnic group with the highest educational levels.

The educated urban elite, especially the civil servants or those in the private sector with contacts and friendships to deal effectively with the government, were the clear gainers from the extensive economic controls over prices and foreign exchange, the lack of transparency of government regulations, and extensive delegation of governmental powers that were found in Madagascar until the mid-1980s or in Malaŵi starting in the 1980s.[5] On a personal level, the conditions permitted civil servants to gain power and income from bribes and those in the private sector who could obtain the scarce licenses and leases to gain monopoly rents. The educated urban elite as a whole also benefited directly from such measures as the lowering of real prices of agricultural products and the maintaining of an overvalued exchange rate and indirectly from the extensive system of controls that increased governmental jobs and bureaucratic power. In Malaŵi the educated urban elite were also the major gainers from the estate policy, at least in the early years, when they could easily obtain such land and ready credit to set up farming operations; later, external shocks led to shifts in ownership of the estates to other groups (chapter 4). Existing information does not permit detailed description of the modalities of rent-seeking and the extent of the short-term gains to the various segments of the educated urban elite. In the long run the gains such measures afforded the educated urban elite were more ephemeral than concrete.

THE TRADITIONAL RURAL ELITE. The traditional leaders in the countryside have seen an erosion of their power, especially in Madagascar. They proved no match for the governmental boards for purchasing agricultural crops, which depressed agricultural prices. Although in Malaŵi these leaders received certain rights to conduct courts according to traditional customs, in both countries their political powers became increasingly restricted as political parties and government bureaucracies penetrated the countryside. If smallholders wanted a representative of their interests, they could not turn to the traditional rural elites but rather had to seek out those of the educated urban elite or of the foreign interests who could understand that many of the smallholders' interests coincided with the long-term development goals of the nation.

FOREIGN INTERESTS. Three types of foreign interests have influenced policymaking in these two countries. *Multinational enterprises* (in Madagascar, only up to 1975) have played a role in very specific policies concerning tariffs and tax treatment of their operations. *Foreign expatriates* have staffed a number of the joint ventures and have served in various roles in the two governments. These foreign specialists have few domestic loyalties, except to the top political leaders, at whose pleasure they serve. Especially in Malaŵi such expatriates have filled some key governmental positions in which loyalty to the top leadership is essential. *Foreign financial institutions*, especially such international organizations as the International Monetary Fund and the World Bank, have played highly influential roles in microeconomic and macroeconomic policymaking in Malaŵi in the 1970s and, to a lesser extent, in the 1980s. In Madagascar the influence of these organizations seems to have been small in the 1970s and much greater in the 1980s, especially with the liberalization program. During the mid-1980s these international organizations tied a series of structural adjustment loans in both countries to such measures as devaluation, dismantlement of domestic price controls, liberalization of controls on foreign trade and agricultural markets, and the balancing of governmental expenditures and receipts. Other conditions included the reorganization of particular governmental bureaus and implementation of investment programs to widen production bottlenecks. The question of the particular interests of these organizations in supplying such policy advice must be left for others to discuss.

PATRIMONIALISM. The polity of both nations essentially has consisted of a government and a mass of people, with few formal institutions acting as intermediaries. The educated urban elite and foreign interests have influenced policy only in informal ways. Associated with such a "naked polity" is generally some type of patrimonial state, that is, personal rule by a leader who maintains power through charisma, by appealing to traditional authority structures, by developing a legitimizing ideology, by dispensing patronage, by exercising force through the army or police, or by rewarding particular groups enough to maintain political legitimacy.[6] Such rewards may be general—for example, when all groups benefit through economic development—or specific policies arranged to benefit particular groups. Clearly this type of naked polity encourages patrimonialism, and patrimonialism in turn acts to perpetuate that political structure.

Is the patrimonial state inimicable or complementary to economic development? In most instances, particularly when patrimonialism involves clientism and corruption, abuse of office, arbitrary administration of laws and insecurity of property, political insecurity, inability to deliver necessary public services, or economic policymaking based solely on short-term considerations, it is clearly detrimental to economic development. Patrimonialism could be associated with a "strong state," however, which could encourage economic development. This can occur, for instance, when a leader has sufficient power to insure continuity in the administration of laws, to develop an effective governmental apparatus for delivering necessary public services for productive enterprises, or to take unpleasant short-term measures with a high long-term payoff. In Malaŵi during the 1970s patrimonialism and economic development were complementary.

In sum, the structure of the polity does not indicate which economic policies a government will pursue. Rather, particular economic policies evolve from concrete circumstances and from the interactions of ideology and interests.

Economics and Politics up to 1979

In very stark terms, ethnicity appears to have played an important role in the policies of both Malaŵi and Madagascar in the 1970s. The agricultural orientation in Malaŵi and the manufacturing emphasis of the Ratsiraka government in Madagascar mainly reflect the circumstance that the educated urban elite in Malaŵi were primarily from a minority ethnic group and in Madagascar, from the dominant ethnic group. This ethnic element appears to have been less important in both nations in the 1980s.

MALAŴI. How did President Banda manage to maintain such a centralized polity and strong state? After a forty-year absence from the country, Hastings Kamuzu Banda entered Malaŵi at a unique moment to lead the struggle for independence. Events surrounding the formation of the federation had discredited the entire older leadership of the major political party fighting for independence. The younger leaders did not know Banda well, but they needed an older and respected man as their leader in order to give legitimacy to their own political efforts. They offered Dr. Banda the leadership of the party and also, as he required, complete power to appoint party officials. Because the country's two most important mass organizations, those for women and for youth, were also party auxiliaries, Banda's powers of appointment extended to them as well. A short time after independence Banda became Life President and the nation became a one-party state, a measure that many Malaŵian leaders advocated before independence (see Short 1974). Because party membership was a requirement for some important jobs, this constitutional change extended the President's appointment powers to the entire state apparatus.

In contrast to many other African leaders, President Banda has not relied on a large army or police to maintain his authority. (Their small numbers should not belie their effectiveness, however.) Much of his political power can be traced to certain more basic factors.

Most obviously, leading his nation to independence gave him enormous political prestige, which his brief imprisonment by the British colonial authorities only enhanced. He broadened his political base by adopting roles of traditional authority and by helping certain disadvantaged groups such as women and children, especially through his control of their mass organizations. Furthermore, he has used his powers of appointment very carefully and has quickly and effectively removed from public life those suspected of plotting against him.[7] The relatively small private sector has provided little alternative as a source of employment for dissatisfied intellectuals or politicians, so Banda's powers of patronage have been an important factor in stabilizing his political position. Such patronage powers also explain why he has been quite willing to see an expansion of state ownership of the means of production in the modern sector and a broadening of the powers of the traditional law courts, whose officials hold tenure at the will of the president, at the expense of an independent English-type judiciary.

President Banda's authority was also strengthened because until the late 1970s his government appeared to bring higher standards of living to a significant portion of the population. Furthermore, the party apparatus has been effective in solving problems and settling disputes—for example, on certain occasions the party has mediated industrial disputes between workers and their employers. Also, the formal powers of the president over the resources of the country were enhanced in such a way as to strengthen his political position; more specifically, the sequestration laws permit the president to expropriate the property of those accused of political subversion, and changes in the land tenure laws gave him the right to override the decisions of traditional political authorities.

With continuity of political power under Banda, Malaŵi's major economic policies, at least until the 1980s, were relatively consistent. Furthermore, the high degree of political centralization allowed the government to take a number of measures that were painful in the short-run but that had a high long-run payoff; for instance, it could raise direct taxes enough to become a net source of investment funds, in contrast to Madagascar, where taxes were primarily indirect and were not raised.[8] Banda's strength has also permitted relative decentralization of management of the parastatals; the outcome in any important difference of policy between them and the president has never been in doubt.

Even more interesting to consider is the choice of the agricultural path of development. When Banda arrived in Malaŵi, he was not beholden to any particular group nor did he represent any particular set of individuals. He never married and had no strong family interests to consider. His choice of an agricultural path of development appears a logical extension of the way he views himself: as a villager whose first duty is to help his fellow villagers (chapter 3). Many of his policies—such as relatively large investments in the rural sector, relatively low import tariffs, labor-intensive investments, and relatively low urban wages—reflected this driving concern to further the interests of the rural sector; producer price policies were an unfortunate exception. These policies found favor in the eyes of various international lenders, which encouraged and helped to finance them.

During the independence struggle, competing conceptions of Malaŵi's future development path could be found within the top political leadership. The most important political clash came to a head in the first few months after independence. The "cabinet crisis" of 1964 brought a number of issues to a head, including the relative power exercised by Dr. Banda, several foreign policy issues, and three economic issues: more rapid indigenization of the civil service, higher salaries for Malaŵians in the civil service, and lower hospital rates. Although these economic policy disputes precipitated the crisis, they were not the crucial issues. All positions the dissidents took were in the interests of the educated urban elite, especially the civil servants; for example, lower hospital rates would benefit urban groups in general more than rural people because most hospital facilities were located in urban areas and were used mainly by city residents. The economic dispute also had ethnic overtones; because of their higher levels of education, ethnic groups from the northern regions (especially the Tonga and Tumbuka) dominated the civil service in the early years after independence. Quite quickly, this dissident group was decisively defeated, removed from office, and exiled, effectively eliminating opposition from the left for a generation. The success of this action also removed from the agenda those economic policy measures young left-leaning leaders undertook in many of the other new anglophone African nations.

From time to time other groups emerged to challenge Banda's rule, but they were dealt with swiftly; the major issues of contention appear not to have concerned economic strategy, although we cannot be sure of this. Nevertheless, the congruence of ethnic interests and differences between urban and rural orientations in the development strategy continued for some years, especially because the northerners had the most to gain from an urban strategy of development not just because of their higher levels of education and their grip on the civil service but also because their region was the least suited to agriculture. In the available information about such struggles, the ethnic rather than the policy differences have received greatest attention.

The Malaŵi government has tried to downplay incidents of interethnic conflict, however, in order to maintain domestic harmony; as a result, information about them is sketchy. Conflict between the northerners and the Chewa simmered in the early 1970s with the arbitrary dismissal or imprisonment of some members of the educated urban elite originally from the north. It flared briefly in the open in 1975 and 1976, when roughly 300 northerners in high- and middle-level civil service positions were dismissed; subsequently many were detained in prison without trial (Legum and Drysdale 1977, p. B-268). The purge appears to have been instigated by Chewa extremists, notably Focus Gwede, the head of Special Branch of the Police (the security police), which apparently was trying to build up its own patronage base. The next year the northerners were released from prison, but Gwede and Albert Muwalo were sentenced to death for a plot against Banda's life (Legum and Drysdale 1978).

Some observers have argued that in recent years the importance of ethnicity has declined, partly because of the equalizing of education among the three regions. For instance, in May 1983 four ministers or former ministers, alleged to be opponents of Banda, were reported killed in a car accident (Legum and Drysdale 1984); the ethnic background of all four was different, and only one was a northerner. In the late 1980s ethnic frictions increased, however, and President Banda removed a number of northerners from public posts. Insufficient information is available to say anything very definite about the present state of ethnic frictions.

President Banda took a series of measures to create an elite to lead the country in the future. One of his first major projects was the creation of a university; he also established an elite secondary school, Kamuzu Academy. His emphasis on estate agriculture appears to have had a similar motive; these policies were a way of gaining the allegiance of certain segments of the educated urban elite, especially politicians and high civil servants, by turning them into a rural bourgeoisie with strong ties to the state (chapter 4). Ironically, the estate owners who finally succeeded in such economic endeavors were a somewhat different socioeconomic group, but they still provided a type of rural leadership that was important for the future of the nation.

Of course, economic motives also played an important role in the estate strategy. More specifically, President Banda seems originally to have viewed the estates not only as a means of rapidly increasing exports but also as a means for harnessing what he believed to be the individualism and the acquisitiveness of the rural population. Moreover, he has viewed the estates as "schools" of modern agricultural techniques that would raise the productivity of those who returned from the estates to small-holder agriculture. Contrary to my own analysis of the subject, Banda claims to see a complete complementarity, not a competitiveness, between the smallholder and the estate sectors.[9] Whatever the original intentions of this strategy, the estate provided a simple and effective method of increasing production without straining the administrative capacities of the government.

Some observers have claimed that in the past Chewa nationalist groups favored an even greater emphasis on the estate strategy than the government, because Chewa controlled the greatest number of the large estates. A survey of estate owners (chapter 4) revealed that 35 percent of the respondents were Chewa, a group composing roughly 28 percent of the population. This was not a gross overrepresentation, especially given the fact that the Central Region, where most Chewa live, is considerably more suitable for estates than either the overpopulated Southern Region or the Northern Region, which has many transportation difficulties. Although ethnic interests may have originally played some role in the estate strategy, these do not now seem important for the continuation of the strategy. At least until 1979, the estates were a leading economic sector, and it is difficult to argue with success.

The willingness of the Malaŵi government to expand individual economic initiative in other areas also reduced the administrative burden on the government. Furthermore, this strategy may have given the economy some flexibility in the face of external shocks (chapter 6).[10]

MADAGASCAR. Madagascar's political situation has been considerably more complex than Malaŵi's. Why did Madagascar, which started along a path similar to Malaŵi's, turn suddenly toward the left? Why did it nationalize the French properties? Why did its development strategy have an urban orientation? Why did the government undertake the invest-to-the-hilt campaign? How did the government maintain control in the face of a dramatic economic decline, and why did it seem to reverse course in 1987?

In Madagascar, in contrast to Malaŵi, independence was not obtained through political struggle but was handed over by the colonial power as part of a larger political design. No single party or person led the nation to independence. Although Philibert Tsiranana was one of his country's founding fathers, he had neither the initial prestige nor the authority of a Banda.

In comparison with Malaŵi, the Malagasy polity has more centers of power, the government has ruled with less formal authority, and the patrimonial rulers have been less able to impose their will either on the government bureaucracy or on economic actors. The president of Madagascar has considerably fewer formal powers than does Malaŵi's president. The educated urban elite in Madagascar has been a larger and more powerful group than in Malaŵi, and both urban and rural groups have been more willing to riot and to create other civil disturbances to press their political demands. Also, the country has had a variety of competing political parties, except for special periods when all party activities have been banned.

The nature of party politics in Madagascar provides more insight into the policy differences between the two countries. Until 1972 the PSD (Parti social démocrate), which was founded by Philibert Tsiranana in 1956, dominated Madagascar politics. The PSD was composed in considerable part of people who had originally been members of PADASM (Parti des deshérités de Madagascar). PADASM had been founded in 1946 and supported by the colonial government as a foil against a more nationalistic party, the MDRM (Mouvement démocratique de la rénovation malgache). Thus large segments of the Malagasy population thought the PSD did not fully represent their interests. Most of the leading personalities in the PSD were côtiers, in contrast to the highland ethnic groups (especially the Merina) that played a large role in the other parties. Tsiranana's program represented in large part a continuation of the economic policies of the colonial government (chapter 10); he did, however, place greater stress on agriculture.

Tsiranana relied on his prestige, his powers of patronage, and his political skills to maintain power. In the early 1970s, however, the nation experienced some short-run difficulties; for instance, a cattle plague and drought in 1971 and a cyclone in March 1972 adversely affected production and rural incomes in many parts of the country, especially the south. These economic problems, a split in the party between would-be successors to Tsiranana, student strikes in the urban areas (following the 1968 precedent of the student strike in France), and his own illness diminished Tsiranana's effectiveness in exercising his authority. To quell the civil disturbances occurring in 1971 and 1972, he had to call in the police and army. Since that time, these organizations have played an important political role, and all the succeeding Malagasy presidents have come from the military. The Merina have been overrepresented in the army officer corps.

Gabriel Ramanantsoa (1972–75), a Merina, was the next president. He formed a government of soldiers and technocrats and took a series of measures embodying the strong nationalist sentiments that were to be extremely costly economically (chapter 9). Although he did not nationalize a great deal of property, his government did set up several new state enterprises that Didier Ratsiraka, his successor, used to take over certain economic activities previously carried out by foreigners. Ultimately, Ramanantsoa proved a weak leader and was forced to resign by the military leadership.

Ratsiraka, a compromise candidate of the military, had a quite different approach toward the governance of a patrimonial state.[11] For this astute politician, ideology was an important tool to gain the support of the educated urban elite and to maintain his political legitimacy. Furthermore, his government had a much different ethnic base than that of Tsiranana. In the Tsiranana government, the Merina, who composed slightly more than a quarter of the population, were underrepresented in cabinet posts (chapter 9). Nevertheless, they held most of the high civil service posts because of their educational level and because the capital of the country is located in the center of the Merina territory. When the Ramanantsoa government replaced the French expatriates in government posts, the educated Merina had the most favorable opportunities to obtain these positions. The Ratsiraka government's nationalization program provided additional opportunities for the Merina to advance themselves, especially because about half of the nation's industrial production originated in Merina-dominated Antananarivo Province.

This shift, from the 1960s to the 1970s, in the relative economic weight of the Merina in relation to the *côtiers* was reflected in changes in the composition of the cabinet. The percentage of Merina in the cabinet roughly doubled after the mid-1970s, and since then they have been overrepresented in relation to their share in the population. Didier Ratsiraka is a *côtier* (of Betsimisaraka origin), however, and according to the impressions of French specialists on Madagascar, he has gradually increased the representation of *côtiers* in the higher positions of the civil service. In other respects as well he appears to have carefully balanced and neutralized competing family, ethnic, and economic interests to maintain his political base.[12]

Madagascar's economic decline has had a political cost for Ratsiraka—a gradual loss of popular interest in and support of the ideology that allowed him in the mid-1970s so effectively to consolidate his country and his own political position. In the mid-1980s he has met with considerably more difficulty in imposing his economic policies on either the government bureaucracy or the private sector; witness his problems in liberalizing agricultural prices or in carrying out other aspects of economic reform (chapter 12).

In sum, whatever impact the nationalist program and the nationalization had for the nation as a whole, they benefited the educated urban elite, a particularly high share of whom were Merina. Additional manifestations of the shift toward urban interests under Ratsiraka were the fall in the real prices paid to agricultural producers (chapter 12); the formation of FNUP, which skimmed off the potential agricultural profits and used them for urban investments such as the construction of universities in each province (chapter 15); and the reduction in relative resources of the Ministry of Agriculture (chapter 10).

In an important sense the invest-to-the-hilt campaign was merely a continuation of the same pro-urban program. In the campaign's beginning phases, Madagascar had relatively loose internal financial constraints. Interest rates in international financial markets were relatively low, Madagascar had a low level of external debt and a good international credit rating, and the coffee boom was not yet over. By drawing upon coffee profits and by borrowing abroad, the country could finance a large investment program without having to raise domestic taxes. Furthermore, technicians of the International Monetary Fund and the World Bank encouraged Madagascar to invest more; they (correctly) saw its low investment rate as one of the major causes for its low rate of economic growth and encouraged external borrowing. These international organizations, however, did not have a significant influence on which projects would receive such financing.

Economics and Politics after the Second Oil Shock: 1979 to the Late 1980s

From the mid-1970s to the mid-1980s Malaŵi experienced three important external shocks: a decline in its external terms of trade, brought about both by the rise in the international price of oil and by a relative fall in Malaŵi's export prices; a disruption of its rail traffic through Mozambique by the activities of the RENAMO insurgents; and a rise in government expenditures necessary to aid the Mozambique refugees and to reduce RENAMO operations on Malaŵi territory. Madagascar had only the oil shock to face. Its relative export prices rose somewhat, and its long-term external terms of trade did not greatly change. It did, however, face some severe domestic shocks brought about by policy failures stemming from the invest-to-the-hilt program.

Since 1979 both Malaŵi and Madagascar have experienced roughly similar economic histories: a rapid rise in debt-servicing and attendant problems; debt rescheduling; and structural adjustment loans from international organizations, which have been conditioned on devaluation and on liberalization of internal price and import constraints. In both countries per capita GDP continued to fall in the first two-thirds of the 1980s (much more in Madagascar than in Malaŵi because of Madagascar's greater policy failures in the late 1970s). Because of dependence on foreign loans and debt rescheduling, neither government has been able to direct economic activities according to its own desires. Each country has responded differently to the situation.

MALAŴI. In the mid-1980s knowledgeable Malaŵians seemed unable—or unwilling—to talk openly about the broad economic picture or about changes in economic strategy. Innovative ideas seemed to be exhausted, and the focus of public attention was on isolated economic problems and special administrative aspects of particular programs. The government had not discontinued unsuccessful economic programs as quickly as it had in the previous decade. The new development plan, *DevPol II*, proposed policies pointing in the right direction, but it is a bland document based on some unrealistic assumptions (chapter 3).

President Banda has not changed his major views on economic policy, but as he has aged, his attention has turned away from the details of economic policymaking.[13] His long-term advisors also have aged, and policymaking has devolved to younger politicians and the civil service. As a result, policy decisions have taken much longer to reach, and the policies chosen have been less consistent than when the Life President played a more active role. For instance, from 1980 through 1987 the top officials were unable to agree on a second long-term plan to refocus development efforts to meet the new challenges of the 1980s.

This devolution of power seems an important explanatory factor underlying the dramatic increase in governmental controls on the economy during the first half of the 1980s. These controls reduced the economy's flexibility in responding to external shocks. Furthermore, policymaking developed a certain urban bias; examples include the maintenance of an overvalued exchange rate; the maintenance of price controls on certain imports, such as automobile parts and fuels, that are important to urban consumers; the inappropriately low producer prices given to smallholders; and the continuation of an agricultural program that did not greatly benefit the smallholder but that required extensive administrative staff.

MADAGASCAR. Madagascar's problems in the mid-1980s were quite different. Although knowledgeable Malagasy seemed quite willing to talk about the large economic picture, they were inattentive to administrative problems because they have been unable—or unwilling—to specify how to implement particular programs or policies. A major problem was policy inconsistency, abetted by the overlap in bureaucratic authorities.

Experts on Malagasy politics have offered several explanations for the apparent reversal in economic policy in the mid-1980s. One is that the top leadership gradually realized the failure of the previous policies and was willing to attempt some dramatic changes, especially if it could obtain funds from international lending organizations in time to improve the economic situation before the presidential election in the fall of 1989. Another is that the policy changes reflected a realignment in the political coalition supporting the president and the rise in power of a group of technocrats from the civil service, armed forces, and private sector (calling themselves the *Garamaso*, a name that has not yet reached the press) who advocate liberalization and are abetted by international lending institutions. A third explanation is that *Procoops*, an enterprise tied to the AREMA party and the president's family, has been able to take advantage of many of the concessions offered in the privatization program, giving it a financial stake in the liberalization (Berg 1989). Others observe that informed public opinion has turned against the previous dirigistic policies and that the governmental liberalization program has merely been getting in front of this ideological change. I have no solid evidence by which to determine the relative validity of these various interpretations of the policy shift. In the 1989 presidential election, Ratsiraka won a third term in office by taking credit for the liberalization, and the single candidate opposing these reforms received the fewest votes. Ratsiraka faces, nevertheless, considerable political discontent, and, in 1989–90, at least two coup attempts were thwarted by his government.

Aside from severe problems in servicing the foreign debt, Madagascar's major economic problems have been internal, mostly arising from inconsistencies of policy and implementation. Because political power is less centralized in Madagascar than in Malaŵi, high Malagasy political authorities face more constraints and in formulating and implementing policy must be more careful to balance interests. Thus policy inconsistencies are more likely to occur; comparison of the liberalization occurring in the two countries in the late 1980s provides evidence for this proposition (Berg 1989, Christiansen and Stackhouse 1989, and Shuttleworth 1989).

The formal liberalization program has been dramatic, and certain measures, such as the devaluation of 1987, have been encouraging. At least until the end of 1987, however, many of these measures were being subverted to a certain degree by informal governmental regulations at various levels ("liberalization without liberalization").[14] Policy inconsistencies were also exacerbated by civil disturbances in various towns during 1986 and 1987, which required taking short-term palliative measures that could have adverse long-term impacts. Impressionistic evidence from 1988 and 1989, however, suggests that many of these problems have been resolved.

Economic Development and Income Distribution

In both Malaŵi and Madagascar income differentials have widened and poverty has increased (chapter 16). Are governmental efforts to achieve economic development, whether or not they are successful, necessarily taken at the expense of income equality? Given the interplay of ideological and economic interests determining economic policies, did the two governments have much choice in the policies they selected?

Policy Alternatives

A great deal has been written about the alleged trade-off between growth and equality. In the context of the two countries under examination, such arguments highly overstate the policy problems facing governmental decisionmakers.

INVESTMENT AND INCOME INEQUALITY. According to an oft-repeated argument, greater income inequality leads to greater savings and investment, which induce faster growth. Previous chapters show that the government sector can increase saving in other ways as well—that is, by the extent to which it administers the parastatals to earn a profit, by the degree to which it can balance its own budget, and by its willingness to raise interest rates to make saving more attractive. During the 1970s Malaŵi's public sector was the source of considerable savings, while Madagascar's was not. Another method of increasing savings is for the government to encourage those groups that tie their economic futures to investment and growth and to discourage those groups that are not interested in economic development. In both countries more effective encouragement of smallholder agriculture would have led to greater economic growth with a special benefit to poor and traditional groups, which under the right conditions were willing to produce for export.

The experiences of Malaŵi and Madagascar show that the effective investment of savings can be more important than the level of savings in itself. As discussed in chapters 3 and 10, the amount of investment required for an addition unit of production (ICOR) rose considerably in both countries, reaching astronomical levels in Madagascar from the mid-1970s to the mid-1980s. The ICOR could have been reduced, for instance, by creating the proper investment environment (for example, by allowing firms freely to import production inputs); by choosing wisely which projects to finance with public investment; and by devising a system of incentives to encourage private investment that will be able to withstand market competition.

SOCIAL AND ECONOMIC EXPENDITURES. Allocating resources from the government budget for social or for economic purposes poses an even more difficult problem. How can expenditures for additional schooling be weighed against expenditures for agricultural extension work? This is clearly a matter in which the influences of ideology and economic interests play a predominant role.

The ability of either government to influence income distribution by direct transfers has been limited, given their fiscal constraints. Malaŵi did not attempt a large-scale social program, and Madagascar's social measures were in certain respects counterproductive. Direct government expenditures in such poor nations realistically cannot substantially change the income distribution in the short run. The government's major impact on income distribution, as shown in previous chapters, has come about from more general programs such as investment in agriculture, appropriate exchange rate and agricultural price policies, or provision of effective agricultural extension. Many of these promote both faster growth and more equal distribution of income. The effectiveness of government social expenditures is also very important; for example, Madagascar's large health expenditures have done relatively little to improve the indicators of the level of health.

THE WAGER-ON-THE-STRONG POLICY. Both countries—but Malaŵi to a much greater extent than Madagascar—consciously adopted policies to widen income differentials in agriculture by encouraging the stronger elements in that sector; neither country intended poverty to increase, however. The Malaŵi government was unable to administer its vast investment programs in agriculture in such a way as to increase production among smallholders to a significant degree. Furthermore, as farms diminished in size, it did not take policy measures to improve their productivity to offset diminishing returns. In Madagascar, the relative decline of investment in agriculture, the turning of the internal terms of trade against agriculture, the overvalued exchange rate with a resulting shortage of agricultural inputs and consumer goods for the farmers, and the disintegration of both markets and the rural transportation infrastructure all contributed to the poverty problem.

The Importance of the Rural Sector

In each country, the increase in income inequalities within the rural sector was the major cause of the widening of income differentials for the economy as a whole and of the rise in poverty. This relationship is certainly not inevitable in poor agricultural nations. For instance, Taiwan achieved economic development with a narrowing of rural income differentials (see Fei, Ranis, and Kuo 1980). In that case, growth in rural industrialization provided an important source of growth in off-farm income; rural policies focused less on projects benefiting only a small share of the rural population and more on various types of labor-intensive agricultural projects, especially for the poorest farmers; and the government avoided policies in foreign trade and other sectors that would result in nonprice rationing of agricultural inputs. If Malaŵi and Madagascar had tried the first two of these measures, they would not have encountered serious ideological or economic objections; the third measure would have conflicted with the interests of the urban elite, however.

In both Malaŵi and Madagascar, the smallholder population is the poorest. Clearly, achieving growth with equity will require support of smallholder production to improve the living standards of this group. Such a general prescription is easier to make than to apply, however. Both nations have experienced administrative failures of programs for smallholders. Some specifics of a program to raise agricultural productivity and production might include permitting agricultural producer prices to reach market levels; providing alternative sources of employment such as labor-intensive rural industries; making physical investments, such as microirrigation works, that will benefit farmers; and creating an organizational infrastructure that will allow farmers easily to receive agricultural inputs and consumer goods, market their crops, and obtain credit and good technical advice. In certain circumstances, encouragement of agricultural estates also might be beneficial.

The challenges of growth with equity in poor, agricultural nations with relatively little arable land per capita, high external debts, and a relative dearth of physical and human capital are daunting. The political and economic constraints on achieving growth with equity are considerable. Nevertheless, as this brief review of alternatives for the two countries suggests, growth with equity is possible, but in nations as poor as Malaŵi and Madagascar this development path requires particular sensitivity to the special problems of agriculture. In the late 1980s leading public figures in both countries appear to have shared this view. Whether these policymakers can overcome the political, administrative, and financial constraints in implementing public economic policies consistent with these views remains to be seen. A favorable international environment, political courage and imagination, and a dogged tenacity are among the important ingredients for success.

Notes

1. Although during the 1950s most orthodox Marxists stressed the universal applicability of the Soviet development path for the third world, these views changed in the 1960s and especially the 1970s. Thus Madagascar's choice of a new development strategy after 1975 did not follow the kind of advice on economic development the Soviet Union was then giving to interested nations. Valkenier (1983) and Hough (1986) have analyzed this shift in general; Pryor (1986), p. 36, observes this Soviet advice in a specific country.

2. Obviously nationalism itself does not imply autarky; certainly, highly nationalistic nations, such as Republic of Korea, have also placed considerable

emphasis on foreign trade. Nationalism does influence how such trade is carried out and controlled. These two countries' heritage of colonial ideas about trade was different. The British elite in Nyasaland were probably much more influenced by Ricardian ideas about the mutual benefits of trade than were the French elite of Madagascar, who were carrying out a very conscious *économie de traite* in order to extract a useful surplus from Madagascar for the benefit of France.

3. The rather shadowy *Club des 48* is one of these family groupings.

4. Finding a proper descriptive term for this group is difficult. The term "elite" should not be taken to mean "social elite"; "middle class" does not fit because this group is certainly not in the middle of the social hierarchy; the term "bourgeoisie" is inappropriate because wealth in the form of ownership of the means of production is often less important than income and authority stemming from high position in some public or private organization. Zolberg (1966) speaks of "bureaucratic gentry, " of which the key element is a person's relationship to a formal political structure. I believe that education, which influences one's relation not only to the formal political structure but also to state enterprises, is more crucial; moreover, "gentry" has an unfortunate fox-and-hounds connotation.

5. This bald assertion is based on highly developed analysis of rent-seeking and directly unproductive profit-seeking activities, as found in such surveys as that by Colander (1984).

6. For this brief discussion I draw heavily on Sandbrook and Barker (1983) and Sandbrook (1986).

7. Although a small group of advisors, such as John Tembo, has remained with President Banda for many years, the turnover of cabinet members has averaged about 4.2 years each. This datum covers the period from 1964 through 1983 and was calculated from raw information used in compiling table 2-2.

8. At independence Banda faced a considerably more dire fiscal situation than Tsiranana, and this undoubtedly focused his mind on the problem. Malaŵi's greater emphasis on direct taxes was undoubtedly also a carryover from colonial times in that the British placed greater emphasis on direct taxes than did the French. To the extent that Malaŵi's tax structure has been more responsive to domestic economic conditions than has Madagascar's (which received a higher percentage of its revenues from import taxes), it could more easily obtain increasing tax revenues during the prosperous 1970s.

9. In my interview with Banda on April 22, 1987, we touched in several different ways upon the complementary versus competitive nature of the estate and smallholder sectors. The judgment reported in the text summarizes both his remarks to me and his ideas expressed in a number of speeches as well.

10. The question of flexibility is examined empirically by Bela Balassa, "Adjustment Policies and Development Strategies in Sub-Saharan Africa, 1973–1978, " in Syrquin, Taylor, and Westphal (1984), pp. 317–40. Balassa's argument is not complete, because his correlations may be less the result of economic controls alone than of the specific nature of the civil service in the countries that were administering such controls.

11. Actually, General Richard Ratsimandrava immediately followed Ramanantsoa as President, but he was assassinated after only a week in office, before he could accomplish anything of interest.

12. President Ratsiraka has maintained his original coalition from the time he took power to the mid-1980s, as manifested by the relatively slow turnover in the cabinet; for instance, from 1977 through 1984, the average cabinet term was 4.8 years. Given the relatively short period under examination, which biases this statistic downward, cabinet turnover appears to have been significantly less than in Malaŵi (footnote 7). This datum was calculated from the raw materials used to compile table 9-2.

13. In our interview President Banda expressed his impatience with many detailed issues of economic policy in which he had previously taken great interest. Gordenker (1976) presents an interesting case study of Banda's deep involvement in economic policy in his early years.

14. Some commentators, such as Hugon (1987), have argued that the liberalization contains some fatal design flaws. This argument is difficult to evaluate because of confusion about which measures have actually been implemented and which are merely "for show."

Appendix

A. Land Tenure in Malaŵi and Madagascar

Malaŵi

TRADITIONAL TENURE ARRANGEMENTS. Traditional forms of land tenure apply to almost all land in the smallholder sector. Tenure customs differ according to ethnic group, type of inheritance (matrilineal or patrilineal), and marriage system (matrilocal or patrilocal, monogamous or plural marriage).

Generally, all people living in a particular local area have a claim on "customary land" without paying a rent. Most of this land cannot be sold easily, although some has been leased to estates. Permission to use a particular piece of land is obtained from traditional political authorities; or, if family land, from family authorities (which, depending on the area, can be the family of one's mother, one's father, or one's spouse). Any claims on land must be validated by actual cultivation, however, and unused land reverts to the authority from which it was received. The rules as to what constitutes "use of land" are complex, particularly when land is fallowed.

Thus land hoarding is difficult except for those in authority. In allocating land, the traditional authorities face a problem. They are under pressure to provide land for claimants without land, but they cannot easily reallocate land in use by others. The literature on tenure does not discuss the decision rules followed in this land allocation process.

Other allocation methods include receiving land from government agricultural schemes, squatting, borrowing land from a friend, and sharing it with members of an age-set. Although a great deal more can be said about the theoretical rules of land transfer in the different ethnic groups, the rules governing customary land vary also according to locality; moreover, according to some people, the rules are changing over time. Some indications of the actual practices followed in Malaŵi are shown in table A-1.

The data in the table show that the share of smallholders obtaining land from the headman declined markedly between 1968 and 1980; this suggests that the unused land available for distribution by traditional political authorities was declining. Supporting evidence is shown by the share of smallholders obtaining land from the headman by age of smallholder; a higher percentage of the older smallholders than of younger smallholders obtained land in this way. To a certain extent, of course, this phenomenon reflects the longer span of time the older farmers lived in the village and the greater trust the headman

Table A-1. Sources of Smallholders' Land-Use Rights, Malaŵi, 1968–69 and 1980–81 Crop Seasons
(percentage of smallholders)

		Relative by birth		Relative by marriage		
Region/age	Headman	Male	Female	Male	Female	Other[a]
All regions,						
1968–69	33.4	29.5	20.7	6.1	6.5	3.8
Northern	29.6	56.2	7.4	4.6	0.7	1.5
Central	28.5	36.0	23.7	4.1	5.5	2.3
Southern	37.9	18.0	22.1	8.0	8.7	5.3
All regions,						
1980–81	26.2	25.3	19.9	9.3	12.9	6.5
Northern	31.7	45.7	6.4	9.1	2.4	5.8
Central	24.5	18.7	21.9	8.7	10.8	5.4
Southern	26.5	18.4	21.2	9.8	16.7	7.3
Age of household head, 1980–81						
Under 30	12.5	30.2	26.8	9.1	16.0	5.3
30–39	19.6	25.8	23.3	10.2	16.0	5.1
40–49	26.6	25.5	20.1	8.0	13.3	6.5
50–59	31.6	23.1	17.3	10.9	10.7	6.5
60 and over	40.5	21.9	12.2	8.3	8.1	8.9

Source of permission to use land

Note: Detail may not add to 100 percent because of rounding.

a. "Other" sources of use include squatting (in 1968–69, this accounted for 1.6 percent of land use), borrowing land, obtaining land from an agricultural scheme or project, and unknown.

Source: Malaŵi Government (1970), p. 4; and Malaŵi Government (1984), p. 9. The data in the latter source (page xiii) for 1968–69 are somewhat different from those found in the former source; aside from some obvious arithmetical errors, the data for the two crop years are less consistent if the latter source is used for 1968–69.

placed in them (especially a male living with the family of his wife). This phenomenon also reflects land shortages, however.

The share of land received from male relatives by birth has declined considerably, while the percentage of land obtained from relatives by marriage—particularly female relatives by marriage—has increased. This suggests that matriliny was not disappearing with economic development, especially in the south, where land was most scarce. Another possibility is that men in this region did not consider it worthwhile to struggle with women for control over very small plots, which could not provide a viable basis for existence. Female-headed smallholdings were more common in the south than in other regions.

LAND RENTING. Although land scarcity has become a problem, landlessness in Malaŵi has been virtually nonexistent, in contrast to some other African nations with considerably lower population densities. Moreover, the tenure rules have kept the rate of tenancy quite low; for instance, a 1965 sample survey of 2,152 smallholder households in the Southern Region, the most populous region, found that only 4 percent of the holdings involved tenancy (Collier 1985).

Land renting has occurred primarily in the estate sector through a system with a complex evolution. As noted in chapter 2, the *thangata* system on the estates, which occurred primarily in the Southern Region, was effectively abolished at independence in 1964. In the Central Region, a "visiting tenant" system arose in the 1920s and continued to flourish after independence. This is a sharecropping system, whereby tenants grow crops (primarily burley tobacco) for a season (four to six months), sell their crops to the landowner at a previously agreed price, and return to their homes elsewhere. The landowner can renew a contract for the next year or cancel it, and roughly 3 to 4 percent of the contracts have not been renewed as estate owners have weeded out inefficient tenant farmers. The tenants supply housing and food for themselves and their families, receive technical advice and credit for any necessary equipment, and sometimes earn supplementary wages working on the estate. Although the visiting tenant system appeared likely to be abolished at the same time as *thangata*, pressures from new Malaŵian estate owners prevented this, and the system still exists. The extent of the system and its impact on productivity are not documented, but other aspects are discussed by McCracken (1984).

RAMIFICATIONS OF THE TENURE SYSTEM. The system of land tenure in Malaŵi has had some extremely important implications for economic development and the distribution of income.

Adoption of Technology. According to Chipeta (1976a), land tenure arrangements have not impeded the adoption of new agricultural technologies, at least for those technologies that do not depend on scale or credit. Because economies of scale are not important for most crops in Malaŵi, the relatively equal division of land has probably had little impact on total production.

Inequality of Land Holdings. The requirement that traditional land must be cultivated by the holder has meant that until recently the inequality of land holdings was considerably less than in many other countries such as Madagascar. Table A-2 presents some measures of such inequality in Malaŵi, which can be contrasted with those for Madagascar in the same table. This relative equality of land holding, combined with the relatively low incidence of land renting, implies that the distribution of income among smallholders should be more equal than in Madagascar. It also means that absentee landlordship of such traditional lands has been virtually absent, as has an important link between urban and rural sectors occurring in such countries as Kenya (as analyzed by Collier and Lal 1986). Based on the data in table A-2, the inequality of land holding did not change greatly over time, although the data on a per worker basis may be incomparable, and private claims on land did not become much stronger.

Table A-2. Inequality of Smallholdings, Malaŵi and Madagascar, Selected Years

Country/year	Average size (hectares)	Gini coefficient	Theil coefficient	Log variance
Malaŵi				
Planted land, 1968–69[a]				
Per smallholder household	1.538	.369	.234	.505
Per smallholder worker	0.557	.294	.147	.323
Planted land, 1984–85[a]				
Per smallholder household	1.144	.381	.246	.523
Per smallholder worker	0.545	.296	.144	.311
Madagascar				
Total land, 1961–62[b],				
per smallholder household	1.039	.445	.360	.646
Planted land, 1984–85[b],				
per smallholder household	1.458	.380	.251	.595

a. The data for Malaŵi cover only smallholder lands in rural areas. In 1968–69 there were 1.62 family workers per household; in 1984–85 there were 2.10. This suggests that the two censuses used a somewhat different definition of family worker. No major differences in the inequality coefficients occur if "man equivalents" are used instead of total family workers (without taking into account sex or age).

b. The data for Madagascar apparently exclude all holdings larger than 10 hectares.

Source: Malaŵi—Pryor (1988b), table A-5. Madagascar—Pryor (1988a), table A-4; and Ministère de la production agricole et de la réforme agraire and FAO (1988b), table VIII.

Efficiency of Factor Allocation. The system has reduced the ability of the society to allocate rural factors of production efficiently. More specifically, it has resulted in large differences among families in labor-land ratios. In a well-functioning rural factor market, such differences in initial endowments can be equalized by transferring land holdings (for example, by buying and selling, renting in or out, and so forth) and by buying and selling labor. The land market in Malaŵi has been sluggish not only because land cannot be easily bought or rented but also because headmen increasingly have had less land to transfer. The labor market has had to bear the major brunt of any adjustment to achieve an efficient allocation of agricultural factors of production. Efficiency requires a degree of labor mobility that has not existed.

At the present time, the static inefficiency caused by the unequal land-labor ratios among the various areas of Malaŵi is not very great. More specifically, if land-labor ratios had been equalized on all land throughout the country in 1980–81 and if Malaŵian smallholding agriculture could be described with a Cobb-Douglas production function, aggregate production would have been about 2.7 to 4.4 percent higher than it was, depending on the assumption made about the fixed coefficients of the production function. (I have followed an analytic technique used by Paul Collier and have varied the fixed coefficients from 0.2 to 0.8; because the data I used differed somewhat different from his, my results are also slightly different.)

The Labor Market and Rural Poverty. The shrinkage in average farm size has required smallholder families with smaller farms to send workers away to earn supplementary wages. Arbitrarily taking 0.1 hectares per household member as a cutoff point for "land scarcity," in 1968 approximately 965,000 people (about 24 percent of the smallholding population) lived on smallholdings below this threshold; by 1980–81 this number had increased to approximately 1,139,000 people, or about 22 percent of the smallholding population in that year. In the twelve years separating the two investigations, land scarcity increased on an absolute scale but decreased on a relative scale. Other cutoff points yield similar results.

The Credit Market. The traditional land tenure system has discouraged the development of a rural credit market. Farmers cannot pledge their land as a security because it cannot easily be transferred to outsiders. Of course, they could pledge their future crops, but this increases the costs of collecting the collateral, if necessary, not to mention the risk to the credit supplier. Thus private credit, if available, has had a higher interest charge.

Land Scattering. In recent years considerable interest has focused on the underlying causes of land scattering, and how much such scattering impedes production (see Pryor 1982). In Malaŵi in 1968 smallholders averaged about three "gardens" per holding, ranging from 2.4 gardens in those holdings of fewer than 0.8 hectares (2 acres) to 4.2 gardens for holdings larger than 4.9 hectares (12 acres). Assuming that the gardens were not contiguous, this is a very low degree of scattering, at least viewed from an international perspective. We do not know if this lack of scattering was attributable to the way the traditional authorities allocated the land, and we have no data on how far these plots were apart. Land scattering does not appear to be a great problem of the tenure system at present, although in the future it may raise some difficulties.

Limitations on Crops. A final important aspect of the tenure situation is the limitations on the kinds of cash crops that the smallholdings and estates can grow, a topic discussed in chapter 4.

CHANGES IN LAND REGULATIONS. Land tenure rules in Malaŵi have been changing during the last quarter-century, particularly as a result of governmental policies and laws. For instance, in 1965 the legislature passed the Malaŵi Land Bill, which gave the Minister of Agriculture the power to lease, assign, or, in some cases, to sell land from customary areas. Furthermore, if the land is leased, it becomes subject only to the control of the minister, who can raise the rent or reallocate the land. See Williams (1978), p. 242; and Paul Brietzke, "Rural Development and Modification of Malaŵi's Land Tenure System," in Page (1973), pp. 53–68.

An additional law passed several years later gave the Minister of Agriculture the power to declare any part of the country to be a "development area" within which the government would directly supervise all lands. Anyone wishing to acquire land in the area would have to apply to the government (ultimately to the president), and the customary sector has no legal powers to resist alienation of its land. These laws, which the president termed "quite controversial" when he introduced them, gave the executive branch of the government enormous formal powers, which it has used to extend the leaseholds held by the estate sector.

LAND CONSOLIDATION. In the late 1960s the Malaŵi government began to encourage consolidation of plots and registration of land titles in government bureaus, a process that was supposed to be an important component of the integrated land development schemes. To encourage registration, the government also provided a mechanism for deed registry by the traditional authorities. Furthermore, in 1967 the legislature introduced a statute providing that a certain fraction of the property of those dying intestate must be distributed according to English law; the complementary fraction would be divided according to the customary law of the community. The degree to which this law has been observed is not known. All of these measures were partly based on the president's belief that "everyone's baby is no one's baby," that is, that modern agriculture requires absolute security of tenure in order to encourage investment. Although the question has not been thoroughly investigated for Malaŵi, traditional land tenure arrangements appear to be quite secure—as long as the land is used (Payr 1977).

As Ester Boserup (1970) has pointed out, attempts at land registration can have several unexpected and unfortunate results in matrilineal societies (p. 61). If carried out in a heedless fashion, the registration processes often shift land rights from females to males, thus destroying matrilineal inheritance rules. Furthermore, if precautions are not taken, such registration can result in the loss of land by those who do not have the resources to engage in expensive legal battles; the British enclosures are an extreme example of this result.

In Malaŵi several counteracting forces have prevented such adverse effects of land registration. First, traditional authorities have carried out a type of title registry for customary land. Second, the formal deed registration process has been moving at a very slow pace, except during special campaigns such as the Lilongwe Land Development Project, 1968–1978, or the Kasungu burley tobacco area since 1980; only 200 titles a year are said to be processed. Third, the political decision made in the late 1960s to strengthen the native courts operating under customary law, rather than relying on a court system operating under the modification of British law, seems to have acted to prevent eradication of traditional land rights. Thus the conflict between traditional land rights and liberal institutions has been attenuated by the administration of the new land law.

One last aspect of the land registration system deserves mention. According to Clement Ng'ong'da (1985–86), individualization of land titles has not yet led to vigorous land markets, and lenders are still unwilling to accept registered land as security.

Madagascar

TRADITIONAL TENURE ARRANGEMENTS. The system of inheritance has strongly influenced the pattern of traditional land holdings in Madagascar. The different Malagasy ethnic groups vary in the relative importance they place on the principles of bilateral and patrilineal descent and inheritance. In most ethnic groups all children share about equally in the inheritance of real and personal property (ambilateral inheritance); in some smaller ethnic groups only sons receive certain rights in the use of the land for farming, although inheritance of other types of property is shared. Land inheritance includes the right to use communal lands and a space in the family tomb located on the land, a concern of great religious importance to the Malagasy. A crucial aspect of the land inheritance system is the system of marriage and of choice of residence, which permits the exercise of certain land rights.

In contrast to the land tenure situation in Malaŵi, the Malagasy need not farm the land in order to maintain their land rights. Although many observers argue that the ambilateral land inheritance system and the importance of the family tomb encourage living and marrying close to the inherited lands of both spouses, a certain amount of population mobility exists, and an intricate system of land lending and renting has given rise to absentee ownership. A young man can serve as a sharecropper to one relative, partly in anticipation of inheriting the land, while renting out his own land to another relative.

A tension exists between the familial and community rights to land use. For instance, a family may be able to farm its land only in particular months; for the rest of the year the land reverts to communal pasture. Such communal rights appear to be more important in Madagascar than in Malaŵi because in Madagascar cattle raising (and the presence of communal pastures) is of greater importance than in Malaŵi and because cultivation of wet rice—Madagascar's most important food crop—often requires considerable communal effort to regulate the irrigation waters.

Nevertheless, under the traditional tenure system some rights of usage appear to be secure, at least so long as the land is farmed by someone in the family—and so long as the peasant community remains relatively stable. Some have claimed that during the mid-1970s, when certain governmental powers were being devolved to the village governments (*fokotany*), land tenure became more insecure because the new powers of the village community were unclear; I have not been able to find much direct evidence on this subject, however. Areas of recent inmigration are also said to experience a different kind of tenure insecurity, especially because the exact claims of the migrants on the land were unclear.

A much different and, in my view, more important problem of security of tenure arose in the early and mid-1980s with the breakdown of domestic order in many rural areas. For the last 300 years, cattle rustling in Madagascar has been serious enough to draw the attention of foreign observers. In the early and mid-1980s, however, the problem became more severe and did not follow the same "rules" as in the past; furthermore, the practice spread to crops, and praedial larceny (the stealing of crops from the fields) began to increase. Many public reports in Madagascar have addressed this problem, but data on its severity are not reported. This breakdown of domestic order can only adversely effect agricultural production.

LAND RENTING. In 1962, 91 percent of the smallholders in Madagascar owned the land they farmed, 5 percent were pure renters, and 4 percent had some kind of joint tenure arrangement through which they owned part of their land and rented the rest (Madagascar, Ministère des finances et du commerce, and INSRE 1966). The overwhelming share of the rented land was owned by Malagasy, not Europeans. By 1984–85 the situation had not greatly changed: 87 percent of the smallholders owned the land they farmed, 5 percent were pure renters, and 8 percent had some other type of tenure arrangement (Madagascar, Ministère de la production agricole et de la réforme agraire, and FAO 1988a). Data on rental contracts by type are only available for 1962; of the renters, 29 percent had a fixed rent and 71 percent had a sharecropping arrangement (with most paying 33 percent of crops or receipts).

Considerable confusion exists about the extent of rented land in Madagascar in the early years of independence. The data presented above seem to be the most reliable. Sevin and Guerin (n.d.) claim that in 1956, 124,000 hectares were rented, of which 110,000 were owned by Malagasy. According to Madagascar, Commissariat général au plan (1962), p. 107, in the 1950s 150,000 hectares were rented in sharecropping arrangements, of which 120,000 went to Malagasy smallholders. Other sources provide still other data.

Before the results of the 1984–85 census were published, some leading agricultural specialists in Madagascar believed that land renting had increased during the past two decades, especially after 1975. They offered three hypotheses: (a) urban investors began buying land, especially when previous land-owning farmers became pauperized; (b) as population pressure increased, farmers began renting from the village *notables* the less fertile lands lying at some distance from the villages; and (c) in the villages, a *kulak* class was emerging. The census results suggest that all three of these conjectures are overdrawn.

Although Madagascar as a whole has considerable arable land, much of it is far removed from population centers and lacks the essential infrastructure to make it suitable for farming; at the same time, considerable landlessness occurs in many villages (see Pavageau 1981).

RAMIFICATIONS OF THE TENURE SYSTEM. The system of land tenure in Madagascar has some important implications for economic development and the distribution of income.

Land Accumulation. The land tenure rules, especially those permitting land accumulation greater than the holder's ability to farm, suggest that the distribution of land among smallholders should be more unequal in Madagascar than in Malaŵi. The data for Malaŵi and Madagascar in table A-2 validate this hypothesis, at least for the early years. Indeed, the inequality coefficients understate the difference between the countries, because the Madagascar but not the Malaŵi statistics omit "middle-sized farms."

I experimented with determining the importance of this bias by recalculating the inequality coefficients based on the 1962 size distribution data of smallholdings (underlying table A-2) and data on the size distribution of middle-sized and large estates in 1969 drawn from Madagascar, Ministère du développement rural (annual, for 1970), p. 88. These results (Gini, 0.547; Theil, 0.998; log variance, 0.676) are much higher than those in the table. When estates are included in the 1984–85 calculations for Madagascar, the results (Gini, 0.408; Theil, 0.467; and log variance, 0.601) are not much different from those in the table.

The somewhat greater inequality of land holdings in Madagascar than in Malaŵi suggests that smallholder incomes should also be more unequal. This appears valid as well (chapter 16).

Efficiency of Factor Allocation. The land rental system permits optimal land-labor ratios to be achieved more easily in Madagascar than in Malaŵi.

Social Implications. Although its land is more privatized than Malaŵi's, Madagascar lacks a strong law of eminent domain, probably because certain lands have important religious significance (as the sites of the family tombs, for example). Therefore, constructing dams and building drainage or irrigation canals has sometimes proven very difficult if such projects impinge on these special land rights.

Land Scattering. Although parcelization of agricultural land was not important in the past, it has increased in the last few decades. In 1962, there were 3.5 parcels per farm, roughly the same as in Malaŵi; by 1984–85 this average had increased to 4.3 (according to Ministère de la production agricole et de la réforme agraire and FAO 1988a, but according to the preliminary census results, the ratio was 6.5; the source of the discrepancy between the two sources is unclear).

The forces underlying this change in land scattering must remain obscure until the census data are analyzed in detail, but some ingenious hypotheses have been advanced. Donald McCloskey has suggested to me that the rising level of praedial larceny has played a causal role. If we assume that fields are difficult to guard because they are far from dwellings and that crop-stealing follows a relatively random pattern, increased parcelization of agricultural lands would represent a rational response by spreading the risks of the depredations over a larger number of fields. Malagasy economists with whom I discussed this conjecture rejected it because the considerable parcelization occurred before the rural disorder. They proposed several less elegant solutions instead: (a) the breakdown in agricultural markets in the latter part of the 1970s (chapter 12) led to greater smallholder self-sufficiency, greater diversification of crops, and greater need for different microclimates for the new crops; (b) the population surge in the last few decades (resulting from a fall in the death rate) has increased the rate of local overpopulation, leading to smaller and more scattered fields, especially as the villagers begin to use less fertile fields far from the village; and (c) parcelization reflects the increase of sharecropping.

LAND REGULATION AND REGISTRATION. As noted in chapter 11, cadastral surveying and registration of land titles have proceeded together. Title registration began shortly after the French occupation, and by the mid-1980s, about 900,000 hectares of individual and communal lands had been listed in the cadastral registries. Land registration could occur either on individual, collective, or governmental initiative, and the process is quite complicated. Since 1974 the government has been increasing the registered land by about 20,000 hectares a year; the goal is to complete the process in the early part of the next century. The much greater individualization of land has permitted the process to proceed considerably faster than in Malaŵi. Although the infringement of liberal land policies on traditional rights may cause conflicts, the literature does not discuss them systematically. The increase in power of the local communities after 1972 has permitted them to block various attempts by individual farmers to register their land, especially if the land is on a relative large farm (10 hectares or more).

An individual can acquire land title mainly by inheriting it or receiving it as a gift from another person, whether or not that land is registered or held under traditional tenure; by purchasing registered land, although land held under traditional tenure is not easily sold; in recently opened areas, by applying for free land from the community council that administers the area, although this option is not available in older areas; or by following a particular bureaucratic procedure with the Services des domaines by which the state, owner of all unclaimed land, may grant an individual ownership of up to 5 hectares gratis if the individual farms the land. The last procedure is particularly complicated and can involve obtaining the approval of eight or more different representatives of local, provincial, and central governments.

B. Foreign Trade Patterns in Malaŵi and Madagascar

The concentration of trade has both geographical and product dimensions. This note discusses both briefly, as well as certain aspects of exchange rates in Malaŵi and Madagascar.

Malaŵi

The generalizations presented below are based on the same data sources as those used in Pryor (1988b), section F.

GEOGRAPHICAL CONCENTRATION OF TRADE. From 1964 through 1981 a little less than half of all Malaŵi's exports went to Great Britain, while another quarter went to Zambia, Zimbabwe, South Africa, and the United States. During the same period, about one-quarter of its imports were from Great Britain, a fifth were from South Africa, and about one-seventh came from Zimbabwe. In recent years the import share from South Africa has risen to about one-third, while the share coming from Great Britain has declined to about one-fifth. British expatriates appear to have played a relatively minor role in Malaŵi's trade since independence, except to buy or sell export crops in the public auctions. On the list of the largest trade partners, however, all are English-speaking nations, mostly of the British Commonwealth.

Although this geographic concentration of trade is disturbing to many observers, it is not unusual for poor developing nations. This can be seen from Michaely's careful comparative study (1984) of the geographical concentration of trade. Malaŵi had roughly the average concentration of both imports and exports as for the comparison nations.

PRODUCT CONCENTRATION OF TRADE. The composition of Malaŵi's exports can be easily summarized using the foreign trade data underlying the computations in Pryor (1988b), section F. In the first five years after independence, tobacco, tea, and groundnuts constituted about 75 percent of all Malaŵian exports; from 1980 through 1984 the same three commodities plus sugar, which was introduced as an export crop in the late 1960s, accounted for about 85 percent of total exports. From 1964 to the early 1980s exports originating in estate production increased from 25 percent to 70 percent; during the same time, the share of estate production in gross crop production was rising from 15 to 40 percent (chapter 4). Thus the remarkable growth of exports can, in most part, be attributed to the increased importance of estate production of a few crops.

In its meeting with aid donors to Malaŵi in 1983, the Malaŵi government once again stated its intentions to diversify exports, particularly into macadamia and cashew nuts, wheat, and coffee (Malaŵi, Minister of Finance and Economic Planning Division, 1983). *DevPol II* repeated the same themes at greater length. Whether the government will finally carry out these worthy and oft-stated intentions remains to be seen.

The change in the structure of Malaŵi's imports over time has been much more dramatic than that of exports. Detailed data are presented in Pryor (1988b), table F-2b, but the major trends can be seen by comparing the first five years after independence with 1981 to 1985, the last five years for which data are available. Transport equipment and "other imports" maintained their shares of total imports. Several imports declined markedly in share. Consumer goods imports fell from

25 percent of total imports to 13 percent, and intermediate products imports went from 15 to 7 percent. In contrast, the share of plant machinery and equipment imports rose from 10 percent to 15 percent of the total imports, raw materials rose from 28 to 38 percent, and oil products increased from 7 to 14 percent. This pattern very clearly shows important import substitution taking place in the manufacture of consumer goods and many intermediate products; at the same time imports of machinery and raw materials to support this burgeoning manufacturing have increased. Other aspects of this import-substitution pattern can be seen by direct examination of Malaŵi's index of manufacturing production.

Three different comparative studies indicate that the concentration of products composing Malaŵi's exports is roughly comparable to that for similar nations. One study also shows Malaŵi's product concentration of imports to be about 1 standard deviation less than the others. Some confusion arises, however, because various studies of product concentration of trade cover different time periods and use different statistical techniques.

Estimates of product concentration by David Wheeler (1983) are the most recent available to me and cover the longest period of time. Michaely (1984), pp. 55 ff., focuses only on 1973. Tuong and Yeats (1974), pp. 203–15, have made estimates for an earlier year. The Wheeler estimates show Malaŵi's export diversification during the 1970s. Tuong and Yeats make the calculation at different stages of aggregation of the SITC data and show that the coefficients (a Hirschman index) changed little for Malaŵi over time.

A BRIEF HISTORY OF THE EXCHANGE RATE. As of the beginning of 1988 Malaŵi had formally devalued its currency three times: in November 1973, in April 1982, and in February 1987. Equally important, however, were the changes Malaŵi made in tying its currency to different baskets, which in some cases had the same effect as a devaluation. From independence to November 1973 the Malaŵi kwacha (MK) (or its predecessor, the pound) was tied to the British pound sterling, even after the dissolution of the Sterling Area and its associated monetary privileges in June 1972 and the float of the pound sterling in the later years of the period (which was accompanied by two de facto devaluations against gold). The link to sterling appeared appropriate at the time because in the first five years after Malaŵi's independence Great Britain absorbed about 56 percent of Malaŵi's exports and supplied about 28 percent of its imports. During the transition period from November 1973 to June 1975, the MK was tied to a currency basket consisting of U.S. dollars and pounds sterling. From June 1975 to September 1983 the MK was tied to the SDR; subsequently the MK was tied to a different bundle of currencies (apparently more closely

416 Malaŵi and Madagascar

related to its trade pattern), which resulted in a de facto devaluation against the SDR.

Madagascar

The generalizations presented below are based on the same data sources as those used in Pryor (1988a), section F.

GEOGRAPHICAL CONCENTRATION OF TRADE. From 1960 through 1984 roughly 39 percent of Malagasy exports went to France; another 21 percent went to the United States; and 5 percent went to Japan, the third largest export partner. About 56 percent of Madagascar's imports during these years came from France; and about 8 percent were from West Germany, the second largest partner. The role of French expatriates in the foreign trade of Madagascar has received considerable comment. Under the Tsiranana and Ramanantsoa governments (1960 to 1975), the high percentage of imports from France can be traced to the dominant role of the largest foreign trade firms, which were French owned. This geographical concentration of imports continued, however, even after these French firms were nationalized.

The geographical concentration of Madagascar's exports was roughly similar to that of comparison developing nations, according to the calculations of Michaely (1984), pp. 73 ff. The concentration of its imports, however, was 53 percent higher (2.4 standard deviations) than the average (at least in 1973). This shows dramatically that the import ties to the former colonizing power had not been fully cut.

PRODUCT CONCENTRATION OF TRADE. Madagascar has exported a broad range of products, which is consistent with its broad range of climates and with having various colonial governors impose different development plans on it. From 1964 through 1984 coffee, cloves, vanilla, sugar, and sisal accounted for about 60 percent of its exports. The structure of imports has changed greatly over the years (Pryor 1988a, table F-3). The shares for energy (especially after the first oil shock), food, and, to a certain extent, industrial equipment have risen; the share for consumer goods has fallen dramatically. Domestic manufacturing of consumer goods has not greatly increased, and little import substitution has occurred, in part because of the overvaluation of the exchange rate (chapter 14).

This concentration of exports and imports can be put in perspective by comparing the results for other countries, using the studies cited in the discussion about Malaŵi. Madagascar's export concentration was about 0.5 to 1 standard deviation less than the average; its import concentration was 1.2 standard deviations below the average. This latter phenomenon is difficult to explain, but it might reflect the government's lack of success in encouraging small factories for producing special goods, leaving Madagascar to import a wide variety of products.

A BRIEF HISTORY OF THE EXCHANGE RATE. From 1950 until April 1, 1982, the Malagasy franc (FMG) was tied at a fixed rate to the French franc. The *Institut d'emission*, which served as a central bank, was established in 1962 and was jointly owned and administered by France and Madagascar. It held its foreign reserves in a special operations account in the French treasury, which guaranteed unlimited conversion of the FMG into French francs. This arrangement was similar to that in other former colonies of France. Although it issued its own currency, Madagascar was considered for public purposes to use the CFA franc.

In 1973 Madagascar left the Franc Zone and established a nationally owned central bank that controlled its own foreign currency reserves. For another nine years, however, the Malagasy government continued to peg its currency to the French franc. After April 1, 1982, Madagascar tied its currency to a market basket of currencies of its major trade partners and then undertook a series of small devaluations in order to try to bring its currency into equilibrium. Not until June 1987, however, did Madagascar carry out a devaluation of significant magnitude.

C. The Road Network in Malaŵi and Madagascar

Table C-1. Road Inventories, Malaŵi and Madagascar, Selected Years
(kilometers)

		Malaŵi		
Year	Total	Paved	Gravel	Earth
1964	10,128	431	742	8,955
1970	10,703	448	751	9,504
1975	10,702	1,242	533	8,927
1980	10,763	1,904	254	8,605
1983	11,542	2,166	529	8,847

		Madagascar		
		Primary and secondary		Estimated
Year	Total	Paved	Gravel and earth	rural roads[a]
1960	27,168	1,290	12,878	13,000
1965	27,122	1,836	12,286	13,000
1970	27,708	3,254	11,454	13,000
1975	27,781	4,464	10,317	13,000

a. The estimate for rural roads varies in different sources; this estimate falls roughly on the median of the various estimates.

Source: Malaŵi—Malaŵi NSO, *Malaŵi Statistical Yearbook 1982*, pp. 95–96. Madagascar—primary and secondary roads (respectively the responsibility of the national government and the provinces): Madagascar, Minister of Finance and Planning (1977); estimated data for rural roads (maintained by the villages): FOFIFA and Ministère de la production agricole et de la réforme agraire (February 1983).

D. The Size of the Government Sector in Malaŵi and Madagascar

Table D-1. Indicators of the Size of the Government Sector, Malaŵi, 1964 to 1985
(percent)

	State-sector workers[a]		Government workers[b]		Central government[c]			
							Public gross fixed capital formation	
Year	Share of labor force	Share of modern sector	Share of labor force	Share of modern sector[d]	Public expenditures/ factor price GDP	Current government expenditures/ factor price GDP	Share of factor price GDP	Share of total gross fixed capital formation
1964	n.a.	n.a.	n.a.	n.a.	27.6	20.7	3.1	32.7
1965	n.a.	n.a.	n.a.	n.a.	24.9	17.7	4.3	37.1
1966	n.a.	n.a.	n.a.	n.a.	26.0	18.2	5.8	36.9
1967	n.a.	n.a.	n.a.	n.a.	25.1	19.2	4.2	32.1
1968	2.6	30.3	1.9	22.4	28.3	19.6	5.3	27.3
1969	2.7	28.9	1.9	20.9	34.5	18.5	5.0	22.3
1970	2.7	28.0	1.8	18.9	35.2	18.6	8.6	32.9
1971	2.9	27.8	1.9	18.0	28.0	16.1	6.3	33.9
1972	3.1	28.2	2.0	17.8	27.0	17.0	6.2	26.5
1973	3.3	27.3	2.1	16.9	27.0	15.5	8.0	36.6
1974	3.3	26.4	1.9	14.8	26.4	15.0	8.5	42.0
1975	3.3	25.2	1.9	14.7	31.2	14.6	13.7	51.6
1976	3.3	23.9	1.7	12.5	25.9	14.2	8.6	36.8
1977	3.2	22.2	1.5	10.8	27.0	13.3	10.5	44.5
1978	3.1	20.1	1.3	8.8	34.2	16.5	15.5	46.7
1979	3.0	19.5	1.3	8.3	38.3	18.9	15.7	53.4
1980	3.3	20.8	1.5	9.6	42.4	18.4	17.2	69.6
1981	3.2	23.2	1.6	11.9	39.7	22.5	12.4	74.2
1982	3.1	22.2	1.9	14.0	37.1	23.2	11.4	71.0
1983	3.1	20.6	1.8	11.9	35.3	20.9	12.3	80.9
1984	3.0	20.8	n.a.	n.a.	36.3	22.8	9.8	67.3
1985	3.0	19.7	n.a.	n.a.	n.a	n.a.	n.a.	n.a.

n.a. = Not available.

a. Excludes parastatals operating under private law; includes primarily government workers and workers in statutory bodies.

b. Paid employees in central and local governments minus paid employees in statutory bodies.

c. Expenditures only of the central government for the fiscal year, which begins in April. Current expenditures include current consumption, grants and subsidies, and interest. Public investment expenditures are by government, statutory bodies, and some parastatals.

d. Includes all wage and salary workers in the NSO labor force survey; the data for 1968 through 1976 are adjusted to make them consistent with the sample after 1976.

Source: Total labor force (includes only workers aged 15 and over)—Pryor (1988b), table B-1; government workers—Malaŵi, NSO, Reported Employment and Earnings, various issues, and Malaŵi, Office of the President and Planning, Economic Report, 1985; public expenditure and investment—Pryor (1988b), tables K-2a and D-2b.

Table D-2. Indicators of the Size of the Government Sector, Madagascar, 1960 to 1982
(percent)

Year	Total expenditures/ factor price GDP	Operations expenditures/ factor price GDP[a]	Investment/ factor price GDP	Investment/ total gross fixed capital investment
1960	14.1	13.3	0.7	7.2
1961	16.2	15.3	1.0	10.3
1962	15.7	14.5	1.2	13.5
1963	17.6	14.3	3.4	30.9
1964	16.6	14.4	2.2	19.8
1965	17.4	15.1	2.3	22.6
1966	16.9	15.1	1.9	14.3
1967	17.1	14.7	2.5	17.7
1968	18.9	14.3	4.6	30.6
1969	19.6	14.5	5.2	32.6
1970	17.7	13.1	4.6	30.1
1971	18.4	13.4	5.1	29.9
1972	20.1	14.1	6.0	44.2
1973	18.5	13.8	4.7	34.7
1974	15.7	11.9	3.8	28.8
1975	16.2	12.8	3.4	27.9
1976	20.3	15.5	4.8	38.6
1977	17.1	13.7	3.5	27.6
1978	23.0	18.9	4.0	28.5
1979	28.1	18.1	10.0	40.3
1980	28.4	17.1	11.3	49.3
1981	22.9	14.7	8.2	47.0
1982	16.7	13.1	3.7	28.6

Note: These data cover only the central government; however, in 1972–73 the central government absorbed most of the budget of the provincial governments. These expenditure series appear consistent but are somewhat different from the expenditures data underlying tables 15-1 and 15-2.

a. Operations expenditures include current and transfer expenditures but omit certain types of price subsidies.

Source: Pryor (1988a), table K-3a.

E. Additional Source Materials for Chapter 1

Table 1-1

The data for Malaŵi and Madagascar come from various tables in Pryor (1988a) and (1988b). For the thirty-one low-income nations most of the data come from appendix tables of various issues of World

Table E-1. Political Conditions in Sub-Saharan Africa

Country	Total military involvement score	Coups	Attempted coups	Reported plots	Marxist regime	Afro-socialist regime	Multi-party state system, 1984–85
Former French colonies							
Bénin	42	6	3	3	Yes		
Congo, Peoples' Republic of	33	3	5	3	Yes		
Burkina Faso	30	5	1	2	Yes?		
Central African Republic	26	3	3	2			Yes
Madagascar	18	2	2	2	Yes		Yes
Niger	18	1	4	1			
Mauritania	16	2	1	3			
Guinea	15	1	1	7		Yes X	
Togo	14	2	0	4			
Chad	9	1	1	1			
Mali	9	1	0	4	Yes X		
Comoros	6	1	0	1			Yes
Cameroon	4	0	1	1			
Gabon	3	0	1	0			
Côte d'Ivoire	3	0	0	3			
Senegal	3	0	1	0			Yes
Djibouti	0	0	0	0			
Total	249	28	24	37	5	1	4
Former British colonies							
Ghana	55	5	6	12		Yes	
Sudan	40	2	7	9			
Uganda	37	3	6	4			
Nigeria	25	4	1	2			Yes
Sierra Leone	16	2	1	3			
Zambia	7	0	2	1		Yes	
Seychelles	6	1	0	1	Yes		
Kenya	5	0	1	2			
Tanzania	5	0	1	2		Yes	
Gambia	4	0	1	1			Yes
Zimbabwe	4	0	1	1	Yes		Yes
Malaŵi	1	0	0	1			
Botswana	0	0	0	0			Yes
Lesotho	0	0	0	0			Yes
Mauritius	0	0	0	0			Yes
Swaziland	0	0	0	0			
Total	205	17	27	39	2	3	6

Note: The meaning of the data and the sources are described in the text. Somalia is excluded from these lists because it belonged partly to Great Britain and partly to Italy.

Bank, *World Development Report* (annual). The per capita GDP data for all nations come from Summers and Heston (1988). Data for several countries are my own rough estimates. The GDP data for each country are weighted by the population. The arable land data for the weighted averages come from Food and Agricultural Organization (annual), volume 37; their comparability with the Malaŵi and Madagascar data is not clear because the FAO estimates and those reported in this study are quite different for the two countries.

Footnote 2, Chapter 1

Table E-1 presents a classification of Sub-Saharan nations of former British and French colonies according to several categories. This table serves as the basis of some generalizations presented without documentation in chapters 1, 2, and 9.

The "total military involvement score" shown in the table is the sum of the coups (multiplied by 5), the attempted coups (multiplied by 3), and the reported plots. These data are taken from McGowan and Johnson (1984), table 1. A "Marxist regime" is defined as one in which the leading political figures declare themselves Marxists and take serious measures to implement such an ideology; an Afro-socialist regime is defined as one in which the leading political figures declare themselves adherents to some type of non-Marxist socialism and take serious measures to implement such an ideology. Some have claimed that Ghana is a Marxist regime; the evidence available to me does not support this designation. Any "X" following a "Yes" means that the political constellation has changed and the rating was no longer suitable in 1984–85. These designations are drawn from Ottaway and Ottaway (1981); Young (1982); and more recent information.

Information on whether the state does not have any legal political parties or has only one is drawn from Worldmark (1985) and Banks (1985).

F. Additional Source Materials for Chapter 3

The data in table 3-3 present an unweighted average of the percentage breakdown of expenditures from the development fund for each year. The data for the two periods are not completely comparable, however, and the data for the early period are adjusted as follows: expenditures for police and for local authorities are excluded from the development budget in the early period because these appear to be current expenditures; "natural resources and agriculture" includes expenditures on agriculture, forestry, fishing, geological survey, and rural development; "transportation and communication" includes all expenditures on roads and bridges and half the expenditures for "public works" (with the other half assigned to "government buildings"); "utilities" includes only expenditures on water and sewerage.

G. Additional Source Materials for Chapter 5

Studies of Agricultural Responses to Prices (footnote 4)

Many works have focused on the economic response of farmers in Malaŵi; and some of these are summarized in World Bank (May 1981a), pp. 172–80. The major studies include: Brown (1970a), (1970c); Channock (1972); Chipeta (1976a); Colman and Garbett (1975); Dean (1966); Gordon (1971); Humphrey (1972); Kydd (1977); Lavrijsen and Sterkenburg (1976); Mills (1973), (1975); Minford and Ohs (1976); and Pearson and Mitchell (1945).

Evidence on Relative Savings in Urban and Rural Sectors

Data on savings in Malaŵi are very rough; the most detailed available data are presented in table G-1. They suggest that in 1968 the marginal propensity to save was higher in the rural than in the urban sector and that any attempt to transfer income from the rural to the urban sector would result in a fall in aggregate savings.

In order to predict changes in saving and investment resulting from a shift in income between urban and rural areas, we would have to have information about financial flows between urban and rural sectors, for which little data are available. A clearer view of credit constraints would also be necessary. For instance, borrowing constituted 4.7 percent of posttax income in the urban area but only 1.2 percent among smallholders. If credit had been more available to the rural sector, both borrowing and repayment of loans probably would have been higher. Whether net savings would have been higher or lower is unclear. On theoretical grounds a greater availability of agricultural credit might have encouraged greater net investment because it would reduce risk. Until more is known about savings and investment behavior of Malaŵian smallholders, we cannot be sure.

Microeconomic Impact of ADMARC Activities

Some calculations by the World Bank for 1977 illuminate the impact of ADMARC's uniform pricing rule. Table G-2 shows World Bank estimates of how much a product would cost at a particular point if costs of exports plus transportation are used as a basis of comparison. Karonga and Chitipa, which are in the Northern Region, received the highest subsidies or lowest taxes. Lilongwe and Salima, in the Central Region, received lower subsidies or higher taxes than the Northern Region. In the Southern Region, which is the most favored part of the country with respect to transportation costs, Ngabu, Phalombe, and

Table G-1. Saving or Investment in Rural and Urban Sectors, Malaŵi, 1968

	Smallholder families, 1968–69			Urban families, 1968[a]	
Midpoint of average annual after-tax income in income groups[b] (MK)	Net capital cash disbursements[c] (MK)	S/Y (percent)	Midpoint of average annual after-tax income in income groups[b] (MK)	Net capital cash disbursements[d] (MK)	S/Y (percent)
58.35	-1.58	-2.7	70.37	0.23	0.3
62.24	-0.96	-1.5	140.43	1.68	1.2
74.09	-0.91	-1.2	188.00	1.01	0.5
78.11	-0.69	-0.9	257.38	4.44	1.7
83.55	-0.08	-0.1	334.59	2.41	0.7
90.08	0.65	0.7	450.48	0.50	0.1
98.98	-2.92	-3.0	671.15	9.16	1.4
106.24	1.69	1.6	1,094.40	-32.90	-3.0
124.21	3.95	3.2	4,114.00	20.54	0.5
162.08	8.29	5.1	n.a.	n.a.	n.a.
381.46	9.73	2.6	n.a.	n.a.	n.a.
Average					
84.31	0.07	-0.0	824.00	3.11	0.3

Calculated MPS
Smallholder families = .038
Urban families = .004

n.a. = Not available.
Note: S/Y = savings over income after taxes; MPS = marginal propensity to save after tax income. The latter statistic was calculated from the data in the table using a linear, least squares regression. Intersectoral flows of funds do not appear to influence these results.

a. Includes only families in the four largest towns.
b. Includes cash and noncash income minus direct taxes.
c. Includes cash expenditures on farm equipment and repairs and work oxen, cattle, and other livestock, minus credit received and "other cash receipts," which consist chiefly of withdrawals from savings.
d. Includes cash expenditures for loans repaid and made, savings, house-building and house-purchasing expenses, minus capital receipts in cash, which include various kinds of loans and withdrawals from savings.

Source: Savings data—Malaŵi Government (1970), tables R-12 and R-13; and Malaŵi, NSO (1970c), tables 3 and 4. Income data—Pryor (1988b), tables I-1 and I-2.

Table G-2. Microindicators of ADMARC's Pricing Policies, Selected Years

	ADMARC trading profits, 1972–84[a]	
Product	Share of sales	Estimated share of farmer receipts
Tobacco	47.7	126.2
Groundnuts	23.2	45.4
Cotton	17.9	38.7
Rice	-15.9	-32.0
General produce	-19.3	-34.0
Maize	-29.2	-21.9
Total	22.6	44.1

Product	ADMARC purchase price/ export price, 1964–84 (average unit values)
Maize	63
Groundnuts	55
Pulses	52
Tobacco	39
Paddy rice	35

Profit (+) or subsidy rates (-) of ADMARC purchasing or selling prices, 1977[b]

Town	Purchase price Maize	Purchase price Groundnuts	Purchase price Rice	Selling price Nitrogenous fertilizer
Karonga	-145.7	+120.0	-88.9	-68.4
Lilongwe	-39.1	+144.0	—	-24.5
Phalombe	-37.1	+144.7	—	-10.9
Ngabu[c]	-41.7	+143.6	—	-12.9
Mangochi	-17.0	+149.3	—	-15.6
Chitipa	—	—	-83.3	—
Salima	—	—	-54.2	—

— = Not applicable.

a. The profit data from 1971–72 through 1983–84 are the average of the individual rates for each year; data for 1978–79 and 1980–81 are missing. The estimated profit markups from the prices paid to the smallholders are estimated from such data for seven years and the data of the ratio of profits to sales for the entire period.

b. The profit and subsidy data reported for 1977 are calculated on the basis of export prices plus transportation costs to the designated locale; the tax or subsidy rate is the ratio of such export prices to the ADMARC price minus unity.

c. Ngabu is sometimes written Mgabu.

Mangochi received still lower subsidies or higher tax rates. If similar comparisons had been made for tobacco, groundnuts, and cotton, a large and differentiated regional tax would have been shown as well.

The data on profit rates for this table come from ADMARC, *Annual Report*, and World Bank (May 1981a), p. 90. Data on the average ratios of ADMARC to export prices come from Pryor (1988b), section C. The other data come from World Bank (February 1981), p. 93, and World Bank (May 1981a), pp. 50–58.

ADMARC *Profits*

The literature on Malaŵi contains various conflicting series on ADMARC profits. The data of Brown (1970b), pp. 37–52, differ from mine; he examined operations in only three crops, and whether he also included administrative costs is unclear. My data in table G-3 also differ from series presented by Robert E. Christiansen, in Fyfe and others (1985), pp. 407–70, in that I followed ADMARC's procedure for accounting for these overhead costs in its published reports rather than following Christiansen's adjustments.

Crop Specialization and Credit Constraints

The perverse crop specialization in Malaŵi is briefly discussed in the text. That discussion rests strongly on some pioneering work by Paul Collier (Collier 1985, and Collier and Lal 1986).

In 1977–78 the gross margins (that is, gross revenues minus the costs of seeds, wood, fertilizer, and other inputs) for local maize, groundnuts, and tobacco were respectively 53, 82, and 99 MK per hectare, and these crops required, respectively, 766, 1,490, and 3,215 work hours per hectare, according to Chipande (1983a). Thus tobacco is considerably more labor intensive than local maize and, other things equal, should have been the crop of choice on farms with small amounts of land per worker. The situation is not complicated by possibilities of double-cropping, because irrigation is available only on a minuscule portion of the arable land. In general, food crops in Malaŵi are said to be less labor intensive than tobacco or other cash crops.

The data in table G-4 do not validate this hypothesis. The smallest farms grow relatively more capital-using crops, and the largest farms grow relatively more labor-using crops (although, of course, the production of capital-using food crops constitutes by far the largest land use for all farms, independent of size). I provide an explanation of this phenomenon in chapter 5, in which the discussion focuses on the ways Malaŵi smallholders face risk.

Table G-3. Macroindicators of ADMARC's Pricing Policies, 1964 to 1985–86

	Total profits		Trading profits			
Year	MK (thousands)	Percentage of GDP	MK (thousands)	Percentage of GDP	Percentage of farmer receipts	Percentage of smallholder value added
1964	730	0.5	n.a.	n.a.	n.a.	n.a.
1965	980	0.6	n.a.	n.a.	n.a.	n.a.
1966	80	0.0	n.a.	n.a.	n.a.	n.a.
1967	-3,628	-1.9	n.a.	n.a.	n.a.	n.a.
1968	116	0.1	n.a.	n.a.	n.a.	n.a.
1969–70	4,030	1.9	3,977	1.9	39.5	n.a.
1970–71	2,667	1.1	2,660	1.1	19.6	n.a.
1971–72	8,892	3.1	8,715	3.0	62.4	n.a.
1972–73	6,075	2.0	6,327	2.0	38.4	n.a.
1973–74	8,463	2.5	8,111	2.4	56.6	7.0
1974–75	10,816	2.5	11,031	2.5	64.3	7.7
1975–76	7,369	1.5	9,977	2.0	48.8	6.3
1976–77	23,739	4.1	22,685	3.9	98.5	11.6
1977–78	17,395	2.5	30,040	4.4	107.8	12.7
1978–79	2,616	0.4	4,181	0.6	13.7	1.7
1979–80	-4,682	-0.6	70	0.0	0.2	0.0
1980–81	-6,197	-0.7	326	0.0	1.1	0.1
1981–82	618	0.1	8,863	0.9	30.7	2.1
1982–83	3,043	0.3	12,219	1.1	29.1	2.6
1983–84	7,914	0.6	6,550	0.5	14.2	1.2
1984–85	4,350	0.3	n.a.	n.a.	n.a.	n.a.
1985–86[a]	-26,028	-1.4	n.a.	n.a.	n.a.	n.a.
Average	—	0.9	—	1.8	41.7	4.8

n.a. = Not available.
— = Not applicable.
Note: The fiscal year ends in March. The denominators of the percentages reported in the table are for the year in which the fiscal year began.
a. Preliminary.
Source: Total profits of ADMARC (and its predecessor agency, the Farmers Marketing Board)—Malaŵi, Minister of Finance, *Public Sector Financial Statistics* (irregular); and Malaŵi, Office of the President and Planning, Economic Planning Division, *Economic Report 1986*, p. 98. Trading profits and total payments to smallholders—ADMARC, *Annual Report;* and World Bank (February 1982), p. 40. GDP and value-added data—Pryor (1988b), section C, and the sources cited therein.

Table G-4. Indicators of Crop Specialization, Malaŵi, 1968–69 and 1980–81

	Farm size (hectares)					
Indicator	Less than 0.81	0.81– 1.61	1.62– 2.42	2.43– 4.85	More than 4.85	Average
1968–69 crop year						
Hectares per "man equivalent"[a]	0.21	0.44	0.66	0.96	1.71	0.56
Share of planted land devoted to food crops (percent)[b]	88.3	86.4	86.6	84.3	82.5	85.4
Cash crop receipts						
Per hectare (MK)	2.55	2.88	3.53	5.56	5.76	4.16
As share of total cash receipts (percent)	27.7	42.7	49.9	58.0	62.7	50.7

	Less than 0.50	0.50– 0.99	1.00– 1.49	1.50– 1.99	2.00– 2.99	More than 2.99	Average
1980–81 crop year							
Hectares per "man equivalent"[a]	0.14	0.29	0.46	0.60	0.75	1.01	0.43
Share of planted land devoted to food crops (percent)[b]	88.9	86.2	81.2	77.9	74.7	74.6	81.5

Note: Because of mixed stands, the differences in cropland devoted to noncash crops of smallholdings of various sizes are probably understated, especially in 1968–69, when most of the planted land was used for mixed stands.

a. "Man equivalents" are calculated from estimates of family composition. A "man" is defined as a male between 15 to 60; a woman in the same age group, as 0.8 man; and all others in the family, as 0.3 man.

b. Food crops are considered to be maize, pulses, cassava, millet, sorghum, and potatoes.

Source: Various tables in Malaŵi Government (1970) and (1984).

The apparent increase in relative cash crop production of the largest farms between the two years may reflect a statistical artifact in that mixed-stand production was much greater in the earlier agricultural year. Therefore, the area devoted to cash crops may have been underestimated.

H. Additional Source Materials for Chapter 9

Estimates of French land holdings in Madagascar are conflicting. Useful data come from France République, Services des domaines et de la propriété fonciere (1922); Madagascar, Ministère des finances et de commerce, and INSRE (1966); Desjeux (1979), pp. 49 ff.; Gendarme (1960); Heseltine (1971), pp. 151 ff.; and Minelle (1959), pp. 340 ff.

A number of surveys focus on the actual land farmed by foreign colonists. For the agricultural year 1955–56 Minelle estimated the actual land farmed by European colonists as 104,000 hectares, or about 6 percent of the total land under cultivation. Survey data for 1956 reported by Heseltine, pp. 151 and 193, showed 6,000 French citizens naming agriculture as their main occupation; a somewhat later survey indicated that these farmers, plus about 1,000 French citizens from Réunion, were farming 89,000 hectares. In the agricultural year 1961–62 an agricultural census (Ministère des finances et de commerce, and INSRE p. 25) placed the area of the farms larger than 5 hectares (citizenship of the owners unspecified) as 7.4 percent of the total cultivated area. In 1970 the Ministère du développement rural et de la réforme agraire (*Annuaire statistique agricole,* 1970) reported 2,849 "grand concessions" (origin of owners also unspecified, but other data suggest that by this time many of these owners were Malagasy) with a total area of 172,464 hectares, or an average of 60.5 hectares, representing about 6.0 percent of total cultivated land. All of these results appear roughly consistent.

Total land area owned by foreigners appears to have been much greater, however. For example, for 1955–56 Gendarme (pp. 129 ff.) shows that 4,149 concessions comprising 691,682 hectares were definitively granted and another 3,665 concessions comprising 243,370 hectares were provisional; his data had to be supplemented by several small estimates of my own. Thompson and Adloff (1965), pp. 330 and 335, place the land granted to large concessions at 900,000 hectares and then note that a 1956 study showed 2.5 million hectares of land had been registered, of which the concessionaires had permanent title to 600,000 hectares and temporary titles to 1.4 million hectares. For support, they cite Gendarme, but how they arrived at a result so different from my reading of his data is unclear.

Lacking access to the original sources, I have no way of reconciling these diverse statements about total land ownership. Clearly, total foreign-owned land was considerably larger than the actual amount farmed. Furthermore, according to the discussion by Thompson and Adloff, foreign concessionaires had developed less than half of the land they owned. In the late 1950s the Tsiranana government rapidly obtained about 250,000 hectares of land by means of a tax on unimproved land; in later years it took still more land in this way.

I. Additional Source Materials for Chapter 16

Sources of Labor for the Increase of Estate Agriculture

According to the data that I could locate, smallholders have been the major source of the employment on the estates, supplemented during the 1970s by some Malaŵians returning from work abroad. I have seen no convincing evidence, as some have claimed, that the growth of the estates has led either to an absolute decline of the men working in the smallholder sector or to an important skewing of the male-female ratio among smallholder workers.

A contrary view is found in three articles: Kydd and Christiansen (1982), Christiansen and Kydd (1983), and Christiansen (1984). Two of these articles present a table showing part-time and full-time employment of males and females in agriculture for 1966 and 1977 and refer the reader to an unpublished article for an explanation of how these estimates were derived. On the basis of these calculations, the authors conclude that the growth of the estates has resulted in a "feminization" of the smallholder sector.

I attempted some estimates on data from the 1966 and 1977 censuses, plus the surveys presented in Malaŵi, NSO, *Reported Employment and Earnings: Annual Report*, which start in the late 1960s, but I have been unable to replicate the results or the conclusions these two articles reached. According to my estimates, from the middle 1960s to the early 1980s the number of female workers in the "modern sector" increased at an average annual rate of about 10 percent, while male workers increased about 7 percent a year. No reasonable estimates about the proportion of part-time workers in the later years (data on this matter are available only for 1966) and about the size of the smallholder sector yield the results that Kydd and Christiansen published on the ratios of males and females in this sector.

Regional and Ethnic Income Differences

In Malaŵi considerable policy concern has been expressed about the "dead North," and the consensus seems to be that the average level of income increases as one moves from the Northern to the Southern Region. These alleged income differences have also been used to explain the net migration from the north to the south (a matter discussed in greater detail in chapter 5).

The Northern Region contains the most unused arable land in the country and has the highest level of education. The better education is explained by the relatively greater number of missionary schools established in that region during the colonial period (starting with David Livingstone). Data on the level of education of the population (for example, average school attainment and level of literacy), which are presented on a regional level, and data on the northerners' share of jobs requiring advanced education or skills both reflect this educational advantage. According to Selby Hickey Joffee (1973), in 1970 northerners held more than half of the professional positions in the civil service; furthermore, they held more than 60 percent of the law degrees and more than 70 percent of the doctorates in the nation. Joffee also details how immediately after independence the government favored the north as a recipient of development expenditures, especially for roads and bridges, even though its inhabitants were not the politically dominant ethnic group. Chapter 17 explores some aspects of this greater level of education of the northerners.

The data in table I-1 reveal that the difference in average family incomes of smallholders in the three regions in Malaŵi was small in 1968–69—a conclusion that differs from the conventional wisdom. The nutrition data discussed in chapter 16 also suggest a lack of significant income differences among the three regions in this early year. By 1984–85 income differences had widened between the smallholders of the Southern Region, where average family income was now lowest, and those of the Central and Northern Regions. The common misperception about the relatively low incomes in the Northern Region has probably arisen because most of Malaŵi's urban areas are in the Southern Region; also the north has less than its share of economic infrastructure such as roads.

An important implication of these results is that a number of the government's policies to subsidize the north were misguided. For instance, ADMARC, the parastatal crop marketing board, has paid the same prices across the entire country, even though transportation costs have been much higher in the north. The data have some other interesting implications as well. The Central Region, which had the lowest average smallholder income in 1968–69, had the highest in 1984–85. The dominant ethnic group in this region is the Chewa, from which the Life President stems. The relatively low agricultural incomes in the Southern Region may relate to its having the highest land densities (Pryor 1988b, section A) and the most rural overcrowding, so

Table I-1. Indicators of Regional Inequalities, Malaŵi and Madagascar, Selected Years

Region and agricultural development district	Average family income of smallholders (MK) 1968–69	1984–85	Urban population, 1977 (percent)	Adult literacy rate, 1977[a] (percent) Male	Female
Malaŵi	86.42	358.2	8.5	40.8	17.4
Northern region	89.16	470.9	6.9	61.5	32.2
Karonga	n.a.	450.9	n.a.	n.a.	n.a.
Mzuzu	n.a.	476.8	n.a.	n.a.	n.a.
Central region	83.79	472.5	6.4	37.9	16.8
Kasungu	n.a.	538.8	n.a.	n.a.	n.a.
Salima	n.a.	430.7	n.a.	n.a.	n.a.
Lilongwe	n.a.	437.7	n.a.	n.a.	n.a.
Southern region	87.57	251.6	10.5	38.4	14.3
Liwonde	n.a.	215.1	n.a.	n.a.	n.a.
Blantyre	n.a.	261.9	n.a.	n.a.	n.a.
Ngabu	n.a.	354.3	n.a.	n.a.	n.a.

Province	Average family income, rural sector (thousands of FMG) 1962	1980	Urban population, 1975 (percent)	Adult literacy rate, 1965[a] (percent) Male	Female
Madagascar	60.9	226.9	16.3	50	29
Antananarivo	76.6	256.0	26.2	77	56
Fianarantsoa	51.8	218.8	10.2	47	23
Toamasina	55.4	178.3	11.8	45	20
Mahajunga	70.7	183.4	15.0	41	18
Antsiranana	51.1	256.1	22.1	48	23
Toliary	69.1	267.6	9.1	25	15

n.a. = Not available.
a. For both countries "adult" includes all those over 14 years of age.

Source: Malaŵi—income data, sources described in Pryor (1988b), section I (income data for all districts are multiplied by the same adjustment coefficient); urban and literacy data, Malaŵi, NSO (1984), vol. I, pp. 26–27 and 142. Madagascar—income data, François and others (1967), p. 37, and Madagascar, Banque de données d'état (1987a), p. 1; other data, Madagascar, INSRE (n.d.[f]), p. 11, and (n.d.[c]), p. 63.

the effects of diminishing returns in agriculture are most apparent there. Another possible causal factor is related to ethnicity and religion; the Liwonde Agricultural Development District in the Southern Region had the highest concentration of Muslims, who are allegedly the least willing to change their traditional farming methods. The reasons underlying the marked change in average smallholder incomes in different areas of the country deserve much closer study.

The lower part of table I-1 shows average family incomes in Madagascar in the rural sector in the different provinces. The range (in percentages) in average income between the poorest and richest provinces was less than between the Agricultural Development Districts in Malaŵi and did not appear to have increased very much over time. Other indicators of regional differences, such as urbanization rates and adult literacy rates, were more unequal than in Malaŵi.

Table I-2 shows that average rural incomes and literacy rates were considerably more unequal among ethnic groups than among regions. Incomes and literacy rates were highest among the Merina, the largest ethnic group, in contrast to Malaŵi, where the largest ethnic groups—the Chewa and the Nyanja—are located in the Central and Southern Regions, where the literacy rates have been lowest (the Malaŵi statistics do not cross-tabulate data on literacy and income by ethnic group).

In Madagascar income, literacy, and ethnic dominance have shown much stronger correlation than in Malaŵi. This, in turn, appears to give regional politics there more intensity. A number of unfortunate location choices for manufacturing plants in the late 1970s were probably the result of these regional tensions (chapter 14).

Changes in Illiteracy by Regions in Madagascar

The recent agricultural census in Madagascar allows some useful glimpses into the regional allocation of educational funds. A comparison of the degree of illiteracy in 1984–85 of the population between six and twelve years old (educated after 1973) and of the population fifteen years and over (usually educated before 1970) implies that educational expenditures have become more regionally equalized. The remarks in chapter 16 are based on table I-3.

Notes on Table 16-4

The World Health Organization publishes tables on the distribution of children according to their body sizes (WHO 1983). These tables permit easy determination of whether the height, weight, or weight-height ratios for any child of a specified age fall 2 standard deviations or 10 percentage points below the median. No standard method has developed for reporting the results of nutritional surveys, however. Because I have chosen to report the results according to percentages of the median, the data presented in standard deviations must be adjusted accordingly. The problem is complicated because the distribution statistics of body sizes of the children from the country under study are not known.

Table I-2. Indicators of Ethnic Inequalities in Madagascar

Ethnic group	Literacy rate, 1965 (percent)[a] Male	Literacy rate, 1965 (percent)[a] Female	Average rural incomes, 1962 (thousands of FMG)
Merina	74	52	81.8
Betsileo	66	44	62.8
Betsimaraka	40	17	49.1
Tsimihety	41	14	58.4
Sakalava	36	18	54.6
Sihanaka	—	—	66.3
Bara	—	—	58.3
Antanosy	—	—	53.5
Antaisaka	—	—	52.3
Antaimoro	—	—	46.8
Mahafaly	—	—	43.6
Antandroy	—	—	41.6
Antaifasy	—	—	41.1
Tanala	—	—	40.8
Ethnic groups of southeast	39	17	—
Ethnic groups of south	14	3	—

— Not available.
a. Includes only those 15 years of age and over.
Source: Literacy rate, Madagascar, INSRE (n.d. [c]), p. 63; income data, François (1967), tome 3.

Methods of varying degrees of sophistication can be used to make this adjustment. For presentation in table 16-6, I have chosen to use a simple proportional adjustment because the cut-off points for either method of reporting the data are not very different. This method can be illustrated by a numerical example. Assume that 30 percent of the children of Country X have a weight less than 2 standard deviations from the WHO median weight. From the WHO tables, this represents 78.427 percent of the median weight. Then 30 x .9803 (that is, 78.43/80.00), or 29.41 percent, of the children have weights below 80 percent of the median.

I have estimated the ratio of 2 standard deviations from the median by calculating an average of this ratio for both boys and girls for ten different age groups from birth up to sixty months. The adjustment factor for weight (2 standard deviations to 80 percent of the median) is .9803; for height (2 standard deviations to 90 percent of the median), 1.0240; for the weight-height ratio (2 standard deviations to 80 percent of the median), 1.0349.

Table I-3. Illiteracy by Sex, Age Group, and Region, Rural Madagascar, 1984–85
(percent)

	Both sexes		Men		Women	
Province	6–12 years	15 and over	6–12 years	15 and over	6–12 years	15 and over
All Madagascar	31.9	38.3	31.4	29.7	32.3	47.0
Antananarivo	24.3	16.9	25.0	11.5	23.5	22.7
Fianarantsoa	27.6	36.7	28.3	26.4	27.0	47.3
Toamasina	28.7	36.5	26.7	28.1	30.6	45.0
Mahajunga	29.6	50.7	30.5	37.8	28.7	63.6
Antsiranana	19.5	41.6	19.2	30.3	19.7	53.1
Toliary	57.4	66.3	60.5	57.1	54.2	75.2

Source: Madagascar, Ministère de la production agricole et de la réforme agraire, and FAO (1988c), vol. 3, table xv.

Bibliography

ADMARC (Agricultural Development and Marketing Corporation). Annual. *Annual Report.* Limbe.

Ahlers, Théodore, and others. 1984. *Etude du secteur rizicole: Rapport final.* Somerville, Mass.: Associates for International Resources and Development.

Althabe, Gérard. 1969. *Oppression et libération dans l'imaginaire.* Paris: Maspero.

Andriamananjara, Rajaona. 1974. *The Investment Code, 1973.* Antananarivo: Imprimerie nationale.

Archer, Robert. 1976. *Madagascar depuis 1972: La marche d'une révolution.* Paris: l'Harmattan.

Arhin, Kwame, and others. 1985. *Marketing Boards in Tropical Africa.* London: KPI Ltd.

Asiwaju, A. I. 1976. *Western Yorubaland under European Rule, 1889–1945: A Comparative Analysis of French and English Colonialism.* London: Longman.

Askari, Hossein, and John Thomas Cummings. 1976. *Agricultural Supply Response: A Survey of the Econometric Evidence.* New York: Praeger.

Baker, Colin. 1972. "The Administrative Service of Malaŵi—A Case Study of Africanization," *Journal of Modern African Studies* 10(4): 543–60.

Banks, Arthur S. 1985. *Political Handbook of the World, 1984–1985.* Binghamton, N.Y.: CSA Publications.

Barber, James Davis. 1972. *The Presidential Character: Predicting Performance in the White House.* Englewood Cliffs, N.J.: Prentice-Hall.

Barker, William J. 1961. *The Economy of British Central Africa.* London: Oxford University Press.

Bastian, G. 1967. *Madagascar: Etude géographique et économique.* Paris: Fernand Nathan.

Bates, Robert H. 1984. *Markets and States in Tropical Africa: The Political Basis of Agricultural Policies.* Berkeley: University of California Press.

Battistini, René, and G. Richard-Vindard, eds. 1972. *Biogeography and Ecology of Madagascar.* The Hague: Junk.

Berg, Elliot. 1989. "The Liberalization of Rice Marketing in Madagascar," *World Development* 17(6): 719–28.

Berthélemy, J. C., and Christian Morrisson. 1987. "Manufactured Goods Supply and Cash Crops in Sub-Saharan Africa," *World Development* 15 (10/11): 1353–67.

Berthélemy, J. C., and others. 1988. *The Supply of Manufactured Goods and Agricultural Development*. Paris: OECD Development Center.

Bettison, David G. 1958. "The Demographic Structure of Seventeen Villages in the Peri-Urban Area of Blantyre-Limbe, Nyasaland," *Communication of the Rhodes-Livingstone Institute* 9. Lusaka.

Bharier, Julian. 1980. "Improving Rural Water in Malaŵi," *Finance and Development* 15(2): 34–37.

Birnberg, Thomas B., and Stephen A. Resnick. 1975. *Colonial Development: An Econometric Study*. New Haven: Yale University Press.

Blades, D. W. 1970. "Foreign/Malaŵi Ownership of Manufacturing Gross Output, 1967." National Statistical Office Research Paper 7. Zomba.

Blanc-Pamart, Chantale, and others. 1984. *La SOMALAC à Madagascar: Production, organisation et économie de riz*. Paris: Ministère des relations extérieures.

Bloch, Maurice. 1971. *Placing the Dead: Tombs, Ancestral Villages and Kinship Organization in Madagascar*. Ann Arbor: University of Michigan Press.

Boeder, Robert B. 1974. "Malaŵians Abroad: The History of Labor Emigration from Malaŵi to its Neighbors." Ph.D. dissertation, Michigan State University. East Lansing, Michigan.

Bose, Swadesh, and others. n.d. "Export Crop Parastatals in Eastern Africa: A Study of Comparative Trading Efficiency." World Bank internal memorandum, Washington, D.C.

Boserup, Ester. 1970. *Women's Role in Economic Development*. New York: St. Martin's Press.

Braun, Gerald, and Heribert Weiland. 1980. "Die Entwicklung der Republik Malaŵi zwischen Freiwillige Abhängigkeit und Autoritärer Grundbedurfnisstrategie," *Verfassung und Recht in Übersee* 13:339–59.

Bray, Francesca. 1986. *The Rice Economies: Technology and Development in Asian Societies*. Oxford: Blackwell.

Brown, C. P. 1970a. "Aspects of Smallholder Decisions Regarding the Allocation of Farm Resources in Malaŵi," *Rhodesian Journal of Economics* 4(3):38–50.

———. 1970b. "The Malaŵi Farmers Marketing Board," *Eastern Africa Economic Review* 2(1): 37–52

———. 1970c. "The Marketing of Primary Produce." Processed.

Brown, Gilbert. 1981. "Malaŵi: Basic Needs." World Bank internal report 3461-MAI, Washington, D.C.

Brunt, M. A. 1983. "Environmental Effects of Development: Malaŵi." Zomba: Food and Agricultural Organization.

Bunge, Frederica M., ed. 1983. *Indian Ocean: Five Island Countries.* Washington, D.C.: Government Printing Office.

Cadoux, Charles. 1969. *La république malgache.* Paris: Editions Berger-Levrault.

Camacho, Martine. 1982. "Bilan de la politique de coopérativisation de l'agriculture," *Terre malgache/Tany malagasy* 21 (August): 155–81.

———. 1986. *Les poubelles de la survie: La décharge municipale de Tananarive.* Paris: l'Harmattan.

Central African Federation of Rhodesia and Nyasaland, Central Statistical Office. 1964. *National Accounts and Balance of Payments of Northern Rhodesia, Nyasaland and Southern Rhodesia.* Salisbury.

Chaigneau, Pascal. 1981. "Madagascar: De la première république à l'orientation socialiste." Thèse pour le Doctorat de 3ème cycle de sociologie politique, Université de Paris X, Nanterre.

———. 1984–85. "Un état à orientation socialiste: Madagascar." Thèse pour le Doctorat d'état ès lettres et sciences humaines, Université de Paris X, Nanterre.

———. 1985. *Rivalitées politiques et socialisme à Madagascar.* Paris: Centre des hautes études sur l'Afrique et l'Asie modernes.

Chamley, Christophe, and others. 1985. "Tax Policy for Malaŵi." World Bank internal memorandum, Washington, D.C.

Channock, Martin. 1972. "The Political Economy of Independent Agriculture in Colonial Malaŵi: The Great War to the Great Depression," *Journal of Social Science* 1(1).

Chenery, Hollis, and Moises Syrquin. 1975. *Patterns of Development, 1950–1970.* New York: Oxford University Press.

Chhibaer, Ajay. n.d. "Taxation and Aggregate Savings: An Econometric Analysis for Three Sub-Saharan Countries." World Bank internal memorandum, Washington, D.C.

Chikhula, Prainy Lucian. 1984. "The Implementation of Basic Human Needs as a Tool of Economic Development: Some Evidence from Malaŵi's Sectoral Growth." Ph.D. dissertation, State University of New York, Buffalo.

Chimango, L. J. 1977. "The Money Lender in Court," *Journal of Social Science* 6: 83–96.

Chimwaza, Beatrice Mary. 1982. "Food and Nutrition in Malaŵi." Ph.D. dissertation, Faculty of Science, University of London, London.

Chipande, Graham H. R. 1983a. "Labor Availability and Smallholder Agricultural Development: The Case of Lilongwe Land Development Programme." World Employment Programme Research Work Paper WEP 10-6/WP61. Geneva: World Labour Office.

———. 1983b. "Smallholder Agriculture as a Rural Development Strategy." Ph.D. dissertation, University of Glasgow.

Chipeta, Chinyamata. 1976a. "Family Farm Organization and Commercialization of Agriculture." Ph.D. dissertation, Washington University, St. Louis, Missouri.

———. 1976b. "The Role of Trade Unions and Employers' Associations in Economic Development and Employment Creation in Malaŵi." Geneva: International Institute of Labour Studies.

———. 1982. *Economics of Indigenous Labor*. New York: Vantage Press.

Chisiza, D. K. 1963. "The Outlook for Contemporary Africa," *Journal of Modern African Studies* 1(1): 25–38.

Christiansen, Robert E. 1984. "The Pattern of Internal Migration in Response to Structural Change in the Economy of Malaŵi, 1966–1977," *Development and Change* 15(1): 125–51.

Christiansen, Robert E., and Jonathan Kydd. 1983. "The Return of the Malaŵian Labor from South Africa and Zimbabwe," *Journal of Modern African Studies* 21(2): 311–25.

———. 1986. "The Political Economy of Agricultural Policy Formulation in Malaŵi." Paper presented to the World Bank, Washington, D.C.

Christiansen, Robert E., and Lee Ann Stackhouse. 1989. "The Privatization of Agricultural Trading in Malaŵi," *World Development* 17(6): 729–40.

Club des amis de la S.T.A.R., ed. 1971. *Nouvelles 1971*. Antananarivo: Imprimerie des arts graphiques.

Colander, David C., ed. 1984. *Neoclassical Political Economy: The Analysis of Rent-Seeking and DUP Activities*. Cambridge, Mass.: Ballinger.

Coleman, G. 1973. "International Labour Migration from Malaŵi, 1875–1966," *Journal of Social Sciences* (University of Malaŵi) 2.

Collier, Paul. 1985. "The Allocation of Factors in African Peasant Agriculture." World Bank internal memorandum, Washington, D.C.

Collier, Paul, and Deepak Lal. 1986. *Labour and Poverty in Kenya, 1900–1980*. Oxford: Clarendon Press.

Colman, D. R., and G. K. Garbett. 1975. "Economic and Sociological Issues in the Development of the Lower Shire Valley." Manchester. Processed.

Conference on Design and Implementation of Rural Development Strategies and Programmes in Malaŵi. 1985–86. Lilongwe.

Constantine, F., and others. 1979. *Les entreprises publiques en Afrique noire*. Vol. I. Paris: Pedone.

Covell, Maureen. 1987. *Madagascar: Politics, Economics and Society*. New York: Columbia University Press.

Dean, Edwin. 1966. *The Supply Responses of African Farmers: Theory and Measurement in Malaŵi*. Amsterdam: North Holland.

Deane, Phyllis. 1953. *Colonial Social Accounting*. Cambridge: Cambridge University Press.

de Bandt, Jacques, Benoît Boussemart, and Jean-Claude Rabier. 1986. "L'industrie malgache: Conditions et scénarios de développement." Antananarivo.

de Bandt, Jacques, Benoît Boussemart, Jean-Claude Rabier, and K. Sipek. 1984. "Madagascar: La gestion du système des prix industriels." Paris.

Deleris, Ferdinand. 1987. *Ratsiraka: Socialisme et misère à Madagascar.* Paris: l'Harmattan.

Dequin, Horst. 1970. *Agricultural Development in Malaŵi.* 2nd. ed. Munich: IFO Institut für Wirtschaftsforschung.

Deschamps, Hubert. 1959. *Les migrations intérieures passées et présentes à Madagascar.* Paris: Berger-Levrault.

Desjeux, Dominique. 1979. *La question agraire à Madagascar: Administration et paysannat de 1985 à nos jours.* Paris: l'Harmattan.

Dethier, Jean-Jacques, and J. Dirck Stryker. 1985. "Comparative Study of the Political Economy of Agricultural Pricing Policies: Madagascar Case Study." World Bank internal report, Washington, D.C.

Dez, Jacques. 1962. "Developpement économique et tradition à Madagascar," *Cahier de l'institut de sciences économiques appliquées* series V(4): 79–108.

Dilg, Karl-Heinz. 1973. *Malaŵi, Voraussetzungen und Möglichkeiten der industriellen Entwicklung: Afrika Industrieberichte 17.* Hamburg: Afrika Verein.

du Bois de Gaudusson, Jean. 1979. "Madagascar: Des enterprises publiques aux entreprises socialistes." In F. Constantine and others, eds., *Les entreprises publiques en Afrique noire.* Vol. I. Paris: Pedone.

———. 1985. "Madagascar: A Case of Revolutionary Pragmatism," *Journal of Communist Studies* 1(3/4): 101–22.

Dumont, René. 1959. "Les principaux problèmes d'orientation et de modernisation de l'agriculture malgache." Manuscript on deposit in the CITE library, Antananarivo.

———. 1961. "Les principales conditions d'un rapid developpement de l'agriculture malgache." Manuscript on deposit in the CITE library, Antananarivo.

Ettema, Wim. 1984. "Small Scale Industry in Malaŵi," *Journal of Modern African Studies* 22(3): 487–511.

Fei, John C. H., Gustav Ranis, and Shirley W. Y. Kuo. 1980. *Growth with Equity: The Taiwan Case.* New York: Oxford University Press.

Fieldhouse, D. K. 1986. *Black Africa, 1945–1980: Economic Decolonialization and Arrested Development.* London: Allen and Unwin.

Fields, Gary S. 1975. *Poverty, Inequality, and Development.* Cambridge: Cambridge University Press.

FOFIFA and Madagascar, Ministère de la production agricole et de la réforme agraire. 1983. "Highland Rice Report." Working paper. Antananarivo.

Food and Agricultural Organization (FAO). Annual. *Production Yearbook.* Rome.

France, Ministère de la coopération. 1963. *Economie et plan de développement, République malgache.* Paris.

———. 1986. "Déséquilibres structurels et programmes d'adjustement à Madagascar." Paris.

François, Patrick J., and Commissariat général au plan, Institut national de la statistique et de la recherche économique. 1967. *Budgets et alimentations des ménages ruraux, Rapport de synthèse.* Paris: Imprimerie SPIT.

Frey, Bruno S., and Freidrich Schneider. 1986. "Competing Models of International Lending Activity," *Journal of Development Economics* 20: 225–45.

Fyfe, Christopher, and others, eds. 1985. *Malaŵi: An Alternative Pattern of Development.* Centre for African Studies, Seminar Proceedings 25, Edinburgh University. Edinburgh.

Gendarme, René. 1960. *L'économie de Madagascar: Diagnostic et perspectives de développement.* Paris: Editions Cujas.

Ghai, Dharam, and Samir Radwan, eds. 1983. *Agrarian Policies and Rural Poverty in Africa.* Geneva: International Labour Office.

Gifford, Prosser, and William Roger Louis. 1971. *France and Britain in Africa: Imperial Rivalry and Colonial Rule.* New Haven: Yale University Press.

Giles, B. D. 1979. "Economists in Government: The Case of Malaŵi," *Journal of Development Studies* 15(2): 216–33.

Glenshaw, Peter, and David Harmon. 1985. *Madagascar: Assessment of the Climate for Private Sector Development and Investment.* Washington, D.C.: International Science and Technology Institute, Inc.

Gondwe, Blackmore C. J. 1972. "L'influence de l'aide extérieure dans l'évolution du Malaŵi contemporain." Ph.D. dissertation, Université de Provence, Aix-en-Provence, France.

Gondwe, Derick Kanyerere. 1977. "The Incidence and Economic Effects of Indirect Taxation in Malaŵi." Ph.D. dissertation, University of Manitoba, Winnipeg, Canada.

Gordenker, Leon. c. 1976. *International Aid and National Decisions: Development Programs in Malaŵi, Tanzania, and Zambia.* Princeton, N.J.: Princeton University Press.

Gordon, J. G. 1971. *A Model for Estimating Future Agricultural Acreage and Production in Malaŵi.* Agrarian Development Studies 4. London: Wye College.

Gulhati, Ravi, and Viaml Atukorala. n.d. "Import Instability and External Reserves in Eastern and Southern Africa." World Bank internal memorandum, Washington, D.C.

Hazlewood, Arthur, ed. 1967. *African Integration and Disintegration.* London: Oxford University Press.

Hazlewood, Arthur, and P.D. Henderson. 1960. *The Economics of Federation.* Oxford: Basil Blackwell.

Heller, Peter S., and Alan A. Tait. 1984. "Government Employment and Pay: Some International Comparisons." International Monetary Fund Occasional Paper. Washington, D.C.

Heseltine, Nigel. 1971. *Madagascar.* New York: Praeger.

Hesp, Paul. 1985. *Producer Prices in Tropical Africa*. Research Reports 23/1985, African Studies Centre. Leiden.

Hewitt, Adrian, and Jonathan Kydd. 1984. "A Study of the Effectiveness of Aid to Malaŵi." Paper submitted to the Task Force on Concessional Loans of the World Bank/IMF Development Committee. Washington, D.C.

Heyneman, Steven. 1981. "Malaŵi: The Development of Human Capital." World Bank internal report 3462-MAI, Washington, D.C.

Hicks, J. R. 1979. *Causality in Economics*. Oxford: Blackwells.

Hirsche, R. 1986. *Rapport final d'une mission de réflexion sur le secteur rizicol malgache*. Vol. II. N.p.: C.C.C.E.

Hirschman, Albert O. 1973. "The Changing Tolerance for Income Inequality in the Course of Economic Development," *Quarterly Journal of Economics* 87(4): 544–65.

Hirschmann, David, and Megan Vaughan. 1984. *Women Farmers of Malaŵi: Food Production in the Zomba Region*. Institute of International Studies Research Series 58. Berkeley: University of California.

Hough, Jerry F. 1986. *The Struggle for the Third World: Soviet Debates and American Options*. Washington, D.C.: Brookings Institution.

Hugon, Philippe. 1976. *Economie et enseignement à Madagascar*. Paris: Institut international de planification de l'éducation, UNESCO.

———. 1986. "La crise économique à Madagascar et l'intervention de Funds Monétaire International," *Canadian Journal of African Studies* 20(2): 186–218.

———. 1987. "La crise économique à Madagascar," *Afrique contemporaine* 144(4/198): 1–23.

Humphrey, David H. 1972. "Preliminary Report on the Smallholder Innovation Research Project." Processed.

———. 1973. "Malaŵi's Economic Progress and Prospects," *Eastern African Economic Review* 5(2): 71–105.

International Institute of Strategic Studies. Annual. *The Military Balance*. London.

International Monetary Fund (IMF). Annual(a). *Balance of Payments Yearbook*. Washington, D.C.

———. Annual(b). *Government Finance Statistics Yearbook*. Washington, D.C.

———. Annual(c). *International Financial Statistics Yearbook*. Washington, D.C.

———. Monthly. *International Monetary Statistics*. Washington, D.C.

———. 1971. *Surveys of African Economies*. Vol. IV. Washington, D.C.

International Service for National Agricultural Research (ISNAR). 1982. "A Review of the Agricultural Research System of Malaŵi." The Hague.

———. 1983. "La recherche agricole à Madagascar: Bilan et perspectives du FOFIFA, Rapport au gouvernement de la Repoblika Demokratika Malagasy." ISNAR Report R13. The Hague.

Jackson, E. F., ed. 1965. *Nyasaland Symposium: Economic Development in Africa*. Oxford: Blackwell.

Jelliffe, Derick B. 1966. "Assessment of Nutritional Status of the Community." Monograph Volume 53. Geneva: World Health Organization.

Jelliffe, Derick B., and E. F. Patrice Jelliffe, eds. 1979. *Human Nutrition: A Comprehensive Treatise*. New York: Plenum Press.

Joffe, Selby Hickey. 1973. "Political Culture and Communication in Malaŵi: The Hortatory Regime of Kamuzu Banda." Ph.D. dissertation, Boston University.

Jolly, Alison. 1980. *A World Like Our Own: Man and Nature in Madagascar*. New Haven: Yale University Press.

Jones, Rachel Mai. 1982. "Financing Education." Paper presented at the Social Science Conference on Developments in Malaŵi in the 1980s, University of Malaŵi.

Jones, Robert A., and Roger J. Robinson. 1976. "Income Distribution and Development: Rhodesia and Malaŵi Compared," *Rhodesian Journal of Economics* 10(2): 91–103.

Kadzamire, Z. D. 1977. "Planning for Development in Malaŵi: 1954–1974," *Journal of Social Sciences* (University of Malaŵi) 6: 60–82.

Kettlewell, R. W. 1965. "Agricultural Change in Nyasaland," *Food Research Studies* 5(3): 229–87.

Kinsey, B. J. 1984. "Conflicts between Growth and Equity Objectives in Planning Rural Development Projects: The Lilongwe Land Development Program," *Journal of Social Science* 11(1): 37–46.

Kornfeld, Guy. 1986. "Monsieur Dider Ratsiraka, Président de la République Démocratique de Madagascar, répond aux questions," *Le nouvel observateur* 1128 (June), insert, p. iii.

Kottak, Conrad Phillip. 1980. *The Past in the Present: History, Ecology, and Cultural Variation in Highland Madagascar*. Ann Arbor: University of Michigan Press.

Kravis Irving B., Alan Heston, and Robert Summers. 1982. *World Product and Income: International Comparisons of Real Gross Product*. Baltimore, Md.: Johns Hopkins University Press.

Kydd, Johnathan G. 1977. "The Supply Response of Smallholder Farmers in Malaŵi," *Journal of Social Science* 6:18–28.

———. 1982. *Measuring Peasant Differentiation for Policy Purposes: A Report on a Cluster Analysis Classification of the Population of the Lilongwe Land Development Program: Malaŵi for 1970, 1977*. Zomba: Government Printer.

Kydd, Jonathan G., and Robert E. Christiansen. 1981a. "The Distribution of Income in Malaŵi in 1977." University of Malaŵi, Center for Social Research, Income Distribution Project, Paper No. 1.

———. 1981b. *Trends in the Distribution of Income in Malaŵi since Independence*. Report submitted to the U.N. Department of International and Social Affairs, Contract CON 20/81. Zomba.

———. 1982. "Structural Change in Malaŵi since Independence," *World Development* 10(5): 355–75.

Lal, Deepak. 1986. "Stolper-Samuelson-Rybczynski in the Pacific," *Journal of Development Economics* 21(1): 181–204.

Lavrijsen, J., and J. J. Sterkenburg. 1976. *The Food Supply of Lilongwe, Malaŵi*. Geographical Institute, Geographical Studies 3. Utrecht: University of Utrecht.

Leamer, Edward E. 1987. "Paths of Development in the Three-Factor, n-Good General Equilibrium Model," *Journal of Political Economy* 95(5): 961–1001.

Lecaillon, Jacques, and Dimitri Germidis. 1977. *Inégalité des revenues et développement économique*. Paris: Presses universitaires de France.

Lefebre, Bureau Francis. n.d. "Madagascar: Règlementation des importations." Manuscript on deposit at the Library of the Maison des sciences de l'homme, Paris.

Legum, Colin, and John Drysdale, eds. Annual. *African Contemporary Record*. London: Africa Research.

Lele, Uma. 1975. *The Design of Rural Development: Lessons from Africa*. Baltimore: Johns Hopkins University Press.

Liebenow, J. Gus. 1981. "Malaŵi: Clean Water for the Rural Poor," *American University Field Staff Reports* 40. Washington, D.C.

———. 1982. "Malaŵi's Search for Food Self-Sufficiency," UFSI Reports 30–32, University Field Service Institute.

Loesch, Dieter. 1983. *Markt oder Staat fuer die Dritte Welt? Wirtschaftssystem und Wirtschaftspolitik in Entwicklungslaender am Beispiel der Republic Malaŵi*. Hamburg: Verlag Weltarchiv.

MacBean, Alisdair. 1966. *Export Instability and Economic Development*. London: Allen and Unwin.

Madagascar Government. Irregular. *Journal officiel de la République Démocratique de Madagascar*. Antananarivo.

———. 1980. *Charte des entreprises socialistes*. Antananarivo: Imprimerie nationale.

Madagascar, Banque des données de l'état. 1987a. "Enquête sur les budgets des centres urbains secondaires, 1980: Dépenses." Antananarivo.

———. 1987b. "Enquête sur les budgets des centres urbains secondaires, 1980: Revenues." Antananarivo.

———. 1987c. "Enquête sur les budgets des ménages—milieu rural." Antananarivo.

———. n.d. "Recensement industriel, Années 1983 et 1984." Antananarivo. Processed.

Madagascar, Commissariat général au plan. 1961. *Economie malgache: Evolution 1950–1960*. Antananarivo.

———. 1962. *Rapport sur le développement de Madagascar*. Antananarivo.

———. 1964. *Plan quinquennal*. Antananarivo.

———. 1969. *Cinquième rapport sur l'exécution du 1er plan quinquennal.* Antananarivo.

Madagascar, Direction générale du plan. 1977a. *Les options fondamentales pour la planification socialiste.* Antananarivo. Abbreviated in text *FundOp.*

———. 1977b. *Premier plan, 1978–1980.* Antananarivo.

———. 1978. *Les stratégies axées sur la satisfaction des besoins fondamentaux.* Série "Etude techniques du plan" 13. Antananarivo.

———. 1979a. *Rapport du séminaire sur la planification régionale.* Série "Etudes techniques du plan" 20. Antananarivo.

———. 1979b. *Revenues des ménages urbains et satisfaction des besoins fondamentaux à Madagascar.* Série "Etudes techniques du plan" 22. Antananarivo.

Madagascar, Institut national de la statistique et de la recherche économique (INSRE). n.d.(a). *Comptes économiques de Madagascar en 1962.* Antananarivo.

———. n.d.(b). *Comptes économiques de Madagascar en 1973.* Antananarivo.

———. n.d.(c). *Enquête démographique, Madagascar 1966.* Antananarivo.

———. n.d.(d). *Enquête sur les budgets familaux, milieu urbain, 1977–79, Résultats provisoires.* Antananarivo.

———. n.d.(e). *Les 415 premiers établissements commerciaux de Madagascar, Années 1968–1969.* Antananarivo.

———. n.d.(f). *Recensement 1975: Série études et analyse.* Antananarivo.

———. Annual(a). *Recensement industriel.* Antananarivo.

———. Annual(b). *Situation économique au 1er Janvier.* Antananarivo.

———. 1971. *Population de Madagascar: Situation au 1er Janvier, 1970.* Antananarivo.

Madagascar, INSRE, and République française. 1970. *Comptes économiques de Madagascar, 1966.* Antananarivo and Paris: Imprimerie technigraphie.

Madagascar, Minister of Finance and Planning. 1977. *Basic Social and Economic Data on Madagascar, 1950–1975.* Technical Studies, document 001. Antananarivo.

Madagascar, Ministère d'état, Chargé des finances. 1971. *Journées nationales de la planification du développement.* Antananarivo: Imprimerie nationale.

Madagascar, Ministère de l'enseignement supérieur. 1985. *Evolution de l'enseignement supérieur à Madagascar de 1960 à 1965.* Antananarivo.

Madagascar, Ministère de la population et la condition sociale. n.d. *Enquête sur les enfants de moins de 6 ans, 1981.* Antananarivo.

Madagascar, Ministère de la production agricole et de la réforme agraire. Annual. *Statistiques agricoles: Annuaire.* Antananarivo.

———. 1980. *L'agriculture malgache en chiffres.* Antananarivo.

———. 1986. *Premiers résultats provisiores du recensement national de l'agriculture et des enquêtes connexes.* Antananarivo.

Madagascar, Ministère de la production agricole et de la réforme agraire and FAO. 1988a. *Projet recensement national de l'agriculture et système permanent des statistiques agricoles.* Antananarivo.

———. 1988b. *Projet recensement national de l'agriculture et système permanent des statistiques agricoles.* Vol. II, *Charatéristiques generales du milieu rural.* Antananarivo.

———. 1988c. *Projet recensement national de l'agriculture et système permanent des statistiques agricoles.* Vol. III, *Cultures et superficies des exploitations agricoles.* Antananarivo.

———. 1988d. *Projet recensement national de l'agriculture et système permanent des statistiques agricoles.* Vol V, *Cheptel et equipment des exploitations agricoles.* Antananarivo.

Madagascar, Ministère des finances. Annual. *Statistiques du commerce extérieur de Madagascar.* Antananarivo.

Madagascar, Ministère des finances et du commerce, and INSRE. 1966. *Enquête agricole.* Antananarivo: Imprimerie nationale.

Madagascar, Ministère des travaux publics. 1985. *Schema directeur du grand Antananarivo: Projet de rapport final de synthèse.* Project MAG 82/011. Antananarivo.

Madagascar, Ministère du développement rural et de la réforme agraire. Annual. *Annuaire, Statistiques agricoles.* Antananarivo.

———. 1979. "Cooperative socialiste révolutionnaire de Lohafasika (Ambatondrazi)," *Bulletin d'information* 29–30: 44–45.

———. 1986. *Premiers résultats provisoires du recensement national de l'agriculture et des enquêtes connexes.* Antananarivo.

Madagascar, Ministère du Plan. 1974. *Plan de développement national, 1974–1977.* Antananarivo.

Maddison, Angus. 1990. "The Colonial Burden: A Comparative Perspective." In Maurice Scott and Deepak Lal, Eds., *Public Policy and Economic Development.* Oxford: Clarendon.

Madu, Oliver V. 1978. *Models of Class Domination in Plural Societies of Central Africa.* Washington, D.C.: University Press of America.

Malaŵi Government. 1964. *Development Plan, 1965–69.* Zomba.

———. 1970. *National Sample Survey of Agriculture, 1968/69.* Zomba: Government Printer.

———. 1983. *Urban Household Expenditures Survey, 1979/80.* Zomba: Government Printer.

———. 1984. *National Sample Survey of Agriculture, 1980/81.* Zomba: Government Printer.

Malaŵi, Minister of Agriculture and Natural Resources. Irregular. *Agro-Economic Survey.* Zomba.

———. 1980. *National Rural Development Programme: National Credit Study—Phase 1.* GITEC Consulting, Lilongwe.

Malaŵi, Minister of Education and Culture. 1984. *Education Statistics, Malaŵi 1984.* n.p.

Malaŵi, Minister of Finance. Irregular. *Public Sector Financial Statistics.* Zomba: Government Printer.

Malaŵi, Minister of Finance and Economic Planning Division. 1983. "International Conference of Partners in Economic Development: Past Performance and Prospects for 1983–1987." Lilongwe.

Malaŵi, Minister of Health, WHO, and UNICEF. 1986. *Report of the Joint Program Review of Maternal and Child Health.* Lilongwe.

Malaŵi, NSO (National Statistical Office). Annual(a). *Annual Economic Survey.* Zomba: Government Printer.

———. Annual(b). *Malaŵi Statistical Yearbook.* Zomba: Government Printer.

———. Annual(c). *Reported Employment and Earnings Annual Report.* Zomba: Government Printer.

———. 1969. *Malaŵi Population Census 1966: Final Report.* Zomba: Government Printer.

———. 1970a. *Compendium of Agricultural Statistics.* Zomba: Government Printer.

———. 1970b. *Compendium of Statistics for Malaŵi, 1970.* Zomba: Government Printer.

———. 1970c. *Household Income and Expenditure Survey for Urban Areas and Agricultural Estates, 1968.* Zomba: Government Printer.

———. 1972. *National Accounts Report, 1964–1970.* Zomba: Government Printer.

———. 1980a. Compendium of Agricultural Statistics. Zomba: Government Printer.

———. 1980b. *Malaŵi Population Census, 1977: Final Report.* Zomba: Government Printer.

———. 1983a. *Annual Economic Survey, 1973–1979.* Zomba: Government Printer.

———. 1983b. *National Account Reports, 1973–1979.* Zomba: Government Printer.

———. 1984. *Malaŵi Population Census, 1977: Analytical Report.* Zomba: Government Printer.

———. 1987. *Malaŵi Family Formation Survey 1984.* Zomba: Government Printer.

Malaŵi, Office of the President and Planning, Department of Economic Planning and Development. 1988. *Statement of Development Policies, 1987–1996.* Zomba: Government Printer. Abbreviated in text *DevPol II.*

Malaŵi, Office of the President and Planning, Economic Planning Division. Annual. *Economic Report.* Zomba: Government Printer.

———. 1971. *Statement of Development Policies, 1971–1980.* Zomba: Government Printer. Abbreviated in text *DevPol I.*

———. 1986. "National Physical Development Plan" (draft). Lilongwe.

Malaŵi, Reserve Bank of Malaŵi. Quarterly. *Financial and Economic Review.* Lilongwe.

Mara, Armand. 1986. *Le Ratsirakisme: Un défi*. Antananarivo: Editions CNAPMAD.

Maxwell Stamp Associates, Ltd. 1986. *Etude de politique industrielle à Madagascar*. London: Association internationale de développement.

May, Ernesto. 1985. "Exchange Controls and Parallel Market Economies in Sub-Saharan Africa." World Bank Staff Working Papers 711. Washington, D.C.

McCracken, John. 1984. "Share-Cropping in Malaŵi: The Visiting Tenant System in the Central Province." In Christopher Fyfe and others, eds., *Malaŵi, An Alternative Pattern of Development*, Centre for African Studies, Seminar Proceedings 25, Edinburgh University.

McGowan, Pat, and Thomas H. Johnson. 1984. "African Military Coups d'Etat and Underdevelopment: A Quantitative Historical Analysis," *Journal of Modern African Studies* 22(4); 633–66.

McMaster, Carolyn. 1974. *Malaŵi: Foreign Policy and Development*. New York: St. Martin's Press.

Meier, Gerald M., ed. 1987. *Pioneers in Development*. Second Series. New York: Oxford University Press.

Michaely, Michael. 1984. *Trade, Income Levels, and Dependence*. Amsterdam: North Holland.

Mills, J. C. 1973. "Technology in the Subsistence Sector of Malaŵi." Paper presented at the University of Edinburgh. Processed.

———. 1975. "Price Responses of Malaŵi Smallholder Farmers: Fast, Slow, or None?" Occasional Paper 2. Chancellor College, Department of Economics. Zomba: University of Malaŵi.

Minelle, Jean. 1959. *L'agriculture à Madagascar*. Paris: Marcel Rivière.

Minford, Patrick, and Peter Ohs. 1976. "Supply Responses of Malaŵi Labor," *Eastern Africa Economic Review* 8(1).

Mkandawêre, R. Mulomboji. n.d. "Customary Land, the state, and Agrarian Change in Malaŵi." Unpublished paper prepared at the Institute of Social Research, Zomba.

Mlia, J.R. Ngoleka. 1975. "Malaŵi's New Capitol City: A Regional Perspective," *Pan-African Journal* 8(4): 397–401.

———. 1987. "Public Decision-Making and the Spatial Organization of Development in Malaŵi." Ph.D. dissertation, Department of Urban Planning and Policy Development, Rutgers University, New Brunswick, N.J.

Morrisson, Christian. 1968. *La répartition des revenues dans les pays du tiers monde*. Paris: Edition Cujas.

Morton, Kathryn. 1975. *Aid and Dependency: British Aid to Malaŵi*. London: Croon Helm and the Overseas Development Institute.

Msukwa, Louis A. H. 1986. "Agricultural Development and Undernutrition: The Case of Malaŵi." Paper presented for the Second Annual Conference on Food Security Research in Southern Africa. Harare.

Mtewa, Mekki. 1986. *Malaŵi: Democratic Theory and Public Policy.* Cambridge, Mass.: Schenkman Books.

Munger, Edwin S. 1969a. "President Kamuzu Banda of Malaŵi," *American University Field Staff Report.* Series 13, no. 1, Central and Southern Africa: 1–32.

———. 1969b. "Trading with the Devil: Malaŵi's Economic Relations with Portugal, Rhodesia, and South Africa," *American University Field Staff Report.* Series 13, no. 1, Central and Southern Africa: 1–17.

Murdock, George Peter. 1959. *Africa: Its People and Their Culture History.* New York: McGraw-Hill.

———. 1967. *Ethnographic Atlas.* Pittsburgh: University of Pittsburgh Press.

Neale Walter C. 1984. "The Evolution of Colonial Institutions: An Argument Illustrated from the Economic History of British Central Africa." *Journal of Economic Issues* 18(4):1177–87.

Nelson, Harold D., ed. 1973. *Area Handbook for the Malagasy Republic.* Washington, D.C.: Government Printing Office.

———. 1975. *Area Handbook for Malaŵi.* Washington, D.C.: Government Printing Office.

Ng'ong'da, Clement. 1985–86. "Land Reform and Land Dispute Resolution in Malaŵi." In Conference on Design and Implementation of Rural Development Strategies. Lilongwe.

Nyasaland Protectorate. n.d. *Development Plan, 1957–1961.* Zomba: Government Printer.

———. 1946. *Report of the Census of 1945.* Zomba: Government Printer.

———. 1962. *Development Plan, 1962–1965.* Zomba: Government Printer.

Nyirenda, A. A., H. D. Ngwane, and D. G. Bettison. 1959. "Further Economic and Social Studies, Blantyre-Limbe, Nyasaland." Communication 17, Rhodes-Livingston Institution, Lusaka.

Organisation for Economic Co-operation and Development (OECD). 1984. *Geographical Distribution of Financial Flows to Developing Countries, 1980/83.* Paris.

Ottaway, David and Marina Ottaway. 1981. *Afrocommunism.* New York: Holmes and Meier.

Pachai, Bridglal. 1973. "African-Grown Tea in Malaŵi: An Experiment in Agricultural Smallholding." In Melvin E. Page, ed., "Land and Labor in Rural Malaŵi," parts I and II, vol 20, *Rural Africana.*

———. 1978. *Land and Politics in Malaŵi, 1875–1955.* Kingston, Ontario: Limestone Press.

Page, Melvin E., ed. 1973. "Land and Labor in Rural Malaŵi," parts I and II, vol. 20, *Rural Africana.*

Palmer, Robin, and Neil Persons, eds. 1977. *The Roots of Rural Poverty in Central and Southern Africa.* London: Heinemann.

Papanek, Gustav F., and Oldrich Kyn. 1986. "The Effect of Income Distribution on Development, the Growth Rate, and Economic Strategy," *Journal of Development Economics* 23(1): 55–67.

Pavageau, Jean. 1981. *Jeunes paysans sans terres: L'example malgache.* Paris: l'Harmattan.

Payr, Gerhard. 1977. "Foerderung und Beratung traditioneller Kleinbauern in Salima, Malaŵi." Afrika Studium 96, IFO Institut fuer Wirtschaftsforschung. Munich: Weltforum Verlag.

Pearson, E. O., and B. L. Mitchell. 1945. *A Report on the Status and Control of Insect Pests of Cotton in the Lower River Districts of Nyasaland.* Zomba: Government Printer.

Petitjean, Bernard. 1978. "Le système agro-industriel et les pays du tiers monde: Le cas de Madagascar," *Tany malagasy/Terre malagache* 18.

Phipps, Brian. 1976. "Evaluating Development Schemes: Problems and Implications, A Malaŵi Case Study," *Development and Change* 74: 469–85.

Pike, John G. 1968. *Malaŵi: A Political and Economic History.* New York: Praeger.

Pike, John G., and Gerald T. Rimmington. 1965. *Malaŵi: A Geographical Study.* London: Oxford University Press.

Pourcet, Guy. n.d. "La dynamique du sous-développement à Madagascar." Thèse de Doctorat d'Etat, Université de Paris X, Nanterre.

———. 1987. "Dépendance alimentaire et urbanisation: Le cas de Madagascar." LAREA, Laboratoire de recherche en économie appliquée, Université de Paris X, Nanterre.

Poirier, Jean, and Jacques Dez. 1963. "Les groupes ethnique de Madagascar." Manuscript on deposit at the CITE Library, Antananarivo.

Price Waterhouse and Malaŵi Development Corporation. 1985. *Investing in Malaŵi.* Blantyre.

Pryor, Frederic L. 1968. *Public Expenditures in Communist and Capitalist Nations.* London: Allen and Unwin.

———. 1973. *Property and Industrial Organization in Communist and Capitalist Nations.* Bloomington, Indiana: Indiana University Press.

———. 1978. *The Origins of the Economy: A Comparative Study of Distribution in Primitive and Peasant Economies.* New York: Academic Press.

———. 1982. "An International Perspective on Land Scattering," *Explorations in Economic History* 19(3): 296–320.

———. 1985a. *A Guidebook to the Comparative Study of Economic Systems.* Englewood Cliffs, N.J.: Prentice-Hall.

———. 1985b. "Climatic Fluctuations as a Cause of the Differential Growth of the Orient: A Comment, " *Journal of Economic History* 45(3): 667–73.

———. 1986. *Revolutionary Grenada: A Study in Political Economy.* New York: Praeger.

———. 1988a. *Income Distribution and Economic Development in Madagascar: Some Historical Statistics.* World Bank Discussion Paper 37. Washington, D.C.

———. 1988b. *Income Distribution and Economic Development in Malawi: Some Historical Statistics*. World Bank Discussion Paper 36. Washington, D.C.

Pryor, Frederic, and Chinyamata Chipeta. Forthcoming 1990. "Economic Development through Estáts Agriculture," *Canadian Journal of African Studies*.

Quisumbing, M. Agnes R., and Lance Taylor. 1989. "Resource Transfers from Agriculture." In Sukhamoy Chakravarty, ed., *Industry and Agriculture in Economic Development*. Vol. 3, *Manpower and Transfers*. New York: St. Martins.

Rabemiafala, Célestine. 1984. "Contribution à l'évaluation de l'état nutritionnel des enfants malagasy de moins de 6 ans à travers le complexe materno-infantile de Tsaralalana (Ville d'Antananarivo)." Thèse, Doctorat de médecine, Université de Madagascar, Antananarivo.

Rabes, Jean, and Maurice Rakotoanost. 1979. "Etudes des migrations de masse à Madagascar." Ministère de développement rural et de la réforme agraire.

Rabier, Jean-Claude, ed. 1986. "Actes du séminaire de politique et stratégie de développement à Madagascar." Université de Paris X, Nanterre.

Rafrezy, Vincent Andrianarivelo, and Iarivony Randretsa. 1985. *Population de Madagascar: Situation actuelle et perspectives d'avenir*. Ministère de la recherche scientifique et technologique pour le développement. Antananarivo.

Rakotomanga, Georges. 1977. *Fokonolism et droit de propriété*. Antananarivo: FOFOPA.

Ralaimihoatra, Edouard. 1962. *Histoire de Madagascar*. Antananarivo: Librarie de Madagascar.

Ramahatra, Olivier. 1986. "Les fondement théoriques des programmes de stabilisation du Fonds Monétaire International à Madagascar." Thèse pour le doctorat ès sciences économiques, Université de Paris X, Nanterre.

Ramanandraibe, Lucile Rasoamanalina. 1987. *Le livre vert de l'espérance Malgache*. Paris: l'Harmattan.

Ranger, T. O., ed. 1968. *Aspects of Central African History*. Evanston, Illinois: Northwestern University Press.

Rarijaona, René. 1967. *Le concept de propriété en droit foncier de Madagascar*. Universiteé de Tananarive, Faculté de droit et des sciences économiques, Série études malgaches 18. Paris: Editions Cujas.

Rasomoelina, Désiré. 1978. "Contribution à l'étude géographique du Moyen Ouest malgache: La vie rural de la cuvette de Belobaka." Thèse pour le doctorat de IIIème cycle, Université de Paris X, Nanterre.

Ratsiraka, Didier. 1975. *Charte de la révolution socialiste malgache tous azimuts*. Antananarivo: Imprimerie d'ouvrages éducatifs.

Razafimahefa, Andriamampandry. 1986. *Naturzerstörung durch Wald- und Weidebraende in Entwicklungsländer: Ursachen, Folgen und Gegenmassnahmen am Beispiel von Madagascar*. Munich: Weltforum Verlag.

Razafimandimby, Simon Joseph. 1987. "Suites de l'impact de la libéralisation de la commercialisation du paddy au Lac Alaotra." Antananarivo.

Razafimpahanana, Bertin. 1972. *Le paysan Malagasy.* Antananarivo.

Razin, A., and E. Sadka, eds. 1987. *Economic Policy in Theory and Practice.* London: Macmillan.

Rose, Torre, ed. 1985. *Crisis and Recovery in Sub-Saharan Africa.* Paris: Organisation for Economic Co-operation and Development.

Rotberg, Robert I. 1965. *The Rise of Nationalism in Central Africa: The Making of Malaŵi and Zambia, 1873–1964.* Cambridge, Mass.: Harvard University Press.

Rotberg, Robert I., ed. 1983. *Imperialism, Colonialism, and Hunger in East and Central Africa.* Lexington, Mass.: Lexington Books.

Rouveyran, Jean Claude. 1972. *La logique des agricultures de transition.* Paris: Maisonneuve et Larose.

Rouveyran, Jean Claude, and Bertrand Chauaney. n.d. "Approche descriptive et quantitative de l'agriculture malgache." Faculté de droit et des services économiques. Antananarivo.

Sah, Raaj Kumar, and Joseph E. Stiglitz. 1984. "The Economics of the Price Scissors," *American Economic Review* 74(1).

Salmond, K. F. 1957. *Investigation into Grain Storage Problems in Nyasaland.* Colonial Office Research Publication 21. London: HMSO.

Sandbrook, Richard. 1986. "The State and Economic Stagnation in Tropical Africa," *World Development* 14(3): 319–32.

Sandbrook, Richard, and Judith Barker. 1983. *The Politics of Africa's Economic Stagnation.* Cambridge: Cambridge University Press.

Schaefer-Kehnert, Walter. 1982. "Success with Group Lending in Malaŵi," *Development Digest* 20(1): 10–16.

Schoffeleers, J. M., and A. A. Roscow. 1985. *Land of Fire: Oral Literature from Malaŵi.* Limbe, Malaŵi: Popular Publications.

Seminaire national sur la vulgarisation agricole, Fianarantsoa. 1983. "Rapport." Antananarivo.

Serdula, Mary, and others. 1987. "Acute and Chronic Undernutrition in Swaziland," *Journal of Tropical Pediatrics* 33 (February): 35–42.

Sevin, G., and M. Guerin. n.d. "La terre: Les rapports de l'homme et du sol." Manuscript on deposit at the BdPa (CITE) Library in Antananarivo.

Short, Philip. 1974. *Banda.* London: Routledge and Kegan Paul.

Shuttleworth, Graham. 1989. "Policies in Transition: Lessons from Madagascar," *World Development* 17(3): 397–408.

Sierra, Katherine. 1981. "Malaŵi: Employment Aspects of Economic Development." World Bank internal report 3453-MAI, Washington, D.C.

Societé d'étude pour le développement économique et social. 1971. *Projections du produit intérieur brut de quatorze pays africains et malgache pour 1985.* Paris.

Spacensky, Alain. 1970. *Madagascar: Cinquante ans de vie politique*. Paris: Nouvelles éditions latines.

Speck, Samuel W. 1967. "African Local Government in Malaŵi: Its Development and Politics under British Rule." Ph.D. dissertation, Harvard University, Cambridge, Massachusetts.

Statesman's Yearbook. Annual. London: Macmillan.

Stratton, Arthur. 1964. *The Great Red Island*. New York: Scribner's Sons.

Summers, Robert, and Alan Heston. 1984. "Improved International Comparisons of Real Product and Its Composition, 1950–1980," *Review of Income and Wealth* 30(2): 207–62.

———. 1988. "A New Set of International Comparisons of Real Product and Price Level Estimates for 139 Countries, 1950–1985," *Review of Income and Wealth* 34(2): 1–25.

Syrquin, Moshe, Lance Taylor, and Larry E. Westphal, eds. 1984. *Economic Structure and Performance*. New York: Academic Press.

Szal, Richard. 1987. "An Agrarian Crisis in Madagascar?" World Employment Program Research, Working Paper 84, International Labour Office, Geneva.

Taylor, Charles Lewis, and Michael C. Hudson. 1972. *World Handbook of Political and Social Indicators*. 2nd edition. New Haven: Yale University Press.

Tew, Mary. 1950. *Peoples of Lake Nyasa Region*. Ethnographic Survey of Africa, International African Institute. London: Oxford University Press.

Thoboni, Maleen. 1984. "Charging User Fees for Social Services: Education in Malaŵi," *Comparative Education Review* 20(3): 402–22.

Thomas, Simon. 1985. "Economic Development in Malaŵi since Independence," *Journal of African History* 14(4): 681–98.

Thompson, Virginia, and Richard Adloff. 1965. *The Malagasy Republic: Madagascar Today*. Stanford: Stanford University Press.

Todd, W. H. W. 1984. "A Comparison of Smallholder Agricultural Development in Kenya and Malaŵi." Occasional Paper 7, Centre of African Studies, Edinburgh University.

Tronchon, Jacques. 1982. *L'insurrection malgache de 1947*. Fianarantsa: EFA.

Tuong, HoDac, and Alexander Yeats. 1974. "A Note on the Measurement of Trade Concentration," *Oxford Bulletin of Economics and Statistics* 36(3): 302–15.

Turcotte, Denis. 1981. *La politique linguistique en Afrique francophone*. Québec: Les presses de l'université Laval.

United Nations. Annual. *Statistical Yearbook*. New York.

———. 1974. *Short and Medium Term Prospects for Exports of Manufactured Goods from Selected Developing Countries*. Antananarivo.

United Nations Educational, Scientific, and Cultural Organization (UNESCO). 1984a. *Madagascar: Rapport d'évaluation générale du système éducatif*. Paris.

———. Division du financement de l'éducation. 1984b. *République démocratique de Madagascar: Priorités, contraintes et perspectives du développement de l'éducation.* Vol. I, ASM/ED/EPP/017. Paris.

United Nations, Fund for Population Activities. 1979. *Report of Mission on Needs Assessment for Population Assistance.* Report 25. New York.

United Nations International Children's Emergency Fund (UNICEF). Annual. *The State of the World's Children.* London: Oxford University Press.

———. 1984. *Situation Analysis of the Child in Madagascar.* Nairobi.

U.S. Agency for International Development. 1986. "Rural Enterprises and Agrobusiness Development Institutions Project (READI)." Lilongwe.

U.S. Council of Economic Advisors. Annual. *Economic Report of the President.* Washington, D.C.: Government Printing Office.

Vail, Leroy, and L. White. 1984. "Variations on the Theme of Ethnicity." Paper presented at the University of Edinburgh, Center of African Studies.

Valkenier, Elizabeth K. 1981. *The Soviet Union and the Third World: An Economic Bind.* New York: Praeger.

von Blackenburg, P. 1966. *The SOMANGOKY Settlement Scheme.* Berlin: Institut fuer ausländische Landwirtschaft an der technischen Universität.

Warner, Dennis R., and others. 1983. "Malaŵi's Self-Help Rural Water Supply Program: A Mid-Term Evaluation of the USAID Financed Projects." Work Field Report 105. Lilongwe.

Wheeler, David. 1983. *Sources of Stagnation in Sub-Saharan Africa.* Second Report to the World Bank, Washington, D.C.

Williams. T. David. 1978. *Malaŵi: The Politics of Despair.* Ithaca: Cornell University Press.

Wolgin, Jerome, and others. 1983. *The Private Sector and the Economic Development of Malaŵi.* U.S. AID Evaluation Special Study 11. Washington, D.C.

Wood, A. W. 1970. "Training Malaŵi's Youth: The Work of the Malaŵi Young Pioneers," *Community Development Journal* 5(3): 1230–39.

World Bank (International Bank for Reconstruction and Development). Annual. *World Development Report.* New York: Oxford University Press.

———. January 1971. "Recent Economic Position and Prospects of the Malagasy Republic." Internal report AE-11a, Washington, D.C.

———. December 1973. "Agricultural Sector Review: Malaŵi." Internal report MAI-235a, Washington, D.C.

———. December 1976. "Madagascar: Economic Memorandum on Current Economic Position and Prospects and Selected Development Issues." Internal report 1099a-MAG, Washington, D.C.

———. July 1979. "The Economic Development of Madagascar: Main Issues." Internal report 167a-MAG, Washington, D.C.

———. 1980. *Madagascar: Recent Economic Developments and Future Prospects.* Washington, D.C.

———. 1981. *Accelerated Development in Sub-Saharan Africa: An Agenda for Action*. Washington, D.C.

———. February 1981. "Malaŵi: Growth and Structural Change, A Basic Economic Report." Internal report 3082-MAI, Washington, D.C.

———. May 1981a. "Malaŵi: The Development of the Agricultural Sector." Internal report 3459-MAI, Washington, D.C.

———. May 1981b. "Malaŵi: The Development of Human Capital." Internal report 3462-MAI, Washington, D.C.

———. May 1981c. "Malaŵi: The Development of Manufacturing." Internal report 3460-MAI, Washington, D.C.

———. November 1981. "Madagascar: Economic Memorandum." Internal report 3389-MAG, Washington, D.C.

———. February 1982. "Malaŵi: Growth and Structural Change: A Basic Economic Report, Statistical Appendix," Internal report 3082a-MAI, Washington, D.C.

———. June 1982. "National Rural Development Program, Review Report." Internal report 3895-MAI, Washington, D.C.

———. 1983. *World Tables*. 3d ed. Baltimore, Md.: Johns Hopkins University Press.

———. February 1983. "Madagascar: Transport Sector Memorandum." Internal report 4057-MAG, Washington, D.C.

———. June 1983. "Madagascar Agriculture and Rural Development: Sector Memorandum." Internal report 4209-MAG, Washington, D.C.

———. October 1984. "Madagascar: Current Economic Situation and Prospects." Internal report 5154-MAG, Washington, D.C.

———. November 1984. "Madagascar: Review of the Public Investment Program." Internal report 5285–MAG, Washington, D.C.

———. December 1984. "Madagascar: Export Crop Sub-sector Review." Internal report 5097-MAG, Washington, D.C.

———. July 1985. "Malaŵi, Economic Recovery: Resource and Policy Needs, An Economic Memorandum." Internal report 5801-MAI, Washington, D.C.

———. March 1986a. "The Democratic Republic of Madagascar: Country Economic Memorandum." Internal report 5996-MAG, Washington, D.C.

———. March 1986b. "Malaŵi: Population Sector Review." Internal report 5648-MAI, Washington, D.C.

———. October 1986. "Madagascar: Population and Health Sector Review." Internal report 6446-MAG, Washington, D.C.

World Health Organization n.d. *Study of the Epidemiological Aspects of Breast-Feeding in Madagascar*. Project 62/MAFA/WHO, preliminary report. Antananarivo.

———. 1983. *Measuring Change in Nutritional Status*. Geneva.

———. 1986. "Country Profile (Health), Republic of Malaŵi." Lilongwe.

WHO, Government of Madagascar, and UNICEF. 1984. "Report of the Joint Program Revue, Maternal and Child Health." Antananarivo.

World Meteorological Organization. 1971. *Climatological Normals.* Geneva.

Worldmark Encyclopedia of Nations: Africa. 1984. New York: John Wiley.

Woronoff, Jon. 1972. *West African Wager: Houphouët versus Nkrumah.* Metuchen, N.J.: Scarecrow Press.

Wright, Fergus Chalmers. 1955. *Agrarian Consumers in Nyasaland and Tanganyka.* Colonial Office, Colonial Research Study 17. London: Her Majesty's Stationery Office.

Wright, Gavin. 1978. *The Political Economy of the Cotton South: Households, Markets, and Wealth in the Nineteenth Century.* New York: Norton.

Young, Crawford. 1982. *Ideology and Development in Africa.* New Haven: Yale University Press.

Zolberg, Aristide R. 1966. *Creating Political Order: The Party State of West Africa.* Chicago: Rand McNally.

Index

Abrahams Report of 1946, 32
Absentee owners, 84
Adloff, Richard, 429, 430
ADMARC. *See* Agricultural Development and Marketing Corporation (ADMARC)
Advance Guard of the Malagasy Revolution (AREMA), 5, 13
Agricultural Development and Marketing Corporation (ADMARC) (Malaŵi): agricultural prices and, 74, 105–09, 113, 141, 176, 426, 427; manufacturing and, 146–47, 148, 154; microeconomic impact of, 423–26; price controls and, 154; product markets and, 98–100
Agricultural extension and research, 55, 77, 78–79, 249–52, 253
Agricultural producer cooperatives, 254–55
Agricultural production: in colonial period, 31; development plans and, 55; in estate agriculture, 44, 45, 85–87; land tenure and, 69–70; in Madagascar, 224, 241, 244–45, 256; in Malaŵi, 44; policies to promote, 10, 399; prices and, 102–03, 268–69; roads and, 322; small-scale agriculture in Malaŵi and, 44, 71–72, 404–05
Agricultural product markets: in Madagascar, 262–67; in Malaŵi, 97–101, 120

Agriculture: Banda and, 389; economic development and, 59, 61; investment in, 10, 71–72, 72–75, 75–77; Madagascar's colonial period and, 230–31; Madagascar's development and, 232, 233, 235–36; Madagascar's management of, 246, 247, 248, 252–53; Malaŵi's master farmer program and, 80; Malaŵi's policy toward, 67–68; nationalism in Malaŵi and, 38–39; subsidies to, 79
Agriculture, estate, 81–85; absentee owners and, 84; Banda and, 390–91; income distribution and, 87–89; labor and, 90, 116, 430; land competition and, 89–90; management problems and, 83; production in, 44, 45, 85–87; production strategy and, 10, 253–56
Agriculture, small-scale: capital-intensive projects and, 72–76, 245–47, 256–57; credit and, 115–16, 276–79; investment in, 75–77; labor-intensive projects and, 77–80, 247–53, 257; labor market and, 117–20; land tenure and, 68–70, 242–44; production in, 44, 71–72; production strategy and, 10, 399; technology and, 77–78, 245, 248–52
Air transport, 165, 324. *See also* Transportation

Army: in Madagascar, 244, 251, 330–31, 369; in Malaŵi, 172
Asians: ethnic friction and, 26–27; incomes of, 371; as lenders, 278; in Madagascar, 200, 203, 323; in Malaŵi, 24; manufacturing and, 151; rice marketing and, 262; sale of retail outlets by, 100; violations of currency laws and, 52; wholesaling and importing and, 210. *See also* Ethnic groups
Associations d'intérêt rural (AIR) (Madagascar), 248

Balance of payments: in Madagascar, 135, 136–37, 234, 287, 291, 294, 300, 301–02, 319; in Malaŵi, 48, 59, 124–40
Banda, Hastings Kamuzu, 61, 67, 99, 190, 433; credit and, 109; economic development and, 39, 53–54, 62–63, 382, 395; economic ideology of, 6–7, 38, 39, 379; estate purchase and, 81, 83, 84–85; ethnic groups and, 26, 389–90; FCR ("food, clothing, roof," or basic needs) doctrine of, 180; government of, 5; nationalism and, 33–34, 37; political power of, 12, 387–91; population policies and, 44; on poverty, 365; rail line and, 163; tenure in office of, 52; unions and, 35, 36
Banks, Arthur S., 422
Banks, 60, 81
Battle of Rice campaign (Madagascar), 244
Beira (Mozambique), 21, 163
Berg, Elliot, 263
Berthélemy, J. C., 266, 268
Birth control, 44, 220
Boserup, Ester, 409
Bowring, Charles, 30
Brazzaville Declaration of 1944, 209
Brietzke, Paul, 408
Brown, C. P., 102, 427
Bureaucracy: elite groups and, 385–86; ideology and, 383–84; infighting in Malaŵian, 61–62; in Madagascar, 236, 328–30

Camacho, Martine, 362
Capital flows in Madagascar's rural sector, 279–80
Capital formation, 61
Capital-intensive projects in small-scale agriculture, 72–76, 245–47, 256–57
Capitalism, 3, 9, 37, 38, 150, 210, 212, 378–81
Capital utilization rate, Malaŵi, 171
Cattle tax, 205–06, 223, 288, 334, 360
Central African Federation, 33
Chaigneau, Pascal, 213, 275
Channock, Martin, 38, 102
Children: anthropometric data on, 366–69; infant mortality and, 44, 183, 366, 369
Chilembwe rebellion of 1915 (Malaŵi), 33
Chimpembere, Henry, 36
Chipande, Graham H. R., 426
Chipeta, Chinamata, 102, 116, 405
Chisiza, Dunduzu, 36, 38
Chokani, Willie, 36
Christiansen, Robert E., 87, 117, 140, 142, 361, 426, 430
Climate: of Madagascar, 198; of Malaŵi, 21
Collier, Paul, 118–19, 426
Colman, D. R., 102
Colonial period: ideological development in, 378–79; in Madagascar, 28, 204–07, 221, 391, 429–30; in Malaŵi, 3–5, 24–25, 27–32, 34–35, 45, 190; small-scale agriculture in, 77. *See also* France; Great Britain
Communications: in Madagascar, 230, 232, 233; Malaŵi's development plans and, 58, 61
Compagnie Lyonnaise, 210
Compagnie Marseillaise, 210
Conseil d'orientation (Madagascar), 309–10
Consumption: agricultural product market and rural, 265–67; and Madagascar's development plan, 234; prices and, 103, 269

Consumption substitution (Malaŵi), 134
Corruption, 171, 385
Credit: cooperatives and, 112; estate agriculture and, 81, 90–91; land tenure and, 90, 111, 276, 405, 407; manufacturing and, 311, 314, 317; markets for (Madagascar), 276–80, 311, 314, 317, 342–44; markets for (Malaŵi), 35, 407; policy in Malaŵi and, 187–89; rural sector in Malaŵi and, 109–16, 120, 407; small-scale agriculture and, 74. *See also* Loans
Crop reservation policy (Malaŵi), 69–70
Crops: double-cropping of, 22; estate agriculture and, 82, 91–92, 97–98; export (Madagascar), 208, 244–45, 256, 263–64; licenses for (Madagascar), 243; Madagascar's development and, 235; in Malaŵi, 22; prices in Madagascar and, 267; private trading in, 263. *See also* Maize; Rice; Tobacco
Crop specialization, 115, 426
Currency: allocation system for, 128; exchange rate and overvalued, 132–33; Madagascar and Franc Zone and, 211, 223–24, 291, 292, 296, 297, 304, 417
Currency devaluation: in Madagascar, 225, 287, 291, 296, 297–98, 300; in Malaŵi, 48, 133–34, 136

Data: agricultural (Malaŵi), 85–87; on economic growth in Madagascar, 219–20; income distribution, 351–52; lack of, 6, 45, 329
Dean, Edwin, 102
Debt: Madagascar's, 224–25, 287, 302–03, 344; Malaŵi's, 47, 179, 187, 188–89
Debt service: Madagascar and, 235, 332, 394, 396; Malaŵi and, 47, 137–38, 174, 179, 394
Default on foreign loan, 121, 138, 225, 235
Defense expenditures. *See* Army

Deficit: budget, 179, 225, 301, 332, 343; trade, 136–37
Deficit spending (Malaŵi), 135
Deforestation (Madagascar), 198
de Gaulle, Charles, 209
Denmark, 137
Depreciation allowance and manufacturing, 150, 151, 311
Desjeux, Dominique, 429
Devaluation. *See* Currency devaluation
Development. *See* Economic development
Development of Malaŵian Trader Trust (DEMATT), 153
Development policies (*Dev Pol*), 54–63, 68, 71, 76, 78–79, 82–83, 92, 103, 109, 114, 128–30, 134, 149–51, 153, 158, 160–64, 172–74, 180–81, 183–85, 187, 231, 232, 356, 395
Dumont, René, 248

Ecological problems (Madagascar), 198–99
Economic development: education and, 329–40; exports and, 304; health and, 60, 61, 185; ideology and, 214, 381; income distribution and, 396–99; in Madagascar, 219–25, 229–37; in Madagascar's colonial period, 206–07; Madagascar's investment policy and, 225–29; in Malaŵi, 39–40, 43–48, 53–63, 170; trade and, 140, 304–05
Economic ideology: administrative and managerial, 383–84; capitalism as, 3, 9, 37, 38, 150, 210, 212, 378–81; in colonial period, 378–79; factors influencing, 378–81; health and education and, 381; in Madagascar, 212–14; in Malaŵi, 36–39; Marxism as, 3, 9, 13, 378, 381; policy and, 377, 378–81; public sector and, 381; socialism as, 9, 38, 212, 213–14, 228, 234, 378–81. *See also* Nationalism
Economic institutions: in Madagascar, 210–12; in Malaŵi, 34–36
Economic interests: Banda and, 387–91, 395; interest groups and, 384–94;

oil shock and, 394–96; policy and, 377, 384–87; political situation in Madagascar and, 391–94

Education: economic development in Malaŵi and, 59, 60, 61; ethnic groups in Madagascar and, 202, 203; expenditures in Madagascar, 331–32; expenditures in Malaŵi, 172–74, 180–83; ideology and, 381; in Madagascar, 211, 337–49; in Madagascar's colonial period, 206; in Malaŵi's colonial period, 34, 36; manufacturing and, 152, 153

Elite groups, 385–86, 387, 389, 392

Emigration: income distribution and, 142, 361; Madagascar and, 204; from Malaŵi, 27, 47, 116–17, 139; into Malaŵi from Mozambique, 48; remittances and, 140, 142, 355. *See also* Migration, internal

Enterprises socialistes (Madagascar), 309

Estate agriculture. *See* Agriculture, estate

Ethnic groups: Banda and, 389–90; elite groups and, 385, 387; income and wage differences among, 359–60, 433; in Madagascar, 200–04; in Malaŵi, 24–27. *See also* Asians

European Economic Community, 153, 246

Exchange rate: economic growth and, 305; Madagascar's, 417; Malaŵi's, 97, 100, 125, 416–17; manufacturing and, 152, 312; trade and, 132–33, 141, 296–300; transportation and, 325

Expenditures: in Madagascar, 328–29, 330–32, 336, 344–45; in Malaŵi, 170, 172–74, 179, 180–83; Malaŵi's and Madagascar's compared, 8–9, 397–98

Export Promotion Council (Malaŵi), 153

Exports: crop, 32, 56, 141, 208, 244–45, 256, 263–64, 267, 269, 271, 272; debt service and, 137; devaluation and, 134, 300; development and, 55, 59, 61, 140, 232, 234, 235; economic growth and, 304; equilibration of balance of payments and, 300–01; estate tobacco, 47, 97; exchange rate and, 296, 297, 298; favored sector approach and, 131–32; foreign exchange and, 129; income and, 141; Madagascar's, 225, 416; Malaŵi's, 48, 391, 414, 415; manufacturing, 150, 152, 160; mineral, 200; parastatals and, 264; prices of, 101, 107, 125, 141, 295, 394; restrictions on, 293; tax treatment and, 131, 176, 293–95; trade openness and, 125, 128; trade orientation and, 287, 288–91; trade strategy and, 10–11

Extension service: development and, 55; small-scale agriculture and, 77, 78–79, 249–52, 253

External shocks, 5, 85, 190, 225, 394–96

Favored sector approach in trade, 131–32, 295–96

FCR ("food, clothing, roof") doctrine (Malaŵi), 180

Federal Republic of Germany, 54, 137, 147, 416

Fertilizer, 100, 112, 114, 115, 312

Finance: absorption effects and (Malaŵi), 135–36; constraints on state-owned farms in Madagascar and, 255; devaluation and (Malaŵi), 133–34, 136; exchange rate policies and (Malaŵi), 132–33, 141; income and (Malaŵi), 134–35; prices and (Malaŵi), 134. *See also* Credit; Investment

Fiscal system (Malaŵi), 186–89

Fokonolona (Madagascar village councils), 235, 253, 254; credit and, 278–79

Ford Foundation, 62

Foreign aid: Madagascar and, 228, 303–04; Malaŵi and, 50, 138–39

Foreign exchange: in Madagascar, 225, 229, 291, 292, 319, 323; in Malaŵi, 128–29, 141

France: as colonial power in Madagascar, 28, 204–07, 391; colonists from, 429; exports to, 416; foreign aid and, 304; investment in rural sector and, 355; Madagascar's withdrawal from Franc Zone and, 211, 223–24, 291, 292, 296, 297, 304, 417; Marxist ideology in, 378, 382; post-independence Madagascar and, 201–02, 208–10, 246, 378, 379, 382

Fundamental Options (*FundOp*) (Madagascar), 233–34, 235

Galliéni, Joseph, 205–06, 210, 211, 223, 334
Garbett, G. K., 102
Gendarme, René, 429, 430
General Farming Company (Malaŵi), 81, 82
Geography: of Madagascar, 5, 197–200; of Malaŵi, 5, 21–24, 163–64
Ghana, 421
Giles, B. D., 62, 170
Gondwe, Derick Kanyerere, 178
Gordon, J. G., 102
Government: efficiency of Malaŵi's, 170–72; employees in Malaŵi's, 170; expenditures of Madagascar's, 328–29, 330–32, 344–45; expenditures of Malaŵi's, 170, 172–74, 179, 180–83; fiscal system of Malaŵi's, 186–89; ownership and Malaŵi's, 35; revenues of Madagascar's, 269, 332–42, 345; revenues of Malaŵi's, 174–79; size of, 419, 420. *See also* Bureaucracy; Parastatal enterprises; Public sector
Government expenditures and revenues. *See* Expenditures; Revenues
Great Britain, 147, 163, 378–79, 382, 414, 415; bilateral loans and, 137, 139; as colonial power in Malaŵi, 24–25, 28–31; economic policy and, 34–35; grants from, 47, 54; land question and, 31–32; sectoral growth and, 45; subsidies and, 174
Greek businessmen in Malaŵi, 52, 151

Grenada, 139
Gross domestic product (GDP): in Madagascar, 219, 221, 225; in Malaŵi, 43, 45, 48; trade as share of Malaŵi's, 125, 126
Gwede, Focus, 390

Hazlewood, Arthur, 33
Health: expenditures in Madagascar, 331, 340–42, 381; expenditures in Malaŵi, 60, 61, 174, 183–85, 381; labor market and, 117–18; Malaŵi's population policies and, 44; in post-independence Madagascar, 211; poverty indicators and, 266–69, 433–35
Henri, M., 279
Heseltine, Nigel, 429
Heston, Alan, 422
Hill Mission (by British government), 54
Hirschman, Albert O., 370
Hugon, Philippe, 297

Ideology. *See* Economic ideology; Nationalism
Illiteracy, 337, 433, 435
Import and Export Company of Malaŵi (IMEXCO), 147
Import licensing, 128, 151–52, 292
Import quotas, 10, 59
Imports: exchange rate and, 114, 296–97, 298, 300; favored sector approach and, 131–32, 295; Madagascar's, 234, 235, 269, 295, 416; Madagascar's rice, 262, 263; Malaŵi government projects and, 136; Malaŵi's, 131–32, 414, 415; Malaŵi's restrictions on, 128–29; manufacturing and, 150, 151, 295, 312, 313, 317; protection and, 310–11; rural areas in Malaŵi and, 100; tariffs in Madagascar and, 293–94; tax treatment and, 129–31, 178, 293–95, 334; trade openness and, 125, 128; trade strategy and, 10, 11
Import substitution, 10, 135, 383, 415; Madagascar's development plan

and, 232; manufacturing and, 160–61, 319
Income: decline of off-farm, 119–20; direct taxes and inequality of, 179; equity question and, 11–12; of estate workers, 87, 88; of ethnic groups, 202; ethnic and regional differences in, 431–33; exports and, 141; inequality, 261, 377, 397–98, 398–99; land holdings in Madagascar and, 243, 257; Madagascar's development plan and, 235; in Malaŵi's colonial period, 31; manufacturing and, 153; monetary and nonmonetary differences and, 353–54; per acre cash, 119; prices and stability of, 106–07, 272; relative shares of labor and property, 352–53; rural-urban gap in, 11, 233, 354–56; smallholder family, 71, 73, 75, 80; taxes and differential in, 98; trade and, 134–35, 300
Income distribution: agricultural prices and, 261, 269, 274; data on, 351–52; economic development and, 396–99; education and, 181–83, 339–40; emigration and, 142, 361; equity and, 11–12, 351, 353, 364–65, 370–71; estimates of, 361–65; government expenditures and, 336, 397–98; in Malaŵi, 57, 87–89; manufacturing and transportation and, 325; poverty and, 351, 362, 365–70; structure of income and, 352–56; trade and, 135, 141–42, 305; wages and, 356–60
Incremental capital-output ratio (ICOR), 52–53, 61, 229, 397
Industrial Development Bank (INDEBANK) (Malaŵi), 147, 148
Industrialization: in Madagascar, 381; in Malaŵi, 30, 35; rural, 398
Infant mortality, 44, 183, 366, 369, 434–35
Inflation, 187, 189, 228, 313, 343
Infrastructure, rural, 72
Interest groups, 14, 384–94
Interest rates: in Madagascar, 228, 343–44; in Malaŵi, 52, 111, 187, 188, 381; public expenditures and, 174; subsidies for, 114
International Development Association, 246
International Finance Corporation, 147
International Monetary Fund (IMF), 48, 386
Invest-to-the-hilt strategy, 9, 225, 228–29, 234–35, 237, 255, 298, 301–04, 311, 312, 318, 344, 345, 369, 394
Investment: agriculture and, 10, 71–72, 72–75, 75–77, 103–06; balance of payments and, 301; economic development and government, 9; government sector in Madagascar and, 329, 330, 336, 344, 345–46; imports and, 136; income inequality and, 397–98; in Madagascar's colonial period, 206–07; Madagascar's economic growth and, 221, 224, 225–29, 232, 236–37, 394; in Malaŵi, 48–53, 56, 170; manufacturing and, 149, 150–52, 165, 310–12, 313, 314–15, 324; rural sector and, 103
Irrigation, 198, 246

Jaona, Monja, 369
Japan, 416
Joffee, Selby Hickey, 431
Johnson, Thomas H., 422

Kandawêre, J. A. K., 76
Kornfeld, Guy, 220
Kydd, Jonathan G., 87, 140, 142, 361, 430

Labor: estate agriculture and, 90, 116, 430; forced (colonial Madagascar), 205; formal and informal exchanges (Malaŵi) and, 116–17; market for (Madagascar), 280–82, 407; market for (Malaŵi), 35, 117–20, 407; government employment of (Malaŵi), 170; managers and, 148; manufacturing and, 152–53, 159, 161, 162; productivity of, 61, 85

Labor-intensive development: credit programs and, 114; in Malaŵi, 59; small-scale agriculture in Madagascar and, 247–53, 257; small-scale agriculture in Malaŵi and, 77–80
Labor market: in Madagascar, 280–82; in Malaŵi, 35, 116–20, 430–31
Labor unions. *See* Unions
Land: accumulation of, 411–12; competition for, 89–90; consolidation of, 408–09; market for, 35; scattering, 407–08, 412–13; use (Malaŵi), 22–23
Land cultivation: constraints on (Madagascar), 241–42; constraints on (Malaŵi), 68; in Madagascar, 199, 208, 243–44, 246; in Malaŵi, 22–23
Land holdings: colonial, 429; credit and size of, 114
Landlessness, 69
Land question: in Madagascar, 207–08; in Malaŵi, 31–32
Land reform (Madagascar), 243
Land tenure: credit and, 90, 111, 276, 405, 407; efficiency and, 407, 412; in Madagascar, 208, 409–13; in Malaŵi, 403–09; in Malaŵi's colonial period, 32; plantation workers and, 89; renting and, 405, 410–11; small-scale agriculture in Madagascar and, 242–44; small-scale agriculture in Malaŵi and, 68–70
Language: in Madagascar, 200; in Malaŵi, 26
Lavrijsen, J., 102
Lewis, Arthur, 353
Lilongwe (Malaŵi), 164
Livestock: cattle tax and, 205–06, 223, 288, 334, 360; in Madagascar, 242, 243; tsetse fly and (Malaŵi), 22
Livingstone, David, 29, 431
Loans: to estate agriculture, 81; *kubwereka*, 111; Madagascar's foreign, 225, 227–28; migrants and, 278; to parastatals, 311; in rural sector, 109, 110, 111, 112. *See also* Credit

Madagascar: agricultural production strategy in, 10, 224, 241, 244–45, 256; colonial period in, 5, 6, 28, 204–07, 391; economic development strategy in, 9; economic growth in, 219–25, 229–37; economic ideology in, 212–14; economic institutions in, 210–12; economic policies in, 3, 7, 213–14, 215, 379; economic similarities between Malaŵi and, 3; economy of, 4, 5, 7–9; ethnic groups in, 200–04; geography of, 197–200; government sector in, 419, 420; historical background on, 3–6; independence of, 207, 208–10; land question in, 207–08; political structure of, 13–14; social indicators and, 3, 4, 6; trade and fiscal policy of, 292–95, 296–304; trade orientation of, 287, 288–92; trade patterns in, 416–17; trade strategy of, 10–11. *See also* Ramanantsoa government; Ratsiraka government; Tsiranana government; *and specific subjects such as* Currency; Imports; Investment; Manufacturing
Maize, 22, 23; subsidy for, 108
Malaŵi: agricultural policy in, 67–68; agricultural production strategy in, 10; colonial period in, 3–5, 6, 24–25, 27–32; economic development strategy in, 9, 53–63; economic growth in, 43–48; economic institutions in, 34–36; economic outlook at independence of, 39–40; economic policies in, 3, 6–7, 38, 39, 379; economic similarities between Madagascar and, 3; economy of, 4, 5, 7–9; efficiency of government in, 170–72; ethnic groups in, 24–27; fiscal system of, 186–89; geography of, 21–24; government sector in, 419, 420; historical background of, 3–6, 27–34; ideology in, 6–7, 36–39; land question in, 31–32; political

structure of, 12–13, 14; social indicators and, 3, 4, 6; trade orientation of, 124–32; trade patterns in, 413–16; trade strategy of, 10–11. *See also* Banda, Hastings Kamuzu, *and specific subjects such as* Currency; Imports; Investment; Manufacturing

Malaŵi Congress Party (MCP), 34, 38, 148

Malaŵi Development Corporation (MDC), 147, 148, 150, 152

Malaŵi Entrepreneurial Development Institute (MEDI), 153

Malaŵi Union of Savings and Credit Cooperatives (MUSCCO), 153

Malnutrition, 362, 367, 369

Manufacturing, 30, 141, 229; development and, 44, 56, 60, 235; exports and, 150, 152, 160; foreign exchange and, 129, 319; growth rate of, 308, 318–21; imports and, 150, 151, 295, 312, 313, 317; import substitution and, 160–61, 319; labor and, 152–53, 159, 161, 162; nationalizations and, 308, 309, 313; ownership and, 146–50; policies toward, 150–54, 308, 310–15, 325; Press Holding Corporation (Malaŵi) and, 148–49; price controls and, 154–57, 308, 316–17, 324; production growth in, 159–62; public sector and, 146–50, 165; small enterprises and, 153–54, 315–16; structure of Madagascar's, 309–10; taxes and, 311, 314; transportation and, 146, 159, 161, 162–65, 166, 312–13; wage controls and, 157–59, 317–18

Market forces, ideology and, 380–81

Marketing: agricultural prices and, 275; development and, 55, 59, 60

Markets: labor (Malaŵi), 35, 116–20; land (Malaŵi), 35; product (Madagascar), 262–67; product (Malaŵi), 97–101, 120; rural credit (Malaŵi), 35, 109–16, 120

Marxism, 3, 9, 13, 378, 381, 421

Maxwell Stamp Associates, 293, 294, 311

McCloskey, Donald, 412

McCracken, John, 405

McGowan, Pat, 422

Medical services. *See* Health

Meritocratic system (Malaŵi), 182

Michaely, Michael, 414, 415, 416

Migrants: and loans, 278; remittances by, 140, 142, 355

Migration, internal: in Madagascar, 281–82; in Malaŵi, 89–90. *See also* Emigration

Military: involvement in Africa, 421; in Madagascar, 244, 251, 330–31, 369; in Malaŵi, 172

Mills, J. C., 102

Minelle, Jean, 429

Mineral deposits, 23–24, 200

Minford, Patrick, 102

Ministry of Trade, Industry, and Tourism (MTIT) (Malaŵi), 150, 151–52, 154, 155

Mitchell, B. L., 102

Mollet, Guy, 209, 213

Monetary policy: in Madagascar, 342–44; in Malaŵi, 186–87

Mozambique: emigration into Malaŵi from, 48; insurgents (RENAMO), 47, 48, 83, 125, 141, 163, 172, 394

Multinational corporations, 146, 157

Muwalo, Albert, 370

National Bank for Rural Development (BTM) (Madagascar), 276

Nationalism: ideology and, 380, 382–83; Madagascar and, 209, 212; Malaŵi and, 31–34, 35, 36–37

Nationalization, 7, 60, 203, 214, 224, 228, 234, 253–54, 256, 257, 264, 298, 308, 309, 310, 313, 318–21, 382–83

National Rural Development Program (NRDP) (Malaŵi), 72, 75, 76; credit and, 112

National Seed Company (Malaŵi), 79

Netherlands, 147

Newspapers, 13–14

Ng'ong'da, Clement, 409

Ohs, Peter, 102
Oil prices, 129
Opération productivité rizicole (OPR) (Madagascar), 248
Ord, Henry, 63
Organization commune africaine et malgache (OCAM), 212
Ottaway, David, 422
Ownership: absentee, 84; in Malaŵi, 35, 60; manufacturing and foreign, 146, 149; public (Madagascar), 214

Pachai, Bridgial, 32
Page, Melvin E., 408
Parastatal enterprises: and investment, 9, 50; in Madagascar, 228, 234, 246, 264, 265, 310, 311, 313, 322–23, 332; in Malaŵi, 60, 79, 91, 100, 146, 147, 389. *See also* Agricultural Development and Marketing Corporation (ADMARC)
Patrimonialism, 386–87
Pearson, E. O., 102
Physicians, 340–41
Plantations. *See* Agriculture, estate
Poirier, Jean, 201
Police in Malaŵi, 172
Political structure, 12–14, 386–87, 421, 422
Politics: Banda and, 5, 12, 387–91, 395; ethnic groups in Madagascar and, 202–03; in Madagascar, 391–94, 396; in Madagascar's colonial period, 206; Madagascar's independence and, 209
Poll tax, 29, 31–32, 205–06, 223, 288
Population: in Madagascar, 5, 200, 220, 221, 356; in Malaŵi, 5, 27, 44, 164–65, 356
Ports, 21, 163, 313, 324
Poverty: estate agriculture and, 87; health as indicator of, 366–69, 434–35; income distribution and, 351, 362, 365–70; rural, 11, 407
Press Holding Corporation (Malaŵi), 48, 81, 82, 83, 99, 147, 148, 149, 152
Price controls, 10, 48, 225, 229, 298, 329; ADMARC and, 154;

manufacturing and, 154–57, 308, 316–17, 325
Prices: ADMARC and, 74, 105–09, 113, 141, 154, 176, 423–26; agricultural (Madagascar), 223, 225, 262, 263, 267–76, 283, 335; consumption effects and, 103; development plans and, 59, 60; domestic, 189, 264; edible oil, 360; export, 101, 107, 125, 141, 394; financial and economic effects and, 108–09; income stability and, 106–07; intersectoral terms of trade and, 102–06; investment and, 103–06; manufacturing and, 161; oil, 129; production and, 102–03; tariffs and, 129; trade and, 131, 134; trade analysis (Madagascar) and, 295, 300; trade openness and reduced, 288; variations over distance and, 107–08
Private sector: investment and, 9, 56, 61, 228; manufacturing and, 314–15, 315–16; reprivatization and, 310; saving (Malaŵi), 51–52; wage controls and, 158–59
Progressive Farmer (*Achikumbe*) Program (Malaŵi), 80
Protectionism, 130–31, 150, 151, 310–11
Pryor, Frederic L., 6, 32, 413, 414, 416, 420
Public sector: balance of payments and, 136–37; financing (Malaŵi), 50–51; ideology and, 381; investment (Madagascar), 228–29; in Madagascar, 7, 234–35; manufacturing and, 146–50, 165; parastatals and (Malaŵi), 9, 50, 91, 100, 146, 147; wage controls and, 158

Railroads: in Madagascar, 197, 205, 207, 323; in Malaŵi, 21, 30, 31, 47, 54, 56, 60, 83, 163; Mozambique insurgents and, 47, 48, 83, 125, 141, 163, 172, 394
Rakotomavo, M., 310
Ramanantsoa (Gabriel) government, 212, 223–25, 233, 237, 250–51, 253–

54, 262, 270, 288, 311, 324–25, 337, 338, 392, 393, 416
Ranavalona III, queen of the Merina (Madagascar), 205
Ratsiraka (Didier) government, 5, 203, 223–25; agricultural production and, 245, 254; devaluation and, 298; development plan of, 233–35; economic ideology and policies of, 7, 213–14, 345, 379; education and, 337, 338; health and, 341; investment and, 9, 236–37; intersectoral terms of trade and, 270–71; land reform and, 243; manufacturing and, 308, 309, 311, 312, 314, 318; nationalist movement and, 212; nationalization and, 416; politics and, 393, 396; prices and, 288; rural markets and, 261; transportation and, 321–22; urban projects and, 214
Razafimandimby, Simon, 275
Razafimpahanana, Bertin, 249–50
Regional policy: Madagascar's development plan and, 232; transportation and, 164–65, 324
Religion, 202, 204
Remittances: expatriates and, 355; by Malaŵians abroad, 140, 142
RENAMO (Mozambique insurgents), 47, 48, 83, 125, 141, 163, 172, 394
Research, agricultural, 79
Revenues: Madagascar and, 332–42, 345; Malaŵi and, 174–79, 189
Rhodesia, 33, 34, 83
Rice: imports, 262, 263; labor exchanges and, 280, 281–82; prices, 271, 273, 275; production, 244; subsidy, 264
Roads: in Madagascar, 197, 205, 207, 321–22, 330, 418; in Malaŵi, 162–63, 418, 433
Rotival, Maurice, 207
Rural sector: capital flows and, 279–80; capital-intensive agricultural projects and, 72–76, 246, 247, 252–53; credit and (Malaŵi), 109–16, 120; development and, 62; education and, 182; elites in, 385–86; ethnic groups in Madagascar and, 203; French investment in Madagascar's, 355; income differences and, 354–56, 364; income gap and, 11, 233, 254–56; income inequality and, 398–99; infrastructure in, 72; investment in, 9; labor-intensive projects and, 77–80; labor market in, 280–82; in Malaŵi, 27; nonmonetary income and, 353; poverty in, 351, 407; savings in, 423; subsidies to, 360; taxes and, 176; transportation and, 100. *See also* Agriculture; Agriculture, estate; Agriculture, small-scale
Rural trade schools, 153

Savings: home banking and, 115; in Madagascar, 226, 227, 228–29, 300, 397, 424; in Malaŵi, 49, 50, 51–52, 56, 269, 397; taxes and, 176
Sectoral growth: investment and, 58–59; in Malaŵi, 43–44
Shuttleworth, Graham, 263
Small-scale agriculture. *See* Agriculture, small-scale
Small Enterprise Development Organization of Malaŵi (SEDOM), 153
Social Democratic Party (Madagascar), 5
Social expenditures, 172–74, 328, 397–98
Social indicators, 3, 4, 6
Social insurance system (Madagascar), 330
Socialism, 9, 38, 212, 213–14, 228, 234, 378–81
Société de l'Emyrne, 210
Société d'intéret national des produits agricole (SINPA) (Madagascar), 262–63, 265
Société Rochefortaise, 210
Soils: in Madagascar, 198; in Malaŵi, 22
SOMALAC development authority (Madagascar), 246–47

South Africa, 137, 139, 163, 414; emigration from Malaŵi to, 47, 116
Spacensky, Alain, 213
Sterkenburg, J. J., 102
Subsidies: agricultural, 10, 79, 108, 109; estate agriculture and, 91; Central African Federation and, 33; investment strategy and, 9; interest rate, 114; rice, 264; to rural sector, 360; to urban sector, 360
Summers, Robert, 422

Taiwan, 139
Tanzania, 139
Tariffs: import, 11, 293–94; in Malaŵi, 10, 34, 57, 129–31; protective, 150, 151; as public revenue, 174–76
Taxes: agricultural prices and, 108; cattle, 205–06, 223, 288, 334, 360; consumption price effect and, 103; development and, 56; direct, 176–77; on exports, 59, 131, 176, 294, 334; hut, 29; on imports, 129–31, 178, 293–95, 334; investment strategy and, 9, 232; manufacturing and, 311, 314; poll, 29, 31–32, 205–06, 223, 288, 334, 360; public investment and, 228; revenues and, 174–76, 189, 332–42, 345; trade and, 129–31, 293–95
Tax holidays (Malaŵi), 56, 150
Technology, agricultural, 73, 74, 85, 120, 405–06; small-scale agriculture and, 77–78, 245, 248–52, 406
Tembo, John, 190
Thangata (labor service tax), 32
Thompson, Virginia, 429, 430
Tobacco, 22, 115, 244; ADMARC and, 108–09; devaluation and, 134; estate agriculture and, 82, 91, 98; export, 47, 97, 141; export taxes on, 131; master farmer program and, 80
Tourism, 128
Trade: balance of payments and, 135, 136–39; credit and, 188; development and, 59–60, 140, 232, 234; favored sector approach to, 131–32, 295–96; financial side of, 132–36, 141; fiscal aspect of Madagascar's, 296–304; income distribution and, 135, 141–42; Madagascar's, 287, 288–92; in Madagascar's colonial period, 211; in Malaŵi, 34–35; nationalism and foreign, 382–83; openness and, 125–28, 288–92; patterns of, 413–17; quantitative restrictions and, 128–29, 292–93; strategy, 10–11; tax treatment and, 129–31, 293–95; urban sector and, 141. *See also* Exports; Imports
Trade unions. *See* Unions
Transportation: development plans and, 55–56, 58, 61; farmers and, 100; in Madagascar, 197, 207, 230, 232, 233, 265, 320–25; maize and, 108; Malaŵi's, 21; manufacturing and, 146, 159, 161, 162–65, 166, 312–13; Mozambique insurgents and disruption of, 47, 48, 83, 125, 141, 163, 172, 394; regional policy and, 164–65, 325; on Zambezi River, 30, 31
Tribalism, 26. *See also* Ethnic groups
Truck transportation, 322
Trypanosomiasis, 22
Tsetse fly, 22
Tsiranana (Philibert) government: 5, 202, 221–22, 430; agricultural production and, 245, 253, 255; capital flows and, 279–80; economic ideology and policy of, 214, 215, 379; education and, 337; import sector and, 295; intersectoral terms of trade and, 269–70; investment and, 236; Madagascar's independence and, 209–10, 231–33; manufacturing and, 308, 311; nationalization and, 416; politics and, 392, 393; rural sector and, 250; socialism and, 213
Tuong, HoDac, 415

Unemployment, 135, 221, 234, 300, 357, 358; education and, 182
Unions: in Madagascar, 211, 317–18; in Malaŵi, 35–36, 134, 357; wage controls and, 157, 159
United States, 137, 139, 414, 416

University of Madagascar, 338
Urban sector: education and, 182; elites in, 385, 389, 392; ethnic groups in Madagascar and, 203; income differences and, 11, 233, 354–56, 364; income inequality and, 351; Madagascar's development policy and, 214, 237; in Malaŵi, 27; rural workers and, 353; savings in, 423; subsidies to, 360; taxes and, 176, 178; trade and, 141

Vaccination program, 185, 341
Vail, Leroy, 31
Vocational Training Institute, Malaŵi, 153

Wage controls, 157–59, 317–18
Wager-on-the-strong: in Madagascar, 241, 250, 398; in Malaŵi, 67–68, 77, 80, 92, 97, 120, 398
Wages: in colonial period, 206; credit to provide, 114; education and, 182; of emigrants, 142; in estate agriculture, 88; foreign trade and, 135, 141; government expenditures on, 332, 359; income distribution and, 356–60; income policy and, 360; in Madagascar, 211, 282, 358–59; in Malaŵi, 36, 57, 356–58; manufacturing and, 161; regional and ethnic differences in, 359–60; replacement of Europeans and, 171
Water supply: 22, 185, 198, 341
Wheeler, David, 129, 131, 294–95, 415
Wilberforce College, 148
Williams, T. David, 128, 408
Wolgin, Jerome, 149
Women: credit and, 114; emigration and, 116
World Bank, 48, 99, 147, 148, 155, 171, 263, 293, 317, 322, 386, 420, 422, 424
World Health Organization (WHO), 367, 433–34

Yeats, Alexander, 415
Young, Crawford, 422
Young Pioneers (Malaŵi), 78, 117, 250

Zambia, 414
Zimbabwe, 414
Zomba (Malaŵi), 164